# REFORMING MONEY AND FINANCE

# REFORMING MONEY AND FINANCE

## Toward A New Monetary Regime

### SECOND EDITION

Robert Guttmann EDITOR

Routledge
Taylor & Francis Group
LONDON AND NEW YORK

First published 1997 by M.E. Sharpe

Published 2015 by Routledge
2 Park Square, Milton Park, Abingdon, Oxon OX14 4RN
711 Third Avenue, New York, NY 10017, USA

*Routledge is an imprint of the Taylor & Francis Group, an informa business*

Copyright © 1997 Taylor & Francis. All rights reserved.

No part of this book may be reprinted or reproduced or utilised in any form or by any electronic, mechanical, or other means, now known or hereafter invented, including photocopying and recording, or in any information storage or retrieval system, without permission in writing from the publishers.

Notices
No responsibility is assumed by the publisher for any injury and/or damage to persons or property as a matter of products liability, negligence or otherwise, or from any use of operation of any methods, products, instructions or ideas contained in the material herein.

Practitioners and researchers must always rely on their own experience and knowledge in evaluating and using any information, methods, compounds, or experiments described herein. In using such information or methods they should be mindful of their own safety and the safety of others, including parties for whom they have a professional responsibility.

Product or corporate names may be trademarks or registered trademarks, and are used only for identification and explanation without intent to infringe.

**Library of Congress Cataloging-in-Publication Data**

Reforming money and finance : toward a new monetary regime /
Robert Guttmann, editor.—2nd ed.
p. cm.
Includes bibliographical references and index.
ISBN 1-56324-770-4 (hardcover : alk. paper).—ISBN 1-56324-771-2 (pbk. : alk. paper)
1. Money—United States.
2. Banks and banking—United States.
3. Debts, External—Latin America.
4. Debts, External—United States.
5. Monetary policy.
I. Guttmann, Robert, 1951–
HG540.R44   1996
332.1′0973—dc20
96-31863
CIP

ISBN 13: 9781563247712 (pbk)
ISBN 13: 9781563247705 (hbk)

To Norman Lewandowski,
who has meant so much to me and my family

# Contents

List of Tables and Figures     xi

Preface     xiii

PART I :    CURRENT ISSUES IN MONEY AND BANKING:
AN OVERVIEW
*Robert Guttmann*

1. **Managing Credit-Money**     3
2. **Regulating Financial Institutions**     8
3. **The International Monetary System**     14

PART II:    MONETARY POLICY: DEBATES AND VIEWPOINTS

4. **Recent Policy Dilemmas of the Federal Reserve**
   Robert Guttmann, *The Federal Reserve as Policy Maker*     27
   Henry Kaufman, *Opportunities and Challenges Confronting Monetary Policy*     34
   Alan Greenspan, *The Fed Aims for Price Stability*     43

5. **The "Soft Landing" Strategy of Greenspan's Federal Reserve**
   Robert Guttmann, *The Federal Reserve's Preemptive Strike of 1994*     50
   Interview with David M. Jones, *Greenspan's Quest for Stability*     53
   Jerry J. Jasinowski, *The Case Against Further Monetary Tightening*     61
   Dimitri B. Papadimitriou and L. Randall Wray, *The Fed: Wrong Turn in Risky Traffic*     67

## PART III: FINANCIAL INSTABILITY AND BANKING REGULATION

### 6   *The Financial Underpinnings of Slow Growth*

Robert Guttmann, *Financial Fragility and Stagnation*    75

Robert Pollin, *Destabilizing Finance Worsened This Recession*    79

Benjamin M. Friedman, *Financial Roadblocks on the Route to Economic Prosperity*    87

### 7   *Banking Crises and Lender-of-Last-Resort Interventions*

Robert Guttmann, *The Management of Financial Instability*    96

James R. Barth, R. Dan Brumbaugh, Jr., and Robert E. Litan, *Bank Failures Are Sinking the FDIC*    101

R. Dan Brumbaugh, Jr., and Kenneth E. Scott, *A Political Logjam Still Blocks Banking Reform*    114

Edward W. Hill and Roger J. Vaughan, *Banking: Real Risks Require Real Reforms*    121

Edward J. Kane, *Taxpayer Loss Exposure in the Bank Insurance Fund*    126

### 8   *The Debate Over Reforming Banking Regulations*

Robert Guttmann, *Why We Regulate Banks*    133

James B. Thomson, *Using Market Incentives to Reform Bank Regulation and Federal Deposit Insurance*    138

Henry Kaufman, *How Treasury's Reform Could Hurt Free Enterprise*    148

Robert I. Adler and Douglas E. Ferguson, *Bank Reform: Medicine Worse Than the Malady?*    155

Albert Gailord Hart, *How to Reform Banks—and How Not to*    161

Wolfgang H. Reinicke, *Turf Fights in Regulatory Reform*    170

Richard Aspinwall, *Conflicting Objectives of Financial Regulation*    179

Wolfgang H. Reinicke, *Consolidation of Federal Bank Regulation?*    182

## PART IV: THE INTERNATIONAL MONETARY SYSTEM AND THE GLOBALIZATION OF FINANCE

### 9   *Global Finance in a Tripolar World Economy*

Robert Guttmann, *The "Triad": Toward a New Multicurrency Standard*    191

Howard M. Wachtel, *Taming Global Money*    198

David Felix, *Financial Globalization and the Tobin Tax*    203

Interview with C. Fred Bergsten, *A New Big Three to Manage the World Economy*    206

William M. Burke, *Rising Sun . . . Falling Dollar*    215

Interview with C. Fred Bergsten, *Freer Trade: Breaking Out All Over the Globe*    221

### 10   *Managing the Global Debt Crisis*

Robert Guttmann, *Debt Reschedulings, Credit Securitization, and the "Emerging Markets"*    228

Benjamin J. Cohen, *What Ever Happened to the LDC Debt Crisis?* 235
Richard N. Cooper, *External Adjustment: The Proper Role for the IMF* 241
José Angel Gurria Treviño, *The Mexican Debt Strategy* 245

## PART V: THE EMERGING MONETARY REGIME

11 **Transition to a New Monetary Regime**

Robert Guttmann, *Defining Monetary Regimes* 253

Henry Kaufman, *Structural Changes in the Financial Markets: Economic and Policy Significance* 258

Bibliography 267
Index 271
About the Editor 274

# List of Tables and Figures

**Tables**

1. Growth of Nominal GNP versus Credit   9
2. The Rise of "Near Money" Deposits and Borrowed Liabilities in the 1970s   11
3. Latin America's Adjustment to the LDC Debt Crisis   18
4. Federal Reserve Purchases of U.S. Treasury Obligations   35
5. Chairman Greenspan's Scorecard: Inflation   69
6. Chairman Greenspan's Scorecard: Capacity Utilization   69
7. Volatile Interest Rates   71
8. Finance, Investment, and Interest Rates for Nonfinancial Corporations   80
9. Household Income and Financing Patterns   81
10. Savings, Lending, and Banking Patterns   83
11. Economic Stability and Long-term Interest Rates   84
12. Estimates of BIF's Crisis Resolution Costs   103
13. Estimated Three-Year Bank Failure Costs Under Alternative Assumptions Concerning Recession Scenarios, Failure Probability, and Resolution Costs   104
14. Number of Banks Losing Money and Paying Dividends   110
15. Calculating Hypothetical BIF Loss Exposure From Asset Breakdown Given by Veribanc's Partition of FDIC-Insured Commercial and Savings Banks   131
16. Yen/Dollar Exchange Rate and Inflation Differential   216

**Figures**

1. Capacity Utilization Rate   37
2. Employment Cost Index   37
3. Short-Term Business Borrowing   37
4. Real Short-Term Interest Rate   56

5. Depository Institutions' Share of Total Nonfinancial Debt   59
6. Actual and Expected Inflation Growth   68
7. Real *Ex Ante* and Real *Ex Post* Interest Rates   68
8. Interest Payments as a Share of Available Earnings, 1946–90   89
9. Interest Payments as a Share of Cash Flow, 1946–90   89
10. National Saving as a Share of GNP, 1951–90   91
11. Investment as a Share of GNP, 1951–90   92
12. Bank Insurance Fund Reserves Relative to Insured Deposits   103
13. Bank Equity Capital Relative to Total Assets   108

# Preface

The 1980s and first half of the 1990s have been a period of revolutionary change in banking and finance. Different financial institutions are developing a dizzying array of new products, while at the same time trying to cope with growing losses from earlier investments. The proliferation of "electronic" money and banking is transforming our payments system as well as financial markets. Congress, in typical piecemeal fashion, has begun to overhaul the regulatory apparatus for financial institutions put into place more than six decades ago. After years of debate, many of the outstanding issues are finally nearing resolution. In the meantime, financial news captures in the headlines with great regularity, whether it is Wall Street's changing fortunes, currency crises, spectacular losses from trading in financial derivatives, the actions of the Federal Reserve, or worries about our budget and trade deficits.

These developments, far-reaching and dramatic as they may be, are not necessarily well understood either by economists or policy makers. For example, the worldwide integration of financial markets and the corresponding dominance of short-term capital flows in and out of different currencies and countries have vastly increased the interdependence among nations. Yet most models guiding policy making still assume an essentially closed U.S. economy.

Change in the real world is necessarily accompanied by change in theoretical thinking. We now face new problems and questions that require answers different from the past. Both theory and policy have to adapt to this rapidly transforming reality. That new thinking is now gradually emerging, in response to the painful realization of mistaken forecasts, through trial and error, and above all in ceaseless debate. This book, an updated and revised version of an earlier edition published by M. E. Sharpe in 1989, is one small contribution to this clarification.

## Objectives of the book

The literature on finance and banking falls basically into two categories. The first is textbooks, which introduce students to the basic concepts in this field. By and large, however, textbooks do not have much to say about the profound changes transforming our financial system. These tend to be discussed in the second category by a small group of monetary economists or financial experts. Writing primarily for a small professional elite, those specialists often use highly technical language and publish their works in relatively obscure outlets.

The objective of this volume is to present a nontechnical analysis of current issues relating to monetary reform and financial restructuring without requiring a lot of knowledge about economics from the reader. Drawing on my experience as a teacher, I have aimed the book principally at students of money and banking—

whether at the intermediate college level or taking introductory courses in graduate school. It can be used either in lieu of a standard textbook or as supplementary reading material. More generally, the book should also prove useful to anyone wanting to know more about the ongoing transformation of the financial system and its profound implications for our economy.

As we shall see, standard theory has very specific notions of money and finance that do not necessarily give satisfactory answers to today's questions. Ultimately, this problem can be overcome only by formulating a more accurate monetary theory. Toward this objective we have to link money creation to credit financing and put financial instability at the center of our analysis. Those steps necessitate the kind of broad treatment of the subject matter presented here. Moreover, by reprinting and analyzing key contributions from leading proponents of the different theoretical approaches, the book retraces the recent evolution of economic thought on this complex subject. This format allows us to identify both theoretical advances as well as remaining limitations. Most important, I try to shed more light on the complex relation between economic theory and policy in order to get a clearer picture of current debates and formulate a policy agenda for institutional reform that can carry us well into the next century.

## Outline

Part I presents an overview of the major issues facing the monetary authorities today. We start in chapter 1 with an analysis of monetary policy. This dimension of economic policy deals with the management of the money supply by our central bank, the Federal Reserve (the Fed). In this context we need first of all to define what constitutes money, bearing in mind that there are different forms of money and that these are subject to their own historic evolution. In chapter 2 we turn our attention to the current restructuring of our credit system, which comprises banks, other financial institutions, and the securities markets. Driving this process is a powerful combination of financial innovations and regulatory changes. Finally, in chapter 3 we focus on the international monetary system, with special emphasis on the repercussions of flexible exchange rates and the global debt crisis.

In Part II we take a closer look at the recent conduct of the monetary policy of the Fed. Specifically, in chapter 4, we analyze the Fed's experiment with Monetarism in the early 1980s and the complex balancing act the U.S. central bank followed after it abandoned monetary targeting in 1982. Since then the Fed has refocused on interest rates, but has done so with an anti-inflationary bias that has kept "real" (i.e., inflation-adjusted) interest rates at historically elevated levels. In chapter 5 we recount the debate surrounding the Fed's preliminary tightening in 1994, which aimed to nip inflation in the bud. That so-called soft landing strategy of the Fed proved quite controversial, not least because it slowed down a recovery that had had an unusually hard time getting going.

Part III deals with commercial banks, the center of our credit system. In chapter 6 we analyze the hangover of excessive indebtedness, fueled by a borrowing binge during the 1980s, which is one of the central reasons why economic growth during the 1990s has been below the historic average. In chapter 7 we analyze the crisis of the U.S. banking system during the early 1990s and the measures taken to deal with this dangerous situation. Finally, in chapter 8, we take up regulatory reform, with special emphasis on the 1991 proposal by the U.S. Treasury to create a new framework of banking regulations.

International monetary affairs are the subject of Part IV. Chapter 9 analyzes recent efforts among leading industrial nations to stabilize volatile exchange rates and contain the centrifugal tendencies that threaten to tear our multicurrency system into three separate currency zones. The global debt crisis and its resolution, which turned some developing countries into "emerging markets" capable of once again attracting foreign capital, are the subject of chapter 10.

The conclusion, presented in Part V, attempts to synthesize the key arguments introduced earlier. Here, in the final chapter, we try to identify the key characteristics of the emerging regime of money and finance and discuss what policy makers can do to bring this transition to a successful conclusion.

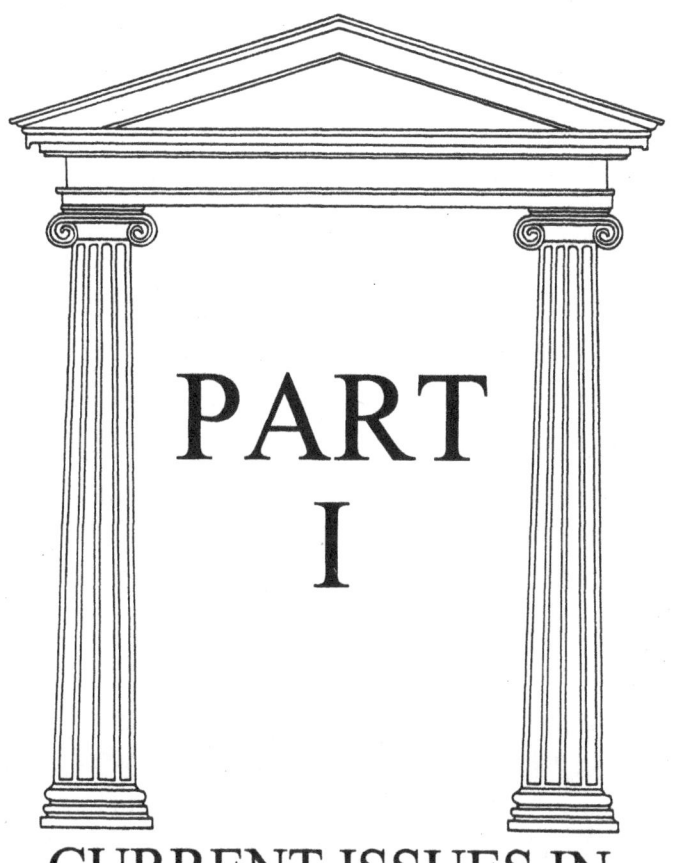

# PART I

## CURRENT ISSUES IN MONEY AND BANKING: AN OVERIEW

Robert Guttmann

# CHAPTER 1

# Managing Credit-Money

## The functions and forms of money

Money plays so dominant a role in our daily lives that we tend to take it for granted. We often forget that money is a *social institution* subject to ongoing change. This complicates the task of defining what exactly constitutes money. In theory, anything can represent money, as long as it is widely accepted as such within its geographic sphere of circulation. This acceptance depends on its capacity to carry out several unique *functions*:

- Money is, above all, used as a *medium of exchange* in market transactions to pay for goods and services. It is able to do this as the socially accepted representative of purchasing power, giving its holders command in the marketplace.
- Money also acts as a *unit of account* which allows all marketed goods and services to be expressed on the basis of a common numerical standard, the money price.
- In addition, money functions as a *store of value*, thereby preserving purchasing power over time and allowing its holders to postpone their purchases until later. This enables money to be saved and lent out to someone else in the meantime, the foundation of our credit system.
- Finally, money also has to settle debts effectively when they come due. Here it functions as *means of payment*.

When analyzing the historic evolution of money as a social institution, we must distinguish between two different types of money. One is *commodity money*, in which the monetary unit (such as our dollar) is defined as a certain quantity of one or more precious metals. The Coinage Act of 1792 introduced a bimetallic standard in the United States based on gold and silver coins ("specie"). This gave way to a gold standard in 1834. With the exception of temporary suspensions to help the government finance wars (e.g., 1862–78, 1914–19), we maintained that gold standard until its abolition during the Great Depression.

Under such a metallic standard, money holders could redeem their dollars in gold or silver at the officially fixed rate of exchange. They also had the unrestricted right to import and export those metals at that official rate. These characteristics of commodity money exerted an automatic discipline on the economy by linking the quantity of circulating money tightly to the nation's supply of precious metals. Always having to face the possibility of people trying to redeem their dollars and get gold, the government could not afford to issue dollars much in excess of its gold reserves without risking monetary instability.

On the international level, the gold standard established fixed exchange rates between different currencies (e.g., dollar, pound, franc, mark, yen), defined by their respective weights in gold. External imbalances in trade and capital flows were automatically corrected.

Countries with balance-of-payments surpluses ("surplus countries") experienced net inflows of gold, followed soon by faster increases in money supply and credit, intensifying inflationary pressures, and consequently deteriorating trade performance. The exact opposite occurred in the case of "deficit countries," where the deflationary effects of gold outflows let to lower imports and higher exports.

Despite its capacity for automatic self-regulation, such a gold standard was ultimately fraught with serious problems. Its international adjustment mechanism via specie flows between countries was actually based on inflationary (or deflationary) destabilization of entire national economies. At the same time, the domestic "gold coverage" requirements for money and credit eliminated the scope for effective countercyclical economic policy initiatives. More generally, the reliance on relatively fixed (i.e., "inelastic") supplies of precious metals imposed a rigid barrier on money creation and thus on economic growth.

To overcome this barrier, the banking system soon began to develop new instruments circulating as money (i.e., a medium of exchange) in our economy. Whether taking the form of inconvertible paper currency of the state's monetary authorities or notes and deposits of private banks, they all had one thing in common. Each of these monetary instruments was issued in the wake of credit extension and represented therefore *credit-money*. In other words, they were all created in direct response to borrowing by economic agents in need of additional liquidity. This credit-linked process of money creation lessened reliance on inelastic supplies of commodity money.

An early example of such credit-money, circulating widely after 1836, were notes issued by state-chartered banks whenever they lent funds to borrowing customers. These *state bank notes,* apart from having limited geographic circulation and becoming obsolete when the issuing bank failed, suffered from a lack of homogeneity.[1] Consequently, the National Banking Acts of 1863/4 replaced them with safer and more uniform bank notes issued by federally chartered banks. Unable to compete with these *national bank notes,* state banks could survive only by offering a new and more attractive form of credit-money. In the 1880s they introduced *demand deposits,* which allowed borrowing customers to write checks on bank deposits payable on demand. These convenient checking accounts soon replaced bank notes as the dominant form of credit-money, a position they have maintained to date.

Apart from this private bank money, credit-money could also take the form of state-issued paper currency. For example, during and after the Civil War (1862–78), the U.S. Treasury issued inconvertible "Greenbacks" which made up for disappearing specie reserves and helped to finance war-related budget deficits. In 1913 Congress established the Federal Reserve and empowered the new central bank to issue notes—today's dollar bills.

The return of the United States to a gold standard after World War I (1919) meant that the issue of Federal Reserve notes and demand deposits was still ultimately restricted by the nation's available specie reserves. This situation lasted until the unprecedented collapse of our banking system during the Great Depression. As part of a broader monetary reform, the Roosevelt Administration took our currency off the gold standard, under the Emergency Banking Act of 1933 and the Gold Reserve Act of 1934.

That step marked the climax of a gradual movement away from commodity money. It freed money creation from the metallic barrier of rigid gold coverage. The issue of credit-money, whether in the form of private bank deposits or as state-issued paper currency, could now respond directly to the liquidity needs of the economy by being tied directly to the lending activity of the banking system. In other words, we had finally established a flexible (i.e., "elastic") supply of currency.

The abolition of the gold standard in 1934 moved the United States to an *inconvertible paper standard;* this provided for an elastic currency based on different forms of credit-money. These different forms represented money by simple declaration (or fiat) of the government. Their effectiveness depended therefore on public confidence, which could be undermined by signs of monetary instability, especially the devaluation of money through inflation. But that new monetary standard had no automatic correction mechanism, such as the gold coverage requirements and specie-flow adjustments of commodity money. Consequently, it had to be a *managed* standard.

## Central bank management of private bank money

This management of the inconvertible paper standard rests with the central bank and its manipulation of the money creation process, which is the domain of *monetary policy*. The Fed has direct control over part of the money supply, its own Federal Reserve notes. But how can it affect money creation by private banks? That depends on its control of the *payments system,* which transfers funds from one location to another for payment in transactions and settlement of debts. The Federal Reserve Act of 1913 authorized the central bank to operate a nationwide check-clearing system; this system was set up in 1918 and later expanded to include both wire transfers and electronic funds transfers.[2]

This check-clearing mechanism forms the core of our payments system. It works by having participating banks keep a fixed portion of their deposits as reserves in accounts with the central bank (or as cash in their vaults). Checks can then be cleared by simply transferring an equivalent amount of reserves from the account of the bank on which the check was written to the account of the bank in which the check was deposited, with the Federal Reserve acting as bookkeeper.

Whenever customers deposit cash or checks in their accounts, the receiving bank gains an equivalent amount in reserves. Of those it has to keep only a small fraction as required reserves. The rest constitutes *excess reserves,* which can be loaned out in the form of new demand deposits. In other words, the ability of private banks to create new money in the process of such credit extension depends on their excess reserves. These in turn are under the direct control of the central bank. The Federal Reserve can manipulate total bank reserves by trading government securities ("open market operations") or lending to banks ("discount loans"). Its reserve requirements determine, then, which portion of that total represents excess reserves.

While each individual bank can extend credit and thereby issue new demand deposits only up to the amount of its excess reserves, the banking system as a whole can create a multiple of those in new money. This *money multiplier* comes into effect when borrowers spend their new demand deposits and thereby transfer reserves from one bank to another. The recipient bank has to keep a certain percentage of those newly gained reserves to cover its additional deposit liabilities, but can loan the rest as excess reserves. A third bank is now gaining those reserves, and so forth. At the end of this chain reaction all initial excess reserves are turned into required ones, and the money creation process will have been exhausted.[3]

## The operating targets of the Federal Reserve

How should the Federal Reserve use its monetary policy tools to manage the inconvertible paper standard most effectively? The answer to this question depends on one's view of the relationship between the money supply and economic activity. This issue is one of the most contentious in economics, with two dominant schools of thought in standard monetary theory "Monetarism" and "Keynesianism," battling each other.

• *Monetarism,* a modern variant of the age-old quantity theory of money, stresses the stable, long-run expansion of the money supply in line with the economy's natural growth capacity as a key prerequisite for full employment and price stability (see Harry Johnson, 1962; Milton Friedman, 1968). Consequently, followers of this approach want the central bank to focus on money-supply measures as its principal operating target. The most important of these monetary aggregates include $M_1$, which consists of currency plus demand deposits (e.g., NOW accounts), $M_2$ which is $M_1$ plus various savings deposits (e.g., consumer CDs, money market funds), and $M_3$ which adds to $M_2$ yet another set of savings deposits (e.g., negotiable CDs, large Eurodollar accounts). It should also be noted that Monetarists tend to blame our economic problems on wrong policy. See, for example, the analysis of the Great Depression by Milton Friedman and Anne Schwartz (1963) as the result of Federal Reserve mistakes.[4]

• *Keynesianism,* based on the writings of John Maynard Keynes (1930, 1936), takes a radically different view of central bank intervention in our economy. In contrast to the fixed policy rule of Monetarism, Keynesians believe in the importance of discretionary monetary policy as a short-run stabilization tool to counteract cyclical fluctuations in economic activity. In this context, they want the Fed to focus on interest rates and other credit conditions as its main operating targets.[5]

## The credit cycle of private banking

Apart from the relatively small portion of state-issued coins and notes, most credit-money is issued by private banks turning their nonearning excess reserves into income-yielding loan assets. Since money creation is thus linked to credit extension by banks, we cannot construct an accurate monetary theory without analyzing how they behave. Any reasonable model of bank behavior in turn has to account for the fact that the issue of credit-money depends on highly variable investment decisions of both lending banks and their borrowing customers.

Assuming the Fed allows sufficient expansion of (excess) reserves in the banking system, the creation of private bank money is ultimately determined by the profit motive. New money is created (in the act of credit extension) only if banks are willing to lend their excess reserves and debtors want to borrow these funds at mutually acceptable terms. This dependence on the profit motive confronts the banking sector as a difficult *trade-off* between safety and profitability. When banks opt for safety, they may decide to increase their capital base, keep more reserves, and/or invest in safer assets. But these safety-oriented strategies come at the expense of more profitable investment opportunities, and vice versa.

Banks and other financial institutions tend to manage this trade-off in an inherently unstable manner. During periods of recovery they share the public's optimistic expectations and eagerly seek to expand their assets in response to strong credit demand. The search for higher returns encourages them often to lend too much and to make investments that would have been rejected as too risky under less euphoric circumstances. Then expectations rapidly turn sour as debtors begin to face debt-servicing problems in the wake of declining income. Mounting losses and risks force lenders into a sudden emphasis on safety. They insist on tougher credit terms and/or reduce their supplies of funds. This tightening comes at a time of great vulnerability for many debtors and reinforces the spread of spending cutbacks. The result is general debt deflation and recession. Thus banks typically behave in *procyclical* fashion.

A second feature of private bank money is that the Federal Reserve does not have full control over the money supply. Its policy tools, whether reserve requirements, discount loans, or open-market operations, enable it to manipulate bank reserves. This management of (excess) reserves determines only the banks' ability to create money. It controls neither their willingness to lend nor the demand for bank loans from debtors, the other two determinants of money creation. These depend instead on the profit motives of lending banks and borrowing customers.

## Financial instability and the "lender of last resort"

The credit cycle of the banking system makes our economy vulnerable to incidences of *financial crisis*. One historic lesson from the 1930s is that this kind of crisis, if not contained, is the economic equivalent of a heart attack. This is so for two interrelated reasons:

• Bank failures have a tendency to spread, especially when they prompt worried depositors to withdraw funds from their bank accounts. Given the practice of fractional-reserve banking, such runs on bank deposits have a tendency to sink even relatively healthy banks and thus may easily turn into a self-fulfilling prophecy: The more banks fail, the greater the panic runs. This process, a standard feature during the era of commodity money, reached a climax in the Great Depression. Over 9,000 banks failed within three years in the United States, and still-solvent banks had to shut down temporarily in order to prevent collapse.

• In addition, such spreading bank panics have a profoundly paralyzing effect on economic activity. As a cause of chain bankruptcies in the banking system, they wipe out savings, destroy much of the money supply, and reduce credit volume. Such disruptions may turn a normal cyclical downturn into a depression.

Given these negative repercussions of bank failures, it was only a question of time before the government was forced to find ways to cope with financial crises. One policy option widely used today is the intervention of government agencies as *lender of last resort* for cash-strapped and failing institutions. It should be noted that the introduction of the Federal Reserve in 1913 was intended to do just that by giving reserve-deficient banks access to its discount window. But this mechanism failed to prevent the collapse of the domestic banking system between 1929 and 1933, because the Federal Reserve limited access to the discount window through excessively restrictive collateral requirements. This debacle was followed after 1933 by a major expansion of the lender of last resort, which succeeded in reducing the number of bank failures and containing instances of financial crisis.[6]

The Glass-Steagall Banking Act of 1933 created the Federal Deposit Insurance Corporation (FDIC). Financed through annual insurance premiums paid by member banks, the FDIC has two important functions. One is to insure bank deposits (currently up to $100,000 per account). This deposit insurance aims to reassure otherwise worried depositors and thereby limit their propensity for panic runs. The other is to organize the orderly removal of failing banks, either by providing financial assistance to merge them into healthy banks or through outright asset liquidation. Companion legislation set up the Federal Savings and Loan Insurance Corporation (FSLIC) to do the same for thrifts. In addition, the Banking Act of 1935 broadened the lending authority of the Federal Reserve by allowing banks to pledge any asset (e.g., their own promissory notes, government securities) as collateral for discount loans rather than just commercial loans to business firms.[7]

While clearly effective, this lender-of-last-resort assistance has also created a significant problem. Its assurance of government bail-outs erodes the disciplining force of market failure and may prompt banks to undertake riskier investments that, if successful, promise higher returns. This *moral hazard* can be overcome by such measures as imposing larger bank capital requirements on risky assets and limiting the size of banks given guaranteed protection. Furthermore, the monetary authorities try to counteract the risk-taking bias of banks by examining them on a regular basis and imposing special regulatory constraints on their behavior.

The first two decades of the postwar period were marked by a remarkable absence of financial crisis in the United States. Barring the occasional FDIC assistance for (mostly small) banks facing failure, no major lender-of-last-resort intervention was necessary until the first "credit crunch" in 1966. This excellent record was due to a variety of fortunate circumstances, including strong balance sheets (i.e., large savings, low debt burdens) of the private sector at the end of World War II and the unprecedented postwar boom. But this situation began to change in the mid-1960s. Since then, the U.S. economy has suffered from increasingly severe recessions (in 1969–70, 1974–75, 1979–82, 1990–92), each of which required more extensive lender-of-last-resort assistance.[8]

## Notes

1. By 1860 there were more than 1,600 different banks operating under the diverse laws of some 30 states, and each bank could issue a variety of notes. This heterogeneity also encouraged counterfeiting on a massive scale. For example, the "Bank Note Reporter and Counterfeit Detector" listed more than 1,000 counterfeit bank notes during that year.
2. Before 1918, checks were cleared by a "correspondent" banking network among thousands of individual banks. In general, large city banks handled payments services for the smaller, usually rural banks within a given area. That elaborate and cumbersome network caused high transfer costs and frequent delays. In addition, many banks redeemed out-of-town checks at discount rather than at par.
3. The maximum size of this multiplier is the reciprocal of the required reserve ratio. In reality, however, the multiplier is made smaller by various leakages. Banks may keep excess reserves rather than loaning them out. The public may make cash withdrawals which disrupt the reserve transfer between banks in the check-clearing process. Moreover, the actual size of the multiplier is affected by shifts of funds among deposits with different reserve requirements. Jerry Jordan (1969) stressed that all these factors are subject to relatively stable behavioral patterns, thus allowing the Federal Reserve to predict the actual multiplier quite accurately.
4. Reagan's election victory in 1980 propelled *supply-side economics* to the forefront. While its neoconservative protagonists share many of the Monetarist arguments, they reject its prescription of stable money supply in the long run as too restrictive and difficult to attain. Instead, supply-siders such as Robert Mundell (1971), Victor Canto et al. (1983), and Marc Miles (1984) call for the return to some sort of gold standard. Such a system, they argue, would give the money supply an objective basis for adjusting automatically to price fluctuations (see our discussion of specie-flow adjustments above). In other words, they favor a "price rule" in lieu of the "quantity rule" of the Monetarists.
5. This ideal of countercyclical monetary policy predates Keynes and the Great Depression. It emerged originally (known as the "Banking School") during the first half of the nineteenth century in Britain, as evidenced by the practices of the Bank of England and the debate with the "Currency School," the predecessor of Monetarism, over the Bank Act of 1844.
6. Between 1890 and 1920 bank failures averaged approximately 100 per year in the United States. That annual average rose to about 600 in the 1920s and an astonishing 2,200 during the early 1930s. But the creation of more effective lender-of-last-resort mechanisms after 1933 succeeded in sharply reducing the number of bank failures, keeping them within an average range of four to nine per annum between 1942 and 1981.
7. In 1973 banks with strong cyclical fluctuations in loans and deposits (e.g., farm banks) gained easier access to the discount window through a "seasonal borrowing privilege." At the same time the Federal Reserve restated its willingness to lend even to nonbank institutions and business firms in emergencies. And in 1980, discount loans became available to nonmember banks, thrifts, and credit unions.
8. Martin Wolfson (1994) provides an excellent analysis of the major lender-of-last-resort interventions over the past three decades, including the 1966 thrift crisis, the collapse of Penn Central and panic in the commercial paper market in 1970, the failure of Franklin National in 1974, the bailout of the Hunt Brothers in 1980, the defaults of Penn Square, Drysdale, and Mexico in 1982, the rescue of Continental Illinois in 1984, the stock market crash of 1987, and the collapse of the thrifts in the late 1980s.

# CHAPTER 2

# Regulating Financial Institutions

## Financial regulations

The financial sector has traditionally been regulated because of its unique position in our economy. Dealing with other people's money, financial institutions have a fiduciary responsibility unlike any other industry. This is especially true for those institutions that have the power to create new money in the form of transaction deposits. In addition, the mobilization of loanable funds in financial markets affects the distribution of capital among different uses and thus plays a major role in resource allocation. But these crucial functions may be jeopardized in light of the inherent instability of the credit system and the widespread repercussions of bank failures. This vulnerability was seen as a justification for extensive government regulation of financial institutions.

There are several types of financial regulation, each with its own specific purpose:

1. *Money creation.* Certain regulations focus on the issue of private bank money and are therefore a necessary component of monetary policy. Balance-sheet restrictions, such as those introduced under the National Banking Act of 1863 or the Depository Institutions Deregulation and Monetary Control Act of 1980, specify which private institutions are given monopoly power over money creation and what types of transaction deposits they can issue. Those institutions (e.g., commercial banks, thrifts) are then subjected to central bank management of their otherwise procyclical money creation process, through policy tools such as reserve requirements and access to discount loans.

2. *Selective credit controls.* In emergency periods the Federal Reserve has used those controls to redirect credit allocation. For example, during World War II and the Korean War it restricted consumption by imposing minimum down-payment requirements and maximum repayment periods for consumer credit purchases. Ever since 1934 it has imposed down-payment ("margin") requirements on credit purchases of stock to prevent excessive speculation in the stock market. In 1980, the Fed used its powers under the Credit Control Act of 1969 to impose special reserve requirements on money-market mutual funds and issuers of credit cards.

3. *Structure regulations.* These aim to shape the financial sector in terms of size distribution and product differentiation among financial institutions. For example, bank charter policies, such as those defined under the National Banking Acts of 1863 and 1864, limited entry into banking. Branching restrictions under the McFadden Act of 1927 protected smaller banks as local monopolies. The Glass–Steagall Act of 1933 separated commercial banking (i.e., deposit taking and commercial lending) and investment banking (i.e., dealership, brokerage, and underwriting of securities) in order to prevent market manipulation and conflicts of interest in

the stock market. Bank mergers were subjected to special regulatory controls under the Bank Merger Act of 1966, while the Bank Holding Company Acts of 1956 and 1970 gave the Federal Reserve control over the activities and geographic markets of those banks operating as bank holding companies.[1]

4. *Safety regulations.* Apart from lender-of-last-resort interventions, financial instability has also been countered by regulations. For example, the National Banking Acts of 1863 and 1864 imposed minimum capital requirements on national banks, restricted the types and maximum amounts of their loans, and introduced obligatory reserve requirements on bank notes and deposits. Glass–Steagall gave the Federal Reserve the power to set maximum rate ceilings on bank deposits (Regulation Q). This aimed to stop destabilizing price competition, where banks bid up deposit rates to attract funds and then invest them in high-yield and correspondingly riskier assets for a positive yield spread. In addition, different regulatory agencies (e.g., Federal Reserve, FDIC) supervise and examine banks on a regular basis.

5. *Regulation of financial markets.* Following the stock market crash of 1929, the U.S. government has regulated the nation's securities markets. The Securities Act of 1933 specified disclosure and regulation requirements for public offerings of new securities. The Securities Exchange Act of 1934 established the Securities and Exchange Commission (SEC) to regulate the securities exchanges, set disclosure standards for companies with securities listed on an exchange, and prohibit certain practices of market manipulation (e.g., insider trading).

Financial regulations always emerge as an urgent policy issue during periods of intense instability. It is therefore not surprising that the collapse of the U.S. banking system during the Great Depression prompted a major regulatory overhaul. The Emergency Banking Act of 1933 and the Gold Reserve Act of 1934 abolished the gold standard in favor of an inconvertible paper standard subject to central bank management. The Glass–Steagall Act of 1933 introduced new bank regulations (e.g., rate ceilings on bank deposits), created the FDIC, and separated commercial and investment banking. The Securities Act of 1933 and the Securities Exchange Act of 1934 provided a new regulatory framework for the stock and bond markets. And the Banking Act of 1935 strengthened the Federal Reserve's monetary policy tools. Together these new regulations, a key component of Roosevelt's New Deal, created a much more stable banking system and thus laid the foundations for the postwar boom.[2]

Table 1  **Growth of Nominal GNP versus Credit**

|  | % per year | | | $billion |
|---|---|---|---|---|
|  | 1960s | 1970s | 1980-85 | (end-1985) |
| Nominal GNP | 6.89% | 10.06% | 8.07% | $3998.1 |
| Debt |  |  |  |  |
|   Corporate | 9.40 | 11.22 | 10.39 | 1505.1 |
|   Household | 8.55 | 11.40 | 10.30 | 3224.6 |
|   U.S. government | 1.96 | 8.83 | 15.84 | 1660.4 |
|   State and local governments | 7.55 | 7.39 | 12.47 | 553.1 |
|   Financial | 14.94 | 16.78 | 15.69 | 248.9 |

*Source:* Federal Reserve Bank of Kansas City, *Debt, Financial Instability and Public Policy,* 1986, p. 16.

## The postwar "debt economy"

One of the most striking features after World War II was the progressively rising trend toward debt financing. The emergence of this *debt economy* must be traced to the immediate postwar years when U.S. industry and consumers, boosted by much strengthened balance sheets, finally had the opportunity to satisfy their pent-up demand. Credit financing of private spending was given additional room to grow, as the war-related bulge in public sector debt was gradually worked down to more normal levels. Debt also proved to be a comparatively cheap source of finance because of historically low interest rates and tax deductibility of interest expenses.

This "debt economy" embraced the entire economic system. Each type of activity became gradually more reliant on debt (see Table 1).

• Budget deficits, ever since Roosevelt's New Deal the cornerstone of stimulative economic policy, have added each year to the national debt.

• Industrial corporations have often preferred debt to equity for two reasons. It can be issued at lower cost than common stock, because investors consider bonds less risky than equity and thus require a lower rate of return. Moreover, increased debt levels also raise the rate of return to shareholders for any given sum of profits by allowing for a proportionately smaller capital base (the leverage factor).

• Consumers, benefiting from high employment levels and large income gains, were willing to borrow in order to buy expensive products after having had to postpone such purchases during the long years of depression and war. Large-ticket consumer items were increasingly turned from luxuries into necessities. Home ownership, apart from its utility as living space, gave consumers an asset with strong appreciation potential, often their only major source of wealth. The dispersion of homeowners into suburbia combined with policy biases (and societal preferences) that favored road construction over mass transit, thus making the possession of cars indispensable for most. And college education, a costly service, became a necessary entry condition for a gradually widening range of occupations.

• Finally, the aggressive expansion strategies of financial institutions provided the engine for this postwar "debt economy." Those institutions constantly sought to increase their business volume by tapping new sources of funds and then finding additional clients to lend to.

The rapid postwar growth of debt in the United States was further supported by the monetary authorities. The Federal Reserve used its monetary policy tools to keep interest rates low. The effective lender-of-last-resort protection of the banking system also helped to expand credit volumes by making financial transactions safer. Finally, a variety of incentives were put into place to boost consumer credit. For example, a larger portion of the nation's savings was channeled into mortgage financing of real estate purchases by giving thrifts special tax and regulatory treatment and by setting up government-sponsored institutions (e.g., Government National Mortgage Corporation) to develop a secondary market for mortgages. Being allowed to operate their own (relatively unregulated) finance companies, automobile manufacturers could offer prospective customers cheap car loans and make this service part of their competitive strategy. Student loans benefited from government subsidies, which lowered their cost and lengthened repayment schedules. Credit cards, increasingly used for retail purchases, were issued and processed within a separate and privately operated clearing system.[3]

## The debt–inflation spiral and regulatory erosion

The absence of any serious recession over sustained periods of time, as was the case in the 1950s and 1960s, relaxed fears and fed buoyant expectations. This prompted private borrowers to take on more debt and to become less averse to risk in their pursuit of higher returns. As the memory of past failures faded, lenders also developed a bias in favor of profitability at the expense of safety. Their increasingly aggressive pursuit of new sources of funds and credit opportunities supported this movement toward higher financial leveraging, i.e., the increased reliance on debt as a source of funds.

Eventually, however, such a gradual trend toward more debt is bound to erode balance sheets. Higher debt-servicing burdens, which after all constitute fixed costs, reduce net income and cause sharper profit fluctuations for any given change in sales volume. Heavily indebted borrowers are more likely to require additional funds just to service their old debt. Such a situation can soon become a vicious circle, especially when interest rates rise and the share of short-term debt grows.

During the 1970s, this balance-sheet erosion became a self-feeding dynamic due to gradually intensifying *stagflation*. This peculiar crisis form, a combination of slow growth and accelerating inflation, caused the "real" (i.e., inflation-adjusted) income of many economic agents to decline. The resulting shortfall in cash flows was often covered by increased borrowing. Rising debt-servicing burdens could then be relieved through accelerating inflation, which devalued the principal. That process became increasingly self-propelled: as income indexation spread, purchases were sped up to beat expected future price hikes, and negative "real" interest rates encouraged further debt financing.

But this debt–inflation spiral could not go on forever. Its results—most notably rising illiquidity and increased reliance on short-term debt—eventually made further debt accumulation increasingly difficult to sustain. Such limitations tended to become acute at the peak of an inflationary boom when the combination of spreading speculation and credit overextension imposed a need for restraint. Amidst these signs of growing financial instability the Federal Reserve could no longer accommodate the debt–inflation spiral and had to abandon its easy-money, low-interest policy. Beginning in the mid-1960s, such switches to a tighter monetary policy (i.e., slower money growth, higher interest rates) occurred at each cyclical peak, in 1966, 1969, 1973, and 1979.

The destabilizing consequences of this self-feeding debt–inflation spiral, however, went beyond a merely cyclical impact and also made themselves felt over the long run. With each cycle, inflation peaked at higher levels, debtors took on more debt, and balance sheets ended up progressively weaker. These forces gradually undermined the financial health of our economy. Even those sectors of the economy initially in a market position to charge extra-high prices and thus benefit from inflation could not maintain their advantage forever. Their windfall gains from inflation attracted a great deal of new funds which allowed them to finance rapid capacity expansion. At the same time, demand for their expensive products began to slow, as eroding purchasing power forced buyers to cut back or to look for cheaper substitutes. These sectors (e.g., agriculture, oil, other commodities) then ended up with growing excess capacity, especially in 1975 and then again after 1981.

This long-run deterioration undermined the existing framework of financial regulations. Some of them simply became counterproductive in the wake of accelerating inflation. For example, whenever unregulated interest rates rose above the deposit-rate ceilings under Regulation Q of the Glass–Steagall Act, banks and thrifts would at times face massive withdrawals by depositors looking for higher returns elsewhere. This problem of *disintermediation* became especially acute during the late 1970s with the emergence of money-market mutual funds (MMMFs) as a very attractive alternative to bank deposits. In addition, consumer credit would often dry up suddenly when inflation pushed market rates above the state-regulated usury ceilings on those loans. Branching restrictions make banks more vulnerable by limiting their customer base, especially in unit-banking states such as Illinois or Texas. To the extent that regulations reduced the scope of banks and thrifts for diversifying their assets, these institutions were confined to relatively narrow segments of the credit market and thus were more likely to overextend their lending capacities.

*Financial innovation* spread throughout the system, increasingly weakening the regulatory framework. Much of this activity aimed to bridge the gap between the growing borrowing needs of many debtors and the disintermediation of savers out of low-yielding assets, especially traditional bank deposits. Moreover, these innovations also undermined the effectiveness of monetary policy. For example:

• In the early 1960s, banks began to develop a variety of *borrowed liabilities*, such as negotiable certificates of deposits (CDs), federal funds, repurchase agreements (Repos), and Eurodollars (see Table 2). These short-term funds freed bank lending from the reserve constraints imposed by the central bank and thus enabled banks to expand profitable loan assets much more rapidly than their deposit liabilities *(liability management)*. In other words, the process of money creation occurred increasingly outside the reach of the central bank.[4]

• The takeoff of Eurobanking after 1966, comprising dollar-denominated deposits and loans outside the United States, gave the larger U.S. banks easy access to additional funds whenever the Federal Reserve tightened at home. By permitting domestic clients to deposit their funds in the Euromarket and then borrow these funds back from their overseas subsidiaries, U.S. banks could also circumvent Regulation Q and thereby reduce the threat of disintermediation.

• In the late 1970s, banks and other depository institutions introduced new deposit instruments, such as Automated Transfer of Savings (ATS) accounts, Negotiable Order of Withdrawal (NOW) accounts, or money-market mutual funds (MMMFs).[5] By combining relatively high interest yields and check-writing powers, these deposits were designed to counter the disintermediation of funds out of zero-interest demand deposits and rate-controlled savings deposits. Frequent shifts between traditional money deposits and those new "near money" instruments made the Federal Reserve's operating targets more volatile.

Banks also made growing use of regulatory loopholes during the 1970s. By switching their charters from the Comptroller of Currency to state agencies, banks

Table 2  **The Rise of "Near Money" Deposits and Borrowed Liabilities in the 1970s**
($ billion)

| | Demand deposits | Saving deposits | ATS NOW | MMMFs | Repos (term) | Eurodollar (net) (term) |
|---|---|---|---|---|---|---|
| 1965 | 132.5 | 256.9 | 0.1 | 0.0 | 0.0 | 1.7 |
| 1970 | 166.3 | 261.0 | 0.1 | 0.0 | 1.6 | 2.2 |
| 1975 | 214.2 | 388.7 | 0.9 | 2.7 | 8.4 | 9.7 |
| 1976 | 224.4 | 452.8 | 2.7 | 2.4 | 14.1 | 14.8 |
| 1977 | 239.6 | 491.3 | 4.2 | 2.4 | 19.4 | 20.2 |
| 1978 | 253.8 | 480.8 | 8.5 | 6.4 | 27.0 | 31.8 |
| 1979 | 261.9 | 423.1 | 17.1 | 33.4 | 30.1 | 44.7 |
| 1980 | 266.5 | 401.4 | 27.6 | 61.6 | 34.7 | 50.3 |
| 1981 | 236.2 | 345.7 | 77.4 | 150.6 | 37.0 | 67.5 |

*Source:* Economic Report of the President, 1985, pp. 304–5.

could opt out of membership in the Federal Reserve System and benefit from the more lenient regulations of state banking commissions. These allowed, for example, lower reserve requirements, and state-chartered banks could count certain income-earning assets as reserves. The number of Federal Reserve member banks declined steadily from 6,221 in 1965, comprising 83 percent of total bank deposits, to 5,568 (72 percent) in 1978. In addition, more and more banks sought to diversify their activities by restructuring themselves into bank holding companies (BHCs). As multibank BHCs, banks could avoid geographic branching restrictions, while the status of one-bank BHCs enabled them to move into related nonbanking activities, such as data processing, investment advice, and limited underwriting. Between 1970 and 1981, the number of registered BHCs rose from 121 banks, which together made up 16.2 percent of total bank deposits, to 3,500 banks, controlling 74.1 percent of deposits.

## *The deregulation of banking*

In response to this regulatory erosion, Congress passed the Depository Institutions Deregulation and Monetary Control (DIDMC) Act in 1980. This major banking legislation addressed many of the problems discussed above.

- The act resolved the membership crisis of the Federal Reserve and strengthened its monetary policy by bringing an additional 33,000 depository institutions (i.e., all nonmember banks, thrifts, credit unions) under its monetary umbrella.
- Various "near money" deposits (i.e., ATS, NOW, money market certificates, credit union share drafts) were legalized and subjected to reserve requirements. This made them officially part of the money supply.
- Regulation Q and usury ceilings were both phased out, thus ending price controls on savings deposits and consumer loans to allow once again full price competition in banking.
- Thrifts were deregulated to diversify their assets and liabilities, enabling them to operate much more like commercial banks. The scope of their diversification was extended further by the Garn–St. Germain (Depository Institutions) Act of 1982.

These provisions of the DIDMC Act of 1980 have accelerated the transition toward a new banking system based primarily on a large array of interest-yielding deposit instruments that combine both transaction and investment components. No longer constrained by Regulation Q, banks and thrifts have offered a whole new generation of deposits carrying money-market rates (e.g., consumer CDs, SuperNOW accounts, money-market deposit accounts). Similarly, variable-rate instruments, such as adjustable-rate mortgages, have increasingly replaced the traditional fixed-rate loans on the asset side.

Since passage of the DIDMC Act of 1980, banks and thrifts have undoubtedly faced much heavier competitive pressures. In addition, these depository institutions have also intensified their search for new and profitable markets in order to make up for growing losses on old debt, and because of the declining profitability in their traditional markets. Yet at the same time the 1980 Act was at best partial deregulation and left many regulatory constraints intact. This clash between intense competition and regulatory restrictions has led to a piecemeal transformation of the banking industry and continued debate over further deregulation.

One aspect worth mentioning in this context is the gradual movement toward *nationwide banking* by means that effectively bypass still existing branching restrictions. This development has been fed by technological change, most notably the spread of electronic fund transfers. Many states have recently concluded reciprocity agreements to give their respective banks access to each other's markets. This has led to the emergence of "superregionals"—usually multi-bank holding companies operating in an interstate region—as the fastest growing segment of the banking industry. In addition, we have witnessed the spread of "integrated banking networks" in which banks in different states allow their respective customers access to each other's automated teller machines. After 1981, banks and other institutions also set up "limited service banks" (LSBs) which can provide many bank services on a national basis.[6] And the rapid increase in bank failures during the early 1980s has forced regulators to relax the Bank Merger Act of 1966 with regard to takeovers and acquisitions of failing depository institutions by out-of-state banks.

Regulators will also have to address a second controversial dimension of restructuring in our banking system—the *product extension* of financial institutions. New technology, such as electronic funds transfers, enables them to offer their customers new or improved financial services. This is especially true for electronically integrated "sweep accounts," such as the Cash Management Accounts or mutual fund families, which allow easy transfer of funds between different types of deposits and credit lines. Thrifts, mutual funds, and investment banks have begun to offer banking products (e.g., credit cards, investment and transaction deposits) and set up LSBs for that purpose. Sears, Merrill Lynch, American Express, Prudential-Bache, and many others are already well on their way to providing customers with a full line of financial services irrespective of state lines.

In response, commercial banks want to extend their product range into hitherto prohibited areas, especially investment banking. The scope of this product extension depends on easing regulatory restrictions. The Garn–St. Germain Act of 1982 gave banks more power to form subsidiaries, including "reverse holding company" structures in which several banks can share ownership of a service company subsidiary, such as a computer processing firm, remote terminal network, or automated clearinghouse. In recent years, many states have allowed their state-chartered banks to expand on a limited basis into nonbank activities, such as securities underwriting, brokerage, real estate development, and insurance. The Federal Reserve, empowered by the Bank Holding Company Act of 1956 to define bank-related activities, has gradually followed suit and expanded the product range of nonbank subsidiaries of BHCs. But with nonbank institutions increasingly offering banking services, banks want much broader diversification to create a competitive, "level" playing field (see chapter 8).

## Notes

1. The structure of our credit system is also fundamentally shaped by the fact that different types of financial institutions are all subject to their own specific regulations, and as such are set apart from each other. Thrifts, for example, followed until recently the rules of the Federal Home Loan Bank Board. Mutual funds are guided by the Investment Company Act of 1940. Pension fund operations are regulated by the Employee Retirement Income Security Act of 1974.

2. For more details on this regulatory framework and its repercussions for the evolution of the credit-driven boom in the 1950s and 1960s, see Robert Guttmann (1984; 1990).

3. In response to the consumer movement of the late 1960s, the government introduced various laws to protect consumers in credit transactions. These included the Consumer Credit Protection Act of 1969 (popularly known as the Truth in Lending Act), the Equal Credit Opportunity Act of 1974, the Fair Credit Billing Act of 1974, the Home Mortgage Disclosure Act of 1975, and the Community Reinvestment Act of 1977.

4. Negotiable CDs are large time deposits that can be sold in a secondary market before maturity. Federal funds are short-term loans from banks with excess reserves to reserve-deficient banks and other financial institutions. Repos are short-term loans with government securities as collateral. Eurodollars are dollar-denominated time deposits at foreign banks or overseas branches of U.S. banks that can be loaned out. For an excellent discussion of "liability management" see Dudley Luckett (1980).

5. ATS accounts are essentially zero-balance checking accounts fed from savings accounts. NOW accounts are demand deposits that pay interest. MMMFs, offered by mutual funds, are savings deposits yielding current money-market rates against which checks (in excess of $500) can be written.

6. LSBs exploited a loophole in the Banking Holding Company Act of 1956 where banking was defined as taking deposits *and* making commercial (business) loans. By omitting one of these activities, LSBs could offer all other banking services on a nationwide basis.

CHAPTER 3

# The International Monetary System

## The "gold dollar" standard of Bretton Woods 1945–73

One of the most important economic developments during the postwar boom has been the growing *internationalization* of capital. The long boom that followed the end of World War II was very much propelled by the dramatic expansion of world trade following the reduction or removal of trade barriers.[1] Accelerating overseas investment by U.S. firms in the 1950s and 1960s gave rise to multinational corporations (MNCs) producing and marketing their goods in a large number of countries. U.S. banks followed their largest corporate clients abroad, thus turning themselves into transnational banks (TNBs). Soon these TNBs set up their own credit and payment system, the Euromarket, which enabled them to operate beyond the nationally confined reach of central banks. Technological improvements in transportation and communications facilitated the global integration of production and financial markets, a trend that began in earnest during the late 1970s. In short, we have today a globally integrated economy in which resources and activities are no longer confined by national boundaries.

This internationalization of capital benefited a great deal from the new international monetary system set up in 1944, near the end of World War II, the *Bretton Woods* system. It was a modified version of the gold-exchange standard first introduced in the interwar period.

• Under this new system the U.S. dollar became the principal form of world money. The United States, at that time the absolutely dominant economic power, agreed to exchange dollars in the hands of foreigners on demand with gold from its specie reserves at an officially fixed rate of $35 per ounce. This convertibility guarantee made the dollar as good as gold in international circulation.

• In addition, the official dollar price of gold formed the basis for defining fixed exchange rates between national currencies.

• Finally, Bretton Woods introduced new international monetary authorities to regulate the system. The International Monetary Fund (IMF) helped member countries with balance-of-payments difficulties undertake appropriate adjustment programs by offering them short-term loans in return for accepting tough austerity measures. And the International Bank for Reconstruction and Development (the so-called World Bank) offered developing countries long-term loans at concessionary terms for strategically important investments.

These features bolstered global economic relations. The return to full convertibility of key currencies in the late 1950s, made easier by the new system of fixed exchange rates, encouraged trade among the United States, Japan, and Western Europe. The IMF and the World Bank played an important role as catalysts for capital transfers to the developing countries, thereby smoothing the transition from their colonization to political independence. Stable currency prices reduced uncertainty in foreign investment decisions and thus helped to spur the global expansion of multinational corporations and transnational banks. In general, the extraordinary growth of world trade and capital flows in the 1950s and 1960s was one of the principal forces responsible for the long postwar boom.

Besides providing the institutional framework for stable and effective monetary arrangements among nations, the Bretton Woods system gave the issuer of world money (in this case the United States) a new form of *seigniorage*. Previously, in the era of commodity money, this benefit was the profit a government could make on the coinage of money. In the modern era seigniorage has taken on a different meaning. When a national currency functions as world money, it has to be transferred from the place of issue—the domestic banking system—into international circulation. This can be done only by having the issuing country run balance-of-payments deficits with the rest of the world. Foreigners willing to hold that currency as an international medium of exchange and reserve are then in fact financing the issuing country's external deficits on a revolving basis. This seigniorage benefit allows the national issuer of world money to run continuous deficits without having to face the normal external constraint of deficit-cutting adjustments.

Given the chronic trade surpluses of the United States as the absolutely dominant global power, the only way dollars could flow into international circulation was through U.S. capital exports. The dollar shortage abroad in the late 1940s required the conscious organization of such capital outflows. Those took the form of major military spending commitments overseas by the United States (e.g., the North Atlantic Treaty Organization), foreign aid assistance (e.g., Truman's Marshall Plan, Kennedy's Alliance for Progress), and opening foreign markets for the investments of U.S. corporations and banks.

Bretton Woods thus offered the world community a "social contract" among nations. The United States was allowed to satisfy the global demand for its capital by means that strengthened its own power, while the other countries received in the process ample supplies of dollars needed for their participation in the global economy. It is also worth noting here that the exclusion of the Soviet bloc from Bretton Woods ultimately had a detrimental effect on the centrally planned economies, forcing them into autarchic development strategies and inefficient barter agreements with other countries.

However, Bretton Woods did not survive. As a matter of fact, it was one of the first victims of the regulatory erosion in the wake of intensifying stagflation discussed above in chapter 2. The system collapsed in August 1971 when President Nixon ended the convertibility between dollars and gold. The realignment of exchange rates under the Smithsonian Agreement in December 1971 lasted only a little more than a year, and in early 1973 the major industrialized countries began to let their currencies float freely in the foreign exchange markets.

The demise of Bretton Woods was caused by several interrelated imbalances that had been building up in the system for years.

• The limited gold supply was soon incapable of supporting the strong demand for global liquidity in the wake of rapidly expanding world trade. In addition, the supply was increasingly redistributed, with the United States facing a steady decline of its gold reserves due to redemptions and occasional speculative runs. Already by the late 1950s its reserves were inadequate to back all dollars in international circulation. That imbalance grew worse each year, with more and more international dollars becoming de facto inconvertible. In that situation the system could survive only as long as foreigners continued to have confidence in the dollar.

• That confidence began to erode in the late 1960s when the overvaluation of the dollar became increasingly evident. Inflation in the United States suddenly began to accelerate above the rates experienced elsewhere, without adequate compensation through sufficiently higher interest rates. In addition, other industrialized countries had finally managed to catch up with the United States in terms of international competitiveness, especially West Germany and Japan. The overvalued dollar only reinforced this process by making U.S. imports cheaper and its exports more expensive. These forces began after 1968 to trigger downward speculative pressure on the dollar.

• Such currency speculation was greatly facilitated by the emergence of the *Euromarkets* in the 1960s. With growing supplies of dollars circulating overseas, it was only a question of time before foreign banks and subsidiaries of U.S. banks accepted dealing in dollar-denominated instruments abroad. In the absence of any regulatory costs, banks could afford to offer better rates on Eurocurrency deposits and loans while at the same time avoiding the reach of their domestic monetary authorities. This unregulated credit and payments system, operating parallel to the official transactions among central banks, made it much easier to shift funds into and out of different currencies and countries. It thus became a very efficient conduit for speculation against the dollar. Between 1968 and 1971 this speculation was mostly absorbed by foreign central bank purchases of dollars, but that process broke down after the United States announced its first trade deficit in nearly a century.

## Flexible exchange rates and currency speculation

Monetarists such as Milton Friedman (1953, 1967) and Harry Johnson (1972) and even some Keynesians (see, for example, James Meade, 1966) predicted that a system of flexible exchange rates would be self-correcting and lead to balanced trade and capital flows. But over the last quarter century that system has behaved quite differently. Exchange rates have moved in multiyear cycles characterized by increasingly large amplitudes ("overshooting") and highly volatile daily price behavior. This instability has in turn exacerbated trade imbalances, whose reversals have taken years of painful adjustment. Moreover, we have witnessed increasingly disruptive and perverse capital flows, such as the net outflows from developing countries and the enormous absorption of foreign savings by the United States in recent years.[2]

The volatility in foreign exchange markets is the result of one of the most remarkable developments over the last decade, the extraordinary growth of *short-term capital movements* across the globe. Huge sums, according to various estimates averaging up to $1400 billion per day, are constantly being moved into and out of different countries and currencies. Only a small proportion of this gigantic transaction volume, perhaps 15 percent, goes toward financing trade and direct investment, the traditional international activities. The predominant share is absorbed by short-term capital flows of corporations and banks adjusting their financial asset portfolios in response to interest- and exchange-rate fluctuations. In other words, they constitute speculative capital ("hot money").[3]

Currency speculation, while certainly possible in a system of fixed exchange rates (see our discussion of Bretton Woods above), became more lucrative after 1973 under the new regime of deregulated currency prices. Since its objective is to earn short-term capital gains from correct guesses about future price movements, this activity thrives on market instability. Moreover, "hot money" transactions have been facilitated by the Euromarkets, which greatly increased the mobility of financial capital around the globe. The introduction of currency futures, options, and swaps enabled market participants to hedge against the price risk from volatile exchange rates. But these new instruments also attracted speculators by allowing them to trade large amounts of currency with little capital. Today, currency speculation is a significant source of profits for many banks and corporations.

Following predicted changes in interest-rate differentials and/or exchange-rate movements, speculative capital flows are nowadays often large enough to make those expectations a self-fulfilling prophecy. For example, market sentiments toward depreciation may spark a sell-off, which drives down the price of this particular currency. Confirmation of expectations and capital losses for those holding onto the devaluing currency prompt additional currency sales, explaining the often observed "bandwagon" effect among speculators.

The self-feeding nature of speculation also arises, because that activity often exacerbates precisely those underlying structural imbalances that gave rise to the expectational bias of speculators in the first place. For example, dollar depreciation makes U.S. imports more expensive and exports cheaper. These price effects operate more rapidly than corresponding volume adjustments in trade. It takes a while before either import quantities are cut back or export volumes grow sufficiently to compensate for those price changes. In the meantime, our total import bill increases (the price rises, while the quantity is slow to fall) and export earnings decline, the *J-curve* effect. This deterioration in the trade balance—coupled with rising domestic inflation fueled by more expensive imports—may add to the downward pressure on the currency.

Whenever countries get caught in such a vicious cycle of accelerating devaluation and growing trade deficits, they have had to stop this process through dramatic policy switches toward fiscal austerity and/or monetary restraint. This happened, for instance, to Britain's Labour government in 1975, the Carter administration in 1979, and the Socialists in France during 1982–83. Those examples illustrate the degree to which currency speculation, with its destabilizing effects on prices and trade, has eroded the sovereignty of national governments in their economic policy options.

## The global debt crisis of the 1980s

One of the dominant economic issues of our times has been the lingering debt crisis of many less-developed countries (LDCs), which erupted into the open with the nearly simultaneous defaults of Mexico and Brazil in the summer of 1982. For nearly seven years that crisis threatened the world economy in several ways.

- Default threw many LDCs into sustained depression, which has eroded their capacity for economic development and social welfare. Mass unemployment and rampant inflation led to considerable political unrest in those countries.
- The combination of very high debt-servicing burdens and capital flight led to net outflows of capital from LDCs to industrialized nations, thus draining poorer nations of much-needed resources.
- Industrialized countries lost a large volume of exports, as LDCs were forced to restrict imports.
- In desperate need to earn more foreign exchange reserves for debt servicing, most LDCs flooded world markets with their commodities in order to increase their export earnings. This contributed to global deflation in commodity markets. Lower prices in the wake of overproduction forced LDCs to produce even more in order to make up for the revenue shortfall, thus feeding deflation pressures.
- The debt crisis exposed many of the world's leading banks to potentially massive losses that threatened their solvency. While most of those banks survived the crisis intact, they ended the decade much weakened. The erosion of their capital base, especially after a $31 billion write-down loss in 1987, forced U.S. banks to cut back their lending activity and thus contributed to a slowing of economic growth.

This global debt crisis, which started after 1973 with the recycling of the surplus of oil-exporting countries (OPEC) to nonoil LDCs in the Euromarket, was a classic case of credit overextension. Ample credit supplies and improved export earnings in the wake of sharply rising commodity prices during the 1970s enabled developing countries to grow very rapidly. This success encouraged them to borrow even more. But those funds were frequently not used for the kinds of investments that could assure adequate income gains for future debt servicing. Much of the debt financed imported consumer goods for a small ruling elite, armaments, or huge construction projects with relatively low economic returns. Many LDCs also suffered enormous waste of funds from widespread mismanagement and corruption. Of course, a large amount of funds did get channeled into industry. But this investment boom in developing countries during the late 1970s only set the stage for overproduction after 1981, because it led to very rapid capacity expansion in key sectors (e.g., oil, chemicals, metals, steel, shipbuilding).

Governments in industrialized countries actively encouraged these Euroloans to LDCs, as domestic political pressure forced cutbacks in their official foreign aid programs. And the banks themselves had good reason to find this recycling activity very attractive. Intense competition put Eurobanks under strong pressure to loan out their rapidly swelling OPEC deposits as soon as possible. Loans to LDCs promised higher returns than domestic lending. Carrying variable rates, these loans also transferred interest-rate risk to the debtors. Moreover, banks considered sovereign debt less likely to default than private-sector debt.

At the same time this initially successful recycling of petrodollars was not followed by effective policy adjustments. In 1979 the global economy experienced its second "oil shock," when the same combination of accelerating inflation, dollar devaluation, and supply disruption at a time of high demand allowed oil producers once again to drive prices sharply higher. Already heavily leveraged, LDCs suddenly faced large trade deficits which they covered by taking on even more Euroloans.

That borrowing spree lasted until the Federal Reserve's dramatic policy switch toward restraint in October 1979 hit those debtor countries with a *double squeeze*. On the one hand, sharply rising U.S. interest rates in its aftermath spilled immediately into the Euromarkets. With most of their old loans carrying variable rates, LDCs suddenly faced huge increases in debt servicing costs at a time of extraordinary borrowing needs. On the other hand, their ability to meet this increased burden declined precipitously. The new Federal Reserve policy helped trigger a global recession that collapsed commodity prices and deflated the export earnings of LDCs. Moreover, once the dollar began to appreciate because of high U.S. interest rates, LDCs had to generate more nondollar funds in order to service a given sum of dollar-denominated debt. That deterioration was further aggravated by massive capital flight. When Mexico declared itself unable to meet its payments obligations in mid-1982, Eurobanks panicked and cut back new loans to LDCs. Suddenly starved of funds, other large debtor nations defaulted as well.

## Finding a new international lender of last resort

The onset of the global debt crisis threatened the solvency of the U.S. banking system.[4] Even worse, when the problem broke into the open, there was no international lender of last resort ready to deal with this crisis effectively. Monetary authorities had to react immediately or face serious problems among our largest banks. And so they did. The successful bailout of Mexico gave birth to a new international lender-of-last-resort mechanism that has been in active use ever since.

This mechanism consisted of several steps. Countries with liquidity problems were first given short-term "bridging loans" by the Federal Reserve, the U.S. Treasury's Exchange Stabilization Fund, other central banks, or the Bank for International Settlements. These were designed to avert outright default by providing those cash-strapped debtor nations with funds until a longer-term solution could be worked out. The second step usually involved an agreement with the International Monetary Fund. In return for accepting austerity programs, which aimed at reducing its borrowing needs by cutting its deficits, the troubled debtor nation was given a small loan from the IMF. More important, such an agreement provided the "green light" for debt reschedulings by private banks, which delayed repayment and in certain cases even provided new loans to assure proper servicing of old debt.

This ad hoc, case-by-case mechanism for crisis management set up in 1982 was essentially designed to give defaulting LDCs enough cash to make interest payments, which then flowed right back into bank income statements. In the process, the repayment of maturing LDC debt was continuously delayed and/or funded out of additional credit. This "rollover," often at higher interest rates and with additional fee income, enabled U.S. banks not only to avoid classifying most LDC loans as nonperforming, but also to *increase* their profits.

But this distortion of income statements eroded confidence in the U.S. banking system, causing with growing frequency sharp declines in bank stock prices and "flights into quality" by bank depositors and creditors. This forced regulatory agencies to institute more effective controls. Following passage of the International Lending Supervision Act in 1983, the Federal Reserve imposed higher minimum capital requirements which limited the banks' ability to increase lending to individual LDCs. Banks were also required to disclose more information about their LDC debt, including data on country exposure. And finally, regulators gradually tightened rules for loss accounting and for setting aside reserves against troubled loans. Until then banks had been given wide latitude in interpreting these rules.

Initially the IMF-led crisis management of the LDC debt crisis set up in 1982 actually aggravated the financial difficulties of many LDCs by placing too much of the adjustment burden on the debtor countries in order to protect the banks. Continuous reschedulings increased the indebtedness of already heavily burdened LDCs. At the same time, the debtor countries had to endure extremely painful adjustments. Their austerity programs produced some desired results, most notably a switch to sizable trade surpluses. But these improvements came at the expense of highly destabilizing long-term consequences. Years of deep recession further weakened the inherently fragile structure of LDC economies. Sharply declining living standards and mass unemployment fueled social unrest. While the debt crisis accelerated the transition from military rule to democracy in many LDCs (e.g., Argentina, Brazil, Peru, Philippines), the newly elected leaders have had to overcome a great deal of political instability and to struggle with entrenched elites opposed to reform.[5] Stabilization programs, while initially capable of positive results, often ended in spectacular collapse. The chaos that followed required new reschedulings and prompted even tougher austerity measures.

As illustrated in Table 3 for Latin America, LDCs had to run large trade surpluses and reduce investment activity to cope with growing debt-servicing burdens.

Table 3 **Latin America's Adjustment to the LDC Debt Crisis**

|  | All as percentage of GDP | |
| --- | --- | --- |
|  | 1977–82 | 1983–85 |
| External debt | 34.3% | 47.2% |
| Interest payments | 3.2 | 5.6 |
| Trade balance (except interest) | –0.8 | +4.7 |
| Net investment | 11.3 | 5.5 |

*Source:* IMF World Economic Outlook.

This wrenching adjustment resulted in sharp declines of real gross domestic product (GDP) per capita, ranging between 6 percent (Mexico) to 17 percent (Argentina, Venezuela) from the 1981 peak to 1985. Despite these sacrifices it became eventually clear that a large portion of LDC debt, having been earlier frittered away unproductively in capital flight and luxury consumption, would never be repaid.

While locking LDCs into a devastating debt–deflation spiral without the prospect of lasting improvement, the IMF-led crisis management helped transnational banks. These could continue to book their LDC loans as income-earning and thus mask losses on de facto defaults. By shifting the burden of additional lending increasingly to others (e.g., multilateral agencies, governments, non-U.S. banks), U.S. banks also managed to reduce their relative exposure. In essence they were allowed to get more debt-servicing income flows than outflows in the form of new loans to LDCs. Already-shrinking LDCs were thus forced to export capital (on top of massive capital flight by their own upper classes) in support of U.S. bank income. This reversal of traditional capital flows not only deepened the plight of debtor countries, but also hurt creditor nations in terms of lost export earnings and eroding public confidence in the financial statements of their banks.

The first stage of the global debt crisis was thus managed in too unbalanced a fashion, placing so much of the burden on the debtors that their temporary illiquidity problem soon grew into a structural insolvency problem amidst depression conditions and growing debt burdens. This process of degradation had the dynamic properties of a downward spiral that could easily spin out of control if it continued for too long. At some point the management of this crisis had to be rebalanced in order to provide some long-term solution for the suffocating debt-burden increases of the post-1981 phase. That point came in 1985 when U.S. Treasury Secretary Baker suggested giving fifteen debtor nations of strategic importance new funds in exchange for structural reforms to deregulate and open up their economies.

This so-called *Baker Plan* proved inadequate because of the refusal of private banks to offer new loans to that group of debtor countries. What the plan did in effect was to redistribute sovereign credit risk from private banks to multilateral lending institutions and thus to the taxpayers of the industrial nations funding these organizations. But the additional funds provided by such official lending institutions as the IMF, the World Bank, or the Paris Club (organizing intergovernmental loans) could not make up for the shortfall of funds from private lenders. Yet at the same time the Baker Plan did facilitate two positive developments of crucial importance. One was the adoption of structural reforms which dramatically transformed the key economies of Latin America and Southern Asia with the help of such far-reaching steps as privatization of public enterprises, price deregulation, removal of protectionist barriers to trade and foreign investment, land reform, and improved fiscal discipline. The other positive result of the Baker Plan was to encourage greater financial innovation aimed at transforming the illiquid LDC loans into more liquid instruments that could be sold off or swapped with other debt (e.g., loan sales, debt–bond swaps, debt–equity swaps).

The inadequacy of the Baker Plan produced a critical moment in 1987 when Brazil, facing renewed debt-servicing problems after the collapse of its stabilization plan, refused to service its debt unless given more relief by its private creditors. This desperate go-it-alone step by Brazil forced the banks to confront the reality of large de facto losses on their LDC loans. Hidden by lax accounting rules until that moment (e.g., book-value accounting for loans, generous treatment of bad-debt losses), these losses were about to explode on their balance sheets because of Brazil's unilateral decision to default. Just before the ninety-day waiting period concerning the recording of nonperforming loans was about to expire, Citibank decided to set aside $2.5 billion in loan-loss reserves. That decision by the largest U.S. bank forced its competitors to follow suit to the tune of $31 billion in reserve set-asides that year alone. This step enabled the banks to make much more aggressive use of the various new market-based devices by which they could rid themselves of LDC debt at a relatively limited loss, such as loan sales and debt-for-bond swaps.

The combination of structural reforms among debtors and debt-reduction strategies of private lenders was institutionalized in the third phase of crisis management. That phase began in 1989 when U.S. Treasury Secretary Brady suggested a new round of agreements between the two sides that would effectively reduce the debt burdens of selected LDCs—particularly those countries where structural reform had made the greatest progress—through much more extensive use of various swapping devices. The latter would replace loans with bonds backed by the creditor governments. The *Brady*

*Plan* reduced the effective debt burden of many debtor nations at a time when their structural reforms finally began to bear fruit. It also greatly accelerated the securitization of LDC debt (i.e., the repackaging of illiquid loans into tradable securities). By the time some debtor nations had restored their creditworthiness as a result of macroeconomic stabilization and structural reforms, this credit securitization enabled mutual funds, pension funds, and other institutional investors from the industrial nations to direct funds towards those debtor nations in lieu of the traditional bank loans that were no longer forthcoming.

In the early 1990s many of the LDCs turned so into booming *emerging markets* whose rapid industrialization and integration into the world economy was financed by long-term investment from multinational corporations and a huge wave of securities purchases by institutional investors from the United States and Europe. The latter source of capital imports proved, however, very fickle. At the first sign of trouble, which arrived when the newly elected president of Mexico botched a peso devaluation attempt in December 1994 (for more detail see chapter 11), the institutional investors withdrew their funds massively from LDC securities.

The speed of this capital flight and its rapid worldwide contagion created a dangerous crisis situation in early 1995, which the existing international lender-of-last-resort mechanism was not well equipped to handle. Unlike the first LDC debt crisis in 1982, this latest crisis no longer centered on banks, which have always been the traditional conduit for lender-of-last-resort interventions by central banks. Moreover, the new lenders, for the most part institutional investors with a short reaction span and capable of dumping massive amounts of securities in seconds, possessed behavioral characteristics that required a much more rapid lender-of-last-resort response than the slower banks and their more illiquid loans of a decade ago.

The latest crisis, which spread from Mexico to other emerging markets in a matter of days, was met by a rescue operation in which the governments of industrial nations, directly and indirectly through the IMF, offered Mexico $50 billion to back its currency and dollar-denominated securities. In other words, in the new world of institutional investors and securitized credit the lender of last resort has to declare its willingness to defend the country (or countries) under attack against a highly organized and concentrated flight of capital. A few months after the bailout of Mexico the industrial nations, cognizant of the changed realities of global finance, decided to enhance the IMF's emergency assistance capacity substantially. Debtor countries would also have to disclose much more extensive and timely information about their macroeconomic condition; this would prevent such sudden panics from recurring by imposing corrective action before the crisis breaks.

## *The United States as net debtor*

While the LDC debt crisis continues to make itself felt in new variations, a second financial crisis capable of threatening the world economy looms on the horizon. The global stock market crash in October 1987 gave us a first taste of the problem. In this context we have to analyze the peculiar growth pattern that emerged from the collapse of the debt–inflation spiral in the early 1980s to drive the post-1982 recovery on a worldwide scale. This pattern is dominated by the record U.S. budget and trade deficits. As a result of these twin deficits, the United States was able to act as a "locomotive" for other countries. Its consumer-led boom after 1982 allowed the economies of Western Europe, East Asia, and Latin America to recover from the depth of the downturn in the early 1980s by pursuing an export-led growth strategy. But this recovery could not be sustained, because it was based on serious imbalances in global trade and capital flows. These tend to feed already considerable tensions, especially protectionist pressures and volatile exchange-rate movements.

Our starting point is the dramatic switch in fiscal policy after Reagan took office in 1981. Massive reductions in both personal and corporate income taxes combined with large, multiyear increases in military spending and selective cuts in antipoverty programs. As a result, U.S. budget deficits, already made larger by lower tax revenues and rising outlays for entitlement programs in response to recession (the so-called *automatic fiscal stabilizers*), started to grow rapidly after 1982.

But Reagan's supply-side predictions of large increases in savings and investments in the wake of lower marginal tax rates failed to materialize. High-income groups used their windfall gains from the tax cuts mostly for additional consumption. The proportion of disposable income put into savings actually declined, reaching a record low of 2.9 percent in 1987 (compared to a long-term average of 6 percent). Corporate investment, after an initial surge to make up for project delays and cancellations during the deep recession of the early 1980s, did not grow much after 1984. This was not surprising in light of large and continued excess capacity in many industries. The impact of Reagan's fiscal policy changes, rather than following the supply-side blueprint, gave us instead fiscal stimulation in the Keynesian tradition as first established in Roosevelt's New Deal. The result was a deficit-driven and consumer-led recovery, rather than the planned savings-driven and investment-led growth.

Once the recovery was safely under way in 1983, its precise course was increasingly shaped by monetary policy. After mid-1982 the Federal Reserve switched to a more accommodating monetary policy based on rapid money growth and gradually declining interest rates. Much of the accelerated money creation between 1983 and 1986 was required to fund huge increases in the volume of financial transactions, the massive refinancing of old debt, and revenue outflows to the rest of the world in the wake of growing U.S. trade deficits. These factors caused the "velocity" (or turnover) of money to decline, a highly unusual phenomenon during a recovery. Consequently, faster money growth during that period did not rekindle inflationary pressures, as predicted by Monetarists.

U.S. interest rates remained at historically high levels for a long time, especially when compared to the much more rapid reduction of inflation. The record-high "real" interest rates of the 1980s had several causes:

- Following the phase-out of Regulation Q in 1980 (see chapter 2), banks and thrifts increasingly competed for funds by driving up deposit rates and then strove to maintain their profit margins by coordinated pricing of their loans.
- This practice of "spread banking" was reinforced by stagnant savings and strong credit demand from consumers, corporations, and the federal government.
- In addition, inflationary expectations died very slowly. Fearing accelerating inflation in the wake of surprisingly strong recovery during 1983–84, bondholders insisted on a high inflation premium.

Nonetheless, nominal interest rates declined gradually, first in response to the more accommodating monetary policy, and then because of lower inflationary expectations in the wake of continuous deflation in global commodity markets. These interest-rate reductions had to be based on a careful balance between two competing forces. On the one hand, interest rates had to fall enough to sustain recovery. On the other, they had to remain high enough (when compared with rates overseas) to attract foreign capital.

With private and public debt rising rapidly in the United States amidst declining savings, we soon came to depend on foreign capital inflows to finance our excess spending. Attracted by higher returns, better growth opportunities, and political stability in the United States, foreign investors gladly obliged. Their inflows, representing increased demand for U.S. dollars, pushed the exchange rate of our currency relentlessly upward. This made our imports cheaper and our exports more expensive. The result was a rapidly deteriorating trade balance.

The large U.S. trade deficits proved quite beneficial in the short run. Domestic inflation was kept in check as our industries faced increased competitive pressures both at home and abroad. Because of cheap imports Americans experienced a significant improvement in their purchasing power, despite only modest wage increases. And the United States, increasingly acting as the "consumer of last resort" for the rest of the world, became the locomotive for global recovery. Its trade deficits allowed other countries to pursue export-led growth without abandoning fiscal austerity and other restrictions on domestic consumption.

After a couple of years of recovery, however, the negative aspects of this growth pattern began to emerge. The extraordinary rise of the dollar in 1983 and 1984 depressed sales for our manufacturing and agriculture sectors at home and abroad. Regions with a strong concentration of these industries (e.g., the Midwest, Southwest) faced brutal decline. But industries without foreign competition, such as many services, construction, and retailing, continued to expand rapidly. This division added to intersectoral imbalances and intensified uneven development among regions. The U.S. economy became increasingly bicoastal and based on services. The crisis of trade-dependent sectors, especially energy and farming, fueled protectionist pressures at home and trade conflicts with other nations. Default of many farm and energy loans made an already shaky banking system even more vulnerable. Thus, acting as a drag on domestic industry and banking, our rapidly rising trade deficits slowed U.S. growth rates from the earlier 5 to 6 percent per annum in 1983–84 to a much more moderate annual level of 2 to 3 percent after 1985.

That slowdown, triggering the automatic fiscal stabilizers, reduced the growth in tax revenues and caused larger outlays for entitlement programs. The resulting increase to our already enormous budget deficits required additional foreign capital inflows, which in turn drove the dollar and our trade deficits even higher. This mutually feeding interdependence between our budget and trade deficits caused the United States in 1985 to become—for the first time since World War I (1914–18)—a debtor nation. Between 1980 and 1989 our net capital position vis-à-vis the rest of the world had moved from a positive $400 billion in net assets to a negative $600 billion in net liabilities.

While many Americans may feel a great deal of unease to realize that the United States has turned from being the once-dominant creditor into the world's largest debtor within a decade, they also need to keep in mind that this country is not in the same constrained position as other debtor nations. Apart from having the largest and most diversified economy, it has also benefited from being the principal issuer of world money and thus having its balance-of-payments deficits automatically financed by foreigners willing to hold dollar reserves (see our discussion of seigniorage at the beginning of this chapter). In other words, the United States has had the unique privilege of being able to borrow from the rest of the world in its own currency.

Even though it has been much easier for the United States than for any other nation to attract funds from abroad, our debtor status is not without burden. We need to service this external debt, which transfers each year 1 percent of our GDP abroad. Such a resource transfer means proportionately less of the income gains generated in the United States go to Americans, one of the key factors why so many of our workers have seen their wage income stagnate or even decline (in inflation-adjusted "real" terms) in recent years. Since those debt-servicing charges show up as a debit item in our services account with the rest of the world, they also tend to feed our current-account deficits which we cover with additional borrowings. Yet at some point foreigners may well become saturated with dollar-denominated assets and refuse to provide us with additional funds. Any such slowdown in capital imports would drive U.S. interest rates rapidly higher and in this way endanger domestic recovery.

Precisely such a situation arose in the second half of 1989, when foreign investors quite suddenly slowed the recycling of their surplus dollars to the United States. Part of this reaction came about because of changed circumstances of creditor nations, especially an investment boom in the European Community in the aftermath of the "single market" initiative of 1987 and retrenchment by Japanese investors with the collapse of their speculative "bubble" economy. More lucrative investment opportunities opened up elsewhere, especially in those LDCs turning themselves into emerging markets. The U.S. economy, on the other hand, had at that point become less attractive for foreign investors already heavily vested in dollar-denominated assets. Nearing its full-employment capacity after seven years of uninterrupted expansion, it had begun to show signs of renewed inflation while the dollar faced continuous devaluation pressures. Both factors posed increased price risks for foreign investors which then-prevailing yields on dollar-denominated assets did not adequately compensate for. As foreign capital inflows began to slow considerably during the second half of 1989, U.S. interest rates began to rise in sustained fashion to the point of triggering a recession by mid-1990.

With the beginning of U.S. recovery in 1992 (while both Europe and Japan remained mired in deep recession), capital flows to the United States resumed at a heavy pace. Today we owe the rest of the world nearly $1 trillion and continue to add to that considerable sum between $100 billion and $150 billion each year. As Clinton's budget reversal in 1993 and the Fed's tightening in 1994–95 illustrate, such a dependence on foreign capital puts added pressure on our policy makers to keep structural budget deficits in check and pursue an anti-inflationary policy of high "real" interest rates—the two principal policy priorities of bondholders at home and abroad. Yet it also seems obvious that the relative degree of freedom enjoyed by the United States on account of its seigniorage benefit is still sufficient to allow for a gradually devaluing dollar and even declining short-term interest rates without necessarily triggering capital flight. While our dependence on foreign capital continues, the composition of our capital imports has improved in recent years to the extent that the share of long-term direct investments coming into this country has steadily increased. Finally, and this may be the most encouraging bit of news, the U.S. economy has become once again much more competitive in light of a cheaper dollar, falling labor unit costs, improvements in product quality, trimmed-down corporate structures, and a strong presence in the new high-tech growth industries of the future.

## Notes

1. This liberalization of trade was achieved through several multilateral agreements to eliminate or lower duties and quotas, such as the General Agreement on Tariffs and Trade in 1947 and the Kennedy Round in the early 1960s. Certain regions, such as Western Europe, Latin America, and Southeast Asia, established free trading zones in the form of common markets.

2. Standard exchange-rate theories, especially the "monetary approach" (see Jacob Frenkel, 1976), all base their equilibrium models on the assumptions of efficient markets and rational expectations. But the overwhelming empirical evidence to the contrary has engendered various new approaches within the established orthodoxy, such as the "overshooting" model of Rudiger Dornbusch (1976), the "random walk" (see David Backus, 1984), and the "rational bubble" model (see Richard Meese, 1986). For a most interesting analysis of the medium-term cycles and short-term fluctuations of currency prices under the present system, see Stephan Schulmeister (1983, 1987).

3. The most reliable estimates of the daily transaction volume in foreign exchange markets come from regular Federal Reserve surveys. See also Ian Giddy (1979), Patricia Revey (1981), Michael Andrews (1984), and Bank of England (1986) for earlier studies of foreign exchange trading which document the takeoff of this market a decade ago.

4. In 1982, U.S. bank claims on non-OPEC LDCs amounted to $103.2 billion or 154 percent of their capital. The nine largest domestic banks had lent an astonishing 227 percent of their capital to LDCs.

5. Even though the specific problems differ from country to country, many LDCs face the same urgent needs for land reform, expansion of social services, infrastructure investments, containment of the military, more effective taxation of the rich, labor legislation, abolition of protected monopolies, and industrial diversification.

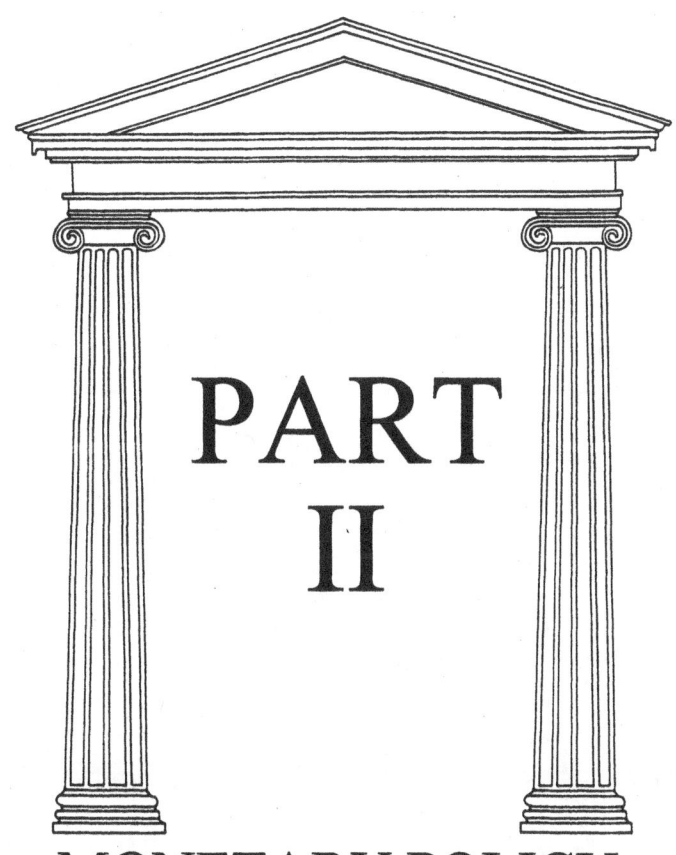

# PART II

## MONETARY POLICY: DEBATES AND VIEWPOINTS

CHAPTER 4 | RECENT POLICY DILEMMAS OF THE FEDERAL RESERVE

# The Federal Reserve as Policy Maker

ROBERT GUTTMANN

The proper conduct of monetary policy is a key issue of contention in economic theory. The controversies surrounding this issue usually focus on two distinct sets of questions. The first concerns the *structure* of the central bank. How should it be related to the rest of the government? Given the money-creation powers of private banks, what kind of relationship should the central bank have with those institutions? To what extent can and should its functions of monetary policy and bank regulation be separated? The second set of questions concerns the *operating targets* the central bank should use when formulating policy. Each variant of monetary theory stresses different targets, and recent U.S. monetary policy has been characterized by a great deal of ad hoc experimentation in this regard.

## The central bank as monetary authority and regulator

The central bank occupies a unique position in government as the monetary authority of the state. This function requires a large degree of institutional independence from the executive and legislative branches, otherwise the central bank cannot resist political pressures by either body for faster money growth to finance expensive government programs. On the other hand, too much independence is often seen to come at the direct expense of its public accountability and democratic control. Given the immense powers of a central bank and the often enormous impact of its policies, it is not surprising that this problem has often been the subject of heated debate among politicians as well as policy makers in the United States.

As the monetary authority, the central bank also has to regulate the creation of private bank money. This raises a second issue concerning its structure: the relationship between the central bank and the commercial banks it regulates. Conservatives such as Milton Friedman (1985) tend to criticize the regulatory powers of the Federal Reserve as excessive and harmful. In contrast, their liberal opponents maintain that the central bank has been "captured" by the banks and therefore tends to favor their interests in its policy choices.

## Earlier failures in central banking

The extent to which the structure of the central bank raises complicated political questions was illustrated dramatically by the failure of earlier efforts to set up a monetary authority in our country. In 1791 Congress chartered the First Bank of the United States; it combined both private bank activities (i.e., making loans, taking deposits, issuing bank notes) and public policy functions (i.e., regulating private bank issue of notes, transferring funds across the nation, acting as fiscal agent for the government). Even though functioning reasonably well, this bank was abolished twenty years later amidst a great deal of political opposition.

State banks complained of unfair competition by the First Bank. They also objected to its practice of disciplining overextended banks by draining their reserves through massive redemption of their note issues. Their opposition won the support of agricultural interests and rural politicians who feared that First Bank would siphon off funds to the cities for industrial investment and curb the "easy money" policies of state banks. Antifederalists considered First Bank unconstitutional. The Second Bank of the United States (1816–36) met with much the same antipathy as its predecessor. The contradiction between central banking functions (e.g., control over currency issue by state banks) and commercial banking business was in this case even more pronounced. Not only did the Second Bank control nearly one-third of all the bank assets, but its private ownership structure invited fraud and corruption.[1]

The shortcomings of the state banks after 1836, most notably their propensity to failure and the unreliability of their bank notes, led to major bank reform during the Civil War. But the National Banking Acts of 1863 and 1864 did not reinstate federal centralized control of banking. Instead, those acts tried to replace state banks with a system of federally chartered ("national") banks and standardized bank notes. Those national banks had to keep minimum reserve requirements against their notes and deposits, ranging from 15 percent for country banks to 25 percent for big city banks. The particular modalities of these reserve requirements created two major problems:

• National banks were required to hold Treasury bonds as security against any note they issued. This made the supply of national bank notes solely dependent on the U.S. government bond market and thus "inelastic" to economic needs.

• In addition, the national banking system allowed legal pyramiding of reserves by permitting country banks to count their deposits in city banks as part of their reserves. City banks competed hard for those deposits, because they could loan them out for additional income. During harvest season, when rural banks distributed large amounts of currency, they exchanged their reserves for cash. With their cash holdings thus depleted, large city banks often had to liquidate loans. This reduction in bank credit would then in turn set off a liquidity squeeze, soon followed by panic sales of financial assets in declining markets.

## How the Federal Reserve works

The Federal Reserve Act of 1913 took account of these earlier failures. For example, it introduced an elastic form of paper currency into the economy, Federal Reserve notes. Moreover, the new central bank was consciously given a decentralized structure, with the twelve *Federal Reserve Banks* set up to represent regional interests and to provide for the credit needs of their regions by issuing currency and determining the discount rates charged on loans to qualifying banks in their district. In the aftermath of the Great Depression, however, the Federal Reserve became more centralized, with much of the decision-making power passing from the regional Fed banks to the seven-member Federal Reserve *Board of Governors* in Washington, D.C. The Banking Act of 1935 set up the Federal Open Market Committee (FOMC), consisting of the seven governors and five presidents of regional Fed banks, to oversee purchases and sales of U.S. government securities.

Ever since that 1935 Act the Federal Reserve has used three monetary policy tools to change (excess) reserves in the banking system:

• It can set *reserve requirements* for different types of bank deposits within specified limits. Lower reserve ratios leave banks with more excess reserves for any given sum of total reserves, and vice versa.

• As the fiscal agent of the government, the Federal Reserve conducts purchases and sales of Treasury securities (i.e., *open market operations*). When the Fed buys securities, it pays for them by adding new reserves to the banking system. Its sales have the opposite effect, since it gets paid with checks that are debited from the reserve accounts of the banks on which they were drawn.

• Finally, the Federal Reserve offers *discount loans* to reserve-deficient banks. Those loans are paid out by simply adding an equivalent amount to the reserve account of the borrowing bank. The central bank can influence demand for these loans by setting the discount rate and eligibility requirements.

Unlike its unsuccessful predecessors, the Federal Reserve was not allowed to engage in commercial activities that competed directly with private banks.[2] While national banks chartered under the Bank Acts of 1863–64 are automatically part of the Federal Reserve System, state banks have a choice of whether or not to join. Since member banks are required to purchase stock of their district's bank, they actually own those regional Federal Reserve Banks. Even though member banks do not enjoy the usual privileges and powers of stockholders in private corporations, they can elect six of their regional bank's nine directors, who in turn pick its president. This blending of private influences into the corporate organization of the Federal Reserve Banks made sure that the central bank kept commercial banking interests in mind.

The Fed's independence from the rest of government was not only assured by this private ownership structure, but also by its budgetary autonomy from congressional appropriations and the rules for the appointment of governors to the Federal Reserve Board in Washington. Governors are appointed by the president (subject to Senate approval) to fourteen-year terms in staggered biannual intervals. Unless some of them resign earlier, each president can therefore only appoint two Fed governors per term. In addition, the four-year term of the chairman does not coincide with that of the president. During the last decade, however, many Fed governors have stepped down before expiration of their term, no doubt because of the comparatively low salaries at the Fed. For this reason, President Reagan was able to pick a whole new board.

As already mentioned, the Fed combines monetary policy tools (e.g., discount loans, reserve requirements, open-market operations) and considerable regulatory powers (e.g., imposing minimum capital requirements and other balance-sheet restrictions). Monetarists and other supporters of the free enterprise system argue that its role as regulator should be reduced, if not entirely abolished. On the other hand, Keynesian and especially Post-Keynesian economists, who worry about financial instability, call for more regulation of financial institutions. But this question goes beyond the traditional ideological split between conservatives and liberals. It has now entered the arena of policy making for two very pragmatic reasons (see also chapter 8).

• One factor is the ongoing regulatory overhaul with regard to financial institutions, which began in the late 1970s and is now rapidly approaching its climax. The problem here is to find the proper balance between market-driven financial restructuring and regulatory constraints on the instability-prone behavior of those institutions.

• The other is the difficult coexistence of several regulatory agencies (e.g., state banking commissions, the U.S. Treasury's Comptroller of Currency, the Federal Deposit Insurance Corporation, and the Federal Reserve) with often overlapping responsibilities and a long history of rivalry. This institutional patchwork needs streamlining to improve the division of labor and coordination among these different regulators. Any resolution of this issue has so far been blocked by the problem of defining what regulatory powers the Fed needs to have in order to conduct its monetary policies effectively.

## Monetary policy strategies in historical perspective

The different variants of standard monetary theory have sharply divergent views concerning monetary policy.

• Keynesians see contracyclical monetary policy as an important tool for reducing the amplitude of business cycle fluctuations. Toward this objective they want the Federal Reserve to focus on credit conditions, especially short-term interest rates.[3]

• Monetarists reject the use of discretionary monetary policy for short-term stabilization purposes, stressing unpredictable time lags and the negative effects of such a "stop–go" policy on the economy. Instead they want the Federal Reserve to focus on the long run and make sure that the money supply expands in line with the economy's natural growth rate (the so-called monetary rule). In addition, they recommend changes in the Fed's operating procedures to improve its control over the money supply.

• Supply-siders stress the importance of tying money issue once again to available gold reserves. In the absence of such a return to the gold standard, they want commodity prices used as the main indicator in the formulation of monetary policy.

For most of the postwar period the Federal Reserve focused primarily on interest rates, reflecting a Keynesian bias. During and after World War II it "pegged" Treasury securities at yields ranging from 0.375 percent to 2.5 percent (depending on maturity) by buying any excess supplies of these debt instruments at prices that maintained yields at those fixed levels. This purchasing policy increased (excess) reserves in the banking system. Because of war-related credit controls, the banks lent these funds mostly to firms involved in war production or bought government securities.

When the domestic economy began to overheat in the wake of the Korean War and inflation suddenly shot up, the Federal Reserve wanted to apply a more restrictive policy. The *Federal Reserve-Treasury Accord* of 1951 ended this "pegging," thereby enabling long-term rates to rise. That agreement freed the Fed to undertake discretionary open-market operations. From 1953 on the Fed followed a "bills only" policy which reflected its primary focus on short-term rates. In 1961 this policy was relaxed in favor of "operation twist" to flatten the yield curve (i.e., difference between short-term and long-term interest rates). Facing a troublesome combination of a weak economy and balance-of-payments problems, the Fed bought Treasury bonds to reduce their yields in the interest of domestic expansion while at the same time selling Treasury bills to raise short-term rates and thereby slow capital outflows. Hence the Fed's concern with interest rates was extended to their maturity structure. In 1966 and 1969 the Fed responded to an overheating economy by adopting temporarily a more restrictive policy that allowed higher rates.

The acceleration of inflation during the 1970s enabled the Monetarists to gain steadily in influence:

• Their first big policy success came in 1971–73 when the Bretton Woods system of a gold-backed U.S. dollar and fixed exchange rates gave way to a system of flexible exchange rates and inconvertible currencies as world money (see chapter 3).

• At the same time Monetarists pressured the Federal Reserve to focus more on bank reserves and monetary aggregates rather than on credit conditions. In 1972, a year of rapidly rising inflation, the Fed finally complied by choosing reserves available for private nonbank deposits (RPDs) as its new operating target and adopting for the first time explicit growth ranges for $M_1$ and $M_2$. This RPD experiment lasted for only three years.[4]

• In March 1975, amidst growing concerns about persistent inflation despite a deepening recession, Congress asked the Fed to specify and disclose annual growth targets for monetary and credit aggregates on a quarterly basis.

• Finally, in October 1979 Monetarism gained its last and most decisive victory in the United States when the Fed abandoned its policy of keeping short-term interest rates below inflation (by "pegging" the Federal funds rate within a fixed range) in favor of tight restrictions on money growth.[5] This dramatic policy switch came amidst a collapsing U.S. dollar and turmoil in global commodity markets, both of which had pushed domestic inflation close to 15 percent per year during 1979.

In March 1980 the Fed reinforced restraint by introducing selective credit controls, especially against consumer debt. The resulting cutbacks in borrowing and spending led to an extremely steep decline of economic activity in the first half of 1980. Attempts to revive the economy in late 1980 proved short-lived, as the conditions of instability and overheating prevailing in 1979 reappeared rapidly. Renewed tightening by the Fed led after July 1981 to the worst postwar recession, propelled by record-high interest rates. Only in August 1982, after more than a year of dramatic "disinflation" and defaults (e.g., Penn Square, Mexico), did the central bank switch once again to a more accommodative policy in support of faster economic growth.

In October 1982 the Fed ended its Monetarist experiment officially when it abandoned monetary aggregates as its policy target. One reason for this change in policy was that the record-high interest rates and slow money-supply growth over the preceding three years had finally broken the inflationary momentum in the economy, but did so only by triggering two back-to-back recessions of remarkable force which by mid-1982 had pushed the economy to the brink of depression. In the face of mounting unemployment, loan defaults, and bankruptcies, the Fed's concern shifted from fighting inflation to counteracting those deflationary forces. The other reason for the abandonment of Monetarism, and the one central bank officials used in their public announcements as justification, was the impossibility to target money-supply measures accurately in an environment of deregulated banking.

Following deregulation in 1980, banks had introduced various interest-bearing checking accounts and other forms of "near-money" deposits (e.g., money-market funds, consumer certificates of deposits). This new generation of private bank money, combining transaction and investment motives, behaved in an inherently unpredictable fashion and thus threw long-established relationships between the monetary base (i.e., currency and bank reserves), the aggregate money supply, and gross domestic product into disarray. Yet the predictability of these relationships, assuming the money supply to be a stable multiple of the monetary base and an equally stable fraction of GDP, is essential to the Monetarist argument in favor of central bank pursuit of slow and steady money-supply growth as the best guarantor of price stability. Once these stability assumptions no longer prevailed in the aftermath of banking deregulation, the Fed had no choice but to abandon the targeting of monetary aggregates prescribed by the Monetarists.

## The Fed's strategic compromise

The failure of the Monetarist experiment forced the Federal Reserve to develop a new monetary policy strategy. Since October 1982 the Fed has resumed its "pegging" of the Federal funds rate (see note 5), thus returning once again to the preferred policy target of the Keynesians. Yet at the same time the U.S. monetary authorities have retained Monetarism's anti-inflationary bias, thus continuing to regard price stability as their overriding policy objective. In practical terms, this has meant that the Fed no longer tries to keep those short-term interest rates it controls (e.g., discount rate, federal funds rate) at the kind of artificially low levels last seen in the 1970s. Instead, rather than following relatively fixed target ranges, the Fed has been adjusting its federal funds rate targets frequently in response to several indicators of future inflation. One is the yield curve, which nowadays tends to get steeper whenever an intensification of inflationary expectations causes bondholders to push long-term rates higher. The second is commodity prices, often an early gauge for future inflation. And the third is the exchange rate, with a rapidly falling dollar making imports more expensive and thus usually creating upward pressure on prices. Even though each of these indicators may behave quite erratically on its own, together they constitute a clear "early warning" signal for future inflation when they are moving in unison. In addition, the Fed also pays attention to signs of inflationary pressures in the "real" economy, most notably labor market conditions and lead times in deliveries of production materials.

This anti-inflationary bias has led policy makers at the Fed to accept historically high "real" (i.e., inflation-adjusted) interest rates in order to keep inflationary pressures subdued. One justification for this high-interest policy has been the need to rebuild and maintain *credibility* in the eyes of bondholders, shareholders, and currency traders who had been burned badly by the inflation-induced devaluation of their financial assets in the 1970s. Only renewed confidence by the financial markets in the anti-inflation stance of the Fed, so its policy makers argued, would allow long-term interest rates to come down from their excessively high levels of the early 1980s. This argument did not begin to bear out before the mid-1990s, when it had become finally obvious to even the most skeptical investors that the devil of inflation had been finally laid to rest by a decade of tight economic policy and accelerating industrial restructuring.

The Fed's post-1982 compromise, combining the Monetarist focus on inflation with Keynesian means of implementation, has also meant that the Fed has refused to follow an automatic policy rule, as the Monetarists push for with regard to money-supply growth. Instead the Fed has since 1982 pursued a discretionary policy centered on timely and frequent adjustments of the target range for short-term interest rates. Whenever the indicators have signalled a heightened potential for reawakening inflation, the Fed has tightened. This rapid response system, a crucial ingredient of its "credibility" strategy, has been nicknamed *soft landing,* since it aims to move the economy to a lower growth path without pushing it into recession. By acting early, even preemptively, the central bank hopes to nip inflation in the bud and thus avoid having to take more drastic measures later that could push the economy into a downturn.

Yet during the same period the Fed has also been willing to loosen its reins considerably whenever slowing growth threatened to create acute conditions of distress. That was the case in 1982 when the onset of a global debt crisis threatened to deepen an already painfully steep downturn, in 1984–85 amidst spreading deflation in global commodities markets, after the stock market crash in 1987–88, and in the wake of the 1990–91 recession. In other words, the Fed has over the last fifteen years pursued a basically countercyclical monetary policy via manipulation of interest rates, as prescribed by Keynesians, but with a strongly Monetarist bias of prioritizing the battle against inflation as the primary policy objective.

## The debate continues

The debate between Monetarists and Keynesians concerning monetary policy has not subsided with the attempts of the U.S. central bank in recent years to adopt a middle ground between the two positions. Keynesian economists and their political allies in the Democratic party have consistently criticized Alan Greenspan, since 1987 the chairman of the Federal Reserve, for his excessively cautious approach. By keeping interest rates high, they argue, the Fed has restricted economic growth below its potential and caused higher unemployment than necessary. In that line of argument, the slow growth and stagnant wage incomes of the 1980s and early 1990s appear to have been caused primarily by the U.S. central bank.

Monetarist protagonists of the Fed's high-interest policy argue, in contrast, that keeping inflation in check must remain the primary policy objective of any responsible central bank. Their position has become influential in the aftermath of more than a decade of accelerating inflation, which had increasingly negative consequences for corporate balance sheets and financial asset values. The turmoil brought on by inflation in the 1970s remains even today a painfully vivid memory among bondholders and other kinds of creditors that assumes the quality of an obsession. Investors now react to the slightest sign of renewed inflationary pressures by charging higher inflation premiums in credit transactions, thus pushing up especially long-term rates to the detriment of securities prices.[6] Ever since the deregulation of interest rates in the early 1980s investors have been in a better position to make their inflation fears count more with policy makers. Their influence has grown a lot since the early 1980s when the government allowed greater market regulation of credit by removing key controls over the interest-rate structure, such as maximum-rate ceilings on bank deposits and loans.

The anti-inflationary bias of the Federal Reserve is not only the logical response to pressures from banks and financial investors, but to those imposed by other external forces. Much higher U.S. budget deficits, whose annual level rose tenfold during the 1980s (from around $30 billion in 1979 to over $300 billion in 1992), created huge borrowing needs by the U.S. government which, competing with the private sector for funds, kept interest rates higher than they would have otherwise been. This so-called *crowding out* process soon gained a global dimension when the United States became a net importer of capital in 1982. Facing declining domestic savings amidst chronically large budget deficits as well as record-high trade deficits exceeding $100 billion a year for most of the last decade, the United States has come to depend strongly on foreign savings. To attract those funds from abroad, the United States has had to offer foreign investors sufficiently high "real" interest rates compared to other countries.

## The recession of 1990–91

The potential dangers of America's dependence on foreign capital became evident for the first time in late 1989 and early 1990 when capital inflows from abroad suddenly slowed to a trickle (see chapter 3). This reversal, caused by saturation of dollar-denominated assets in the hands of foreigners as much as by external events (i.e., redeployment of European funds in the wake of the European Community's implementation of a single market, retrenchment by Japanese financial institutions, the end of capital flight from Latin America), coincided with "tight money" conditions imposed by the Fed. Worried about full employment and a rise in inflation, the Fed had started to push up interest rates in early 1989 in an effort to slow economic growth before any inflationary overheating would trigger a recessionary adjustment. But this so-called *soft landing* scenario turned into a low-altitude crash of the U.S. economy when foreign capital inflows began to decline precipitously despite higher U.S. interest rates. Underestimating the extent and duration of this capital-flow reversal, the Fed kept credit conditions too tight for too long. By mid-1990 the U.S. economy had slipped into a recession.

That downturn soon revealed a dramatic degree of *financial fragility* in the U.S. economy, centering in particular on a troubled banking sector burdened by bad-debt losses (see chapter 6 for more details on this crisis). Having been politically burned by the mismanagement of the thrift crisis, which ended in an expensive taxpayer bailout, the Bush administration had reason to fear a potentially even more costly banking crisis. This nightmare scenario was averted when the Federal Reserve reversed its "tight money" course and pushed interest rates aggressively lower throughout 1990–91. By late 1991, U.S. short-term interest rates had fallen to their lowest levels in nearly thirty years. With long-term rates much more resistant to declines, banks reaped the rewards of an extraordinarily steep *yield curve* in the form of much-enlarged yield spreads between their short-term liabilities and their long-term assets. Such a Fed-induced boost in their profit margins allowed many troubled banks to rebuild their capital base and thereby avert potential failure. As noted by Kaufman (see reprint below), the monetary accommodation provided by the U.S. central bank during the recession also facilitated extensive refinancing operations to ease the debt servicing burdens of otherwise heavily leveraged private-sector debtors. Lower U.S. interest rates had the additional positive consequence of easing pressure on other central banks and making it easier for many developing countries to exit from their decade-long debt crisis.

## The Fed's preemptive strike of 1994

The positive spillover effects of low interest rates eventually triggered a recovery in the United States. Initially, however, the upswing was very slow and uneven. Throughout 1992 and much of 1993, production barely grew, unemployment remained stubbornly high, wages did not rise, and the stock market was stuck in a narrow trading range. Depressed conditions in Europe and Japan provided further impetus for the Fed to continue its accommodating stance.

For Henry Kaufman, as elaborated in his testimony to the House in July 1993 (reprinted below), these constraints were not just cyclical in nature, but reflected structural (and thus more long-term) changes in the economy fueled by globalization of economic activity and rapid technological advances. In his opinion those forces precluded inflation from rising above its remarkably persistent range of 2 to 3 percent. The combination of an accelerating industrial restructuring process and depressed labor-market conditions justified continued emphasis on low interest rates. For Kaufman this objective would be best achieved by international coordination among key central banks (i.e., Fed, Bank of Japan, German Bundesbank) aimed at simultaneous interest-rate cuts.

Ignoring Kaufman's warnings concerning any premature tightening of monetary policy, Fed Chairman Alan Greenspan called for precisely such a course when the U.S. economy finally showed signs of accelerating recovery in mid-1993. In his Congressional testimony of July 1993 (see the reprint below), Greenspan noted the first signs of accelerating inflation in the wake of strengthening recovery and warned that those might soon prompt an appropriate response by the Fed. Addressing the obsolescence of traditional Monetarist prescriptions for slow growth of monetary aggregates in light of their sudden unreliability in a deregulated banking environment, Greenspan proposed in this testimony an alternative policy target that would allow the Fed to pursue its overriding objective of price stability more effectively. The Fed, he declared, would from now on focus on the "equilibrium structure of real (i.e., inflation-adjusted) interest rates." His interpretation of that elusive variable, stressing in particular that real rates on the short end had fallen to near zero and the yield curve needed flattening, was at that point a barely masked reference to the Fed's intention of tightening, first announced in the "asymmetric directive" adopted by its policy-making Federal Open Market Committee in May 1993. We shall see in the following chapter how this renewed incidence of tightening by the Fed played itself out.

## Notes

1. See Charles Kindleberger (1978, p. 124) for a discussion of the Second Bank's fraudulent practice which made it in effect a "speculative bubble" bound to burst.

2. Recent advances in computer and telecommunications technology have allowed private investors to offer new kinds of payments services, such as credit card systems, automated clearinghouses for preauthorized bill payments, or points-of-sale systems linking retail outlets and banks. Moreover, Congress required the Fed in 1980 to start charging for its payments services in order to encourage private competition. But since then the central bank has maintained its dominant market share by charging low prices and attracting enough volume to remain the lowest-cost supplier. There is a strong argument in favor of continued Federal Reserve control over our payments system. After all, it is the only institution capable of creating additional reserves to prevent disruption in the flow of payments.

3. Post-Keynesian economists, trying to salvage Keynes' original ideas from their "bastardization" into an orthodox equilibrium framework, favor even stronger measures, especially selective credit controls, which Keynes (1930) himself approved of. See in this context Basil Moore (1983) and Stephen Rousseas (1986).

4. The RPD experiment was not successful, since this target proved highly elusive and did not relate in stable fashion to the monetary aggregates. For this reason the FOMC stopped specifying RPD targets in early 1976 and chose once again the Federal funds rate (on short-term interbank loans) as its principal target.

5. Federal funds are short-term loans from banks with excess reserves to reserve-deficient banks and other depository institutions. As such they are a very sensitive indicator of changes in bank reserves. The presence of large excess reserves means low demand for these funds relative to supply, causing the rate to fall. The opposite holds for tight reserve positions. The Federal Reserve "pegs" the Fed funds rate within a specified target range through corresponding reserve adjustments. For example, whenever the rate nears its upper target limit, the Fed adds reserves (through open market purchases). This policy illustrates that the Fed cannot control interest rates and bank reserves (i.e., the money supply) at the same time.

6. Interest rates and the prices of bonds and stocks are inversely related. They move automatically in opposite directions for several reasons. Most important, the prices of bonds and stocks are based on the present value of future cash flows expected from these claims. The discounting of these cash flows to present value depends on prevailing interest rates. When these go up, present values of future cash flows (and thus the market value of securities) fall automatically. Securities prices also decline, not least because higher interest rates represent larger business costs and thus the prospect of lower future profits upon which market valuations of securities prices are based. Finally, higher interest rates also reduce the demand for securities in the financial markets by making it more expensive for investors to borrow funds with which to finance securities purchases.

HENRY KAUFMAN

# Opportunities and Challenges Confronting Monetary Policy

*With the credit creation process still moribund, coordinated monetary accommodation would make a valuable contribution to invigorating growth and would be an acceptable risk to take.*

Mr. Chairman, I am pleased to accept your invitation to give my views on the conduct of monetary policy in the United States before this Committee of the Congress.

Over the most recent business cycle, monetary policy has had to contend with extraordinary economic and financial circumstances, which posed great challenges to the formulation and implementation of appropriate policies. Even now, with a moderate economic recovery under way, a number of unconventional elements continue to complicate this task. An unusually large number of business corporations and households have grown wary of debt, and they are trying to reduce their liabilities. Many financial institutions, which experienced a close brush with financial difficulty or saw their competitors narrowly evade adversity, have become more averse to taking risks in their lending and investing. Moreover, profound changes in the workings of our financial markets have had the largely unpredicted side-effect of severing what had been thought of as dependable linkages between the monetary aggregates and the behavior of the economy at large.

The implication of these developments is that our central bank no longer has a reliable measuring rod with which to calibrate monetary policy. It has no choice but to rely on judgment. Therefore, the issue at hand is how it should exercise judgment in the complex period ahead, when we can look forward to modest, but not dynamic, economic growth in the United States, a far more troubled economic and financial environment in Europe and Japan, and sometimes contradictory impulses acting on the rate of inflation.

## Accomplishments of monetary policy during the recent cycle

The Federal Reserve currently has considerable latitude to exercise judgment, because its credibility has been enhanced by recent monetary policy accomplishments. It is worthwhile to take note of them:

*First,* interest rates have been lowered significantly. While it's possible to express misgivings about whether the Federal Reserve always pursued monetary accom-

HENRY KAUFMAN is President of Henry Kaufman & Company, Inc. He delivered this statement before the Committee on Banking, Housing, and Urban Affairs of the United States Senate, July 1, 1993. Reprinted from *Challenge,* September–October 1993, pp. 11–19.

modation with sufficient alacrity, it is undeniable that the central bank has managed to bring down short-term interest rates to around 3 percent, from over 10 percent in 1989 and 6 percent in April 1991, when the statisticians say the last recession ended. This slide in short-term interest rates has had a constructive effect on the long-term bond market as well. By the beginning of this week, the yield on 30-year U.S. Treasury obligations, which is now the bellwether for the U.S. fixed-income markets, had declined below 6.75 percent, from over 9 percent in 1989 and 8.25 percent in April 1991.

To be sure, the decline in short-term rates exceeded that of intermediate- and long-term rates by a large margin, producing an exceptionally steep, positively sloped yield curve. But that positively sloped yield curve has provided considerable benefits to the American economy and financial system. Specifically, it has helped in the financial rehabilitation of banks, savings and loans, and other financial institutions which had suffered from excessive lending to the troubled commercial real estate sector or to highly leveraged corporations. By taking advantage of the upwardly sloped yield curve to make profitable investments without having to absorb additional credit risk, these institutions were able to repair their financial positions. Higher profitability permitted them to rebuild their capital ratios and regain access to the equity and bond markets, which had been all but closed to most financial institutions as recently as two years ago. The consequence has been to greatly reduce the number of actual and potential failures of financial institutions, requiring less of a call on the resources of the Federal Deposit Insurance Corporation funds, and ultimately less of a burden on taxpayers. Without the kind of interest rate decline that the Federal Reserve has instigated, we would be looking at a far more vulnerable financial system, even less able to lend and invest than the one we have now. Accordingly, overall economic prospects would be far gloomier than they are.

*Second,* gradual declines in interest rates across the maturity spectrum have been supportive of large-scale bond issuance by corporations, by financial institutions, and by state and local governments. This has permitted the refinancing of higher-cost existing debt, thereby lowering interest expenses. It has also been supportive of sizable issuance of new equity by large and small enterprises, which has reduced leverage and strengthened balance sheets. This outpouring of new issues of bonds and stocks would not have been possible without significant declines in interest rates.

Table 4  **Federal Reserve Purchases of U.S. Treasury Obligations** ($ billion)

| | | Coupons | | | |
|---|---|---|---|---|---|
| | Bills | Total | Less than 5 years | Over 5 years | Total |
| 1989 | −11.3 | 3.3 | 3.5 | −0.2 | −8.0 |
| 1990 | 13.1 | 1.0 | 2.7 | −1.7 | 14.1 |
| 1991 | 19.0 | 12.0 | 10.1 | 1.9 | 31.0 |
| 1992 | 11.5 | 19.4 | 11.7 | 7.7 | 30.9 |
| 1993 (To Date) | 7.0 | 8.1 | 3.1 | 5.0 | 15.1 |

*Source:* Federal Reserve Bulletin.

*Third,* lower interest rates have been conducive to a record amount of refinancing of existing mortgages. This has allowed millions of homeowners to improve their financial positions, through a combination of lower interest payments and faster repayment of mortgage principal. As a result, over time, the household sector will be able to be more active as consumers and thus to contribute to economic growth.

*Fourth,* while it is true that monetary policy acts mainly on the short end of the maturity spectrum, so that its impact on longer-term interest rates is largely indirect, it should be recognized that the Federal Reserve has encouraged the downtrend in longer-term interest rates more directly through useful modifications in the technical aspects of its open market operations. Specifically, from time to time over the past couple of years, it has added permanent reserves to the banking system by acquiring sizable quantities of U.S. Treasury coupon issues, in addition to its periodic purchases of Treasury bills. As Table 4 shows, the Federal Reserve bought just $14 billion of U.S. government obligations in 1990, of which 93 percent were Treasury bills and just 7 percent were in longer-dated securities. In 1991 and 1992, however, these purchases rose to $31 billion per year and, by 1992, some 65 percent consisted of coupon issues. Especially noteworthy have been the sharp increases in the takedown of governments with maturities over five years, an increase that has accelerated so far this year.

It should also be noted that the new financing initiatives undertaken by the U.S. Treasury this year will also tend to promote lower longer-term interest rates in the United States. Treasury has reduced the magnitude of new issuance of long-term bonds and has announced that it will cut back substantially on future 30-year bond issues by moving to two yearly auctions from four. This is a policy direction I have long favored, not so much because it will reduce the Treasury's overall borrowing costs, but because it will open up opportunities for the private sector to issue debt for very long-term maturities. That will allow business corporations to make desirable longer-term commitments, augmenting their financial resources to fund additional plant and equipment expenditures, research and development activities, and other business expansion. It is notable that, in the past few months, Boeing, Conrail, and Ford Motor Credit have come to the market with noncallable 50-year bond issues, while Texaco has issued 50-year bonds noncallable for 20 years. These are rare events in the fixed-income markets, and it is heartening that they were all well received by investors. The modification in U.S. Treasury debt-management practices is not the principal reason why these long-term issues were successfully brought to market, but it was helpful.

## U.S. economic setting

Let me now turn to the outlook for the U.S. economy and for the inflation rate, which primarily sets the backdrop against which Federal Reserve monetary policy must be formulated. From my perspective, there is little likelihood of an imminent acceleration in the pace of business activity or pickup in inflationary pressures that would justify an immediate tightening of monetary policy. All in all, we seem to be bottoming out cyclically in the inflation rate. In this context, the recent decision by the Federal Open Market Committee to adopt a so-called asymmetrical directive can be interpreted as an attempt to quiet inflationary expectations by reemphasizing the central bank's commitment to subdue inflation. But from a practical policy perspective, it was premature. The basic economic case for a move toward monetary restraint is not yet in place. I would draw your attention to the following factors:

*First,* while there are some elements of moderate strength in the business situation, notably demand for cars and light trucks and outlays for new business equipment, the manufacturing sector as a whole is not on solid footing yet. Durable goods orders are fading, and order backlogs are slipping. Lingering problems in manufacturing are especially evident with regard to job prospects. In contrast to an overall rise in payroll employment for the private business sector, employment in manufacturing has fallen this year, and surveys of business hiring intentions—such as the National Association of Purchasing Managers monthly report—indicate that more companies are planning to reduce staff than are planning to add to staff. I understand that there are some analysts who note that average weekly hours worked in manufacturing have climbed to near record levels and that this may be a precursor of new hiring.

I do not share that view. The relatively high figure for average weekly hours in manufacturing probably reflects a change in the composition of manufacturing employment due to corporate restructuring. Permanent layoffs of support personnel result in a diminishing proportion of salaried staff who work a shorter average work week, and a commensurately higher proportion of hourly workers who tend to have a longer average work week. Restructuring can be expected to have a lasting effect in lowering the number of jobs in manufacturing and perpetuating an unaccustomed frailty in labor markets in the United States.

*Second,* as I mentioned, business investment spending on new equipment has been a relatively strong component of gross domestic product (GDP) over the past several quarters. But its continuation is now questionable in view of the withdrawal of the proposed incremental investment tax credit. Defense-related capital goods orders are conspicuously weak, reflecting the continuing downsizing of the military, but even orders for nondefense capital goods are languishing.

*Third,* U.S. export prospects are diminishing. That is because of the continuing slowdown in the European economies, the extraordinary economic and political uncertainties in Japan, and the increasing degree of international competition in Asian and Latin American markets. I will return to the question of how serious is the economic malaise in the other industrial countries later in my statement. For now, I merely want to stress that merchandise exports cannot be counted on as an important source of stimulus for our domestic economy, as long as the economic growth of our main competitors abroad remains inert.

Taking these factors together, I see little danger that manufacturing output will increase so rapidly in the coming months as to raise the rate of capacity utilization to a level that would bring about a pronounced acceleration of inflation (see Figure 1).

*Fourth,* even outside the manufacturing sector, which accounts for only about one-fifth of total employment, the American labor market remains quite soft, notwithstanding the slight pickup in private sector employment this year. The growth in payroll employment

Figure 1

**Capacity Utilization Rate**
(and Y/Y % change in CPI)

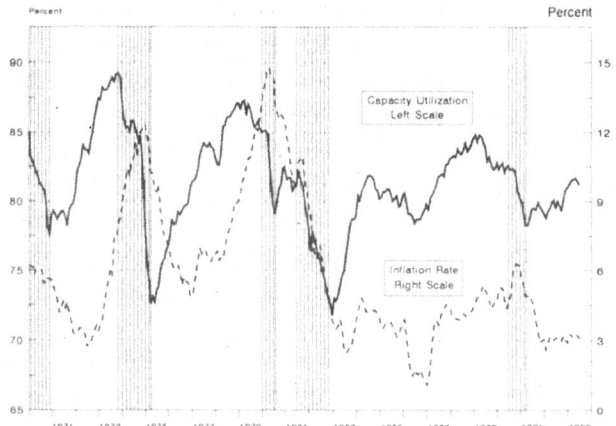

still lags well behind that in previous business expansions, and there seems to be a growing concentration of joblessness among higher-pay groups, such as middle management personnel and professional staff. Newly graduated college students and others leaving school report exceptional difficulty in attaining suitable employment. Thus, it is highly likely that the subdued wage and compensation behavior will continue to retard inflation (see Figure 2).

Figure 2 **Employment Cost Index**

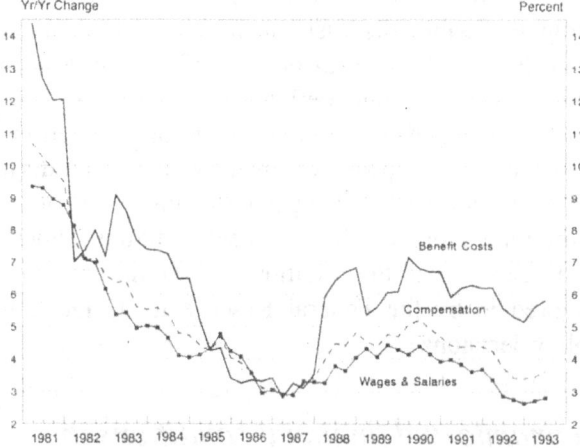

*Fifth*, there are still formidable drags on economic activity stemming from the overbuilding of commercial real estate and the financial consequences of excessive lending to this area. Real estate values continue to fall in important regional markets, most notably southern California, and new commercial building remains depressed in many areas of the country. No amount of jawboning by officials in Washington will change the economic reality that real estate development must endure a long period of adjustment before effective demand is brought back into conformity with overbuilt supply.

*Sixth*, home building has moved ahead, particularly of single-family houses, but the increase in home construction is lagging well below cyclical dimensions. There is little likelihood of a surge in fresh housing-related credit demand—as distinct from mortgage refinancing that generates little net new credit demand—that could pressure credit markets any time soon.

*Seventh*, indeed, there is little evidence of a general rise in net credit demands almost anywhere in the economy. Neither overall commercial bank lending nor short-term business credit (which includes commercial and industrial loans made by banks plus nonfinancial commercial paper) has demonstrated sustained growth over recent months (see Figure 3).

Figure 3 **Short-Term Business Borrowing**
(C&I loans and nonfinancial commercial paper)

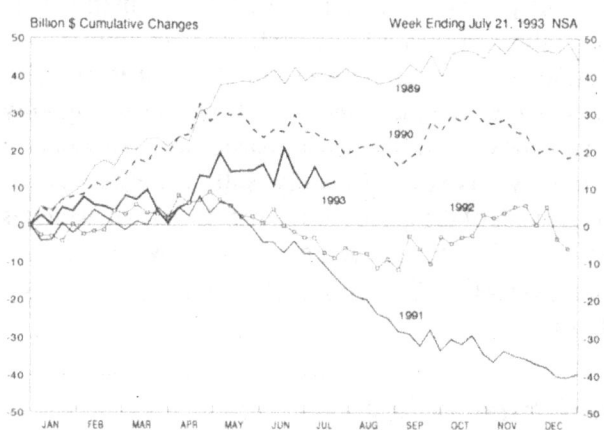

Why is this important? Because it shows that business is staying within itself. Businesses are able to finance virtually all contemplated activities—including work in progress, inventories, and planned plant and equipment expenditures—from internally generated funds. It also suggests a relative paucity of new risk-taking ventures requiring debt finance. While this caution is probably compatible with the continuation of moderate economic growth, it is hardly an early precursor of either a robust expansion of business activity or of a substantial lift in the rate of inflation.

*Eighth*, recent behavior of the monetary aggregates, while erratic, is not suggestive of an inflationary break-out. The growth of the targeted monetary supply, $M_2$, remains well below the lower boundary of the Federal Reserve's target band. During the past several weeks, there has been a spurt in the growth of transactions balances, but these possibly reflect problems associated with seasonally adjusting tax payments and with accounting for the monetary consequences of the bulge in mortgage refinancing. In addition, there have been large increases in currency in circulation, which quite likely reflect the expanding use of U.S. dollars in areas of the world wrestling with political or economic instability, such as the former Soviet Republics. These factors have been responsible for the more rapid growth in $M_1$, the narrowly defined version of the money supply. But I doubt that much of this growth signifies sharply increased spending intentions by consumers and businesses here in the United States. The central bank has de-emphasized the importance of the monetary aggregates, and that seems appropriate to me.

*Ninth,* world commodity prices are weak. Far more important than the price of gold or some other precious metal, which the media like to dwell on, is the price of oil. The price of benchmark West Texas Intermediate has fallen to $18.60 a barrel. A year ago, it was $22.50. Other important commodity prices are also quite depressed; the *Journal of Commerce* commodity price index has slipped back sharply after a temporary rise early this year. Generally, soft commodity prices are a result of the global economic slowdown, which is a powerful factor in suppressing worldwide inflation, and eventually will be decisive in lowering world interest rates.

## U.S. fiscal policy

Monetary policy is not made in isolation; obviously, the evolution of U.S. fiscal policy has critical importance for the central bank. Let me briefly make three general comments about the fiscal outlook that I believe are particularly relevant for the conduct of monetary policy.

*First,* as the Clinton administration's budgetary proposals make their way through the congressional approval process, it is evident that fiscal policy will likely produce little or no near-term stimulus to the economy and, on balance, may have a modestly restrictive cast. For monetary policy, the fiscal year 1994 budget as it is now shaping up should not pose any problem and, in fact, appears to be compatible with the continuation of monetary accommodation.

*Second,* the emerging medium-term fiscal approach depends more on tax and other revenue increases to achieve budgetary restraint than on spending reductions. In addition, the higher taxes are front-loaded in time, while the spending reductions incorporated in the program are back-loaded. For the financial markets, the problem is naturally the danger of backsliding on intended spending cuts in the outer years. Therefore, financial market participants will be eager to see whether the Congress is going to be resolute in assuring that those intended reductions are tamper-proof. There is a strong case for explicit mechanisms within the scope of the budget authorization to make them tamper-proof. The Federal Reserve would probably welcome this as much as the market.

*Third,* I subscribe to the view that meaningful budgetary control over the long term is not possible without a reasonable amount of tax increases. Reducing the deficit solely from spending cuts is probably not acceptable; nor is it desirable. Critics sometimes lose sight of the fact that, to those people whose benefits are cut, that cut is the economic equivalent of a rise in taxes. But I want to urge caution on the composition of tax increases, because there is a dark side to nearly every tax. Many kinds of taxes are inherently inflationary, and it would be wise to proceed with great care when contemplating imposing any of them. I emphasize this point because it would be a great disappointment—as well as a source of public disillusionment—if our government went through the painful process of coming to grips with our vexing budget deficit problems only to fail to secure the hoped-for benefits of improved economic performance and lower real interest rates. That disappointment could easily happen if the imposition of new taxes turned out really to worsen inflation, since a significant rise in the inflation rate would have to be factored in by the Federal Reserve in its monetary policy decisions.

## Economic and financial conditions in major industrial countries

I now want to comment on the international economic and financial landscape and its implications for U.S. monetary policy. For a variety of reasons, the global economy is not doing well, and prospects for an early rebound are dim. Some of the impediments to satisfactory economic revival are specific to individual countries. Thus, like the United States, the United Kingdom also has to contend with a shrinking defense sector and with the legacy of vastly overbuilt commercial real estate. Its recovery from a long recession has been shallow. Germany has to deal with the unprecedented challenge and heavy budgetary expense of integrating a territory with an entirely alien economic and financial culture into a modern, competitive state. The upshot has been unacceptably high inflation, stringent monetary policy to bring it down, and a deep recession. Italy has to restore business and consumer confidence in the wake of extraordinary political events. Japan has to surmount the formidable economic, financial, political, and psychological consequences of the bursting of an overinflated speculative bubble, the emergence of a U.S.-style recession, and now the breakup of decades-old modalities of governance.

But putting aside the differences, there is a distinctive common thread running through the restrained economic prospects of the major industrial countries. In a nutshell, except for Japan, fiscal policy in the usual cyclical sense is inoperative, while monetary policy is encumbered everywhere.

Fiscal policy is inoperative as a practical matter in Europe because of large budgetary deficits that have been built up at all levels of government. It is indisputable that, despite the widespread slump in European business activity, the inclination is toward greater fiscal restraint. The German government is considering ways of bringing its deficit under better control. The overall deficit, including Germany's federal, state, and local governments, has been swollen by huge subsidies to the new eastern states, and lately by the recession, to an estimated 5 percent of GDP this year. When the deficits of state-run enterprises—such as the railways—are added in, the deficit swells even further, to the neighborhood of 8 percent. In France, the overall public-sector deficit is likely to approach nearly 6 percent of GDP, and the new government in France is pressing ahead with plans for fiscal retrenchment through a combination of revenue increases and expenditure restraints. Following the remarkable referendum of April, Italy also has a new government, which is faced with a towering public-sector deficit in the vicinity of 10 percent of GDP, and which is firmly committed to achieving a significant reduction. And governments in many other European countries are also seeking to pare spending and not to launch stimulative programs. Most Europeans believe the government commands too large a portion of economic resources and are reluctant to see that share expand, even for the stated purpose of stimulating economic recovery.

Only Japan has any scope for a significant fiscal expansion. But no one knows how political forces will shake out following the impending general election, or whether the stubborn resistance to meaningful tax cuts on the part of powerful segments of the previous government hierarchy and the ongoing bureaucracy will be shaken. This leaves the bulk of the proposed fiscal expansion in the area of public works expenditures, which are notoriously hard to put into effect in a timely and efficient manner, especially at a time of political uncertainty. It would not be surprising if the actual stimulative impact for the first year of the program turned out to be below the magnitudes initially outlined by the Japanese government.

## Challenges confronting monetary policy

By default, therefore, it is monetary policy that has been left with the full burden of reviving the industrial economies of Europe, as it has in the United States, and monetary accommodation still has a critical role to play in Japan as well. This is not all bad. Monetary policy has the great advantage of flexibility and reversibility. Implementation can be modulated, depending upon the evolution of business activity. More important, monetary accommodation can be put on hold or even reversed, once conditions in the economy start to pick up some momentum. Fiscal policy is a cruder instrument.

But throughout the industrial world, monetary policy is encumbered. There are four reasons for this:

*First*, a number of factors inhibiting an adequate economic rebound are of greater than cyclical dimension. The downsizing of the military is one. Restructuring is another. Pressure to restructure is spreading from North America to Europe and to Japan, as an increasing number of corporations recognize that they are operating in a far more competitive marketplace than in the past and have no choice but to cut costs forcefully. This process leads more businesses to outsource—to manufacture and even to provide services—where labor costs are low. The capacity to do this has vastly improved with cheaper and more technologically advanced transport and communications networks, the lifting of political barriers, and the emergence of large new trading blocs. These developments have also encouraged labor in economically distressed, and in impoverished, parts of the world to become more mobile. Millions of people have thronged into western Europe to improve their economic lot, and more hope to migrate. This will have a profound impact in keeping labor costs lower than they otherwise would be, limiting the bargaining power of organized labor, and fostering certain forms of social unease. How is monetary policy to respond to these developments? There is no historical parallel to serve as a guide.

*Second,* financial impairment is widespread. In many of the key industrial countries, financial institutions that had participated in the excessive lending to commercial real estate or highly leveraged companies in the previous expansion are still disabled. Even those that have been able to improve their profitability, their capital ratios, and their overall financial health are not eager lenders. Managements are chastened. Lending officers are mindful of the criticism they received and have seen their lending authority cut back. There is little evidence of financial institutions seeking actively to expand their lending; they are content to sit back and wait for borrowers to appear. But judging from our experience so far in the United States, borrowers are more interested in curbing outstanding indebtedness than in incurring new debt. Here again, to deal effectively with this problem, the monetary authorities cannot rely primarily on cyclical monetary analysis.

*Third,* the much more deregulated financial markets we now have also tend to make it more difficult to gauge the effect of any stated degree of monetary accommodation. While the process of deregulation has proceeded unevenly and imperfectly, both within and across nations, the common feature is that there is far less segmentation of credit markets. There are also far fewer protected market niches that, in the old days, used to more or less guarantee a dependable stream of earnings to different types of financial institutions. What this means is that banks and other financial institutions are more inclined to increase profits without taking additional credit risk in order to improve their overall financial conditions. As a result, wherever a steeply, positively sloped yield curve has emerged—the customary symptom of an accommodative monetary policy—banks and other financial institutions have stepped up their acquisitions of marketable securities, particularly government obligations, in what started out as a cyclical response. But this reaction seems to go farther and last longer than in previous interest rate cycles. Under these circumstances, we do not know what level of interest rates below today's levels will ignite dynamic credit creation.

*Fourth,* central bank attitudes may also constrict the potential stimulative impact of monetary policy. Central bankers remember earlier periods when monetary accommodation was overdone, and inflationary pressures were effectively validated. They do not want to repeat that mistake. They are also mindful of the sensitivity of the bond markets to any hint of renewed inflation. In a world in which the average unemployment rate in Europe is in double digits, yet inflation rates, relative to unemployment, remain high in many countries, this is no idle concern. Central banks are thus inclined to err on the side of caution in bringing about lower short-term interest rates.

## Monetary policy options

The essence of the policy dilemma in dealing with the global economic and financial situation is that fiscal stimulation is generally not feasible, considering the budget deficits already in place, but that the central banks of the major industrial countries are hesitant to exercise stronger leadership. The need is for a coordinated effort on the part of the major central banks to bring down world interest rates, but naturally, central bankers don't want to leave the impression that they have abandoned their fight against inflation. So they are inclined to hold back, rather than to take the lead.

How much help would bolder monetary policy be at the present time? In my judgment, a great deal. With the credit creation process still moribund, coordinated monetary accommodation would make a valuable contribution to invigorating growth and would be an acceptable risk to take. In fact, the bigger risk would be for central banks to temporize in deference to the conventional argument that more determined monetary easing would disturb the financial markets. Under current conditions of extensive corporate restructuring, widespread softness in labor markets, and mild growth in money and credit, financial markets would readily accept additional monetary accommodation and would not construe it to be necessarily inflationary. By contrast, far more disturbing to the markets would be a breakdown in the process of international economic cooperation and in the liberal trading system that lies at the heart of the process. Such a development, by threatening a progression of trade restrictions and retaliatory counter-restrictions, would carry with it the true danger of an escalation of world inflation.

I am aware that there is an element of risk in moving

in the direction of a greater monetary accommodation. But there is a greater risk in standing aside and essentially acquiescing to inward-looking trade policies. The question is: Which is the more acceptable risk under current economic and financial conditions? My position is that central banks should use the flexibility they have to bring down interest rates, but be prepared to bring rates back up expeditiously when economic activity responds and the inflation rate begins to show signs of a more pronounced lift. Ultimately, this means being prepared to reject the inevitable criticism, whether from politicians or the business community, of *any* move toward restraint.

## Implications for federal reserve monetary policy

The policy challenge facing the Federal Reserve differs from that of most other major central banks in that, unlike other countries, the United States has entered a business recovery, albeit a moderate one, and has to weigh what is needed to sustain economic expansion against what is desirable for continuing downward pressure on the rate of inflation.

I believe that, in the global context that I have described, the Federal Reserve should be able to pursue these joint objectives for at least the time being by maintaining the present degree of monetary accommodation. It may also find the opportunity to take advantage of the coming global de-escalation in interest rates to edge the federal funds rate somewhat lower, particularly if the U.S. dollar continues to display the kind of strength in the foreign exchange markets that it has in recent days. By following this policy course, the central bank will retain the flexibility to react to a change in economic conditions, in particular a more pronounced lift in the rate of inflation.

What I do not favor is a preemptive move toward restraint on the pretext that this would somehow shore up the Federal Reserve's "credibility" in the financial markets and, in so doing, relax market concerns about inflation prospects. I have great doubts about conditioning policy on something as ill-defined as the notion of "credibility." It is a policy argument that has an unfortunate tone of self-righteousness, rather than a firm analytical grounding. As a policy position, it is especially bizarre at the present time when, if anything, the financial markets have shown themselves to be quite comfortable with the overall stance of monetary policy.

The best evidence of this is displayed in the yield curve, which has become notably flatter this year. For example, the spread between the yield on three-month Treasury Bills and the yield on 30-year Treasury Bonds has diminished from 440 basis points in January to about 355 basis points this week. This is suggestive of a mild lessening in long-term inflationary expectations, even as the Federal Reserve has pursued a steady policy of monetary accommodation.

I also reject the proposition that a modest rise in the level of the federal funds rate would have little significance for the economy, and that such a preemptive move by the Federal Reserve would be costless. To the contrary, a higher federal funds rate would translate into higher interest payments by businesses and households—specifically those with adjustable-rate mortgages—a higher dollar in the foreign exchange markets, and some downward pressure on share prices. All would weaken growth prospects.

I also take issue with the assertion that a small increase in the federal funds rate this summer would be welcomed by the financial markets and would, accordingly, lead to a decline in bond yields. Perhaps. But equally likely is that the bond market would interpret such a rise in the federal funds rate as the first of a number of future increases, and market participants might easily react by pushing bond yields higher. Maybe such a preemptive move would reassure the financial markets that the central bank was determined to quell inflation and so would reduce inflationary expectations. But it is also likely that the market would suspect that the Federal Reserve was in possession of information not yet publicly disclosed, indicating the upcoming inflation news was going to be sour. Under that scenario, the rise in the federal funds rate could magnify inflationary expectations, precipitating a sell-off of bonds.

A more systematic analysis of the present inflationary potential within the U.S. economy does not justify either exaggerated inflationary expectations or a preemptive tightening by the Federal Reserve. Inflation as depicted in the most commonly watched measure, the Consumer Price Index, is exaggerating actual price pressures. Inflation is not found in the business community, and it is not revealed in speculative activity in the great majority of product markets. There is no evidence whatsoever of a surge in credit demand on the part of those wishing to finance speculative holdings of inventories, commodities, or real estate, in contrast to the conditions that prevailed during the previous run-up in the rate of inflation in the late 1970s. There is no evidence of a tightening in labor markets that would presage an escalation of wage settlements. To the contrary, as I have detailed, labor markets are soft. And if we look at the stock market, we see a rather nondescript pattern, with the market as a whole holding within a rather narrow trading range, but with the shares of individual companies susceptible to heavy punishment when earnings turn out to be less than what had been hoped for. This is not symptomatic of a business setting characterized by generalized inflation.

The time will come—no one knows precisely when, perhaps in 1994, perhaps not until 1995 or 1996—when the business recovery will have matured, excess capacity will have been worked off, labor markets will have become tauter, the economic recovery abroad will have begun, commodity prices will have turned higher across the board, real estate prices will have firmed, and credit demands will have become conspicuously stronger. Then, we will want the Federal Reserve to act with dispatch and determination to resist forcibly any buildup of inflationary pressures. But none of those circumstances prevails today.

ALAN GREENSPAN

# The Fed Aims for Price Stability

*To allow a market economy to attain its potential, the unnecessary instability engendered by inflation must be quieted.*

Thank you for this opportunity to discuss the Federal Reserve's semiannual monetary policy report to the Congress. My remarks this morning will cover the current monetary policy and economic settings, as well as the Federal Reserve's longer-term strategy for contributing, to the best of our abilities, to the nation's economic well-being.

As the economic expansion has progressed somewhat fitfully, our earlier characterization of the economy as facing stiff headwinds has appeared increasingly appropriate. Doubtless the major headwind in this regard has been the combined efforts of households, businesses, and financial institutions to repair and to rebuild their balance sheets following the damage inflicted in recent years as weakening asset values exposed excessive debt burdens.

But there have been other headwinds as well. The build-down of national defense has cast a shadow over particular industries and regions of the country. Spending on nonresidential real estate dropped dramatically in the face of overbuilding and high vacancy rates, and has remained in the doldrums. At the same time, corporations across a wide range of industries have been making efforts to pare employment and expenses in order to improve productivity and their competitive positions. These efforts have been prompted in part by innovative technologies, which have been applied to almost every area of economic endeavor, and have boosted investment. However, their effect on jobs and wages through much of the expansion also has made households more cautious spenders.

In the past several years, as these influences have restrained the economy, they have been balanced in part by the accommodative stance of monetary policy and, more recently, by declines in longer-term interest rates as the prospects for credible federal deficit cuts improved. From the time monetary policy began to move toward ease in 1989 to now, short-term interest rates have dropped by more than two-thirds and long-term rates have declined substantially too. All along the maturity spectrum, interest rates have come down to their lowest levels in twenty or thirty years, aiding the repair of balance sheets, bolstering the cash flow of borrowers, and providing support for interest-sensitive spending.

The process of easing monetary policy, however, had

ALAN GREENSPAN is Chairman of the Board of Governors of the Federal Reserve System. He presented this testimony before the Subcommittee on Economic Growth and Credit Formation of the Committee on Banking, Finance and Urban Affairs of the U.S. House of Representatives, July 20, 1993. Reprinted from *Challenge,* September–October 1993, pp. 4–10.

to be closely controlled and generally gradual because of the constraint imposed by the marketplace's acute sensitivity to inflation. As I pointed out in my February testimony to the Congress, this is a constraint that did not exist in an earlier time. Before the late 1970s, financial market participants and others apparently believed that, while inflationary pressures might surface from time to time, the institutional structure of the U.S. economy simply would not permit sustained inflation. But as inflation and, consequently, long-term interest rates soared into the double digits at the end of the 1970s, investors became painfully aware that they had underestimated the economy's potential for inflation. As a result, monetary policy in recent years has had to remain alert to the possibility that an ill-timed easing could be undone by a flare-up of inflation expectations, pushing long-term interest rates higher, and short-circuiting essential balance sheet repair.

The cumulative monetary easing over the last four years has been very substantial. Since last September, however, no further steps have been taken, as the stance of policy has appeared broadly appropriate to the evolving economic circumstances.

That stance has been quite accommodative, especially judging by the level of real short-term interest rates in the context of, on average, moderate economic growth. Short-term real interest rates have been in the neighborhood of zero over the last three quarters. In maintaining this accommodative stance, we have been persuaded by the evidence of persistent slack in labor and product markets, increasing international competitiveness, and the decided absence of excessive credit and money expansion. The forces that engendered past inflationary episodes appear to have been lacking to date.

## Disturbing indications of inflation

Yet some of the readings on inflation earlier this year were disturbing. It appeared that prices might be accelerating despite product market slack and an unemployment rate noticeably above estimates of the so-called natural rate of unemployment—that is, the rate at which price pressures remain roughly constant. In the past, the existing degree of slack in the economy had been consistent with continuing disinflation.

However, the inflation outcome, history tells us, depends not only on the amount of slack remaining in labor and product markets, but on other factors as well, including the rate at which that slack is changing. If the economy is growing rapidly, inflation pressures can arise, even in the face of excess capacity, as temporary bottlenecks emerge and as workers and producers raise wages and prices in anticipation of continued strengthening in demand. Near the end of last year, about the time many firms probably were finalizing their plans for 1993, sales and capacity utilization were moving up markedly and there was a surge of optimism about future economic activity. This may well have set in motion a wave of price increases, which showed through to broad measures of prices earlier this year.

Moreover, inflation expectations, at least by some measures, appear to have tilted upward this year, possibly contributing to price pressures. The University of Michigan survey of consumer attitudes, for example, reported an increase in the inflation rate expected to prevail over the next 12 months from about 3.75 percent in the fourth quarter of last year to nearly 4.5 percent in the second quarter of this year. Preliminary data imply some easing of such expectations earlier this month, but the sample from which those data are derived is too small to be persuasive. Moreover, the price of gold, which can be broadly reflective of inflationary expectations, has risen sharply in recent months. And at times this spring, bond yields spiked higher when incoming news about inflation was most discouraging.

The role of expectations in the inflation process is crucial. Even expectations not validated by economic fundamentals can themselves add appreciably to wage and price pressures for a considerable period, potentially derailing the economy from its growth track.

Why, for example, despite an above-normal rate of unemployment and permanent layoffs, have uncertainties about job security not led to further moderation in wage increases? The answer appears to lie, at least in part, in the deep-seated anticipations understandably harbored by workers that inflation is likely to reaccelerate in the near term and undercut their real wages.

The Federal Open Market Committee (FOMC) became concerned that inflation expectations and price pressures, unless contained, could raise long-term interest rates and stall economic expansion. Consequently, at its meeting in May, while affirming the more accommodative policy stance in place since last September, the FOMC also deemed it appropriate to initiate a so-called asymmetric directive. Such a directive, with its bias in the direction of a possible firming of policy over the intermeeting period, does not prejudge that action will be taken—and indeed none occurred. But it did indicate that further signs of a potential deterioration of the inflation outlook would merit serious consideration of whether short-term rates needed to be raised slightly from their relatively low levels to ensure that financial conditions remained conducive to sustained growth.

Certainly the May and June price figures have helped assuage concerns that new inflationary pressures had taken hold. Nonetheless, on balance, the news on inflation this year must be characterized as disappointing. Despite disinflationary forces and continued slack, the rate of inflation has, at best, stabilized, rather than easing further as past relationships would have suggested.

In assessing the stance of monetary policy and the likelihood of persistent inflationary pressures, the FOMC took account of the downshift in the pace of economic expansion earlier this year. This downshift left considerable remaining slack in the economy and promised that the adverse price movements prompted by the acceleration in growth late last year likely would diminish.

## Slowdown greater than expected

While a slowdown from the unsustainably rapid growth in the latter part of last year had been anticipated, the deceleration was greater than expected. A surprisingly precipitous drop in defense spending, a sharp deterioration in net exports, a major blizzard, and some inevitable retrenchment by consumers converged to yield only meager gains in output in the first quarter. But growth apparently picked up in the second quarter, and nearly one million net new jobs were created over the first half. Smoothing through the quarterly pattern, the economy appears to have accelerated gradually over the past two years, to maintain a pace of growth that should yield further reductions in the unemployment rate. Consequently, the evidence remains consistent with our diagnosis that the underlying forces at work are keeping the economy generally on a moderate upward track. However, as I have often emphasized, not all the old economic and financial verities have held in the current expansion, and changes in fiscal policy will have uncertain effects going forward. Thus, caution in assessing the path for the economy remains appropriate.

Financial conditions have improved considerably, lessening the need for balance sheet restructuring that has been damping economic activity for several years now. By no means is the process over, but good progress has been made. Debt service burdens, eased by lower interest rates and lower debt–equity ratios, have fallen substantially in both the business and household sectors. On the other hand, the economies of a number of our major trading partners have been quite weak, constraining the growth of demand for our exports.

Although expectations of a significant, credible decline in the budget deficit have induced lower long-term interest rates and favorably affected the economy, the positive influence thus far is apparently being at least partly offset by some business spending reductions as a consequence of concerns about the effects of pending tax increases.

## Uncertainty about new federal budget

It seems that the *prospective* cuts in the deficit are having a variety of substantial economic effects, well in advance of any *actual* change in taxes or in projected outlays. Moreover, uncertainty about the final shape of the package may itself be injecting a note of caution into private spending plans. In addition, uncertainty about the outlook for health care reform may be affecting spending, at least by that industry.

To be sure, the conventional wisdom is that budget deficit reduction restrains economic growth for a time, and I suspect that probably is correct. However, over the long run, such wisdom points in the opposite direction. In fact, one can infer that recent declines in long-term interest rates are bringing forward some of these anticipated long-term gains. As a consequence, the timing and magnitude of any net restraint from deficit reduction is uncertain. Patently, the overall economic effect of fiscal policy, especially when combined with the uncertainties of the forthcoming health reform package, has imparted a number of unconventional unknowns to the economic outlook.

Assuming, however, we constructively resolve, over time, the major questions about federal budget and health care policies, with the further waning of earlier restraints on growth, the U.S. economy should eventually emerge healthier and more vibrant than in decades. The balance sheet restructuring of both financial and nonfinancial establishments in recent years should leave the various sectors of the economy in much better shape and better able to weather untoward developments. Similarly, the ongoing efforts by corporations to pare expenses are putting our firms and our industries in a better position to compete, both within the U.S.

market and globally. And after a period of some dislocation, the contraction in the defense sector ultimately will mean a freeing up of resources for more productive uses. Finally, a credible and effective fiscal package would promise an improved outlook for sustained lower long-term interest rates and a better environment for private sector investment. All told, the productive capacity of the economy will doubtless be higher, and its resilience greater.

Over the last two years, the forces of restraint on the economy have changed, but real growth has continued, with one sector of the economy after another taking the lead. Against this background, Federal Reserve Board governors and Reserve Bank presidents project that the U.S. economy will remain on the moderate growth path it has been following as the expansion has progressed. Their forecasts for real GDP average around 2.5 percent from the fourth quarter of 1992 to the fourth quarter of 1993, and cluster around 2.5 to 3.25 percent over the four quarters of 1994. Reflecting this moderate rise and the outlook for labor productivity, unemployment is generally expected to edge lower, to around 6.75 percent by the end of this year, and to perhaps a shade lower by the end of next year. For this year as a whole, FOMC participants see inflation at or just above 3 percent, and most of them have the same forecast for next year.

In addition to focusing on the outlook for the economy at its July meeting, the FOMC, as required by the Humphrey-Hawkins Act, set ranges for the growth of money and debt for this year, and, on a preliminary basis, for 1994. One premise of the discussion of the ranges was that the uncharacteristically slow growth of the broad monetary aggregates in the last couple of years—and the atypical increases in their velocities—would persist for a while longer. $M_2$ has been far weaker than income and interest rates would predict. Indeed, if the historical relationships between $M_2$ and nominal income had remained intact, the behavior of $M_2$ in recent years would have been consistent with an economy in severe contraction. To an important degree, the behavior of $M_2$ has reflected structural changes in the financial sector: The thrift industry has downsized by necessity, and commercial banks have pulled back as well, largely reflecting the burgeoning loan losses that followed the lax lending of earlier years. With depository credit weak, there has been little bidding for deposits, and depositors, in any case, have been drawn to the higher returns on capital market instruments. Inflows to bond and stock mutual funds have reached record levels, and, to the extent that these inflows have come at the expense of growth in deposits or money-market mutual funds, the broad monetary aggregates have been depressed.

In this context, the FOMC lowered the 1993 ranges for $M_2$ and $M_3$ to 1-to-5 percent and 0-to-4 percent, respectively. This represents a reduction of one percentage point in the $M_2$ range and a half percentage point for $M_3$. Even with these reductions, we would not be surprised to see the monetary aggregates finish the year near the lower ends of their ranges.

## Monetary aggregate estimates no longer reliable

As I emphasized in a similar context in February, the lowering of the ranges is purely a technical matter; it does not indicate, nor should it be perceived as, a shift of monetary policy in the direction of restraint. It is indicative merely of the state of our knowledge about the factors depressing the growth of the aggregates relative to spending, of the course of the aggregates to date, and of the likelihood of various outcomes through the end of the year. While the lowering of the range reflects our judgment that shifts out of $M_2$ will persist, the upper end of the revised range allows for a resumption of more normal behavior, or even some unwinding of $M_2$ shortfalls. The FOMC also lowered the 1993 range for debt of the domestic nonfinancial sectors, by a half percentage point, to 4-to-8 percent. The debt aggregate is likely to come in comfortably within its new range, as it continues growing about in line with nominal GDP. The new ranges for growth of money and debt in 1993 were carried over on a preliminary basis into 1994.

In reading the longer-run intentions of the FOMC, the specific ranges need to be interpreted cautiously. The historical relationships between money and income, and between money and the price level, have largely broken down, depriving the aggregates of much of their usefulness as guides to policy. At least for the time being, $M_2$ has been downgraded as a reliable indicator of financial conditions in the economy, and no single variable has yet been identified to take its place.

At one time, $M_2$ was useful both to guide Federal Reserve policy and to communicate the thrust of monetary policy to others. Even then, however, a wide range of data was routinely evaluated to assure ourselves that M was capturing the important elements in the financial system that would affect the economy. The FOMC never singlemindedly adhered to a narrow path for $M_2$, but persistent and sizable deviations of that aggregate from expectations were a warning sign that policy and the economy might not be interacting in a way that would produce the desired results. The so-called P-star model, developed in the late 1980s, embodied a long-run relationship between $M_2$ and prices that could anchor policy over extended periods of time. But that long-run relationship also seems to have broken down with the persistent rise in $M_2$ velocity.

$M_2$ and P-star may reemerge as reliable indicators of income and prices once the yield curve has returned to a more normal configuration, borrowers' balance sheets have been restored and traditional credit demands have resumed, savers have adjusted to the enhanced availability of alternative investments, and depositories finally reach a comfortable size relative to their capital and earnings. In the meantime, the process of probing a variety of data to ascertain underlying economic and financial conditions has become even more essential to formulating sound monetary policy. This general approach obviously has its weaknesses. When examining many indicators, some can always be found that counsel against actions that later appear to have been necessary.

In these circumstances, it is especially prudent to focus on longer-term policy guides. One important guidepost is real interest rates, which have a key bearing on longer-run spending decisions and inflation prospects.

In assessing real rates, the central issue is their relationship to an equilibrium interest rate, specifically the real rate level that, if maintained, would keep the economy at its production potential over time. Rates persisting above that level, history tells us, tend to be associated with slack, disinflation, and economic stagnation—below that level with eventual resource bottlenecks and rising inflation, which ultimately engenders economic contraction. Maintaining the real rate around its equilibrium level should have a stabilizing effect on the economy, directing production toward its long-term potential.

The level of the equilibrium real rate—or, more appropriately, the equilibrium term structure of real rates—cannot be estimated with a great deal of confidence, though with enough to be useful for monetary policy. Real rates, of course, are not directly observable, but must be inferred from nominal interest rates and estimates of inflation expectations. The most important real rates for private spending decisions almost surely are the longer maturities. Moreover, the equilibrium rate structure responds to the ebb and flow of underlying forces affecting spending. So, for example, in recent years, the appropriate real rate structure doubtless has been depressed by the headwinds of balance sheet restructuring and fiscal retrenchment. Despite the uncertainties about the levels of equilibrium and actual real interest rates, rough judgments about these variables can be made and used in conjunction with other indicators in the monetary policy process. Currently, short-term real rates, most directly affected by the Federal Reserve, are not far from zero; long-term rates, set primarily by the market, are appreciably higher, judging from the steep slope of the yield curve and reasonable suppositions about inflation expectations. This configuration indicates that market participants anticipate that short-term real rates will have to rise as the headwinds diminish, if substantial inflationary imbalances are to be avoided.

While the guides we have for policy may have changed recently, our goals have not. As I have indicated many times to this committee, the Federal Reserve seeks to foster maximum sustainable economic growth and rising standards of living. And in that endeavor, the most productive function the central bank can perform is to achieve and maintain price stability.

## Counterproductivity of inflation

Inflation is counterproductive in many ways. Of particular importance, increased inflation has been found to be associated with reduced growth of productivity, apparently in part because it confounds relative price movements and obscures price signals. Compounding this negative effect, under the current tax code, inflation raises the effective taxation of savings and investment, discouraging the process of capital formation. Since productivity growth is the only source of lasting increases in real incomes and because even small changes in growth rates of productivity can accumulate over time to large differences in living standards, its association with inflation is of key importance to policy makers.

The link between the control of inflation and the growth of productivity underscores the importance of providing a stable backdrop for the economy. Such an environment is especially important for an increasingly dynamic market economy, such as ours, where technology and telecommunications are making rapid advances. New firms, new products, new jobs, new industries, and new markets are continually being created, and they are unceremoniously displacing the old ones. The U.S. economy is a dynamic system, always renewing itself. It is extraordinary that the system, overall, is as stable as it is, considering the persistent process of change in the structure of our economy. For example, a frequently cited figure is the two million new jobs that have been created since the end of 1991. This is a net change, however, which masks the many millions who found, lost, and changed jobs over the same period. Currently, people are being hired at a pace of approximately 400,000 per week, with job losses running modestly below that figure. Such vast churning in the nation's labor markets is a normal and, ultimately, productive process.

Central planning of the type that prevailed in postwar Eastern Europe and the Soviet Union represented one attempt to fashion an economic system that eliminated this competitive churning and its presumed wastefulness. But when that system eliminated the risk of failure, it also stifled the incentive to innovate and to prosper. Central planning fostered stasis: In many respects, the eastern-bloc economies marched in place for more than four decades.

Risk-taking is crucial in the process that leads to a vital and progressive economy. Indeed, it is a necessary condition for wealth creation. In a market economy, competition and innovation interact; those firms that are slow to innovate or to anticipate the demands of the consumer are soon left behind. The pace of churning differs by industry, but it is present in all. At one extreme, firms in the most high-tech areas must remain constantly on the cutting edge, as products and knowledge become rapidly obsolete. Many products that were at technology's leading edge, say, five years ago, are virtually unsalable in today's markets. In high-tech fields, leadership can shift rapidly. In some markets where American firms were losing share just a few years ago, we have regained considerable dominance. In one case, U.S. firms have seized a commanding lead in just two years in the new laptop computer market, and now account for more than 60 percent of U.S. sales last year, triple the figure for Japanese firms.

More generally, it appears that the pace of dynamism has been accelerating. As one indication, the average economic life expectancy of new capital equipment has been falling. The average life of equipment purchased in 1982, for example, was 16.5 years. By 1992, that figure had declined to 14.5 years, a drop more than twice as large as that over the preceding decade. In addition, telecommunications technology is obviously quickening the decision-making process in both financial and product markets.

In such a rapidly changing marketplace, the agile survive by being flexible. One aspect of this flexibility has been the spread of "just-in-time" inventory controls at manufacturing firms. Partly as a result of innovations in inventory control techniques, the variability of inventories relative to total output appears to be on a downtrend.

The possibility of failure has productive side effects, encouraging economic agents to do their best to succeed. But there are nonproductive and unnecessary risks as well. There is no way to avoid risk altogether, given the inherently uncertain outcomes of all business and household decisions. But many uncertainties and risks do not foster economic progress, and, where feasible, should be suppressed. A crucial risk in this category is that induced by inflation. To allow a market economy to attain its potential, the unnecessary instability engendered by inflation must be quieted.

A monetary policy that aims at price stability permits low long-term interest rates and helps provide a stable setting to foster the investment and innovation by the private sector that are key to long-run economic growth. In pursuing our objectives, we must remain acutely aware that the structure of the economy has been changing and growing ever more complex. The relationships between the key variables in the economy are always shifting to a degree, and this evolution presents an ongoing challenge to the business leader, to the econometric modeler, and to those responsible for the conduct of economic policy.

Clearly, the behavior of many of the forces acting on the economy over the course of the last business cycle has been different from what had gone before. The sensitivity of inflation expectations has been heightened, and, as recent evidence suggests, businesses and households may be becoming more forward-looking with respect to fiscal policies as well.

I believe we are on our way toward reestablishing the trust in the purchasing power of the dollar that is crucial to maximizing and fulfilling the productivity capacity of this nation. The public, however, clearly remains to be convinced: Survey responses and financial market prices embody expectations that the current lower level of inflation not only will not be bettered, it will not even persist. But there are glimmers of hope that trust is reemerging. For example, issuers have found receptive markets in recent months for fifty-year bonds. This had not happened in decades. The reopening of that market may be read as one indication that some investors once again believe that inflationary pressures will remain subdued.

It is my firm belief that, with fiscal consolidation and with the monetary policy path that we have charted, the United States is well positioned to remain at the forefront of the world economy well into the next century.

# CHAPTER 5 | THE "SOFT LANDING" STRATEGY OF GREENSPAN'S FEDERAL RESERVE

## *The Federal Reserve's Preemptive Strike of 1994*

ROBERT GUTTMANN

Greenspan's congressional testimony of July 1993, containing a startling announcement of a new policy target (see chapter 4 above), made it clear that the Fed was ready to slow down the U.S. economy in order to prevent its overheating. The chairman of the Fed, however, did not act immediately upon his pronouncement, as the U.S. economy unexpectedly cooled off for a few months. But by late 1993 activity suddenly reaccelerated to boom levels, and in February 1994 the Fed began the promised tightening with the first in a series of modest rate hikes. Over the next year the central bank would push up the Federal funds rate and/or discount rate seven times to twice their pretightening levels. The Fed characterized this policy course as a preemptive strike against future inflation that would reinforce its "credibility" as an inflation fighter and thus convince financial markets to accept lower long-term interest rates. Ironically, when the Fed began to raise short-term rates, bondholders and currency traders acted in precisely the opposite way. Suspecting the central bank of having acted on some "inside" information about inflationary pressures, these financial investors pushed long-term rates quite a bit higher. Instead of flattening, the entire yield curve simply shifted upward. Eventually, as the Fed continued pushing short-term rates up in the face of slowing growth, the fears in bond, stock, and currency markets subsided and the long-expected decline in long-term rates finally took hold. In the meantime, however, the bond market in particular suffered from a steep and sustained decline in prices, which triggered a series of spectacular losses by investors using complex derivatives tied to the performance of bonds and stocks (e.g., the bankruptcy of Orange County).[1]

### Targeting real short-term rates

Greenspan's preemptive strike against renewed inflation, mediated by the new policy target of real short-term rates, is given an appropriate historic and analytical context by Wall Street economist David Jones in a March 1994 interview with *Challenge* reprinted below. For Jones the tightening of the Fed implied a shift from an "accommodating" to a "neutral" stance defined by real short-term rates of 1.5 to 2 percent. He viewed that action as a necessary step toward maintaining price stability which had a good chance to succeed. While conscious of the deflationary nature of ongoing structural adjustments in the U.S. economy (i.e., debt burdens, corporate downsizing, government deficits), Jones also believed that cyclical forces, in particular the investment-based and export-driven nature of this recovery, would be strong enough to counteract the structural constraints. If that were the case, then the Fed's preemptive tightening would not impair the recovery, but put it on a stronger footing after a temporary slowdown had pushed long-term rates lower.

A less sanguine view of the Fed's interest-rate hikes of 1994–95 was taken by Jerry Jasinowski, president of the National Association of Manufacturers (see reprint below). Jasinowski, reflecting the majority view of his association, argues against premature tightening on the grounds that the threat of renewed inflation has been substantially lessened by the structural changes in the U.S. economy during recent years. Computer-based automation of production and outsourcing have increased capacity more than traditional measures would indicate. Intensifying global competition restricts the ability of corporations to raise prices. Changes in the labor market—in particular growing use of part-time, contingent, and temporary workers—make it easier for industrial firms to manage their labor costs. Most important is the cumulative effect of these structural changes on productivity growth, which is accelerating, especially in manufacturing. To the extent that policy makers underestimate these changes, they are inclined to overestimate the currently prevailing natural rate of unemployment required for price stability which economists define as *full employment*. In other words, the economy could easily tolerate lower unemployment rates (specifically, 5.3 percent instead of the official 5.7 percent) before there is reason to fear inflation. From that perspective, the Fed's interest-hikes of 1994 were premature and caused unnecessary hardships.

Dimitri Papadimitriou and Randall Wray attacked the Fed's policy shift of 1994 from a different angle. In an empirical study (see reprint below) these two economists associated with the Jerome Levy Institute (Bard College, New York) concluded that the Fed's new policy target, real short-term interest rates, was a highly unreliable variable for policy making and as a predictor of future growth conditions. The same was in their opinion true for expected inflation, a nebulous and thus inherently imprecise measure, which the Fed has often used in recent years to justify tightening. Had either variable been used as a target variable in previous decades, instability would have been worse. Given the high social costs of fighting inflation, in terms of higher unemployment, lost income and financial instability, it would be better for the Fed to drop these counterproductive policy targets and ease its anti-inflationary stance to a more reasonable level. Monetary policy should aim at low interest rates, which, together with lender-of-last-resort interventions, help keep the economy more stable.

## Which direction for monetary policy?

The critics of the Federal Reserve are certainly justified in arguing that the Fed tends to overstate the threat of inflation in light of the structural changes transforming the U.S. economy. The interest-rate hikes of 1994 were thus premature and may have imposed unnecessary costs in terms of lost income and jobs. Federal Reserve officials, in particular those appointed by Clinton (e.g., Blinder), may have come to a similar conclusion in recent months. When the interest-rate hikes finally slowed growth to a crawl in early 1995, the U.S. central bank once again reversed course and pushed short-term rates gently lower to keep the recovery afloat. The Fed's principal constituency, financial investors, also relaxed their inflation worries as economic activity slowed down. With long-term rates drifting lower, bond and stock markets experienced a powerful boom that took the Dow Jones from 4,000 to 5,600 in barely a year.

The Fed's "soft landing" strategy of 1994, using rate hikes to preempt a potentially inflationary boom and thus extending the life of the current recovery, can nonetheless be regarded a success. David Jones' prediction that the U.S. economy was strong enough to take the dose of restraint dished out by the central bank proved ultimately correct. Modest growth and low inflation have continued to provide a relatively stable framework for the recapitalization of American corporations and modernization of their productive capacity. U.S. manufacturing industries continue to enjoy a revival of productivity growth and an increase in global market shares.

In sum, the Fed has in recent years managed to combine Monetarist and Keynesian prescriptions for monetary policy in a flexible and rather effective manner. Its officials have moved away from the traditional Monetarist fixation with stable money-supply growth and focused on interest rates instead. They also have seemed inclined to favor countercyclical intervention over fixed policy rules. Yet at the same time they have by and large maintained the Monetarist emphasis on price stability that the central bank adopted first in 1979. The question is how high interest rates need to be in order to assure a stable and low inflation rate of 2–3 percent, and it is here that an important debate between the two sides is taking shape. The Keynesians and their political allies in the Democratic party clearly would like to see lower interest rates than the Fed or financial asset-holders have been willing to accept during the last decade. Greenspan and his Monetarist majority on the Fed's policy-making body argue that it is better to err on the side of caution and keep inflation in check before it has a chance to heat up. Implicit in their argument is the notion that inflation is a worse evil than slow growth. As long as the Fed's preemptive "soft landing" strategy keeps the U.S. economy going, albeit at a moderate pace, there is little that its Keynesian critics can expect to change.

## Note

1. These investors had assumed continued declines in interest rates and were surprised when the policy reversal by the Fed pushed interest rates broadly higher across the entire maturity spectrum. Given the highly leveraged nature of most transactions using derivatives, their wrong bets translated into large losses.

INTERVIEW WITH DAVID M. JONES

# *Greenspan's Quest for Stability*

Q. As you and I begin this conversation, the excitement in your trading room next door suggests some heavy activity in the financial markets. The markets seem to be reacting as much to leadership at the Federal Reserve and the White House as to actual developments in the economy. What do you make of this?
A. I could tell you three stories. The first is about how a friendship evolved between an urbane, cultured, introverted, well-dressed New Yorker named Alan Greenspan and a Southern, backslapping, Elvis Presley–loving, Arkansas politician. You couldn't find two men more far apart in terms of political and economic philosophies.

Alan Greenspan is a devoted free-market capitalist. He was, in his earlier days, a member of the cult of Ayn Rand, who was a fervent advocate of capitalism in its purest form. Therefore, Greenspan believes: the less government, the better; and he emphasizes free markets and private initiative. Clinton is just the opposite. He believes: the more government, the better; or, at least, if you need to solve social problems: the more government, the better.

On the surface, theirs is a very curious relationship. Yet, what is interesting is that the relationship between Clinton and Greenspan is much closer than was the relationship between Bush and Greenspan, even though Greenspan is the true-blue Republican. Even more striking, the relationship between Greenspan and the top three advisers in the Clinton Administration has been very cordial. Greenspan has the highest respect for Treasury Secretary Lloyd Bentsen, Budget Director Leon Panetta, and head of the new National Economic Council Robert Rubin; but Greenspan had much greater difficulty with the Republican Bush Administration's Treasury Secretary Nicholas Brady and Budget Director Richard Darman.

Q. What was the nature of that disharmony?
A. For Greenspan, the problems with Treasury Secretary Brady weren't really the result of personal dislike. He seemed to think Brady was a nice enough guy personally. Rather, Brady was weak on economic policy. His problem was ineptness on policy issues. After all, Brady was never meant to be a significant policy maker. He was just a friend of Bush, and that's why he became Treasury Secretary. Darman was the kind of guy who was difficult to trust, because he was always involved in political intrigue; he was always going through these machinations over who is up or who is down, and who is winning or who is losing. Greenspan apparently just had no time for such a Machiavellian character.

DAVID M. JONES is Executive Vice President and Chief Economist, Aubrey G. Lanston & Co. Inc. This conversation is based on an interview conducted by Richard D. Bartel, editor of *Challenge*, on March 29, 1994, in New York City. Reprinted from *Challenge*, July–August 1994, pp. 19–26.

What happened was amazing. Brady discontinued the traditional weekly breakfast with Fed Chairman Greenspan. This had been a long tradition, dating back as far as the Roosevelt Administration, with Marriner Eccles at the Fed (1934-48) and Henry Morgenthau Jr. at the Treasury (1933-45). But relations quickly improved between the true-blue Republican Greenspan and this Democratic Clinton Administration. As far as I know, they had never met until December 1992, when Greenspan went to Little Rock after the Clinton electoral victory to talk about economic policy.

Q. For the famous economics summit?
A. This was a personal meeting on December 3, 1992, which was scheduled for an hour for talks between Greenspan and President-elect Clinton, but it turned into a two-and-a-half-hour meeting. The two hit it off remarkably well. Greenspan convinced Clinton at this meeting that Clinton's economic program had to meet the test of credibility in the bond market. Only if Clinton followed credible deficit-cutting actions could he hope to exert downward pressure on stubbornly high long-term interest rates and stimulate economic activity. Actually the meeting went so long that Greenspan tried to rush back to the airport and got caught in a traffic jam in, of all places, Little Rock, because of a lumbering freight train. So he missed his plane.

To me, this is a fascinating and revealing story about two men—both fundamentally, intellectually very bright—who love details, even though they approach the economy from utterly different political perspectives and strikingly different backgrounds. Greenspan has the highest respect for Clinton's command of economic issues; it is, to me, professorial. He's able to talk extremely intelligently. His only problem is that he can't pick priorities. And when he does, there is the old question about how much of a resolve he has to follow through. But his intelligence is something no one has ever challenged. This first story, then, is one about the personal relationship between the Fed Chairman and the President.

Q. And the second story focuses on what?
A. Chairman Greenspan, early in his second term, has initiated a major new monetary policy approach that bears his own stamp of identity. During most of his first term (1987-91), the Fed watched a broad array of indicators of financial market conditions, including the money and credit aggregates, money market rates, bond yields, yield spreads, equity prices, and foreign exchange rates, among others. But Greenspan faced the problem of how to explain his policy strategy to the administration, to Congress to which he must be accountable, to the financial community, and to the general public. He can't stand up and say, the Fed watches everything. So he switched last year to a new approach based on the concept of real short-term interest rates. For all intents and purposes he junked the $M_2$ monetary aggregate as an intermediate policy indicator.

Q. But when Greenspan became Fed Chairman in 1987, didn't he follow Volcker's lead, with a focus on the monetary aggregates?
A. Exactly. Remember Volcker started out with $M_1$ and then shifted to $M_2$ because of technical problems. Then Greenspan started with $M_2$. But it was the credit channel that operated most powerfully to push the economy over the edge into the 1990-91 recession. In early 1990, there was a major credit crunch, which I call the "silent" credit crunch or the "grassroots" credit crunch. That wasn't an "old-fashioned" credit crunch.

Q. By "old-fashioned," you mean the credit crunches that occurred when the banking system was still restrained by Regulation Q interest rate ceilings?
A. Yes. When Fed tightening occurred, rising money market rates would typically trigger disintermediation flows out of commercial bank deposits into money market instruments. Regulation Q ceilings restricted the interest rates that banks could pay on time and savings deposits. When market rates—say, on Treasury bills or commercial paper—rose above the bank rate ceilings, savers shifted their funds from the banks to the open market instruments. That loss of deposits would cause a sharp curtailment of bank lending, particularly cutting back on mortgage loans. In those days—before 1980—the Fed could raise rates above the Q ceilings and quickly cause the economy to stop in its tracks. That was the old-fashioned credit crunch.

That's not so today. Federal Reserve tightening has more complicated results now. In early 1990, bank regulators began to jump on the backs of the banks, calling for more caution and higher quality in their loans, and for increased capital. This was prompted by the collapse of many S&Ls, and the regulators feared the same problems would overwhelm the banks. In compliance, the banks cut off credit to builders, developers, and others. Remember, this was happening against the background of Fed easing, not tightening. The Fed had eased six times in the second half of 1989; then it held steady in early 1990, but began to ease again starting in July 1990. It began to ease much more aggressively, particularly in 1991, and it continued in 1992.

Q. By that time, weren't the banks cleaning up their assets and trying to build up their financial position, so they could begin lending again?
A. Yes, but what I'm looking at here is an important policy transition that Greenspan was undertaking. It was hard for all of us to identify that credit crunch and its causes. That crunch had a significant effect in depressing the economy, in addition to the Persian Gulf war and other things. What I'm pointing to is that, around that time, Greenspan began using $M_2$ as a proxy for the availability of credit in the banking system. He was starting to analyze monetary conditions more from the credit side, rather than from the side of bank liabilities and money. He had the quarterly surveys of bank loan officers that were telling him that banks were toughening the terms of credit, as the regulators pressed them.

The Fed brought the federal funds rate down twenty-five times from June 1989 through September 1992, from 9.75 percent to 3 percent—the lowest level in three decades. That brought bank CD rates down to a level that caused everybody to get out of low-yielding CDs into money market and bond-mutual funds. As a result, the Federal Open Market Committee (FOMC) could no longer use $M_2$ as an intermediate policy indicator or an early warning indicator of inflation. In response to that problem, Greenspan, as Fed Chairman, had to decide on a new indicator or strategy for guiding policy.

So the FOMC began to examine a variety of de facto intermediate indicators, including some indicators from the real sectors of the economy that Greenspan had followed in his earlier career as an economic consultant. For example, he watched the "supplier-delivery lead times," among other exotic indicators, that show the tendency of business to accumulate inventories. He also followed some direct measures of inflation: commodity prices, producer prices.

But he sought something to focus on as a single policy instrument, and he finally came up with real, short-term interest rates. Certainly, he wasn't the first to use real, short-term interest rates. His fellow policy makers are driven crazy by that concept, because it ultimately requires a seat-of-the-pants judgment. If you subtract inflation expectations from the nominal federal funds rate, you have an estimate. But inflation expectations can't be measured directly. How do you measure inflation expectations? Do you use the inflation rate of last year, or some estimate for the coming year?

Q. So, how does Greenspan solve that tricky puzzle?
A. He argues that real, short-term rates reached a low point last year when the nominal federal funds rate fell to 3 percent, minus a 3 percent expectation for the inflation rate. Real rates were zero, and he felt policy was very accommodating for a zero real rate of interest. He felt policy could continue to be accommodative so long as he helped to make the banking system healthier. Also, the public could refinance their debts. Families could refinance their mortgages at lower interest rates and thereby reduce their monthly payments, and businesses could raise new equity in the markets to repay outstanding debt and to refinance their debt at lower rates. Alan Greenspan says he was happy to maintain a "quite accommodative policy" to facilitate these balance sheet improvements. There have been times in our history when real short-term rates were negative. For this Fed Chairman, it is a matter of religion—a tenet of faith—that real, short-term rates never turn negative under his tenure.

Q. But the United States has had negative, short-term rates at other times, when the economy passed through a recession trough. What's wrong with that?
A. Greenspan looks back at the late 1970s, when we had negative short-term rates, and that's when the inflation rate exploded to two digits. Now, one can argue that inflation went to two digits in the 1970s, because of oil price shocks and agricultural price shocks, among other things, but Alan Greenspan doesn't accept such reasoning. The last time real short-term rates were negative was in Arthur Burns's tenure as Fed Chairman. Burns was basically all talk and no action in the fight against inflation.

As Greenspan explained in his January 31, 1994, congressional testimony, the Fed cannot overstay accommodative policy when the foundations of growth grow stronger. He was ringing a gong for everybody that said: He's ready to start tightening; and he did that on February 4th.

Q. But he did that in July 1993 too, didn't he?
A. That's when he started to talk tough and when he introduced the concept of real, short-term rates. But he didn't act on that concept until early this year, in part because everyone thought inflation was resurgent in the first four months of 1993, but then cooled off unexpectedly. He wasn't disturbed until the following occurred: He saw 7.5 percent growth in the fourth quarter of 1993; he was looking for a strong acceleration in the fourth quarter 1993 growth in final demand; and he believed the momentum would carry into this year. Accordingly, Greenspan decided, in February 1994, to move short-term rates up from an "accommodative" stance to a "neutral" Fed stance.

Q. How are the financial markets supposed to translate that decision into movements of interest rates?
A. The financial markets had trouble in deciding what is a neutral, real, short-term rate. This question also bothered fellow Fed policy makers, including Fed Vice Chairman David Mullins. It was not easy for anyone to figure out the level of real short-term rates that corresponds to a "neutral" Fed stance on monetary policy. Just what level should we look for in the nominal federal funds rate? The answer is kind of tricky. You can only guess at it. To my way of thinking, you have to look at historical experience with real, short-term rates, as measured by the federal funds rate less inflation expectations over the past two or three decades.

Q. But how do you estimate those inflation expectations?
A. The best estimate of inflation expectations seems to be the Fed's own estimate of the consumer price index that is projected in the Fed Chairman's Humphrey-Hawkins testimony before Congress. Or, you could use some distributed lag of actual consumer price increases over the past year or two. Subtract that inflation expectations number—now roughly 3 percent—from the nominal federal funds rate. So Greenspan's going to go from zero—which is "accommodative"—to "neutral." The average real rate over the last two decades is 1.5 to 2 percent (see Figure 4).

Q. Isn't that strongly biased by the unusual experience with very high money rates in the 1980s?
A. Oh yes. The high rates of the 1980s did give it an upward bias. As I see it, the real rate for a normal

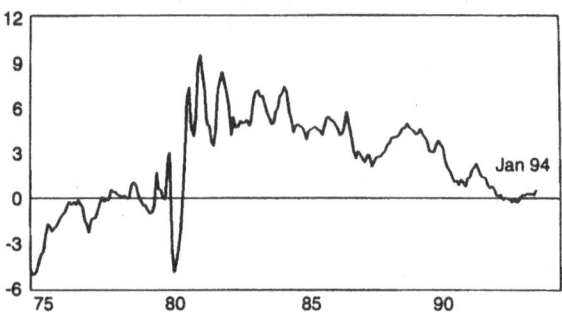

Figure 4. **Real Short-Term Interest Rate**
(Fed funds rate minus year-over-year % change in CPI %)

*Source:* Calculated by Aubrey G. Lanston & Co. from Federal Reserve Board figures.

economic expansion stands somewhere between 1 and 2 percent. This is a "neutral" Fed policy stance, which neither stimulates nor depresses economic growth.

Q. So, based on your expectations, the FOMC will continue to increase the federal funds rate?
A. This economy is now showing strong, self-sustaining economic growth, and indicators of higher orders and higher production and employment point to an upswing in the manufacturing sector. Therefore, I expect that the Fed will tighten the federal funds rate further—to perhaps 5 percent by the end of 1994.

Q. With Mullins and Angell (February 1994) gone from the Board, and Clinton's appointments of Allan Blinder and Janet Yellen about to come into play, how will Greenspan's strategy prevail?
A. Both Mullins and Angell were inflation hawks. Now Greenspan will be facing two Clinton appointments—Blinder from the Council of Economic Advisers and Janet Yellen from the University of California at Berkeley. Both are basically dovish on inflation; they favor growth as a primary objective, and holding down inflation as a secondary objective. Alan Greenspan favors the opposite: holding down inflation as a primary objective and growth as a secondary objective. That's a big difference on policy goals between the Fed Chairman and President Clinton—two new appointments to the Federal Reserve Board.

Q. What does this do to your second story about Greenspan's new strategy?
A. There's another parallel in this process of making monetary policy. The second story is that of a parallel between the nature of economic growth now and that

of the period between the mid-1950s and mid-1960s. During this earlier period, we had strong investment-led growth with high productivity and relatively low labor costs and inflation. At that time, Fed Chairman William McChesney Martin, Jr. (1951–70) followed a procedure of "leaning against the wind." Today, there are a lot of parallels with that earlier period. Then we had real growth without a lot of inflation, as we do now. We now enjoy relatively high productivity growth, which we had in the late 1950s. We now have a chance for sustained growth without serious inflation, just as we had during the golden age of growth in the early 1960s.

Q. But there is a remarkable difference in the two periods. Much of the growth in productivity during the 1990s is related to the shedding of labor in corporate downsizing. We are undergoing an historic, global economic transformation that is driving a restructuring of the U.S. economy.
A. Very true. Now we also have a big budget deficit, and we had a balanced budget then. Certainly, there are differences; but the similarities offer great hope for the present. Today, the first stage of business investment goes along with what you've pointed out—investment in equipment largely to get rid of labor. That business equipment spending has been running at two-digit growth rates in recent quarters. The second stage makes me optimistic. The economy is operating at relatively high levels of capacity utilization, coupled with relatively good profits. Therefore, I'm anticipating significant increases in plant and equipment spending over the next six to twelve months for purposes of expanding productive capacity. This is the job-creating type of investment.

Q. What's more, the United States is now the low-wage producer among the advanced countries, and we've just experienced a decline in unit labor costs.
A. Exactly. So you can't point to a better export platform in the world than the United States. And that is an advantage, not just for U.S. businesses. BMW, Mercedes, and Japanese auto companies, among other foreign businesses, see the opportunities here and are investing in U.S. production facilities. By contrast, in the 1960s, investment was mostly by U.S. firms. The scope for productive investment here has a global dimension that will greatly enhance both the quality and quantity of investment and overall U.S. growth. I see investment as a leading component of GDP growth.

Q. Not long ago, Fed Governor Lawrence B. Lindsey cited a study about the vulnerability of household consumption because of the heavy burden of debt.
A. Yes. But I don't buy his argument, since it doesn't explain much of what is going on now. How does he explain the fourth quarter of 1993 with that theory?

Q. How do you explain it?
A. By simply saying that he underestimates how much gain people got from falling interest rates and from refinancing their mortgages and other debt. That gave households higher net income.

Q. But now, if interest rates are going back up?
A. I won't argue against that ultimate negative effect on consumption. But the negatives will be offset by the positive effects. I concede that consumers have not reduced debt loads very much, and that means the economy has less cushion on the down side. But the multiplier principle says that strong investment-led growth will lead to strong income growth. This will be the key to strong real growth in 1994 and, perhaps, most of 1995 as well.

Q. But, the 30-year bond yield is up over one percentage point since the end of 1993.
A. It's not going to stay at that level. From the lows in October last year of 5.78 percent, the 30-year bond yield broke 7.5 percent in May and then retreated to lower levels. About two-thirds of those moves reflect economic forces—a strengthening economy and rising inflationary expectations; and the Fed is tightening in the background. One-third of that rise reflects domestic questions about the Clinton Administration's effectiveness. In the spring there were doubts about the Administration's credibility: Can it cut defense and budget spending? Would Whitewater blow up or blow over? Then, there are the trade difficulties and general relations with Japan. The dollar crashed, and foreign investors sold dollar bonds heavily—on the theory that the Clinton Administration would talk the dollar down and the yen up, in order to make Japanese exports more expensive. If the political air clears, long-term rates should stabilize.

Q. Now that businesses and households have made their balance sheet adjustments and debt refinancings, the economy returns to the old scenario of income and profit growth, with spending streams generated out of that income.

A. In my view, we're going to have adequate income and profit growth. The internal dynamics of this expansion are good enough to produce sufficient income to support solid consumer and investment spending at least through 1994 and the first half of 1995. What will come in the second half of 1995 and into 1996 is debatable. Most likely, some slowing of economic activity will occur at that time.

Q. So, in the next one to two years, you emphasize the strength of the cyclical recovery rather than structural adjustment?

A. That's exactly the way to say it. Look, the structural adjustment is still going on. The economy is still in a downtrend in a secular, structural way with the deflationary downsizing of major corporations and shifts in consumer preference to Timberland shoes instead of Gucci loafers, to four-wheel-drive vehicles instead of Porsches. Despite the structural change and downsizing, the current cyclical upswing is strong enough, starting in the second half of last year, and continuing at a moderate pace this year and the first half of next year, to overwhelm that secular downtrend. I won't deny that our tendency toward recessions will be stronger than in past decades, when the secular trends were stronger, as in the 1980s and the 1970s.

Q. Your view is not unlike the scenario in the Council of Economic Advisers' Report this year. They see essentially a problem of long-term adjustment dragging the economy down, with the cycle superimposed on it.

A. Right. The Administration was forced to cut the oversized deficit. The fiscal restraint from that deficit reduction is part of the structural adjustment.

Q. Now think about the emphasis on jobs, because it's essentially the lower-income quintiles where the job stagnation exists.

A. That's right. I'm not challenging anyone on that issue.

Q. So if this were a good old recovery of the 1950s or early 1960s, we'd create jobs at the low end of the spectrum. Many of those jobs offered prospects of future advancement and increases in real income. But the problem is that the current U.S. recovery doesn't assure such job growth among low-income workers.

A. I'm not trying to say that this recovery repeats the old-fashioned variety. I'm not drawing a perfect analogy to the 1950s or 1960s. And this is where my third story begins: It is about the nature of the current recovery and its underlying strength in investment spending. The economy is coming back on a growth track, and that is related to the strategy worked out among Rubin, Greenspan, and the president. If the Fed starts a series of moderate tightening steps early on, the Administration will be able to reinforce its anti-inflation credibility, and be able to keep inflation expectations low. With the financial markets reassured, that will limit how much long-term rates will go up. As a result, this expansion can be extended at least well into 1995, if not longer. I honestly believe that there is a good chance the economy can still stay on track.

Greenspan's approach is essentially the right course, and I think he has a better than even chance to succeed in limiting how much long-term rates go up, and extending the life of the expansion. That's point number one.

Point number two is that it's going to be a good-quality growth experience, despite our structural problems—whether they be debt burdens, corporate downsizing, or government deficits. The counterforce to those problems will be a strong cyclical expansion, paced by business capital spending and stronger export growth.

Q. How strong is strong?

A. Our growth potential is probably somewhere between 2.5 percent and 2.75 percent, if we look at long-term trends in productivity and labor force growth. During the decade of the 1990s, productivity growth will be 1.4 percent per annum, up from 0.7 percent in the 1980s. This will be derived from the two-pronged investment surge I mentioned before—labor-saving equipment and an expansion of plant capacity. With respect to the growth of the labor force, based on BLS estimates for immigration, birth rates, and death rates, I expect labor supply to expand at something like 1.2 percent; so potential GDP growth should be about 2.6 percent per year.

Given that long-term potential for trend growth, the cyclical upswing will raise actual GDP growth to within a range of 3.5 percent to 4 percent this year and 3 to 3.5 percent next year. That should reduce the unemployment rate down within a range of 5.5 percent to 6 percent by early 1995. Simultaneously, the capacity utilization rate should rise significantly to above 85 percent. To some extent, of course, our demand will spill over into higher imports from Japan, Germany, and other countries that are in recession, or are beginning to recover and have unused capacity.

Against that background, we are likely to have only a very moderate acceleration of inflation, because the cyclical upswing is working against all the secular forces that are deflationary. In my wildest nightmare, I couldn't picture more than 5 percent inflation. Now, I admit that Nixon put price controls on at 4 percent in 1971; but if you compare the present and near-term inflation rate to 13-to-14 percent inflation in the late 1970s, that's a pretty favorable cyclical comparison.

*Q* But there was a very significant difference in what caused that surge in prices. You have to account for the two oil-price shocks. That's not monetary inflation but supply-side shock; half the rise in the inflation in that period was directly related to soaring oil prices. And when the oil-price collapse came, the decline of inflation again happened to be related to the collapse of oil prices.

Apart from what caused the CPI to jump, once we reach the critical level—whatever that is, at 3 percent, 4 percent, or 5 percent—what do we do about the substantial erosion of Federal Reserve effectiveness in controlling inflation?
A. Commercial banks are the point of contact for Fed monetary policy. A declining share of commercial banks and other depository institutions in total credit extended reduces Federal Reserve effectiveness. Commercial banks, as a percentage of total nonfinancial debt in this country, rose to a peak of about 55 percent in 1975 and have been falling sharply to less than 35 percent at present. Since 1975, more and more credit has been pushed directly through the capital markets. The banks are happy with the steady fees they earn from originating, pooling, and selling mortgages and other loans off their balance sheets. Their capital ratios look great as they sell off those loans. But greater bank reliance on securitization means that the Fed's point of

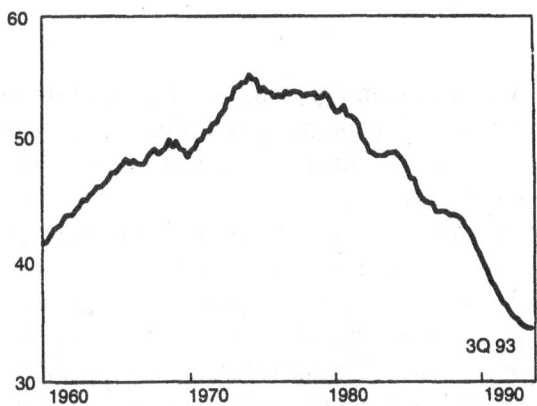

Figure 5. **Depository Institutions' Share of Total Nonfinancial Debt**

*Source:* Calculated by Aubrey G. Lanston & Co. from Federal Reserve Board figures.

contact—the banking system—is a smaller share of the total credit extended (see Figure 5). Therefore, the Fed may have to be more aggressive when it tightens and eases than it would otherwise be, because it has a looser and more difficult grip on the control of credit flows.

This new and more complex world in which the Federal Reserve must operate brings me to another point. Greenspan actually would like the inflation rate to come down even further—down to zero, or something like 1 to 2 percent as measured by the CPI. But he'll accept stability in a rate of inflation that hovers close to 3 percent.

*Q* Well, what if we get into a situation that we were in during the late 1970s and early 1980s—another oil-price shock or some other external price shock.
A. There is an easy answer. With all the downsize risk in the U.S. economy—heavy household debt burdens, corporations restructuring and downsizing, and Europe and Japan undergoing their own structural adjustments—such an inflation shock would be followed by a deep recession.

Q. Really then, as far as Federal Reserve stabilization policy is concerned, the strategy of the game is essentially the same under Greenspan as under his predecessors: You fight inflation by creating economic slack and a larger pool of unemployed workers, and unutilized plant capacity.
A. There's no alternative, at least in the short run. Anti-inflationary monetary policy has worked extremely well, but it always works with pain in the short

run. But remember, in the longer run, stable prices are a prerequisite to sustainable economic growth.

*Q.* But this strategy gives no consideration to the real economic costs of forgone production, jobs, income, and wealth. What about the huge costs of the recession you choose to create?

A. That's fiscal policy's job, and I am not in charge of the political mechanism. If a society wants to reduce the social costs, that is up to Congress to create an appropriate fiscal policy. Of course, the government safety nets would cushion the blow to the unemployed. There are the automatic stabilizers and other special programs in terms of fiscal policy. But the Chairman of the Federal Reserve doesn't have responsibility for regulating fiscal policy.

Q. But doesn't triggering the government safety nets and activating fiscal stimulus mean a burgeoning public sector deficit? That was the policy mix of the 1980s that the Bush and Clinton Administrations inherited. Bush didn't turn it around and Clinton is now doing so.

A. Yes, we are now caught in the wake of too much debt expansion in the 1980s, and now we're being forced to reduce the budget deficit in the 1990s. The consequences are easy to see. The economy will struggle to sustain expansion and the danger of recession will always lurk around the corner.

Q. You seem to be in the camp of those economists who believe we can have moderate growth without accelerating inflation.

A. But it must be a manageable rate of inflation—with consumer price increases at a pace of less than 3 percent. Such rates of inflation won't significantly influence consumer and business decision making. Businesses won't start to build inventories on the speculation that prices will be spiraling upward, and consumers won't buy in anticipation of price appreciation.

Q. What caused the speculation boom of the mid-to-late-1980s, with waves of corporate mergers and acquisitions, real estate speculation, and the banks and other financial institutions deeply involved in it?

A. That was a financial bubble, not a real-sector problem. Business inventories stayed in line, for example. In the normal cycles of the past—the 1950s, 1960s, and 1970s—imbalances in the real sector spilled over to become imbalances in the financial sector. That, in turn, generated inflation, prompting the Fed's tight money and a recession.

By contrast, the 1980s was an unusual decade. Business managed inventories more tightly than ever, and the real economy didn't develop significant imbalances. Instead, a speculative financial bubble developed, as business borrowed for takeovers and consumers speculated in real estate.

*Q.* Since that kind of financial bubble can emerge again, how can the Fed get a handle on it to prevent it or control it?

A. It's very difficult. There's nothing more disturbing to a Fed chairman than pumping liquidity into a system and have it go into financial bubble, instead of into the real sector. The Federal Reserve cannot direct or channel where the funds go.

Q. So the only way you can break the bubble is to break the back of the economy? Isn't there a more efficient and less costly way of affecting the speculative bubble?

A. Up to this point, the economic science hasn't got us any farther. We can only hope to keep business and consumer inflationary psychology under control in order to discourage how much resources go into a financial bubble. If nobody sees an opportunity for a big price payoff from speculating in business inventories, real estate and houses, or commodities, speculative fever cools down. But I don't think you can extinguish it completely.

JERRY J. JASINOWSKI

# *The Case Against Further Monetary Tightening*

*The most serious threat to the expansion is not that there will be a renewed burst of inflation. Rather, it is that the Fed will fail to perceive the structural changes working to keep inflation low, and will turn the screws too hard.*

The Federal Reserve's decision to raise short-term interest rates a full 75 basis points in November 1994 reflects the hope that it can head off any future increases in inflation by slowing down the growth rate. But, while the goal of low inflation and steady growth is commendable, one may disagree with the Fed's timing and with some of its policy targets.

I argue that inflation will remain in check, while productivity is likely to stay high. This means, in essence, that the economy can continue to achieve healthy growth rates without serious inflationary pressure.

As recently as 1989, the unemployment rate fell to 5.3 percent, causing the inflation rate to rise to 4.4 percent. This paralleled the experience at the peak of prior business cycles when lower unemployment and high capacity use led to inflationary pressures. But a series of changes during the early 1990s (particularly in manufacturing) has changed the way the economy works. If Wall Street, and their supporters on the Fed, got out to Main Street more often, they would see that there has been a productivity revolution in plants and on factory floors across the nation.

Many analysts continue to anticipate further increases in rates, perhaps another 100 basis points in 1995. The bond markets have contended that these increases are necessary to hold back inflation. They have further argued that current real long-term interest rates—about 5 percent—pointed to a large "expectations premium." I believe that the bond market's expectations of inflation are unrealistic, in view of the changes in the economy.

## *Industry's perspective*

Certainly, the industrial community takes a different view. From its standpoint, the threat of inflation is unclear, and further tightening moves are neither necessary nor desirable. A crucial issue for monetary policy has to do with whether the current business cycle is qualitatively different from previous ones. The bond market and the Fed appear to take the view that no major

JERRY J. JASINOWSKI is President of the National Association of Manufacturers. Reprinted from *Challenge,* January–February 1995, pp. 9–14.

structural changes have taken place, and that monetary policy should continue to emphasize the same targets it concentrated on in the late 1980s. Based on recent developments in the manufacturing sector, I would argue that the economy is undergoing deeper structural transformations which have raised potential output and reduced inflationary pressure. In other words, *we can now produce more with less inflation than in the past.*

By a large majority, the National Association of Manufacturers (NAM) Board of Directors opposes further increases in interest rates at the present time. In a September poll, fully 49 percent of the NAM Board argued that the Federal Reserve should hold interest rates at or near then current levels. On December 8, 1994, a poll of the NAM Executive Committee echoed this view, with 50 percent arguing that the Fed should hold rates at current levels, and 34 percent arguing that any increases should be delayed until late 1995. By that time, there will be more evidence of how much the economy has slowed down. Some leading CEOs felt that interest rates were nearing levels above which they would begin to choke off demand and generate a sharp slowdown. Rising interest rates were and are perceived as a danger, because the response of the economy to higher rates is not linear. If short-term rates were raised another 50 basis points, the loss in GDP in 1995, relative to trend, would be about $26 billion. A rise in short-term rates of 100 basis points would lower GDP by about $66 billion.

## *The evidence on inflation*

What the Federal Reserve should do is, of course, critically bound up with the perceived direction of inflation. For 1995, just over one-half of the NAM Board of Directors sees inflation in the range of 3 percent or slightly above. Indeed, 29 percent of its members project inflation at below 3 percent. Our econometric forecast is even more sanguine. We project the GDP deflator at only 2.9 percent in 1995.

Industrialists have also staked out a different position on the factors likely to lead to inflation. Arguments that there is a serious risk of higher inflation break down into four areas: (1) capacity pressures; (2) material input costs; (3) international prices; and (4) unit labor costs. We polled the Board and analyzed all four categories.

• *Capacity Use.* The NAM Board does not view capacity pressure as a serious inflationary threat. While overall capacity use is close to where it was at the time of the last increase in inflation in 1989, it is lower than during previous business cycles, when utilization rates of 88 percent or more have been recorded. The possibility that the economy might be overheating has been raised by high rates of industrial capacity use. Since inflation typically rises at the peak of the business cycle, it tends to be correlated with high utilization of capacity. But industry actually has more capacity than the official measures. One reason has to do with the capital stock. The official estimate of that capacity increased by only 2.8 percent in 1993, despite the fact that equipment investment in manufacturing increased by more than 15 percent. After taking depreciation into account, capacity should have increased by 4 percent. A second problem has to do with outsourcing. Many manufacturing firms are now outsourcing many inputs (including service inputs) to other companies rather than conducting them in-house. This means that the capital stock in industry alone is too narrow a measure of the true capacity to produce. The capital stock of the sectors that supply manufacturers should also be taken into account. The outsourcing issue is particularly important for firms that rely on worldwide suppliers. In essence, their capacity is augmented by the global capital stock.

Perhaps the most important aspect of the capacity issue, however, is the improvement in productive efficiency made possible by computerization. The contribution of computers to output has been significantly raised by the innovative ways in which they are used. For instance, computers have been used to control inventories, link factories with suppliers and customers, and facilitate design of new products. In this way, their contribution is considerably greater than the value of the computer stock alone would imply. Nonetheless, the official capacity measures are based on the capital stock alone, rather than on qualitative improvements in the production process.

In a recent poll, the NAM Executive Committee ranked process improvements associated with computerization as the primary factor raising capacity, followed by other technological improvements and outsourcing. Still, there was greater evidence of tightening capacity in some sectors, especially paper products, motor vehicles, and chemicals. Thus, despite the generic reasons for believing capacity to be greater than the official measures, pressure may raise prices in particular industries in 1995.

• *Material Input Costs.* A second issue has to do with

commodity- or material-input prices. The NAM Board sees more of a threat from material-input prices than from any other factor. However, material-input costs (less than 10 percent of total costs) are not usually transmitted to final product prices. In the last few years, industrialists have increasingly tended to resist input price increases by controlling costs. Stated another way, they have tended to engineer input costs out of final product prices in order to avoid risking a loss in market share.

The NAM Board strongly confirms that costs are not, for the most part, being passed forward. Forty-two percent of the Board (the largest share) responded that input costs will be only partially passed through to prices. Fully 34 percent responded that costs would not be passed through at all. Only one-fourth expect to pass costs through. The implication is that recent volatility in crude-goods prices will not translate into large increases in finished-goods prices.

A related issue is whether commodity prices can serve as a barometer of future inflation, irrespective of whether they are passed through. This does not stand up under scrutiny. Statistical studies have demonstrated that commodity prices are much more volatile than more widely based measures, and tend to give "false positive" signals on inflation. Even if commodity prices are taken as reliable indicators, however, they are not currently forecasting higher inflation. For instance, the producer price index for crude materials decreased by 2.9 percent during the last twelve months.

- *International Prices.* Concern has been voiced in some circles that the low exchange rate will lead to higher import prices, and that these will cause domestic inflation. The NAM Board does not see this as a risk. Although Europe is finally recovering from a long recession, there is still enough slack overseas. Sluggish world prices are holding American prices down.

The whole international-price argument ignores the fact that manufacturing has become more globalized during the last decade. This globalization is disinflationary in the long run as well as in the short run for several reasons. Increased competition prevents price increases. For a long time, the conventional wisdom was that American firms were partially protected from worldwide competition, and that they could engage in semiadministered pricing in the domestic market. While this may have been true before the early 1970s, it is certainly not true today. The global economy is extremely competitive, with many third-world countries now competing in advanced industries. What this means is that prices are set by the global market. Industrialists can hope to remain profitable only if they produce more efficiently. They cannot boost their margins by raising prices.

A case in point: Tracy O'Rourke, the CEO of Varian—a diversified high-tech manufacturer on the west coast—recently reported to me that he has doubled his sales in the last three years without a single price increase. This impressive performance was not achieved easily. In his own words, "every sale is a dogfight over prices."

Another reason why globalization is disinflationary has to do with outsourcing. Modern industrial corporations are linked via computer to suppliers all over the world. When domestic markets are tight, they can often find a lower price by outsourcing their components.

- *Unit Labor Costs.* The NAM Board assigns a low risk to wage pressures. Unit labor costs have been very docile in the last few years. During the twelve months ending in the third quarter of 1994, unit labor costs increased by only 0.9 percent in nonfarm business, and declined by 2.9 percent in manufacturing.

A final argument as to why inflation may accelerate has to do with *demand pressure*. While we didn't poll the NAM Board on this, their rather guarded outlook for 1995 shows growth slowing down. Of the major forecasters polled in the *Consensus Economics* surveys, the majority predict GDP gains in the area of 2.8 percent. For demand pressures to become significant, a number of things would have to happen simultaneously. Consumers would have to continue to draw down their savings and increase their debt, despite high interest rates. Construction would have to pick up, despite an oversupply of apartments and office space. Exports would have to come on line faster, due to a stronger recovery overseas. Business would have to build up inventories excessively.

While we are actually quite optimistic about exports, we expect that, after a strong fourth quarter 1994, consumers will retrench in the first half of 1995. In other words, while growth may be strong enough for demand to pull prices upward in 1995, it is more likely that growth will slow down to a more moderate and sustainable pace.

The lower inflation rate in manufacturing has actually been in evidence for quite some time, although it has only recently been recognized. Over the last fifteen years, the inflation rate has been significantly lower in goods than in services. For instance, in 1982–93, the prices of services increased, on average, about twice as rapidly as the prices of goods at the retail level—4.8 percent per year versus 2.4 percent. This trend will continue in the 1990s.

## Factors leading to price stability

Rather than confine the debate to inflation directly, I argue that structural changes in the manufacturing economy have raised potential output to such an extent that we can look forward to a long period of noninflationary growth. These changes are:

- *Faster Productivity Growth.* The clearest indication is the acceleration in manufacturing productivity growth since the early 1980s. While productivity in the nonfarm economy failed to recover after the initial slowdown in the mid-1970s, starting roughly in 1983, productivity actually accelerated above trend in the manufacturing sector.

According to the most recent Bureau of Labor Statistics (BLS) data, manufacturing productivity averaged 2.9 percent growth per year in 1983–93—not bad by any means. But these figures, which are based on GDP, probably understate the true rate of productivity growth. An earlier series based on GNP shows manufacturing productivity growing by 3.1 percent per year in 1979–90. Industrial activity is so internationalized now that GNP is probably a better measure for the manufacturing sector than GDP.

The earlier figures also reveal that most of the acceleration was accounted for by multifactor productivity. By implication, it reflects technological advance. Much of this has been the result of computerization of the production process. This, in turn, argues that potential output—the long-term growth path consistent with stable inflation—may be edging upward. The Fed seems to be operating with the assumption that this is no more than 2.5 percent annually. While recent increases in productivity—2.9 percent in the nonfarm business sector in the most recent quarter—may be largely cyclical, it is probable that the service sector will soon start to achieve higher long-term productivity due to process improvements from computerization. If so, potential output may be higher than the Fed's target.

- *Global Markets.* A second reason to expect stable prices has to do with the fact that American industry is increasingly focusing on global rather than merely national markets. As noted earlier, the globalization of the production process has increased capacity. But more important, unlike the early 1980s, American industry is now highly competitive in world markets. The low dollar and strong productivity improvements have given the United States a comparative advantage in many industrial sectors. The result is that, as the rest of the world recovers, we can look forward to a sustained boom in merchandise exports.

During prior periods when the dollar was low and growth rates were strong abroad (for instance, 1978–80 and 1987–91), exports surged by almost 11 percent per year in real terms. The turning point for net exports (heretofore a drag on the recovery) should come in the fourth quarter 1994. In 1995–96, trade should add $20 to $25 billion per year to GDP. The fact that the trade gains will come primarily in merchandise means that manufacturing productivity will rise automatically. Output will grow faster than hours. The increase in the manufacturing share of output will in turn raise nonfarm productivity. Potential output will grow more rapidly.

- *Wage Competition.* Related to the idea of the noninflationary long-run growth rate is the natural rate of unemployment. Here too, the Fed may be too pessimistic. Up to early 1993, the natural rate was generally estimated at 5.7 percent. When the BLS revised the unemployment rate upward last February, quite a few analysts simply raised their estimate of the natural rate by the same amount. But this makes no sense, because all the extra workers previously missed by the BLS are employable. They compete for jobs. Furthermore, the last time full employment was achieved (in 1989), the unemployment rate dropped as low as 5.3 percent. The demographics do not argue for any increase in the natural rate since this time.

Another reason why the natural rate should be viewed as lower than 5.7 is the increasing prevalence of part-time, contingent, and temporary employment. Most of these workers would prefer to regain full-time permanent jobs. Consequently, while they are measured as fully employed, they are likely to compete with the unemployed for available jobs. This competition will keep wages down.

There are other factors working to hold unit labor costs in check. Workers are justifiably worried about job security, in the face of many restructurings. They are unlikely to make aggressive wage demands. At the same time, there is an increasing trend toward nonwage compensation, in the form of stock options, incentive payments, and bonuses. In essence, this means that wage costs will increase less rapidly, and workers' total compensation will become more dependent on the profitability and productivity of firms.

## Measurement bias

While the Consumer Price Index (CPI) is the most widely used measure of inflation, it is also one of the least reliable. The expenditure weights in the CPI are currently based on 1982–84. If they were based on 1993, the rate of inflation would be four-tenths of a percentage point lower. For instance, in 1993, the CPI rose by 3.0 percent, while the implicit-price deflator for personal consumption rose by 2.6 percent. Part of the problem is that the CPI is weighted toward sectors (such as medical services) with high inflation rates and does not include items (such as personal computers) that have been going down in price. Indeed, Fed Chairman Alan Greenspan acknowledged this during the question-and-answer session following his December 7, 1994 testimony to the Joint Economic Committee.

The tendency of fixed-weight indexes to overstate inflation is not limited to the CPI. In 1993, the implicit-price deflator for GDP rose by 2.5 percent, while the fixed-weight deflator (based on the 1987 expenditure weights) rose by 3.1 percent. In the most recent quarter, the implicit-price deflator rose by 1.9 percent while the fixed-weight deflator rose by 3.2 percent. Inherent in inflation measures as a whole is the problem that price indexes are based on posted prices rather than on actual transactions. Consequently, they tend to miss sales, discounts, or the effect of negotiations between buyers and sellers.

It is also possible that the BLS is underestimating the unemployment rate, despite the revisions to the household survey last February. The labor-force participation rate and the employment-to-population ratio for males both fell during the last recession. They have not yet regained their prerecession levels of 1989. Since this cannot be explained solely by retirement, it is likely that the BLS household survey is missing workers who will return to the labor force, and that the unemployment rate is higher than the current estimate.

## Lags in monetary policy

One further reason not to raise interest rates so quickly is that the effect of the previous increases has yet to be fully reflected in economic activity. The lag between interest rates and real activity is generally estimated at about six to nine months. The Fed's major moves on interest rates did not come until the summer, with the result that it will not be until the first quarter of 1995 that their effect will really be in evidence. In the face of continued strong growth in the third and fourth quarters, some analysts have expressed surprise at the seeming resilience of spending in the face of such high real borrowing costs. This resilience, however, is more apparent than real. The recent spurt of growth does not actually indicate insensitivity to rising rates, but rather is the lagged effect of unusually low rates in 1992 and 1993.

Given the lags, a reasonable strategy for the Federal Reserve would be to wait to gauge the results of its previous decisions. This would argue for holding rates at or near current levels until the second quarter. One reason why the Fed might not do so, however, is that the slowdown will probably be gradual. In fact, many forecasters expect the economy to be on a "glide path" in 1995, slowing from a strong first half to a more moderate second. Recent numbers showing buoyant employment and incomes in the fourth quarter support this scenario. If so, the Fed will have little evidence that the slowdown is materializing, and may be tempted to raise rates immediately.

If short rates are raised by another 50 basis points, the implied growth rate for 1995 will fall to 2.9 percent. Larger rate hikes—e.g., 100 basis points—would pull the growth rate down to about 2.7 percent, with most of the slowdown coming in the second half.

## Bond market pessimism

If some of the statements from the bond market are taken at face value, it would suggest an almost incredible pessimism about the ability of the economy to achieve noninflationary growth. For instance, the bond market has been issuing warnings about inflation since early 1993, but so far it has failed to materialize. Some analysts have claimed that the natural rate of unemployment is well over 6 percent. If true, wages would now be rising explosively. But, as noted earlier, unit labor costs are increasing slowly in nonfarm business and are declining in manufacturing. The best that can be said of this perspective is that it is unrealistic. It completely fails to recognize the technological advances that have made it possible to achieve higher growth and simultaneously control costs. At worst, it is a paranoid response. Bond traders live in a world that is seriously out of touch with the dramatic changes occurring in the real economy.

The level of real long-term interest rates—over 5 percent—is partially attributable to this lack of realism. There are, of course, other causes, including the recent escalation in household debt and the continuing federal deficit. The federal deficit (now about 3 percent of GDP) accounts for about 30 percent of borrowing, and households currently account for more than one-half. With investment likely to exceed saving by an estimated $135 billion in 1994, the United States is still facing a capital shortage. The best chance to reduce long-term interest rates would be another round of deficit reduction by the federal government.

## Faster growth without inflation

What all this boils down to is a very favorable long-term outlook for noninflationary growth. With American industry highly competitive in world markets, exports will pick up and keep the economy growing. Industrial exports will boost productivity both in manufacturing and the nonfarm business sector. But the main source of productivity gains will come from technological advance—much of it the result of computerization.

Productivity gains are one reason why inflation will remain low. But there are others. Industrial capacity is higher than measured. Increases in the prices of material inputs are not being passed through. Competitive pressures have led industry to avoid price increases. Changes in labor markets will prevent wages from accelerating. Under these circumstances, the most serious threat to the expansion is not a renewed burst of inflation. Rather, it is that the Federal Reserve will fail to perceive the structural changes working to keep inflation low, and will tighten too much.

Even without accepting the evidence of fundamental changes in the U.S. economy, the Fed's collective interest-rate increase (the largest since 1981) was a mistake. Much of the impact of the Fed's previous hikes in interest rates has yet to work its way through the system.

Americans paid a high price for the wrenching economic changes in the 1980s. In the wake of corporate downsizing, thousands of Americans lost their jobs. Many more have undertaken difficult retraining programs to keep their jobs. Now, U.S. industry is lean and mean. It can compete with anyone in the world. By raising interest rates excessively now, Wall Street and the Fed are punishing the U.S. economy for what it did right. They're asking business and labor alike to pay the price. That may sound fair in the topsy-turvy world of *Alice in Wonderland*, but it doesn't in the real world today.

DIMITRI B. PAPADIMITRIOU AND L. RANDALL WRAY

# The Fed: Wrong Turn in Risky Traffic

*The moderate inflation achieved recently does not entail significant costs. Indeed, the benefits to be gained by eliminating this inflation cannot be expected to exceed the costs that would be engendered by higher unemployment, greater uncertainty, and lost output. Given the current state of the economy, it is far more important to focus on full employment than on inflation.*

In the past decade and a half, U.S. monetary policy has deviated radically from that of the postwar period. It has embarked on a series of policy experiments focused almost exclusively on price stability. Beginning in 1979, under Chairman Volcker, the Fed pushed interest rates above 20 percent and unemployment above 10 percent. That resulted in the deepest recession since the Great Depression. Similarly, under Alan Greenspan, the Fed pushed interest rates to nearly 11 percent in the first quarter of 1989 (when inflation was less than 5 percent) and contributed to a long recession. More recently, the Fed has tightened six times in ten months to fight perceived inflationary pressures. In our view, the pursuit of stable prices by the Fed since 1979 has contributed to high levels of unemployment, low productivity growth, and reduced economic growth—all of which was experienced by the U.S. economy during the 1980s and 1990s.

In the summer of 1993, Chairman Greenspan announced that the Fed would drop monetary aggregates as targets of monetary policy and would, instead, target a real interest rate. This announcement was met with nearly universal surprise and was rejected by most economists as unworkable. In later testimony, Greenspan advocated inflation expectations as the target of monetary policy. During the past year, the radical shift in policy announced by Chairman Greenspan in four separate testimonies, as well as the six occasions on which the Fed raised short-term interest rates, violated the goals of monetary policy as laid out by the chairman himself in June 1994. At that time, he said:

> Most importantly, we can reinforce ongoing trends in the private sector that enhance our productive potential by helping to create a stable environment for sustainable noninflationary economic growth. Stability in economic conditions boosts confidence and makes long-range planning by businesses and households much easier.

Unstable interest rates, uncertainty over actions to be taken at the Federal Open Market Committee (FOMC) meetings, and unstable exchange rates generated by rudderless central bank policy have all reduced

DIMITRI B. PAPADIMITRIOU is Executive Director of the Jerome Levy Economics Institute of Bard College. L. RANDALL WRAY is Research Associate at the same institute and Associate Professor of Economics at the University of Denver. Reprinted from *Challenge*, January–February 1995, pp. 15–21.

Figure 6  **Actual and Expected Inflation Growth**

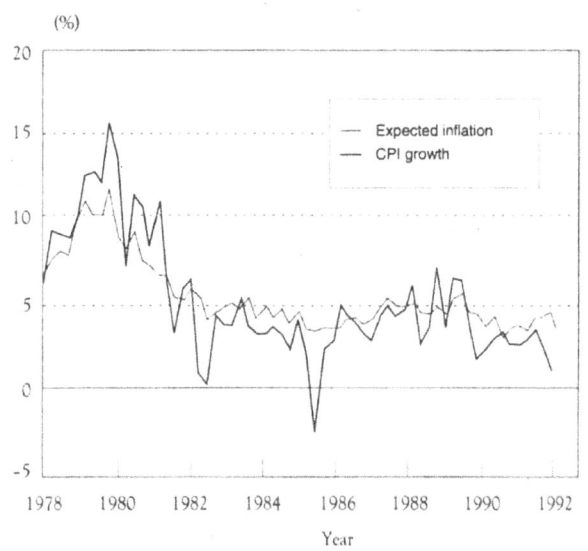

*Note:* The figure represents the inflation rate as measured by quarterly changes in the consumer price index and expected inflation as measured by the University of Michigan's expected inflation series one-year forward forecast.
*Source:* The Forecasting Center of the Jerome Levy Economics Institute.

Figure 7  **Real *Ex Ante* and Real *Ex Post* Interest Rates**

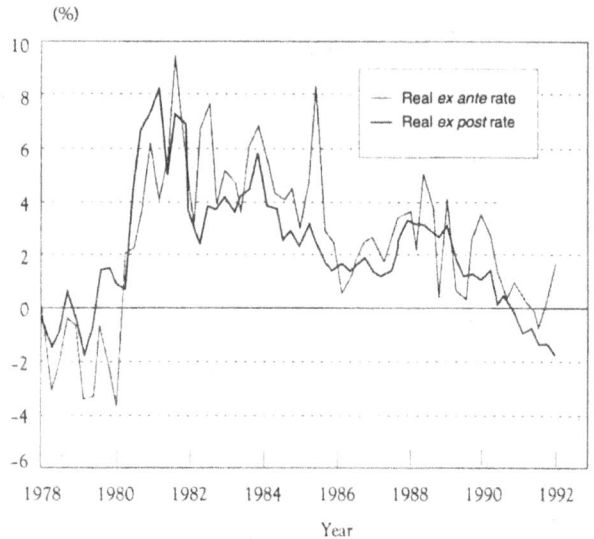

*Source: National Income and Product Account* and the Forecasting Center of the Jerome Levy Economics Institute.

stability, confidence, and the ability to engage in long-run planning. Finally, there is, so far, no evidence that the Fed's moves since February 1994 have lowered inflation expectations. The policy has caused investors to shun the long-term end of the market. The yield curve will remain steep, because high long-term rates are required to compensate holders of long-term bonds for the capital losses they would suffer when the Fed tightened further.

## Would random policy be better?

While the Fed's policy clearly failed by Chairman Greenspan's own test, we analyzed the data since 1959 to determine how well Chairman Greenspan's proposals would have fared, had they been adopted in the past (see Figure 6).

If the Fed had adopted a real interest rate target in the past, how often would it have correctly read economic conditions? Over the entire examined period, the real *ex post* short-term interest rate averaged just less than 1.5 percent, with a maximum of nearly 9.5 percent and a minimum of –5.5 percent (see Figure 7). Assuming that the average real rate of 1.5 percent is a proxy for Chairman Greenspan's "equilibrium" real rate, then a real rate above this should indicate an economy facing disinflationary pressures. And a rate below this should presage dangers of accelerating inflation.

Table 5 is a "scorecard" for Chairman Greenspan's proposed policy. Assume that he plans to implement a tight policy when the real interest rate drops below 1.5 percent to fight inflationary pressures and to implement an easy policy when the real interest rate is above 1.5 percent. As this table shows, there were sixty-five quarters in which Greenspan would have adopted an easy policy. However, forty-eight of these quarters were followed by accelerating inflation (defined as a rise of inflation by one percentage point or more within the following four quarters). Chairman Greenspan's policy would have been *mistaken* 74 percent of the time. Indeed, as the table shows, he would have adopted the incorrect policy 96 percent of the time between 1959.2 and 1971.1, 50 percent of the time between 1971.1 and 1983.1, and 66 percent of the time between 1983.2 and 1993.3. There were seventy-three quarters in which the real rate fell below 1.5 percent. This suggested to Greenspan that tight money policy would be required. However, thirty-seven of these quarters were followed by declining inflation. This policy would have been incorrect 100 percent of the time between 1983.2 and 1993.3, 28 percent of the time between 1971.2 and 1983.1, and 60 percent of the time between 1959.2 and 1971.1—for an overall score of incorrect policy responses 51 percent of the time.

In addition, the real interest rate often misinterprets the "tightness" of the economy as measured by the

| Table 5 | | Chairman Greenspan's Scorecard: Inflation | | | |
|---|---|---|---|---|---|
| Period | Number of quarters with STr >1.5% | Number of quarters with inflation > 4.7% | Number of quarters with inflation < 4.7% | Number of quarters followed by accelerating inflation | Chairman Greenspan adopts wrong policy (%) |
| 1959.2–1971.1 | 23 | 2 | 21 | 22 | 96 |
| 1971.2–1983.1 | 12 | 8 | 4 | 6 | 50 |
| 1983.2–1993.3 | 30 | 4 | 26 | 20 | 66 |
| Period | Number of quarters with STr <1.5% | Number of quarters with inflation > 4.7% | Number of quarters with inflation < 4.7% | Number of quarters followed by accelerating inflation | Chairman Greenspan adopts wrong policy (%) |
| 1959.2–1971.1 | 25 | 8 | 17 | 10 | 60 |
| 1971.2–1983.1 | 36 | 28 | 8 | 26 | 28 |
| 1983.2–1993.3 | 12 | 4 | 8 | 0 | 100 |

*Source:* Authors' calculations based on National Income and Product Account and The Levy Economics Institute Forecasting Center.
*Note:* STr is the real short-term rate as measured by subtracting the inflation rate (as measured by the rate of increase in the consumer price index) from the three-month Treasury bill rate. Owing to data limitations, it was assumed that the inflation rate will not rise above 2.3 percent within four quarters following 1993.3. Inflation is measured as the quarterly rate of change in the consumer price index.

| Table 6 | | Chairman Greenspan's Scorecard: Capacity Utilization | | | |
|---|---|---|---|---|---|
| Period | Number of quarters with STr >1.5% | Number of quarters with cap. util. > 82% | Number of quarters with cap. util. < 82% | Number of quarters followed by falling cap. util. | Chairman Greenspan adopts wrong policy (%) |
| 1959.2–1971.1 | 23 | 16 | 7 | 9 | 61 |
| 1971.2–1983.1 | 12 | 0 | 12 | 7 | 42 |
| 1983.2–1993.3 | 30 | 9 | 21 | 3 | 90 |
| Period | Number of quarters with STr <1.5% | Number of quarters with cap. util. > 82% | Number of quarters with cap. util. < 82% | Number of quarters followed by falling cap. util. | Chairman Greenspan adopts wrong policy (%) |
| 1959.2–1971.1 | 25 | 15 | 10 | 8 | 68 |
| 1971.2–1983.1 | 36 | 22 | 14 | 19 | 47 |
| 1983.2–1993.3 | 12 | 0 | 12 | 4 | 67 |

*Source:* Authors' calculations based on National Income and Product Account and The Levy Economics Institute Forecasting Center.
*Note:* Cap. util. is capacity utilization. STr is the real short-term interest rate as measured by subtracting the inflation rate (as measured by the rate of increase of the consumer price index) from the three-month Treasury bill rate. Owing to data limitations, it was assumed that capacity utilization will not fall below 78.8 percent or rise above 82.8 percent within four quarters following 1993.3.

capacity utilization rate (see Table 6). Chairman Greenspan claims that when the real short-term interest rate is below "equilibrium," bottlenecks will follow as capacity utilization rises, thereby generating inflation. In other words, when the short-term interest rate is below 1.5 percent, capacity utilization is expected to rise, generating inflationary pressures that can be lessened if the Fed adopts a tight policy. Similarly, when the real interest rate is above 1.5 percent, capacity utilization is expected to fall. We examined the four-quarter period following each real interest-rate observation to see whether a real rate below 1.5 percent predicts rising capacity-utilization rates and whether a real rate above 1.5 percent indicates falling capacity-utilization rates. We defined a rise or fall as an increase or decrease of capacity utilization by two percentage points or more over any quarter within four quarters of the period under observation.

As Table 6 shows, when the real rate was above 1.5 percent, the chairman would have chosen the wrong policy 61 percent of the time between 1959.2 and 1971.1, 42 percent of the time between 1971.2 and 1983.1, and 90 percent of the time between 1983.2 and 1993.3—for an overall average of 71 percent incorrect policy choices. In other words, in most cases, relatively high real interest rates did not foretell falling capacity-utilization rates, so that an easy policy was not indicated. On the other hand, when the real rate was below 1.5 percent, the chairman would have chosen the incorrect policy 68 percent of the time between 1959.2 and 1971.1, 47 percent of the time between 1971.2 and 1983.1, and 67 percent of the time between 1983.2 and 1993.3—

for an overall average of 58 percent incorrect policy responses. These tests, then, lead us to conclude that real interest rates do not correctly predict future capacity-utilization rates and cannot be used to guide monetary policy designed to affect capacity utilization with a lag of up to a year.

However, our tests assume the Fed did not actually adopt the "correct" (that is, Chairman Greenspan's) policy. For example, if the Fed adopted a tight policy each time the real rate fell below 1.5 percent, this would (according to Chairman Greenspan's theory) prevent inflation so that Table 5 would report a policy error (because the low real interest rate would not be followed by inflation). If the Fed actually (perhaps unknowingly) followed Chairman Greenspan's rule, then Table 5 might report a score of 100 percent wrong policy responses. If the Fed had actually adopted perverse policy (that is, the opposite of Chairman Greenspan's rule), then Table 5 could report no policy errors. But, through close examination of actual Fed discount rate policy, we found that the Fed has, in the past, adopted "perverse" policy a bit more than 40 percent of the time and "correct" policy a bit less than 30 percent of the time. This indicates that the incorrect policy responses of Tables 5 and 6 cannot be attributed to the Fed's unknowing adoption of Chairman Greenspan's policy, because the Fed's past policy appears to be nearly random with respect to Greenspan's prescription.

Greenspan has also claimed that expected inflation is a good predictor of future inflation. Indeed, expected inflation seems to be the only guide analyzed by the Chairman that has yet to be dismissed. But commentators have noted that expected inflation is frequently not a good predictor of future inflation. In 1980, respondents to surveys predicted inflation would average 9 percent over the next decade. Actual inflation turned out to be only half of that. Any policy based on longer-term inflation expectations during the 1980s would have seriously overestimated inflationary pressures. Indeed, the evidence suggests that, rather than expected inflation predicting inflation, inflation expectations are adaptively formed on the basis of current inflation along with past inflation. At best, expected inflation is a good predictor only over the very short run (see Figure 4 above).

To determine whether expected inflation would serve as a useful target for monetary policy, we looked at data since 1978 on expected inflation, actual inflation, and Fed policy to see whether an increase in inflation expectations could be used as the basis of policy actions to be taken in advance of accelerating inflation. We examined whether an increase in inflation expectations had, in the past, correctly anticipated future inflation. We next examined whether the Fed had knowingly or unknowingly followed this policy in the past. We found that instances of accelerating actual inflation were predicted by rising expected inflation (within the previous four quarters) only 24 percent of the time. In most cases, expected inflation did not correctly anticipate inflation. We also found that, in the majority of cases where the expected inflation guide does not predict the accelerating inflation that actually occurs, the acceleration of inflation cannot be attributed to easy-money policy.

## Alternative approach to monetary policy

The period from World War II to the late 1960s or early 1970s has frequently been called the "golden age" of U.S. economic history. It is beyond the scope of this article to review in detail all the factors that contributed to the superior economic performance. We will focus, instead, only on the Fed's aggregate monetary policy. The key difference between the early postwar period and the late postwar period is the degree of commitment of the Fed to stable, and generally low, interest rates. In 1951, the Fed abandoned the interest rate peg and gradually abrogated its commitment to low and stable interest rates over time. Still, until 1966, the Fed maintained the discount rate below 4 percent and the three-month Treasury bill rate well below 5 percent. In 1966, the Fed (apparently due to fear of forthcoming inflation) pushed the discount rate to 4.5 percent and the Treasury bill rate above 5 percent. That resulted in the first postwar financial crisis. After 1966, the Fed embarked on a series of attempts to "fine-tune" the economy through the use of tight-money policy each time there was fear that inflation would accelerate. In late 1969, from 1973 to 1974, from 1978 to 1985, and from 1988 to 1990, the Fed pushed short-term rates higher. In each case financial crises and/or recessions ensued.

The transition to attempts at fine-tuning has led to much greater interest-rate instability (see Table 7). From mid-1959 to 1966, the standard deviation of the three-month Treasury-bill rate was 0.61, while that of long-term government securities was only 0.14. For the Treasury bills, the standard deviation increased to

Table 7  **Volatile Interest Rates**

| Period | Mean | Stand. dev. | Max. | Min. |
|---|---|---|---|---|
| 1959.2–1993.3 | | | | |
| Long-term governments (composite) | 7.25 | 2.61 | 14.00 | 3.00 |
| 3-month T-bills | 6.18 | 2.80 | 15.09 | 2.32 |
| 1959.2–1965.4 | | | | |
| Long-term governments (composite) | 4.04 | 0.14 | 4.35 | 3.80 |
| 3-month T-bills | 3.18 | 0.61 | 4.30 | 2.32 |
| 1966.1–1977.4 | | | | |
| Long-term governments (composite) | 6.08 | 0.84 | 7.27 | 4.44 |
| 3-month T-bills | 5.59 | 1.27 | 8.39 | 3.43 |
| 1978.1–1993.3 | | | | |
| Long-term governments (composite) | 9.51 | 1.87 | 13.60 | 6.15 |
| 3-month T-bills | 7.91 | 2.96 | 15.09 | 2.98 |

*Sources:* The Levy Economics Institute Forecasting Center; National Income and Product Account.

1.27 for 1966 to 1978, and to 2.96 for 1978 to 1993. For long-term securities, the standard deviation rose to 0.84 and 1.87 for these periods. While Chairman Greenspan refers to the costs of uncertainty generated by inflation, we believe that the costs generated by unstable interest rates (and exchange rates) may be as important, if not more important. Indeed, the explosion of the derivatives market, which entails substantial costs and risks, is evidence that markets believe interest-rate instability is costly.

We emphasize our belief that active Fed policy is sometimes warranted. We agree that the Fed must retain some discretionary power to take aggressive action when it becomes necessary. But the escalation of its intervention into the economy that has occurred under the leadership of Chairmen Volcker and Greenspan has raised uncertainty, increased instability in domestic financial markets, contributed to instability of the dollar in foreign-exchange markets, generated costs of hedging, and increased interest rate and default risk. It certainly has had deleterious consequences for economic growth. A comparison of the results of Fed policy before and after 1966 suggests that policy directed at stabilizing interest rates more successfully accomplishes the goals outlined in the 1946 Employment Act and the 1978 Full Employment and Balanced Growth Act.

Previous to Chairman Volcker's experiment, the Fed employed a tight-money policy to fight perceived inflationary pressures, usually in response to expansionary fiscal policy. For example, the Fed's move to a tight policy in 1966 was in the context of a high-employment economy with rising government defense expenditures during the Vietnam War. Tight policy during the early 1980s was frequently justified as necessary to reduce inflationary pressures thought to result from the large and rising government deficits. But the recent tightening has occurred while government deficits have been falling and after the president and Congress reached agreements that will substantially reduce fiscal stimulus. Thus, unlike previous periods in which tight-money policy could be justified on the basis of fiscal policy being excessively stimulative, the current tightening comes while fiscal policy is widely believed to be moving to reduce the stimulus.

The evidence also suggests that Chairman Greenspan's proposed targets (whether real interest rates or expected inflation) would have led to incorrect policy much of the time in the past. There is no reason to expect these will perform any better in the future. By Chairman Greenspan's own admission:

• Our understanding of the economy is imperfect and the measurement of important variables like inflation is imprecise;
• no observable variables are sufficiently well-correlated with inflation to allow their use in policy formation;
• the impact of monetary policy on the economy is subject to long, uncertain, and variable lags;
• economic theory does not provide unambiguous guidance for the formation of monetary policy;
• there is no consensus regarding how the Fed can stabilize prices even if, as Chairman Greenspan claims, there is growing consensus that central-bank policy should stabilize prices.

However, we do not agree that this should be the sole goal of monetary policy. Nor does Congress agree. It has twice directed the Fed also to pursue full employment.

The Fed has moved to tighten policy this year while citing a variety of arguments to justify its actions. But recent statements have suggested that Fed policy is based on hunches rather than on any specific indicators. Governor LaWare admitted to Keith Bradsher of the *New York Times,* "I get a feel for what I think is going on based on the information—not only the anecdotal information in the press and the statistical information assembled and compiled by the staff here, but also from the general tone of the markets. I'm probably least sensitive to the money figures because I don't know what they mean anymore."

Noted monetarist Jerry L. Jordan admits: "In the last thirty years, economists have uncovered little additional information about how monetary policy works, except for the finding that expectations of future policy are vitally important in the process." David Jones, a longtime Fed watcher, says that "policy has become more intuitive over the last year." Bradsher reports that "Fed officials in effect rely on educated hunches of what they should do, rather than following the dictates of computer models or a couple of key indicators." And finally, Governor Lindsey's statement to Bradsher summarizes the problem faced by the Fed: "I came on believing what I had been taught—and taught as a professor—which was $M_2$. I don't think I can use it anymore. [Instead] we look at a whole raft of variables. We ignore nothing and focus on nothing."

The Fed's stance from mid-1992 to February 1994 was the correct policy. By holding the discount rate at 3 percent, the Fed allowed short-term rates to fall quickly, and long-term rates gradually declined. The economy began to recover from a prolonged recession. Firms and households were able to refinance at lower interest rates. They reduced debt loads, thereby allowing them to undertake new spending. Unemployment fell. The government interest burden declined and the federal budget deficit was reduced. Financial institutions and markets recovered. And the dollar held steady in foreign-exchange markets (although it fell against the yen, which is exactly what it should have done given the large U.S. trade deficit with Japan). The experience since February 1994 stands in stark contrast to the relative tranquility of that period. The tighter monetary policy was a mistake, and it would be an even greater mistake to tighten further.

## Vain pursuit of zero inflation

The experiment of targeting monetary aggregates has been a failure. Chairman Greenspan has proposed replacing monetary aggregates with either real interest rate or expected inflation targets. We have cast some doubt on Chairman Greenspan's choice of either a real interest rate or expected inflation target for monetary policy. We have also argued that, had the chairman adopted such targets in the past, this would not have helped to stabilize the economy. We also cast doubt on the use of expected inflation data series as the basis of policy formulation. Chairman Greenspan has argued that current conditions indicate inflation will soon accelerate, and will impose intolerable costs on society. It is apparent that the only justification for frequent changes of policy is, to a great extent, the Fed's intuition regarding what will lower inflation expectations and the Fed's hypothesis that lower inflation expectations are necessary to prevent a future acceleration of inflation. We see little evidence that inflation is likely to accelerate. Globally, manufacturing is operating far below capacity. Real wages are falling in the United States and in other developed economies. Labor productivity has risen rapidly in the United States. Many Eastern European countries are set to increase exports. Unemployment rates are high among most OECD nations. And low-wage, high-unemployment countries in the developing world can increase exports to meet any rise of world demand. Most important, we do not agree that the moderate inflation achieved recently entails significant costs. Indeed, the benefits to be gained by eliminating this inflation cannot be expected to exceed the costs that would be engendered by higher unemployment, greater uncertainty, and lost output. Until economists obtain a clearer estimate of the costs of inflation, of policies that can be used successfully to fight inflation, and of the costs of fighting inflation, pursuit of zero inflation as the ultimate goal of monetary policy must be seen as an insupportable, risky, and excessively radical proposition.

What is most apparent from recent policy statements is that the Fed's policy has become increasingly rudderless. The Fed appears to be "flying blind." It has chosen target variables that reflect "hunches" that inflation will rise. The result is a series of destabilizing policy changes that disrupt financial markets and have negative impacts on the "real" sector (that is, on employment and investment decisions). Rather than watching inflation or other economic variables, Wall Street is watching the Fed. It is trying to guess what the Fed might do next. Even the noted monetarist, William Poole, argues: "It's a very dangerous game to play, to drag out whatever indicator is pointing in the right direction."

Inflation has been, is, and is likely to be, well within acceptable limits. Fed policy should be refocused on providing a stable financial sector (through lender-of-last-resort policy and maintenance of low interest rates). This will help to provide an environment in which employment can rise. Given the current state of the economy, it is far more important to focus on full employment than on inflation.

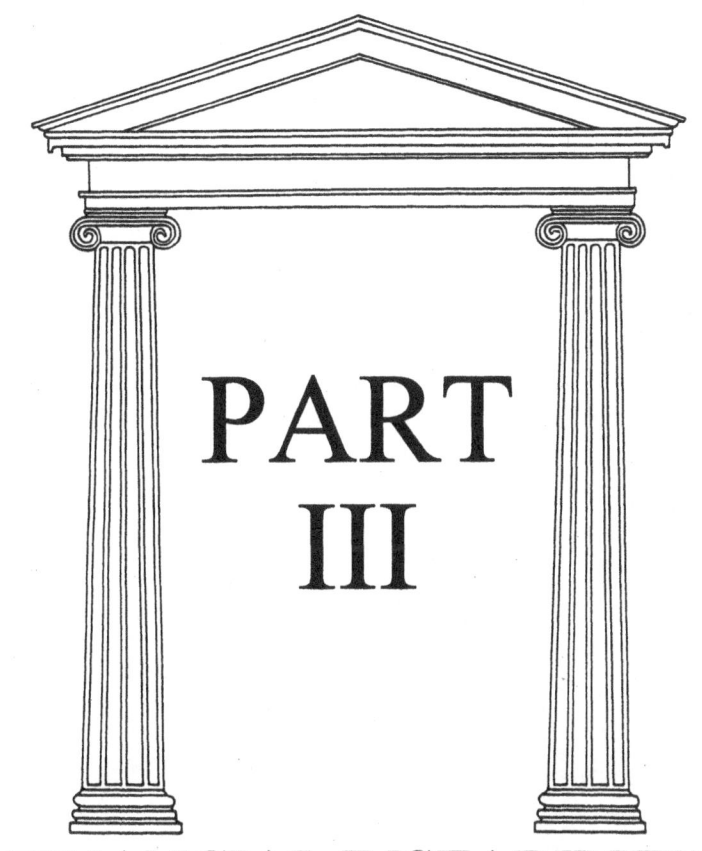

# PART III

# FINANCIAL INSTABILITY AND BANKING REGULATION

# CHAPTER 6 | THE FINANCIAL UNDERPINNINGS OF SLOW GROWTH

# *Financial Fragility and Stagnation*

ROBERT GUTTMANN

The recession of 1990–91 could have been much worse, had it not been for the exceptionally accommodative policy stance of the Fed during those two difficult years. This accommodation allowed a large number of borrowers to refinance their debts at lower rates and gave troubled banks the opportunity to rebuild their depleted capital base. In this way the U.S. central bank managed to prevent a serious financial crisis from spinning out of control. But the breathing space provided by monetary easing did not remove the underlying conditions of financial instability that had triggered the credit crunch in the first place, and the weight of these conditions continues to be felt across the U.S. economy. It is that financial-constraint aspect of our current slow-growth pattern that we focus on in this chapter.

## *Financial instability and business cycles*

Our economy, as dynamic as it may be in terms of spreading technological progress and thriving on innovation, is also inherently unstable. Its growth is subject to cyclical fluctuations, with recessionary adjustments occurring in fairly regular intervals. One of the principal forces underlying that cyclical growth pattern is financial in nature. The tendency toward industrial overproduction, which is clearly the main reason why our economy experiences recurrent downturns, tends to get reinforced by credit overextension. The same optimism seen during boom periods, which motivates producers to overestimate their future sales capacity, also prompts lenders to extend too much credit and make loans that under less euphoric conditions would have been considered excessively risky. Given the intertwined and mutually feeding nature of industrial overproduction and credit overextension, it is not surprising that recessionary market adjustments tend to be triggered by incidences of acute financial crisis. Whatever form those manifestations of credit overextension may take, be it a spectacular debt default or a stock-market crash, they may at that point trigger recession by forcing a broad retrenchment in credit supplies. More generally, we can say that the business-cycle dynamics characterizing the growth pattern of our economic system are reinforced by a parallel *credit cycle* which at first feeds boom conditions to the point of overextension and then imposes retrenchment on overextended agents.[1]

Throughout the postwar period this credit cycle has had a clearly marked presence in the U.S. economy. Whenever the booming economy would run up against its capacity limits, the ensuing signs of accelerating inflation would prompt lenders and savers to demand higher nominal interest rates as compensation for being repaid in devalued dollars. Commercial banks, however, could not partake in that practice because of maximum-rate ceilings on their deposits which the Fed did not allow to keep track with inflation.[2] As inflationary pressures pushed market-determined interest rates above the artificially low deposit-rate ceilings for banks, those intermediaries would face massive withdrawals of funds by depositors seeking higher returns elsewhere. Such *disintermediation* forced banks to cut back their lending, a reaction often reinforced by state-imposed "usury" ceilings on consumer loans which made that type of credit less profitable during periods of rising interest rates.

Government regulation of bank pricing thus provided an automatic cooling-off mechanism against accelerating inflation by shutting down bank lending at the peak of business upswings. After 1966 we saw such *credit crunches* at each cyclical turnaround—in 1969, 1973–74, 1979, and then again in 1981. When the government deregulated bank deposit and loan rates in the early 1980s, it also removed this automatic type of credit crunch from the business-cycle dynamics of the U.S. economy. No longer constrained by interest-rate ceilings, banks are now in a position to counter any disintermediation by offering higher rates and maintain profit margins by pushing up their loan rates.[3] With this kind of market regulation, known as *spread banking*, the only limit to credit expansion is the ability as well as willingness of banks and their borrowing customers to enter into credit transactions under mutually acceptable terms. Of course, the process of credit overextension may in such a deregulated environment go on much longer than in the era of government-imposed credit crunches. At the same time it is also likely to be a more gradual process, because market regulation of interest rates makes it easier for the suppliers of funds to charge higher risk and inflation premiums. The bias towards higher interest rates, which deregulation has brought about, makes any build-up of inflationary pressures much less likely than before when the Fed kept key interest rates in the banking system artificially low.

While financial deregulation may well have stabilized the business cycle, it has by no means abolished credit crunches. As the downturn of 1990–91 clearly illustrated, this phenomenon is still very much with us as a trigger of recessionary adjustments. That latest credit crunch also showed us how in the postderegulation era, when a growing proportion of bank loans carry variable rates, any sustained tightening by the Fed tends now to ripple more rapidly through the credit system as a much larger group of borrowers faces suddenly higher debt servicing burdens in the course of rising interest rates. In 1990 the Fed probably underestimated this magnified impact of any tightening in the new regime of variable-rate loans and thus ended up raising interest rates too much for too long. Its policy makers have certainly learned from that experience, as their gradualist "soft landing" strategy of 1994–95 has shown.

## Long-term increases in indebtedness

The recession of 1990–91 was certainly characterized by a rather intense credit crunch that began to unfold in late 1989 and then grew into a fairly broad retrenchment of bank lending by mid-1990. How much of that was simply due to the impact of deregulation in terms of lengthening the process of credit overextension is hard to say. What is more obvious is that much of the intensity of that credit crunch was the result of a long-term build-up in debt levels across all sectors of the U.S. economy which left borrowers saddled with historically high debt servicing burdens and lenders exposed to greater bad-debt losses.

Such a gradual increase in debt levels over several business cycles has been first identified by Hyman Minsky (1964) as a major aspect of the long-wave phenomenon known as the *Kondratieff cycle*.[4] During the expansion phase of such a long wave borrowers are inclined to take on more debt over time, or in the words of financial economists increase their *leverage*, because debt supports higher levels of spending and is therefore an inherently attractive tool of expansion. To the extent that previous levels of indebtedness succeeded in raising their income levels, borrowers will be more inclined to risk higher debt levels the next time around. Lenders, wishing to increase their financial income, will be inclined to accommodate those wishes and increase their supplies of funds. Minsky explained such a supracyclical increase in leverage not only by the propensity of borrowers and lenders to incur greater risks in their efforts to maintain income growth, but also as a result of the shallow and short recessions encountered during such expansion phases which force only minor reductions in debt levels. As borrowers increase their debt levels from cycle to cycle, they incur higher fixed costs in the form of debt servicing charges and thereby rigidify their cost structure. This renders them more vulnerable, as it becomes more difficult for them to counter declining revenues with cuts in costs. This vulnerability, which Minsky (1982) characterized as *financial fragility*, becomes acute and potentially dangerous when debtors have to borrow new funds in order to service their old debts.[5]

In this section we present evidence that the U.S. economy reached such a point of financial fragility during the 1990–91 recession, after a spectacular build-up of debt levels during the 1980s across all sectors of the U.S. economy. Robert Pollin (see reprint below) analyzes this trend for each sector. Concerning the industrial sector, he notes that the transition in the latest long wave from postwar boom to a period of sustained stagnation occurred in the early 1970s when corporations encountered a sharp erosion in their profitability, which in turn prompted a slowdown in their capital spending as well as a significant markdown in the market value of their net worth by the stock market. At that point we saw a first leap by corporate America toward higher levels of debt financing, consisting mostly of what Pollin termed *compensatory finance* with which to counter the decline in internal sources of funds from profits and shareholders. That was followed in the 1980s by yet another hike in leverage, this time prompted by corporations seeking to exploit depressed stock market conditions and acquire existing assets cheaply in one of history's greatest merger and takeover waves. This use of debt may be categorized as *speculative finance*. Neither type of finance represents in Pollin's eyes productive finance capable of generating sufficient long-term increases in income. Nor are they interest-elastic. Their excessive use is therefore bound to create a situation where debt servicing charges rise faster than income gains, a precursor of financial fragility. Similar conditions prevailed among households, where the middle class was forced into much higher levels of compensatory finance to counter wage stagnation and rising housing prices while the rich engaged heavily in speculative finance for capital gains from trading of financial assets or real estate.

With regard to government debt Pollin notes that the record budget deficits of the Reagan–Bush era (1980–1992) were probably not the principal reason for the exceptionally high real interest rates during that period. More important factors include the higher risk premiums charged by lenders in credit transactions and the deregulation of interest rates that made this response possible in the first place. In so denying the validity of the conservative crowding-out argument, Pollin concludes further that the often-cited decline in savings was neither factual (if one includes business savings) nor did it seem to have prevented the public and private sectors from going on a decade-long borrowing binge at the same time. More troubling to Pollin than any alleged crowding-out problem is the increasingly tenuous linkage between savings and productive investment due to dramatic changes in the banking system as well as the eroding capacity of budget deficits to stimulate productive activity in the private sector.

Pollin's argument, namely that the various sectors of the U.S. economy have reached dangerous levels of indebtedness, is further developed by Benjamin Friedman (see reprint below). The Harvard economist analyzes the rapid increase in corporate leverage during the 1980s as a side-product of an ultimately counterproductive speculative merger boom with negative consequences for corporate balance sheets and income statements. Concerning the huge U.S. budget deficits, Friedman presents us with his version of the crowding-out problem whereby the combination of declining domestic savings and exploding government borrowing crowds out productivity-enhancing investment activity.

According to both authors the levels of indebtedness reached in the private sector as well as by the federal government became so burdensome because little of the debt had been used for productive purposes to generate durable productivity and income gains. This unproductive borrowing binge created by the late 1980s a dangerous debt overhang that made the subsequent downturn of 1990–91 so much more difficult to deal with. Acute conditions of financial fragility forced cash-strapped consumers to scale back their purchases, overleveraged businesses to cut costs drastically, and banks to reduce lending in the face of large bad-debt losses. To the extent that these financial-squeeze conditions have continued to prevail beyond the cyclical downturn of the early 1990s, they have slowed the subsequent recovery. Both Pollin and Friedman see much of today's corporate downsizing and wage stagnation directly related to excessive accumulation of relatively unproductive debts in the previous decade.

As Minsky (1964) noted, a debt overhang of such proportions used to throw the economy into a depression. Today, however, such depressionary debt-deflation processes are counteracted by a variety of institutional constraints which stabilize financially fragile economies. The large role of the government in our "mixed" economy, reinforced by its capacity for deficit spending, prevents a collapse of profits. Equally important is the government's intervention as *lender of last resort* to manage financial crises and contain their impact. Deposit insurance, for instance, makes sure that bank losses do not spill over to the public. After a banking crisis is contained by deposit insurance, the central bank is in a position to inject liquidity into the banking system to ease the squeeze.

These institutional arrangements to manage financial crises in the United States, which were put into place during Roosevelt's New Deal (i.e., Glass–Steagall Act of 1933, Bank Act of 1935), have so far prevented any recurrence of depression. Yet at the same time it is also clear that our most recent bout with financial fragility in the late 1980s and early 1990s has exposed some inherent weaknesses of our lender-of-last-resort mechanisms. For instance, the deposit insurance approach currently in use may be less effective in dealing with a systemic banking crisis than the holding company approach last used in the United States during the 1930s, when the government-run Reconstruction Finance Corporation (RFC) injected new capital into insolvent banking institutions. Instead of beefing up the depleted capital of troubled banks, the U.S. central bank offers emergency funds from its discount window that tie up performing bank assets as collateral. And its open market operations, while useful against a liquidity crisis and instrumental in postcrisis relief, cannot deal with a solvency crisis among banks suffering massive bad-debt losses. In light of prevailing conditions of financial fragility, these limitations of our various lender-of-last-resort mechanisms have become an important matter of debate among U.S. policy makers and form the subject of our next chapter.

## Notes

1. The discussion of different theoretical perspectives concerning financial crisis by Wolfson (1994) makes it clear that all these paradigms stress the cyclical nature of this phenomenon as a trigger of recessionary adjustments.

2. The Glass–Steagall Act of 1933 had given the Fed the authority for such rate ceilings on all kinds of bank deposits (Regulation Q) in order to contain damaging price competition in banking, which could lead to excessively risky behavior among banks. In addition, states had been empowered under so-called usury laws to set maximum interest rates banks could charge on consumer loans (e.g., mortgages, credit cards). Price regulation thus applied for most commercial banks in the United States to both deposit liabilities and a significant portion of their loan assets.

3. Price competition among banks (and relative to money-market funds) can be quite intense on the deposit side, with banks often bidding up rates to attract funds. At the same time banks follow an oligopolistic markup pricing strategy on the asset side. All their loan rates are tied to the *prime rate,* the interest rate banks charge their best corporate customers. And the banks tend to adjust their prime rates in coordinated fashion at the same time, usually after similar changes of the discount or Federal funds rates by the Fed.

4. Soviet economist N. Kondratieff (1926) presented a variety of empirical indicators to highlight the existence of 40-to-60-year cycles in the evolution of capitalist economies. In these so-called *long waves,* a period of sustained and rapid expansion would typically be followed by a couple of decades of much slower growth.

5. Minsky distinguishes three stages of debt financing, depending on the relation between income gains and debt servicing charges. In *hedge financing* revenues are sufficient to cover all commitments associated with the debt. In *speculative financing* only interest payments are covered, but not the principal to be paid at maturity. The most dangerous position is *Ponzi financing* where the shortfall of revenues relative to debt-related cash-flow commitments is such that the borrowers need to take on new debt just to cover the old debt.

ROBERT POLLIN

# Destabilizing Finance Worsened This Recession

*Systemic financial difficulties lie at the root of our economy's surprisingly severe recession and unfavorable longer-term prospects. To avoid a replay of the 1980s we must reverse the rise of speculative and compensatory finance and promote the productive use of financial resources.*

In March 1990, only four months before the recession began, the *Wall Street Journal* reported that "60 percent of macroeconomic forecasters surveyed by the National Association of Business Economists don't expect a recession in the next three years."

Even by November 1990—when, as the National Bureau of Economic Research (NBER) now tells us, the recession was already four months old—the *New York Times* reported that an NBER forecasting model was itself still predicting that economic growth would rise sharply to around 4 percent over the upcoming several months, and that the likelihood that the economy would be in recession by February 1991 was 3 percent.

Once the recession was officially recognized, the mantra among forecasters was "short and mild." By now, "long and deep" resonate far better. Even more disturbing are the prospects for the postrecession economy: that the unfavorable trends that characterized the 1980s—slow growth of GNP, a worsening income distribution, low productivity growth, and pervasive financial instability—are likely to continue after the recession ends.

It is clear now that systemic financial difficulties—the debt overhang and credit crunch, continued high real interest rates, and unraveling systems of intermediation and regulation—lie at the root of the economy's surprisingly severe recession and unfavorable longer-term prospects. Many explanations have been advanced for these financial problems, among them that the savings rate is too low, federal deficits are too large, banking regulators were too lax and are now too stringent, and the private sector has borrowed excessively. These explanations at best offer partial truths, and as such, mislead more than they illuminate.

The financial system's basic problem is rather that credit has been utilized insufficiently to finance *productive* spending—spending that enhances the productive capacity of firms and individuals—and disproportionately to finance *speculative* and *compensatory* spending—borrowing to purchase existing assets with

ROBERT POLLIN is Associate Professor of Economics at the University of California-Riverside. Reprinted from *Challenge*, March–April 1992, pp. 17–24.

| Table 8 | Finance, Investment, and Interest Rates for Nonfinancial Corporations | | | | |
|---|---|---|---|---|---|
| Cycles | 1960–69 | 1970–73 | 1974–79 | 1980–81 | 1982–90 |
| Pretax profit rate (pct.) | 12.2 | 8.1 | 5.9 | 6.0 | 8.6 |
| Market value of equities/net worth at replacement cost (pct.) | 96.1 | 83.6 | 41.4 | 43.8 | 62.7 |
| Growth of capital expenditures (pct.) | 6.2 | 4.3 | 4.1 | 0.4 | 2.2 |
| Borrowed funds/capital expenditures (pct.) | 30.2 | 38.7 | 28.8 | 30.1 | 37.2 |
| Internal funds/capital expenditures (pct.) | 93.8 | 82.8 | 87.7 | 82.8 | 100.7 |
| Real interest rate (average of commercial paper and bond rates) | 2.6 | 2.3 | –0.1 | 1.8 | 5.8 |

*Sources:* National Income and Product Accounts; Flow of Funds Accounts of Federal Reserve System; Balance Sheets of U.S. Economy; Citicorp Economic Database.

*Note:* Profit rate calculated according to method described in R. Pollin, "Alternative Perspectives on the Rise of Corporate Debt Dependency," *Review of Radical Political Economics*, Spring and Summer, 1986.

the expectation of capital gain, and to compensate for declining income streams or other internally generated funds. The ascendancy of speculative and compensatory borrowing, in turn, is linked to even deeper difficulties: the stagnation of productivity and profitability, the decline of real wages, and the worsening distribution of income.

## *Destabilizing finance 1: corporations*

The distinctions between compensatory, speculative, and productive finance are apparent in the case of nonfinancial corporations. The basic evidence is shown in Table 8, which, as with succeeding tables, reports data over the four full business cycles since 1960. (Cycles are based on annualizing NBER quarterly peaks; peak years are those in which NBER quarterly peaks fall within the first two quarters of that year or the last two quarters of the previous year.) Beginning with the data on corporate profitability, we see that from a 1960s peak of 12.2 percent, corporate profitability fell in the early 1970s to 8.1 percent. The ratio of market value of equities to net worth at replacement cost—what we may call a *proxy q ratio*—fell with it, from 96.1 to 83.6 percent. This ratio reflects the stock market's perceptions of future corporate profitability. Capital expenditures also fell over this period, but not by as much as the decline in profitability. Thus, corporate borrowing relative to their capital expenditures rose sharply from 30.2 to 38.7 percent.

This first upward shift in debt financing is an instance of *compensatory* credit demand: in the face of declining internal sources, corporations financed capital expenditures increasingly from debt. To a small degree, this tendency may have been promoted by the decline of real interest rates, falling on average from 2.6 to 2.3 percent. But such a sharp increase in debt financing cannot be attributed primarily to the interest rate decline.

In the second half of the 1970s, profit rates fell even further and the *proxy q* ratio plunged: the stock market here is valuing the current cost net worth of firms at only 41 cents on the dollar. The growth of capital expenditures again fell, now to 4.1 percent. In this period, however, corporations did not increase borrowing to sustain capital expenditures, even though real interest rates were negative. They primarily cut back capital expenditures, but also relied to a somewhat greater extent on internal funds.

Beginning in 1982, as is by now well known, a fundamental shift occurred in corporations' finance and investment strategies. Their commitment to financing capital expenditures remained weak. For the full period, capital expenditures grew by only 2.2 percent; and *all* of that growth was due to a 35 percent increase in spending between 1983–84. Otherwise, capital expenditures declined by an average of 1.5 percent annually.

But new vistas for *speculative* finance had emerged in this period. With the net worth of corporations for sale at an average of 44 cents on the dollar as of 1982 (as shown in the market value/net worth ratio), firms borrowed to an unprecedented degree to buy up existing assets rather than create new capital stock. The debt/capital expenditures ratio thus jumped to 37.2 percent, despite the paltry growth of capital expenditures itself. At the same time, the ratio of internal funds to capital expenditures rose to an average of over 100 percent. This means that, in the aggregate, *none* of the growth of debt over 1982–90 was necessary to finance new capital expenditures; *all* of it was devoted to mergers and buyouts.

In addition, this surge in speculative borrowing corresponded with the runup in real interest rates to an average of 5.8 percent, a level unprecedented over the past 100 years of U.S. history. Thus, even more than during the surge of compensatory finance in 1970–73, the rise of speculative credit demand over 1982–90 was essentially interest-inelastic.

As to the consequences of this investment and finance pattern, profitability did increase somewhat over this period, but almost entirely through redistributive effects (from lower taxation and a falling wage bill—a redistribution from stakeholders to shareholders) with little overall gain in productivity. And gains were not nearly adequate to outweigh the growing burden of debt. By the time the recession began, corporate interest payments absorbed 44 percent of pretax earnings, a level more than double the average figure for the 1960s and 1970s. Loan defaults, business failures and restructurings—signposts of the debt overhang—rose sharply in the 1980s and into the recession.

But this debt overhang is not merely a matter of excess, but rather the result of more fundamental problems—stagnating profitability and the subsequent decline in firms' market value. In the early 1970s, falling profitability induced both a cut in capital expenditures and a rise in compensatory finance. But as neither profitability nor market values improved significantly, investors increasingly perceived greater opportunities through swapping ownership claims on existing assets rather than creating new productive capacity. Yet corporate income streams did not rise commensurate with the mounting debt burden that financed mergers and buyouts. Conditions were in place for the subsequent sharp contraction.

## Destabilizing Finance 2: Households

We can explain the household debt situation through a similar focus on the causes and implications of compensatory and speculative finance.

Households obviously differ tremendously in terms of age, wealth, income, consumption patterns, and degree of financial security. Nevertheless, the increase in debt financing from the mid-1970s onward, and especially in the 1980s, occurred broadly across household types: by income quintiles, about half the total increase in household debt was due to the top 20 percent of the income distribution and the other half to the lower 80 percent. In the aggregate, as Table 9 shows, net household borrowing rises from 6.1 percent of disposable income in 1970–73 to 8.0 percent in 1974–79. Borrowing then fell off in the 1980–81 cycle, but rose again over 1982–90, to 8.3 percent.

In part, this broadly based increase in debt financing was supply-driven, through more aggressive loan marketing by intermediaries. The proliferation of credit cards, as one element of this new marketing strategy, has weakened the bureaucratic and psychological bar-

| Table 9 | Household Income and Financing Patterns | | | | |
|---|---|---|---|---|---|
| Cycles | 1960–69 | 1970–73 | 1974–79 | 1980–81 | 1982–90 |
| Net borrowing/disposable income (pct.) | 5.5 | 6.1 | 8.0 | 6.1 | 8.3 |
| Outstanding debt/total assets (pct.) | 12.7 | 13.7 | 14.5 | 14.3 | 16.2 |
| Median family income (thousands of 1982 dollars) | 28.6 | 34.2 | 34.5 | 32.8 | 34.3 |
| Incomes for lower 40% (thousands of 1982 dollars) | 16.3 | 16.8 | 16.7 | 15.5 | 15.8 |
| Real mortgage rate | 3.9 | 3.2 | 0.9 | 2.9 | 7.6 |
| Past due mortgages (pct.) | 2.9 | 3.6 | 4.5 | 5.1 | 5.3 |
| Personal bankruptcies per 10,000 population | 8 | 8 | 9 | 13 | 19 |

*Sources:* Flow of Funds Accounts of Federal Reserve System; Balance Sheets of U.S. Economy; Citicorp Economic Database; Bureau of Census Current Population Surveys; Administrative Office of U.S. Courts.

riers that once inhibited ordinary households from taking on debt. But what of the demand side? Here explanations diverge according to income classes.

During the 1980s, the upper 20 percent, and especially the top 1–2 percent of households experienced both sharply rising incomes and greater access to financial markets. These developments encouraged the rich to borrow for the purpose of investing in financial markets and real estate. With ample access to credit, one could risk other people's money in the pursuit of large and rapid returns. Thus, while the ratio of debt/total assets rose for households in the aggregate over the period shown (Table 9), disaggregated data show that wealthy households matched their increasing indebtedness with larger asset acquisitions.

But of course such speculative investment opportunities are accessible to only a select few. The majority of nonwealthy households borrowed for compensatory purposes, especially those in the bottom 40 percent of the income distribution for whom the rise of household debt was sharpest in the 1980s. We need to review patterns on real wages, incomes, and housing costs to understand the sources of this demand.

The average real wage fell by 18 percent between 1972–90. But because of the rise of two-earner households, most household incomes did not fall as severely. As Table 9 shows, median family incomes have basically stagnated since the early 1970s, while for the lower 40 percent of families, the average income of $15,800 is 6 percent below the level of 1970–73.

And while most real incomes for the nonrich were

stagnating or declining, the costs of housing, as measured by the shelter component of the CPI, rose by 13.3 percent more than the overall rate of inflation between the 1970-73 and 1982-90 cycles. This is especially significant since shelter costs, through the financing of mortgages and durables, are directly linked to the demand for credit. In addition, shelter is the least flexible item in the family budget and thus the first claim on its income. As the sociologist Michael Stone has explained, once a household is committed to a particular dwelling, it is more difficult to move in response to financial difficulties than to switch food stores or even consumption patterns in an effort to reduce other living costs.

Poor and middle-income households thus increased their mortgage and consumer borrowing to attempt to maintain stable living standards while incomes stagnated or fell and housing costs rose. And here again, sharply rising real interest rates did not dampen this compensatory credit demand. As Table 9 shows, mortgage rates averaged only 0.9 percent over 1974-79, but rose to an average of 7.6 through 1982-90.

It has been argued that the household sector's rising debt/income ratio does not seriously threaten overall financial stability since debt servicing has not risen as rapidly as outstanding debt. This relatively slower growth in debt servicing occurred for two reasons: because the average repayment period on consumer loans has increased since the mid-1970s, reducing the annual burdens for a loan; and because longer maturity mortgage loans, including home equity loans, are being increasingly substituted for consumer loans, since interest payments on mortgages remain fully tax deductible while deductions on consumer loans are being phased out.

Nevertheless, despite this slower rise in average servicing burdens, from disaggregated data we see that the *dispersion* in the proportion of servicing obligations among high-debt and low-debt households had also widened. That is, servicing burdens increased significantly for households with high debt levels and fell correspondingly for households carrying relatively little debt. This is what underlies the observation that, as an average, no significant increase has occurred in households' servicing burdens. But in terms of the financial system's stability, the favorable conditions for low-debt households do not symmetrically counterbalance the worsening situation for the heavily indebted. After all, a chain under tension will snap through a single weak link.

The direct measures on financial distress support the idea that heavily indebted households were indeed facing growing repayment difficulties through the 1980s. As Table 9 shows, delinquencies on mortgage loans and personal bankruptcies were at peak levels between 1982-90, conveying patterns of distress normally associated with a recession rather than the lengthy Reagan/Bush expansion. These unfavorable patterns have continued into the recession, becoming characteristic features of the financial malaise.

## Rising deficits and declining performance

The other major source of credit demand over the 1980s was the federal government. There are, of course, intensive debates seeking to explain the association between the rise of deficits and declining economic performance. The mainstream crowding-out view holds that the large deficits are the *cause* of declining performance, since deficits absorb the savings that could be channeled to other sources, toward capital expenditures in particular. Thus, while private borrowers may still have access to funds, the federal borrowing requirement has forced interest rates to a prohibitive level.

But the evidence before us demonstrates several problems with this view. The first, as we have seen, is that the growing deficits have not inhibited private sector borrowing. To the contrary, private borrowing increased in the 1980s along with the federal deficits. And while federal deficits no doubt exert upward pressure on interest rates, this surely cannot serve as a full explanation for the rise of real rates. At the least, we would also need to explain both the factors influencing credit supply, including the goals and constraints governing Federal Reserve policy; and, perhaps most neglected, the factors influencing the private sector's largely interest-inelastic credit demand. After all, even after the unprecedented increase in the federal government's borrowing requirement over the 1980s, the private sector still accounted for two-thirds of total domestic borrowing.

Capital expenditures did, of course, decline over the 1980s. But this resulted not from either quantity or price constraints on the availability of loanable funds, but rather through the decisions of firms to invest less and increasingly to finance nonproductive activity relative to creating new capital stock. Thus, as Benjamin Friedman has written, persistent large-scale deficits "did increase the funds business had available to finance new investment, but business simply had other plans for how to spend them."

Structural changes in the economy since the 1960s, as illustrated in the changing financial patterns for both corporations and households, have also transformed the way the economy responds to federal deficit spending. Thus, the impact of a 1990 deficit is substantially different from that of, say, a 1970 deficit of equivalent magnitude.

The first point here is that the stagnation of pretax profitability and real household incomes, beginning in the early 1970s, was the motivating force behind the taxpayers' rebellion of this period: increasing take-home pay became another form of compensation for the stagnation of pretax incomes. As we now know, the beneficiaries of the subsequent cuts have been the corporations and the wealthy, not households generally. But the consequence has nevertheless been an unprecedented increase in high employment deficits.

At the same time, the economy's structural changes meant that the deficit's capacity to stimulate demand weakened over time. Part of this is due to the well-known effect of a country simultaneously running trade and budget deficits. The United States, in these circumstances, exported part of the demand stimulus of its deficit to its trading partners by importing more from abroad.

But additional factors have also been crucial. For one, the decline of the profit rate and the market value of firms has attenuated any capital expenditure inducement from a given injection of federal deficit spending. Declining profit expectations dampened animal spirits, and thus larger demand boosters became necessary to embolden investors' enthusiasm. And when investors did become aroused, low market values created an incentive to buy existing firms rather than create new capital stock.

Finally, financing the deficit has led to an upward redistribution of income. This weakens the deficit's demand stimulus because the wealthy have lower marginal propensities to consume. It is not inevitable that financing the deficit should induce an upward distributional bias. But it follows from two conditions that prevailed in the 1980s. The first was the highly skewed ownership pattern of government debt, with wealthy individuals, corporations, and intermediaries—foreign as well as domestic—owning the overwhelming proportion of federal government bonds. But even with

| Table 10 | Savings, Lending, and Banking Patterns | | | | |
|---|---|---|---|---|---|
| Cycles | 1960–69 | 1970–73 | 1974–79 | 1980–81 | 1982–90 |
| Personal savings/GNP (pct.) | 4.6 | 5.8 | 5.4 | 5.1 | 3.4 |
| Gross business savings/GNP (pct.) | 11.9 | 11.2 | 12.6 | 12.7 | 12.6 |
| Gross private savings/GNP (pct.) | 16.6 | 17.0 | 18.0 | 17.8 | 16.0 |
| Domestic lending/gross private savings (pct.) | 62.4 | 77.5 | 92.5 | 86.2 | 123.0 |
| Reserves/loans for banks (pct.) (assuming constant res. requirement) | 7.6 | 5.0 | 3.5 | 2.8 | 2.6 |
| Bank loans/total loans (pct.) | 23.9 | 24.7 | 18.1 | 13.5 | 15.0 |

*Source:* Citicorp Economic Database.

this, positive interest returns to owners of government debt must also persist for a redistributive effect to occur. Such was not always the case in the 1970s but emphatically was so in the 1980s. As a result, a larger share of government spending flowed to the wealthy, either directly or through their ownership of corporations and intermediaries.

Through these and related structural changes since the 1960s, both cyclical and high employment deficits have been growing over time, but their capacity to stimulate demand has weakened while their negative collateral effects, including their upward redistributive effect, gain strength.

## Declining savings rates are a distraction

It is true that private savings rates have fallen over the 1980s relative to GNP, as Table 10 shows. This decline has been substantial for personal savings, a pattern that is easily explicable within the scenario of financial stress and compensatory credit demand described earlier.

But other factors need to be emphasized. The first is that business savings comprises roughly 70 percent of total private savings, and this ratio did not fall over the most recent cycle. Thus, total private savings, including both personal and business savings, was still at its low point over the 1982–90 cycle, at 16.0 percent. Yet this is only slightly below the 16.6 percent figure prevailing in the 1960s, the most prosperous decade of the postwar period.

But there is a still more basic point to raise. We are

concerned with savings rates primarily as they influence the economy's capacity to supply credit. The fact is that savings flows from households and businesses—the "ultimate savers" as opposed to the banks, brokerage houses and other financial intermediaries—have only a weak influence on the availability of credit or interest rates. This is because, as James Earley has written, the actions of ultimate savers "take place in a different terrain from the process of lending and borrowing." That is, acts of savings by households and businesses are decisions to hold cash or, more customarily, purchase financial assets, rather than spend. But what kinds of financial assets are available to them, and how those assets are to be utilized for loans, is almost entirely the result of decisions by the intermediaries. Thus, as Earley puts it, the connections between savings and credit supply are inherently loose.

These connections have slackened exceptionally since the mid-1960s, when the entire system of financial intermediation was transformed. Indeed, for profit maximizing intermediaries, a major purpose of innovation has been precisely to increase their independence from raw material suppliers—ultimate savers as well as central banks.

The weakening of links between ultimate savings and credit supply since the mid-1960s can be seen clearly in Table 10. In the 1960s, domestic lending absorbed an average of 62 percent of private savings. The ratio then advances strongly in the 1970s, and after declining in 1980–81, rises to an average level of 123 percent during 1982–90. That is, the proportion of lending to private savings doubles over this period, to a point where, on average, domestic lending *exceeds* private savings by 23 percent.

It is not the case, moreover, that this relative increase in lending is responsible for the high real interest rates over 1982–90. A rise in the lending/private saving ratio will exert upward pressure on interest rates within a given financial environment. But innovation changed the institutional environment beyond recognition between 1960 and 1990. Thus, as Table 10 also shows, even after controlling for changes in reserve requirements, the reserve/loan ratio for the banking system falls from 7.6 percent in the 1960s to 2.6 percent over 1982–90. Moreover, the banks' proportion of total lending also falls, from 24 to 15 percent between the 1960s and the 1982–90 cycle. These figures reflect much greater flexibility both in the velocity at which reserves can circulate and in the variety of institutions

| Table 11 | Economic Stability and Long-term Interest Rates | | |
|---|---|---|---|
| | 1890–1929 | 1947–79 | 1980–89 |
| Real interest rate (average of commercial paper and corp. bond rates) | 3.4 | 0.7 | 5.9 |
| Bank failures (per 10,000 banks) | 100.5 | 4.0 | 78.0 |
| Business failures (per 10,000 firms) | 97.3 | 42.3 | 90.8 |

*Sources:* Historical Statistics of the United States; Citibank Economic Database; Statistical Abstract of the United States, various editions.

capable of attracting savings and issuing loans. Linkages between interest rates, lending, and savings have weakened in the process.

In short, it is simply a distraction to try to understand current financial distress through looking at savings flows. Especially unwarranted is further hand-wringing over the insufficient thriftiness of American families.

## Increasing risk and high interest rates

Without doubt, a number of factors are responsible for the exceptionally high level of real interest rates in the 1980s. Two influences are the rise in aggregate credit demand—including the compensatory and speculative demand of the private sector as well as federal government borrowing—and the requirements necessary for maintaining the value of the dollar in a financial market. However, an additional consideration needs to be addressed. It is that, considered within the long-term historical experience, the level of real interest rates over the 1980s is consistent with the increasingly risky environment that has prevailed in recent years. As Table 11 shows, the elevated interest rate levels in the 1980s represent not only a sharp break with the rest of the post–World War II era, but also a reversion to levels of the prewar period. (To avoid misleading comparisons, the prewar period is represented here as exclusive of the Depression years.) More specifically, rates averaged 3.4 percent between 1890 and 1929, fell dramatically to an average of 0.7 percent in 1947–79, but then, in the 1980s, rose to an unprecedented 5.9 percent.

What the table also shows is that comparable changes occurred in the overall riskiness of the economic environment over these periods. As two indicators, we consider the bank and business failure rates. The bank failure rate was 104.8 per 10,000 institutions during 1890–1929, then fell to 4.0 in 1947–79. In the 1980s, it rises to 78.0.

Business failures show a less extreme, if still dramatic, change. The failure rate averaged 100 per 10,000 businesses in 1890–1929 and fell to 42.3 between 1947 and 1979. In the 1980s, in a near-complete reversion to the prewar era, the failure rate rose to 90.8 per 10,000 firms.

Thus, from these data, the interest rate level over the 1980s appears to be a rational response to the sharp decline in observed stability over these years. Indeed, the degree of riskiness for lenders in the 1980s may well be historically unique, in that, unlike the prewar period, it combines high levels of instability with persistent inflation.

## Socializing investment is stabilizing

Achieving a desirable policy path, of course, presupposes a clear understanding of the problems at hand. I have argued that the fundamental problems facing the U.S. macroeconomy today—and thus the basic sources of the unexpectedly long and severe recession—are not the federal deficit, inadequate saving, the unprecedentedly high real interest rates, or the excessive debt buildup within the private sector. The most basic concerns are rather the decline in productive investment spending associated with the relatively low returns on capital expenditures and the stagnating or declining living standards for the majority of households. These developments are reflected in the financial sphere through the rise in compensatory and speculative credit demand and the declining use of financial resources for productive purposes. Over the 1980s, the rise of speculative and compensatory finance, along with the weakening countercyclical effects of federal deficits and the loosening of constraints on intermediaries, created a fragile financial structure, one whose vulnerabilities were bound to worsen the effects of any downturn, regardless of its origin.

A primary goal of policy should therefore be to reverse the rise of speculative and the need for compensatory finance and to promote the productive use of financial resources. No single policy lever is sufficiently potent to achieve these aims; a new approach to policy is needed. Some suggested elements of this approach follow.

A transaction tax for short-term holdings of real estate and financial assets should be implemented to discourage speculative credit demand by both corporations and households. While mergers and buyouts have predictably declined during the recession, such activity could revive during the recovery if the economic landscape fostering such activity does not change.

Keynes supported such a transaction tax in the *General Theory* "with a view to mitigating the predominance of speculation over enterprise in the United States." More recently, the idea has been revived by such figures as James Tobin and Warren Buffett. Buffett's proposal is a 100 percent tax on all gains from the sale of stocks or derivative securities held for less than one year. The securities market would remain liquid because investors could sell securities at any time. The point would be to eliminate profiteering from short-term asset holdings.

The limitation of the transaction tax is that it would inhibit speculative finance but not necessarily promote long-term investment. To a significant extent, corporations evidently consider productive investment as insufficiently profitable. This suggests the need for increased public investment, both to improve profit opportunities by lowering the costs of production and to subsidize activities in which social rates of return are higher than private rates.

More specifically, this means substantial increases in public spending on infrastructure, child care, public education, housing, and renewable energy. In addition to the long-term benefits of such spending, its immediate effect (if programs were implemented at a reasonably large scale—$60–120 billion this year) would be to jolt the economy out of stagnation. Public investment spending, in other words, is a quick-fix remedy with long-term benefits.

The financing of these programs should have five sources: an increase in revenues through the stimulating effects of such policies; the transaction tax (although its main purpose is to change behavior, not raise revenue); the transfer of funds out of military spending; a decline in interest rates, which will reduce interest payments on government debt; and raising taxes on the wealthy.

Perhaps the greatest challenge for the public investment program is how to forge plowshares from our now elephantine military economy. For all its bad features—and there are many, ranging from the wasteful to the nefarious—military spending has also promoted both the stability of aggregate demand and technical innovation. We must, of course, seize the transcendent opportunity for disarmament. But public investment policy must then also reproduce elsewhere both demand stabilizers and a nurturing environment for nonmilitary research and development.

On taxes, Lawrence Mishel and David Frankel have estimated that tax reforms between 1977 and 1990 produced an increase in aftertax income of $45,565 for the richest 1 percent of families, while the bottom 80 percent of families all suffered a tax increase. It will not be possible to revitalize the economy as long as its basic institutions so egregiously foster inequality. Moreover, if public investments are to be targeted at lowering costs for businesses, owners and managers of businesses will have to accept higher personal taxes as the *quid pro quo*.

These proposals to inhibit speculative finance and support productive investment by both public and private sectors will yield another major benefit: they will create an environment favorable to a large, sustained decline in real interest rates. Several factors will contribute to this result.

• First, borrowing for productive purposes will substitute for speculative and compensatory borrowing, and this will promote financial stabilization. As Hyman Minsky has long argued, financial instability results when debt commitments systematically outstrip income flows. Relative to the effects of speculative and compensatory borrowing, financing productive activity by its nature will increase the extent to which incomes rise in step with debt financing.

• In addition, recall that during the 1980s, none of the growth of corporate debt financed fixed investment in the aggregate; all of it went to finance mergers and acquisitions. This means that if speculative finance is discouraged, corporations could borrow more for capital expenditures without exerting upward pressure on interest rates. In other words, a free lunch is here to be grabbed: productive borrowing can substitute for speculative finance, so the aggregate demand for funds need not rise, and probably could fall.

• Finally, increasing public sector borrowing specifically while private speculative and compensatory borrowing falls means that the proportion of government debt held by U.S. creditors will rise. This also will contribute to financial stabilization, as federal debt is nondefaultable (although its value can, of course, depreciate through inflation). Indeed, the high proportion of government debt held by U.S. creditors in the early postwar years—beginning at 62 percent of total debt outstanding in 1947 and not falling below 30 percent until 1964 (a figure still not attained as of 1990)—was one factor contributing to the financial tranquility of that period.

And if financial stabilization can be promoted in this way, a corollary will be to strengthen the effectiveness of monetary and regulatory policy. Conventional monetary and regulatory policies are well equipped to maintain the boundaries of prudent and equitable activity within a generally stable financial environment. But, as the last fifteen years have shown, they are poorly suited themselves to stabilize a system being destabilized by powerful macro forces. The one exception is lender-of-last-resort policies executed either at the Federal Reserve discount window or through deposit insurance bailouts. But such efforts contribute to stability only in the narrow sense of preventing a fragile system from descending into a crisis.

More effective regulatory strategies should also emerge through focusing on the links between speculative and compensatory borrowing and financial instability. Bank and S&L examiners have been criticized for laxity over the 1980s. Now, perhaps to atone for previous errors, they have reportedly become too stringent. But the aim of regulators should be neither laxity, stringency, or even the golden mean between these. The regulatory system rather needs to promote productive finance and equity and to discourage speculative finance. That is, the financial system should be geared not toward financing either less or more, but to financing *better*.

Taken as a whole, the foregoing proposals obviously entail, in some fashion, the disinterring of ideas about state-organized economic planing. At present, such concepts are so disreputable as to appear absurd. But economic planning is not synonymous with Stalinism, nor must it imply the ascendancy of rent-seeking over efficiency. Certainly the Japanese and Korean economies have not suffered through extensive government participation. In a U.S. context, planning could bring not only the dynamic efficiency gains experienced in East Asia, but also a deepening of democracy itself, insofar as popular representatives become empowered to participate in the basic investment and financing decisions that determine overall well-being.

At the conclusion of his *General Theory*, Keynes called for a "somewhat comprehensive socialization of investment" to overcome what he regarded as capitalism's outstanding faults, "its failure to provide for full employment and its arbitrary and inequitable distribution of wealth and incomes." Do we now possess the democratic will to pursue this Keynesian course, or must we stand complaisant before the continued assaults of the *status quo*?

BENJAMIN M. FRIEDMAN

# *Financial Roadblocks on the Route to Economic Prosperity*

*The heavy debt-service burdens created by the wave of corporate speculation in the 1980s sharply squeezes our economy's prospects in the 1990s. We now need financial resources for more investment—in new factories, new machinery, new research, new infrastructure, and a better educated work force—not more consumption.*

Nobody who lives in the United States and keeps his eyes and ears open could miss the rising level of popular discontent over today's weak economy. Election-oriented opinion polls, the statements of assorted business leaders, posturing by members of Congress, and the evident disarray within the Bush Administration all convey the same message. Americans are more worried about their economic prospects, and the nation's, than they have been for a long time. The recession—and more specifically, the absence of any visible recovery—has become the central focus of rapidly spreading discontent. Politicians of both parties are therefore scrambling to be first in line with one or another traditional antirecessionary action like a job-creating public works program or a tax cut to spur consumer spending.

All this frustration and even anger is difficult to explain simply in terms of what has happened (at least thus far) in the recession. From the summer 1990 peak to last spring's low point, the nation's total output fell by 1.2 percent after allowance for inflation. The average decline in the previous seven U.S. business downturns was 2.6 percent. More specific indicators of economy-wide business activity tell roughly the same story. Unemployment has only just recently edged above 7 percent of the labor force, and it is still up by just 2 percent from the twenty-year low point touched only briefly in early 1989. Not so long ago any unemployment rate with a six in front of the decimal point would have been hailed as a solid success representing effective "full employment." Use of the country's industrial capacity is off by about 5 percent from its recent peak, again a decline that is fairly modest by the standard of business downturns since World War II. Nobody welcomes a recession, to be sure, but why has the public reacted so sharply to what on most counts has been among the mildest downturns of the postwar period?

BENJAMIN FRIEDMAN Is William Joseph Maier Professor of Political Economy at Harvard University. This paper draws on Professor Friedman's recent research and writings, including especially *Day of Reckoning: The Consequences of American Economic Policy under Reagan and After* (Random House, 1988) and *Implications of Corporate Indebtedness for Monetary Policy* (Group of Thirty, 1990). Reprinted from *Challenge,* March–April 1992, pp. 25–34.

The most likely answer follows from taking a somewhat broader perspective. As of year-end 1991, total economic output in the United States stood only 2.8 percent above the level reached at year-end 1988, for an average real growth rate of merely 0.9 percent per annum over the three years. This performance marks the second-slowest growth sustained over any three-year period since the demobilization immediately following World War II. (The only slower three-year growth record was during the back-to-back recessions of 1980 and 1981–82.) In short, the U.S. economy is moving ahead barely if at all, and increasing numbers of Americans are well aware of that failure.

This stagnation at the outset of the 1990s is in large part the predictable—indeed, widely predicted—consequence of two major economic and financial legacies of the 1980s. First, under the burden of the record federal budget deficits of the past ten years, which have consistently absorbed nearly three-fourths of the nation's net private saving, the United States has systematically underinvested in practically all of the makings of a vigorous economy. The average working American therefore has less capital behind him—older factories, fewer machines, a more decrepit infrastructure than if the country had followed a normal economic trajectory, and he is presumably less productive as a result. Second, because corporate business has followed the government's lead by borrowing in record volume during a period of record low (for the postwar period) investment in new earning assets, the economy's private sector has built up a further barrier to renewed expansion in the form of leverage that is for many companies difficult, and for some impossible, to service. This private debt burden has, in turn, impaired the ability of banks and other lenders to provide credit to fund the ordinary requirements of economic expansion.

Viewed in perspective, therefore, the current stagnation of U.S. economic growth is understandable enough. But because this degree of economic stagnation is so unfamiliar—and also because it has appeared immediately after the artificially faster growth performance created by the inflated borrowing of the Reagan years—both popular opinion and the ensuing political response have reacted as if the country's problem were simply a traditional business recession caused by insufficient aggregate spending. This confusion is potentially dangerous, in that the policy actions that would be appropriate in the event of a serious recession due to weak aggregate demand are not the same as the steps required to turn around the current, more serious, stagnation. In some respects, the two sets of potential actions even run directly counter to one another. Hence a deeper understanding of the economy's situation, given the "facts on the ground" inherited from the 1980s, is especially important at this point.

## "Credit Crunch," Corporate Debt, and Banks

Only a person who had been living in a closet could be unaware of the extraordinary wave of debt-financed transactions that swept over much of corporate America in the 1980s. To a greater extent than at any time since World War II (perhaps ever), U.S. businesses undertook mergers, acquisitions, stock repurchases, and leveraged buyouts. As a result, the indebtedness of U.S. corporations engaged in nonfinancial lines of business rose to postwar record highs, not just in dollar terms but also compared with ongoing economic activity. The nonfinancial corporate sector's outstanding debt, measured as a percentage of gross national product, had fluctuated narrowly around 30 percent from 1960 through 1980. By year-end 1989, before the recession began, it stood at 39 percent. Among unincorporated nonfinancial businesses, significantly including real estate partnerships, outstanding debt relative to GNP had slowly crept from 9 percent in 1960 to 16 percent in 1980. By 1989 it was 24 percent.

From an economic perspective, however, what was remarkable about the business borrowing of the 1980s was not just the record dollar volumes and the changing debt-to-income relationships but the purpose for which so many companies borrowed. In a debt-financed merger or acquisition, one company borrows to acquire the existing assets of another. In a leveraged buyout, a newly created entity borrows to acquire an existing company's assets. In a debt-financed stock repurchase, a company borrows simply to buy in its shares from whichever stockholders want to sell.

In short, none of these transactions creates any new earning assets. From the perspective of the corporate sector as a whole—and in the case of stock repurchases, even from the perspective of the single firm—each is simply a substitution of debt for equity within the firm's capital structure. Between 1984 and 1990, the volume of equity retired in this way by U.S. nonfinancial corporations exceeded the entire gross proceeds of all new equity issues by $641 billion.

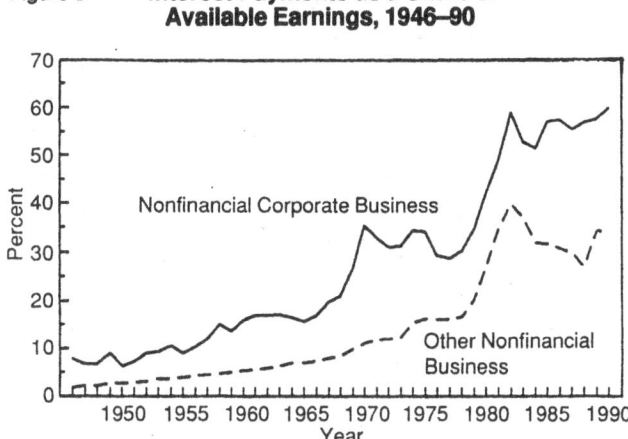

Figure 8  Interest Payments as a Share of Available Earnings, 1946–90

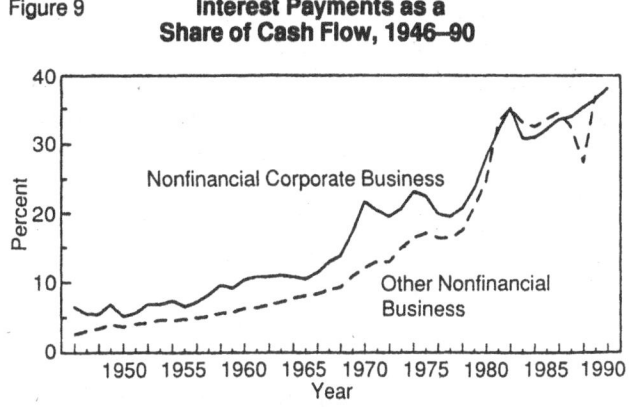

Figure 9  Interest Payments as a Share of Cash Flow, 1946–90

One implication of this massive debt-for-equity swap was, of course, an erosion of corporate balance sheets. In a basic sense, that is what financial leveraging is all about. Standard book-value balance sheet measures showed a sharp increase in debt–equity ratios, and a decline in net worth, for many companies and in the aggregate. Corresponding market-value measures, which are presumably more relevant for most purposes related to economic analysis, showed less deterioration because of most companies' rising stock price. Throughout the 1980s, the market-value debt–equity ratio for the U.S. nonfinancial corporate business sector as a whole fluctuated mostly in a range that was well above the levels of the 1950s and 1960s, yet below the peaks reached in the 1970s. Even the stock market crash in October 1987, for example, did not carry aggregate market-value leverage back to the postwar peak reached when the market fell sharply in September 1974.

More so than increasing balance sheet leverage, however, the result of the corporate borrowing wave of the 1980s that has the greatest implications for the U.S. economy's prospects in the 1990s is the increase in debt service burdens (see Figure 8).

The share of earnings, measured before interest and taxes, that U.S. nonfinancial business corporations pay out in interest rose from less than 10 cents on the dollar in the early 1950s to more than 20 cents by the late 1960s. In the first half of the 1970s, as rapid inflation drove nominal interest rates higher while two recessions depressed earnings, the interest share rose above 30 cents. Then, at the outset of the 1980s, the combination of even more rapid inflation and the worst recession since the 1930s pushed it past 50 cents on the dollar.

The main import of the record borrowing done by U.S. corporations since then—again, largely borrowing to achieve higher leverage, not to create more earning assets—is that the share of earnings absorbed by interest payments has remained well above 50 cents on the dollar ever since, despite the decline in nominal interest rates and despite an eight-year economic expansion that carried corporate earnings in 1989 to more than double the recession-depressed level of 1983. The experience of unincorporated nonfinancial businesses resembled that of corporations until the early 1980s, but since then interest-to-earnings ratios have fallen somewhat for these borrowers. Interest payments have remained at or near record levels compared with cash flow for both corporate and noncorporate businesses, however (see Figure 9).

The distinction between balance sheets and debt service ratios, as a measure of the legacy of the business borrowing wave of the 1980s, is essentially the familiar distinction between stocks and flows. In principle, a firm's outstanding debt is the present value of the future stream of payments it is obligated to make, including interest and principal. Similarly, the market value of a firm's equity is supposed to represent the present value of its future stream of earnings, net of such obligatory payments as debt service and taxes. In a perfect capital market—"perfect" in the economist's abstract sense, that is—the correspondence between these respective concepts would be such that whether the stocks or the flows constituted the appropriate focus of any particular analysis would be mostly a matter of convenience.

Actual capital markets are not perfect, however. One reason why the relevant flows may matter in ways not captured by the corresponding stocks is simply that speculative asset markets may misprice the relevant claims. Prices established by the market at any given time may reflect factors other than market participants' collective best judgment of the most likely prospects for uncertain future outcomes. Moreover, those judgments may be wrong, in any case. That the stock market "forecasts" strong earnings growth for either an individual company or business as a whole does not necessarily mean that strong growth will ensue.

Further, while prices in the market at best reflect properly discounted values of accurately expected entire streams of future earnings and payments against them, most businesses have to meet the payments for which they are liable in real time—year by year, quarter by quarter, month by month. A company can cover an insufficiency in one period with excess proceeds from an earlier period only to the extent that it has retained that excess within the firm, rather than distributed it in dividends or paid it out through some form of transaction that substitutes debt for equity. A company can cover an insufficiency in any one period with excess proceeds from a *future* period only to the extent that some lender is willing to advance credit against that future excess. If capital markets were perfect—again, "perfect" in the economist's sense—a firm's ability to borrow against future earnings would simply reduce back to the same issue of whether the appropriately discounted streams of anticipated earnings and payments net to positive present value. But in the actual context of an imperfect market for credit, there is no assurance that every firm with positive net present value can always borrow.

Flows do matter, therefore, and in particular the large interest obligations (compared with earnings) that U.S. corporations incurred in the 1980s in principle can—and probably do—affect what activities businesses undertake. A positive view of such influences, sometimes called the "back against the wall" view of corporate behavior, is that high debt service burdens induce corporate managers to achieve operating efficiencies that they would not otherwise attempt. When the alternative is default and potential bankruptcy, eliminating unnecessary staff or renegotiating long-standing relationships suddenly becomes a more acceptable way of doing business. Hence eliminating a firm's "net free cash flow" raises the expected trajectory of future earnings, thereby increasing the present value of the firm and also increasing lenders' willingness to advance it credit. Under this interpretation, the leveraging of corporate America in the 1980s should have enhanced the economy's prospects for growth in the 1990s.

An alternative, more negative view is that high leverage induces corporate managers to sacrifice longer-run objectives—that is, to forego initiatives that would raise the net present value of the firm's expected earnings stream, and therefore in a perfect capital market would raise the market value of the firm as well—in favor of ensuring adequate short-run cash flow to meet current obligations. For example, there is ample evidence indicating that highly indebted firms undertake less research and development than otherwise comparable firms with lower leverage. Similarly, there is growing evidence that highly indebted firms do less capital spending than their less leveraged counterparts. Given the links connecting both research and investment to productivity, these developments suggest that the widespread leveraging U.S. corporations did in the 1980s has left a *diminished,* not a strengthened, basis for the economy's growth in the 1990s.

Moreover, when so many companies step up their leverage, and to so great an extent, the result can be to alter the economic environment in ways that go well beyond just the sum of individual-firm effects calculated on an all-other-things-equal basis. An important part of the reason why the relationship between flows of interest payments and flows of earnings matters in the first place is that credit markets are imperfect. Not every firm seeking to finance a project with positive expected present value can always do so. The behavior of lenders—banks, insurance companies, finance companies, and even investors in the open market for fixed-income securities—is a key part of the story.

There is reason to believe that in the United States in the 1980s the leveraging of business borrowers was of sufficient prevalence and magnitude as to impair the ability of many of these lenders to play their customary role in the economy's credit intermediation mechanism, and hence further compound the problems ordinarily confronting leveraged firms by rendering the credit markets more imperfect. Business bankruptcies and defaults rose sharply in the wake of the 1981–82 recession—hardly a surprising outcome, given the severity of the downturn. What is historically unusual, however, is that the number of bankruptcies and the volume of defaulted liabilities (measured relative to GNP) remained at postwar record highs until late in the decade, and even then never fell back to anything like prerecession levels.

A fundamental feature of debt markets, which the discussion of U.S. business leveraging has too often overlooked, is that each transaction has both a borrower and a lender. When a borrower defaults, some lender takes a loss. When a borrower's likelihood of meeting its obligations erodes, the expected value of some lender's claim declines. These losses and declines in value represent reductions in the net worth, or capital, of lenders. In a financial system in which many lenders are themselves highly leveraged intermediaries that must meet minimum capital requirements, these losses and declines in value therefore impair their ability to extend new credits or renew old ones. Especially when the intermediaries in question represent the only plausible source of credit for specific would-be borrowers—for example, in the case of small businesses with just one or a few well-developed banking relationships—borrowers' ability to obtain credit is impaired as well. In short, the entire market becomes more imperfect.

Nearly every major category of lender in the U.S. credit markets has suffered at least some deterioration along these lines since the mid-1980s. Many commercial banks have had to take huge losses against what were already strained capital positions, and there is evidence that the banks whose capital has fallen most have cut back most on lending. Many insurance companies have experienced analogous reductions in their "surplus" accounts. Some major finance companies have suffered losses large enough to make their parent companies rethink the amounts of capital they are prepared to commit and the conditions under which they are prepared to commit it. Market buyers for newly issued "junk bonds" have simply disappeared altogether.

In sum, the legacy of the business leveraging movement of the 1980s is not only an overburdened nonfinancial business sector, less able to finance new capital formation internally and less prepared to seek new credit, but also a financial system less prepared to provide credit when it is sought. The combination does not bode well for the economy's ability to achieve productivity growth, and hence to provide high-value-added jobs, in the 1990s.

## Federal Government Debt and Deficits

President Ronald Reagan took office in 1981 and promptly began to implement the three-part fiscal program on which he had successfully campaigned. Its key elements were across-the-board cuts in personal income tax rates (in the event amounting to 25 percent), a large buildup of military spending, and protection of such nondefense spending programs as medicare and

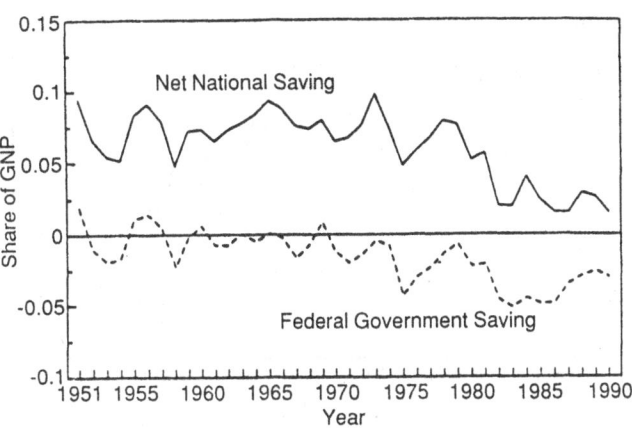

Figure 10  National Saving as a Share of GNP, 1951–90

social security.

As most (though certainly not all) economists had predicted, this combination led to a decade of record-size federal budget deficits despite the fact that the nation was neither at war nor in any kind of sustained economic downturn (see Figure 10). The borrowing that the U.S. Treasury had to do to cover this chronic excess of spending over revenues approximately tripled the national debt over the course of the decade, or about doubled it after allowance for inflation. By year-end 1990 the federal government's outstanding interest-bearing indebtedness amounted to more than 46 percent of gross national product, a level last seen (on the way down) in 1960.

Of course, no one expects the U.S. government to default on its obligations. The issues raised by the extraordinary surge of government borrowing in the 1980s are therefore fundamentally different from those raised by the increase in business borrowing. Yet the two are related in that each has left a legacy with which the U.S. economy must cope as it moves through the 1990s. The immediate reason why large government deficits sustained under conditions of full employment are damaging is that they absorb private saving that would otherwise be available to finance either new capital formation at home or net investment abroad. The United States has traditionally been a low-saving country compared with most other advanced industrialized economies, with U.S. net private saving averaging 7–8 percent of national income in recent decades. In the 1980s the federal deficit averaged 3.8 percent of national income. Moreover, only a small part of this budget gap for the decade as a whole reflected any direct impact of economic weakness. Even with both revenues

Figure 11 **Investment as a Share of GNP, 1951–90**

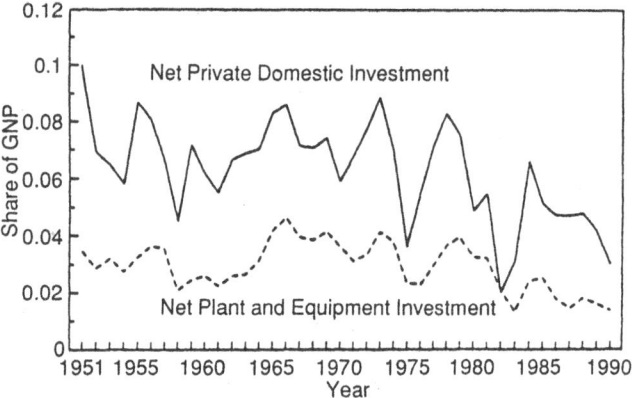

and expenditures calculated on a high-employment basis, the deficit still averaged 3.2 percent of national income over the decade.

To make matters worse, private saving in the United States also declined, relative to income, in the 1980s. This lower saving rate—in the face of historically unprecedented peacetime government deficits—constituted an important economic phenomenon in its own right, in that it directly contradicted the "Ricardian" notion that individuals act to offset government deficits by saving more either on their own account or via the private businesses that they own. Instead, U.S. net private saving declined from the usual 7–8 percent of national income to just 5.2 percent on average for the decade, thereby compounding rather than offsetting the government's dissaving. Overall national saving (including saving by the private sector as well as by federal, state, and local governments) as a share of national income therefore declined from the 7.3 percent average of the prior three decades to only 2.5 percent in the 1980s (see Figure 10).

Given the basic relationship between an economy's saving and its investment, it is hardly surprising that the share of U.S. income devoted to investment also declined in the 1980s (see Figure 11). Overall private domestic investment in the United States fell to a lower share of GNP than in any decade since World War II. Conversely, the share of national income devoted to personal consumption expenditures rose, almost continually, to record highs.

Spending on new business plant and equipment, the component of investment most directly connected to productivity and hence ultimately to wages and living standards, declined relative to income fairly steadily throughout the decade (Figure 11). Net investment in plant and equipment fell from 3.2 percent of GNP in 1981, about equal to the prior postwar average, to a postwar record low of 1.4 percent in 1990. Gross of depreciation, the share of income devoted to plant and equipment declined from a postwar peak of 12.1 percent in 1981 to 9.6 percent, back down at the average for the 1950s, in 1990. Nor did these comparisons merely reflect the onset of recession at the end of the decade. The net plant and equipment share held below 2 percent throughout 1986–90, and the gross share stayed below 10 percent throughout 1987–90.

Moreover, the United States was able to achieve even this meager investment performance only by becoming a major capital importer. In a closed economy the decline in investment relative to income would have exactly matched the decline in saving. By contrast, in the 1980s the United States was able to use inflows of foreign capital to achieve an investment ratio that, while shrunken to be sure, nevertheless exceeded what the combination of reduced private saving and increased government dissaving would have financed. Given the relationship between an open economy's capital account and current account, however, the capital inflows that facilitated this extra investment corresponded to a major decline in many U.S. firms' ability to compete against foreign producers in markets both at home and abroad. This decline in competitiveness, together with the broader implications of the nation's abrupt change from a modest capital exporter to a substantial capital importer, has also constituted an important phenomenon in its own right (politically as well as economically).

In the context of implications for the U.S. economy's growth prospects in the 1990s, however, the essential point is that even with the added investment financed by large capital inflows, the investment rate in the 1980s still fell well short of prior experience. As a result, the economy's ratio of capital to labor also failed to grow in line with prior experience. In 1989 the United States had $39,500 of privately owned plant and equipment for every private-sector worker, not all that much more than the corresponding level of $35,900 (measured in 1989 prices) in 1979. By contrast, between 1948 and 1979 the private economy's capital–labor ratio had risen from $19,000 of capital per worker (again in 1989 prices) to $35,900. The source of the contrast was not that employment growth sped up in the 1980s—it about matched the prior three decades' average experience—but that growth of the capital stock slowed. If the United States had merely invested enough in the 1980s to keep its stock of plant and equipment growing at the pace that had prevailed on average during 1948–79, by 1989 there would have been not $39,500 but $44,100 of capital for each worker.

Business plant and equipment, of course, is not the only form of capital that contributes to an economy's productivity. Infrastructure of the kind that governments typically provide—highways, airports, port installations, research facilities—can also enhance productivity. So can investment in human capital through education or on-the-job training. If the United States in the 1980s had slighted investment in business capital in order to rebuild its basic infrastructure, or to improve its education system, there would be ample room to debate whether new capital in these other forms might have been as beneficial as the foregone business capital formation, or perhaps even more so.

But in fact U.S. investment in these other forms of capital suffered in the 1980s as well. The share of federal government spending devoted to physical investment outside the defense establishment averaged just 1.2 percent in the 1980s, lower than at any other time since World War II. The same is true of spending at the state and local government level. As a result, the nation's total stock of government-owned capital grew by only 1.7 percent per annum on average in the 1980s, well below the 2.6 percent per annum average for 1948–79. Education has also received a shrinking share of U.S. resources in the last decade. Not surprisingly, given demographic trends, overall spending on primary and secondary education declined relative to GNP in the 1980s. Spending on higher education held about steady as a share of GNP.

In sum, during the 1980s the United States underinvested in just about all of the makings of a strong, growing economy. As a result, overall productivity growth continued to be disappointing despite the reversal of several factors to which many researchers have pointed as potentially important contributors to the post-1965 (and especially post-1973) productivity slowdown. In the 1980s, the age and experience level of the average American worker were rising, energy prices were mostly either steady or falling, and the share of business capital spending devoted to meeting environmental and health-safety regulations declined. Yet productivity in the economy's nonfarm business sector rose on average at only 1.1 percent per annum during 1980–90, not even as fast as the 1.3 percent per annum average pace for 1965–80, much less the 2.7 percent per annum achieved during 1948–65. Even in the expansion years of the 1980s viewed in isolation—that is, from the business cycle trough in 1982 to the prerecession peak in 1989—overall productivity growth was just 1.6 percent per annum.

The chief area of U.S. economic activity that did achieve unusual productivity gains in this period was manufacturing. Here output per man-hour advanced at 3.2 percent per annum on average during the 1980s overall, or 3.8 percent per annum during 1983–89, nicely ahead of even the 2.9 percent per annum pace posted during 1948–65. As one might expect in an era marked by such a paucity of new investment in factories and machinery, however, this superior performance in the 1980s came primarily through shedding labor. What stands out about the recent performance of U.S. manufacturing is not that output expanded more rapidly than in earlier eras but that employment shrank. Manufacturing output, both over the 1980s as a whole and during the 1983–89 expansion taken in isolation, grew less rapidly than during 1948–65. But, while manufacturing employment rose at 1.0 percent per annum during 1948–65 (and at 2.0 percent per annum during 1965–80), it *declined* by 0.9 percent per annum during 1980–90. The 1980s thus became the first decade since the industrial revolution in which fewer U.S. workers had jobs in manufacturing at the end of the decade than at the beginning.

The experience of the manufacturing sector in particular is relevant not only because it is (perversely) the one major example of high U.S. productivity growth in the 1980s but also because of the role manufacturing (along with construction on a much smaller scale) has historically played in providing high-value-added, and therefore high-wage, jobs for Americans without college educations. Despite the weak position of labor in the manufacturing sector in the 1980s, in 1990 the weekly pay of production or nonsupervisory workers was 28 percent higher in manufacturing than in the nonfarm business sector as a whole (manufacturing included), and more than twice the pay level in such major job sectors as retail trade. With barely nineteen million Americans employed in manufacturing at the 1990 business cycle peak, versus twenty-one million at the 1979 peak, it is hardly surprising that the wage of the average worker in private business declined by 7 percent compared with inflation, or that wage inequalities between workers with and without college educations widened dramatically, over the decade.

## Policy Prescriptions

The first essential step in devising an effective public policy to address the U.S. economy's current problems is to recognize just what the problems are. No sudden change in policy now can instantly remove the impediments to prosperity left as the legacy of the 1980s. Stagnation due to a decade of overborrowing and underinvestment is different from a conventional insufficiency of aggregate demand. Hence today's quest by almost every politician for a way to "jump start" the economy is misguided.

In today's context a traditional antirecessionary fiscal expansion would probably buy a modest addition to real growth in the near term at the expense of further damaging the U.S. economy's longer-run prospects. Even excluding the spending due to the bailout of the savings and loan industry, the federal government's structural deficit still remains in the range of 3–4 percent of national income, greater than at any time in U.S. peacetime history except for the height of the Reagan period and the one-shot tax rebate episode in 1975. More to the point, the entire volume of net saving done in 1991 by all U.S. businesses and households combined amounted to just 3.9 percent of national income. In other words, even apart from the effect of the recession in lowering tax revenues and adding to spending, the federal government is already absorbing substantially all of the nation's available private saving.

A parallel way to make the same point is to note that in 1991 consumer spending accounted for 67.5 percent of total economic activity, including the private sector as well as the government. A consumption share of this magnitude stands well above the 62–63 percent that used to be the standard norm for the U.S. economy in the 1950s, 1960s and 1970s, or even the bloated 65.5 percent average share that resulted from the personal tax cuts of the 1980s. The notion that business is faltering because consumers are not spending enough is not just wrong but wrongheaded.

What America needs is more investment—in new factories, new machinery, new research, new infrastructure, and a better-educated work force—not more consumption. Over the medium to longer run, fiscal stimulus in the form of either across-the-board tax cuts or directionless "jobs" programs would only cut more deeply into the already shrunken share of income that the nation now devotes to investment in its future in any of these aspects. More consumer spending fueled by tax cuts, or greater government spending, would instead mean more government borrowing to absorb an even greater share of already scarce private saving, leaving even less to finance needed investment.

The contrast between the fiscal policy actions that might usefully address the stagnation now affecting the U.S. economy and those actions that would be appropriate under conditions of a major deficiency of aggregate demand is all the more important because the experience of the 1980s gives little hope that any fiscal steps taken now would prove temporary. To give the argument its due, after the business recession of the past year or so there is some merit to the ever louder call for an all-purpose boost to government spending or a consumer-oriented tax cut. But in light of the chronic fiscal imbalance that has bled all aspects of America's investment for the past ten years, that merit hinges crucially on the removal of any stimulus to consumption or noninvestment government spending once the economy has returned to approximately full employment of its resources.

In today's political climate temporary fiscal stimulus has about as much credibility as the tooth fairy. Any realist knows that whatever tax cut or spending increase Congress and the president put in place in 1992 will still be at work, raising either private or government consumption at the expense of investment, in 1995 and perhaps far beyond. For just this reason, the guiding principle behind any fiscal action taken at this point should be to adopt only measures that will still be useful several years hence.

Given these constraints, four sets of actions now seem most appropriate:

1. Congress should change the tax code to eliminate the long-standing bias in favor of debt over equity financing by private business. Just how big a role tax incentives played in spurring the corporate leveraging wave of the 1980s remains a topic for serious quantitative research. But now that the consequences of this experience have demonstrated that high leverage in sufficient degree can have important negative externalities, there is little point in waiting until the results of that research are in hand to eliminate distortionary tax features whose qualitative effect has long been clear a priori.

2. Congress should adopt serious banking reform, reform designed to allow banks to attract adequate capital to support lending in support of genuine economic expansion. In light of the experience of federal

deposit insurance during the last decade, however—not just in banking but also in the thrift industry—the most sensible way to expand banks' ability to earn profit and hence attract capital, while limiting the government's exposure to potential losses, is probably some form of the "narrow bank" plan. In such a system, some banks would issue insured liabilities and hold only very safe assets, while others would engage in a much broader range of activities financed by issuing only uninsured liabilities. Meaningful bank reform in this context would also presumably include interstate banking. As the experience of some regions (for example, New England) in the 1990–91 recession has illustrated, businesses, homeowners, and other would-be borrowers sometimes pay a large price for their local bankers' protection from competition.

3. Congress should undertake stimulative fiscal action, but only in forms that either add directly to investment activity (broadly construed) or encourage the private sector to do so. Among potential spending measures, this means additions to the forms of public infrastructure that enhance productivity, in contrast to mere porkbarrel job creation, as well as programs to improve deteriorating education systems. The federal government can and should undertake some of these steps on its own. Others are most efficiently accomplished via support provided to the states. Indeed, in many states increased federal support is now crucial merely to keep in place key programs that build infrastructure or educate tomorrow's work force. Among potential tax actions, this emphasis on stimulating investment means limiting any major tax cuts to measures such as restoring the investment tax credit, which the 1986 Tax Reform Act abolished. (Some potential tax changes that would be useful in this regard—for example, integrating the treatment of dividends at the corporate and personal levels, or switching from the current corporate income tax to a business cash flow tax—would not only increase investment incentives but also reduce artificial incentives to excess leverage in business financial structures, and if appropriately designed could even do both without any loss of revenue.) After the recession—and presumably after the election—Congress and the president should return to the hard challenge of reducing the government's chronic drain on saving. But to avoid this effort's defeating its own purpose, they should do so without either cutting into the government's own already diminished investment activities or imposing tax increases that would reduce private investment incentives.

4. The Federal Reserve System should maintain an easier monetary policy, especially as long as the economy has a clearly visible margin of unused labor and capital resources. Easier monetary policy does more than just provide useful stimulus to spending in the near term. It also works in the right direction from the perspective of what the U.S. economy needs in the longer run. The persistent problem of the past ten years has been an extraordinary imbalance of macroeconomic policies, as an overly expansionary fiscal policy has ground away against restrictive monetary policy. The result was to drive real interest rates to record high levels and depress productive investment to the lowest share of national income in half a century. Now that an increase is in order in the overall degree of expansion provided by fiscal and monetary policies combined, the case for achieving that additional expansion primarily via easier monetary policy is strong. The fact that the Federal Reserve can readily reverse any monetary easing once it is no longer in the economy's best interest, while Congress and the president almost surely could not reverse any major expansionary fiscal actions, only makes an easier monetary policy all the more appealing at this point.

CHAPTER 7 | BANKING CRISES AND LENDER-OF-LAST-RESORT INTERVENTIONS

# *The Management of Financial Instability*

ROBERT GUTTMANN

Financial instability, both in its cyclical manifestations as a trigger for recessionary adjustments and in the course of long waves as a key force behind stagnation and restructuring, is an endemic feature of capitalist economies. Ever since the Great Depression, which started with a stock-market crash in 1929 and eventually culminated in the collapse of the entire credit system, we have taken those manifestations of crisis quite seriously and used government intervention to deal with them. Roosevelt's money and banking reforms of 1933–35 imposed a number of regulatory restrictions on America's financial system that provided for more stable securities exchanges and tightly circumscribed banking activities (see chapter 1). Commercial banks, for instance, were prohibited from engaging in price competition, nationwide branching, or bank-related activities such as investment banking. In return they had, as the only type of financial institution capable of money creation, the privilege of access to deposit insurance, to emergency funds from the Fed's discount window, and to the Fed's payments services (e.g., check clearing, fund transfers).[1]

This combination of institutional restraint and lender-of-last-resort assistance worked exceedingly well until the peak of the stagflation crisis in the late 1970s. At that point commercial banks as well as thrifts suddenly faced rather large losses due to disintermediation of funds into nonregulated alternatives (e.g., money-market fund shares) and negative yield spreads between their short-term liabilities and their long-term assets. It was in 1980, in the midst of the worst credit crunch in the postwar period, that Congress passed the Depository Institutions Deregulation and Monetary Control Act (DIDMCA) to phase out rate ceilings on bank (as well as thrift) deposits and loans so that these depository institutions could effectively counter any disintermediation of funds and better defend their yield spreads. The thrifts, which had been hit particularly hard by the post-1979 hike in interest rates due to their especially pronounced maturity mismatch between liabilities and assets, were given additional regulatory relief by DIDMCA in terms of product diversification. Their deregulation was extended in the Garn–St. Germain Depository Institutions Act (DIA) of 1982.

## The thrift debacle

The government's decision to give thrift institutions greater freedom in terms of product and price competition had unintended consequences that ultimately proved disastrous. When lawmakers deregulated the thrifts in 1980–82, many of those institutions had already suffered severe losses in income, asset values, and capital. Government officials had underestimated the extent of these losses which the book-value and historic-cost accounting rules of *Generally Accepted Accounting Practices* (GAAP) used by the thrifts tended to obscure. That problem, which also plagued commercial banking, became more pronounced after the Reagan administration slashed supervision and enforcement budgets of thrift and bank regulators. Failure by the government at that point to deal with the rapidly growing number of potential or actual insolvencies encouraged weaker thrifts to use the new-found powers of product diversification as an opening for the pursuit of high-return, high-risk financing strategies that would, if successful, allow them to grow out of their troubles.[2]

To bring more capital into the industry, thrift regulators had eased takeover provisions which enabled many speculators to acquire thrifts cheaply and then use the low minimum capital requirements of these institutions to launch highly leveraged transactions. Due to widespread use of deposit brokerage, those so-called *go-go thrifts* were in a position to access deposits from across the nation on a large scale by offering attractive yields. Since those were insured by the government, depositors did not care where their funds went and what they were used for. The extraordinary growth of these new thrifts attracted more capital, further boosting their expansion.

It did not take long for the combination of weak thrifts trying to grow out of their troubles and aggressive go-go thrifts to create a situation where unfavorable movements in interest rates would seriously hurt a large number of overextended institutions. Already in 1984, during a period of rising interest rates, it became clear that deregulation had aggravated the systemic-risk conditions of the thrift industry. At that point thrift regulators, with the tacit support of lawmakers and administration officials, decided on a strategy of *regulatory forbearance* which was designed to hide economic losses through a variety of accounting gimmicks and thereby enable de facto insolvent thrifts to remain open.[3] In this way, it was hoped, the small FSLIC would be spared the task of having to clean up the mess and incurring large losses in the process. As the losses of thrifts mounted, accounting relief and the warehousing of failed institutions came to operate on an ever-growing scale. By 1987 it was obvious that even under the relaxed GAAP and RAP rules thrift losses had reached proportions beyond the limited capacity of the FSLIC, and Congress authorized, in the Competitive Equality Banking Act (CEBA), a recapitalization of the thrift insurance fund. Still, forbearance continued while thrift losses grew unabated.

In 1989 the situation had become so grave that lawmakers finally decided to tackle the thorny issue head on. In the Financial Institutions Reform, Recovery, and Enforcement Act (FIRREA) of 1989 they abolished the Federal Home Loan Bank Board in favor of a less captured regulator, the Office of Thrift Supervision (OTS) placed within the U.S. Treasury. The insolvent FSLIC was replaced by a Savings Association Insurance Fund (SAIF) which was put under the control of the FDIC, next to a newly created Bank Insurance Fund (BIF). The FDIC was also put in charge of the Resolution Trust Corporation (RTC) which FIRREA created to dispose of hundreds of insolvent thrifts. This bailout operation could cost taxpayers anywhere from between $160 billion and $300 billion in the span of a decade.

## The commercial banking crisis of 1991

As most authors presented in this chapter emphasize, similar developments took place during the 1980s in the commercial-banking sector, albeit on a proportionately lesser scale. Excessive risk-taking, accounting relief, and regulatory forbearance left many banks close to insolvency, yet in a position to stay open and engage in high-risk gambles. While commercial banks tended to be better diversified and capitalized than the thrifts, there were enough bank failures throughout the 1980s to deplete the FDIC's capital position. FIRREA failed to provide the newly created BIF with sufficient capital even though it had become quite clear that many commercial banks, especially the larger money-center banks, would soon suffer additional losses from souring real estate deals and leveraged buyouts after already having taken big hits in 1987 from write-downs of LDC debt and sectoral debt (e.g., farm loans, energy loans). Once the economy had slid into a recession by mid-1990, a replay of the thrift debacle seemed imminent.

The three banking specialists James Barth, Dan Brumbaugh, and Robert Litan focus in their article (see below) on the underlying causes for the banking crisis of 1990–91, the first time the entire banking sector of the United States has faced a systemic-risk threat of sector-wide paralysis since the Great Depression. As they point out, the problems of commercial banks are essentially structural in nature.

- For one, the banks are losing market share to relatively unregulated and more cost-efficient nonbank alternatives. Depositors can put their funds into money-market funds or cash-management accounts at investment banks that give them more direct and easier access to a larger array of investment opportunities than commercial banks can offer. Those nonbank deposit alternatives even provide check-writing privileges on a limited scale.

- Commercial banks are seeing even more market erosion on their asset side. Their best borrowers, large corporations, have abandoned them and prefer instead to issue commercial paper or other securities which offer many competitive advantages over loans. This trend has especially hurt the large money-center banks. Even their consumer-credit divisions find themselves locked in deadly competition with consumer finance companies, mortgage banks, thrifts, and a host of credit-card issuers. Loss of traditional customers has prompted many banks to look for alternative lending sources whose prospects for higher yields are linked to greater risks. More of their loans, especially in the high-risk areas of commercial real estate and leveraged buyouts, have consequently gone sour.

- Commercial banks have joined the trend in favor of direct finance via securities markets, which on its own threatens to marginalize their role of indirect intermediation finance in the credit system, by bundling their loans into collateralized securities. Such *securitization* of credit improves the liquidity position of banks and allows them to limit interest-rate risk, but it also undermines their original function of financial intermediation between liquid deposits and illiquid loans which justified their positive yield spread. As loans become more liquid, a trend further encouraged by the rapid growth of secondary markets for the resale of loans at market value, the banks lose their unique profit legitimation of obtaining higher yields for funding illiquid loans. As the spreads between liquid liabilities and increasingly less illiquid assets decline, banks become more inclined to compensate for their profit erosion with potentially profit-rich innovations in their financing positions that often carry unforeseen risks. The phenomenal increase in off-the-book derivatives transactions by banks is a good example of this trend.

Squeezed on both sides of their balance sheets and in their income statements (although pressures there are lessened by misleading GAAP rules and a high degree of discretion concerning loss accounting), banks have only limited response options. A legacy of regulatory restrictions on their activities and portfolios, which date back to the New Deal and in light of modern technology or global competition are quite anachronistic, deprive these institutions of adequate diversification possibilities and keep them locked out of many reasonably rewarding investment opportunities.

In light of these constraints, commercial banks have ended up less profitable, less capitalized, and more prone to risk than they should be for our domestic economy to function well. As Dan Brumbaugh and Kenneth Scott emphasize (see below), these structural weaknesses of the banking system have been reinforced by a flawed regulatory approach consisting of outdated restrictions that encourage risk-taking while sapping the competitiveness of banks vis-à-vis less-constrained nonbank institutions. Add to this a cyclical downturn amidst conditions of a generalized debt overhang, and you have the ingredients for a major banking crisis.

## The restructuring effort of 1991

As Barth, Brumbaugh, and Litan illustrate quite convincingly by evaluating alternative crisis scenarios, the problems of major commercial banks had reached such an intensity by 1991 that even a mild recession would soon threaten the solvency of the newly created BIF and thus paralyze the FDIC. Similar estimates of projected FDIC losses are presented here also by Edward Hill and Roger Vaughan as well as Edward Kane. If no action was taken in light of such imminent losses, the FDIC would surely be driven to an intolerable level of regulatory forbearance, possibly with the same kind of negative repercussions that we encountered in the thrift debacle, or give way to a massive taxpayer bailout.

Facing the unpalatable prospect of having to choose between two fiscally disastrous and politically unpopular strategies, the Bush administration and key lawmakers in Congress began to consider a major regulatory overhaul for commercial banking. The 1991 reform proposal by the Treasury, which initially seemed to have majority backing in both chambers of Congress, linked a removal of outdated regulatory restrictions on bank activities and portfolios to a reform of the deposit-insurance system (see chapter 8). Had this proposal become law, it would have strengthened banks by allowing them to branch nationwide, engage in a much larger variety of bank-related activities, and draw equity capital from industry and commerce for rapid recapitalization. But, as is well described in the piece by Brumbaugh and Scott, turf battles and special-interest lobbying pressure sank the Treasury proposal.

What the lawmakers passed instead, the so-called Federal Deposit Insurance Corporation Improvement Act (FDICIA) of 1991, was a much narrower piece of legislation that focused solely on deposit-insurance reform. The law provided the FDIC with additional capital and cash infusions from the Treasury that were backed by higher deposit insurance premiums and liquidation of collateralized assets respectively. It also established a system of early-warning signals, based on risk-weighted capitalization measures, to guide FDIC interventions before a bank became insolvent. If the FDIC sees the capital erosion of a bank reach dangerous proportions, it can now demand corrective action or apply sanctions in order to prevent insolvency. Before passage of the 1991 law, the FDIC had to wait until a bank had become insolvent before it could intervene. Earlier intervention would presumably limit the risk exposure of the FDIC. The FDICIA provided in addition for early-closure provisions to remove failed banks expeditiously. Finally, it also abandoned the "too big to fail" doctrine first adopted in 1984 to restore a modicum of market discipline among bankers while at the same time reducing FDIC losses from bank failures.

Brumbaugh and Scott (see below) criticize the FDICIA on several grounds. For one, the law left a fairly large degree of uncertainty concerning the newly installed risk-weighted capital standards by continuing to rely on inherently biased GAAP rules for bank accounting and allowing delays in the consideration of interest-rate risks. Those concerns are also voiced by Kane in his piece, while Hill and Vaughan note increased interest-risk exposure of banks due to their large-scale buying of Treasury securities in recent years. Second, the act's "least-cost" provisions for FDIC interventions leave that regulatory agency with too much discretion, thus raising the prospect for continued regulatory forbearance (especially if the Treasury assistance for the FDIC proves inadequate). The authors stress the need for less discretion and more automatic response modes in the application of sanctions against deteriorating banks, a sentiment also shared by Barth, Brumbaugh, and Litan, who propose a concrete mandatory-action plan the FDIC should pursue to save weak banks or remove them promptly once they have become insolvent. Finally, sharply higher deposit insurance premiums, through which healthier banks are forced to subsidize weaker banks, may prompt the former to pursue higher-risk assets in compensation. Hill and Vaughan voice the same worry, as does Kane.

Edward Kane assesses the FDICIA from a slightly differently angle. For him, the primary problem with the act lies in its enforceability. He sees numerous indications that bank regulators are hostile to the Congressional intent behind the law of limiting deposit-institution losses through prompt FDIC intervention. Regulators, for example, oppose any reduction in their discretion with regard to troubled banks. These sentiments leave one doubtful as to what extent the days of regulatory forbearance are over. The temptation to delay coping with bank insolvencies in the (usually false) hope of loss avoidance is surely still there, nowadays reinforced by public anger against the thrift bailout and politicians' obsessions with the budget deficit. Kane also worries that the FDICIA's provisions for weighting minimal capital standards by interest-rate risk rest on flawed assumptions about how likely interest-rate changes may impact on bank capital. These flaws, aggravated by continued reliance on the GAAP standards of book-value accounting, make it very difficult for the FDIC to identify the true extent of troubles among weakening banks. That evaluation bias feeds the regulators' temptations to engage in regulatory forbearance.

## *The future of commercial banking*

There is a general consensus among the authors presented here that the U.S. banking system is in the midst of a massive restructuring and that the legislators missed a golden opportunity to give this process a clearer direction when they failed in 1991 to enact the Treasury's broad deregulation guidelines. It seems equally obvious that the breathing space provided by FDICIA passage and sharply lower short-term rates in 1991–93 is of only temporary duration. Commercial banks are likely to face continued restructuring pressures from weakened balance sheets and excess capacity.

Hill and Vaughan foresee a splintering of the commercial-banking sector amidst its overall shrinkage. Money-center banks have been forced to abandon their dream of turning into *financial supermarkets* on a profitable basis within the current regulatory structure. The weaker ones among them should be merged into stronger institutions, followed by a radical streamlining of their marginal operations. This trend has in effect already begun in quite spectacular fashion, as evidenced by the relaxation of bank-merger restrictions by regulators and the recent wave of multibillion-dollar mergers between money-center banks (e.g., Manufacturer's Hanover and Chemical). The more profitable money-center banks, which have successfully exploited regulatory loopholes to pursue new avenues of revenue growth in bank-related activities outside the reach of regulators, will specialize in arranging complex financial transactions for their corporate customers on a global scale. Those merchant banks may want to hand in their bank charters and so escape the regulatory costs pertaining to commercial banking (e.g., rising insurance premiums). They should have little difficulty replacing their deposit funds with money-market instruments that provide large amounts of funds in a short period of time. Traditional commercial banking will be left to the superregionals which will mass-market their banking products in regional markets. Smaller banks will pursue niche banking or exploit their comparative advantage of local connections, frequently turning into loan boutiques that function as the small-business equivalent of consumer finance corporations.

These differentiation trends notwithstanding, it seems inevitable that commercial banks will want to compete more effectively with securities markets and nonbank institutions by offering a greater variety of financing instruments and engaging in a wider range of activities. This prospect brings us back to deposit insurance and regulatory reform of commercial banking. What most authors in this chapter argue is the need to separate the diversifying banking institution of the future into two parts: a "narrow bank" matching insured deposits with safe and liquid investments (e.g., government securities), and separately capitalized subsidiaries engaging in riskier bank-related activities that are financed by uninsured funds. Such a dual structure would limit the risk exposure of the FDIC to the relatively safe core of the multiproduct banking institutions and shield it from their riskier layers through effective "firewalls." That kind of structure would also encourage market-based risk evaluation and coverage mechanisms (e.g., private deposit insurance), which would enhance discipline among bankers.

Speculation among academic specialists as to the precise nature and structure of future banking rests heavily on the kind of regulatory regime that banks and other financial institutions are likely to face at the beginning of the new millenium. The failure of the Treasury's reform proposal and various "narrow bank" initiatives does not mean that these issues have gone away. On the contrary, they are in more urgent need of resolution than ever. It is for this reason that we must now focus our attention on the implications of the original Treasury proposal or any alternative for banking reform.

## Notes

1. Thrifts, which could be considered a narrowly focused type of commercial bank specializing in savings deposits and real-estate finance, were given their own regulatory framework (the Federal Home Bank Board), which included emergency funding by the FHLBB and deposit insurance administered by the Federal Saving and Loan Insurance Corporation (FSLIC).

2. After 1982, thrifts got heavily involved in the financing of land development and commercial real estate projects while also engaging more actively in speculative finance through greater use of repurchasing agreements or financial derivatives.

3. These accounting gimmicks, euphemistically categorized under the rubric of *Regulatory Accounting Practices* (RAP), allowed for delays in the booking of losses, advancing of gains, accounting profits in the wake of mergers, artificial boosting of net worth, and the hiding of asset depreciation (see Guttmann, 1985).

JAMES R. BARTH, R. DAN BRUMBAUGH, JR., AND ROBERT E. LITAN

# *Bank Failures Are Sinking the FDIC*

*Even before gauging the downside effects of the current recession, the Bank Insurance Fund may run out of cash at any moment. Federal policymakers have no choice but to reform the system now.*

This nation faces an almost unprecedented situation in having most of its largest banks operating on—or conceivably, over—the edge of insolvency. Debating on which side of the line they currently fall is unproductive. The key fact is that many of these banks not only currently have weak balance sheets by any reasonable standard, but they also are highly exposed to additional deterioration in their capital positions due to their significant involvement in high-risk lending, the "kryptonite" of the banking system (loans so toxic they can threaten even big banks). Perhaps most disturbing of all, even for those institutions that survive the current economic downturn, the fundamental structural changes occurring in the banking industry will impel them to take greater risks in the future, unless the laws currently governing the banking business are substantially modified.

Not since the creation of deposit insurance in 1933 have the U.S. banking industry and its deposit insurer been as troubled as they are today. Indeed, it is conceivable that for the first time since 1933, bank insolvency costs could rise so high that they would not only deplete the resources of the Bank Insurance Fund (BIF), but would also exhaust the financial ability of healthy banks to pay for the insolvencies.

## Overview of current problems

Enormous uncertainties surround any attempt to project the actual costs of future bank insolvencies. The uncertainties stem to a significant degree from the fact that banks rely on historical, or book value, accounting, which allows institutions tremendous flexibility to understate selected asset deterioration and to magnify selected asset improvement. Essentially, this accounting camouflages the true economic declines in banks' economic earnings and capital.

Regulatory laxity and forbearance have caused further deterioration by condoning, if not abetting, high-

JAMES BARTH is Lowder Eminent Scholar in Finance at Auburn University, Alabama. DAN BRUMBAUGH, JR. is a San Francisco-based financial institutions consultant. ROBERT LITAN is a Senior Fellow in the Economic Studies program at The Brookings Institution, Washington, D.C. Reprinted from *Challenge*, March–April 1991, pp. 4–15.

risk business strategies followed by weak banks. Meanwhile, legislative restrictions against geographic expansion and affiliations with nonbanking enterprises have impeded adaptation by strong banks to changing market conditions.

What makes the current weakness in the U.S. banking system so troubling is that the problems now appear to be centered in the largest banks—those with assets above $10 billion. These largest banks have had the lowest ratios of reported income-to-assets, and equity-to-assets, of any size category throughout the 1980s. Many have very thin capital margins and are reporting declining book value capital ratios. Even small losses as a percentage of assets at these banks alone would easily exhaust the resources of the BIF.

When the BIF closes or reorganizes troubled banks, it suffers substantial losses—indicating that by the time the regulators take action, the banks are deeply insolvent on a market value, or economic, basis. More than anything else, this pattern confirms that historical accounting principles can lead to substantial overstatements of a bank's economic net worth, especially for banks that admit themselves to be weakly capitalized by book value accounting measures.

Market forces are making it progressively more difficult even for healthy banks to earn sufficient returns to attract new capital. This is because the type of financial intermediation performed by banks gradually is being replaced by the securities markets, in two important ways: (1) through the flight of high-quality bank borrowers to the commercial paper market; and (2) the "securitization" of residential mortgages and consumer loans (packaging these into bundles to be sold to the market in the form of securities, with proportional claims on these packages or "trusts"). Increasingly, banks (especially the largest banks) have no other way to regain the "spreads" they once earned except by taking more risks. The rising loan losses in the industry reflect these developments.

The BIF is the victim of the negative trends affecting the banking industry. Of special concern to Congress and the executive branch, the BIF itself has found it increasingly difficult to predict accurately its losses and the size of its reserves, a situation that complicates budget planning.

We anticipate even further complications ahead. Net interest margins earned by banks have been falling. Banks are seeking profitability by increasingly investing in high-risk loans and assets. Erratic and inadequate provisioning for loan losses have propped up the earnings and capital of many banks, but have not been able to obscure the downward trend in both financial statistics.

Barring some unexpected beneficial economic development, many more banks—including perhaps some major banks—will become insolvent, even by historical accounting standards, in the period immediately ahead.

## BIF insolvency

Even before taking account of any downside effects of the recession, the BIF may have a liquidity problem at any time. If the administration and the Congress wish to avoid putting the FDIC in a position where it is forced to grant forbearance to troubled banks that merit resolution, a way must soon be found to come up with additional cash.

It hardly needs underscoring that the worst kind of forbearance practiced in the 1980s for thrifts—whereby hundreds of institutions actually reporting themselves to be insolvent were permitted to "gamble for resurrection" *without* meaningful supervision—had disastrous results. In addition, any optimism about the effectiveness of forbearance for banks must be tempered by the fact that weakly capitalized banks in recent years have failed at a much higher rate than banks with strong capital positions. Indeed, the banking industry as a whole will continue to face increasingly intense competitive pressures from other financial institutions and the securities markets, which will narrow available profit opportunities for most banks, let alone those that may fall into insolvency or be severely weakened by additional loan losses.

In sum, the federal government faces the risk of additional bank failure costs—if not now, then eventually—if the FDIC is forced by a shortage of cash and reserves to refrain from closing or reorganizing insolvent banks on a timely basis.

At year-end 1989, the FDIC reported its reserves, or the equivalent of its net worth, at $13.2 billion, or just 0.7 percent of total insured deposits held in U.S. commercial banks. Figure 12 illustrates that at this ratio, the fund was in the poorest condition in its history, and well below the 1.25 percent target for the BIF set in the Financial Institutions Reform, Recovery and Enforcement Act of 1989 (FIRREA). Early in 1990, the FDIC projected that the BIF would break even. But the FDIC's latest forecast for 1990 is that the BIF will lose

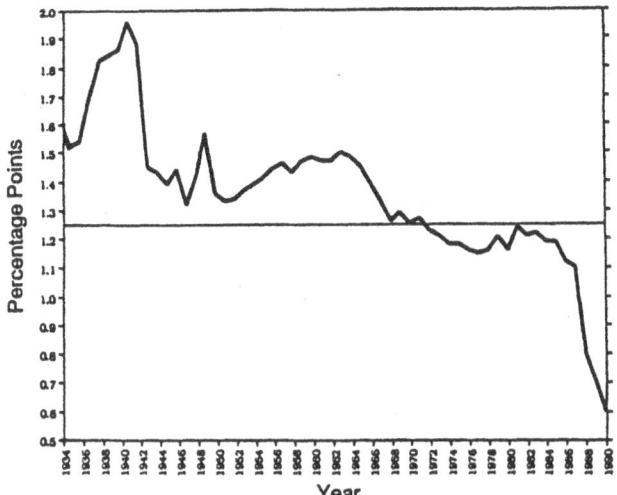

Figure 12  **Bank Insurance Fund Reserves Relative to Insured Deposits**

Source: FDIC.

another $3 billion, bringing its reserve level at the end of this year down to about $10 billion, or about 0.5 percent of insured deposits.

To help staunch the flow of red ink the FDIC announced at the end of the summer that beginning in 1991 it would raise bank insurance premiums from 15 to 19.5 basis points. As part of the budget agreement reached in October 1990, the administration projected that the FDIC would raise bank insurance premiums still further, to 23 basis points, the same level as for thrift deposits.

## Recession effects on bank failure costs

It is very difficult to estimate the effects of a recession on the BIF with great precision. Recessions vary in intensity and length. They can also have very different regional impacts. Accordingly, we have estimated the potential effects on the BIF of three possible recessions, differing in their severity. We assume, however, that in each case the recession is triggered primarily by the recent (and possible future) increases in oil prices, which have depressed consumer spending and induced the Federal Reserve to pursue a tighter monetary policy to contain the resulting inflationary pressures. We therefore assume in each recession scenario that banking conditions will not deteriorate any further (indeed, they should improve) in three key Southwestern states whose economies are heavily dependent on oil production: Louisiana, Oklahoma, and Texas.

We constructed these three recession scenarios by

Table 12  **Estimates of BIF's Crisis Resolution Costs**

|  | Base case assumptions ($ billion) | High |
|---|---|---|
| Mild recession | 1.1–3.5 | 2.5–12.2 |
| New England style | 3.2–10.3 | 4.5–26.3 |
| Texas style | 4.7–15.3 | 6.6–45.1 |

projecting how the distribution of banks across our different capital categories (each with its own probability of resolution) would change if all banks outside the Southwest *uniformly* experienced the same deterioration in their capital ratios as the reductions *surviving banks* already have experienced in Texas and New England (see Table 12). Specifically, in our "worst case" scenario, we assume that all non-Southwestern banks suffer the same 1.5 percentage point drop in their capital ratios as the average surviving bank in Texas suffered between 1986 and 1988. Our "New England-Style" scenario assumes that all non-Southwestern banks suffer a 1.0 percentage point reduction in their capital ratios, or about the same degree of equity deterioration as the average surviving banks in Connecticut and Massachusetts experienced between mid-1989 and mid-1990. Finally, our "mild" recession scenario assumes a 0.5 percentage point across-the-board deterioration in the capital ratios of all non-Southwestern banks, or a recession with half the severity of the "middle" scenario.

When combined with the resolution probabilities and cost ratios previously discussed, these various recession "shocks" produce additional failures and associated costs. Table 13 displays the results from these simulations, together with a projection assuming no recession, for each of the combinations of failure probability and resolution cost assumptions discussed above. The difference in resolution costs attributable to any of these recessions can be easily calculated by subtracting the "no recession" cost estimate for each combination of assumptions from the cost estimate for the appropriate recession scenario.

Thus, for example, the table illustrates that the additional three-year resolution costs of a mild recession under the base case Congressional Budget Office (CBO) failure probabilities and resolution costs is estimated to be $1.1 billion above the $12.2 billion of losses already embedded (on a probabilistic basis) in the banking system. Using the same assumptions but equalizing the probability of resolution for small and large banks, the additional cost of a mild recession is estimated at

Table 13  **Estimated Three-Year Bank Failure Costs Under Alternative Assumptions Concerning Recession Scenarios, Failure Probability, and Resolution Costs as of June 30, 1990** ($ billion)

|  | No recession | Mild recession | "New England Style" recession | "Texas Style" recession |
|---|---|---|---|---|
| CBO failure probability | | | | |
| CBO resolution costs | | | | |
| base | 12.2 | 13.3 | 15.4 | 16.9 |
| high | 26.4 | 28.9 | 30.9 | 33.0 |
| CBO failure probability | | | | |
| 1985–89 resolution costs | | | | |
| base | 13.0 | 14.6 | 17.8 | 20.9 |
| high | 25.2 | 31.4 | 38.0 | 51.8 |
| CBO failure probability | | | | |
| 1989 resolution costs | | | | |
| base | 18.5 | 20.4 | 24.6 | 28.6 |
| high | 39.2 | 48.9 | 59.0 | 81.0 |
| 1988–89 failure probability | | | | |
| CBO resolution costs | | | | |
| base | 15.8 | 17.9 | 21.6 | 23.8 |
| high | 38.3 | 42.7 | 49.4 | 49.2 |
| 1988–89 failure probability | | | | |
| 1985–89 resolution costs | | | | |
| base | 26.5 | 19.4 | 24.4 | 28.6 |
| high | 35.9 | 43.6 | 53.2 | 65.5 |
| 1988–89 failure probability | | | | |
| 1989 resolution costs | | | | |
| base | 23.9 | 27.4 | 34.2 | 39.2 |
| high | 56.8 | 68.6 | 83.1 | 101.9 |
| 1989 failure probability | | | | |
| CBO resolution costs | | | | |
| base | 15.8 | 17.6 | 20.5 | 21.8 |
| high | 30.8 | 34.1 | 39.0 | 38.6 |
| 1989 failure probability | | | | |
| 1985–89 resolution costs | | | | |
| base | 15.2 | 17.7 | 21.9 | 25.2 |
| high | 28.4 | 35.0 | 42.7 | 55.1 |
| 1989 failure probability | | | | |
| 1089 resolution costs | | | | |
| base | 22.4 | 25.5 | 31.3 | 35.3 |
| high | 44.7 | 55.0 | 66.6 | 86.0 |
| Average of all scenarios | | | | |
| base | 17.0 | 19.3 | 23.5 | 26.7 |
| high | 36.2 | 43.1 | 51.3 | 62.5 |

*Source:* Authors' calculations based on data in *Bank Source*, W.C. Ferguson & Co.

$2.5 billion (above the base estimate of $26.4 billion). Similar calculations reveal the following ranges of *incremental* three-year resolution costs across all of the assumption combinations:

The bottom rows of Table 13 present the average three-year resolution costs over all assumption combinations for each of the recession scenarios, as well as the baseline "no recession" scenario. Given the significant uncertainties pertaining to which combination of assumptions will prove to be the most accurate indicators of actual future bank failure costs, we believe these averages represent the most useful set of failure cost projections for each of the recession outcomes.

In brief, the averages demonstrate that under so-called base case assumptions—that is, assuming continued differentials between the probabilities of resolving large and small troubled banks—the average incremental cost of the three recessions are $2.3 billion (mild), $6.5 billion (New England), and $9.7 billion (Texas). If, however, the large and small troubled banks are resolved with the same frequency during the next three years (our "high-cost" assumption), then the corresponding average incremental three-year failure costs are $6.9 billion (mild), $15.1 billion (New England), and $26.3 billion (Texas). Put another way, the average cost estimates in the table suggest that under base-case assumptions, the *total* bank failure costs during the next three years will range between $17 billion and almost $27 billion, but under the high-cost assumptions, will range between $36 billion and $62.5 billion. To be sure, the foregoing cost estimates for the various recession scenarios could overstate the actual cost if the current recession truly has temporary effects and no banks engage in any of the "gambling for resurrection" behavior that so many thrifts displayed in the 1980s. However, if there is gambling for resurrection, then the delay in closing insolvent banks could produce resolution costs substantially larger than those just shown.

Indeed, there are two reasons why the above estimates are conservative even in the absence of forbearance. First, they assume that the various recessions affect all banks equally and uniformly. In fact, however, the weakest banks may very well suffer the greatest impacts because the same factors that have contributed to the current weakness—heavy asset concentrations in commercial real estate and highly leveraged transactions loans—are also likely to be sources of substantial additional deterioration in capital ratios in any recession. Second, the reductions in equity-to-asset ratios that define our recession scenarios are drawn from the experiences of the average *surviving* banks in Texas and New England. This "survivorship-bias" understates the actual degree of deterioration in capital ratios in these states, since the averages reported earlier do not reflect the substantial erosions of capital in banks in these states that have failed.

In the end, given the likely downward biases in our cost estimates, it is our judgment that the BIF *most likely* faces bank resolution costs in the next three years between the middle and high end of our cost ranges. Assuming, therefore, that the current downturn amounts to no more than what we labeled a "mild recession," bank resolution costs during the next three years should range between $31 billion and $43 billion, a level that would clearly exhaust the resources of the BIF given the January 1991 premium rate (19.5 basis points).

## Structural trends, systemic weaknesses

After the current recession and the lending ills that preceded it are over, will the banking industry's health and that of the BIF simply return to "normal," or are there deeper structural problems with both institutions that should concern federal policy makers? The evidence strongly supports the latter view. In brief, the commercial banking industry has been gradually losing its raison d'être: to serve both as a safe haven for investors' funds and to finance the borrowing needs of individuals and businesses. The reasons are simple.

Banks have been facing increasingly stiff competition for their funds from nondepositories: mutual funds; insurance companies; pension funds; and the securities markets. At the same time, securities markets have been gradually replacing banks as sources of finance.

Banking used to be a much easier business. When inflation was low, all but the wealthiest customers put their money in banks at low, regulated interest rates, and most individuals and companies had nowhere else to turn for funds except to their bankers. In such a world, banks found it was simple to earn a "spread" between the interest rates they paid depositors (none to checking account customers) and the rates they charged their borrowers. Indeed, from 1950 through 1970, the industry's return on assets rose steadily.

Two major developments in the last twenty years produced a sea change in the environment in which banks compete. First, the explosive jump in inflation in 1973–74, and again in 1979–81, induced depositors to look for other investments that promised returns well above the regulated interest rates banks were limited to paying. Ultimately, of course, the double-digit interest rates available on Treasury securities and money market mutual funds in the late 1970s and early 1980s forced Congress to allow banks and thrifts total freedom in the interest rates they could pay their depositors. Yet, now that their deposit rates have been deregulated, banks have found that they must pay more for funds.

Second, powerful advances in computer and information technology made it possible for alternative investments, such as money market mutual funds, to develop. Equally, if not more important, technological advances helped launch the "securitization" of finance, which has enhanced banks' liquidity but is gradually eroding the "spreads" that banks were accustomed to earning on their deposit funds.

Residential mortgages were the first loans to be "securitized." In retrospect, mortgages were easy to securitize because both the instruments and the underwriting process for originating them were highly standardized. Between 1975 and 1988, the volume of mortgage securities outstanding grew by a factor of more than 40, from less than $18 billion to almost $770 billion. By the end of 1988, over 35 percent of all residential mortgages in the United States had been securitized.

Securitization has since spread to other loan instruments, principally auto and credit card loans. In addition, banks have been increasingly active in selling their business loans. From mid-1983 to mid-1990, the volume of outstanding loan sales by commercial banks jumped from $27 billion to $190 billion.

From one perspective, the development of the deeper secondary markets for bank (and thrift) loans that securitization and loan sales have made possible has been a major positive force. In the past, banks generally were stuck with the loans they made until those loans matured. But when banks today need liquidity, or, in the current environment of capital shortage, when they need to shrink their asset base in order to comply with prevailing capital standards, they need only sell some of the loans they have originated. Moreover, banks now have new opportunities for profit, since they have the authority to securitize the loans they make. They can package loans into pools; and they can distribute the resulting securities to other buyers.

But securitization also has had powerful, and much less recognized, negative implications for banks and thrifts as well. Depository institutions arose because they transformed "liquid" deposits into "illiquid" loans to borrowers who effectively had no other options for obtaining finance. Indeed, it was by taking the risk of holding illiquid loans in portfolio that banks and thrifts could charge a sufficient spread over their cost of funds to earn respectable returns on the capital shareholders provided to them.

However, by turning formerly illiquid instruments into liquid securities, securitization and the increasingly deep loan sales market essentially undermine the traditional function banks performed. Banks can no longer charge the spreads they once earned because many of the loans they make are now illiquid. Put another way, securitization widens the demand for formerly illiquid loans—from depositories to pension funds, insurance companies, mutual funds, and individuals themselves—and thereby reduces the interest rates on these loans.

It is now generally understood, for example, that the securitization of residential mortgages has effectively lowered mortgage interest rates, below what they would otherwise be, by 50 to 100 basis points. The drop in mortgage rates has been so substantial that most thrift institutions—required by law to invest most of their funds in residential mortgages—can no longer profitably hold fixed-rate mortgages unless they gamble on the movement of interest rates. This constitutes a desperation strategy forced upon the thrift industry by law; it produced the initial thrift crisis of the 1980s, which persists to this day.

As nonmortgage loans held by banks are increasingly converted to securities, the commercial banking industry will be plagued with similar problems, although perhaps at a slower pace. Banks of all sizes have already suffered an erosion of their "spread" (or net interest margin). The traditionally safest borrowers—blue-chip corporations—essentially have deserted banks as sources of funds, finding it cheaper instead to borrow directly by issuing commercial paper. By 1989, the ratio of nonbank commercial paper outstanding to commercial and industrial (C&I) loans held by banks was over 75 percent, up from less than 10 percent thirty years ago.

With their best customers gone and their margins under increasing pressure, banks have chased riskier loans in an effort to maintain their former returns to shareholders. The result is that loan losses as a share of total industry-wide loans have been rising not just during the past several years, *but for the past three decades.*

Indeed, the drop in banks' net income would have been even greater and noticed earlier if regulators had not permitted banks to camouflage the deterioration of certain loans, beginning with less-developed country (LDC) debt in 1982. In addition, reported earnings have been made more volatile by the collective decisions of banks and their regulators not to make appropriate provisions for loan losses at the time when those assets actually declined in value.

Large banks, in particular, have suffered the most. After all, the blue-chip customers that used to borrow from banks used the largest banks, so one would expect to see those institutions experiencing the greatest difficulties with problem loans. At mid-year 1990, nonaccrual loans held by the largest banks (those with assets above $10 billion) represented almost 2.5 percent of their total loans; in contrast, the same ratio at the smallest banks (those with assets less than $100 million) was just above 0.7 percent.

### Shrinking banking industry

The combination of stiffer competition for deposit funds and the gradual replacement of bank intermediation with direct intermediation performed by the securities markets has enormous implications for the financial marketplace.

• First, these forces help explain why *the banking industry will continue to shrink, relative to other types of financial intermediaries.* There has been a dramatic shift in the share of financial assets held by banks during the past four decades, from over 50 percent in 1950 down to just barely more than 30 percent in 1989. Most of the slack has been taken up by mutual funds and pension funds.

These trends should continue. As both banks and thrifts react to deteriorating asset quality and the recently implemented capital requirements, the share of financial assets held by depositories should continue to shrink.

It is important to view this long-run development with favor, rather than with alarm. The economic forces that created and drove the expansion of nondepository financial institutions benefit the U.S. economy. The proliferating number of financial competitors and the expanding array of financial products they offer are largely the products of greatly improved computer and telecommunications technologies. The resulting products and services are provided more efficiently and at lower cost.

These benefits tend to be obscured by the deterioration, first, of the savings and loans and then more recently, of commercial banks. Some tend to equate the troubles among these institutions with a reduction in financial services offered. Yet, nondepository institutions clearly seem to be taking the place formerly occupied by banks and thrifts in the U.S. financial sector.

Similarly, it is tempting to tie the welfare of the largest banks, which as we have pointed out, have been under severe pressure, with the welfare of the entire banking industry. While clearly large banks—as measured by concentration ratios—are important, they have become progressively *less* important in the overall banking system. This no doubt reflects the inability of these institutions to grow, given the squeeze rising loan losses have put on their capital positions.

• Second, the increasingly intense competitive environment helps explain why *banks have been taking on more risk.* The rising loan losses in the industry, already discussed, make this point self-evident. Banks became less liquid in the 1980s, reducing the share of their assets in cash and investment securities from roughly 36 percent at the beginning of the decade to just 27 percent by the end. An increase in loans took up the slack, rising from 54 percent of total assets to 61 percent. Meanwhile, the composition of bank loan portfolios shifted markedly. C&I loans, the largest component of loans in 1980 at 21 percent, finished the decade at 19 percent.

In contrast, real estate loans grew from 15 percent to 23 percent over the same period, replacing C&I loans as the most important lending category.

Moreover, within the real estate loan category, banks shifted toward the riskiest borrowers. The share of construction and development loans doubled, from 2 percent to 4 percent of total loans. In addition, loans secured by nonfarm, nonresidential real estate—or commercial mortgages—also nearly doubled, from 3.5 percent to 6.5 percent. Though these percentages may seem small, each percentage point, given the size of the commercial banking industry, represents over $20 billion. Moreover, at the same time that banks were rushing into commercial real estate lending, so too were savings and loans. In combination, the two types of depositories gave rise to the enormous overhang of excess supply that is now depressing commercial real estate prices in many major metropolitan markets today and is likely to continue to depress them for some time.

Ironically, in the search for more risk, banks, in effect, have been chasing their own tails. As they lose their best customers, banks turn to increasingly risky lending. As those loans turn sour, and banks seek to meet capital requirements, they try to shrink by intensifying their securitization of assets and selling their loans. But, as noted above, while securitization affords added liquidity, it also lowers spreads. With lower margins, banks are thus encouraged to seek out even riskier borrowers who promise compensating, higher returns. But riskier borrowers eventually mean even more loan losses. And so the vicious cycle continues.

## Challenge for federal policy makers

Unless something is done soon to reduce these risks or to require private actors to share more of their costs, the BIF will face higher costs of picking up the pieces of an increasing number of bank failures.

To be specific, federal policy makers have three options for preventing the explosion of deposit insurance costs in the future.

• First, they can raise bank capital standards even higher, as Fed Chairman Alan Greenspan suggested this past summer. The rationale is straightforward: If banks must, for whatever reasons, accept more risks, then they should have more capital to stand between them and the BIF.

The long-run deterioration in bank capital ratios

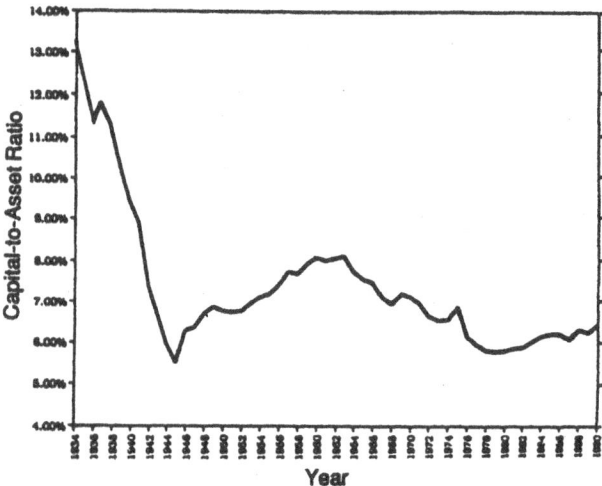

Figure 13  **Bank Equity Capital Relative to Total Assets**

Source: Authors' calculations.

certainly lends support to this view. Figure 13 shows that despite the apparent recent upward trend in the 1980s, the capital-to-asset ratio in the banking industry in 1989 (6.4 percent) was roughly half the level of 1934 during the Great Depression. Furthermore, the largest banks have the weakest capital ratios. Indeed, the average reported capital ratio of the five largest banks stood at just 4.3 percent at year-end 1989; by comparison, the average capital ratio of mutual savings banks was 7.1 percent, and for credit unions, 7.6 percent.

The dramatic decline in the capital ratio indicates that deposit insurance has replaced capital as the depositor's major source of protection against banking losses. Moreover, the reported (non-risk-weighted) capital ratios overstate the degree of capital protection because many of the large banks have substantial off-balance-sheet commitments.

• Second, if banks are being driven by market forces to make riskier loans, then policy makers can prevent further risks to the deposit insurance by narrowing the list of bank-eligible assets. One of us (Litan, 1987) has advanced such a "narrow banking" proposal in the context of broader powers—that is, as the *quid pro quo* solely for those banking organizations that want to enter new nonbanking businesses or affiliate with firms so engaged. Such enterprises would therefore be required to extend their risky, nonmarketable loans through nonbank affiliates, funded by uninsured debt and equity (as are finance companies today). Others, including FDIC Chairman William Seidman, have discussed narrowing bank powers for all banks (in particular, prohibiting them from commercial real estate lending), whether or not they are affiliated with a broader range of activities.

• The third option is for federal policy makers to keep the existing capital standards and bank powers, but provide a much more automatic system of regulatory intervention. Ideally, such a system would be supplemented with market-like devices to impel regulators to act in a timely fashion to prevent weak banks from taking more risks.

Among these three options for the banking system *as a whole,* we prefer the last.

In the end, whichever one of these options for containing risk in the banking system is taken—more capital, narrow banking, or early intervention—the industry will continue to shrink relative to other types of financial institutions. But as we have discussed, this trend has been a feature of the financial marketplace for at least the past four decades and almost certainly for the foreseeable future. Policy makers should not attempt to get in the way of these market forces. Indeed, if no action is taken to contain the rising risks in the banking industry, not only will the federal government face mounting losses for bank failures, but the economy will suffer from a severe misallocation of scarce investment capital. The major cost of the thrift disaster is the $150 billion-plus that was diverted toward the construction of now empty buildings and undeveloped real estate; clearly, these resources would have been far better used if they had been invested in productive plant and equipment. The past and future lending mistakes of banks have the same effect.

## *Reform: discipline and opportunity*

It is useful to classify reform suggestions into two categories: (1) those that provide needed additional *discipline* against excessive risk-taking by the managers and owners of insured depositories that also put the federal government, as the deposit insurer, at risk; and (2) those that provide banks with additional *opportunities* for enhancing profits and reducing cost that will help cure the long-term structural ills that threaten the viability of the banking industry, as presently configured.

Several enhancements would significantly reinforce current discipline against excessive risk-taking. Discipline has been substantially undermined in recent years. Not only deposit insurance itself, but the willingness of federal regulatory and monetary authorities to guarantee even uninsured deposits (the so-called, but inappropriately named "too big to fail" doctrine), plus regulatory forbearance, have all contributed to undermining discipline.

At the top of our list of recommended enhancements to discipline is a system of graduated, mandatory interventions by regulators, based on bank capital-to-asset ratios. Such an approach is embodied in the Comprehensive Deposit Insurance Reform and Taxpayer Protection Act of 1990 proposed earlier this year by Senator Donald Riegle, Jr., and in the recent floor statement on the same issue by the Chairman of the House Banking Committee, Rep. Henry Gonzalez. In particular, under such a system, regulators would be *required* to suspend a bank's dividends if its capital ratio fell below some positive level and at a still lower, but positive level, to assume conservatorship over the institution. In addition, we have strongly urged the FDIC to be provided with sufficient access to cash to implement a timely closure policy. Nevertheless, in the event the FDIC is forced by a lack of cash to engage in regulatory forbearance, we also strongly urge that any bank otherwise meriting closure should have its dividends suspended, its growth limited, and conceivably its management significantly changed.

Timely intervention under any mandatory intervention scheme, however, depends on the accuracy of the financial data on which bank capital-to-asset ratios are computed. In this regard, current generally accepted accounting principles (GAAP) can significantly overstate the value of bank capital, especially for weak banks. In theory, market-value accounting (or "marked-to-market" accounting) eliminates this problem. However, a vigorous debate is now under way (for example, between Chairman of the Federal Reserve Alan Greenspan and SEC Chairman Richard Breeden, among other actors) over the practical difficulties of valuing bank assets that are not readily traded and thus have no precise market value. There is also debate over the problems of valuing intangible bank assets such as franchise value (or, more generally, good will). While we agree that bank accountants ultimately should aim toward adopting market-value principles for bank valuation, at the present time we also agree with those who charge that the practical problems with the technique render it difficult to replace current GAAP procedures entirely.

Accordingly, we recommend that until such time as market-value accounting is sufficiently well developed and accepted by the financial community and regulators to replace GAAP, regulators continue to use GAAP as the primary means for reporting banks' financial condition. However, at the same time, we believe that the investment community, depositors, regulators, and policy makers would be well served if banks were required to *supplement* their GAAP-based financial statements with statements resting more on market-oriented values. We understand that the Financial Accounting Standards Board is currently considering a market value accounting proposal, and if so, we support its consideration.

In essence, the debate over proper bank accounting standards boils down to when regulators should take various intervention measures. We believe it is possible to provide more automatic triggers of such actions without resolving this valuation debate. The answer lies in introducing private market assessments of the conditions of banks, and then requiring regulators to use those assessments as the primary, if not exclusive, bases for taking such actions as suspending dividends or assuming conservatorships.

Two such methods are available, at least for larger institutions (those above, say, $1 billion in assets): (1) requiring such banks to maintain some portion of their total capital in the form of subordinated debt; and/or (2) requiring the FDIC to obtain reinsurance from the private market on a small *pro rata* portion of its insurance risk for these banks.

Currently, banks are *permitted* to count subordinated debt toward their "Tier 2" risk-adjusted capital standard. The first proposal would *require* that banks constantly maintain, perhaps on a quarterly basis, some fraction of Tier 2 capital as subordinated (uninsured) debt, with maturity of at least one year. As numerous academic scholars have pointed out, unlike an equity capital requirement that banks can generally meet by continued earnings growth (rather than through new equity issues), a subordinated debt requirement (at least for the larger banks that are capable of accessing the debt market), would continually subject these banks to a market test. Regulators, in turn, could base their decisions whether to take various regulatory measures based on the "spread" between the interest rate on a bank's subordinated debt and Treasury securities of comparable maturity. The "spread" would measure the perceived riskiness of the bank. At the limit, if a bank could not sell its required issue of subordinated debt at any price, that would be a conclusive signal for regulators to place the bank in conservatorship. The regulators should perhaps also be required to do this if the interest rate spread on the subordinated debt exceeds a certain threshold, say 500 basis points.

A mandatory reinsurance plan for the FDIC, such as the one recently proposed by Sen. Alan Dixon (S. 3040), would accomplish the same objective. Briefly, Dixon has proposed that the FDIC be required to obtain reinsurance on a small portion (10 percent) of its total risk in insuring the deposits of large banks (those with assets above $1 billion). In principle, the Dixon plan would "kill two birds with one stone": It would allow the private marketplace both to set "risk-based" premiums and also to determine when the regulators should close or place the bank in conservatorship.

There are competing advantages and disadvantages to the subordinated debt and mandatory reinsurance alternatives. On the one hand, the advantage of the mandatory reinsurance plan is that its market signals would be based on the collective decisions of actors whose principal business would consist of monitoring and assessing banks, rather than on decisions by a diverse body of subordinated debt holders whose financial interests in the safety of banks generally would not be as strong. On the other hand, a mandatory reinsurance plan will only work if sufficient capacity to provide that insurance is forthcoming to develop a competitive market; such conditions might not obtain for some time. In addition, regulators would have to supervise and regulate the solvency of the reinsurers themselves; this degree of oversight would not be needed for a subordinated debt requirement.

Since it is not clear at this point how fast a competitive market in reinsurance would develop, we favor the immediate implementation of a subordinated debt requirement for large banks, with an instruction to the regulators that they develop intervention "triggers" based on spreads between interest rates on bank subordinated debt and Treasury securities. At the same time, we believe that the FDIC ought to be encouraged to begin selling off portions of its risk so that it can get a private reinsurance market off the ground. Eventually, this market may mature sufficiently to serve as another source of automatic direction for regulatory intervention.

Regardless of the mechanism used for triggering regulatory action, such action must be made more automatic than it has been in the past. At a minimum, for example, regulators must become more aggressive about compelling banks to cut or suspend dividends

| Table 14 | Number of Banks Losing Money and Paying Dividends | |
|---|---|---|
| | Total number | Number with capital < 6% |
| 1989 | 37 | 29 |
| 1988 | 12 | 9 |
| 1987 | 41 | 39 |
| 1986 | 9 | 7 |

when earnings drop and capital is weak. Sizable numbers of large banks that were losing money paid dividends in 1987 and 1989, years in which most large banks made major additions to their loan loss reserves. In addition, most of the larger banks that paid dividends yet lost money in the years 1986–89, had capital ratios below 6 percent, or the threshold above which bank failure rates seem to be quite small (see Table 14).

By year-end the Comptroller of the Currency intends to implement a complicated new system for calculating when banks may not pay dividends. As we understand it, however, even under this new system, banks that lose money will still be able to pay dividends without regulatory approval: (1) if they pass a minimum capital test; and (2) as long as the dividend does not exceed the combined retained earnings of the current and previous two years. Moreover, even if it flunks these tests, the bank may pay dividends if it obtains permission from the regulators.

We believe a more restrictive dividend policy is in order, especially at this time when so many banks need to shore up their capital positions. In brief, we believe that any bank losing money in the current year should simply be prohibited from paying dividends, regardless of its capital ratio. In addition, regulators should curtail or even suspend dividend payments by banks that show a profit but nevertheless have capital ratios below some threshold level.

## Opportunity: structural reform

At this writing, it is expected that the Treasury Department's deposit insurance reform package will also include so-called structural reform provisions. Specifically, current interstate restrictions on bank branching and holding company expansion will be removed, and the Bank Holding Company Act will be significantly modified to permit banks to affiliate with a broader range of financial (if not commercial) enterprises. Without delving deeply into these two issues, we wish here to make several points.

• First, there is an overwhelming consensus among academic experts who have studied the matter that banks, not just bank holding companies, need the ability to operate nationwide. Virtually no other business in the United States is so geographically restricted as the banking business. These restrictions must be removed if the overall health of the banking system is to improve.

At a minimum, allowing banks to branch nationwide would permit them to diversify their risks and thus reduce the deposit insurance liabilities of the federal government. It is difficult to believe that nine of the top ten banks in Texas that failed during the 1980s would have failed had they been part of larger nationwide operations. Similarly, had Continental Illinois been able to branch beyond the confines of Chicago, and thus diversify its funding sources, it is at least conceivable that the deposit run that helped trigger the bank's collapse would not have taken place, or if it did, would not have had the same disastrous effects.

Geographic diversification also would accelerate the much needed consolidation of the banking industry and the shedding of excess capacity. The current geographic restrictions, however, frustrate this shrinkage, preventing banks in different parts of the country from consolidating their back and front offices to cut costs.

The only "justification" for the existing geographic restrictions, if there ever was one, was to prevent banks from amassing excessive economic and political power. Today, however, this concern is an anachronism now that no U.S. bank ranks even among the top twenty largest banks in the world.

• Second, we believe that banks should have the ability to affiliate with other types of enterprises in order to permit them to realize so-called economies of scope in delivering combinations of services. We recognize that there is limited evidence of how significant these economies are. But perhaps the best evidence that they exist is now being provided by many major European banks, which in preparing for so-called EC 1992 already have acquired or affiliated with major European insurers and securities firms.

At the same time, however, it is critical that the government not extend the "safety net"—deposit insurance and the Federal Reserve's discount window—to nonbank activities. The last thing the federal government needs now is to socialize even more private sector risk.

We see three broad approaches for preventing this outcome:

1. Constructing so-called legal "firewalls" between banks and their affiliates;
2. Requiring banks that want to broaden their affiliations to have additional capital (beyond the level already required), a suggestion recently advanced by Fed Chairman Alan Greenspan; and
3. Limiting the investments of banks that affiliate with a wider range of enterprises to "safe" assets (government and private securities with well-developed secondary markets), or "narrow" or "safe" banking.

## Big, troubled banks

The problems of large banks require special attention. Four options short of liquidation—an uninviting prospect that few endorse—are available for dealing with the problem:

1. *Hope and pray, or "forbearance."* The first approach, and the one most likely to be implemented, is simply to hope that the largest banks are really (if barely) solvent and that the current economic downturn will be sufficiently short and mild not to tip these institutions over the edge. To be sure, this so-called forbearance policy was pursued in the thrift industry with disastrous results. The big banks are not expanding wildly, with the regulators' permission, as did the thrifts; on the contrary, many are shrinking. Thus, a case can be made that like the forbearance policy pursued in the early 1980s after the LDC debt crisis first emerged, forbearance this time around could permit the large banks time to recover.

The flaw in this line of argument, of course, is that although the big banks have reported recovery since the 1980s, their financial data have hidden substantial loan losses that they have begun to recognize only recently. In addition, as we have stressed throughout this report, many of these institutions face still additional losses because they are engaged in high-risk lending. Everything we know about the trends in the banking industry point to new forms of risk-taking in the years ahead, once the banks feel secure enough to begin doing so. In short, the forbearance option carries with it big, some would say unacceptable, risks.

2. *Suspend dividends.* Many of the larger banks have thus far failed to raise loan loss reserves to realistic levels—close to the current levels of nonperforming loans. If this were done, many of these banks would

have extremely thin capital margins measured at book value. This, of course, is what the stock market has been saying when pricing the shares of these institutions at well below book value.

With such thin margins for error, many large banks should simply not be paying dividends. Although some large banks recently have cut their dividends, the regulators should go even further. The only argument against doing so is that such a step will unsettle the markets. But to refrain from suspending dividends while banks also refrain from issuing new stock to shore up their capital, is to permit these institutions to gamble with "Hail Mary" passes in the hope of recovery. The rest have been attempting to sell off their crown jewels, leaving behind little earning power for the future. At the very least, it is better to suspend dividends instead.

3. *Rescue through governmental intervention.* A third option we have recently heard mentioned in some quarters is to repeat what was done when Continental Illinois Bank failed in 1984, but on a much larger scale: Have the government inject capital (in the form of preferred stock) into the larger troubled banks on the condition that they change management, cut costs, and streamline their operations.

Although this option theoretically could lower costs to the BIF if the banks receiving these capital infusions actually recovered, it raises a series of troublesome issues. First, it might not work. Although Continental Illinois improved after the FDIC purchased preferred stock in its holding company, the bank is now laden with substantial volumes of high-risk loans that pose future risks. In short, the verdict is not yet in on the Continental rescue.

Second, it would be highly ironic if the United States were to move toward more state involvement in its banking sector in an age when many developing countries are either thinking about or actually moving (in the case of Mexico) in the other direction. One of the major reasons our government has urged the governments of other countries to privatize their banks is to entrust the market, rather than the government, with the critical credit decisions that banks make. Yet effective nationalizations of our major banks could put our government in precisely this position.

Third, the government will develop an inherent conflict of interest if it both acquires major ownership interests in a number of important banks, while simultaneously regulating and supervising all banks.

Finally, we fear that heavy government involvement in the banking industry could siphon off the needed political momentum for reforming the nation's banking laws. We suspect that Congress would not be too hospitable to removing geographic and product-line restrictions that hamper banks if the government at the same time is seen as being forced by events to rescue the major banks.

4. *Implement mergers and financial reform.* If suspending dividends paid by banks won't sufficiently rebuild their capital, then policy makers ought to be aggressively pushing the larger banks into mergers with healthier partners as the principal way of protecting the BIF and ultimately the taxpaying public. The problem with this approach, however, is that there are only a few healthy U.S. banks with sufficient capital that could purchase most or all of the major troubled banks. To be sure, regulators could push the U.S. banks into the hands of the foreign banks (mostly European) healthy enough to make these acquisitions, but we suspect that this is hardly a preferred outcome for a nation that once prided itself on its financial prowess.

One minimum step that would facilitate mergers and acquisition of troubled banks by healthy U.S. banks, would be to eliminate the outmoded restrictions on interstate branching. Such restrictions prevent banks from diversifying their deposit and lending risks, and from efficiently shedding excess capacity. With interstate branching, a major regional bank would find it less costly to purchase part, or all, of another troubled regional or money bank. There would be no need for duplicate management at the bank and holding company levels, and the combined bank would have a larger lending limit that would better enable it to compete for borrowers against much larger foreign institutions.

A more ambitious step would be to permit commercial and industrial companies to invest heavily in, or even to own, commercial banks, as we have already discussed. To put it bluntly, if commercial enterprises could be interested in purchasing troubled banks, they might be able to save the BIF from paying for a much more costly bank-to-bank merger, or even a liquidation, down the road.

There is little doubt that many commercial firms already heavily engaged in financial activities have the wherewithal to make substantial investments in major banks. These include: American Telephone & Telegraph Company; Ford Motor Company; General Electric Company; General Motors Corporation; International Business Machines Corporation; and Sears, Roebuck and Company. The capital of the largest banks pales in comparison to that of the commercial companies already engaged in financial services.

It is not clear, of course, to what extent commercial enterprises would help rescue part, or all, of the major troubled banks if allowed to do so. In addition, the mixing of banking and commerce threatens to extend the federal safety net to commercial activities, unless at least one of the three mechanisms listed above for walling off the bank from its affiliates is adopted. Nevertheless, given the serious situation in which many large banks find themselves, coupled with the risks they pose to the BIF, we believe that it is time for policy makers to begin seriously considering whether and to what extent to permit entry into the banking business by commercial firms. At the very least, Congress should consider permitting commercial enterprises to buy or invest in only *troubled and failed banks*.

All of the options for dealing with the present difficulties of large banks—including doing nothing at all—carry certain risks. We urge the Congress and the administration at least to begin debating the options.

R. DAN BRUMBAUGH, JR., AND KENNETH E. SCOTT

# *A Political Logjam Still Blocks Banking Reform*

*After twelve years of a seemingly endless banking crisis, the elements to solve it are clear, well understood, and ready to implement. But political interest groups so whittled down 1991 reform law that more Congressional bailouts and taxpayers' exposure may still lie ahead.*

Anyone who has ever whittled can sympathize with President Bush and the Senate and House Banking Committees over the fate of the Federal Deposit Insurance Corporation (FDIC) Improvement Act of 1991. They began with sweeping plans to recapitalize the FDIC, to overhaul major parts of the deposit-insurance system, and to improve the condition of depository institutions by tearing down barriers to bank ownership, prohibitions on bank affiliations with securities and insurance companies, and restrictions limiting operations across state lines.

After often-bruising debates in six different Senate and House committees, endless sorties by legions of financial-industry lobbyists, and several floor fights, the Congress produced emergency borrowing for the FDIC and modest deposit-insurance reform. Like a whittler who started with a large block of wood and a grand design and ended up shaving it down to a toothpick, the president and the banking committees are regrouping for another try. Barring the closure of one of the nation's largest troubled banks, which would drain much of the FDIC's newly borrowed reserves, congressional strategy will focus again on deposit-insurance reform and the scope of depository operations.

The deposit-insurance reforms adopted in the 1991 banking act and those most likely to be prominent in the next round were remarkably foreshadowed in a 1989 report, *Restructuring America's Financial Institutions,* by the Brookings Task Force on Depository Institutions Reform. We served on the task force with economists George J. Benston, Jack M. Guttentag, Richard J. Herring, George G. Kaufman, and Robert E. Litan. A comparison and contrast between the report's recommendations and what the Congress has and is likely to produce provides an up-to-the-minute critique of many of the likely deposit-insurance reform proposals. We also offer our own suggestions for future reform.

R. DAN BRUMBAUGH, JR., an economist in San Francisco, is coauthor with James Barth and Robert Litan of *The Future of American Banking* (M.E. Sharpe, Inc., 1992). KENNETH SCOTT is Ralph M. Parsons Professor of Law and Business at Stanford Law School. Reprinted from *Challenge,* March–April 1992, pp. 35–41.

## What needs to be fixed

As the Brookings task force described, there are two sets of crucial defects. In the first set, pertaining to the deposit-insurance system, there are four basic flaws that need to be fixed. The first is that deposit insurance creates moral hazard by encouraging risk-taking, especially by depositories whose capital has eroded. By protecting all insured depositors from loss, as well as most uninsured creditors, deposit insurance effectively eliminates depositor or creditor discipline and relies instead on shareholders and regulators to limit risk-taking. The problem has been compounded because the deposit-insurance premium has been fixed, until recently, without regard to risk. When depositories' capital erodes, moreover, as it has dramatically for both savings and loans and much of the commercial-banking industry, shareholders themselves have incentives to take great risk: it's essentially heads they win, tails the FDIC loses.

The second major flaw is that regulators have been unable or unwilling to detect and prevent excessive risk-taking. The current information systems, primarily regulatory reliance on book-value or historical cost accounting numbers based on generally accepted accounting principles (GAAP), do not provide regulators with timely asset values needed for effective detection of the true economic condition or deterioration of depositories. So, while often groping in the dark, regulators rely on depository portfolio and activity restrictions to limit risk-taking. Risk-taking is not effectively constrained, however, because within broad asset categories enough discretion exists for managers to take enormous risks when they so desire.

The third major flaw is that when depositories slide toward insolvency, regulators have been unable or unwilling to intervene fast enough to prevent staggering losses to the deposit-insurance funds. By essentially relying on GAAP in assessing solvency, regulators are often unaware that "GAAP solvent" depositories are at or over the brink of market-value insolvency. Depositories do not even need to be clever at covering up their insolvency. Often all they need to do is recognize capital gains and defer capital losses.

Fourth, and finally, when insolvent depositories are seized and reorganized, all depositors and creditors are usually bailed out—not just insured depositors. This bailout problem applies largely to depositories considered "too-big-to-fail," or more accurately "too big to be permitted to cause loss to uninsured depositors or creditors." The fear most often cited by regulators to justify this kind of bailout is that in its absence depositors at other depositories might run and possibly cause a systemwide financial crisis. Regardless of whether this is a legitimate worry (we think it is overblown), the bailout further reduces market discipline at large depositories and it simultaneously places smaller depositories at a competitive disadvantage.

There is a second set of two basic flaws in the legal framework of the depository institutions themselves. The first and foremost is that U.S. banks and savings and loans have been forced to carry a lot of quite unnecessary risk, by being prevented from fully diversifying their borrowers and customers in terms of business lines and regions of the country. U.S. banking has been more fragmented, and correspondingly more vulnerable to limited, local economic downturns, than that of any other major Western country. The result has been far higher failure rates over the last half century than any other comparable nation has experienced.

Further weaknesses have developed as a byproduct of portfolio and activity restrictions. Portfolio restrictions and restrictions on scope of operations—for example, on the ability to branch nationwide—have impeded the ability of federally insured depositories to adapt to competition. Depositories essentially have been placed in a regulatory vise while nondepository and nonfinancial firms have developed competing products around the globe.

The second design defect, more strongly applicable to savings and loans although also a growing problem for banks, is a maturity imbalance between assets and liabilities, creating enormous interest-rate risk. Savings and loans traditionally funded long-term, fixed-rate mortgages with savings deposits withdrawable on demand. If market interest rates rose sharply, the cost of deposits would go up accordingly; however, the earnings on assets would not. Consequently, the institution would operate at a loss. Or, in balance-sheet terms, the value of the old fixed-rate mortgages would go down and the institution's net worth would plunge. In 1980 and 1981, this process drove the entire U.S. savings-and-loan industry into economic insolvency, and the problem persists today. Such a structure of financial intermediation is a prescription for ultimate disaster.

## 1980s legislation; perspective for 1990s

Any reform of our depository system should be tested by how the reform addresses the set of flaws associated directly with deposit insurance and the second set of flaws that hobble depositories' ability to compete and diversify risk. By these standards, how does the legislation of the 1980s fare? The Financial Institutions Recovery, Reform, and Enforcement Act (FIRREA) of 1989—the last of four pieces of legislation in the 1980s—represents a transition point between the legislative approach of the 1980s and the approach that is evolving in the 1990s.

The FIRREA purported to change the deposit-insurance system by abolishing the Federal Home Loan Bank Board and the Federal Savings and Loan Insurance Corporation (FSLIC) as the chief federal regulator and insurer, respectively, of savings and loans. The act created the Office of Thrift Supervision (OTS) to replace the Bank Board, and placed it within the Treasury Department. The act also created the Savings Association Insurance Fund (SAIF) to replace the FSLIC and placed it under the FDIC, which also was to administer the newly created Bank Insurance Fund (BIF). These reforms were at best a modest shift in direction and essentially ignored all the flaws identified by the Brookings task force and others. Although touted as improving regulatory efficiency, similar goals could have been achieved with a change in personnel and mandate at the Bank Board. The goal may actually have included little more than making the OTS less responsive to industry pressures (but more responsive to pressures from within the administration) than the old Bank Board, coupled with some empire building at the FDIC.

Before FIRREA, federal legislation in the 1980s was almost exclusively limited to a somewhat panicky patchwork of solutions to the savings-and-loan crisis. The 1980 Depository Institutions Deregulation and Monetary Control Act began to deregulate interest rates in order to let the savings and loans staunch the deposit outflows caused by skyrocketing market interest rates. The Garn–St. Germain Act of 1982 primarily began to expand or deregulate allowable activities for savings and loans, in order to provide them with profitable alternatives to the fixed-rate mortgage and thus diversify their risk.

These were efforts to make savings and loans more competitive. Yet, because these new powers were given to unhealthy—indeed, generally already insolvent—savings and loans, the effect was in part to exacerbate moral hazard. Because the deregulation of allowable activities per se was perceived by Congress as the problem, some provisions of FIRREA were a backlash. FIRREA, for example, provided substantial penalties for savings and loans that did not place most of their assets in "housing-related" assets, primarily home mortgages. In this regard, FIRREA was actually a step backward.

Finally, in addition to the regulatory shuffling, FIRREA began the taxpayer bailout of the FSLIC. The Competitive Equality Banking Act (CEBA) of 1987 had begun the process of recapitalizing the FSLIC, initially through a complicated borrowing designed to be repaid without taxpayer dollars. Each of these acts provided too little funding for the FSLIC to close all insolvent savings and loans, and did so while the examination and supervision apparatus could not adequately contain savings and loan risk-taking. This compounded the moral hazard problem. Under the circumstances, an insolvent FSLIC also had an incentive to allow savings and loans to gamble for resurrection, in order to resurrect itself.

Meanwhile FIRREA completely ignored the developing crisis among commercial banks. Indeed, by giving the FDIC control of the SAIF and also of the newly created Resolution Trust Corporation (RTC), designed to dispose of failed thrifts, FIRREA stretched an already overloaded bank deposit-insurance agency. Nor did FIRREA address more than superficially the closure policies of the deposit-insurance agencies. The "too-big-to-fail" doctrine, for example, was never mentioned; nor was the issue of closing troubled depositories before they imposed losses on the insurance funds.

To address these and other issues, the Treasury Department in February 1991 published an official proposal for bank reform that was the genesis of the administration's legislative proposal and the two bills initially supported by the House and Senate Banking Committees. To promote prompt closure of insolvent banks, it recommended that the FDIC be able to borrow more funds from the Treasury, to be paid back by the banking industry. To bring more capital into depositories and promote diversification, it recommended that industrial companies be able to own depositories. To diversify geographic risk, it recommended that depositories be able to branch nationwide. To provide opportunities for product diversification, it recommended that well-capitalized depositories be able to enter the securities and insurance businesses.

The Treasury Report began a legislative process that

would focus for the first time on some of the flaws enumerated by the Brookings task force. The House and Senate Committees proposed legislation that actually responded to the fundamental issues. Then in a long and agonizing process, every manner of lobbyist, special interest, fractious committee and subcommittee, and floor fight after floor fight, whittled away at the legislation.

## FDIC Improvement Act of 1991

In the tradition of the 1980s, the FDIC Improvement Act of 1991 provided a $30 billion unsecured line of credit to the FDIC from the Treasury Department to cover losses at failed banks. It required the Treasury and the FDIC to schedule bank deposit-insurance premiums to ensure repayment of the borrowing. The act also provided the FDIC with authority to borrow up to an additional $40 billion in "working capital" to be collateralized by assets taken in by the FDIC from failed banks. The assets are ultimately to be sold to repay the working capital. No one knows whether the funding is adequate or whether the banking industry will in fact be able to repay the borrowings.

Much of the remainder of the act attempted to reform aspects of the deposit-insurance system. The act required all depository regulators to review their minimum capital standards every other year to ensure that they were sufficient to minimize losses to the insurance funds. It specifically required the regulators to set a "leverage" ratio of capital-to-total-assets and a "risk-based" ratio of capital-to-risk-adjusted-assets. The latter was required to have an interest-rate risk component within eighteen months. Whether these requirements are meaningful remains to be seen. Since 1980, tinkering with capital requirements has been nonstop; the requirements currently include both leverage and risk-adjusted versions that are lower than the minimum capital requirement that existed for savings and loans in 1980.

The act did address the closure mechanism to be used in the future by the FDIC. The act broadly tied closure, supervisory, and enforcement actions to five levels of capital from "well capitalized" to "critically undercapitalized." In general, as capital declines the more rigorous supervision is to become. And ultimately the regulators are supposed either to take control (by appointing a conservator) or to seize and close (by appointing a receiver) any bank or thrift that fails to maintain capital above the "critical capital" level.

Superficially, these provisions of the act are similar to the first of the two reform proposals recommended by the Brookings task force. The task force recommended that depositories be sorted into four capital-to-asset categories from "adequately capitalized" (with capital-to-asset ratios greater than 8 percent) to "solvency endangered" (with capital-to-asset ratios less than 3 percent). As with the new banking act, the lower the ratio the tougher would be the regulatory sanctions.

Not so superficially, however, the act's provisions operate in a manner dramatically different from the task-force recommendations. For the purpose of defining capital, for example, regulators are required to adopt accounting standards that are consistent with and no less stringent than Generally Accepted Accounting Practices (GAAP), notwithstanding that GAAP has been employed without exception by deteriorated savings and loans and banks to obscure much deeper market-value problems. In contrast, the Brookings task force would have required regulators to measure and monitor the market value, not the accounting value, of a depository's capital.

The act, moreover, sets the "critical capital" level at no less than 2 percent equity capital to total assets (and gives regulators the power to set the remaining minimum levels for the other categories). The difference between 2 percent capital based on GAAP and the Brookings' 3 percent based on market values can be substantially greater than one percentage point. Two percent GAAP capital can actually obscure deep market-value insolvency. Thus, whether the act provides an "early closure" mechanism as advertised, or a fig leaf behind which to continue to hide regulatory forbearance, is a legitimate question.

The task force also would have required that as the capital ratios decline the regulator's discretion in applying sanctions would be greatly reduced. The task force said, for example, that a "solvency-endangered" depository would have to implement "expeditiously" the capitalization plan that was required of all "inadequately capitalized" depositories (the group just above "solvency endangered"), or sell the depository, or be put in conservatorship by the FDIC. Swift, unambiguous resolution would have been mandatory.

In contrast, the act provides so much discretion that it appears to anticipate forbearance. The act requires a capitalization plan (at the as-yet undefined "undercapitalized" level just above the "critical" level) and requires conservatorship or a receiver if a depository fails to maintain capital above the "critical" level—unless an alternative is viewed more likely to protect the insurance fund against losses. In most cases a depository that falls below the "critical" level for more than one year would have to be closed—unless regulators determined that the depository was viable, had positive capital, improving income, falling bad loans, and was substantially complying with its capitalization plan. Although to the uninitiated that may seem quite a task, with GAAP accounting it is not necessarily much of a hurdle.

Skepticism seems justified as well about the part of the law that supposedly abandons "too-big-to-fail." The act allows the FDIC to continue to pay off uninsured depositors and creditors, but if they are protected the FDIC is required to show that it may have avoided a greater loss in the process. Whether this merely will continue the "too-big-to-fail" doctrine under a new terminology is an open question, to which the FDIC's recent full bailout for CrossLand Savings in New York City would suggest an affirmative answer. Operationally this process will be spelled out by the FDIC in "least-cost" provisions that the law requires the FDIC to develop. "When?" you might ask. The regulations do not become effective until January 1, 1995. Thus, we may truly abandon "too-big-to-fail" in about three years. The net effect is that deeply troubled big banks will almost surely receive regulatory forbearance for years to come, and perhaps indefinitely.

If the condition of depositories improves or if the funding provided to the FDIC proves adequate, the capital standards, "early" closure provisions, and "abandonment" of "too-big-to-fail" may appear to work. If, however, the banking industry continues to deteriorate or if the funding provided to the FDIC proves inadequate, the act seems likely to perpetuate the status quo of forbearance in the face of deterioration. In other words, there should be a healthy suspicion that in the absence of future unexpectedly beneficial developments in banking and the economy, the legislation provides loopholes through which regulators can continue to drive a convoy of trucks carrying forbearance.

The problem is reliance on discretionary actions by regulatory agencies that function in a political environment that is loath to commit additional funds—even if taxpayer dollars are not explicitly required. In the past, the result has been that prolonged periods of discretionary forbearance bought time for regulators, Congress, and the president. The FDIC Improvement Act of 1991 appears to continue, or at least provide future opportunities to continue, that costly practice.

## Defining the transition issues: 1991–1992

It took two sets of problems, working together, to produce the disaster of the current multi-hundred-billion dollar magnitude. (1) There were structural weaknesses in our system of depositories—most crucially, quite unnecessary risk from a woeful hobbling of depositories' ability to compete in a changing market and a limitation on opportunities to diversify assets by industry and geographically. (2) There were also design defects in our deposit-insurance scheme—fixed premiums, ineffectual capital requirements, poor prevention of excessive risk-taking, tardy closure of insolvent depositories, and protection of uninsured depositors and creditors. All of this took place with supervisory agencies operating with great discretion in a political arena. That meant inaction when action was most needed.

The 1991 Act has addressed this second set of design flaws, but in a way that still relies completely on the depository regulatory agencies to do the right thing at the right time. That is exactly what they did not do in the 1980s, and the political reasons for choosing forbearance are just as strong now as they were then. The administration's and the House and Senate Banking Committees' effort to attack the first set of structural weaknesses in our depositories failed after much struggle. All the proposals involving additional portfolio options and activities were defeated in the course of passage of the 1991 Act. Thus, opportunities for added geographic and product diversification and new competition are temporarily dormant, at best.

The process of the failure in 1991 turned on a turf battle among industry lobbies that made the practical problem quite clear. Remedying the structural defects in depositories, with a broader range of activities and branching, means more competition for other businesses such as insurance agents, securities firms, and rural banks. Any business will always oppose new competition, using "public-interest" arguments. The argument repeatedly invoked in the 1991 debate, for example, was that giving depositories additional investment powers and geographical scope would merely give them new ways to impose excessive risk on the insurance funds and ultimately the taxpayer.

## A new option for banking

Thus, the goal should be to reduce regulatory discretion that leads to forbearance, and simultaneously to alleviate fears that allowing depositories to compete and diversify will result in excessive risk-taking. Two ways to do that were provided in our 1989 Brookings report. That report suggested, as described above, a tiered system of capital requirements, supervisory restrictions, and ultimately of mandatory (with little or no regulatory discretion) recapitalization or takeover of institutions at the point at which they become barely market-value solvent. Although a version of that proposal has now been enacted, it leaves so much discretion in the hands of regulators that excessive risk-taking by deteriorated depositories may be not only possible but likely.

The Brookings task force, recognizing the possibility of excessive regulatory discretion even where it is explicitly discouraged, therefore offered a second proposal. It would require insured deposits to be backed by readily valued assets of at least the same amount, reducing the insurance funds' risk to a minimal level. Our suggestion for the 1992 legislative round would be a new option: a depository that chooses to adopt this second proposal would be afforded the extended authority and branching that were discussed throughout the 1991 debates. As a result, there would be no added risk to the insurance funds, and that result would be far less dependent on supervisory judgment and discretionary action.

In this proposal, insured deposits could be backed by readily valued assets in either of two ways. The depository issuing the deposits could be restricted to investing only in securities that are actively traded on well-organized markets. This is sometimes called the "narrow-bank" approach. Alternatively, and more simply, the depository could be required to collateralize fully all its insured deposits with readily marketable assets, with the rest of its activities unconfined. For convenience, our discussion will focus on this "collateralized" approach.

With either the "narrow-bank" or "collateralized" approach, because the assets are actively traded, their value could be determined accurately on a daily—or hourly—basis. If the assets' value falls below the amount of insured deposit liabilities, the bank or parent holding company would either put in more assets or the bank would be closed immediately. There would be no opportunity for extended arguments over valuation or time for the accumulation of massive insolvencies.

Obviously, depositories now invest in many non-traded assets, such as commercial and industrial loans, consumer loans, and real-estate mortgages. These would have to be funded with uninsured borrowings or investment pools, as to some extent they are now anyway. These uninsured borrowings would bear more risk and carry higher returns. Customers would divide their funds as they preferred, between no risk (and minimal return) insured deposits and higher risk (and return) other forms of depository investments. Checking accounts could be confined to the insured-deposit category.

The other activities of a depository that opted for the collateralized approach would present no risk to the insurance fund, which would be fully protected by the collateral pool of assets, whose value it could monitor continuously. Indeed, there would be no reason to charge such a depository more than a very small premium, to cover some administrative expenses and the possibility of a fraud loss exceeding the depository's capital and fidelity bond coverage. The volatility of the assets a depository chose to put into its collateral pool would determine the amount of additional collateral required.

## Critique of the 1991 "core-bank" version

The basic concept we are proposing has, in one form or another, a fairly long lineage. For different purposes, in the realm of monetary policy, it was urged by Henry Simons and Milton Friedman many decades ago, under the rubric of 100 percent reserve banking. More recently, it has been written about by several of the Brookings report authors. And under the name of "core bank," the idea was advanced by Representative Charles Schumer (Dem., N.Y.) during the consideration of the 1991 Act.

The Schumer amendment, drawn from Lowell Bryan, a banking consultant, had two main elements. One was a limit on what depositories could pay on deposits, to 105 percent of the rate on Treasury securities of comparable maturity. The other was a limit on loans to a single borrower, to 6 percent of a depository's equity capital (as compared with 15 percent for national banks under current law).

At first glance, those provisions do not seem much related to a "core-bank" concept, but that was the intended purpose. The limit on loan size was supposed to force all "high-risk" activities outside the insured depository, to uninsured affiliated finance and investment companies. Only those uninsured affiliates could pay depositors and investors the higher rates appropriate to higher-risk assets. The insured core bank could, within its lending limit, continue to make mortgage, corporate, and consumer loans. If it incurred losses and was threatened with approaching insolvency, it would be prevented by the deposit-rate ceiling from attracting a large volume of new funds by offering higher interest. This would supposedly make the weak depository illiquid, allowing the Federal Reserve to refuse it liquidity support and force it to close.

The Bryan approach to core banking, however, is illogical and ineffectual. Loan size is not the same thing as loan risk; large loans can be to very strong borrowers, and small loans to marginal credits. The correlation between size and risk is poor. If the goal is really diversification, moreover, the 6 percent limit does not achieve it. The number of individual borrowers is an exceedingly primitive measure of diversification, which depends more on whether the borrowers are all in the same type of business or same part of the country. The failure of almost all the saving and loans and banks in Texas, for example, was not due to too few borrowers.

Likewise, a low deposit interest-rate ceiling does not keep a depository from investing those deposits in high-risk assets. Nor does the weakness of a depository's capital level mean its assets are illiquid, or that it will be faced with a heavy outflow of deposits. After all, depositors have no particular reason to withdraw, no matter how insolvent it may be, if they are covered by the FDIC. That is part of the lesson of the 1980s. All the deposit-rate ceiling would mean is a slow rate of growth for core banks. Whether their capital is strong or weak, the effect is the same.

Although the specific Bryan formulation is nonsensical, there are many possible variants. The "narrow-bank," "collateralized," or "core-bank" concept underlying the Schumer amendment, is worth serious consideration. That is especially true if it is coupled with an attack on the real cause of inadequate diversification in depository portfolios: the outmoded activity and geographical restrictions imposed in the financial world of a half-century ago.

If that consideration is undertaken in the next round of congressional hearings, there are two issues that need to be examined. The first is how worried we should be about bank runs or panics, as they pertain not to insured deposits but to uninsured deposits. The argument used by regulators and even some economists, most often to justify "too-big-to-fail," is that if a bank (or its uninsured affiliate) got into trouble, customers would race to withdraw their deposits from other banks or affiliates. Why? Because the customers cannot distinguish one from another, so one failure causes them to leave the rest. This proposition is supposed to be founded on nineteenth-century experiences. Both the reading of history, and the assumption that the relevant conditions are the same today, are controversial and controverted. But the issue is important and needs to be taken seriously.

The main reason for taking that first issue seriously is the second one: if one or several banks or their affiliates were to fail, how likely is it that Congress would respond to some constituent pressure by bailing out the uninsured depositors or investors? It is wholly predictable that investors who chose federally uninsured deposits for their higher return would subsequently assert that they never dreamed they bore higher risk. Although happy to take in the higher returns, if the risk materialized they would claim it was unfair that they should take a loss.

This rationalization does not work in the stock and bond markets, but has worked very nicely recently in state thrifts in Ohio, Maryland, and Rhode Island. Unless ways are utilized to reduce the likelihood of such a congressional bailout, the taxpayer exposure underlying deposit insurance would have been worsened, not removed. Again, there are possible solutions, but the political dimension of the problem must be recognized candidly.

So our conclusion is not that there are simple little cures to our seemingly endless banking crisis. After we have lost some $200 billion in a debacle that has been well known for twelve years, we ought to be prepared to acknowledge the magnitude and complexity of the situation. On the other hand, our counsel is not one of despair. The elements of a stronger banking system, and perhaps even of a deposit-insurance scheme that does not itself create crises, are understood. It remains to be seen whether the political system, long semiparalyzed by interest-group deadlock, can find a way out. The 1991 legislative struggle, frustrating though it was, suggests that the necessary ingredients are in fact at hand.

EDWARD W. HILL AND ROGER J. VAUGHAN

# Banking: Real Risks Require Real Reforms

*Mounting problems in the banking industry loom. Can we avert them?*

America currently has two banking industries: one, with about 10,000 members, is healthy, profitable, and competitive; the other, with fewer than 2,000 members, is undercapitalized, unprofitable, and dying. The future of American banking as a whole depends on how quickly politicians and regulators deal with the latter.

Unfortunately for healthy banks and taxpayers, Washington and the banking industry itself seem to be suffering from chronic denial that a massive problem exists.

Federal banking regulators continue to minimize the number of banks that must be closed, pinning their hopes on a much-delayed economic recovery or upon the magical powers of deregulation, and eerily replaying the behavior of savings-and-loan regulators a decade ago.

Yet, regulators are not alone in repeating the steps taken in the savings-and-loan minuet. The banking lobby itself is closing ranks around its weaker members, sacrificing the interests of its larger constituency—healthy bank holding companies—in a vain and doomed attempt to prolong the lives of the industry's crippled giants.

We called our recently published book *Banking on the Brink* not only because we identified nearly 2,000 banks on the brink of failure, restructuring, or merger, but also because we believe that *the industry stands on the brink of radical change*. It is being transformed by both fierce competition from nonbanks and the technological revolution sweeping through the world's capital markets.

## Dramatic change coming

The industry is poised to shrink dramatically, with its survivors falling into one of three categories: retail banks, merchant banks, and loan boutiques.

EDWARD W. HILL is an associate professor and economist at the Levin College of Urban Affairs at Cleveland State University, and ROGER J. VAUGHAN is an economic consultant based in Santa Fe, N.M. They are the authors of *Banking on the Brink: The Troubled Future of American Finance,* recently published by Washington Post Company Briefing Books. Reprinted from *Challenge,* January–February 1993, pp. 13–17.

Even more significant is that this transformation will restructure the geography of banking. *The all-purpose financial supermarket that many of New York's money-center banks tried to become is quickly fading,* and with it the overwhelming influence of New York, Chicago, and Los Angeles as banking centers. These cities will continue to house merchant banks, arranging complex financial transactions for large corporate customers in global markets and earning their income from fees instead of loans. Because these merchant banks do not need deposits to fund their operations, they will be unwilling to submit to high insurance premiums and inconvenient regulations. In fact, many merchant banks already are contemplating turning in their bank charters, choosing instead to operate as financial corporations. These institutions could offer money-market mutual funds rather than checking accounts and could borrow on the commercial paper market instead of using brokered certificates of deposits.

So, who will meet America's day-to-day banking needs? It will be the *new breed of retail banks,* emerging from a group of successful superregional banks. These retail banks will live on their ability to mass-market banking services—from checking accounts and ATMs to credit cards, home mortgages, and home equity loans. The winners in this category will be those banks that keep costs low, are well capitalized, and take advantage of economies of scale in advertising, marketing, and credit scoring.

Retail banks now have more in common with Wal-Mart than they do with J.P. Morgan, and their continued expansion will likely resemble the hub-and-spoke strategy used by airlines. Retail giants are currently, or soon will be, located in so-called second- and third-tier cities often in the heart of the Rust Belt, where costs are much lower than in yesterday's financial centers. They can be found in Albany (KeyCorp), Pittsburgh (Mellon Bank Corp. and PNC Financial Corp.), Cleveland (Society Corp. and National City Corp.), Columbus (Banc One Corp. and Huntington Bancshares, Inc.), Detroit (Comerica Inc. and N.B.D. Bancorp Inc.), Minneapolis (First Bank System Inc. and Norwest), and, possibly, St. Louis (Boatmen's Bancshares Inc.).

Other major headquarters cities include Charlotte (NCNB Corp. and First Wachovia Corp.) and San Francisco (BankAmerica Corp.). Although Cincinnati has two excellent retail banks in Fifth Third Bancorp and Star Banc Corp., both are currently too small to be considered giants. The endangered banking species are smaller regionals lacking either a large market or large market share, or those banks that attempt to combine retail and merchant banking within the same corporate structure.

Bank management, as recent events have shown, cannot control a fully diversified supermarket-type institution. Merchant banks and superregionals can't serve everyone. Smaller businesses will need their own loan boutiques: small lending institutions familiar with their industry or local community. Loan boutiques, such as Commerce Exchange Bank in Beachwood, Ohio, and Chicago's South Shore Bank, will operate as a small-business analogy to consumer finance corporations.

## Evolution requires extinction

There is little question that the banking industry will continue to shrink over the decade. It already plays a much smaller role in the financial system than it did two decades ago, with growing international financial markets replacing many of the traditional functions of banks. This shrinkage will generate a fierce public-policy debate over the banking industry in terms both arcane and confusing. Fortunately, the lay person needs only to remember two simple questions to keep his or her bearings in the coming storm of verbiage: How will the banking industry shrink? Will healthy banks be able to retain their current international competitive strength, or will the burden of supporting their weaker competitors drag them down as well?

If what you hear in the upcoming discussion about banks and banking does not ring true when you consider these questions, hold on to your wallet. The great banking debate, if it is to have any meaning, should be about how to shrink the industry at the least cost to the taxpayer. Keeping crippled banking giants alive neither shrinks the industry nor minimizes taxpayer cost.

Despite what you may hear, *there is a mounting problem in commercial banking,* resulting largely from bankers' overindulgence in commercial real estate during the 1980s. But if we act promptly, the problem may be less of a shock to taxpayers and to healthy banks than if we deny and delay.

According to our analysis in *Banking on the Brink,* there are now roughly 2,000 troubled banks and 300 troubled bank holding companies, with combined book assets of more than $1 trillion. Perhaps 1,200 or so of these banks are likely to either fail, become victims of forced mergers, or reorganize themselves. This is not a radical estimate; the FDIC has roughly 1,000 banks on its own secret list of "problem banks," and it publicly admits that between one-quarter and one-half of these banks will fail within two to three years.

And yet, banking industry spokesmen blandly insist that all is well, pointing to this year's record profits as proof. Unfortunately, the very basis of these profits is creating future problems. Why? Because most of the earnings of weak banks are the result of the industry's plunge into government securities. Banks are able to profit from the difference (or spread) between the low rates they pay to depositors and the higher rates they earn on "riskless" government securities in the face of weak borrowing demand.

No sensible observer thinks that these interest-rate spreads can continue indefinitely. The bond markets are already making allowances for a rise in short-term interest rates; so, weak commercial bankers may soon be caught in the same vise that crushed thrift executives a decade ago.

As spreads narrow (and they must), bank earnings will plummet. When this happens, weak banks' true problems—the reduced valuations that should have been assigned to commercial real estate loans—will become painfully obvious. At the same time, confident assurances from bankers that the government securities they hold will be easy and profitable to sell will ring hollow.

In a market suddenly flooded with bank-held securities that have lost value, ask this question: Who will buy and at how much of a loss to the selling banks? This mismatch is most apparent in weak commercial banks eager to book quick earnings to offset their defective commercial real estate loans.

About these banks, Boston College's Edward Kane has said, "This is not only the same road that the thrifts traveled, it is the same rut in the road." As Federal Reserve Chairman Alan Greenspan recently told a Japanese audience, America is bogged down in the worst recession since World War II. The principal culprit is a continuing slide in asset prices. Nowhere is this slide more apparent than in the commercial real estate market, in which even the "appraised" values—to which banks mark down nonperforming real estate loans—often are well above realistic market values. The U.S. Comptroller of the Currency reported in October that banks were receiving 50 cents on the dollar of the appraised value of real estate they owned.

Given time, the overwhelming majority of banks will work through this problem, as they did earlier problems with other forms of high-risk lending. But weak banks with weak managers face insolvency.

## The cost of delay

The core of the banking crisis lies in 54 bank holding companies, *14 with more than $10 billion apiece in assets and another 40 with assets between $1 billion and $10 billion each.*

If the portfolios of each of these holding companies had been given honest market valuations, it is likely that none could have demonstrated a positive net worth at the end of 1991. Several are too poor to write off their bad loans, too weak to survive without deposit insurance, and too large to be swallowed by even the most gluttonous competitor.

Yet, over the course of the past year, *industry analysts have claimed that these banks were staging a turnaround. This is almost certainly wrong.* The improvement that has occurred in bank stock prices, and the ease with which even relatively weak banks raised new equity, is largely the result of three external factors: the Federal Reserve's decision to lower reserve requirements, the FDIC's decision to bail out sick banks before they became truly insolvent, and falling interest rates, allowing banks to cut their cost of funds even more rapidly than their loan rates.

None of this changes the underlying problems facing weaker banks. This year's record bank profits, applauded by the industry's cheerleaders, have done little or nothing for sick banks. Strong banks have grown stronger and weak banks weaker.

Congress and the administration must decide when and how these crippled giants will be liquidated, restructured, or merged with healthy and willing partners. And the longer Washington delays, the higher the ultimate bill. Had Washington acted to resolve the banking crisis at the start of 1992, for instance, it would have cost the Bank Insurance Fund (BIF) about $50 billion, most of which could probably have been covered by the fund's resources.

The cost and consequences of this delay will be tremendous. The banking problem can easily grow to $75 billion. Weak multibank holding companies are likely to transfer their remaining profitable assets (for example, credit card operations, or leasing businesses) from sick to healthy affiliates. They would then be in a position to approach regulators and demand a suspension of the cross-guarantees that require them to back their sick affiliated banks with all their capital.

Regulators would then face a real nightmare. Either they bail out investors in the holding company along with depositors in the sick bank, or they force the entire bank, sick and healthy affiliates alike, into receivership.

Delay might also drive strong banks, such as J.P. Morgan or Bankers Trust, to abandon their banking charters altogether and operate instead as nonbank financial institutions. Why should they tolerate steep fees and unpredictable special levies for insurance they do not really need? After all, their sound credit ratings allow them to raise funds directly in the commercial paper market at competitive prices, without paying FDIC premiums or submitting to the burden of outdated regulations.

Or, more frightening still, what if healthy banks were to engage in risky lending behavior in reaction to higher insurance fees? After all, they are charged as if they are wild-eyed risk-takers. Why shouldn't they behave that way and get their money's worth? Stockholders of healthy banks should wonder why they must subsidize their less competent competitors at the behest of federal regulators.

In either case, if healthy banks give up their charters or become large risk takers, the outlook for the bank insurance fund and taxpayers is bleak. If many banks start opting out of the federal insurance system, the FDIC will be forced to increase fees on the remaining weaker banks, further hindering their ability to recover while encouraging still more banks to return their charters. Or, if healthy banks begin taking larger risks, the fund will eventually face larger and larger losses. Either is a nightmare scenario, and neither is inconceivable.

## Reverse triage

Now that we have weathered the "December surprise" that Ross Perot referred to during his presidential campaign, it may yet be called the "December Dud." Because of the small number of banks that closed, the temptation will be to sit back and relax, and to listen to the blandishments of industry spokesmen and regulators that all is under control and that the worst is past. Unfortunately, the December closings will mark not the end of "the banking problem" but the continuation of a slowly rising tide of bank failures. These failures will be precipitated by the FDIC's new and tougher capital standards, but their underlying cause remains the long-postponed recognition of massive real estate losses. As the economy recovers, the inevitable rise in interest rates will ensnare desperate bankers who have both invested heavily in long-term Treasury bonds and have not written down their problem real estate.

In the months since the publication of *Banking on the Brink*, regulators, trade associations, industry lobbyists, and even key staffers of Senate committees have savagely attacked our conclusions. Many in the press have focused only on our worst-case projections, ignoring our most likely range of estimates. Beyond these quibbles over accounting techniques and estimation methods, however, is a more basic question, namely: What is commercial real estate worth in today's market?

Our answer is that it is worth not nearly as much as bankers and regulators would have us believe. Given the faint hopes for a short- or mid-term turnaround in commercial real estate values, or a sudden and sharp rise in economic activity (miraculously unaccompanied by a rise in interest rates) this ugly fact threatens the viability of poorly capitalized banks.

It is true that the vast majority of American banks are quite healthy. But they are being systematically bled by regulators determined to prop up weak banks so as to maintain a system with fundamental flaws. These same regulators backed away from attempts to create a real system of risk-related FDIC insurance premiums in 1992, under a full-court industry lobbying effort. The result is that income is being transferred among banks, with weak banks paying too little for their insurance and well-managed banks paying too much. Taking from the rich and giving to the poor hurts not only healthy banks but the economy as well.

Congress, the White House, and regulators are searching, with increasing desperation, for a miracle cure that imposes neither a direct cost to the taxpayer nor an increase of the deficit. They hope, for example, that by relaxing antitrust laws, two sick banks can merge their way back to health. Unfortunately, this policy is more likely to create crippled giants that can survive only by hiding behind the FDIC's doctrine of too-big-to-fail.

The best U.S. bankers recognize this, calling instead for the banking system to winnow out its lesser members, rather than waiting for the FDIC finally to act when a bank's losses become too big to ignore.

Another much-touted cure is to require banks to carry deeper reserves. But rational private investors will not provide sufficient funds to shore up weakly capitalized banks. Why? Because investors not only recognize that these banks have paid dismal dividends for more than a decade, they also know that bank accounting practices make it impossible to measure the true value of bank capital. This makes the enforcement of meaningful capital standards extremely difficult.

## What to do?

So far, Congress and the White House have placed their full faith in further deregulation. But while the expansion of banking powers—interstate banking, the sale of nonbank products such as insurance, and the ownership of banks by nonbanking companies—is laudable, it must take a back seat to three more urgent actions.

- *They must close problem banks.* Given sufficient time, some troubled banks might recover. But for each that does, others will fall into even deeper trouble. It is preferable to err on the side of caution by closing, restructuring, or merging all banks that fail to meet strict, market-based standards of net worth.
- *They must improve bank accounting.* Murky but legal bank accounting procedures allow banks to disguise large asset losses. Our study highlights the enormous discrepancy between conventional bookkeeping and the actual market value of bank assets. Adopting market-value accounting will allow regulators to close banks as soon as they are insolvent. It will also allow bankers to manage operations, and to enter into mergers and acquisitions more efficiently.
- *They must narrow deposit insurance.* Because depositors have no reason to care whether their bank is well-managed, bad banks are free to keep repeating their mistakes. We recommend that depositors with a total of more than $100,000 in a bank (including certificates of deposits, brokered deposits regardless of size, payroll accounts, and interbank deposits) be required to purchase private deposit insurance. Once a vigorous private insurance market develops, this statutory amount could be lowered to $80,000 or even $60,000.

Private insurers will charge depositors in different banks varying premiums based on the bank's capitalization, portfolio diversity, and strength of management. As these premiums begin to affect the real interest rates earned by depositors, money will begin to flow out of weak and badly managed banks and into good banks without harming small depositors. After all, that was the original purpose of public deposit insurance. Although it may be preferable for banks to purchase this private insurance, thereby saving on transaction costs, who purchases the insurance has no impact on the economics of the proposal; this is a "Coasian" problem [a conflict that can be settled more effectively by private parties using market-based incentives than by government intervention—Ed.]. What does make a difference is that private insurance is purchased and that markets are at the core of risk assessment and rate setting.

The premiums charged by private insurers also should be used to run the FDIC's insurance program on a sound actuarial basis (for the first time). FDIC premiums should be automatically linked to private market rates, not rates negotiated by highly paid lobbyists or through political pressure. Needless to say, this cannot be done in the halls of Congress or in the boardroom of the FDIC. Weak banks will fight these proposals down to the last dollar in their lobbying budgets.

Still, while many powerful economic arguments can be leveled against deposit insurance, it remains a political fact of life. The question is how to live with it.

Politicians must recognize that bank failure is an inherent part of the financial system, and that no regulation can alter that fact. This means redesigning deposit insurance so that when failures occur they can be readily absorbed without a direct spillover to the taxpayer. It also means designing a deposit insurance system that does not prolong the life of inefficient banks.

For the public, the challenge lies in admitting that the deposit insurance system cannot be kept in its present form without incurring enormous costs. Banks have tripped four times since the mid-1970s and they will assuredly stumble again without real reform. That means learning to live with coverage limits as well as a system that rewards strong banks and punishes poorly managed ones.

For bankers, it means learning to live without the heavy subsidy that federal insurance provides for their deposits, while accepting new restrictions on risk taking, at least at insured depository institutions.

For stockholders, it means forgoing the subsidies provided by the federal government through the too-big-to-fail doctrine, deposit insurance, and various accounting gimmicks devised by the Fed and the FDIC.

For regulators, it means forcing banks finally to come clean about the condition of their portfolios.

The truth may not set them free, or spare the taxpayer the final bill for the banking mess, but it's a start.

EDWARD J. KANE

# Taxpayer Loss Exposure in the Bank Insurance Fund

*In simple terms, the root problem in deposit insurance today may be described as a scandal in bank and government accounting.*

One needn't read U.S. newspapers very carefully to see that the media is embarrassed about having allowed a steady diet of baloney dished up by federal officials to dissuade them from grasping the slowly unfolding story of the FSLIC mess. A continuing official propensity for confusing both the press and the public is suggested by the cynical transformation of FSLIC into a handful of successor institutions and funds, one of which (the Savings Association Insurance Fund) has been assigned the reassuring acronym SAIF.

In order to forestall a replay, reporters and editors seem to be sounding the rebellious 1960s rock anthem: "We won't be fooled again." This time, the press is eager to entertain rumors and allegations about hidden weaknesses in the Bank Insurance Fund (BIF). Banks and banking regulators are defending themselves against unpleasant charges in a less than congenial environment, one in which a feisty press accords them considerable disrespect.

## The assault on Vaughan and Hill

One set of allegations that bankers and regulators seemed to enjoy refuting emanated from an October 1992 critique of the BIF published by the Washington Post Co.—*Banking on the Brink* by economists Roger Vaughan and Edward Hill.

Descriptions of this $220 book in the popular press have emphasized a $100 billion worst-case scenario rather than the book's far from excessive projection that the BIF is probably between $45 billion and $59 billion short of net reserves. Additional attention has been drawn to the authors' findings that as many as 2,000 unhealthy banks were in deep trouble (a number twice the FDIC's estimated number of problem banks), and that a taxpayer bailout of the fund was inevitable.

The authors' worst-case figure was produced by subjecting an array of troubled banking assets to 80 percent writedowns. Emphasizing the severity of this assumption, an *American Banker* columnist panned the book, and industry spokespersons cried foul. One characterized the exercise as "unfair" and "irresponsible." Another professed to be amazed that "something so

EDWARD J. KANE is James F. Cleary Professor in Finance at the Carroll School of Management of Boston College. Reprinted from *Challenge,* March–April 1993, pp. 43–49.

one-sided got so much play." On its own behalf, the FDIC arranged a press conference to identify weaknesses in the Vaughan-Hill analysis and to characterize these authors' assumptions as "extreme" and "unsubstantiated."

The FDIC's characterization of the Vaughan–Hill procedures is both literally correct and fundamentally unfair. Like most other official statements about the BIF, it is a misleading half-truth. Unreliable accounting measures of bank and BIF economic performance and economic condition require every careful analyst to experiment with a range of less than fully substantiated assumptions, as a way of extracting economic truth from self-serving accounting reports of bank condition. The desirability of such sensitivity analyses makes one suspect the moderation and probity of critics who suggest that exploring the effects of a range of unsubstantiated assumptions is an unfair or inadmissible analytical method.

## Accounting coverups

In simple terms, the root problem in deposit insurance today may be described as a scandal in bank and government accounting. In tough times, the valuation and itemization principles that accountants and regulators use contain reporting options that encourage the hiding of large opportunity losses from public view. They also allow the recording of discretionary nonrecurring profits in ways that can overstate current profits and net worths for years on end. The rosy bias in these readings, and in the projections based on them, have much in common with the rigged scales dishonest butchers use to overcharge their clients. With a show of apparent precision, they systematically and repeatedly mismeasure the obligations deposit insurance is putting on the taxpayers' bill.

I want to emphasize that by feigning ignorance about the extent of these hidden losses and of their long-term economic consequences, Federal Reserve and Treasury officials are doing a disservice to taxpayers. They are moving the BIF along the same ruts in the same road that led FSLIC to ruin. As thrift regulators did during the 1970s and early 1980s, gambling banking regulators are bifurcating their industry, forcing its healthy members to support a substantial number of hopelessly crippled competitors. They are effectively authorizing a risk-loving horde of living-dead or "zombie" institutions to prey on financial markets.

When past S&L regulators decided to cover up the extent of FSLIC losses in the 1970s and 1980s, and to defer hundreds of needed insolvency resolutions, they cited four plausible excuses that, by passing FIRREA and FDICIA, Congress has made inoperative. These four time-honored excuses were:

• Regulators' authority to move against economically insolvent "zombie" institutions that were able to show positive accounting net worth depended on examiner writedowns that were difficult to defend both in the courts and in the political arena.
• Regulators did not have enough borrowing authority to cover the asset writedowns their insurance fund would have to absorb (the RTC still faces this problem today).
• Given the uncertain nature of taxpayer backup, regulators had some reason to fear the admittedly remote possibility that rationally based runs on troubled banks and thrifts by uninsured depositors might degenerate into a costly national crisis.
• Regulators could not be sure either that Congress would repair deficiencies in insurance-fund reserves with taxpayer funds or that its individual members would not strongly pressure them to go easy on zombie institutions for political reasons.

With these reliable excuses for delay stripped away, faint-hearted banking regulators are now forced to offer a less convincing excuse for delaying writedowns. They have to claim that it is a good gamble to wait for truly *eager* private buyers to come along to take over each of hundreds of troubled deposit-institution franchises and their weakest assets. To defend this claim, they have to exaggerate the financial and macroeconomic dangers of insisting on prompt recapitalizations. They also have to ignore the interest costs of waiting, along with the perverse effects on bank investment incentives this strategy introduces, and to dismiss or mischaracterize empirical evidence about how much this strategy cost taxpayers in the S&L insurance mess.

The fundamental question is what defects in bureaucratic incentives render regulators deeply reluctant to resolve deposit-institution economic insolvencies when and as they develop. What career advantages and benefits to reputation make them so willing to pretend that plainly nonrecurring and easily reversed accounting profits booked as a result of a nonrepeatable, election-year decline in interest rates have restored hundreds of terminally weak banks and thrifts to long-term health? The economic condition of crippled banks today parallels that of an AIDS victim who has been lucky enough to get over a bout of pneumonia. Although each crippled bank has received a welcome gift of time, its condition remains seriously distressed.

Leaving a weak bank's insolvency unrepaired is unfair to taxpayers. This is because taxpayers hold the bag for the downside of every interest-rate gamble and other speculative wagers that economically insolvent zombie institutions manage to put on the table. The rapid expansion of bank positions in government securities and the size of nonrecurring profits reported in securities trading in 1992 should have scared regulators into developing truly effective rather than sham procedures for disciplining interest-rate risk-taking.

## Regulator efforts to discredit FDICIA

Ever since William Clinton became president-elect, we have heard a great deal about FOBs (Friends of Bill). Employment files for FOBs are each said to carry a number that inversely orders the strength of the friendship. According to the ordering used, First Lady Hillary Rodham Clinton would be FOB1. This, of course, is the reverse of the ordering that would obtain in the British royal family. Focusing on enmity rather than friendship, I have been developing a file on FOFs (Foes of FDICIA). So far, the lowest numbers in my file have been won by a few Federal Reserve and Treasury officials, with some miscreant ex-regulators and banking trade-association spokespersons close behind.

In my experience, spoiled children are the ones who complain the loudest about parental discipline. For taxpayers, "Skeptics of the Bill" would probably make a more telling acronym. Administrators' objections to FDICIA's curtailing of their discretion to forbear are not burdened with logic. They ask us to let good possibilities outweigh bad probabilities. They emphasize the good ways agency officials could use the lost discretion, while refusing to acknowledge the temptations that have *repeatedly* led them and their predecessors astray in abuse of this discretion.

At this very moment, officials are pushing the BIF down the same ruts in the same road that FSLIC took in 1983. Their continued willingness to help put off bank asset writedowns and to delay the resolution of economically insolvent deposit institutions places a losing bet for taxpayers, a bet that is nonetheless welcomed by the weakest and loudest segment of the industry. At the same time, it should be recognized that trade-association lobbying positions are apt to be biased in favor of weak institutions. This is so because a financial industry's weakest members can and do earn profits from building up a disproportionate and life-sustaining degree of clout in industry trade associations.

Because delay is costly, it breaks faith with other taxpayers and with the spirit of the FDIC Improvement Act of 1991 (FDICIA). The central thrust of the 1991 legislation is to insist that, when and as an insured institution's capital position declines, its managers are confronted with a mandate to recapitalize their firm promptly or else. The virtue of this exit-policy mandate is that it subjects a weakening firm to the same sort of discipline that its creditors would impose if they weren't insured against loss by the FDIC. It is important to understand that recapitalization does not imply the disappearance of a bank's assets, nor even of its franchise. What it *does* imply is a timely repricing of bank assets and a market testing of the value of keeping a troubled institution in play.

Identifying timely demands for recapitalization as regulatory excess that dictates a mindless shrinking of the banking industry is part of a nasty public-relations campaign that bank trade associations and some federal regulators are waging against the FDIC Improvement Act of 1991. This campaign uses all three of the non-pecuniary tools of the unprincipled special-interest lobbyist—mischaracterization, distortion, and exaggeration. The campaign erroneously characterizes *transitional* costs from changing regulatory patterns as if they were permanent burdens. In addition, it exaggerates FDICIA's curtailment of regulatory discretion as far more restrictive than it truly is. It distorts the extent to which recapitalization pressure is apt to aggravate the nation's financial problems, alleging that it will worsen already waning shortages of credit and put unhealthy pressure on weak institutions.

The central purpose of FDICIA is to inhibit the doubling and redoubling of deposit-institution losses which have already occurred. The campaign ignores survey evidence indicating support of this regulatory principle and of other regulatory strategies embodied in FDICIA by a substantial majority of ordinary bankers. The FOFs (Foes of FDICIA) characterize the idea of restricting regulators' discretion not as a strategy for protecting strong institutions and unwary taxpayers from gambling by weak institutions, but as a recipe for whipping up actuarially avoidable losses in weak institutions.

Accounting loopholes make the economic value of bank capital difficult to quantify. As long as lobbyists can hold market-value accounting at bay, the tripwire system of capital discipline needs to be supplemented by secondary triggers that can provide timely signals of a hidden worsening in an insured institution's enterprise-contributed net worth.

Parallels exist between the detailed regulatory standards the act requires regulators to develop and covenants in private contracts conveying renegotiation rights in situations where changes in a borrower's condition are hard to observe and can occur suddenly. Recognizing this parallel clarifies the view that regulators have an *obligation* to waive covenant violations when close investigation demonstrates the violations to be inconsequential. Nevertheless, the call for standards is being depicted as a completely misguided strategy of a regulatory micromanagement. On my campus this October, I heard one regulator characterize the FDIC Improvement Act as an "oxymoron of the first order," full of "asinine provisions," requiring unnecessary regulatory standards. One week earlier, Treasury Secretary Brady opined to conferees at the annual meeting of the American Bankers Association that the burden of regulatory compliance "had reached a level that is intolerable" and called for the reestablishment of "a balanced approach to lending and risk-taking." One wonders whether he means by a "balanced approach," the one FSLIC managed to promote.

By and large, federal regulators are carrying out their responsibilities under the act in an unfriendly spirit. I will cite two examples of this. First, FDICIA requires that regulators incorporate interest-rate risk into the risk-based capital regulatory framework. Interest-rate risk refers to the danger that future movements in market interest rates will induce a net adverse revaluation of the asset and liability positions an institution holds. In July, in response to the FDICIA requirement, federal bank regulators issued a proposed rule that fails to develop either an effective measure of a bank's exposure to interest-rate risk or an effective framework for limiting the extent to which these exposures pass through to the net reserves of the BIF.

Although user-friendly computer software for interest-rate-risk analysis is in use at many banks and available from private vendors (such as Fiserv), the proposal emphasizes pencil-and-paper simplicity in reporting requirements. It seeks to estimate the effect on the net value of an institution's on- and off-balance-sheet positions if interest rates moved 100 basis points in either direction. To this end, it assigns each position an "approximate" price-volatility risk weight established by the banking agencies. Finally, the agencies plan to use the resulting measures only to identify and subsequently discipline banks that are taking high levels of interest-rate risk relative to their peers.

Given the billions of dollars at stake and the availability of modern information technology, it is outrageous to let simplicity in reporting procedures outweigh the need for banks and regulators to examine how a bank's true exposure to the range of likely interest-rate changes impacts its capital, by raising the required rate of return on equity. It is equally important to calculate the value of the loss exposure that each bank's interest-rate risk imposes on the BIF. Because interest rates tend to rise and fall in cyclical fashion, potential upward and downward swings in prospective interest rates seldom appear symmetric. Although short-term and long-term rates tend to move in the same direction, swings in these rates do *not* tend to affect asset and liability value equally. Near the start of a recovery, in particular, the range of possible interest-rate increases far exceeds the range of probable decreases, and nasty declines in long-term asset values can occur with great suddenness.

Worst of all, the proposal makes no effort to incorporate the cumulative interaction of *past* interest-rate risk-taking and actual interest-rate movements into the capital ratio that triggers FDICIA's trip-wire system of regulatory discipline. Given the damage interest-rate risk did to FSLIC, it is a disgrace that authorities have not installed an adequate system for measuring interest-rate risk by this time. If such a system were in place, it would clarify the urgency of recapitalizing a number of seriously distressed banks as soon as possible. Today, some of these banks are blithely telling us that their bet is okay because long rates are going to fall this year even if short rates rise. I offer the following riddle:

Q. Which item does not belong on the following list: gonorrhea, AIDS, herpes, interest-rate risk.

A. Gonorrhea. Why? Because it is the only one that federal authorities are both willing and able to tell taxpayers how to eliminate.

Mandated under FDICIA, the proposed regulatory structure for measuring and controlling interest-rate risk illustrates the growing conflict between the chairmen of the congressional banking committees and top federal banking regulators. This tension reinforces the theory that regulatory forbearance aggravated the FSLIC mess and is underscored by these parties' respective attitudes about coming clean concerning the size of the shortage in the BIF's explicit reserves.

Consider the contrast between two statements made in March 1991 as comments on the sizable adjustments then being made in FDIC loss estimates for the Bank Insurance Fund: The first, uttered by Chairman of the House Banking Committee, Henry Gonzalez, was, "We must avoid a rerun of the shifting numbers, the gimmickry, and the outright deceit that marked so much of the savings and loan crisis." FDIC Public Relations Officer Alan Whitney offered the second. He said, "[All estimates] were based on the best information available at those times. It is clear that economic conditions changed over the time."

The confusion is also exacerbated by the open ridicule that top Federal Reserve and Treasury officials have heaped on specific elements of FDICIA and by their open contempt for the act's attempts to reduce regulatory discretion. They seize virtually every opportunity available to reinforce industry concerns about excessive regulatory burdens and to communicate their own reluctance to implement various of its provisions (e.g., use of stock-market values in assessing soundness and the need to set loan-to-value standards for mortgage loans). Such comments constitute a *second* line of FOF mischaracterizations, exaggerations, and distortions, deserving of congressional review.

Several FDICIA initiatives have been unfairly characterized as bank-bashing exercises. One initiative that seems to me to ask authorities to treat divergences between the market value of a bank's stock and the book value of its net worth as a covenant-like signal of hidden problems has been openly mocked by the Federal Reserve. The Fed's request for public comment on this initiative frames the issue as if Congress had asked bank regulators to control bank stock-prices. The questions the Fed posed are laden with sarcasm and plainly invite respondents to hold the provision up to ridicule.

Federal banking regulators are, so far, stubbornly refusing to acknowledge what Congress has clearly grasped—that the lessons of the S&L insurance mess apply to the banking regulators and the BIF. In asking for detailed regulatory norms, Congress is not "bashing" banks. It is telling regulators to develop enforceable standards of regulatory performance. Such standards would force regulators to leave a clear "audit trail" for regulatory decisions that effectively waive taxpayer covenant rights. Taxpayers and Congress need just such standards and audit trails to make top regulators accountable for deposit-insurance losses that accrue *during* their watch (as opposed to losses that are realized at their discretion).

## *The false test of a "December surprise"*

Reluctance to disclose problem situations or to take tough disciplinary actions against an agency's regulatory clientele lies at the heart of the deposit-insurance problem. This is what makes the situation a "mess" rather than a "crisis." The need for regulatory action is hidden and the cumulative effects of repeatedly deferring needed actions are misrepresented. The result is that public-policy experts end up debating *whether* action is truly needed rather than focusing on hammering out effective programs of action. Fears of a "December Surprise" similarly misframed the central issue in the mess. Treated as a test for industry weakness, this idea focused on the sideshow of forecasting regulators' highly politicized decisions about whether and when to "fail" or recapitalize economically insolvent banks, rather than on measuring and controlling the *unbooked losses* to which the BIF exposes the federal taxpayer.

This summer, I estimated that, as of December 31, 1991, BIF's net loss exposure might amount to $53 billion. Applying the same estimation methods to June 30, 1992, data for banks, as computed by the bank-analysis firm Veribanc, Inc., BIF's position improved to between $45 and $50 billion.

However, on the basis of net-worth and earnings data, Veribanc sorts banks into categories patterned after the colors of the standard traffic light. The 1,067 doubtful banks that fall into what Veribanc calls its "red," "yellow," and very-light "green" categories correspond roughly to the 1,044 "problem banks" identified by the FDIC. As Table 15 shows, the bulk of BIF's unbooked loss exposure lies in two seriously distressed "yellow" categories. As does a yellow traffic light, their condition should signal a halt to toleration of their weakness. Many of these banks are deeply insolvent economically, even though their accounting ratios are not yet desperate enough to force federal regulators either to demand recapitalization or to impose other mandatory disciplines. The danger of their future average deterioration from per-

Table 15

**Calculating Hypothetical BIF Loss Exposure
From Asset Breakdown Given by Veribanc's Partition of
FDIC-Insured Commercial and Savings Banks, as of June 30, 1992**

| Veribanc category | Number of banks | Assets (in $bn.) | Hypothetical rate of case resolution | Hypothetical assets to be resolved (in $bn.) | Hypothetical rate of BIF loss | Hypothetical BIF loss exposure (in $bn.) |
|---|---|---|---|---|---|---|
| Red: no stars | 143 | 34.4 | 0.9 | 31.0 | 0.3 | 9.3 |
| Yellow: no stars | 99 | 28.8 | 0.9 | 26.0 | 0.3 | 7.8 |
| Yellow: one star | 155 | 225.0 | 0.6 | 135.0 | 0.2 | 27.0 |
| Yellow: two stars | 639 | 166.8 | 0.6 | 100.0 | 0.2 | 20.0 |
| Green: no stars | 28 | 8.1 | 0.4 | 3.2 | 0.2 | 0.6 |
| Green: one star | 3 | 54.4 | 0.4 | 21.8 | 0.2 | 4.4 |
| All "doubtful" banks | 1,067 | 517.5 | | 317.0 | | 69.1 |
| Green: two stars | 1,277 | 54.4 | 0.005 | 0.3 | 0.2 | 0.1 |
| Green: three stars | 9,801 | 2,650.7 | 0.001 | 2.7 | 0.2 | 0.5 |
| All banks | 12,145 | 3,222.6 | | 320.0 | | 69.7 |
| Less BIF's reserve for its estimated liability for unresolved cases | | | | | | −15.2 |
| BIF's unbooked loss exposure | | | | | | 54.5 |

*Note:* The hypothetical rates of needed case resolution and of BIF loss are offered as indicative guesses. Detailed analysis of past transitions across partitions of bank assets would be needed to establish econometric estimates of these variables.

verse risk-taking incentives leads me to offer an alternative—a larger estimate of BIF's unbooked loss exposure of $54.5 billion.

The electorate must understand that there could have been a surprise this December only if it came from the policies of the new president and new Congress. It could *not* come from the tangible capital trigger set by FDICIA. Scheduling a life-and-death exam one year ahead and making the right answer to the test question known in advance gave zombie firms ample opportunity to cram effectively for the test. Those that could not recapitalize themselves in a straightforward manner have been drawing on whatever accounting options they could find to nudge their capital ratio above the 2 percent threshold. Troubled banks' interest in locating on the edge of the regulatory tripwire minefield explains why the seriously distressed "yellow" categories are so full. Exercising sharp accounting options is, of course, easier when test administrators are anxious not to see too many weak "students" embarrass themselves.

This fall, Veribanc found that banks were rapidly migrating from the list of "critically undercapitalized" institutions it maintains. By late October, a more aggressive closure policy and regulatory relief had reduced the list to 41 banks, with $10.6 billion in assets. Interestingly, several escapees made it over the wall because of special agreements with the agencies that served to qualify selected categories of debt instruments as regulatory capital. By early December, the list had been compressed to about 20 banks with only about $6 billion in assets. In October, Veribanc estimated that only another 146 banks with $38 billion in assets were probably in the "undercapitalized" or "significantly undercapitalized" regulatory zones that trigger lesser disciplines.

Not observing a spurt in bank failures or recapitalizations, either in the wake of the November 3 election or when FDICIA's 2 percent capital threshold kicked in, tells us more about regulatory faintheartedness than about the extent of economic insolvency in the banking industry. In the meantime, and probably for months to come, a disturbing number of undercapitalized deposit institutions are free to book short-funded positions in Treasury securities without recapitalizing themselves. Indeed, the weighting pattern used in the risk-based capital system encourages this. These positions are speculative gambles on the course of future interest rates, for which taxpayers are unconscionably being made to hold the downside. Even if the managers and stockholders of these institutions end up winning their bets, taxpayers are financing their speculations on an interest-free basis.

Top regulators' penchant for discussing hardheaded insolvency resolution as a policy that would "close down the industry" disgracefully distorts the recapitalization issue. Just as in a private restructuring, no government supervisor should liquidate an insolvent institution whose franchise can be shown to be valuable enough to continue it in operation. If a troubled (yet viable) firm's stockholders refuse to recapitalize the enterprise, their position should be closed out. While supervisors search for new private investors to take over the bank, the FDIC should routinely seek to offset BIF's loss exposure with a carefully balanced claim on the firm's future cash flows.

## BIF accounting profits

Anyone who has helped a loved one face cancer knows that denying the existence of a problem is prototypically less painful in the short run than confronting that problem head-on. But, it is dramatically less beneficial as well. Any thinking person should be disturbed by the economic benefits the FDIC and banking trade-association spokespersons claim for FDIC projections of the net "accounting income" that BIF can generate from future premium receipts. These projections are being used to allege that the BIF can recapitalize itself over time by charging relatively safe banks an excessive price for FDIC services. In turn, the allegation that BIF's capital shortage will vanish over time by itself is being used to justify a policy of benignly neglecting the economic insolvency of hundreds of weak banks.

Analyses of BIF loss-exposure that forecast large amounts of future net premiums are conceptually flawed. Premiums and additions to reserves should be calculated net of the insurer's loss exposure in each client. Economic theory indicates that setting premiums high above their value to low-risk bank clients is bound to increase BIF's contingent loss-exposure. As the Shadow Financial Regulatory Committee has emphasized, burdensome premiums create a virtually irresistible incentive for low-risk institutions to expand their risk-taking to make sure that the value of the insurance services they receive from BIF equals or exceeds the charge the FDIC levies on them. This insight clarifies that, in equilibrium, the present value of BIF's future net premiums must be zero. Moreover, it is easy for an institution to expand its risk-taking, e.g., by securitizing or collateralizing strong assets or by mismatching the futurity of an institution's assets and liabilities. This means that any transitional benefits to BIF reserves from raising premiums are bound to dissipate quickly.

Putting off the insolvency resolution of crippled banks and using accounting gambits to suggest the possibility of a painless recapitalization for BIF are faithless actions worthy of protest by strongly capitalized institutions and other informed parties. For BIF to become truly self-financing, it is not enough to rebuild its reserves in an accounting sense. Although it can price and police its services to avoid *future* losses, outside resources must be tapped to overcome the imbedded losses arising from the effects of *past* forbearance policies. Resources to cover past losses can be collected only through taxes of some kind.

If temporarily very profitable survivor banks are truly going to be asked to share the recapitalization burden with the general taxpayer, Congress had best plan to enact a one-time special tax assessment against bank income or assets.

CHAPTER 8 | THE DEBATE OVER REFORMING BANKING REGULATIONS

# *Why We Regulate Banks*

ROBERT GUTTMANN

The U.S. banking crisis of 1990–91 triggered a national debate over the future of banking and the regulatory framework that should guide the industry's restructuring process. The debate has centered on the Treasury's proposal in February 1991 to deregulate banking by eliminating the Glass–Steagall restrictions on bank activities and tightening deposit insurance. Even though much of that proposal was eventually defeated in Congress, with only limited deposit-insurance reform passed in the end (FDICIA 1991), the idea of radically changing the regulatory framework for banks to direct the restructuring process in that vital sector of our economy has not died with the failure of this governmental initiative. U.S. commercial banking, while temporarily relieved by economic recovery and improved profit margins, is still a sick industry structurally. A large number of thrifts and banks remain seriously weakened by bad-debt losses, thin capitalization, and excess capacity. Depository institutions as a whole face serious competitive threats from foreign banks and domestic nonbank institutions, both of which are increasingly capable of invading the traditional market turf of commercial banks. In this battle banks are hampered by anachronistic regulations dating from the New Deal or before which leave them at a competitive disadvantage and unable to restructure properly. As lawmakers and regulators struggle with this issue, they have to make any possible alternative to existing banking regulation coherent with the emerging global banking framework.

## *Market regulation versus government regulation*

A radical approach in favor of returning commercial banking to the discipline and incentives of the marketplace is put forward at the onset of this chapter by James Thomson, an economist and high-ranking official with the Federal Reserve Bank of Cleveland. Writing in early 1990, when the government was in the midst of a review of deposit insurance mandated by FIRREA in 1989, Thomson suggests a free-market approach to banking as the best alternative to the current system of taxing and subsidizing banks through government regulations that date back sixty years or more and have lost much of their meaning in today's world of banking. Thomson's plan would let banks engage in whatever bank-related activities they deem profitable. Deposit insurance would be dramatically lowered, and the Fed would be allowed to offer discount loans for liquidity purposes only (i.e., no open-assistance lending to insolvent institutions). Closure rules would be determined by market forces abandoning weak institutions. Market incentives would be reinforced by more realistic market-value accounting and timely disclosure of pertinent information by banks and regulators alike. Government regulation would be limited to minimum capital requirements, disclosure requirements, outside audits, and market-value accounting rules.

Thomson provides two rationales for such a market-oriented reform. One is that the existing federal safety net for banks has had perverse results, especially the moral-hazard problem of excessive risk taking by weaker institutions and the high social costs of regulatory forbearance, which have substantially weakened the industry as a whole. In his eyes these problems are innate when one replaces market regulation with government intervention of the kind that thwarts the disciplining, resource-allocating, and signalling functions of the marketplace. From that perspective it makes little sense to undertake piecemeal reform that leaves the basic regulatory framework in place. Much more fundamental change is necessary! His other rationale for a return to market regulation is that commercial banks are not so special that they need to be protected and constrained by the government. Arguing this point on the basis of the allegedly high social costs of bank failures, Thomson concludes that there is little empirical evidence suggesting such a negative externality in today's competitive and globalized financial-services environment. On the contrary, market-determined closure processes may very well unfold more rapidly and at lower ultimate cost to society than the current socialization of bank risks and losses by the government.

This view is rejected by other authors presented here. Robert Adler and Douglas Ferguson, for instance, take explicit issue with the notion that market regulation works well in the case of commercial banking. For them, the bankers' unrestrained pursuit of profit is bound to lead to credit overextension and a conscious repression of realistic risk assessments, as already witnessed during the 1980s in the aftermath of bank and thrift deregulation. In the absence of proper lender-of-last-resort mechanisms, the banks' excesses could still trigger a systemwide crisis of confidence by the public with potentially disastrous consequences for the economy. Arguing from a different angle, Henry Kaufman also considers banks special institutions whose very nature requires government supervision and regulation. Unlike Thomson, he sees the specialness of banks embodied in their function of *money creation,* which determines their activity of financial intermediation. Other nonbank intermediaries are not in a position to replace this role of commercial banks. The government has to regulate commercial banking activities if it wants to manage the money supply, interest rates, and credit allocation effectively. Albert Hart, in his paper presented here, shares that same view.

## Assessing the Treasury proposal for banking deregulation

While most of the authors, with the exception of Thomson, favor continued reliance on (reformed) government protection and regulation of commercial banking, they exhibit less agreement as to the precise nature of regulatory reform. The key point of reference for their differences in opinion and approach is the Treasury's 1991 bank reform proposal. Before exploring those differences, we should note that there is widespread consensus concerning at least one of the key provisions in that proposal, the establishment of nationwide banking through elimination of geographic branching restrictions. This regulation is clearly outdated in light of today's fund-transfer technology and nationally integrated financial markets, with many banks already quite capable of operating on an interstate basis. Moreover, branching restrictions leave banks less diversified, subject them to greater risks of failure, and impair their necessary shakeout process.

Henry Kaufman takes issue with the Treasury's proposal to merge commercial banks with industrial enterprises. For one, such cross-ownership would lead to an excessive degree of concentration in terms of both economic and political power to the detriment of entrepreneurial initiative and against the democratic aspirations of the electorate. Moreover, the tightly intertwined relationship thus created between bankers and corporate managers would inevitably lead to conflicts of interest that could compromise sound banking practices. Abusive interference by corporate headquarters would force the banking subsidiary to undertake imprudent actions that help the parent company at the expense of a larger public interest. The regulator's idea of "firewalls" to keep the interests of the corporation and its banking subsidiary apart will not work, a point also stressed by Adler and Ferguson. Either the firewall is so effective that it weakens the incentives for corporations to invest in banks, or it is de facto permeable. Kaufman believes that firewalls cannot work in any case, given the inability to control intracompany communication channels and information flows. He suggests that, given the intertwined nature of banking and other corporate operations in any such bank–industry combine, the government would have no choice but to extend its safety-net provisions to the entire conglomerate, if the latter ever faced financial difficulties. The result would be the evolution of a perniciously lopsided industrial policy geared toward the country's largest corporations and controlled by a financial–industrial–governmental elite that benefits from such a *corporatist state* at the expense of the rest of American society.

Adler and Ferguson use similar arguments to oppose the Treasury's proposal for a merger between investment and commercial banking. Apart from the difficulties associated with the creation of effective firewalls, these two Wall Street economists emphasize the inherently procyclical nature of both types of banking activity. During recessions banks would face losses not only from defaulting loans but from declining securities markets. We may add that there are very large differences in corporate culture between commercial banks and investment banks. It is difficult to balance the divergent interests of loan officers and free-wheeling dealmakers or traders under one and the same roof, and commercial banks may find their forays into investment banking fraught with unforeseen problems.

In this context it is worth noting, as do several of the authors included in this chapter, that the regulatory structure and type of banking found in other countries does not serve as a reliable model for anyone else and cannot be simply replicated in the United States. Each country has its own distinct cultural practices, institutional specificities, political contexts, and policy traditions which together give that country's regulatory framework its distinct (and inimitable) characteristics of application. So we cannot just import Germany's universal-banking structures and expect the same results without taking into account how the government interacts with banks there. The same holds true for Japan's bank-industry combines known as *keiretsu*.

Yet irrespective of the specificity of domestic banking regulations, U.S. government officials have to keep in mind that whatever regulatory framework they design for domestic banking operations will have to be coordinated with international developments that are being shaped by the irreversible global integration of banking and financial markets. This issue affects our policy makers on two levels. For one, the emerging financial integration on a global scale requires increasing harmonization of regulations between countries, culminating in multilateral agreements for uniform regulatory standards (such as the Basle Agreement in 1988 pertaining to risk-based minimum capital requirements for banks). Moreover, U.S. policy makers have to negotiate reciprocal-access rules for banks and other financial institutions in the context of multilateral trade-liberalization negotiations for services under the auspices of the World Trade Organization. Here the existence of rule differences between, say, the United States and the European Union creates difficulties. Under "national treatment" principles insisted on by the United States, we would place new restrictions on the U.S. operations of foreign depository institutions which those institutions have been hitherto exempted from or which they do not face in the European context. The global aspects of regulatory reform for banking therefore need careful consideration and a lot of negotiating so that any proposal for domestic reform fits into the emerging global framework of banking regulations.

## Reform of the federal safety net

There is general agreement among our various authors here that the government's safety net for depository institutions, as currently structured, does not work. By keeping insolvent institutions open, the FDIC and Federal Reserve end up penalizing healthy institutions, raising the social costs of bank failure, and undermining discipline against excessive risk taking. This burdensome practice of regulatory forbearance needs to be stopped, and the moral hazard curtailed.

Other than Thomson's suggestion for a radical scaling-back of the federal safety net for banks, most of the authors favor a continued role for relatively extensive deposit-insurance coverage and active use of the Fed's reliquification channels (i.e., discount window, open market purchases of government securities, repurchasing agreements) as the central lender-of-last-resort mechanisms capable of assuring financial stability. Yet at the same time there is a consensus to limit these mechanisms more carefully by making their availability conditional on "good behavior." Henry Kaufman wants a rating system for banks based on outside audits and full deposit-insurance restricted to banks with top ratings. Albert Hart goes a step further with his innovative idea of offering safety-net provisions only to depository institutions that have entered into a contractual obligation with regulators to rebuild their capital base and abstain from certain unsound banking practices. Such capital buildup contracts should be accompanied by more broadly based reserve requirements, taking account of the spread of new means-of-payments instruments (e.g., negotiable certificates of deposit, repurchasing agreements), as well as a resumption of interest-rate ceilings on bank deposits to limit excessive risk taking by banks and increase the government's leverage in maintaining lower interest rates. Several authors point also to the relationship between bank holding subsidiaries and their bank subsidiaries as an area that needs regulatory clarification.

## *Regulatory streamlining*

A good number of contributions in this chapter, most notably the two articles by Wolfgang Reinicke, stress the cumbersome and counterproductive U.S. regulatory apparatus dealing with our financial-services industry. That apparatus consists of several overlapping agencies (e.g., FDIC, Federal Reserve, the Treasury's Comptroller of Currency, the Securities and Exchange Commission, and state banking commissions) competing with each other for turf and power. The multitude of regulatory agencies encourages higher regulatory cost burdens for the regulatees and greater uncertainties as to the precise meaning of specific regulations which various agencies interpret differently. This chaotic situation is aggravated by conflicts between the different regulatory agencies as to the precise nature of their role in any regulatory reform. Because they deal solely with specific segments of the banking industry, they tend to entertain a myopic view that expresses the narrow interests of their clients rather than seeing the issue of banking reform from the macro perspective it deserves. This regulatory fragmentation has encouraged regulatory forbearance, either because regulators want to extend their relative power or because they have been captured by their clients. It has also made any broad consensus for regulatory reform much more difficult, as competing and adversarial regulatory bodies clash in their myopic visions that reflect narrow turf concerns and divided private interests. The time has come to streamline this fragmented structure of regulatory agencies.

Two different approaches to regulatory streamlining can be distinguished. The first is presented by Richard Aspinwall, chief economist of Chase Manhattan, who notes that banking regulation involves several distinct functions that may enter into a variety of unforeseen conflicts with each other. He recommends a regulatory structure whereby these functions are each concentrated in one specific agency and mediated by a supra-organizational mechanism for conflict resolution. For him such a function-based division of responsibilities among different regulators forced to resolve their conflicts is better than the current arbitrary fragmentation or the Treasury's proposed centralization of banking regulation in one agency where such conflicts between different regulatory objectives are internalized and may reach the point of paralysis.

Wolfgang Reinicke, on the other hand, favors the Treasury's idea of centralizing the major regulatory and supervisory activities pertaining to depository institutions in the hands of a single, independent Federal Banking Commission (FBC). Reinicke answers the critics of this proposal count by count, including a rejection of the argument made in the piece by Henry Kaufman that this central supervision task should be placed with the Federal Reserve in support of its intervention obligations as lender of last resort and in the conduct of monetary policy. For him it seems entirely sufficient to have representatives of the Treasury and the Federal Reserve serve on the FBC board to facilitate inter-agency coordination. What neither Kaufman nor Reinicke approve of is the political compromise in the Treasury proposal that would place supervisory responsibility over state-chartered bank holding companies in the hands of the Fed. If the U.S. central bank has any supervisory role to play it is with regard to the largest (and predominantly federally chartered) banks whose actions have a significant impact on the effectiveness of monetary policy and are more likely to trigger a financial crisis with potentially dangerous contagion effects.

In sum, the banking system is undergoing a massive restructuring process that creates the need for a new regulatory framework. The overhaul that is required would involve the establishment of nationwide banking, a clarification of the relationships between commercial and investment banking as well as between banks and industry, a more effective federal safety net, as well as a streamlined structure of regulatory oversight. Whether or not these objectives are achievable in light of serious political barriers remains an open question. It usually takes a crisis to pull all the divergent interests together toward action. The crisis of 1990–91 opened the issue of regulatory reform and provided limited reform of the federal safety net (including the Basle Agreement of 1988 which phased in uniform and risk-weighted capitalization requirements for banks across the industrialized world). Market pressures have made nationwide banking inevitable, a fact recognized now by both parties in Congress and thus a matter of legislative consensus. Regulatory loopholes have allowed commercial banks to expand into investment banking via separately capitalized subsidiaries, but have done so in a highly uneven fashion. Corporate forays into commercial banking, mostly through the loophole of so-called *limited-services banks,* have been on hold since 1987 and await clarification. Regulators still stonewall their streamlining. It is only when they finally agree to set their narrow interests aside in favor of a broader public interest, that the law will finally catch up with the realities of contemporary banking.

JAMES B. THOMSON

# *Using Market Incentives to Reform Bank Regulation and Federal Deposit Insurance*

## Introduction

Reform of the financial services industry became a hotly debated issue in the 1980s, and this debate continues to rage in the 1990s. Much of the debate has been generated by a growing recognition that fundamental reforms are needed in our banking and thrift regulatory systems to respond to market-driven change in the financial services industry. Deposit-insurance reform has taken center stage in the political arena, as the Financial Institutions Reform, Recovery and Enforcement Act (FIRREA) of 1989 formally commits $159 billion of taxpayer money to resolve the thrift crisis and mandates that a study of federal deposit insurance be undertaken.

The overall objective of reform in the financial services industry should be to maximize the efficiency and stability of the banking and thrift systems while minimizing the exposure of the federal safety net—and hence the taxpayer—to losses generated by insured banks and thrifts. A plethora of reform proposals have been advanced by the banking industry, bank regulators, and the academic community. Their reform proposals typically can be divided into proposals that rely on increased regulation and less discretion for bank management,[1] and proposals that rely on market-oriented solutions and increased management discretion within supervisory guidelines.[2]

The purpose of this paper is twofold. First, it presents the case for adopting market-oriented reforms to the regulatory system and to the financial safety net.[3] Second, it summarizes the literature from one perspective and presents a cohesive view on the topic. Section I reexamines the issue of whether banks are special and the issue of stability in banking markets, both regulated and unregulated. In addition, section I looks at principal-agent problems associated with bank regulation (Kane, 1988b). Section II proposes reforms to our sys-

JAMES B. THOMSON is an assistant vice president and economist at the Federal Reserve Bank of Cleveland. The author thanks Edward Kane, George Kaufman, and Walker Todd for helpful comments and suggestions. Reprinted from Federal Reserve Bank of Cleveland *Economic Review,* 26 (1), 1990 (First Quarter), pp. 28–40.

tem of regulatory taxes and subsidies. Conclusions are presented in section III.

## I. Stability in banking markets

Those who propose reforms that rely on an increased role for regulation in determining limits on bank powers and activities—and hence a reduced role for management discretion, shareholders' control, and market discipline—assume that financial markets are inherently unstable or that banks are "special" in the sense that the social costs of bank failures significantly exceed the private costs (Corrigan, 1987; Tallman, 1988). Therefore, proponents of increased regulation are willing to trade efficiency for stability. Moreover, in principle, increased regulation protects the public purse from losses by restricting the participation of insured depository institutions in activities that are deemed to be excessively risky.

The reforms outlined in this paper assume that the opposite is true; that, left to their own devices, financial markets are stable in the sense that in the long run they exhibit an orderly process of change, and that, if there is tradeoff between efficiency and stability, it exists only in the short run.[4] Moreover, it is the system of regulatory taxes and subsidies, in our view, that makes banks "special," not any intrinsic characteristic of banking.[5]

**Are Banks Special?** The "banks-are-special" argument typically is based on one of two notions: either that bank failures have a high social cost or that all runs on individual banks are contagious and, therefore, the banking system is unstable. Since the issue of banking-system stability is dealt with in the following section, we will concentrate on the social cost of bank failures here. To argue that banks are special because there are high social costs associated with their failures, one must demonstrate two things: first, the social costs associated with their failures are significantly greater than the private costs of bank failures (that is, there is an economically significant externality associated with the failure of a bank); and second, the social costs of bank failures are significantly higher than the social costs of failures of other firms.

What has been the cost of bank failures? Benston et al. (1986, ch. 2) show that for the entire period from 1865 to 1933 (the time period between the National Banking Act and the creation of the FDIC), total loses were $12.3 billion, or about 1 percent of total commercial bank assets. Losses to depositors were only about $2.4 billion, or about 0.21 percent of commercial bank deposits. Even in the Great Depression (1930–33), the losses to depositors were only about 0.81 percent of total commercial bank deposits. So, in an environment of no federal deposit insurance and lighter regulation, the private costs of bank failures appear to have been small.

The issue of the "specialness" of banks rests on social costs, however, and not on private ones. Unfortunately, the social costs of bank failures are difficult to quantify, because measures of the size of the externalities associated with bank failures are highly subjective or do not exist.

The first of these externalities is the loss of banking services in the community or the disruption of special banking relationships. Banking relationships are considered valuable, because one service performed is information intermediation. In the first case, rarely does a community lose all of its banking services when an individual bank fails. Kaufman (1988) argues that in those few cases where the only bank in the area fails, it is often replaced by another bank or financial institution, often in the same location. Furthermore, liberal chartering of new banks and the relaxation of intrastate and interstate branching restrictions should take care of this problem when it does arise.

Second, most firms have relationships with more than one financial institution, and many of the lending officers of the failed institution find jobs with other banks in the area, often with the bank that replaces the failed institution (Benston and Kaufman, 1986). Moreover, as Schwartz (1987) argues, it is difficult to believe that financial institutions interested in acquiring the liabilities of a failed bank would not also be interested in capturing their creditworthy customers, especially if banking relationships have value.

The second externality may be the disruption of the payments system.[6] Because banks are the conduit for payments in this country, the failure of a major depository institution could cause the failures of other banks on the payments system, topple the payments system itself, or at least shut it down for an unacceptable period of time. However, there is no reason that the failure of any institution, not even a large one, should result in the collapse of the payments system.

Even today, the loss on assets associated with large bank failures is typically small, certainly not approaching 100 percent.[7] Therefore, banks with payments-related exposure to the failed institution should realize only a small loss, and the threat of loss from payments-systems defaults should cause banks to limit their exposure to other banks that are considered to be excessively risky. After all, banks routinely do this today in the federal funds market. In addition, the lender of last resort can immunize the rest of the payments system from the failure of a single bank by lending (with a "haircut") to banks against their claims on the failed institution until those claims are realized.[8] The Federal Reserve's role in providing liquidity to financial markets during the October 1987 stock market crash illustrates how a properly functioning lender of last resort can prevent spillover effects from bank failures or from crises in individual financial markets.

The third component of social costs is the causal relationship between declines in the banking industry and in the level of general economic activity. Do declines in the banking sector cause declines in economic activity, or is the opposite true? A review of the historical evidence by Benston et al. (1986, ch. 2) and Schwartz (1987) suggests that bank failures are caused by the declines in general economic activity, whether the declines are national or regional.

Therefore, although there are economic and social costs associated with individual bank failures, these costs do not appear to be significantly larger than those for other firms. As Saunders and Walter (1987) point out, the costs of individual bank failures are much different from the costs to the economy from a collapse of the banking system, and those who argue that bank failures have high social costs often fail to recognize the difference. Thus, the argument that banks are special because of social externalities associated with their failures does not appear to be valid.

***Bank Runs and Stability*** Opponents of market-based banking reforms argue that the very nature of bank and thrift deposit liabilities (that is, they are redeemable at par on demand) makes free-market banking systems inherently unstable.[9] They argue that, without federal deposit guarantees, the banking system is subject to contagious bank runs. As the argument goes, deposit insurance removes or reduces the incentives for bank runs and thus stabilizes the banking system. Regulation, in turn, is needed to protect the federal deposit insurance agency, and ultimately the taxpayer, from the moral hazard embedded in federal deposit guarantees.[10]

To analyze this claim of instability, one needs to distinguish between rational and irrational bank runs. Kaufman (1988) argues that a rational bank run is one that occurs because depositors have good information that their depository institution has (or may) become insolvent. This type of run should not be contagious and, in fact, is the method the market uses to weed out the weak institutions. Because rational bank runs are essentially a market-driven closure rule, they act as a form of market discipline on bank management and shareholders (Benston and Kaufman, 1986).

Kaufman (1988) describes an *irrational* bank run as one that occurs because poorly informed depositors mistakenly believe that their depository institution has (or may) become insolvent. Institutions that are truly solvent can stop an irrational run by demonstrating their solvency. Although these runs theoretically could be contagious, it is unlikely that they would be (except, possibly, to other insolvent institutions) because other banks and thrifts have incentives to provide liquidity to solvent institutions experiencing runs. In fact, private bank clearinghouses performed this function prior to the creation of the Fed (Gorton and Mullineaux, 1987).

Moreover, a properly functioning lender of last resort can prevent irrational bank runs from becoming systemic bank runs by providing liquidity to solvent institutions experiencing runs. In so doing, the central bank further relieves pressures on solvent institutions, while removing any potentially destabilizing effects of irrational bank runs, yet without precluding rational bank runs on insolvent institutions (Meltzer, 1986) and Schwartz (1987, 1988). One should note that bank runs were historically a statewide or systemic problem primarily in unit banking systems, where regional and therefore industry diversification of assets was artificially restricted by regulations. Thus, irrational bank runs may simply be an unintended side effect of branching restrictions, rather than a natural source of instability in free-market banking systems.

By suppressing or overriding market closure mechanisms, federal deposit insurance has reduced or removed one of the self-correcting forces that ensures the efficiency and long-run stability of banking markets. Kane (1985, ch. 3) and Thomson (1986, 1989) argue that the way federal deposit insurance is priced and administered results in government subsidy of the risks undertaken by insured banks and thrifts. This, in turn, leads to perverse incentives for risk taking by insured institutions and decreases the stability of the financial system.

***Moral Hazard and Regulation*** To mitigate the moral hazard (that is, the incentives for the insured to increase their risk in order to maximize the combined value of their equity and deposit guarantees) intrinsic in deposit insurance guarantees, strict regulations were adopted that limited the scope of activities in which banks could participate and the types of products (both asset and liability) they could offer. In other words, regulations were used as a tax to offset the perverse effects of the subsidy inherent in federal deposit insurance (Buser et al., 1981). These regulations sought to alleviate the moral hazard problem by removing a large degree of management and shareholder discretion in the operation of depository institutions.

An unintended side effect has been that these regulations have made managers and shareholders less responsive to market incentives and have reduced the flow of capital from poorly managed institutions to well-managed ones (because all institutions are equally insured). This system most assuredly resulted in fewer bank failures from the mid-1930s through the late 1970s, but did so at the expense of the long-run stability of the financial system, as evidenced by the escalation of problems in the banking and thrift industries in the 1980s.[11] The movement of capital from marginal firms in an industry to the strongest and best-managed firms is another of the self-corrective forces that would ensure the long-run stability of our banking system.

While regulation may reduce the moral hazard associated with deposit guarantees, Kane (1988b, 1989b) shows that principal–agent problems cause other forms of moral hazard to arise.[12] In the principal–agent framework, bank and thrift regulatory agencies are viewed as self-maximizing bureaucracies whose primary task is to act as the agent for taxpayers to ensure a safe and sound banking system and to minimize the taxpayer's exposure to loss. In addition, regulators must cater to a political clientele who are intermediate or competing principals. Furthermore, regulators are sometimes motivated by their own self-interest.[13]

In Kane's (1989e) principal–agent framework, political pressures and self-interest considerations create perverse incentives for regulators that may cause them to "paper over" emerging problems in an industry instead of dealing with them early and forcefully. They hope that, by buying time to deal with each crisis, the ultimate cost of resolving it will be smaller. Policies such as "too big to let fail," capital forbearance programs, and the adoption of regulatory accounting principles (RAP) for thrifts are some of the more visible manifestations of the problem (Kane, 1989b).

***Regulation and Stability*** Government-regulated systems, such as those operative in our banking and thrift industries, attempt to achieve stability by setting up a delicate and complex web of regulatory taxes and subsidies. In the case of banks, regulation has attempted to achieve stability by limiting competition between banks and nonbank financial institutions, both through prohibitions on activities banks can engage in (Glass–Steagall restrictions) and by subsidizing the banking system (through federal deposit insurance). Regulators are charged with the task of stabilizing the banking system by delivering the optimum mix of regulatory subsidies and taxes.

As Kane (1985, ch. 5) points out, the ability of regulators to deliver an optimum mix of regulatory taxes and subsidies becomes increasingly difficult over time as competitive forces in financial markets gradually erode existing regulations and alter the size and mix of regulatory taxes and subsidies.[14] Existing regulations often are weakened, or are made completely inappropriate, or become counterproductive. In addition, subsidies inherent in fixed-rate deposit insurance, access to discount-window credit, and free finality of payments over the Federal Reserve's wire transfer system increase in size. This effect is accentuated by exogenous shocks to the financial system, such as surges of inflation or technological changes.

These market-driven changes in our system of regulatory taxes and subsidies are the beginning of the ongoing process of regulation, market avoidance, and reregulation: a process that Kane (1977, 1988a) calls the "regulatory dialectic." The response of government-regulated systems to market-driven changes in the size and mix of regulatory taxes and subsidies is to accommodate the shocks. Changes to the regulatory structure tend to lag developments in the marketplace and are typically piecemeal, usually with the purpose of either validating market innovations or reregulating areas where market forces have made existing regulations obsolete.[15] This may include regulations designed to limit or prohibit new activities that are deemed too risky (for example, thrifts' investments in high-yield bonds), the removal of regulations that are unenforceable or politically costly to continue (for example, deposit-rate ceilings), or the modification of existing regulations (for example, risk-based capital standards for banks and RAP accounting standards for thrifts).

Essentially, the regulatory response is to deal with the symptoms of a shock without making the structural adjustments necessary to allow the banking system to adjust fully. This often results in policies aimed at protecting the regulator's weakest client firms at the expense of the efficient firms in the industry and, hence, the stability of the banking system. An example is the capital forbearance policies adopted by both the thrift and bank regulators during the 1980s (Barth and Bradley, 1989, table 3; Caliguire and Thomson, 1987; and Thomson, 1987a). Moreover, regulatory interventions in the banking system tend to thwart market-oriented forces often enough that normal market outcomes are difficult to achieve within the limited scope of activities that the regulators are willing to permit. Consequently, increased subsidies from the public purse become necessary to permit regulated entities to achieve the returns on equity that enable them to remain competitive. This system minimizes the number of failures of individual, regulated firms in the short term, but increases the efficiency loss and the aggregate public exposure to loss in the long term. Kane (1989b) points to the current thrift debacle as a vivid example of this type or regulatory behavior.

The result is a set of financial institutions that are special and unique only in terms of the regulatory taxes and subsidies to which they are subject. In other words, it is the restrictions on organizational form, where they can do business, and what businesses they can be in, coupled with access to federal deposit guarantees, to the Federal Reserve's discount window, and to the Federal Reserve-operated payments system that make depository institutions special. Additionally, banks and thrifts are less efficient and less able to adapt to changes in the economy than they would be if they were more subject to market incentives, and the resulting banking system is less stable in the long run than one governed by market principles.

## II. Market-oriented reforms

The alternative to increased regulation is a system of reforms that relies more heavily on market forces to shape the structure of the financial services industry.[16] Market-oriented reforms, such as a reduction in the scale and scope of the federal safety net, improved information systems (including the adoption of a timely, solvency-based closure rule for banks and thrifts), would increase the efficiency and long-run stability of the banking system. Rather than blocking or attempting to circumvent market forces, these reforms would rely on market forces to reestablish the tradeoff between risk and returns in financial services, so that those who benefit from the gains of risky strategies would also bear the losses when these strategies did not pan out. Therefore, there would be less of a need for regulations, as distinct from reliance on market forces, to protect the public purse from losses.

In its most extreme form, market-oriented reforms would establish a free-market banking system with no remaining vestiges of the federal safety net (discount-window access, deposit insurance, and direct access to the Federal Reserve payments system). The market would determine the structure and scope of financial intermediaries' activities, and market-determined closure rules would prevail. The role of the government would be limited to collecting and disseminating information and to enforcing property rights by resolving contractual disputes. However, reforms to the federal safety net necessary for a free-market banking system are unlikely to be implemented. Kane (1987), echoing Downs (1957), argues that subsidies, like those embodied in the financial safety net, tend to become viewed as entitlements by the subsidized industry. Industry trade associations and other special interest groups lobby Congress vigorously to protect their narrow interests, while society's interests are sufficiently diffuse that they cannot defeat special interest lobbies.

One caveat to note is that the following proposed reforms have transitional or "switching" costs that must be dealt with. This is especially true of deposit-insurance reforms. These transitional costs would be less of a problem if the reforms were applied to an industry that is already healthy. Obviously, this is not the case for either our banking industry or the thrift industry.

It must be recognized that the transitional costs, which include the cost of recapitalizing, reorganizing, or closing insolvent and unsound institutions, cannot be avoided forever regardless of whether reforms are adopted. Moreover, as demonstrated so vividly by the thrift crisis, the sooner these costs are dealt with, the smaller they are likely to be (Kane, 1989b, ch.3; Barth and Bradley, 1989). Therefore, the realization of the switching costs should not be seen as an impediment to reform, but rather as an important first step in implementing any set of reforms. FIRREA represents a partial realization of these switching costs; however, considerably more needs to be done before a comprehensive package of deposit insurance and regulatory reforms can be implemented.

***Deposit-Insurance Reform*** Restoring market discipline as an effective constraint on bank and thrift activities is the main purpose of deposit-insurance reform. The coverage and pricing of federal deposit guarantees must be changed so that the federal bank and thrift insurance funds do not subsidize risk in the financial system.

To restore market discipline to banking, federal deposit insurance coverages must be limited, and remaining coverage must be correctly priced.[17] At the very least, deposit insurance should be cut back to strict observance of the current statutory limit of $100,000. Furthermore, this limit should be applied per depositor, rather than to each insured deposit account. Coverage should not be extended in any circumstance to explicitly uninsured depositors, unsecured creditors, or stockholders of banks and their parent holding companies. In other words, the failures of all insured institutions should be handled in a manner that reduces the regulators' and insurers' incentives to minimize insured deposit payouts while maximizing long-term exposures to uninsured claims.

Kane (1985, ch. 6) proposes that strict enforcement of the current limit would require some changes to the failure resolution policies of the FDIC and might require statutory constraints on the authority of the FDIC to rescue large insolvent financial institutions.[18] These constraints would preclude the use of failure-resolution techniques such as open-bank assistance and purchase-and-assumption transactions, which provide de facto coverage to de jure uninsured claimants.[19] Such changes would give the "too big to let fail" doctrine the decent burial it deserves and would restore some measure of market discipline to banking.

However, truly to reap the benefits of deposit-insurance reform, the statutory limits on coverage should be reduced to levels significantly below the current $100,000 ceiling. Kane (1986) and Thomson and Todd (1990) suggest that a reduction in the limit from $100,000 to $10,000 (indexed to the Consumer Price Index) would be consistent with a social desire to provide a safe haven for the savings and transaction balances of small savers while reestablishing large depositors as a source of discipline on banks' risk taking. Thomson and Todd (1990) point out that a $10,000 ceiling exceeds the average (arithmetic mean) insured deposit account in both banks and thrifts (about $8,000) and that depositors with balances in excess of $10,000 already have access to U.S. Treasury bills, which are close substitutes for federally guaranteed bank deposits.

In addition to lowering the insured deposit ceiling, several authors have suggested that a coinsurance feature could be added for additional deposit balances above the full-insurance level.[20] For example, if the deposit insurance ceiling were set at $10,000, the FDIC could provide 90 percent coverage for balances between $10,000 and $50,000 and 70 percent coverage for balances in excess of $50,000. Other, apparently more drastic, variations on this theme are possible; the original (1933) interim deposit insurance scheme provided for only 50 percent coverage for balances in excess of $50,000, for example. Presumably, if mandatory closure rules were adopted, private insurance markets would develop to provide coverage for the coinsurance deductible portion of the deposit for those depositors who desired full protection.

An important feature of coinsurance is that it would establish minimum recoveries on deposit balances in excess of the fully insured limit. This would remove an important constraint on the FDIC's ability to resolve bank failures quickly without extending forbearances to uninsured depositors. With coinsurance, the federal deposit guarantor would not need to estimate in advance the losses to the uninsured depositors. It would simply apply the coinsurance haircut to depositors' balances. If the institution's total losses did not exceed the haircut amount, the receiver would rebate to the uninsured depositors their share of the difference. Thus, coinsurance would alleviate financial hardship for uninsured depositors by paying them a predetermined portion of their deposits up front.

***The Role of the Discount Window*** For deposit-insurance reform to be truly effective, the Federal Reserve should avoid using its discount window to support the solvency (capital replacement) of, or to delay the closing of, an insolvent bank or thrift (Kane, 1987). Benston et al. maintain that solvency support or capital replacement lending by Federal Reserve Banks is simply another way for regulators to extend de facto guarantees to uninsured depositors and other creditors of depository institutions: it provides an opportunity for those claimants to liquidate their claims at par, thereby increasing the ultimate cost (loss upon liquidation) to either the lender of last resort, the deposit insurance fund, or the receiver.

This loss arises because, if good assets are pledged to the lender of last resort to fund early redemption at par of some (usually the largest) uninsured claims, then the pool of good assets remaining to cover eventual payments to insured depositors and other uninsured claimants is reduced. The effect of this practice is analogous to the effect of a leveraged buyout (LBO) announcement on outstanding corporate bonds of the LBO target: the pool of assets available to cover outstanding bonded debt service is reduced to cover LBO debt service. Rating agencies have no choice but to downgrade outstanding bond issues, and those bonds decline in secondary market value.

To preserve the use of the discount window for purposes other than *liquidity* support for solvent institutions (the originally intended and the only theoretically sound purpose, according to Todd, 1988a), the following guidelines should be followed. First, the discount window should be available only to demonstrably solvent institutions, with the loans fully secured by sound and fairly evaluated collateral. Heavy and frequent borrowers at the window should be required to demonstrate their solvency, and loans should not be extended or renewed once an institution is determined to be insolvent.

Second, discount-window advances should be made at unsubsidized rates with a penalty for loans made to heavy or frequent borrowers. Finally, the discount window should not be seen as a substitute for the maintenance of a reasonable amount of liquidity by even solvent financial institutions, except in extraordinary circumstances.

*Information and Market-Value Accounting* Kane (1989b, ch. 6) asserts that better information systems are needed to increase the effectiveness of both government regulation and market-oriented regulation of depository institutions. Currently, our regulatory system suppresses information about depository institutions, which results in information flows to market participants that are both noisy and "lumpy."[21] Noisy and lumpy information flows do not allow markets to make several small corrective adjustments as new information comes in: instead, they cause the market to make larger and more dramatic adjustments as market participants attempt to process new information. This, in turn, leads to the appearance that markets overreact to new information as it arrives.

To improve the informational efficiency of markets, several authors have advocated the use of market-value accounting (Kane, 1985, chs. 5 and 6, 1987, 1988a; Benston et al., 1986, ch. 8; Benston et al., 1989; Benston and Kaufman, 1988). Traditional accounting systems like GAAP (generally accepted accounting principles) and RAP result in unnecessary noise in the information system because they allow firms to carry assets and liabilities at their par value (usually, historical cost) and do not reflect the subsequent changes in their market value. Therefore, Thomson (1987a) argues that GAAP and RAP may not be good measures of the true solvency of a bank or thrift, that both GAAP and RAP tend to be high-biased measures of solvency problems, and that the degree of error in GAAP and RAP measures increases as solvency deteriorates.

Berger et al. (1989) correctly point out that market-value accounting systems themselves are not perfect, as there are many assets and liabilities on the balance sheets of banks and thrifts for which estimates of market value are not readily available. However, Benston and Kaufman (1988) and Mengle (1989) argue that it is possible to adjust assets and liability values for changes in interest rates and that, as markets develop for securitized bank assets, the ability to make reasonable, market-based adjustments to the value of similar assets in bank portfolios increases. Market-value accounting is not a panacea and still results in noisy information streams. Nonetheless, it is a less noisy information stream than the one that flows from both GAAP and RAP. Over time, market-value accounting should become less noisy as financial markets evolve.

In addition to the use of market-value accounting, Benston et al. (1986, ch. 7) suggest that the regulatory community move from suppression to timely dissemination of information. FIRREA takes an important step in this direction as it mandates that cease-and-desist orders, supervisory agreements, and other regulatory actions are to be published by the appropriate supervisory agency. Hoskins (1989) goes even further in advocating that banks and thrifts should have the right to release their examination ratings and report to the public.[22] Finally, annual audits by independent accounting firms should be required for all financial institutions. For small, well-capitalized institutions for whom this rule could prove to be a financial hardship (for example, consolidated entities with less than $100 million in assets), outside audits could be required only every second or third year.

Both of these changes in the current information system would increase the effectiveness and efficiency of market-based oversight of depository institutions and would increase the stability of the financial system. Markets would be better able to discriminate among financial institutions and to force corrective action much sooner than is currently possible, thereby reducing the probability of bank runs (Pennacchi, 1987). Consequently, systemic stability would be improved, as the size and the volatility of the market reaction would be smaller. Better information systems also would reduce the ability of regulators to conceal problems in the financial services industry as they emerged.

***Deregulation and Timely Closure of Insolvent Institutions*** Under a market-based incentive system, the role for supervision and regulation would be radically different. Regulators would be assigned the task of enforcing a few basic rules (for example, minimum capital requirements, periodic reporting and public disclosure requirements, outside audits, and market-value accounting), and monitoring efforts would be directed at ensuring that those rules were observed. Any individual or financial institution able to meet these minimum guidelines would be granted a bank charter. Institutions that failed to meet these guidelines would be required either to close or to adjust their operations to comply.[23]

This approach, proposed by Benston and Kaufman (1988) and Benston et al. (1989), recognizes that a bank's management has the skills, information, and incentives to make optimum use of its resources, while bank regulators do not. As long as supervisors tolerated failure (either through market closure or a solvency-based closure rule), any financial service or activity could be performed by any financial institution, as long as it could do so within the minimum operation guidelines.

Unlike the current approach toward bank regulation, which often seeks to suppress market forces, this approach attempts to complement and enhance market discipline. Allowing managers and stockholders to make the decisions governing the operation of their institution, including scope of activity and institutional structure, would make them more responsive to market incentives. The perverse incentives currently facing managers and owners of weak and barely solvent institutions would be neutralized by supervisory interference as the condition of the institution deteriorated.[24] The most extreme case of supervisory interference would be closure or forced sale of institutions that deteriorated to the point where they violated the minimum operating standards.

This approach would lead to a more efficient and stable financial system than pure regulation. Fewer resources would be expended in the enforcement and evasion of outdated rules by regulators and regulatees, respectively, and those who took the risks would bear the consequences of those decisions. Organization forms and activities would be dictated by markets.

Since market forces would be allowed to operate unfettered, efficiency and stability would be enhanced: private capital would be reallocated by market forces to the best-managed institutions and away from the weak and poorly managed ones, which would be allowed to fail. Timely release of information to markets under the supervisory approach would allow financial distress in an institution to be detected more quickly, constraining the growth of marginally solvent and insolvent institutions. Market recognition of financial distress would lead to an orderly outflow of funds and an increase in the cost of funds for troubled institutions, which, in turn, would lead to more orderly and timely closure of insolvent institutions and a reduction in their ultimate failure-resolution costs.

## III. Conclusion

At the August 9, 1989, signing ceremony for FIRREA, President Bush proclaimed, "We will keep the federal deposit insurance system solvent and help serve those millions of small savers who make America great" while "ensuring the taxpayers' interests will always come first."[25] Accomplishing both of these objectives will require great effort in any case, but might be impossible without market-oriented reforms of the financial structure such as those described here.

Moreover, as Kane (1989c, 1989e) argues, the Bush plan from which FIRREA evolved was not based on a comprehensive theory of how the losses in the thrift industry occurred and were allowed to grow so large. Consequently, because the Bush plan (and, by inference, FIRREA) fails to correct the incentive-incompatibility problems in the current deposit-insurance contract that caused the current thrift crisis, there is a high probability that taxpayers will be faced with another deposit-insurance crisis in the near future.

It is hoped that the study of federal deposit insurance mandated by FIRREA, and currently under way at the U.S. Treasury Department, will address the fundamental structural flaws in the federal safety net and, in particular, in federal deposit insurance. The purpose of any reforms to the federal safety net and to our system of bank regulation should be to increase the efficiency and long-run stability of the banking system while protecting the public from financial loss. The market-oriented reforms put forth in this paper would go a long way toward achieving these goals.[26]

## Notes

1. Reform proposals that rely on increased government regulation include Corrigan (1987) and Keehn (1989). These authors propose the use of regulation as a substitute for market discipline, and hence reforms to the federal safety net. Corrigan and Keehn would allow bank holding companies to engage in virtually any financial activity so long as there is legal separation between the nonbanking activities and the insured banks in the holding company. In principle, this would capture some of the efficiencies of an integrated financial services industry without increasing the size and scope of the safety net. However, Kane's (1989b) application of principal-agent theory to regulatory agencies calls into question the substitutability of regulation and market discipline.

2. Proposals that rely on increased market discipline include Cates (1989), Ely (1985, 1989), Kane (1983, 1985, 1986), Benston et al. (1986, ch. 9), Benston and Kaufman (1988), the Federal Reserve Bank of Minneapolis (1988), Hoskins (1989), Thomson and Todd (1990), and Wall (1989).

3. For an opposing view, see Campbell and Minsky (1987), Guttentag and Herring (1986, 1988), and Randall (1989).

4. The trade-off between efficiency and stability in the short run can occur only when there are no principal-agent problems associated with bank regulation or, in other words, when bank regulatory are "faithful" agents as defined by Kane (1989b). Otherwise, the trade-off between efficiency and stability would not hold even in the short run. The author thanks Edward Kane for this analysis.

5. For a comprehensive look at the arguments and evidence as to why banks are not special, and a list of articles on the subject, see Saunders and Walter (1987).

6. Payments-system concerns are the motivation for the safe-bank proposals of Litan (1987) and others.

7. Although loss rates have ranges as much as 50 percent of assets in small-bank failures, the failure of these banks is not a threat to the payments system.

8. Lending with a haircut refers to the practice of making short-term collateralized loans for less than the estimated market value of the collateral. That is, the lender estimates the value of the collateral and then "takes a little off the top." This is usually done when the market value of the collateral is measured with uncertainty.

9. The theoretical foundation for this viewpoint is found in Diamond and Dybvig (1983). In their model of a simple economy, Diamond and Dybvig find that government deposit insurance improves social welfare by removing the possibility of systemic bank runs. However, McCulloch and Yu (1989) show that private contracts could perform the same function as deposit insurance in the Diamond and Dybvig world. Furthermore, McCulloch and Yu find that neither the private contracts nor government deposit insurance can improve social welfare in the Diamond and Dybvig world if private capital markets exist outside the official banking sector.

10. For a detailed discussion of bank runs and their positive implications for economic stability, see Kaufman (1988).

11. Schwartz (1987, 1988) argues that the sixty years of relative stability in our financial system were due to price stability and not to either deposit insurance of bank regulation. She argues that one cost of price-level instability is troubled depository institutions, regardless of whether they are regulated.

12. For a general discussion of agency costs and principal-agent problems and their application in corporate finance, see Jensen and Meckling (1976) and Jensen and Smith (1985).

13. Of course, throughout this paper, it is assumed that all politicians and bureaucrats firmly believe that their actions are motivated exclusively by the public interest. The analysis provided here emphatically does *not* accuse public servants of intentionally acting in bad faith but, rather, assumes that they do not always articulate or understand their real motives.

14. Regulatory subsidies arise because banks and thrifts are not charged the fair value of the risk-bearing services provided to them by the federal safety net. Regulatory taxes represent the reduction in the value of a bank or thrift due to constraints placed on its profit-maximizing function through regulation.

15. The difference between the market and regulatory adjustment process is equivalent to the difference in exchange-rate adjustments under floating and fixed exchange rates. Under floating exchange rates, supply and demand factors in markets cause nearly continual adjustment of the exchange rate. Under a fixed-exchange-rate regime, the official exchange rate is maintained for long periods of time, with large adjustments made periodically.

16. This section draws heavily on Benston et al. (1986), Benston and Kaufman (1988), and Kane (1985, 1986, 1987, 1989a, 1989b, 1989c, 1989d).

17. Merton (1977, 1978) shows how option pricing can be used to model and value deposit guarantees. Using Merton's results, Thomson (1987b) shows how information regarding the market prices of uninsured and partially insured deposits can be used to construct risk-based deposit-insurance premiums for insured deposit balances. Ronn and Verma (1986) show how option pricing can be used to derive estimates on the value of deposit insurance using stock-market data and different closure assumptions.

18. For expressions of skepticism that regulators would allow big banks to fail, even if explicit deposit-insurance coverage were reduced or, in advance, said to be strictly enforced, see Trigaux (1989) and Passell (1989).

19. The failure-resolution policies of the FDIC are the process through which implicit guarantees are issued to uninsured depositors, general creditors, subordinated creditors, and even stockholders. For a discussion of FDIC failure-resolution policies, see Benston et al. (1986, ch. 4), Caliguire and Thomson (1987), Kane (1985, ch. 2), and Todd (1988b).

20. Coinsurance was a feature in the original FDIC Act (see Todd, 1988a). Kane (1983) suggested coinsurance as part of a six-point deposit-insurance reform proposal. Baer (1985) sug-

gested it as part of a proposal for mixed private and public coverage of deposits. More recently, Cates (1989), the Federal Reserve Bank of Minneapolis (1988), and the Federal Reserve Bank of Cleveland (Hoskins, 1989) have embraced the concept of coinsurance.

21. The information flows are lumpy in the sense that large amounts of information are arriving at discrete intervals, as opposed to smaller amounts of information arriving nearly continuously.

22. Mandatory release of examination ratings and reports by the regulators is a sufficient, but not necessary, condition for the timely dissemination of information about the condition of insured institutions. If banks and thrifts are allowed to release their examination ratings and reports to the public, then institutions with high ratings would have incentives to signal their condition to the market.

23. Prior to 1933, the solvency test applied in bank closing cases was *either* incapacity to pay obligations as they matured or balance-sheet insolvency. Since then, the Office of the Comptroller of Currency has tended to use *only* the former "maturing obligations" test, although the statutory basis for the latter "balance-sheet" test remains intact. Compare 12 U.S.C. Section 191 (balance-sheet or maturing obligations) with Section 91 (usually interpreted as "maturing obligations" only).

24. The Benston and Kaufman (1988) and Benston et al. (1989) proposals set up different trigger points for increasing supervisory interference as the institution slides towards insolvency and allows regulators to close the institution before it becomes insolvent.

25. See "Bush Remarks: 'First Critical Test' Has Been Passed," *American Banker,* August 10, 1989, p. 4.

26. The reforms set forth in this paper are aimed at increasing market discipline primarily through increased depositor and stockholder discipline on insured banks and thrifts. Another way to increase market discipline on banks is through the use of subordinated debt (see Baer, 1985; Benston et al., 1986, ch. 7; and Wall, 1989) and surety bonds (see Kane, 1987). For conflicting evidence on the ability of subordinated-debt holders to discipline bank risk taking see Avery et al. (1988) and Gorton and Santomero (1990). Ely (1985, 1989) would use banks to discipline each other through a system of cross-guarantees of their liabilities.

HENRY KAUFMAN

# *How Treasury's Reform Could Hurt Free Enterprise*

*The bank reform proposals will alter our economic and financial system for the worse. They open a back door to an insidious industrial policy, creating a financial-industrial-government elite that could lead to a corporatist state.*

The U.S. Treasury has recently put forth a series of proposals to modernize our financial system. Although I certainly agree with the Treasury's stated goal to devise a regulatory environment that will help assure the long-term health of deposit institutions, I have some differences with their recommendations.

Over the last few years of severe financial adjustments, deposit institutions—both commercial banks and thrifts—have experienced great trauma. Some institutions have failed. Many others are still short of capital, have questionable assets, and are experiencing losses. A few commentators assert that deposit institutions as a class of financial intermediary have no future—that in some sense they will become financial dinosaurs.

Of course, extrapolating trends from the worst decade for banking since the 1930s is bound to produce dour expectations. But that exercise is essentially backward looking. It doesn't take into consideration several prospective developments that will be more favorable for deposit institutions.

## Positive developments

For one, the securitization of corporate debt, which did much to bypass deposit institutions, will probably taper off because the illusions created by this approach have now been exposed. In the heyday of the 1980s it seemed that virtually all debt, regardless of credit quality, could be transformed from nonmarketable to marketable form, be deemed highly liquid, and trade in an active secondary market within narrow spreads between bid and asked quotations. In the crevices of financial thinking of some participants at the time grew the astonishing misconception that the risks in holding high-risk debt were thus reduced, that an obligation could be quickly sold if the credit quality of the issuer deteriorated abruptly, and that somehow the obligation would bounce around in the market with no one having to bear a significant loss. This illusion has now been pierced,

HENRY KAUFMAN is President of Henry Kaufman and Company, Inc. This article is based on a speech given at the Bank & Financial Association's 21st Annual Banking Symposium, March 27, 1991. Reprinted from *Challenge,* May–June 1991, pp. 4–10.

and few junk issuers have access to the market.

The lesson is that securitization can flourish only where credit quality is either high or improving noticeably. This is not now the case in the United States. Last year only 52 percent of all corporate bonds outstanding had a credit rating of "A" or better, as compared to 72 percent in 1982 and 83 percent in 1972. That ratio is bound to fall further as the recession proceeds, and it will take some years to reverse the process. The implication is that more business financing will have to be consummated directly with financial intermediaries, and strong deposit institutions will have first choice when it comes to short and medium-term lending to the better credits.

Not all forms of securitization, however, weaken the competitive position of deposit institutions. For instance, the securitization of credit-card receivables provides a useful alternative financing technique for card issuers. More important, both commercial banks and thrifts should continue to benefit from the securitization of mortgages. Most of them can compete successfully in one, two, or even all three aspects of mortgage finance—origination, servicing, and holding mortgages as investments.

## Nonbanks no substitutes for banks

Taken together, the likely changes in market conditions over the next several years will tend to arrest the decline in market share of deposit institutions. But from a broader, conceptual viewpoint, I would make a stronger contention. I maintain that a well-functioning group of deposit institutions is *indispensable* for the well-being of our economy, because other financial intermediaries do not have the capability to replace them.

Consider the key features of other major institutional groups. Deposit institutions have about $5 trillion in assets. The next largest financial intermediaries, the insurance companies, have assets amounting to nearly $2 trillion, followed by pension and retirement funds with $1.9 trillion. Far behind are finance companies with $600 billion and open-end mutual funds and money market funds with about $500 billion each.

Both insurance companies and pension and retirement funds are generally long-term lenders and investors, reflecting the longer-term nature of their liabilities. Today, quite a few insurance companies must limit their growth because of asset quality problems. Corporate pension and public retirement funds are, therefore, in a strong position to achieve attractive returns as long-term lenders and equity investors. However, corporate pension fund growth will slow in the 1990s. And the spectacular growth of the public retirement funds will probably not be repeated in this decade because the financial problems confronting many state and local governments will greatly retard their ability to increase public payrolls. In any event, banking-type assets are not a good fit with the liability side of pension funds.

In contrast, finance companies have posed a competitive challenge to deposit institutions. This has been primarily in business lending, rather than in consumer lending, where banks have actually gained market share in recent years because of the tax advantages of home equity loans. However, these incursions into business lending by finance companies will probably slow. Finance companies have experienced a drop in the credit quality of their loan portfolios. Some have substantial positions in highly leveraged transactions, including the large troubled loans. Quite a few finance companies, just like deposit institutions, have had their own credit ratings downgraded.

Money market funds, a direct competitor to deposit institutions, will probably continue to gain ground over the near term until the thrift crisis is finally resolved and the financial problems of some banks wane. But these shocks to confidence will be behind us within a few years. Capital positions and profitability of surviving institutions will improve and deposit insurance will remain in force. Money market funds must still limit the return they can offer to the returns available on high quality obligations in the short-term market. A slowing in the growth of the A1- and P1-rated paper market will pose a constraint, and greater risk taking by certain money market funds may create problems that will remind investors that they are holding uninsured funds.

## Fundamental issues

I do not mean to suggest here that deposit institutions and, for that matter, other financial intermediaries, will have smooth sailing into a new era of financial viability. Much will depend on how we restructure the financial system, on what philosophical underpinnings will guide these reforms, and on the path of the next economic recovery.

Whatever the philosophical basis for reform, one thing is clear: Government policy toward financial institutions should not return to the reckless approach of the last decade. It was grounded on the naive and ultimately incorrect belief that highly deregulated institutions would make a positive contribution to the economy, without introducing new elements of risk. The differences between the role of financial institutions and that of commerce were unfortunately forgotten. At the heart of these differences lies this reality: A highly competitive struggle among financial institutions involves the bidding for a limited volume of money and credit. That total amount of credit creation is controlled by the central bank. Because of the effective limit the Federal Reserve places on credit creation, extreme competition among financial institutions leads to financial cannibalism and speculative excesses that are to the detriment of all. We could, of course, accept this cannibalism with its attendant failures and let the powerful survive. But such thoroughgoing market discipline would not be without cost. It would put at risk private savings, precipitate financial shocks, and thus potentially unleash periodic economic and financial upheavals.

The alternative is, first, to recognize the special role of financial institutions and the defined limits within which they are required to habitate and, second, to impose sufficient guidelines for their correct behavior.

It is critical that the reformers of our financial system take into account the special role of deposit institutions. Banks, unlike any other institutional group, are at the heart of our payments mechanism, without which our credit structure and financial markets could not function. All other financial intermediaries are in actuality utterly dependent on this payments mechanism.

Deposit institutions are also the group through which the Federal Reserve directly carries out monetary policy. As a result, banks are subject to considerable cyclical swings in the size and composition of their assets and liabilities. Banks are required to maintain noninterest-bearing reserves at the Fed. The official safety net is thus generally restricted to the banking system. But, were it not for the unique role of deposit institutions in being the provider of credit to their customers, when other sources of credit dry up, the Federal Reserve would one way or another be forced to extend its reach into all kinds of private-sector institutions and transactions. Otherwise, the system would be subjected to the danger of a financial gridlock.

To be frank, in our new world of finance, quite a number of institutions and markets are piggybacking or getting a free ride from the banks. I could never understand why investors in money market mutual funds are permitted to write checks on their investments even though the funds do not have to maintain reserve requirements on the balances. Nonbank credit-card issuers could not function without banking. All credit instruments deemed to be highly liquid and marketable are in one way or another dependent on some sort of banking service. The central role of banking in recent years has been disdained by some observers who are dazzled by all the new credit instruments, trading practices, and the globalization of markets. But I have to wonder how any of them could flourish without the solid backstop of a sophisticated banking system.

This essentiality of banking needs to be recognized on many levels, from the pricing of banking services to the crafting of new legislation to modernize the regulatory structure covering financial institutions.

## The U.S. Treasury proposals

With this background in mind, let me evaluate the key features of the U.S. Treasury's proposals for improving the banking system.

*Nationwide Banking* The proposal to allow nationwide banking is long overdue. The fragmented banking arrangements in the United States reflect our historical financial roots but not what is required to finance the modern, interrelated commercial and financial society we now have. Today, there are no more significant pockets of captive savings. Our money and capital markets reach into all regions of the country and are closely linked internationally. Major credit cards and mutual funds are national and international in scope. Differences in financing terms among regions of our country have been systematically reduced through the securitization of debt and *de facto* national banking operations. It no longer makes any sense, if it ever did, to retain legal barricades whose only substantive effect is to hamper efficient deposit banking.

I would be opposed to nationwide banking if it would result in massive banking concentration that would establish monopolistic positions. But in the current circumstances that will not happen. This is because many of the very large money center banks are short of capital and still have a substantial volume of marginal assets to write down. They do not have the financial capacity to participate in banking consolidation. Therefore, what is likely to emerge is an increased number of large banks. That top tier will consist of the existing money market banks, together with the largest regional banks and thrift institutions that have already been rapidly expanding, and a new group of well-capitalized regional institutions that have not yet aggressively pursued acquisitions. A reduced, but still substantial, number of small and medium-sized deposit institutions with special competitive strengths will also survive and prosper alongside these nationwide franchise builders. In all, banking competition will remain lively, and banking concentration ratios will be far short of what they are today in such industrial countries as Canada, the United Kingdom, and Germany.

***Deposit Insurance Proposals*** Unlike the Treasury's nationwide banking proposal, I do not favor its proposal to limit the deposit insurance maximum to $100,000 per individual and $100,000 for retirement accounts. Nor would I ban deposit insurance on brokered deposits. These recommendations are defective. While superficially they would seem to limit the direct liability of the insurance fund, they leave open the key question: "At what cost?"

The costs are actually quite high. First, the proposal would reduce the value of the deposit-taking franchise just at a time when deposit institutions are under pressure to increase capital. Second, by continuing to support the "too big to fail" doctrine the Treasury is discriminating in favor of big banks, thus leaving the deposit insurance funds with enlarged indirect liabilities.

The issue here should not be confined to how *legally* to limit the liabilities of the deposit insurance fund but rather how to achieve safe and sound banking practices that will over time minimize the need to draw on the insurance fund. The Treasury's position is an awkward attempt at compromise in the long-running debate over how to discipline banks—through the marketplace or through regulations. Deposit insurance obviates most efforts at market discipline. Small depositors are protected and thus do not evaluate the soundness of their banks. Large depositors have the ability to distinguish between sound and questionable banks, but the "too big to fail" doctrine protects them and thus dilutes market discipline. Large depositors, therefore, in big banks are protected and only large depositors in small banks that fail are sometimes hurt.

To reconcile this issue of government versus market discipline, I propose that all deposit institutions be rated—either by one of the private-sector bond rating agencies or by an official supervisory agency. To be eligible for full insurance coverage, deposit institutions would be required to maintain at least an AA rating. Falling below this rating would mean the loss of full insurance coverage twelve months later, unless the institution initiated remedial action prescribed by regulators. Phasing in the new deposit insurance eligibility requirements might take five years.

The benefits would be great. The too-big-to-fail doctrine could be scrapped, since all insured institutions would have to follow more conservative lending practices. Early intervention by the regulators in case of management failure would be encouraged, a proposition that the Treasury itself is supporting. And taxpayers wouldn't have to rescue overextended deposit insurance funds. Risky ventures would be undertaken by sophisticated investors who can weigh the risks and rewards and accept losses without a government bailout.

***New Financial Powers for Well-Capitalized Banks*** The Treasury's proposal to grant banks new powers has some questionable aspects. The government would allow well-capitalized banks to sell insurance and mutual funds, and it would permit bank subsidiaries to underwrite and trade stocks and bonds. The emphasis here seems to be on permitting this expanded activity so long as the institution is strongly capitalized. In other words, the government will sanction the activity if the financial integrity of the institution is assured.

This, however, is only one responsibility of the government. The other is to prevent harm arising out of financial conflicts of interest. This the Treasury proposal does not do. Institutions that are both lenders and investors, on the one hand, and underwriters and traders of securities, on the other, have an inherent conflict of interest. How can they possibly propose to maintain diligent objectivity on new offerings due for public distribution when concurrently they may have in their portfolios the debt or the equity of the issuer?

The Treasury's proposal neglects how such conflicts of interest contributed to the financial excesses of the 1980s. Many junk bonds were sold by investment banks with part of the proceeds going to repay a bridge loan granted by the same investment banker. Today many of these bonds sell at deep discounts and are of questionable value. These practices undermine the very essence of the role of financial institutions—objective credit judgments leading to the most productive and efficient distribution of capital. Just because an institution is well capitalized does not necessarily protect us against such abuses.

***Commercial Ownership of Banks***  The most subtle proposal, but the one with the most far-reaching consequences for the long term, is the government's plan to allow commercial and industrial corporations to own commercial banks. This will eventually alter our economic and financial system for the worse, because it will hurt free enterprise and lead to a corporatist state.

Over a period of time, the joining of industry and banking will produce mammoth entities. These combines will have a strong influence on the flow of credit and thus on business competition. A large corporation that controls a big bank will give in to the temptation to use it for extending credit to those who can benefit the whole organization. The captive bank will attract low-cost funds through insured deposits and will deploy them to finance retailers, jobbers, manufacturers, and individuals who further the distribution of the parent's products and services. The bank will be inclined to withhold credit from those who are, or could be, competitors to the parent corporation. Thus, the cornerstone of effective banking—independent credit decisions based on objective evaluation of creditworthiness—will be undermined.

*The merging of banking and commerce also will be detrimental for monetary policy for two reasons:*

- The first reason is that no matter how many times the authorities may say the opposite, in an emergency the safety net that now covers large banking institutions deemed to be "too-big-to-fail" will have to be extended to shield their parent corporations as well. Otherwise, the bank will inevitably be vulnerable to huge withdrawals of deposits.

Some may claim that this risk can be avoided through strict firewalls between a bank and its parent. That is naive. There are practically no benefits from a passive relationship between a bank and business corporation. Therefore, the only kind of linkage between a large corporation and a large bank that is likely to happen is an intimate one. Ultimately, the government will have little choice but to extend the safety net to the combined entity. Naturally, there will be a *quid pro quo*. Government will demand—and get—supervisory authority extending beyond the bank to the parent corporation.

- The second reason for the detrimental impact on monetary policy is that when large commercial firms control big banks, support for a steady antiinflationary monetary policy will wane. There is a basic difference between banking and industry. Banks are the channel through which the central bank tries to achieve its objectives. By contrast, business corporations are the targets. It is their profits that are restrained or enlarged through monetary policy. Consequently, it is in their nature to have more of an inflationary bias than independent financial institutions.

As for our long-term economic growth potential, the creation of giant banking-industrial combines will have numerous detrimental consequences. It will create a powerful self-perpetuating elite. It is folly to believe that government would stay aloof from this elite group. Through the back door will come an insidious form of "industrial policy."

This industrial-banking-governmental leadership group will become highly protective of existing organizations. For many corporations and very wealthy families, the emergence of a corporatist state in which there is an elitist control over the economy may be quite desirable. Economic inefficiencies can be covered up. Downside economic risk can be limited through the safety net.

However, for most Americans, this antigrowth and elite-managed industrial policy would incite envy and dull economic aspirations. Economic renewal and vitality would be retarded as our traditional treatment of healthy, free-wheeling markets gave way to discriminatory treatment of emerging businesses and the overall discouragement of market disciplines.

For the ordinary shareholder, the conglomeration of banking and business is another way of subverting the shareholder's role. If a corporation has sufficient excess cash to invest in a bank to control it, the better alternative would be to return that cash to the shareholders. They can then make their own decisions about whether to invest in a bank. This preferable alternative would encourage economic democracy rather than erode it.

***Regulatory Amalgamation***  The Treasury's proposal to simplify and centralize somewhat the regulatory structure for depository institutions is an important step in the right direction. Multiple official supervision has led to differences in reporting, examination, and accounting standards to the detriment of the safety and soundness of deposit institutions. It has also tended to focus legislative bodies on the activities of specific institutions without adequate regard for what impact that proposed legislation would have on the financial system as a whole.

The amalgamation of the Office of the Comptroller of the Currency and the Office of Thrift Supervision would tend to encourage a convergence of banking and thrift regulation, and that could lead to the issuance of a single banking charter. That would help in simplifying the regulatory structure.

However, the Treasury's proposal to split responsibility for the supervision of bank holding companies between the Federal Reserve and the Treasury is not well thought out. One of the few elements of today's regulatory structure that has clarity is the Federal Reserve's oversight of all bank holding companies. Dividing this responsibility, so that the Fed retains oversight of holding companies of state-chartered banks while moving oversight of holding companies of national banks over to the Treasury, will lead to needless disparities in regulatory treatment. The idea appears to be a political compromise without any apparent economic rationale behind it.

I believe that in today's world of complex and highly innovative institutions, the central bank can cope with the task of pursuing an effective monetary policy only if it has intimate knowledge of the workings and activities of banking institutions, especially those of the largest ones. Today that is possible, because of the Fed's oversight of bank holding companies. This intimate knowledge of the banking business would be partially obscured under the Treasury proposal.

My preference would be to centralize all deposit banking supervision under the Federal Reserve. After all, when banking institutions start to hemorrhage, the central bank is responsible for judging the risk to the system and the need to intervene as lender of last resort. This does not mean that other key agencies of government should play no role in the supervisory process. A new supervisory group should be established in which the Fed would hold a senior position while others such as the U.S. Treasury would be important members. Nevertheless, in this way, the link between monetary and supervisory performance would be clearly established and the official body most responsible for it—the Federal Reserve—could be held accountable.

***Strengthening the Role of Bank Capital*** Emphasizing the central role of capital for banking institutions, another feature of the Treasury's proposals, is as a general matter highly constructive. The Basle Agreement of 1988, however, is still the major policy initiative in this whole area. It set forth capital requirements based on differential asset risk and it limited asset growth for inadequately capitalized institutions. As a result, the basic prudential guidelines for growth and for the makeup of assets and liabilities are now in place.

Unfortunately, neither the Basle Agreement nor the proposals of the Treasury put forth capital requirements for other major financial institutions such as insurance companies, investment banks, securities dealers, finance companies, just to mention some. These institutions, therefore, are free to benefit from the tougher capital requirements imposed on banks. This is inequitable. In a highly integrated financial world, international agreement on uniform capital standards for large institutions in each institutional group—as well as uniform trading, reporting and accounting standards—is a necessary prerequisite if financial cannibalism and excesses are to be avoided.

Now the thrust of the Treasury's proposals is in a different direction: They offer the carrot rather than just the stick. That is, the proposals provide rewards for good behavior. Well-capitalized banks would be subject to more moderate supervision and allowed to expand the scope of their activities, while undercapitalized banks would be subject to more intrusive supervision and tough restrictions. This is a laudable approach, especially to the extent it will restrain weaker institutions. But as I have stressed earlier, allowing banks to diversify into new activities should not be based on capital capacity alone. Disappointingly, the Treasury has made no suggestions that would directly help to increase bank capital. In view of the volatility of markets and credit quality problems, deposit institutions should at a minimum be allowed to accumulate more reserves. In this connection, I have long urged that deposit institutions—and for that matter all of the major financial intermediaries—should value their assets at the lower of cost or market. This is a departure from some of the recent lax accounting standards, but it is not mark-to-market accounting, either. What it will do is enable deposit institutions to enlarge their capital by building up sizable valuation reserves, without tax consequence, when asset values rise. It would reward those who managed well and discipline those who did poorly.

Realistic and conservative accounting standards should be welcomed by everybody—bankers, government leaders, investors, and the public at large. They will strengthen the deposit institution, allowing it to move successfully through adverse economic conditions and enabling it to maintain steady credit standards for borrowers regardless of the immediate business climate. No one benefits from abrupt lurches from excessive credit availability to excessive credit denial.

Accounting fictions should never be reintroduced, not even to keep fragile institutions alive. In fact, keeping fragile institutions alive—whether through permissive accounting standards or through direct financial aid—is a major policy error, which ultimately produces perverse effects. By keeping uneconomic competitors afloat, the policy raises the costs of funds to healthy banks, lowers the rate of return on assets for healthy banks, depresses overall profitability in the banking business, and therefore greatly retards the building up of bank capital. It sacrifices healthy institutions (and the taxpayer) for the temporary relief of those institutions which have failed.

## Prospects

All in all, I feel that the 1990s will gradually and irregularly be an improving decade for deposit institutions. The reckless financial behavior of the 1980s is behind us, although the costs it imposed will be with us for a long time. The whole episode is leaving a salutary imprint on public attitudes and on our government. The financial buccaneers, who recklessly bid for funds to invest in weak assets, are in disrepute. Our official regulators and new legislation will tilt much more to closer supervision rather than toward laxity in order to limit future excesses. It was a close call, but the financial system has withstood the brunt of the damage and it has held.

For the economy, the debt legacy of the 1980s means that economic recovery over the next few years will probably be of below-cyclical proportions. This is the price that we have to pay to overcome the debt excesses of the past.

Nevertheless, a slow growth period will have many beneficial aspects. It will lay a solid foundation for a longer period of sustainable economic growth because inflationary pressures will not quickly reignite. Moderation of inflation will, in turn, encourage a further decline in interest rates. For deposit institutions, this would suggest the persistence of a positively sloped yield curve, a very helpful development for banking profits.

As for deposit institutions themselves, for the first time in the entire post–World War II period they will fall into two distinct groups. The one will be adequately capitalized, and the other will not. The well-capitalized group will have excellent opportunities to finance the new economic recovery, while the other group will be convalescing. Some of its weaker members will be liquidated.

As the speculative element in the marketplace is eliminated, the group of well-capitalized institutions will have improved control over pricing their services and over their costs. They will improve their profit margins, stabilize their earnings, and increase their share of markets. They will enjoy a better equity price for their shares and have access to both the public debt and equity markets. They will be able to finance growth and undertake some of the new powers that may become available. The other group, still convalescing and capital restrained, will have limited access to costly new debt and equity capital. The pressure on them to shrink or merge with financially stronger institutions will remain in force for some time.

This is the way it should be, anyway. Otherwise, financial sinners would dominate us all and prudence and integrity would have no reward.

ROBERT I. ADLER AND DOUGLAS E. FERGUSON

# *Bank Reform: Medicine Worse Than the Malady?*

*A cure for banking's ills will not result from limiting federal deposit insurance and allowing commercial banks to engage in investment banking. Such legislative "therapy" would further cripple the patient.*

The American banking system is, of course, ailing. Belatedly, after first ignoring the symptoms and then loudly protesting the discomfort, the administration and Congress are wrangling over measures intended to cure the sick patient. Some components of the proposed therapy, though, may threaten the health of the nation's financial system and, ultimately, the soundness of the American economy.

Two key elements in the administration's prescription pose particularly grave risks of severe side effects: the curtailment (some even suggest elimination) of federal deposit insurance; and granting commercial banks the authority to engage in investment banking. While a superficial rationale appears to provide a sugar coating for both pills, an analysis of the active ingredients reveals the potential toxicity.

## Alleged discipline of the marketplace

The proposal to reduce sharply or to eliminate the protection provided by the FDIC rests on the implicit premise that the insurance is itself to blame for the malady. In the view of some, it removes the "discipline of the marketplace" by eliminating the incentive for depositors to be selective regarding the financial strength of the institutions to which they entrust their funds. Insurance, though, is not the problem; that would be akin to blaming the messenger for the bad news. The fundamental source of the plague of bank failures is a credit problem. Far too many bankers have amply demonstrated their inability to discern and to manage properly the risk in their loan portfolios. They have virtually tumbled over each other in their rush to maintain or increase their market share and to expand their balance sheets as fast as, or faster than, their competitors. In the process, they eagerly extended loans to Latin American and other developing countries, hardly pausing to ask how much debt the recipient nations could bear; to speculative real estate development often without much

ROBERT I. ADLER, CFA, is Vice President and Senior Investment Officer of BHF Securities Corporation in New York. DOUGLAS E. FERGUSON, CFA, is President of Ferguson Investment Consultants, Inc., North Tarrytown, New York. Reprinted from *Challenge*, November–December 1991, pp. 51–55.

thought to the economic viability of each new project; and to leveraged buyouts, vastly underestimating the risk that a recession might impair operating cash flow or make it tougher to repay loans with the proceeds from divestitures.

In other words, bankers, like many speculators in securities or tulip bulbs, tend to jump on the latest fad, perhaps under the assumption that some greater fool will bail them out. After all, what is the more likely motivation for a credit committee to approve a highly risky loan: because the depositors are protected if it turns out to be a mistake? or because the year-end bonus will be bigger, or the stock options worth more, if the deal works out? The question virtually answers itself.

Given those circumstances, the target of the "discipline of the marketplace" doctrine is misplaced. The FDIC was designed not to protect any one bank or banker from the consequences of failed policy, bad luck, or even outright fraud. Rather, it was intended to shield the depositors who, notwithstanding the contentions of the most ardent free market advocates, are simply not equipped to evaluate the quality of loan portfolios, the mismatch between asset and liability durations, bogus accounting practices, or even the caliber of local (much less corporate headquarters) management. In fact, the recent past has provided ample evidence that even the so-called "pros" can be misled by the appearance of propriety in financial reports. For example, a major accounting firm had certified the financial statements of Reverend Jim Bakker's PTL just months before the scandal erupted; another had provided the audit of Charles Keating's Lincoln Savings & Loan upon which five U.S. senators relied when they went to bat for him with the regulators; and the financial press has all too often reported a sharp drop in the market price of a bank or S&L stock only after a surprise announcement of a huge write-off that even the knowledgeable and sophisticated banking industry analysts had failed to anticipate. If the pros missed it, how can the banking public be expected to find it?

Moreover, quite apart from whatever damage deposit insurance may or may not have done to the legacy of Adam Smith, it has been over the years a vital element in the public confidence in the American banking system. The sense of safety and stability was, in turn, a driving force in building the liquidity, and hence the availability of credit, that was a key source of the nation's economic growth. To weaken this perception of security might well lead not merely to a shifting of deposits from weaker to stronger banks, as some "marketplace discipline" proponents suggest, but to a significant withdrawal of funds from the system. The general public, if sufficiently worried and/or confused about the health of banks and concerned about the limitations (or absence) of federal deposit insurance, could revert to cookie jars or mattresses as repositories for cash. More ominously, foreigners might decide to dispense with the analytical process of selecting the "stronger" banks and instead choose other venues, such as Germany or Switzerland, for their deposits. That outflow of funds from the United States could seriously weaken the dollar, perhaps even eliminating its role as a reserve currency, with the possible consequences of severe inflation, soaring interest rates, and sharply curtailed credit availability.

The FDIC has served its purpose well. Its presence has served to avert a panic that, in the face of stunning problems, might easily have led to runs on the banking system. If it is now running out of funds, it is not because it has mismanaged its assets, but because the banks have mismanaged theirs. It could prove tragic if, in an attempt to restore the health of the banking system, the surgery were to be performed on the wrong organ. Let us not risk validating the old cliché: "The operation was a success, but the patient died."

## Alleged new income sources

Another potentially pernicious idea is the proposal to scrap the Glass–Steagall constraints and allow commercial banks to enter the investment banking business. In theory, this would create a new source of income for the banks, thereby improving profitability and bolstering capital, while making the American banking system more competitive in the global marketplace with the so-called universal banks in other nations.

The intent, of course, is admirable. Before rushing pell-mell along the road paved with such good intentions, though, one should carefully examine the possibility of very deep potholes.

First of all, it is by no means certain that the cycles inherent in commercial and investment banking will offset rather than compound each other. After all, investment bankers have, in the past, just as eagerly succumbed to the temptations of greed and to poor management of risk as have the commercial bankers. In an inherently risk-oriented business, they have not infrequently leveraged their firms to a high degree and committed their leveraged resources to investments of (at best) doubtful quality. And it should hardly come as a surprise that the most acute pressure on the investment bankers' profitability and asset values is felt in the depths of recession—just the point in the cycle when commercial banks, too, are being squeezed. It would be indeed ironic if, just when the commercial bank is compelled to boost its reserves for nonperforming loans, its newly consolidated investment banking subsidiary has to write down the value of the bridge loans it made as a merchant banker and/or take a major loss in its trading accounts or underwriting positions.

Secondly, investment banks as well as commercial banks may carry contingent liabilities and other off-balance-sheet risks. Once again, an unfavorable economic environment is likely to trigger these obligations, compounding rather than ameliorating the financial strains in a combined organization. Dr. Henry Kaufman, in a recent *Wall Street Journal* editorial page comment, warned that off-balance-sheet liabilities in the banking system may prove to be the source of the next "credit crunch," whenever that might be. To the extent that the nation's financial well-being is jeopardized by contingencies, that jeopardy would be intensified by bringing investment banks into the commercial banking fold.

Several influential voices, among them Mr. E. Gerald Corrigan, President of the Federal Reserve Bank of New York, have advocated granting investment banking authority to commercial banks but object to the combination of banks with industrial companies because of the implied protection of the federal "safety net," consisting, among other things, of deposit insurance and the privilege of borrowing directly from the Fed, for the commercial company associated with a bank. But if the safety net is implicit in the case of an industrial or other commercial enterprise, why wouldn't an investment bank be similarly entangled? After all, industrial companies deal essentially with their own funds and have only their own interests at stake. Investment banks, on the other hand, deal heavily in Wall Street's favorite commodity: other people's money. They thus bear a degree of fiduciary responsibility that doesn't pertain to industrial concerns. If there is any whiff of concern that an affiliated industrial company might somehow claim access to the safety net, shouldn't one be at least equally concerned about an affiliated investment bank with its thousands of clients and volatile credit needs?

There is yet another aspect of the combination that raises a threat to the integrity of the American financial system: the potential for breeches of confidentially. It is maintained by some that a so-called firewall would protect the capital markets from abuses stemming from misuse of proprietary information available to commercial bankers. But the permeability of such walls in the investment banking community has already been amply demonstrated; the potentially enormous rewards have far too often proved to be an irresistible temptation. Information has been leaked, or even bought and sold, by printers, lawyers, journalists, and others, as well as investment bankers. There have been blatant cases of fraud, with briefcases full of cash exchanged for proprietary information. If crooks are not deterred by the securities industry's well-known legal framework and the clear risk of severe civil and criminal penalties, what would stop the unscrupulous, the adventurous, the ignorant, or the merely greedy from attempting to profit from the sensitive information obtainable through banking relationships?

Furthermore, investors may have to contend with greater constraints on the free flow of perfectly legitimate information. There have already been too many instances—including the case involving Donald Trump that even earned headlines in the nonfinancial press—of pressures on security analysts to amend their opinions because of relationships between the employers and their corporate clients. Large commercial banks have a far greater number of corporate clients, with a much greater likelihood of overlap between their client base and the analytical coverage by the associated broker's research department. If the president or chief financial officer of a large company calls his or her friendly banker to express displeasure at the negative report issued by an analyst and threatens to take the account across the street to the competitor if nothing should be done about it, just how impregnable would that firewall be? And is the diminution of analytical objectivity not a significant cost, albeit probably not quantifiable, to the American financial markets?

Of course, the firewall might just work. Perhaps a method can be found to insulate completely the two businesses from each other: totally separated, nonconsolidated balance sheets, absolute separation of personnel at all levels, a prohibition on communication in either direction regarding companies or securities, and so on. But if the separation is so rigidly maintained, where would be the synergy? And if there is no synergy, why accept the risks of the consequences of failure?

In sum, it seems eminently possible that the profit cycles and other problems intrinsic to both industries might intensify rather than offset or ameliorate each other. Should that be the case, what remedy would the Fed, or Treasury, or Congress then have to find in order to rescue the system?

## Flawed international comparisons

The case for these far-reaching changes in the complexion of the American banking industry is often supported with an embarrassed admission that Japanese, German, and other foreign banks have far surpassed ours in sheer size, as measured in asset totals, and in corresponding global reach. The comparisons, though, are superficial at best and grossly erroneous at worst.

First of all, it should be noted that banks (along with many other branches of commerce) in these countries have for decades enjoyed the benefits of protected franchises. They have been shielded by governmentally supported policy not only from external competition, but even from the full effects of domestic competition. They are permitted to coordinate policies and practices among themselves and with their governments and/or central banks in a manner that would be a blatant violation of antitrust laws in the United States. In many cases they have built substantial equity positions in major corporations, assuring continuity of banking relationships without threatening profit margins with rate wars or other costly methods. Nor, in fact, have they felt impelled to develop innovative financial products; they, and their markets, were sufficiently well shielded by "administrative guidance" as well as the regulatory environment that they could grow and prosper with conventional instruments. Such a noncompetitive climate would rightly be opposed by American regulators and legislators.

More specifically, Japanese banks did not "benefit" from the absence of deposit insurance or their successes in the securities industry. In fact, Japan does have a minimal deposit insurance system—but it has yet to be drawn upon, because the Japanese government enlists the "voluntary" aid of other banking institutions to support any stricken bank; the recent case of Toyo Shinkin, virtually buried under a gigantic fraud, is a prime example.

And commercial and investment banking in Japan are clearly separated, as they are in the United States, so no example can be taken from that quarter. Japanese bank expansion worldwide has been made possible not by stock brokerage commissions or underwriting fees, but by the growth of the deposit base, which in turn reflects the enormous success of Japanese industry both at home and abroad. This has resulted in a veritable flood of funds into its banking system and into its foreign subsidiary banks serving the overseas interests of its clients. The growth has been augmented, of course, by the strength of the yen versus the dollar over the nearly two decades since currencies were freed from the fixed exchange rates established at Bretton Woods.

Nor is Germany an appropriate paradigm. German banks are actively engaged in the securities business as investment bankers and brokers, but it is important to keep in mind the circumstances under which those functions were originally combined with commercial banking. The currency reform of 1948 effectively eliminated all personal accumulations of monetary wealth, and the capital markets accounted for only a tiny fraction of the financing process. Available funds had to be channeled into rebuilding the nation's infrastructure, meeting basic needs such as housing, transportation, and other components of a more comfortable standard of living, and financing the recovery of industry and commerce. The banks were then the major repository of new savings, and as such became the prime source of capital for both equity and credit financing. This in turn enabled the banks to gain major equity stakes in most large corporations, leading inescapably to locked-in banking relationships that are anathema to the American concept of competitive markets.

Furthermore, it would be foolish to assume that the German banking system has been immune to the abuse of privileged information. The apparent absence of scandal in the past stems less from purity of motive than to the absence of legal constraints. Of course, control of major corporations by their "house" banks makes assaults by outside raiders all but impossible. But there have been many cases in the past of stock price moves in advance of public announcements, and of evident front-running or other forms of price manipulation by the banks, even before the eruption of the scandal involving securities traders at Deutsche Bank, which may ultimately compel Germany to enact laws and establish monitoring systems similar to ours. In fact, the German public generally assumes that stock market profits are made by those "in the know," and they hardly consider such behavior scandalous. Indeed, many are bemused at Americans who become upset over it. It may not be farfetched to suggest that this attitude may be at least a partial explanation for the fact that only some 3 percent of the German public (excluding the former East Germans) are stock owners, compared with about 21 percent in the United States. Does this sound like a system to be emulated here?

Finally, although there is no government-sponsored deposit insurance program in Germany, it would be flagrantly false to suggest that depositors are simply left to the "discipline of the marketplace." A substantial portion of that country's banking assets are held by quasi–public sector institutions (e.g., the "Sparkassen," or savings banks, and the cooperative commercial banks), which offer implicit governmental protection for all deposits. In the private sector, the commercial banks cooperated to establish an insurance fund in response to a crisis that threatened to undermine confidence in the stability of all institutions.

In 1974, the German banking system shuddered with the collapse of Bankhaus I.D. Herstatt, then one of the better known and most highly regarded private banks. There was no form of deposit insurance, and the Bundesbank failed to make immediately clear its role as the nation's "lender of last resort." As a result, the large private-sector banks saw the possibility of a run on the system and a shift of assets to the public-sector institutions. The financial markets were calmed, after a relatively short period of turmoil, when the major institutions decided jointly to protect Herstatt creditors. The protection was later converted to a permanent arrangement by the establishment of a fund financed by all members of the private banking trade organization.

In other words, German private banks in 1974 recognized the value of one of the benefits promulgated some forty years earlier in the United States: confidence in the security of one's funds is the bedrock for confidence in the nation's financial system. Does anyone seriously contend that the abstraction of "market discipline" would be worth jeopardizing that confidence?

## Therapeutic alternatives

These comments are intended to focus attention on the possible hazards posed by two specific measures ostensibly designed to fortify the American banking system, not to suggest a course of therapy that would instantly restore the system's erstwhile vigor. To identify the hazards, though, seems to require that at least some thought be given to possible alternatives that could help strengthen the banking institutions without endangering the health of the broader financial structure.

First of all, barriers to interstate banking should be eliminated. Regional mergers are already punching large holes through state borderlines, and the rationale to maintain the legal constraints grows weaker with each new combination. If size is an issue, perhaps the larger banks will be able to compete more effectively in the global arena; after all, the major German and Japanese banks are nationwide in scope and attract a far bigger share of their respective nation's banking assets than even the biggest American banks. Perhaps, too, the efficiency that comes with size would improve profitability and thus lead to improved capital ratios. And finally, geographic diversification may do far more to ameliorate sensitivity to cyclical swings than would the addition of the risks inherent in investment banking.

Second, the audit process should be amended to ensure absolute independence of judgment and an obligation to report signs of deterioration or any grounds for suspicion of flawed controls or fraud to a central authority such as the Federal Reserve Board or the FDIC and, in due course, to the public. For example, the auditors might be assigned by the central authority, rather than by the bank's Board of Directors, and be changed every three or five years; this may prevent the accountants from growing too close to management to be truly objective, or too dependent on relationships to risk losing a client. Another option might be the institution of periodic, surprise audits, as the Securities and Exchange Commission already imposes on brokers and mutual funds. A mandate from outside the bank might provide the motivation to find and reveal, rather than conceal, the problems that could, if ignored too long, subvert the bank's health.

Third, the cost of premiums for deposit insurance should be clearly related to each bank's balance sheet quality. Commercial insurance companies base their premiums upon perceived degree of risk; why shouldn't the FDIC? The independent auditors could be required to evaluate the soundness of the assets and the resultant danger to depositors, and the premium for deposit insurance would then reflect not only asset size but also the measured risk. Bankers might well be less tempted to issue unsound loans or otherwise stretch credit standards if the cost of insurance would essentially equalize the profit margins that would otherwise be expected from the higher interest rates.

And, finally, explicit accounting standards—regarding elements such as capital strength, balance sheet measures, assumption and quantification of risk, diversification of assets—should be established, and penalties for violations should be sufficiently onerous, and the probability of escaping them unscathed sufficiently low, to deter opportunists. In other words, the banker who may be tempted to play fast and loose with his bank's finances must realize that the consequences not only will be borne by the depositors, the taxpayers, and/or by other credit institutions, but will entail immense personal cost. And with an effective audit mechanism providing a reliable early warning system, the perceived risk may forestall attempts to circumvent the regulations.

The ills of the banking system have already caused the nation far too much pain and expense. It is perhaps gratifying that serious efforts are finally being devoted to the diagnosis and search for a cure. Unfortunately, though, no therapy can be tested in advance for safety and efficacy. The wrong medicine could do serious damage to an already weakened patient. Congress and the administration would be well advised to consider extremely carefully the possible ramifications of the course of action they propose before committing to it not only the banks, but the well-being of the entire nation.

ALBERT GAILORD HART

# How to Reform Banks— and How Not to

*The Treasury's proposed bank reform falls far short of adequacy and must be dubbed a pseudo-reform. We need a system of capital-rebuilding contracts that will bring fresh capital into the banks.*

To restore the public's badly shaken confidence in the U.S. banking system is urgent, everybody agrees, in face of the recession that began in 1990. The backwash from the Gulf War seems likely to make our economic situation still weaker—and to make a bank reform that will restore confidence both more urgent and harder to achieve.

## Official proposal for pseudoreform

The U.S. Treasury published on February 5, 1991, an official proposal for bank reform. Although it includes some forty "specific recommendations," this proposal falls far short of adequacy, and must be dubbed a *pseudoreform*. What the Treasury recommends can be summed up as follows:

1. Bring more capital into banking, and for this purpose authorize investment in banks by industrial companies.

2. Make banking more efficient by consolidation into far fewer institutions, with an average size much greater than at present, and for this purpose authorize nationwide banking organizations.

3. Reduce the number of federal agencies that regulate banks, place each operating bank and its holding company under the same regulator, provide regulators with full and precise information on each bank's condition, and enhance regulatory powers.

4. Tighten the rules of deposit insurance so as to: (a) focus on small depositors; (b) minimize the burden on federal taxpayers from bank losses; and (c) expose well-informed large depositors and nondeposit creditors to enough risk so that their vigilance will remedy the bias of shaky banks toward unduly risky assets.

5. Sweeten (3) and (4) for commercial banks: (a) by encouraging banks to enter the businesses of investment banking and insurance; (b) by continuing to protect all deposits in banks "too big to fail" under the guise of "least costly resolution method" and (c) by "forbearance" from requiring banks to charge off all their bad loans or to set up adequate loss reserves on doubtful assets.

ALBERT GAILORD HART is Professor Emeritus of Economics at Columbia University. Reprinted from *Challenge*, March–April 1991, pp. 16–24.

Let us put aside, temporarily, the reality that these proposals are insufficient for the task of bank reform. Taken within their own, independent context, the first four itemized recommendations are highly appropriate. But the whole concept of sweetening conditions of operation for commercial banks (5) would do more harm than good. And forbearance (5c) would essentially nullify the concept of tightening rules of deposit insurance (4).

The idea that banks can be put in good shape by letting them horn in on the overcrowded business of investment banking is perverse. On the record of the postwar period, such an intrusion promises losses rather than profits for banks. Whenever banks go into a new line where experience as commercial bankers is not the key to success, they flounder.

Witness the Florida real estate disaster when banks went into real estate investment trusts; the loan losses (incurring failure at Continental Illinois) when the banks engaged in syndication of loans based on oil and related real estate in the Southwest; and the evaporation (that still plagues us today) of "sovereign loans" in the Third World. The further mess created by the banks' involvement in corporate takeovers in the 1980s is just beginning to become clear to outsiders, but will prove at least as expensive as those just mentioned.

The idea that confidence in banks can be restored—and the flow of bank losses reduced—by "forbearance" on the part of regulators (5c) is equally perverse. Financial realities are facts of which sophisticated investors take notice, and fictions are recognizable as fictions.

Announcements of bank losses are not descriptions of current events. Rather, they are *acknowledgments* of losses (in Third World loans, for instance) that actually happened some years ago, and are only gradually working their way through a slow-motion accounting process.

When this process is carried through for more old loans, when real estate losses are sifted, and when losses from the collapse of high-leverage business borrowings are recognized, the book value of bank equity will be sharply reduced. In many banks it will drop below zero. In a *New York Times* Op-Ed of January 1991, Edward Kane, who was one of the first to frame a meaningful picture of the savings and loan calamity, warns us that "Banks are looking a lot like S&Ls." He estimates that by objective standards, the FDIC is already insolvent to the extent of $30–60 billion, and that the bill will swell unless there is prompt remedial action.

The financial world is aware that bank losses have been understated and bank profits exaggerated. Hence most banks are priced on the stock market far below their book value. The fact that typical bank stocks sell for several dollars, rather than for a few cents per share, may indicate some fairly widespread assumptions about the "resolution" of problem banks. One such assumption is that the federal government will sometimes shore up failing banks in a way that enables their shareholders to realize more than a token value in a merger. Another is that banks that fail are likely to pay substantial amounts in dividends before they go under. A third is that some bank assets may gain in value in the next year or two, either through a drop in interest rates, or through inflation, which can enable some debtors now in default to catch up (in depreciated dollars) with their overdue payments.

It is not confidence-building to let the public know that the facts of the banking situation are officially regarded as too discouraging to publish. To report the truth and announce a workable program to put banking on a sound footing is what the situation calls for. Down with financial fakery and flummery!

## More than pseudoreform needed

An adequate reform program must include three fundamental elements that are missing from the Treasury proposals:

• Subject all issuers of means of payment to banking controls, so as to relieve banks from unfair competition.
• Impose interest ceilings and standardized reserve requirements on all banks, so as to restore Federal Reserve control over the quantity of effective money.
• Terminate deposit insurance, access to Federal Reserve rediscount windows, and "too big to fail" protection except for banks that sign and fulfill "capital buildup contracts" of the sort explained below.

These apparently radical, but essential, reforms are firmly based in the logic of money and finance.

Traditionally, banks have had special treatment *because they "create money" by lending*. In casual talk, banks are said to lend out the money entrusted to them by depositors. But in fact, banks lend money that was not in existence before the loan.

Each loan adds an asset to the bank's balance sheet, without reducing any other asset. It also adds a liability to the balance sheet—a demand deposit at the disposal of the borrower—without reducing the bank's deposit liability to any other depositor. Nobody ever gets a monthly statement that tells him

> The balance in your account was *increased* during the month by the amount of the checks and currency you deposited;
> Furthermore, the balance in your account was *decreased* during the month by the *sum* of two elements: The amount of the checks you drew during the month *plus X dollars as your share of the loans we made during the month!*

Never! The money the borrowers get is not transferred from the balances of other depositors, but is created by the act of making the loans.

For generations, the great bulk of payments in the U.S. economy have been made through checks drawn against "demand deposit" accounts at commercial banks. These demand deposits constituted the great bulk of the stock of U.S. means of payment—measurable from the early 1920s to the early 1960s by the monetary aggregate called "$M_1$."

Reliance on demand deposits as the means of payment has been at the root of monetary policy. By setting minimum reserve requirements against demand deposits, and by managing the supply of bank reserves, the Federal Reserve was able to restrain the creation of additional money in boom times through restraint on bank lending. In slack times, the Fed was able to ease the terms on which businesses and households would get loans if they chose to borrow and could offer adequate collateral.

As money creators, banks were obliged to accept limits to their extension of credit, and to accept examination to make sure their asset management was scrupulous. They were compensated for carrying this burden of public responsibility in several ways:

1. Only "member banks" had access to the discount window at Federal Reserve Banks and to important Federal Reserve services;
2. Only banks were allowed to hold demand deposits;
3. Each bank was able to build a clientele of "customers" who kept deposits in the bank and relied upon the bank as a source of credit;
4. After the debacle of the early 1930s, banks were sheltered from competition by ceilings on the interest rates that they and their major nonbank competitors were allowed to pay to depositors. For demand deposits, until the last few years, interest payments were banned.

## Radical change in means of payment

The way means of payment are created and held has changed drastically in the last few decades. The result is that commercial banks face unfair competition from other financial institutions. These competitors are now enabled to create means of payment, and to hold means of payment for their clients, without subjecting themselves to a corresponding burden of responsibilities.

Savings institutions began in the 1960s to offer a new means of payment—the NOW account, used by households to pay for their purchases by writing "negotiable orders of withdrawal." These are treated as fully equivalent to checks. Banks (first in the Northeast, not much later in the rest of the country) were authorized soon afterward to offer NOW accounts too. Such arrangements are often called "checking savings accounts."

For businesses, one of the main functions of "money" has been taken over by "negotiable certificates of deposit" (CDs), for which banks other than the issuer make a market. CDs pay a rate of interest in the same range as short-term U.S. government securities. This function is the holding of liquid precautionary reserve funds.

Most business firms used to feel it prudent to keep demand deposits (even though they paid no interest) in excess of expected transaction needs. Such a holding enabled the firm to face delays in its receipts or to seize some unexpected business opportunity, and to count on being able to borrow from its bank. Besides, the scale on which the firm could count on borrowing from its bank was related to the average size of its demand-deposit balance. But a holding of interest-bearing CDs can now be turned into cash at any moment, and borrowing power can be assured by getting a guaranteed line of credit. Thus prudential holdings of demand deposits have become unnecessary.

For large enterprises, the payment functions of money have been taken over in large part by "repurchase agreements" (RPs). Such enterprises can arrange with their banks that every day all, or most, of their demand deposits will get transformed at the close of business into "overnight RPs"—which will be transformed back into demand deposits at the opening of the next business day. Thus the enterprise's funds are always available to cover its checks, but appear as demand deposits only thirty hours a week.

An overnight RP purports to be a contract under which the depositor buys from a bank a stated amount of U.S. government securities, which the bank agrees to buy back next day. But the fictitious character of this arrangement can be seen in bank balance sheets, which always report the situation as of the close of the bank's business day. The securities in question appear as *bank assets* and the RPs as *bank liabilities*. The Federal Reserve calculates its reserve requirements on demand deposits as of the close of business. Thus although RPs in fact serve customers just as do demand deposits, they escape from reserve requirements.

One of the big things wrong with U.S. banking is the fact that nonbank institutions have muscled in on the business of providing means of payment. Upon request, any money-market fund that holds U.S. securities or CDs will provide customers with checkbooks or, on a mere telephone say-so, will transfer funds for the customer by wire or by Telex.

The same arrangement can be made with a mutual fund whose assets are largely corporate stocks, or with a broker who holds stocks on a customer's account. A homeowner who sets up a credit line for a home equity loan can even draw checks on the value of his house. But no reserve requirements or subjection to examinations by regulators are imposed on these nonbank institutions.

Monetary statisticians generally treat these changes as bringing about a sharp increase in the "velocity of circulation" of money in the old sense of currency plus demand deposits ($M_1$). But the source of a large proportion of payments is not in $M_1$ but in some other asset held by the payer. It is more illuminating to say that the stock of means of payment (effective "money") includes large amounts of supposedly nonmonetary claims in addition to $M_1$.

The Federal Reserve has gone partway toward recognition of the monetary facts by treating as an interesting monetary aggregate not only $M_1$ but also "$M_2$" (which consists of $M_1$ plus a number of other items, mostly described as "nontransaction components"). The Fed, however, has no policy handle on $M_2$, let alone on the wider aggregates ("$M_3$") and "liquid assets," which some monetary economists see as more closely related than $M_1$ or $M_2$ to the actual flow of payments.

## Bank failures and federalization

Banks whose book equity drops below zero have traditionally gone into liquidation, with the FDIC making sure that *insured* deposits are paid off in full. But banks deemed by the authorities to be "too big to fail," and smaller banks deemed to be "too expensive to liquidate" now go through a different process which can appropriately be called *federalization*.

When a private bank is federalized, the FDIC takes over all its assets and all its liabilities through a new corporation, in which the FDIC owns all the stock. The bank's offices are reopened immediately for "business as usual." At the outset of federalized operation, customers will find familiar faces at tellers' windows and at loan desks—though top managers may be replaced instantly by FDIC nominees.

The resulting government-owned bank is supposed to be put back into the private sector through sale to another bank or to a nonbank company willing to become its owner. But to arrange such a sale is expensive and time consuming.

A federalized bank with negative net worth (liabilities exceeding its properly valued assets) is presumably worth less than nothing to a potential private buyer. Besides, the buyer is not allowed to buy the bank for two cents, but is called upon to show good faith by investing a substantial amount (in the hundreds of millions for a bank "too big to fail") of his own capital.

To make the federalized bank worth buying, some government agency has to invest hundreds of millions of government capital. This investment takes place partly through FDIC purchase of shares in the "new" corporation, partly by having the FDIC or the Resolution Trust Company (RTC) buy nonperforming assets at face value from the federalized bank. Looking ahead, the private buyer can insist on a promise that any time in the next several years he will be able to sell back to RTC at face value any initially acceptable assets which turn out to be nonperforming.

At the beginning of 1991, the Boston-based Bank of New England (BNE) was federalized as insolvent and "too big to fail." By way of exception to regular procedures, its top management was retained. The reason for this exception was that FDIC had *already* installed a new top management a year earlier—refusing to continue regulatory "forbearance" for the old management—and felt that new management was doing as well as possible in handling the bank's problems.

The nature of the BNE's difficulties will illustrate how federalization can become unavoidable, and why it is so hard to put a federalized bank back into the private sector. The key problems arose because BNE had taken it upon itself to become a pioneer in a new line of commercial-bank business—one that had much in common with the recent antics of savings and loan associations.

This new line was rapid expansion into loans on real estate for a high percentage of the "value" assigned by puffed-up appraisals. Such lending was combined with the financing of construction (malls, office buildings, condos) for which long-term financing had not been arranged, and for which no occupants were in sight. The resulting transactions in overpriced real estate provided a pretext for high appraisals of other real estate when loans were applied for in the New England area.

In consequence of the exaggerated expectations set up by the lending operations of BNE and its imitators, a "gridlock" has largely frozen real estate markets in New England. Many households and companies inclined to relocate cannot do so because no buyer can be found for the property they already hold. As construction jobs now in process are completed (or abandoned), the building industry tends to grind to a halt.

Unsound real estate loans and resulting gridlock are not limited to New England. Similar puffed-up appraisals, excessive percentages of "value" loaned, and exaggerated expectations among holders of real estate can be observed in New York and New Jersey. Parallel problems have been shaping up in other regions—notably California, the Northwest, and the mountain states. Most major metropolitan areas are reporting dangerously high vacancy rates in office buildings, new condos and rental apartments, and commercial space.

The "overhang" created by the large and growing holdings of foreclosed properties by the Resolution Trust Company, with the prospect that this inventory will keep on growing, is a major burden on the U.S. economy. And the RTC has been showing irresolution in its announcements and withdrawals of plans for massive sales of these properties.

## Difficulties of reprivatization

It is too soon at this writing (early February 1991) to tell whether the BNE can quickly be reprivatized. FDIC and RTC tell the press they are negotiating with such possible buyers as First Interstate and Bank of America. Whether either of these (or any other bank with experience in handling large branch-banking operations) can bring up the required hundreds of millions of additional private capital and take on formidable new management problems is doubtful.

The official reform proposals described above look with hope to industrial and other nonfinancial corporations as sources of bank capital, and seek to make sure such corporations are authorized to finance bank holding companies. But most of the industrial and nonbank companies (such as American Express and General Motors) that might be interested, may have shot their bolt by acquiring bankrupt savings and loan associations. Their experience with entry into the financial domain has been disappointing so far. Besides, they now have cash-flow problems within their own industrial domain.

It seems likely that a number of other large and medium sized banks will turn up insolvent in the next year or two. Under the rule "too big to fail," they will get federalized. The process of reprivatization generally takes many months. If insolvencies come close enough together so that FDIC has several large federalized banks on its hands simultaneously, the problem of finding private buyers may become insuperable.

An additional difficulty is that to put a federalized bank in shape to sell requires a large infusion of federal capital and a heavy commitment to buy additional assets that later become nonperforming. The Treasury and Congress are very unhappy about the fiscal effects and the publicity entailed by such provision of federal capital. In such a situation, a funding deadlock may result in a decision to go on running federalized banks that have negative net worth but are supported by the *implicit* obligation of the federal government to its depositors and creditors.

If the U.S. economy does not show a powerful upswing in 1991 (or at latest, early 1992), a clustering of federalizations is all too probable. It is quite possible for a federalized bank to go on taking care of its depositors and its well-secured private debtors. But in case a sizable part of the banking system comes to be operated as a quasipermanent federalized sector, the temptation to use this part of the banking system to finance an irresponsible fiscal policy may prove overwhelming.

## Real reform creates opportunities

Healthier alternatives are created once we treat as banks all providers of means of payment, set sensible reserve requirements and interest ceilings, and face the fact that shaky banks cannot be rescued by letting them enter new lines of business already crowded with more experienced competitors.

• First, it becomes possible to reverse the major policy error of allowing high interest rates to be paid on bank deposits that are effective means of payment. Interest ceilings, it is true, have some of the characteristics of a tax on depositors for the benefit of banks. But it is good public policy to "tax" depositors in exchange for the benefits they will get from a restoration of effective control over the nation's stock of money. Imposing interest ceilings on banks will remove a powerful pressure on interest rates, and increase the Federal Reserve's ability to help stabilize the U.S. economy.

Banks and savings institutions, in the absence of interest ceilings, have been in a position to "buy money" by outbidding other borrowers, and have had a sense of unlimited lending power. Incurring a high cost of funds, and left free by lax regulation to pretend that the high contractual interest rates offered by substandard borrowers yielded an income just as solid as that from lower-rate gilt-edged securities, they adopted risky lending policies of much the sort that generated real estate inflation and gridlock in New England.

Stopping the scramble of banks (and of savings institutions now to be treated as banks) to "buy money" will make it much easier for the Federal Reserve to pull interest rates down. We should be skeptical about the extent to which such an interest shift will actually stimulate investment in housing and in new plant and equipment. But to have future returns "capitalized" at lower discount rates should check the fall of market prices on financial and tangible assets.

• Second, with the real reforms outlined in this article, it becomes possible to build up bank capital by cutting dividends, and by making the unavoidable shakedown of the glut of banks and bank offices yield real operating economies. There is already a healthy tendency to break down barriers to banking across state lines, and to developing healthy branch banking within states. The geographic density of retail branches and of single-office banks is such that substantial economies can be achieved by reducing the number of retail bank offices, without depriving customers of convenient access or subjecting them to any monopolistic squeeze.

• Third, the proposed real reforms make it possible to get out of the trap of the "too big to fail" rule. Banks can be given notice that beyond a deadline not too far in the future (perhaps the end of 1992), their liabilities will be guaranteed if they have entered upon a contract with the regulating authorities that will assure an actual buildup of the ratio of bank capital to liabilities. And a deadline (perhaps the end of 1996) can be set, beyond which uninsured liabilities will no longer have federal guarantees.

## Proper reserve requirement structures

In the pseudoreform proposals of the Brady report, there are elaborate schemes for reserve requirements that would vary from bank to bank and from time to time, according to capital/asset ratios and to the apparent risk structure of assets. But to serve the purposes of making the stock of effective money controllable, a much simpler three-layer system, to apply uniformly to all banks, is more appropriate.

Since demand deposits in the broad sense (including such means of payment as RPs, credit card availabilities, and credit-institution obligations transferable by check or by wire without notice) constitute the bulk of the country's effective money, the bulk of the aggregate reserve requirement must be assigned to demand deposits as well.

This does not necessarily mean that the reserve requirement must be a high percentage of demand deposits. But as will appear below, paying interest on reserve balances is a mechanism by which part or all of the "tax" on users of demand deposits could be replaced. Hence, to set demand-deposit requirements at, say, 10 percent, and make reserves interest-bearing, is probably the best arrangement.

For time deposits, a fairly high requirement would be in order if these deposits were left actually available for payments without notice—as they have been in recent years. But setting a clear boundary between "money" and other creditorship requires a rule by which withdrawals from time deposits must pass through a stage of perhaps a month, during which the funds in questions are *on notice of withdrawal,* and held at zero interest. Time deposits *not* on notice will have a rather low degree of "moneyness," and should carry a correspondingly low reserve ratio—perhaps 1 percent.

## Effective build-up contracts

We court needless dangers by running the policy of "too-big-to-fail" without any design for growing out of that policy. True, there is at last an international accord for setting minima for ratios of bank capital to assets and liabilities. But the agreed ratios are too low to enable most large U.S. banks to dispense with guarantees. And so long as forbearance is a major tool of U.S. policy, neither capitalization nor assets can be measured in a meaningful way for U.S. banks.

Key provisions for build-up contracts designed to enable banks to stand alone without guarantees within a few years from now can be sketched as follows:

1. *Effacing fictitious "capital."* Bank capital in the United States has been seriously eroded by the growth of bank holding companies. These have been widely perceived as sources of bank capital. But historically, they have acquired operating banks by paying off shareholders in cash, thus *removing* capital from banks.

As the authorities seem at last to have grasped, the actual operating banks (as distinct from banking groups and their holding companies) must be required to have adequate capital. Bank holding companies will be a useful part of the reformed financial structure. But they must operate in a way that enables them to draw in capital from nonbank sources and put it into operating banks. Hence the positive value assigned to letting industrial companies own stock in bank holding companies. It might be appropriate to allow such stock also as an asset for pension funds.

Under guarantee contracts, fictitious capital based on "buying money" through short-term subordinated borrowings and short-term preferred stock issues can be banned. Besides, medium-term and long-term debt of other banks can be banned as a bank asset. Thus it becomes feasible to prevent a network of interbank obligations being used to count the same "capital" over and over.

2. *Barring false dating of "profits."* Banks have been using a number of devices to book hypothetical future profits as if they were realized current profits. They do this, for example, with "up-front" fees for mortgages and other long-term loans, sweetened for debtors by lower interest during the period of the loan.

Another popular technique is the sale-and-leaseback arrangement on a bank's headquarters building. The higher the bank puts the "rent" it will pay on the space it continues to occupy, the higher is the "value" of the building to an insurance company or pension fund that becomes the owner. Thus the bank's accounts for the current period (year or quarter) show a "profit" from sale of the building, ignoring the higher future costs in the form of contractual rent payments.

A third ploy for booking hypothetical profit is to treat as current income the entire flow of contractual interest from a "junk bond" that is likely to default within a few years. Interest rates on junk bonds are far above gilt-edged rates. This means the market is saying that when a junk bond borrower promises to pay 11 percent while U.S. Treasury issues of the same maturity yield 7 percent, the difference (of 11 percent–7 percent = 4 percent) is a measure of the probable loss from default or postponement of promised interest and principal payments, rather than part of the bond holder's income.

A properly drafted capital-buildup contract can stop such fakery. It can ban the use of "points" and other up-front charges, and can likewise ban writing rents above market levels into sale-and-leaseback contracts. The buildup contract can also commit banks to put into a special reserve for each junk bond issue held, quarterly, the difference between the contractual interest rate on that issue and the market yield on gilt-edged securities of the same maturity. When the junk bonds are actually sold or redeemed, the difference between the amount realized and the book value (minus the special reserve) can be taken into profits, yielding a reward for good selection among available junk bonds.

3. *Setting capital-buildup targets.* Each bank's contract can embody specific targets for capital/liability ratios, and bar the bank from paying dividends to stockholders (or bonuses to managers) unless these targets are being met. The targets for the mid-1990s should be high enough (perhaps authentic operating bank capital exceeding 15 percent of total liabilities) so that large depositors will be glad to go on banking with the institution when sometime in the mid-1990s the authorities cease to stand behind uninsured liabilities. To meet the targets, each bank will have to induce individual savers or nonbank companies to invest in the bank's new shares or long-term debt.

4. *Extirpating evasive institutional structures.* U.S. banks have engaged for some years in a number of shady practices, made feasible by use of organizational offshoots actually or nominally outside the United States. Such practices became epidemic when bankers discovered, in the early 1960s, that handling Eurodollar operations through a branch in London or some other outside center could put much of the activity of a U.S. bank beyond the effective reach of U.S. banking authorities—without bringing it very far into the domain of the Bank of England or other non-U.S. authorities.

Presently bankers discovered that "shell" branches

could be set up, purportedly located in places where bank controls were nonexistent, or could be molded for the convenience of banks based in the United States. Actual decisions could be made at a U.S. headquarters and entered by teletype in books of record kept at the branch location. Thus a "Nassau desk" at the Chase Bank in New York was in the position of trading with a branch purportedly in the Bahamas—but actually downstairs in the Chase headquarters on Nassau Street in Manhattan, New York, N.Y., U.S.A.

Customers whose deposits and loans were booked at the shell branches (or at more authentic branches in London, Singapore, or Hong Kong, where actual decision makers were present) were largely extra-U.S. subsidiaries of U.S. companies in manufacturing, commerce, communications, insurance. Operations were moved a step further outside U.S. banking controls by classifying these customers as foreigners.

A further step was official authorization to set up "international facilities" located in U.S. centers. The job of "Nassau" could now be carried out entirely in New York City, without the subterfuge of having an official set of accounts typed out in the Bahamas. The rationalization offered by a leading proponent of this scheme was that it was "unseemly" for "great American banks to have to resort to small islands" to avoid controls. He seems not to have noticed that Manhattan is a small island too.

Capital-buildup contracts can be framed so as to ban these subterfuges. Operations now outside U.S. supervision (or, at most, supervised in part by exiguous overseas bank-examination offices) can be regulated by making sure that overseas subsidiaries are real bank offices, and that they are linked into U.S. banking groups as subsidiaries of operating banks rather than of holding companies. Thus banks can be barred from escaping U.S. reserve requirements, loan limits, and capitalization requirements, and from the disclosure rules that apply to domestic dealings. Incidentally, it becomes possible to close some of the major channels (for example in, or purportedly in, Panama) by which drug money is laundered and transferred abroad.

5. *Equalizing treatment of foreign banks operating in the United States.* Foreign banks have established a large presence in this country. Their U.S. branches have been well received by depositors and borrowers even though they are not covered by the "too big to fail" policy. Their customers base their confidence largely on an impression that "of course" these branches will be backed to the hilt by their home offices in Japan or Great Britain in case their U.S. assets turn out badly.

To obviate unfair competition with U.S. banks, it is appropriate to require these branches to meet the same capitalization requirements and loan limits that apply to U.S. banks. Since they may not need "too-big-to-fail" protection, they may not need capital-buildup contracts in the usual sense. But if necessary, all banking organizations of substantial scale (whether or not covered by "too big to fail") can be required to have buildup contracts.

## Abating the risk of severe depression

Unless a system of capital-buildup contracts is set up in 1991, we are compounding the risk that the present recession (or the ensuing recession, if we are lucky this time around) may turn into a major depression. This risk has three major aspects:

First, *risk of an early crisis from financial panic:* We are not exactly in a panic at this writing. But there is a panicky undertone. Though most commentators take the line that the U.S. economy will enjoy an upturn by the middle of 1991, nobody feels sure of it.

The continuance of "too big to fail" as a main reliance for sustaining the U.S. banking system enhances the risk of panic. Estimates of the General Accounting Office as well as such outside expert opinions as that of Edward Kane (cited earlier), indicate that it will take a federal appropriation of several tens of billions of dollars to give assurance that the FDIC and RTC can fulfill their promises. Congress has an understandable reluctance either to appropriate funds on this scale or to give the FDIC and RTC a blank check. Thus, a legislative logjam is not unlikely, and could prove very disturbing to financial markets.

Second, *risk of a wave of bankruptcies:* There is wide awareness recently of numerous small-business and personal bankruptcies, and of conspicuous big-business bankruptcies. Bankruptcy (or a last-ditch effort to stave off bankruptcy) has heavy social costs. It intensifies layoffs of employees, and it stands in the way of installation of new plant and equipment, and of research and development to bring forward new products and new processes.

To bring about constructive reorganization of endangered companies requires new relationships with creditors. If banks—one of the most important groups of creditors—are forced to be completely stiff-necked, it becomes much harder to negotiate constructive reorganizations. Under the present flabby arrangements—even with the changes indicated in Secretary Brady's pseudoreform proposals—the only way to give banks flexibility is federalization.

We get frequent reports that important debtors are struggling to get concessions from their creditors, or to renegotiate lines of credit. There are rumors that many more bankruptcies are in the offing. If these rumors are confirmed by experience, many people will try to run for cover. With a system of capital-buildup contracts in place, prospects of limiting damage from bankruptcy can be much enhanced.

Third, *risk of adverse developments in the "real" economy:* Most decision makers in the U.S. economy are still planning on the assumption that activity in our economy will take a favorable turn later in 1991. If there is no such favorable turn, we will presently hear more and more reports that plant-and-equipment projects are being scaled down, that research-and-development is slowing, and that employers are less willing to hold onto highly qualified employees till activity goes up again.

The fact that the Bundesbank feels obliged to push up German interest rates is disquieting. Optimism that the opening of free markets in the Soviet Union may buoy the world economy is fading, and the prospects for strong markets for the West in East Europe seem less bright. The likelihood that the German economy will act as a "locomotive" to pull along the economies of the other Organisation for Economic Cooperation and Development (OECD) countries seems to be dropping.

Predictions that the winding up of hostilities in the Persian Gulf will rapidly restore full activity in the U.S. goods-and-services economy do not warrant a mere lick-and-a-promise approach to bank reform. With U.S. construction activity held back by the overbuilt condition of real estate and the overhang of foreclosed properties, and with vigorous economic expansion in Eastern Europe no longer a near-term prospect, United States recovery may prove later and weaker than we hope. Even if recovery hopes are fulfilled, furthermore, the fragility and artificiality of the U.S. debt structure remain threatening. To abate the wastage of potentially productive capital through financing of projects whose prospects are dim, and to reduce the risk that financial weakness may intensify future downswings, we must have a bank reform that cures the incentive bias toward excessive risk, and which restores the power to control growth in the stock of effective money.

Authentic monetary reform along such lines as are proposed in this article will bring to bear much more effective ways to put fresh capital into the banks, and to reduce their excessive costs. The proposed system of capital-rebuilding contracts offers much better security against panic in 1991 or in 1992 (or later) than we can have under the pseudoreform proposed by the Treasury. The real reform of banking outlined in this article avoids trying to build confidence by telling the public that the facts about bank difficulties are too unpleasant to publish.

## The need for action

Despite the unavoidable focusing of public and congressional attention on the Gulf War, domestic problems cannot be allowed to slide. Second only to the problem of electoral reform, real reform of banking and private finance has a claim to top place on the 1991 congressional agenda.

Financial fakery and flummery are worn out as methods of dealing with our shaky banking position. The threatened federalization of a large slice of the banking system would do serious damage—above all to fiscal responsibility. To go on stalling and prevaricating is to intensify our implicit commitment to inflation as a "default solution" for our banking problem as for other debt problems. And unfortunately, inflation is a non-solution. It is a way to regenerate most of these problems at a higher price level and with weakened confidence in government.

To redefine banking as provision of means of payment and introduce capital-buildup contracts as a key feature of U.S. bank policy will be far from painless. But it offers a chance to get out of the situation where time after time our policy makers find they can choose only between different ways of doing wrong. The nation needs to work itself into a situation where, for a change, policy makers face options that include ways to do right.

WOLFGANG H. REINICKE

# Turf Fights in Regulatory Reform

*The politics among the regulatory agencies may well prevent structural reform of the U.S. banking system. Restoring the international competitiveness of U.S. commercial banks is as much a political problem and task as it is an economic one.*

In *all* advanced industrial democracies, the debate on the regulation of financial institutions is an extremely complicated one, full of complex and technical questions. But in a close study of the U.S. case, one is struck by the particularly intense political and economic conflicts that surround the debate over regulatory reform. Moreover, a close examination of such controversies suggests much of it is a reflection of the inherently conflictual nature of the policy-making process. That process is often highly subjective, and does not really promote a public policy debate that works to ensure the long-term mandate of an efficient, stable, and sound financial system in the United States.

## Private-sector conflicts

Until the late 1970s, the U.S. financial markets were highly segmented and well protected. The instruments of protection were price, geography, and product regulation. This type of regulatory structure—which has its roots in the nineteenth century and is often described as a cartel—collapsed during the 1970s and 1980s when the various mechanisms of protection crumbled. As a result, the U.S. financial markets experienced a dramatic transformation. Financial *and* nonfinancial institutions began to invade each others' turf through product innovation, deregulation, or loopholes in the current regulatory system.

Today's financial market is characterized by a multitude of financial and nonfinancial institutions that often provide the same services, although they carry different "brand names." For example, recent estimates show that by the end of 1991, commercial banks will provide more home mortgages than the savings-and-loan industry. The outcome is a highly competitive market environment, which has only been intensified by foreign competition and the process of securitization. This increasingly competitive environment has led to a process of consolidation among financial institutions, due to mergers and acquisitions, and/or institutional failure. Consolidation is likely to continue at an even faster rate in the future.

These two trends—an increasingly competitive market environment and the resulting move toward consol-

WOLFGANG H. REINICKE is a Research Associate at The Brookings Institution. This article is based on a project on U.S. commercial banks and the internationalization of finance, and constituted part of Dr. Reinicke's testimony on April 11, 1991, before the U.S. Senate Committee on Banking, Housing, and Urban Affairs. Reprinted from *Challenge*, November–December 1991, pp. 42–50.

idation—have led to a high degree of conflict among private-sector institutions trying to defend and/or enlarge their market share as the dissolution of the cartel continues. Given the degree to which the cartel has already been dissolved, however, there is at this point little or nothing policy makers can do to make it stop. Considering the various public- and private-sector interests and the way in which they are currently distributed in the U.S. financial policy network, policy makers and regulators are unlikely to reerect the walls that once separated commercial from investment banking. Neither will they be able to force nonfinancial corporations to divest themselves from the group of 173 grandfathered nonbank banks. The experience of earlier attempts by the legislature and regulators to halt this move toward functional consolidation attests to that fact. Public policy should, instead, *stabilize* this consolidation process in order to minimize the associated social and economic costs. It should proceed to develop a financial system that internalizes the underlying changes in the market structure while providing for adequate soundness and stability of the individual institution as well as protection and safety for the consumer.

## Fragmented regulatory structure

The private-sector conflicts aimed either to preserve or to dissolve the cartel—in other words to influence regulatory policy. Consequently, these conflicts were quickly projected into the public domain. The projection of private-sector interest into the realm of public policy is nothing new, nor is it unique to the United States. All democracies—albeit to different degrees—are characterized by a continuous, sometimes conflictual dialogue over the role of public policy in a market economy. But when regulators in the United States attempted to stabilize the consolidation process in financial markets in order to minimize the social and economic costs associated with it, they were caught in the multilayered, decentralized structure of their own regulatory system.

More specifically, the coexistence of multiple regulatory agencies in a financial system creates overlap among the regulators at the federal level and between federal and state levels, leading to the emergence of different regulatory regimes. This forces regulators to compete with each other in a market for regulation, reversing the traditional role of public policy. Rather than being a complement to the financial markets by providing the general framework within which financial institutions can freely compete, financial regulation is developing into a market itself and thus becoming an endogenous factor in the decision-making process of private-sector institutions.

This is *not* the proper role of public policy. Financial market regulation should not be the reflection of competing private-sector interests, nor should it be the result of competing regulatory regimes in a single integrated market. On the contrary, public policy must remain exogenous to private-sector competition. *It should not be its consequence, it must be its cause.*

The regulatory overlap and competition among regulators has increased sharply in recent years as a result of the continued functional integration of financial markets and the continued pressure for institutional consolidation. This has heightened the conflict in the public sector, especially among regulators. The process of functional integration has led to jurisdictional turf battles among regulators. The pressure for market consolidation has led to a struggle for institutional legitimacy as regulators fear a decline among their constituencies. Together, jurisdictional turf battles as well as the struggle for institutional legitimacy have led to a new, separate set of policy incentives on behalf of regulators, besides the long-term mandate to ensure financial system stability.

Institutional survival of regulators, under conditions of functional integration and market consolidation, produces policy incentives that for the most part are short term in that they react to market developments. To be more specific, to maintain their status, individual regulatory agencies cannot contemplate the interests of the financial system as a whole, but must at all costs embrace the preferences of that very individual segment of the financial industry they regulate. Unless they can defend or even enlarge the market share of their constituency and thereby their own regulatory turf, they will not be able to endure over time.

Unfortunately, these two sets of incentives—the long-term mandate of financial system stability and the short-term interest in ensuring institutional survival—are not always compatible and more often conflicting. In fact, they have produced the following policy pattern. Short of a major financial crisis in which the long-term public policy mandate outweighs the particularistic interests of the regulatory agencies, the short-term incentives continually dominate the policy-making process of financial market regulation in the United States, as witnessed during the last decade. It is this predominance of a short-term set of interests that not only explains the perpetual conflict, but also the *ad hoc* and reactive nature of financial regulation, whereby individual regulators constantly try to adjust to the pressures of the marketplace.

## Suitable policy in a global environment

One striking example of the reactive nature of public policy in the domain of U.S. financial markets is the fact that in much of the literature on financial regulation in the United States, it has become almost conventional wisdom that government regulatory forces will always lag behind market forces and there is nothing that policy makers—regulators and the legislature alike—can do about it, but to accept it. And clearly the experience of financial regulatory policy during the last decade attests to this phenomenon.

But the predominance of market forces in determining regulation merely reflects the predominance of the short-term incentive structure on behalf of regulators. Such an incentive structure generates policy outcomes that by definition must lag behind and be *reactive* as they respond to market dynamics. This does not *a priori* rule out a proactive, anticipatory public policy legislated by U.S. policy makers. The conflict between the short-term institutional interests and the long-term policy mandate needs to be resolved. In fact, unless the long-term mandate of financial regulation clearly outweighs the short-term institutional interests of individual regulatory agencies, it would be less costly in social, economic, and even political terms to have no regulation at all. This is demonstrated by the experience of the S&L crisis.

There are primarily two policy responses required to deal with this. First, if continued decentralization is unavoidable for historical and political reasons, policy makers must create, at the very least, a level playing field for the various regulatory regimes with built-in institutional mechanisms, whose design will preserve this level playing field among the regimes *over time*. Second, wherever possible, policy makers should work toward the structural consolidation of the regulatory system. The fewer the number of government agencies, the lesser the regulatory overlap and the lower the chance that short-term institutional competition will override long-term public policy. In other words, unless policy makers are willing to induce the necessary functional and institutional consolidation in the U.S. financial markets, the regulators, given their incentive structure, will be unable to stabilize the consolidation process in the private sector.

Apart from eliminating the dual-incentive structure of the regulators outlined above, institutional consolidation and the principle of regulatory harmony could alleviate several additional problems—all related to the problem of structural fragmentation—which have increased over the last decade:

1. It would avoid competition in laxity among regulators and the ability of individual institutions to engage in regulatory arbitrage. The pattern and process of the repeal of the Glass–Steagall Act confirms the arbitrary and *ad hoc* policy-making process that a fragmented system creates.

2. It would avoid the system's difficulties in handling failed or problem banks. Such difficulties usually relate to (a) the reluctance on behalf of the agencies to take effective action against banks with problems, since this often causes the banks to change supervisors; (b) the need for the regulators to coordinate their efforts, which requires time and effort; and (c) the different supervisory goals and instruments of the agencies.

3. It would avoid the division of supervisory responsibility. In some cases one agency is responsible for the holding company and other agencies are responsible for the various subsidiary banks.

4. It would make the agencies more economical and efficient, as many of the existing forms of duplication would be eliminated.

5. It would make regulators more accountable to Congress and the public. To quote Senator William Proxmire, former chairman of the Senate Committee on Banking, Housing, and Urban Affairs, "I think it's far easier for this committee which has oversight on all of these agencies to act if we have a single agency on which to concentrate rather than if we have three disparate agencies, each doing things at different times in different ways. So our oversight would be improved, too."

There is one very fundamental and frequently leveled criticism levied against the consolidation of the regulatory structure into, for example, a single, independent federal agency. Opponents hold that such an action would create an all-too-powerful superagency eliminating all the necessary checks and balances that were so carefully crafted during the first three decades of this century. Such criticism is unfounded and must be rejected. First, Congress can deal directly with any problems of excessive power without recourse to several regulatory agencies. Second, and more important, an analogy between the fragmented regulatory system and the constitutional principle of separation of powers is false because the three regulatory agencies perform the same functions. One agency does not check or veto the actions of another.

There are good reasons to believe that a fundamental overhaul of the regulatory structure is a politically feasible task at this particular time. First, most private-sector interests have expressed general support for the consolidation of the regulatory structure at the federal level. As one bank executive recently commented, "We are examined by the Federal Reserve, the FDIC, and the state. There is very little consistency among the regulators, very little interchange of information, sometimes completely different interpretation of regulations." Second, in principle all regulatory agencies agree that the time has come to streamline the system. The fact that they resist a possible elimination of *their* regulatory powers is a separate matter for Congress and the Executive to decide. Third, and probably most important, political and economic forces *external* to the American political process will force the issue of institutional reform and regulatory harmonization onto the policy agenda quickly, overriding the concerns mentioned above.

At the international level, the emergence of a single global financial market has already begun to induce a process of regulatory harmonization. The most prominent and successful example is the Basle agreement on risk-based capital adequacy standards. In the United States, which until 1985 did not even have uniform capital adequacy standards for commercial banks, the pressure to come to an international agreement was an important element in precipitating an unprecedented amount of cooperation among regulators at the domestic level. As early as 1980, U.S. regulators realized that unless they were able to create one single U.S. standard, they would not be able to participate effectively in the negotiating process at the international level. In fact, once domestic regulations were harmonized, the U.S. became the leader in pushing for the international agreement.

The two aspects of a continued consolidation and increasing pressures for global harmonization will inevitably force policy makers to address the issue at some point in the not too distant future. But rather than waiting until pressures lead to a hasty, uncoordinated response both at home and in the international economy, policy makers should step forward, demonstrate political will, and make the necessary political decisions that will enable the regulatory system to meet the domestic challenge that lies ahead, and thereby allow the United States to lead the move toward a fully integrated, yet *stable* global financial system.

## Domestic structure in global competition

The role of the institutional structure of a financial system is important beyond ensuring effective and efficient mechanisms of regulation. The rules and the legal framework within which domestic financial institutions have to operate also determine their ability to compete internationally. The importance of domestic regulations in determining the global competitiveness of banks has increased dramatically during the 1980s, as national financial markets have progressed from a state of mere interdependence, to one of actual integration. Different national regulations in a single globally integrated market lead to competitive inequalities for those institutions that are subjected to more stringent regulations. Certainly, the dynamics of global competition should not be the *sole* determinant in devising a new set of regulations for banks in any particular country. Still, given the high degree of integration among individual nations, regulations in foreign financial markets can no longer be ignored. Nowhere has this argument been applied more often and more effectively than in the debate over the repeal of the Glass–Steagall Act.

It is striking, however, that the efforts to enhance the competitiveness of commercial banks have almost exclusively concentrated on individual financial institutions. Few have focused on the importance of the broader institutional framework within which banks operate as they engage in both commercial and investment banking activities. For example, for many advocates of enlarged powers for U.S. commercial banks, the German universal bank (or some adaptation of it) has become the model institution that would enable U.S. banks to regain their competitiveness. However, the regulatory structure within which German banks operate has been totally ignored, as well as the high degree of institutional cooperation that exists between the German private and public sector. Yet it is precisely this framework that explains much of the German banking system's stability as well as the banks' success in international financial markets.

Briefly, German banks are supervised by a single regulator that operates in close cooperation with the Bundesbank. All banks adhere to the same set of regulations that are applied rigorously, including very stringent standards on entry and examination. Given the high degree of centralization, the authorities are well placed to devise a proactive regulatory system that guarantees systemic stability and is responsive to the interests of individual financial institutions as well as the entire system, especially under the currently stressful conditions of rapid domestic and international change. This is a key factor in determining worldwide financial-system competitiveness. Modernizing individual institutions along the lines of German universal banks without parallel reform of the regulatory structure is therefore unlikely to generate the ultimate goal—an internationally competitive banking system. In fact it may leave the U.S. banking system even more exposed than before, creating greater instability and risks for the individual consumer and the nation's economy than under the present system.

The establishment of a single financial market in the European Community (EC) by 1993 is another good example that demonstrates the importance that European financial systems attach to the complementary nature of institutional and systemic reform. The creation of an internationally competitive financial market was considered a cornerstone of the EC's 1992 program. By early 1993, universal banking will be allowed across all EC member countries. However, broadening the powers of financial institutions was not the only—nor even the primary—concern. The principal goal of the Second Banking Directive was the establishment of a common prudential and regulatory framework at the European level within which national financial institutions can freely operate. This framework includes common yet stringent standards for bank entry, common prudential rules, and, most important, the "single passport" that enables banks to operate freely throughout the entire community. The Second Banking Directive thus explicitly recognizes the close link between microinstitutional reform and macrostructural institutional adjustment.

While a number of issue areas still need the attention of European Community institutions, substantial progress has been made. The European financial market, in less than five years, has become more open, more liberal, and has achieved a higher degree of institutional integration and regulatory harmonization than has the United States. Together, these three elements make Europe an internationally competitive and attractive marketplace for borrowers and lenders alike, ensuring a steady supply of scarce investment capital.

## Turf fights evident in Treasury report

Will the United States be able to forge a truly nationally integrated and internationally competitive financial system? The Treasury Report has recognized the close link between the regulatory structure of the banking system and its international competitiveness. But little systematic attention has been given by the administration to the reform of the institutional structure of bank regulation in the United States.

The Treasury report has recommended a division of the responsibility of supervising most depository institutions between the Federal Reserve and the newly created Federal Banking Agency (FBA). The FBA would be given regulatory jurisdiction over all *federally chartered* banks and thrifts and their holding companies. The Federal Reserve would be given regulatory jurisdiction over all *state-chartered* banks and thrifts and their holding companies.

The Treasury has explained the rationale for this particular form of realignment by arguing that the sharing of bank holding company supervision responsibilities with the Treasury through the FBA ensures regulatory accountability in the administration. In addition, according to Secretary Brady, it would be "confusing" to go to one regulator, and the Treasury's proposal would be the "natural, logical way to do it."

From the perspective of regulatory efficiency and necessary consolidation, however, this division seems entirely arbitrary. While two agencies are clearly better than four, why are two institutions needed to perform essentially the same function? A holding company does not differ in any major way, regardless of whether a state or national bank is its primary institution. Second, according to the staff of the Federal Reserve, the central bank would be overwhelmed by "small-bank matters" at the expense of broader financial matters, such as monetary policy. Third, the Treasury reform plan continues to put a major burden on policy cooperation in the area of bank regulation among two powerful agencies. Both agencies have numerous other policy functions not always in complete congruence with the policy principles of a bank regulator.

Clearly, the Treasury's proposal to restructure the institutional framework of bank regulation does not pass the test of securing the proactive, long-term public policy mandate needed for stability of the financial system. Thus, it cannot generate the economic and political benefits that consolidation of the bank regulatory structure will bring. Unless the administration can provide a more convincing set of arguments for the particular nature of its restructuring proposal, one must come to the conclusion that the design of the proposal is a reflection of the fact that turf fights among the various agencies have been carried over into the actual debate over structural reform. Not surprisingly, therefore, the Treasury's role as the regulator of the nation's financial institutions would strengthen considerably. Even though the new institution has a different name, the FBA is nothing but a renamed, significantly more powerful version of the Office of the Comptroller of the Currency. As was to be expected, the two other Federal bank regulators have strongly objected to this new division of labor. The Federal Reserve has already announced that it will fight the Treasury plan to strip it of its power on the grounds that it needs to retain oversight of the biggest banking companies. It is those banks, the central bank argues, that are most likely to create systemic problems presenting a threat to its ability to execute effective monetary policy.

As regards the FDIC, the agency would lose oversight over 7,500 state-chartered banks and be left with the responsibility of insuring the institutions. This particular proposition correctly identifies the different functions of the charterer and insurer of a bank and the possible conflicts that might arise if such a dual set of policy objectives were to be pursued by a single institution. This may not necessarily apply to the FDIC, whose sole purpose is to insure the institutions. It is more likely to apply to the regulator, whose goals are broader than insurance. But the Treasury proposal would require the FDIC to obtain permission from the Federal Reserve or the FBA before it could examine banks. This eliminates an important supervisory safeguard: The insuring agency *must* at all times have unqualified access to all troubled banks for examination, and have the ability to examine any other bank in conjunction with its primary regulator. Certainly the experience of the S&L crisis demonstrates the necessity of institutional independence of the insurer from the regulator. It therefore comes as no surprise that the FDIC has also announced its opposition to the plan. According to L. William Seidman, former chairman of the FDIC, the proposal is an invitation to "regulatory civil war."

## Single, independent regulator needed

Given the refusal of the agencies to allow any stripping of their respective regulatory powers, Congress and the president must intervene in this intra-agency turf battle. A single federal charter with an independent insurance agency would meet the above criticisms of the administration's recommendations and at the same time fulfill the goals of efficiency, lower costs, and regulatory consistency while improving the safety and soundness of the depository institutions. In addition, a single independent, federal regulatory agency would be accountable to both Congress and the Executive, guaranteeing the continued presence of checks and balances.

The Treasury is likely to resist such a proposition. However, the strongest opposition to such a proposal is likely to come from the Federal Reserve. This is especially the case for the execution of monetary policy. The Federal Reserve has long argued that significant supervisory and regulatory responsibilities are required for the effective conduct of monetary policy. More specifically, the Federal Reserve argues (1) that information about the banking industry, and ability to influence that industry, are essential to the formulation of monetary policy, and (2) that the Federal Reserve has lender-of-last-resort responsibility for the banks.

As to the first objection, information about the banking system does not have to come from direct bank supervision. As long as the central bank has clear, prompt, and unquestionable access to examination reports, direct supervision is not required. Such access could be legislated by Congress. As one former governor of the Federal Reserve said, "the supervisory work of the Federal Reserve has nothing whatsoever to do with the formulation of monetary policy. . . . I have never seen a single individual in the Federal Reserve System who formulated monetary policy on the basis of his knowledge of banks gained through examinations only by the Federal Reserve."

Regarding the second objection (that the Federal Reserve has lender-of-last-resort responsibility), aspects of bank supervision no longer play any role at this particular stage in the demise of an individual bank or a system-wide banking crisis. Unless it can be demonstrated that only the Federal Reserve possesses qualities as a regulator that could have prevented it from being forced to act as a lender-of-last-resort, and that the other agencies either failed to have or could not acquire, the argument does not stand up to close scrutiny.

In addition, there are several other reasons why the Federal Reserve should *not* supervise banks or bank holding companies. First, too much of the Federal Reserve's time is diverted from monetary policy. But more important, at the same time not enough is spent on supervision. A survey of Federal Reserve governors' participation in votes on bank regulation clearly upholds the notion that they do not divert their attention to matters of bank supervision. According to this survey, taken during 1975, all seven members of the board were present for only 10 percent of the votes and only four members were present for more than one-fourth of the 283 decisions on bank supervision.

Finally, the dual incentive structure of the Federal Reserve's policy responsibilities has also inhibited its ability to enforce consumer protection laws. As one close observer expressed it, the central bank's "primary responsibility to the supervision of monetary policy has significantly interfered with its ability to focus on the very real needs of consumers."

To sum up: First, one of the fundamental principles of a new regulatory structure should be a uniform set of rules, patterned according to the various types of activities in which financial institutions are engaged, and not according to the institutions themselves. There is no specific provision for this in the administration's proposal.

Second, the new regulatory structure should avoid redundancy and inefficiency. The Treasury's recommendations do not follow this basic guideline. In fact, the proposal may increase inefficiency by dividing jurisdictional oversight of bank holding companies between two bank agencies.

Third, one of the key lessons that the savings-and-loan crisis has taught is that a regulatory system must be free from undue Executive or Congressional influence. With regard to the administration's proposal this means that an executive branch agency (such as the Treasury) should not be in the business of bank regulation and supervision. A single, independent regulatory agency with a single federal bank charter will be most effective in applying uniform standards to depository institutions. It clearly avoids redundancy and inefficiency; it is sufficiently independent while at the same time accountable to Congress and the Executive.

Fourth, a consolidated structure can be established to incorporate those other actors in the broader policy network who have a legitimate interest in the safety and stability of the banking system as part of their fiscal and/or monetary policy objectives. If the Federal Reserve and the Treasury insist on receiving timely and accurate information about the state of the banking system, a single federal regulator could be administered by a five-member board headed by a chairman and vice chairman, both appointed by the president and approved by the Senate, and by one representative from the Federal Reserve, the FDIC and the Treasury. Another way of encouraging policy cooperation among these three institutions would be to establish a principle of interlocking membership. Obviously, even such a consolidated structure does not guarantee that conflicts among the various actors in the financial policy network would not arise. If such conflicts remain unresolved under such a structure, an interagency institution modeled on the Federal Financial Institution Examination Council may well be needed to resolve the remaining conflicts.

Finally, regarding the FDIC, this agency must both remain independent and have access to troubled banks, as long as the insurance agency remains a publicly administered institution.

## Caution in using foreign banking models

There are some additional institutional factors—domestic *and* international—that U.S. policy makers should take into account when examining the experience of a foreign country (such as Germany) as they debate the future of the U.S. financial system and its regulatory structure. In the public domain there exists a series of additional institutional factors that explain Germany's considerable success in preserving a safe, sound, and internationally competitive banking system. For example, one principal element is the German system of deposit protection. The insurance system is administered on a private basis through the Bundesverband Deutscher Banken (Federal Association of German Banks). Considerable importance is placed on the private nature of the insurance system, mostly for legal, but also for practical reasons. For example, the fund is not liable to cover losses automatically under all circumstances. Neither the banks nor their creditors have a right to demand payments. At the same time, the private nature of the fund also allows the Bundesverband Deutscher Banken to arrange to come to the aid of a financially troubled bank in conjunction with the other banks and the regulators.

Altogether, this flexibility, the informal but close cooperative relationships with the regulators, and the fact that banks are to a considerable extent responsible for the resolution of their own difficulties, work to explain the success of deposit insurance in Germany. At the same time, it must be mentioned that the German authorities show such reluctance to intervene and act as a "lender-of-last-resort" because the strong supervision and stringent regulations mentioned earlier make failure of the large German banks highly unlikely. A policy of "too big to fail," while possible, is remote.

Moreover, as the failure of Schröder, Münchmeyer, Hengst & Co. demonstrated, banks are likely to suffer considerably under a system of private insurance that minimizes the problem of "moral hazard" and fails to instill the necessary discipline, as well as a control mechanism among banks. Thus while it is unlikely that in the near term, the United States would consider the establishment of a private insurance system, it is important to be aware of this component of the regulatory structure. It is a central factor in explaining the fact that Germany, since the reform of its system in 1974, has experienced only fifteen bank failures, totaling approximately $240 million (at current exchange rates) paid out in refunds to depositors.

Other important aspects of the German banking system, though not directly related to the institutional structure, are the practice of close monitoring and stringent reporting requirements. More specifically, the close examination of data on asset quality, capital adequacy, earnings, quality, and concentration of loans is considered essential in preventing bank failure. In addition, there are stringent bank licensing requirements, which include adequate professional qualification of the management and a minimum amount of startup capital. Still, other elements not directly related to the regulation of banks may well contribute to explaining greater stability of a banking system. For example, in Germany mortgage banks can lend only up to 60 percent of a home's value, while mortgages of up to 95 percent have been available in the United States. This makes banks less vulnerable to a sudden rise in delinquent mortgage loans.

Finally, there are other factors unique to the German system that cannot be implemented by law but are a part of Germany's national financial culture. For example, the close relationship between finance and industry dates back to the Industrial Revolution. Even if this relationship is found to be an element of competitive advantage, it could not be recreated by legislation. Close formal and informal cooperation between regulators and the regulated also encourages early detection of problems and makes preventive regulatory action successful. Similarly, and contrary to the United States, the fear of large concentrated financial conglomerates is much less widespread in Germany than in the United States.

Thus while the centralized structure of Germany's regulatory system must be seen as its core, there are a series of additional factors—institutional and otherwise—that provide additional support to government authorities and that policy makers in the U.S. should consider.

## Global framework missing in U.S. reform

Any comprehensive reform proposal that acknowledges the importance of the regulatory structure of a financial system must also take into account developments in foreign financial markets as well as the emergence of a global regulatory framework for banks and bank holding companies. Given the degree to which national financial markets have become integrated during the 1980s, any reform proposal can no longer consider only the domestic regulatory environment. Clearly, one purpose of the Treasury's recommendations is to make U.S. commercial banks more competitive by allowing individual institutions to engage in the same activities as universal banks. And European banks have lauded the administration's proposal as a positive step toward greater stability that will benefit the international banking system. Yet with regard to the regulatory structure, the administration's bill has been less sensitive. It requires foreign banks to establish separately capitalized subsidiaries before they could engage in securities underwriting and other newly permitted activities.

Foreign banks are strongly opposed to this for a few reasons. They have argued that it would disrupt the global banking system as well as harm the U.S. financial market, and it might also discourage foreign banks from entering the U.S. market. According to the Institute of

International Bankers in New York, "both U.S. and international banks operate in major financial markets around the world through branches so that the entire capital strength of the institution supports its funding and other transactions. If other countries were also to require local incorporation, there would be a balkanization of capital strength and a loss of efficiency in world financial markets."

Given that the Federal Reserve's recent ruling to expand Regulation K, which will allow U.S. banks to expand and broaden their securities activities in foreign markets, this dispute is likely to grow. Thus, it appears certain that if this particular aspect of the administration's plan remains unchanged, European countries and especially the European Community will reopen the debate over reciprocity and almost certainly take retaliatory measures. Policy makers should be aware of such a possibility.

Last, a comprehensive approach to an overhaul of the U.S. regulatory system must also take into account the emergence of a global institutional regulatory framework under the auspices of the Committee on Bank Regulation and Supervisory Issues at the Bank for International Settlements in Basle. The Basle Committee is currently beginning to consider the issue of how to regulate the relationship between banking and commerce, one of the most controversial aspects of the administration's proposal. Even though an international accord regulating the relationship between banking and commerce may be years away, Congress should be kept informed about developments in the Basle Committee on a regular basis since domestic regulations would have to adjust to the standards of such an international agreement, which consequently might influence the current debate. But whatever the outcome, both of the above issues demonstrate the additional complexity that the globalization of financial markets has created for national regulatory authorities. At the same time, domestic financial regulation can no longer be considered in a national vacuum, but should work toward the achievement of an internationally accepted standard.

Congress, the Executive, and the regulators must all demonstrate the political will and leadership to combine reform at the individual institutional level with a comprehensive overhaul of the financial regulatory system.

Indeed, Congress should make the individual institutional reform conditional upon the establishment of a regulatory structure that is its logical counterpart. The administration has argued that consolidation should not be set in motion until other elements of the reform proposal are in place. The opposite is the case. Only once an adequate regulatory framework has been agreed upon, should Congress expand the powers of commercial banks. If this particular policy sequence is followed, policy makers will no longer be liable to charges of deregulation or reregulation. Combining both policy steps would amount to real, comprehensive, and lasting reform of the American banking system.

This reform does not have to follow the European or even the German model of bank regulation precisely. But it must be comprehensive enough to reflect the dramatic changes in the U.S. financial marketplace. Unless policy makers are willing to take such steps, U.S. commercial banks will not be able to compete effectively in the global marketplace, and the banking system will not become any more safe, or stable.

RICHARD ASPINWALL

# Conflicting Objectives of Financial Regulation

Financial regulation has multiple objectives. These include safety and soundness, competitiveness, fair treatment, disclosure, resource allocations, avoidance of abuses, and monetary management. Because these objectives often conflict, there must be a means for explicit and open resolution of conflicting objectives with elements of regulatory activity. Currently, the resolution process is obscured from view. The public rarely knows the full considerations that underlie regulatory actions or failures to act. Even more rarely are the tradeoffs inherent in a decision (or a nondecision) made known.

The major S&L and banking losses of the past decade and a half led to the enactment in 1991 of the Federal Deposit Insurance Corporation Improvement Act (FDICIA). It is designed to increase bank regulatory accountability in at least three ways: (1) prompt corrective action in the event of declining capital positions; (2) least-cost, prompt resolution of those depository institutions failing to maintain minimum capital; and (3) reforms in valuation procedures offering more transparency in assessing the condition of institutions and the performance of regulatory agencies. Whatever are the prospects that future regulatory performance will meet the FDICIA objectives, that act did not address resolution among conflicting objectives of financial regulation.

Failure to address conflict resolution is also a common feature of proposals for consolidating functions of bank regulatory agencies as well as the agencies themselves. This failure surfaces with some regularity. The need for "streamlining," such as functional specialization and reduction of overlapping jurisdictions, is often cited as a justification for action. Another is reduced regulatory autonomy—for example, a recent legislative proposal by Henry B. Gonzalez, chairman of the Committee on Banking, Finance and Urban Affairs. If the record on efforts for agency reorganization is any guide, however, inertia and vested interests will continue to be difficult obstacles for proponents of change to overcome. Indeed, even changes in regulation per se often require severe financial dislocations before action is taken.

## Delineating objectives

The following classifications represent a menu of regulatory objectives and apply to all institutions offering financial services to the public. These objectives also

---

RICHARD ASPINWALL is Senior Vice President and Chief Economist of the Chase Manhattan Bank. Reprinted from *Challenge*, November–December 1993, pp. 53–55.
  Suggestions on an earlier draft from Robert Eisenbeis and Edward Kane are acknowledged with gratitude.

cover the full range of financial functions, which include credit, investment and deposit instruments, funds transfer, securities transacting, investment underwriting and distribution, mutual-fund management and distribution, pensions, and insurance.

- *Safety and soundness*—covering capital rules and oversight, early intervention and resolution, deposit insurance, on-site examinations, securities investor protection, single-borrower limits, brokered deposit restrictions, clearance and settlement of market transactions, and pension benefit guaranty;
- *Competitiveness*—covering new charters, permissible functions, permissible geographic locations, and mergers and acquisitions;
- *Fairness of customer treatment*—covering information about credit and deposit terms, terms of other transactions (including securities purchases and sales), dispute resolution, and nondiscriminatory availability of services;
- *Disclosure and reporting*—covering accounting policies, balance-sheet valuation techniques, content and format of regular reports, special reports (e.g., under ERISA), and event disclosure;
- *Avoidance of conflicts and abuses*—covering treatment of fiduciary standards and avoidance of conflicts of interest, improper self-dealing, tie-in practices, and insider abuses;
- *Allocative preferences*—covering special programs for services (for example, credit and transactions services) to be furnished to designated sectors;
- *Monetary management*—covering elements of control mechanisms claimed to be required in the conduct of monetary policy.

Using the current U.S. regulatory oversight as a starting point, the only objective of the seven where accountability for action is relatively unambiguous is monetary management. This is, of course, the province of the Federal Reserve.

Proponents of functional reform want all oversight of a given kind of financial service (for example, securities underwriting) concentrated in a single agency. This approach should be resisted on two grounds. First, as usually employed, the term "function" is static and often fails to cover close substitutes. Indeed, failure is predictable, if there are returns to regulatory avoidance. Second, functional specialization presupposes scale economies of oversight. Skepticism is warranted on this score. If experience is any guide, reorganization of government agencies typically is accompanied by expanded employment and higher costs, not the opposite.

## *Regulatory complexity*

Regulatory objectives are not only more numerous than is commonly recognized, but their complexities are often masked in superficial and innocuous language as well. Consider the Federal Reserve's own description: "In its role as the central bank and as lender of last resort the Federal Reserve has a basic responsibility for the financial stability of the economy. Intrinsic to this responsibility is a concern for the strength and stability of the banking system and for the consistency of the banking structure with needs of monetary policy."

The terms "concern for," "strength," "stability," and "consistency" imply that the Federal Reserve should or will undertake actions that will improve conditions. This suggests the possibility that nonbanks (i.e., those outside the direct purview of Federal Reserve supervision) could be at a disadvantage. It also suggests that actions in one direction could impair results sought in another. Although the means by which even these three are reconciled are not disclosed by the Federal Reserve, it is often presumed that, in matters of monetary policy, that function had priority.

But the process is more complex. The Federal Reserve's list of objectives omits a number of items. Experience in recent years provides numerous examples of the range of conflicts. These include: income and balance-sheet disclosure (and, more recently, market valuation) versus the exposure of the deposit insurance fund to disclosure of adverse change; CRA performance versus permission to branch; capital sufficiency versus permission for a bank to expand by acquisition; and the forgone income tied to reserve requirements versus monetary control. While this process may not extend to a formal cost-benefit calculus, factors (and their weights) leading to a conclusion should be disclosed.

Conflict resolution has become more complex because of the increased responsibilities placed on regulators of financial institutions and also the widening range of activities being undertaken by the institutions themselves. Regulation of financial services is not confined to banks; nor is regulatory oversight confined to bank regulatory agencies. With the possible exception of prompt corrective action under FDICIA, Congress rarely specifies priorities among objectives it sets for regulatory agencies. Consequently, regulators generally are left to do so themselves. They may proceed on the basis of inferred congressional priorities at the time the legislation was enacted, current congressional preferences, or their own objectives. One of the latter may be empire building, especially among permanent staff members of a regulatory agency. While information processing and response by an agency are not independent of the external operating environment, they tend to reflect preferences emanating from an organization's past behavioral patterns and traditions—its "culture."

## Trade-off accountability

Delineating regulatory objectives is quite distinct from regulatory "ownership" of a given financial function. Better articulation of regulatory objectives should be accompanied by clear-cut accountability for results. Organizationally, this may entail a separate bureau within a given agency or separate agencies. There are numerous ways in which these principles might find organizational expression. Some are:

• Separate chartering and powers responsibilities from supervision and capital oversight functions;
• place "truth in . . ." responsibility covering all suppliers of financial services in a separate bureau, such as the Federal Trade Commission;
• separate all public reporting, disclosure, and accounting oversight in a single bureau;
• separate attention to conflicts and abuses in a single policing entity, such as the Securities and Exchange Commission;
• separate oversight for allocative preferences in the agency responsible for the services being fostered, such as the Department of Housing and Urban Development.

Steps along these lines probably would generate new contesting between agencies or bureaus—a condition to be encouraged, not to be avoided. Uncertain public preference standards (as reflected in conflict) would create impetus for resolving action by the Congress, not by an agency. Shortcomings in regulatory performance would be more visible, since the internal trade-off process would no longer afford protection to regulators.

In summary, changes in the organization of financial regulation should reinforce explicitly the need for more public disclosure of the ways in which conflicting regulatory objectives are reconciled. Inadequate disclosure impairs accountability. Internalizing conflict resolution also may lead to wasteful avoidance tactics on the part of the regulated and undisclosed (and congressionally unintended) priority systems on the part of regulators. Accordingly, new proposals for change in regulatory agencies should be subjected to the test of how conflict resolution will be improved.

WOLFGANG H. REINICKE

# Consolidation of Federal Bank Regulation?

*The time has come to streamline the system. The mandate of Congress is to act in the public interest.*

Until the late 1970s, the U.S. commercial banking system consisted of a series of highly segmented, well-protected markets. The instruments of protection were price, geographic, and product regulation. This type of regulatory structure, which created a set of well-defined, functionally different institutions, had its roots in the nineteenth century and is often described as a cartel. It began to collapse during the 1970s and, in particular, in the 1980s when the various mechanisms of protection crumbled. As a result, the U.S. commercial banking system has experienced a dramatic transformation. Beginning in the late 1970s, financial and nonfinancial institutions began to invade each other's turf through product innovation, deregulation, or loopholes in the current regulatory system, subject to administrative rulings and subsequent judicial consent.

## Financial intermediation in the United States

Today's financial marketplace is characterized by a multitude of financial and nonfinancial institutions that carry different names, even though many provide the same services. For example, as of 1990, commercial banks have consistently issued more home mortgages (about 28 percent of the market) than the savings and loan industry, and home mortgage companies have almost doubled their share from 30 percent to 53 percent. The outcome is a highly competitive domestic market environment that has only been intensified by foreign competition and securitization. This increasingly competitive environment has led to a process of consolidation among financial institutions due to mergers and institutional failure. In the banking industry alone, a total of 4,372 mergers took place between 1980 and 1991. One thousand, four hundred, forty-nine banks,

WOLFGANG H. REINICKE is a Research Associate at the Brookings Institution. This article is derived from a forthcoming book, *Banking, Politics and Global Finance: American Commercial Banks and Regulatory Change* (Edward Elgar), and constituted part of Mr. Reinicke's testimony on March 4, 1994, before the U.S. Senate Committee on Banking, Housing, and Urban Affairs. The author is grateful to Ullrich Heilemann for his helpful comments on an earlier draft. Reprinted from *Challenge*, May–June 1994, pp. 23–29.

totaling over $228 billion in assets, failed between 1980 and 1992, resulting in a 17 percent decline in the total number of insured banks.

This consolidation trend will continue, probably at an even faster rate. Commercial banks will circumvent existing geographic and product restrictions in an effort to maintain, or at least slow down, their decline in market share, while Congress will eliminate some of the outstanding impediments in support of a fully integrated, multiproduct national banking system. This is likely to reduce the number of independent banking organizations even further. At the same time, the challenge from nonbank financial service firms will not subside, and will further erode the overall market share of commercial banks.

## The role of public policy

The principal purpose of public policy should be to guide and stabilize this dramatic change at home and abroad, to ensure the competitive position of U.S. commercial banks in the domestic and global marketplace, and to minimize the associated social and economic costs. As such, regulation should promote a financial system that has internalized the underlying changes in the market structure—domestic and international—and, at the same time, provide for adequate soundness and stability of the banking system, the individual institution and, most important, protection and safety for the consumer.

The projection of private-sector interests into the realm of public policy, particularly during these times of rapid change and adjustment, is nothing new; nor is it unique to the United States. All democracies (albeit to different degrees) are characterized by a continued, sometimes conflictual dialogue over the role of public policy in a market economy. But when federal regulators in the United States attempt to stabilize the process of change and consolidation in the financial marketplace in order to minimize the social and economic costs associated with it, their experience tells us that they are often caught in the multilayered, overlapping structure of their own regulatory system. Almost 60 percent of all banking organizations have two or more federal regulators, and close to one-half of all bank and thrift assets are held by banking organizations with three or four regulators.

The existence of multiple regulatory agencies in the U.S. financial system creates institutional overlap among the regulators at the federal level and leads to the emergence of different regulatory regimes. This forces regulators to compete with each other in a market for regulation and reverses the traditional role of public policy. Rather than being a complement to the financial markets by providing the general framework within which financial institutions can compete freely and fairly, financial regulation is developing into a market unto itself and thus has become an endogenous factor in the decision-making process of private-sector institutions. As one industry representative recently stated, "If the Comptroller is giving me a hard time, it's nice to know that I can go to the state bank department and they will welcome me with open arms."

According to what some have called a "regulatory dialectic," financial institutions will always try to circumvent regulations through innovations and loopholes. However, to *encourage* such behavior through a particular regulatory structure does not seem the appropriate role for public policy. Clearly, private-sector input into the *formulation* of policy is one important ingredient. But financial market regulation and supervision should not be the reflection of competing private-sector interests, nor should it be the result of competing regulatory regimes in a single integrated market. Public policy should be the *cause for competition* in the financial marketplace; it should not be the *consequence of competition*.

The regulatory overlap and competition among regulators has increased sharply in recent years, as a result of the continued functional integration of financial markets and the continued pressure for institutional consolidation described earlier. This has heightened the conflict in the public-sector domain, especially among regulators. Functional integration has prompted jurisdictional turf battles among regulators, and the pressure for market consolidation has prompted a struggle for institutional legitimacy, as regulators fear a decline in the number of institutions they can regulate and supervise. Together, jurisdictional turf battles and the struggle for institutional legitimacy have led to a new, separate set of policy incentives on behalf of regulators, in addition to the long-term mandate to ensure financial soundness of individual institutions as well as systemic stability.

More specifically, institutional survival of regulators, under conditions of functional integration and market consolidation, produces policy incentives that, for the most part, are short term as they react to immediate market developments. To maintain their status and clientele, individual regulatory agencies cannot merely contemplate the interests of the financial system as a whole, but must, at all costs, embrace the preferences of that very individual segment of the financial industry they regulate. Unless they can defend or even enlarge the market share of their constituency, and thereby their own regulatory turf, they will not be able to endure over time.

Unfortunately, these two sets of incentives—the long-term mandate of institutional soundness and financial system stability, and the short-term interests to ensure institutional survival—are not always compatible and more often conflicting. In fact, they have produced the following policy pattern: Short of a major financial crisis in which the long-term public-policy mandate outweighs the particularistic interests of the regulatory agencies, the short-term incentives continually dominate the policy-making process of financial market regulation in the United States, as witnessed during the last decade. And it is this predominance of a short-term set of interests that explains not only the perpetual conflict but also the ad hoc and reactive nature of financial regulation, whereby individual regulators constantly try to respond either to the short-term pressures of the marketplace or to a regulatory adjustment by a competing regulator.

One striking example of the reactive nature of public policy in the domain of U.S. financial markets is the widespread perception that public policy will always lag behind the market forces and there is nothing that policy makers—regulators and the legislature alike—can do about it but accept it. Clearly, the experience of financial regulatory policy during the last decade attests to this phenomenon. Yet, given the dynamic that has been outlined above, the predominance of market forces in determining regulation merely reflects the predominance of the short-term incentive structure on behalf of regulators. As such, it does not, *a priori,* rule out a proactive, preventive, and thus anticipatory public policy legislated by Congress and administered by a regulatory agency.

The current incentive structure among regulators generates policy outcomes that, by definition, must lag behind and be *reactive,* as they respond to short-term market dynamics. Thus, as long as the conflict between the immediate institutional interests and the long-term policy mandate has not been resolved, one should be careful to accept those arguments that characterize market forces as wholly insurmountable.

In fact, the example of other nations' financial systems, as well as developments in international financial markets, suggests that public policy can indeed be *proactive* and anticipatory. Indeed, one might argue that unless the long-term mandate of financial regulation clearly outweighs the short-term institutional interests of individual regulatory agencies, it would be less costly in social, economic, and even political terms to have no regulation at all. Focusing on the long-term health and stability of the financial system supports the dictum that *prevention is better than the cure.* It is also less costly, as has been so aptly demonstrated by the experience of the Savings and Loan debacle.

In sum, the decentralized, multilayered, and overlapping structure of financial regulation in the United States is one important, though not the only, reason for the problems the U.S. banking system has experienced during the last decade. As such, the current reform effort by the Treasury and Congress deserves serious consideration and attention from the public. In addition to dealing with what has been described by all parties involved in the debate as a costly, burdensome, inefficient, and archaic system, it also addresses the broader public-policy concerns that have been outlined here and equips the U.S. banking community with a regulatory structure that can meet the challenges ahead. A single, independent Federal Banking Commission (FBC), which is the central element of the reform, and which includes among its members a representative from both the Treasury and the Federal Reserve, consolidates and concentrates the experience and expertise of both institutions, ensures continued diversity of opinion, and meets their legitimate interest in participating in the broader long-term policy-making process that determines the future structure of the U.S. banking system. At the same time, it relieves policy makers of the constant short-term challenge to respond to the pressure that emanates from both functional and institutional consolidation discussed earlier. As a result, regulators can address the underlying structural problems and future challenges of the U.S. banking system and create framework conditions that ensure its health and international competitiveness.

## Responding to critics

One of the most frequent criticisms states that reform would create an all-too-powerful superagency, which would eliminate all the necessary checks and balances that were so carefully crafted during the first three decades of this century. Such criticism is unfounded and must be rejected.

First, it is widely acknowledged that the regulatory structure was not carefully crafted. To the contrary, it was developed on an ad hoc basis, reacting to various crises that occurred throughout this century, and reflected the multitude of functionally different institutions and markets that no longer exist.

Second, Congress can deal directly with any problems of excessive power without recourse to several regulatory agencies.

Third, an analogy between the fragmented regulatory system and the constitutional principle of separation of powers is false because the three regulatory agencies perform the same functions. One agency does not check or veto the actions of another. It *cannot,* and the history of administrative rulings over the Glass–Steagall Act attests to that. Indeed, the current proposal will introduce a system of checks and balances; it will distinguish among the insurance, regulatory, and lender-of-last-resort functions and does not allow one to compromise the other, as was the case in the Savings and Loan crisis.

Fourth, the composition of the commission as envisioned in the reform proposal will ensure the presence of several viewpoints on questions of regulatory policies and supervisory practices.

Fifth, the bulk of policy making, with respect to the U.S. banking system, should be conducted by the three branches of government that continue to guarantee the presence of checks and balances. The fact that Congress has shown little or no leadership in moving ahead with regulatory reform of the nation's banking laws does not, and cannot, justify the fact that regulators themselves become the principal source of policy making. If anything, consolidation would make regulatory activity more accountable to Congress and the public. To quote Senator Proxmire, former chairman of the Senate Banking Committee, "I think it's far easier for this committee, which has oversight on all of these agencies, to act as if we have a single agency on which to concentrate rather than if we have three disparate agencies with different people to be confirmed who are each doing things at different times in different ways. So our oversight would be improved, too."

## A monolithic structure

Another and related criticism is that the proposed commission would be a "monolith," a "monopoly bank regulatory agency," and that this would be costly to the broader efficiency and flexibility of our financial system. First, as to efficiency, a single commission improves efficiency by reducing inconsistent interpretations of the same laws and rules, consolidating bureaucratic waste and overlap, and reducing costly and repetitive examinations. According to the Office of Management and Budget (OMB), the current reform proposal would reduce government spending by between $150 and $200 million a year—about 15 percent to 20 percent of today's costs. This does not include the savings accrued by the private sector as a result of reducing unnecessary layers of bureaucracy. Furthermore, of primary importance, markets should be efficient and flexible. To put that burden on regulators misses the point and defies their purpose.

In addition, *regulatory quality, not quantity, counts* in determining the flexibility and global competitiveness of the U.S. financial system. In other words, what is important is not the number of regulatory agencies, but the nature of actual regulations and the manner in which they are enforced. In fact, when it comes to some of the central issues in current regulatory policy in the United States, the presence of multiple regulatory agencies would not make any difference. All agree that the time has come to revise the current structure of geographic and product regulation.

It is surprising that the Federal Reserve would join those who have suggested that the independent FBC would turn into a monolith and exercise monopoly power. Not only has the Federal Reserve, with broad support from all branches of government, long been an advocate of its own independence in order to conduct monetary policy, but the thought of having that independence compromised by a parallel body equally entitled to determine interest rates or operate a discount window among which banks could choose seems not just utterly unrealistic; it would defeat the very purpose of sometimes difficult and even controversial decisions and remove the Fed's accountability as the single institution responsible for the conduct of monetary policy. If monopolies in the domain of policy making are so inefficient, then why, and in my view appropriately so, do we have a single agency responsible for the conduct of monetary policy?

It has also been argued that history suggests that competition among regulators has tended to moderate incentives to be lax in supervision. The history of the Glass–Steagall Act during the last twenty years suggests the opposite. In fact, as early as the 1960s, then Comptroller of the Currency James Saxon unilaterally allowed commercial banks to enter the securities business, against the will of the Federal Reserve and the FDIC. At the time, he could be stopped only by the courts. However, since the early 1980s, the Glass–Steagall Act has been dismantled through slow, costly, and arbitrary administrative actions of one individual regulator, often against the fierce opposition of another. This does not mean that Glass–Steagall should not be repealed. To the contrary, given the reality of the U.S. financial marketplace, such a move by Congress is long overdue. But the fact that many have argued that it has been repealed *de facto* but not *de jure* not only raises questions about the apparent ability of the present structure to ensure checks and balances, but also about the process of regulatory policy making itself.

Another argument that has been made is that, under the reformed regulatory structure, banks would be less able to take on international competition. Little evidence for that is available; if anything, however, it points in the opposite direction. For example, contrary to the impression that some critics have tried to give, bank regulation—the rule-making function—in Germany and Japan rests with one single agency. It is true that there is close informal, and, in some cases, formal cooperation, particularly on matters of supervision, between their regulators and the respective central bank, but this is exactly what the reform in the United States is trying to achieve by including a member of the Federal Reserve in the FBC. But again, it is not the structure of regulation that is the most important element in determining international competitiveness but the regulations themselves and, equally important, the management, skill, and strategic choices of the banks themselves.

As to global bank regulation, which is currently discussed and decided in the Basel Committee on Bank Regulation and Supervision, the United States, like the other members of the committee, should be represented by both the FBC and the Fed, given the evolving nature of this relatively recent but rapidly expanding policy forum. This would best be achieved if the representative from the Fed on the commission participated in the discussions.

Critics of reform also charge that the proposal would effectively end the dual-banking system. It is difficult to see how that would be the case. States would remain the primary regulators and examiners of the banks they charter, thus preserving the integrity of the dual-banking system. The fact that the knowledge and experience from state-level supervision will become an integral part of the FBC's policies actually *strengthens the principle of duality*, as the experience and expertise of state examiners is being given greater weight. Getting the FDIC out of the regulation business, on the other hand, does not really tamper with the present degree of duality, since the FDIC is a federal and not a state agency. At the same time, it deals with the long-recognized conflict-of-interest problem inherent in an agency that internalizes both regulatory and insurance functions.

On a more general note, the dual-banking system will not live or die because of the presence or absence of a particular regulatory structure. The fate of the dual-banking system will be decided in the financial marketplace, where the demise of geographic and product regulations may undermine its existence. The excessive emphasis on the future of the dual-banking system in the debate over structural reform is thus misplaced, and it obscures the *real* source of the problems and challenges for the dual-banking system.

## Streamlining the structure

The Federal Reserve has argued that streamlining the regulatory structure would seriously impede its other responsibilities, such as the handling of financial crises, acting as a lender of last resort, managing the payments system, and conducting monetary policy. First, the times when banks dominated our financial system are long gone. Today, the banking industry accounts for only 25 percent of the nation's total financial assets. Of those, the Fed currently supervises only 15 percent. Concentrating on a narrow set of institutions would thus be misleading, and of course, the Fed does not do that but focuses on the much broader concept of financial markets.

In addition, assuming for a moment that a banking crisis has erupted and the Fed has to move in as a lender of last resort, aspects of bank supervision no longer play any role at this particular stage. Unless it can be demonstrated that only the Federal Reserve possesses the expertise and experience as a regulator or supervisor that could have prevented the crisis, the argument does not stand up to close scrutiny. As long as the central bank has clear, prompt, and unquestionable access to all data collected from the banking system, including the examination reports (*all* of which is guaranteed in the current reform proposal), regulatory power and direct supervision are not required. The German regulatory structure, for example, which is renowned for its efficiency and effectiveness, is characterized by a single regulatory agency that shares a common database with the Bundesbank, Germany's central bank.

This also holds true for the conduct of monetary policy. As former Governor J.L. Robertson of the Federal Reserve stated, "... the supervisory work of the Federal Reserve has nothing whatsoever to do with the formulation of monetary policy.... I have never seen a single individual in the Federal Reserve System who formulated monetary policy on the basis of his knowledge of banks gained through examinations only by the Federal Reserve." It would seem that the burden of proof in this matter rests with those who oppose reform. But apart from frequent assertions, it has not yet been convincingly demonstrated how any useful information is obtained from the supervisory process that could not be obtained with another agency doing the supervision. The *critical* condition for adequate and timely policy decisions are the criteria that guide the data-collection process itself and the immediate access by those who need the information. It is far less important *who* collects the information. If the current collection system continues to satisfy these conditions under the new structure, it should be left untouched. If not, it needs to be revised.

Furthermore, if a convincing case can be made that close day-to-day contact is vital for the execution of monetary policy, this does not necessarily have to be linked to regulation, as the Japanese financial system has demonstrated. Moreover, some former Fed officials have actually criticized the supervisory role of the Fed as being detrimental to monetary policy. According to Governor Bucher, "[S]upervision is too important a function to be the Federal Reserve's part-time job." Similarly, Governor Robertson stated that the central bank "should be permitted to devote all of its time and effort to the task of [monetary policy], without diverting attention to bank supervisory matters that demand concentrated full-time attention by people especially qualified for the job." And, indeed, this has been confirmed. A survey of Federal Reserve Governors' participation in votes on bank regulation upholds the notion that they do not divert their attention to matters of bank supervision. According to this survey taken during 1975, all seven members of the board were present for only 10 percent of the votes, and only four members were present for more than one-fourth of the 283 decisions.

## Political controversy

In fact, it is not inconceivable that there is a conflict between regulation and monetary policy. Both policy domains involve political controversy, not the least because of the Federal Reserve's independence. When bold innovative action might be necessary with respect to regulation, the political side effects of making such policy decisions might well lead the central bank to defer, or at least postpone, such action. The history of the Glass–Steagall Act points in that direction. Indeed, according to officials from the Bundesbank, they do *not* want to get involved in regulatory issues and share responsibility, as this may *interfere with their independence* in the conduct of monetary policy. Drawing again on the experience of the Bundesbank, whose conduct of monetary policy has won much praise around the world, there seems to be no causal linkage between broad regulatory powers and the conduct of monetary policy. The exceptions are regulations concerning capital adequacy, where the Federal Bank Supervisory Office is required to reach an agreement with the Bundesbank. Applied to the FBC, one might consider granting the Federal Reserve veto power on such an aspect of regulation.

Finally, given the continued dramatic change in the financial marketplace, one should question the actual relevance of bank regulatory structure on monetary policy. First, as already stated above, the Fed supervises only 15 percent of the depository institutions' assets. Second, and more important, the *real* challenge to the Fed's ability to conduct monetary policy comes from the securitization and disintermediation that all financial markets have experienced over the last decade. This has complicated the tasks of central banks in assessing and controlling systemic risk, in responding to financial crises, and in executing monetary policy. According to Fed Chairman Alan Greenspan, "the liabilities of depository institutions will not be as good a gauge of financial conditions as they once were." For example, mutual fund holdings, most of which are not regulated by the Federal Reserve, totaled just over $2 trillion by the end of 1993. As a result, money-market mutual funds alone now make up about 10 percent of $M_2$. At current trends, total investments in mutual funds will surpass $2.3 trillion in savings and time deposits at banks and thrifts.

## Relevance and challenge

The previous analysis suggests that the arguments that have been presented against reform do not hold up to close scrutiny. There is not one concrete example that would support some of the broader philosophical points made by the opponents of reform. To the contrary, the evidence points in the opposite direction. Unfortunately, the current debate once again indicates the same dynamic that has been outlined above, and that has derailed every single attempt at reform over the last twenty, even forty years, independent of the majorities in Congress or the political persuasion of the administration. Short-term institutional interests to preserve turf continue to dominate over the long-term goal of building a regulatory structure that provides the foundation for a sound, stable, and globally competitive banking system in the United States. If one is looking for an example of gridlock, this is a perfect case. It is supported by the fact that numerous officials (including several from the Federal Reserve), once they are no longer affiliated with a particular regulatory institution, *do* advocate the consolidation of the system in the direction currently suggested. Most recently, this was demonstrated in an impressive way, when eight former regulators endorsed the Treasury's reform proposal. Moreover, in principle, all regulatory agencies agree that the time has come to streamline the system. The fact that some resist a possible elimination of *their* regulatory powers is a separate matter, even understandable from their perspective. The mandate of Congress, however, is to act in the public interest, which is the purpose of this reform effort.

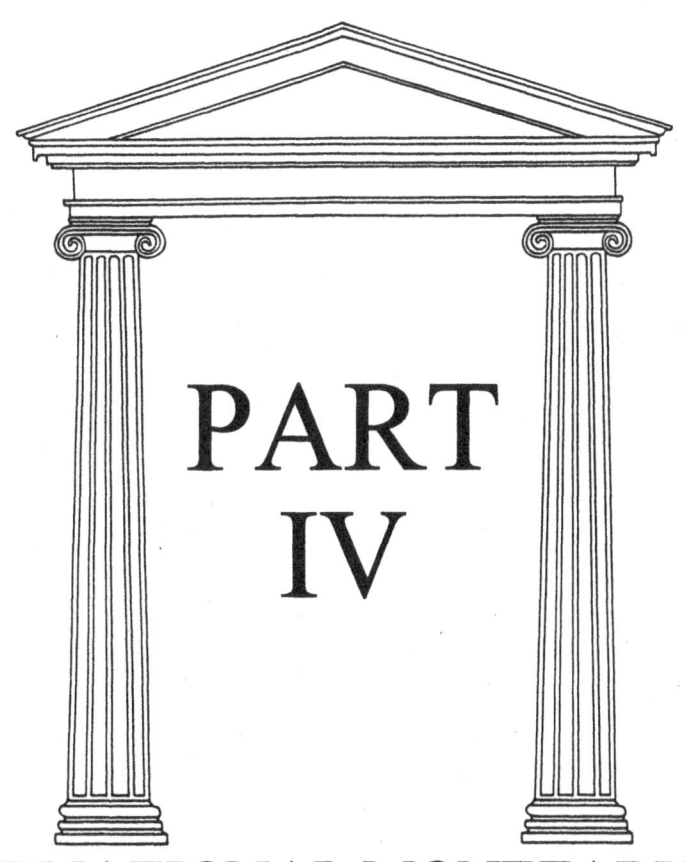

# PART IV

## THE INTERNATIONAL MONETARY SYSTEM AND THE GLOBALIZATION OF FINANCE

# CHAPTER 9 | GLOBAL FINANCE IN A TRIPOLAR WORLD ECONOMY

## *The "Triad": Toward a New Multicurrency Standard*

ROBERT GUTTMANN

One of the more important qualitative changes in the workings of our economic system in recent years has been its accelerating *globalization*. This process has had a number of specific manifestations and channels, be they the growing dependency of national economies on foreign trade, the transformation of multinational corporations into global production networks, or the level of direct and portfolio investments undertaken across borders. But nowhere has this globalization tendency found more depth and intensity than in the area of financial capital.

### The globalization of finance

Far more than is the case with exchange or production, the credit system has become truly globally integrated over the last couple of decades. The world's banks have turned into transnational organizations capable of transcending geographic boundaries and escaping the reach of national regulators by operating an integrated global banking system known as the *Eurocurrency market*.[1] Multinational corporations accumulate cash flows from their operations all over the world and centralize these funds for their yield-enhancing redeployment in global financial-asset portfolios. Institutional investors, such as pension funds or mutual funds, do the same for their cash-rich clients. Thanks to the revolution in telecommunications and computer technology, securities markets operate increasingly as electronic auction places that are rapidly getting integrated with each other. This integration involves both cross-listing of securities as well as global trading capacity in each other's markets through computerized trading and settlement facilities. In sum, borrowers can tap savings anywhere across the world, liquid capital flows freely across borders, financial-asset portfolios are organized globally, and banks operate beyond the reach of domestic regulators.

The central nervous system of this emerging globalized credit system is the *currency market*. This huge market has been revolutionized by the creation of an interbank fund-transfer network named CHIPS (for Clearing-House Interbank Payments System) for the Eurocurrency market and the introduction of financial derivatives (in particular currency futures).[2] CHIPS, run by a private consortium of leading money-center banks, processes most foreign-exchange transactions, whose volume has risen exponentially over the last quarter of a century to a daily average of $1,400 billion. It should be noted that only between 10 and 20 percent of these vast sums traded daily in the world's currency markets correspond to the traditional cross-border activities of trade and long-term foreign investments. The rest consists of short-term capital flows, so-called *hot money*, through which multinational corporations, banks, and institutional investors adjust their global financial-asset portfolios to changing interest-rate differentials and exchange-rate volatility. What we are talking about here is the historically most developed form of *financial speculation* to date, fed by volatile interest and exchange rates.

This speculative activity, the engine behind the globalization of finance, has in no small part been encouraged by deregulation of money and banking—first the appearance of stateless private bank money in the form of Eurocurrencies in the 1960s, then the collapse of Bretton Woods' fixed exchange rates in the early 1970s, followed by the deregulation of interest rates after 1979 and the removal of capital and exchange controls during the 1980s. This deregulation has facilitated the kind of near-perfect mobility of financial capital that we encounter today. It has also made exchange rates and interest rates that much more volatile as those two prices of money became less managed by governments and more subject to free-market regulation. Multinational corporations and financial institutions use hedging devices (e.g., currency futures) to protect their cash-flow commitments against these heightened price risks, while as speculators they may use those same instruments to benefit from correctly anticipated price movements. Hedgers in search of loss avoidance and speculators looking for trading profits ("capital gains") will shift their funds whenever they expect changes in exchange rates or in relative interest-rate differentials. What they do in effect is a form of *arbitrage,* an activity defined as the profitable exploitation of price differentials for the same object in different markets or of its price movements over time.

## The emerging triad of currency zones

The remarkable expansion of currency trading has evolved in a context where the once-absolute dominance of the U.S. dollar has steadily eroded in the aftermath of Bretton Woods' collapse in 1971. Today the dollar's global market share as key currency has dwindled to barely about 50 percent (from over 90 percent in the late 1960s). While the dollar is still the principal form of world money and may well continue in this position due to the system's inherent preference for a single international monetary standard, it now has to contend with more serious rivals such as the German mark and the Japanese yen. These two currencies in particular have sharply risen in importance, especially in a regional context. Neither Germany nor Japan, both highly trade-dependent economies, want to see their currencies reach world-money status for fear that the currency appreciation typically associated with such a process would hurt their export-dependent industries too much. But both nations have developed at the same time strong economic ties with their neighbors, and in this regional integration process their respective currencies have become the anchor for emerging *currency zones*.

• The European Monetary System (EMS), set up in 1979 to shield European currencies from the interminable fluctuations of the dollar, has been dominated by the mark. The planned *Economic and Monetary Union* (EMU), which will succeed the EMS as a single-currency system for the European Union based on a new currency named *Euro,* is still likely to be overshadowed by German actions and preferences.

• Japan propelled its currency to dominance in East Asia's Pacific Rim during the late 1980s due to its massive capital exports in the region in the form of loans, portfolio investments, and above all direct investments. In contrast to the European situation, the yen's status as East Asia's dominant currency lacks any formal institutional grounding, and its relative position may have weakened in the first half of the 1990s due to Japan's crisis-induced retrenchment. We must also consider the fact that the dollar still plays a major role in the region due to the export orientation of many local economies and their success in attracting U.S. direct and portfolio investments (e.g., Korea, Hong Kong, Singapore, Taiwan, Malaysia, Thailand). This presence of the dollar is reinforced by America's extensive security commitments in the region. The battle between Japan and the United States in the Pacific Rim will take more concrete and explicit shape over the next decade when the recently launched *Asia Pacific Economic Cooperation* (APEC) initiative gets off the ground in earnest.

• The Americans have responded to the challenge of mark- and yen-dominated regions by pushing for regional integration with their neighbors, Canada and Mexico, under the *North American Free Trade Agreement* (NAFTA) framework. This free-trade agreement may soon include Chile, with whom negotiations are already under way. The United States would like to extend its provisions eventually to the entire Western Hemisphere, a so-called *Free Trade Area of the Americas* (FTAA), and thereby create a dollar-dominated zone of regional integration stretching from the South Pole to the Arctic Sea.

The emergence of such a *triad,* three integrated regions each dominated by a leading industrial power (United States, Japan, Germany), is threatening to spur centrifugal tendencies in the world economy. In the absence of a cold war, which used to cement relations between those three leaders into a common front against the Soviet Union, conflicts of interest between the three have come to the fore as their once-unassailable security alliance gives way to economic competition. Those conflicts must be contained, lest they tear the global economy into three adversarial, increasingly protectionist blocs vying for power with each other. Such a situation would in the end benefit no one, since the negative externalities and opportunity costs it entails are potentially so high that any adversarial tripolar arrangement becomes a negative-sum game. The only way to avoid such a regression to global conflict is through multilateral agreements that commit the three powers and their respective allies to measures and mechanisms that keep their markets open and foster cooperation with each other.

## Restricting "hot money" flows

The issue of global financial speculation is taken up in this chapter by Howard Wachtel. The American University economist traces the origins of this new phenomenon back to the 1960s when the Eurocurrency market grew into a convenient conduit for currency speculation against rigidly fixed exchange rates that had been set more than two decades earlier at Bretton Woods. The ability of Euromarket participants to bypass national banking regulations and attack unrealistic currency prices had major repercusisons. It destroyed the gold-backed dollar standard of Bretton Woods, forced exchange rates to become "flexible" (i.e., market-determined), and prompted removal of regulatory restrictions on domestic banking operations. This broad wave of deregulation during the 1970s was enthusiastically welcomed by most economists. The Monetarists in particular had argued for a long time (see, for instance, Friedman, 1953) that flexible exchange rates would enforce equilibrating adjustments in external imbalances speedily, thereby reducing the incentives for short-term capital flows. Governments would then be able to pursue domestic economic-policy objectives better shielded from exchange-rate considerations and other external constraints. These predictions would now finally be put to a real-life test.

The rosy picture drawn by the economic orthodoxy in favor of market regulation of currency prices has not been borne out by reality. Exchange rates have proven increasingly volatile, both on a short-run basis (with daily price fluctuations in excess of 1 percent not uncommon) as well as over the longer run (with multiyear cycles in exchange-rate movements exceeding 50 percent in either direction the norm). Wachtel points out that such volatility of the most strategic price category in international transactions, besides invalidating all of Friedman's optimistic predictions, is bound to be detrimental to the stability of the world economy.

• Highly unstable currency prices invite massive speculation for capital gains and necessitate elaborate hedging against price risk. These activities are essentially unproductive (apart from creating a lot of jobs in the financial-services sector) and costly.[3] Their amazing spread in recent years has raised the costs of international transactions to the detriment of trade and long-term capital flows. And the increasingly attractive pursuit of financial income through global portfolios has diverted a lot of corporate funds from long-term investment projects that would benefit the economy more.

• The huge volume of short-term capital flows engendered by exchange-rate volatility has actually had the perverse effect of widening external imbalances by undercutting adjustment processes.[4] And those flows tend to be self-feeding as individual actors in this fast-moving market observe what others do and form their expectations together in mimetic fashion. In that sense speculation is, unlike the individual arbitrage model of Friedman (1953), an inherently destabilizing activity prone to excessive overshooting in one direction before being violently corrected to move in the other direction. Such a pattern invites greater instability in the world economy, in particular the triggering of financial crises with significant contagion potential (as we have seen recently in the case of the European Monetary System in 1992/93 and the Mexican peso in 1994/95).

• The dominance of currency speculation (and hedging) has created what Wachtel qualifies as a *supranational economy,* thriving on price instability and imposing its logic of free-market regulation on governments as never before. For example, the speculators have extended their field of operations to interest-rate movements, especially in terms of relative differentials adjusted for risk. If one country's interest rates are deemed too low relative to others and in light of underlying economic performance criteria, capital will move out of that country and thus drive up interest rates there. It has therefore become impossible for any central bank to use the interest rate as a policy variable for domestic stabilization purposes without endangering exchange-rate stability for its currency. This new external constraint imposed by the supranational economy on governments, crystallized in the fear of sudden and potentially overwhelming capital flights, has undermined their intervention capacity in a much broader sense. The collective sentiment of agents operating in the global currency, bond, and stock markets in favor of low inflation, high real interest rates, continued financial deregulation, and much smaller budget deficits has become the key concern of governments worried about maintaining their "credibility" in the world's financial markets. If they pursue other policy objectives, which the market agents of "hot money" dislike, they may pay dearly with a currency crisis that can be ended only with a reversal of policy (as happened to Britain's Labor Government in 1975, Carter in 1979, or France's Mitterrand in 1983).

Wachtel deems it necessary to tame global "hot money" with regulatory restraints by the monetary authorities, beginning with an extension of reserve requirements to Eurocurrency deposits. He reminds us of Keynes' accurate warnings not to let the two prices of money, the exchange rate and the interest rate, become subject to market regulation. Finding ways to regulate these two prices effectively should therefore be a matter of some urgency for policy makers. Wachtel suggests that governments commit themselves to keeping exchange rates of key currencies within a reasonable range, subject to occasional adjustments should circumstances require such a step. This proposal for *target zones*, an idea taken up in greater detail below by Bergsten, should be supported by coordination of interest-rate policies between the leading economic powers.[5]

The principal rationale for this suggestion is that there will be much less incentive to speculate (or hedge) when exchange rates are more stable and interest-rate differentials more accurate. Speculation may even become a stabilizing factor, when the agents of "hot money" understand that prices are moving toward government-set limits and that therefore greater gains are to be made from betting on a correction in the reverse direction. Another very interesting idea to restrain global financial speculation, which in recent years has gained renewed interest, concerns the imposition of a uniform transaction tax on foreign-exchange dealings in the major financial centers of the world.[6] As David Felix argues, the rate on this tax need not be high (he recommends 0.5 percent) to seriously erode the profitability of currency speculation. Even at low rate levels, such a tax would yield large revenues for participating governments which could be spent for global stabilization purposes (e.g., long-term lending for economic-development projects in less-developed countries).

## Target zones and macroeconomic stabilization

The world economy, driven by the inherently unstable modus operandi of globally integrated financial capital and the centrifugal forces of its tripolar configuration, needs careful management to withstand these pressures. Yet one of the most important characteristics of this world economy, in contradistinction to the traditional national organization of economic systems, is the absence of a supranational state capable of such management. The deeply rooted sense of sovereignty among the various nation-states and their populations, forged in most cases over centuries of often difficult nation building, continues to prevail and prevents such a supranational state from emerging in the near future. Yet nation-states have at the same time also experienced a dramatic erosion in their de facto sovereignty over domestic policy. The possibility of massive capital flight constrains policy options, competition for scarce capital supplies across the globe forces the opening of once-closed economies, and the intense battle for global market shares necessitates new cross-border alliances. Amidst these pressures governments have come to realize across the globe that they cannot manage their own economies unless there is a modicum of cooperation and coordination between them.

The modalities of such supranational management of international relations is taken up in the two *Challenge* interviews with Fred Bergsten, one of America's most influential international economists, which we have reprinted in this chapter. Even though his first interview in 1990 may appear a bit outdated today, especially with regard to his overly optimistic assessments of European integration and Japan's dominance of high-tech industries, it introduces the major outlines of his coordination strategy which the second interview in 1995 elaborates further. Both times Bergsten argues that the world economy is evolving towards three regional blocs (Americas, Europe, and Pacific Rim) and that multilateral initiatives are required for each dimension of relationship in this tripolar configuration.

Bergsten starts his first interview with a brief discussion of the need for new global security arrangements in the aftermath of the cold war to contain rogue states and old conflicts. Here the United States, as the only country that is both a global economic as well as military power, still has a fundamental leadership role to play, as exemplified in the Gulf War of 1990–91 and subsequent U.S. peace initiatives in the Middle East and Europe. The growing importance of economic matters in the geopolitical arena is clearly evident in the willingness of various countries to pay others for their security interests, as witnessed in the Gulf War.[7]

Bergsten then turns his attention to trade, where he sees two parallel developments whose interaction needs careful attention. On the one hand, we are witnessing regional integration initiatives through which the leading economic powers of their world construct "zones of influence" that they dominate, such as the European "single market" and "single currency" projects or America's NAFTA. Neighboring countries on the fringes of these blocs, in Latin America, Northern and Western Africa, Eastern Europe, and South Asia, are accelerating integration of their local economies for eventual participation in these blocs. Within that tripolar context there are clear signs of interbloc conflict and protectionism, especially in America's bilateral relations with the European Union and Japan. On the other hand, we can see a continuous and consistent effort by the industrial nations to negotiate multilateral and globally applicable trade liberalization rules, from GATT's tariff-reduction agreements in the 1950s (e.g., Dillon Round) to the ambitious Uruguay Round concluded in 1994.[8] These agreements are of crucial importance, because they provide a nondiscriminatory level playing field for everyone, extend the benefits of increasingly open markets, and offer a chance for peaceful resolution of commercial conflicts. The key question is how to reconcile and connect the regional bloc formation initiatives with the evolving multilateral framework for world trade.[9]

One of the more remarkable trends in the world economy is the explosion of foreign investment activity by multinational corporations, turning themselves into global production networks. Bergsten feels that this activity should also be put on a legally sounder and politically safer footing through a global investment code. A beginning was made in this direction during the Uruguay Round negotiations on the subject of so-called trade-related investment measures (TRIMs), such as local-content and export-performance requirements which newly industrializing countries often try to impose on multinational corporations, as well as global protection of "intellectual property rights" which guide the transfer of technology between nations. In 1995 the members of the Organization for Economic Cooperation and Development (OECD), comprising the world's industrial nations, agreed to launch negotiations toward a multilateral agreement on investment that would extend the WTO principles of nondiscrimination (national treatment, most-favored nation status) to this activity and establish an international legal framework for investment-related issues (i.e., cross-border transfers, expropriation, performance requirements, conflict resolution between private investors and national governments). Since the investment issue will surely also emerge in the APEC context, the OECD framework may lay the foundations for a global investment accord in the next WTO round.

The final dimension of Bergsten's multilateral framework to manage the emerging tripolar world economy concerns international monetary reform. Such reform is essential, because neither the fixed-rate regime of Bretton Woods nor the flexible-rate regime introduced in 1973 has worked. In the absence of an effective regulatory mechanism governing currency prices, the world economy tends towards excessive instability and protectionist pressures. Both tendencies are likely to be particularly pronounced in our emerging multicurrency regime where speculators, hedgers, and other investors are constantly reevaluating their choices between three competing key currencies.

Bergsten recommends an intermediate solution, a regime of target zones for exchange rates of the key currencies which would allow for fluctuations of plus or minus 10 percent from a set level. The key central banks would coordinate their foreign-exchange interventions in defense of these target zones, provide each other with credit lines and swap facilities to increase their collective intervention capacity, and meet regularly to see whether their price ranges need adjusting. Such a system was put into place by the Group of Seven (United States, Japan, Germany, France, Italy, Britain, and Canada) in the *Louvre Agreement* of 1987. But that system has not really worked all that well. Cooperation on currency prices has been sporadic, usually in response to major shifts in exchange-rate alignments that have caused currency markets to become disorderly (e.g., dollar decline against mark and yen in early 1995 after the Mexican peso crisis). The annual G-7 summits have proven too unwieldy for any serious discussions of international monetary relations. Broader coordination of macroeconomic policies has been confined to occasional synchronization of interest-rate adjustments to counteract recessionary pressures spreading across the globe (e.g., after the stock-market crash of October 1987).

Bergsten would strengthen the Louvre Agreement by leaving the management of the target zone to the three leaders (United States, European Union, Japan) and instituting a G-3 mechanism of regular consultation. More important, he wants a much deeper level of G-3 coordination of macroeconomic policies in which corrective policy adjustments would automatically become an issue for negotiation if certain preestablished performance criteria warranted such action. This point is absolutely vital, because trade balances are in large part determined by such domestic macroeconomic variables as the savings–investment relation or government budgets. America's chronic trade deficits, for instance, are primarily due to our inadequate savings (relative to investment) and structural budget deficits. Japan's large trade surplus is caused by precisely the opposite conditions. If we want to reverse this pattern, which is desirable not least because of our continuous dependence on capital imports turning us from being the world's leading creditor nation to its largest debtor nation within a decade, then we have to correct the policy mix between Japan and the United States.

William Burke gives us a historic account of key developments in the United States and Japan as well as in the complicated relationship between these two countries to show how difficult it is to coordinate macroeconomic policies with each other. The particular conditions in each country, which have created the current misalignment in policy mix, are deeply rooted in cultural traditions, historic experiences, and political preferences. America's consumer-driven economy and Japan's societal organization toward thrift and productivity have developed over many decades and are likely to resist rapid change. Nor do the two governments, each in its own way captured by dominant private interests at home, find it easy to let their domestic economic policies become subject to international negotiations. As long as neither side simultaneously corrects its current-account balance through fiscal and monetary policy adjustments, the exchange rate between yen and dollar will continue to see the kind of exaggerated movement witnessed during the last decade.

## Notes

1. The Eurocurrency market, which took off in the late 1960s and has since grown to over $2 trillion, involves bank deposits and loans in a currency kept outside its country of issue (e.g., U.S.-dollar deposits in London-based bank accounts). Two-thirds of this *Euromoney*, as it is often referred to, consists of dollars whose market share has gradually declined in favor of Euromark, Euroyen, and other Eurocurrency accounts. This form of stateless money is tied to domestic checking accounts, whose property titles change with each Euromarket transaction in that currency abroad. But in the absence of reserve requirements applying to these transactions there is no regulatory limitation to the creation and circulation of Euromoney accounts.

2. Financial derivatives are credit instruments whose value and cash-flow commitments are determined by the behavior of the underlying financial markets to which they are tied. There are tradable derivatives, such as currency futures or stock-index futures, as well as nontraded derivatives specifically tailored to individual portfolio contingencies, such as interest or currency swaps.

3. Hedging involves direct payments made to hold option or futures contracts, which are passed on to others via higher prices on goods, services, and assets traded internationally. Apart from the same kind of transaction costs, speculation engenders negative externalities (e.g., greater price volatility, shortened investment horizons), which burden the global economy more indirectly.

4. Two examples may suffice to illustrate this perverse effect. One is the *sliding J-curve* effect, in which speculators continuously drive down a currency as the anticipated improvement in the trade deficit fails to materialize due to the fact that import- and export-price responses to such currency depreciation tend to occur much more rapidly than counteracting volume adjustments in the opposite direction. The other example concerns the interaction between current and capital accounts in the balance of payments. If a country runs a sizable current-account deficit financed by capital imports, it will incur higher debt servicing charges that, when booked as a debit item, will serve only to increase the current-account deficit.

5. The original theoretical argument in favor of such target zones and macroeconomic policy coordination was presented by J. Williamson (1987).

6. This particular idea was first voiced by Tobin (1978) and is therefore often referred to as the Tobin tax.

7. While the United States received payments from Arabian Gulf states, Western Europe, and Japan for defending their vital

interests of secure oil supplies, it was the United States who paid the Ukraine and North Korea for abandoning their ambitions to become nuclear powers.

8. The Uruguay Round, concluded with the Marrakesh Agreement between 116 nations in April 1994, established zero-tariff markets for key industries, reduced tariffs across the board in many other sectors, phased out quotas, limited export subsidies, strengthened intellectual property rights, extended open-market rules for the first time to services, textiles, and agriculture, and replaced GATT with a stronger World Trade Organization (WTO).

9. This can happen through negotiations between the respective blocs, as has been attempted by the United States in 1995 with its APEC and Trans-Atlantic Trade and Investment Initiative proposals, or it can take the form of bilateral approaches, as in the sectoral "framework" agreements between the United States and Japan. It should be noted that each of the last three major GATT rounds (Kennedy Round in early 1960s, Tokyo Round of mid-1970s, and Uruguay Round of late 1980s) were prompted by increasing steps in Western Europe toward greater regional integration. This trend leads one to conclude that the establishment of an economic and monetary union in Europe will probably trigger yet another multilateral negotiation round under the auspices of the WTO early in the next decade.

HOWARD M. WACHTEL

# Taming Global Money

*The nation-state has been weakened in its influence over economic performance. An emerging supranational economic order is imposing a unified ideology of free markets on an historical setting to which it is ill-suited.*

Of all the changes in the global economy over the past generation, none have occurred with such alacrity as those in global money and finance. And in no other policy sphere have governments lagged further behind in introducing effective supervision and regulation.

Walter Wriston, who (as chairman of Citicorp) was in on the creation of this new world financial order, has written that this was a "new system ... not built by politicians or economists ... which in turn has allowed [the] creation of a new international monetary system. This state of affairs does not sit too well with many sovereign governments because they correctly perceive [it] as an attack on the very nature of sovereign power."

As political sovereignty is challenged by privatized global finance, economic performance in the industrial economies suffers. The results are: higher unemployment, as wealth forsakes capital formation for financial speculation; lower trade volumes to cover the higher costs of foreign-exchange risk; and higher real rates of interest, as countries position their interest rates competitively to stabilize foreign-exchange values.

The Federal Reserve Board of New York estimates that, after allowing for resales, some $650 billion in foreign-exchange transactions are completed each day in New York, Tokyo, and London. Only about 18 percent support either international trade or investment—the ostensible reasons for foreign-exchange markets. The other 82 percent is speculation, the sole purpose of which is to buy enormous volumes low and sell higher in order to make a small unit profit, but a large overall profit. These profits appear as ephemeral jottings on a computer screen.

A globalized money system that recognizes no geographic boundaries threatens the most fundamental economic raison d'être of the nation-state—the ability to control its money supply and influence the value of its money. Using the marvel of modern computer power and telecommunications technology that recognizes no national boundaries, this foreign-exchange system comprises the essence of a *supranational economy*—one that is governed by the fundamental tension between the unbounded economic geography of a private global money system and the bounded political geography of nation states. While recognizing that this technological and institutional genie cannot be put back into the bottle, it is essential, nevertheless, that boundaries be placed on the effect of its operations. There are two compelling reasons for boundaries: (1) a potential for vast finan-

HOWARD M. WACHTEL is Professor of Economics at The American University and is the author of *The Money Mandarins: The Making of a New Supranational Economic Order*, M.E. Sharpe, 1990. Reprinted from *Challenge*, January–February 1995, pp. 36–40.

cial instability; and (2) the undermining of the twentieth century's governing project of social democracy.

## The Scope of the Problem

Several criteria for the policies that will be proposed for dealing with this problem ought to prevail:

- They should be kept simple;
- existing national policies should be extended where feasible;
- existing venues and organizations for international collaboration should be used and no new ones created; and
- no new international treaty arrangements should be promulgated.

With these criteria in mind, I suggest we extend all existing national monetary controls, regulations, and supervision to this global money system. It escapes all such government policies now. Much of this unregulated money flows through the *Eurodollar system* and comes under no national regulatory authority. The system takes its name from, and is defined by, the phenomenon of currencies used outside the borders of any country. It is, therefore, outside the jurisdiction of its nation of origin.

The birth of this system goes back to the late 1940s, when the Soviet Union placed its dollar holdings in a French bank to avoid the possibility of having these accounts frozen, should the United States employ this strategy to wage the cold war. The funds grew slowly, and their potential was not realized until the United States imposed capital export controls in the 1960s. Banks and their multinational corporate customers then found ways around the exchange controls by using the Eurodollar system. The system reached maturity in the 1970s by being the principal receptacle of some $350 billion in surpluses earned by OPEC countries.

About 85 percent of this surplus is made up of dollars, with German marks and Japanese yen being the two other principal currencies. Technically, these currencies should be regulated in the jurisdiction in which they are used—a practice ignored for fear that the operations would be moved to an unregulated venue, if a government began to regulate their activities. We do not even have a good accounting of the dollars in the Eurodollar markets. A rough estimate is that it is nearly $2 trillion. But no agency of the United States government regulates or monitors its movements.

## Central Banking Reform

Effectively, the Federal Reserve Board has abdicated its central function of control over the portion of the money supply that is influenced by the Eurodollar system. The principal control instrument is the power to set reserve requirements. These are set-asides against deposits that banks are required to sequester. For the dollars that circulate inside the United States, banks are required to set aside such reserves. This is what limits the expansion of the money supply, affords the Federal Reserve control over this crucial monetary function, and allows it to influence interest rates. But no such reserve controls exist for Eurodollars. The growth of this component of the money supply lies solely in private bank hands. Here, banks can theoretically lend out all their deposits, even though they tend to hold small reserves—less, however, than is required on domestic accounts. The ability to hold less idle reserves is what makes the Eurodollar system so attractive to banks. They can make all their deposits work for them, thereby receiving larger profits. Because of these profits, they can charge lower interest rates than on domestic borrowing. The policy of extending reserve requirements to Eurodollars, therefore, would place them on an equal footing with domestic dollars. It would eliminate what is now an incentive for banks to hold and invest dollars outside the United States where they can earn higher profits, charge lower rates of interest, and escape regulatory and tax obligations.

The banks' arguments against such a policy change is that the United States does not have sufficient worldwide influence to effectively implement it and that German marks or Japanese yen would replace dollars in the Eurocurrency markets. In regard to the first point, when one government consistently controls 85 percent or more of the market, it has a "monopoly" position that allows it to dictate terms to the market. As to the second point, Germany and Japan have neither the desire nor the capacity to become the world's reserve currency. The real reason banks oppose this policy change is the loss of a major profit center. But this should not be the basis of a public banking policy, the purpose of which is to promote sound banking and economic stability.

Reserve requirements on Eurodollars (combined with other policies) could encourage investment inside the United States and reduce the incentive now offered to investors outside the United States. The Eurodollar system presents the classic supranational dilemma for public policy. If banks are offered an unregulated and lower-taxed arena outside their nation of origin, and give up no domestic supports at the same time, they will opt to do business there rather than in the regulated and higher-taxed domestic economy. Without precluding banks from operating in the Eurodollar system, it is the job of our government to equalize the domestic and international structures in which banks do business. Otherwise, the outcome is predictable. Banks will protect their Eurodollar environment by investing outside the tax and regulatory scope of the U.S. government. The increasingly aggressive flight of capital from the United States in the past two decades is, in no small measure, induced by the skewed incentives provided by this abdication of public-policy responsibility.

## World Trade

We shall see lower volumes of investment inside the United States and more investment outside as one outcome of the privatized and unregulated global financial system. A second outcome represents the higher costs placed on international trade and the resulting lower volume of world trade than would be the case if public-policy boundaries were placed around foreign-exchange speculation. With speculation in foreign exchange comes risk for anyone dealing in future transactions that require conversion of currencies. This is as true for the lone tourist as it is for a large international-trade enterprise. The higher the volatility, the greater the risk and the higher the cost of covering the risk. The volatility in exchange-rate fluctuations in the 1980s and 1990s has been far greater than anyone anticipated after the end of the Bretton Woods fixed-rate regime between 1971 and 1973 and the introduction of market-determined exchange rates. And with this volatility comes risk, higher costs of internationally traded goods, and a lower volume of world trade.

Risk is a cost that is added to the price of internationally exchanged products. The cost occurs when firms have to enter the futures markets to hedge their projected foreign-exchange transactions. While this adds to the employment and income generated in the peripheral financial sectors of the economy, the goods-production economy suffers as these higher costs are passed on in higher prices. And higher prices mean fewer goods and services sold and produced and lowered employment in those sectors. There is, consequently, a distributional shift in employment that arises from foreign-exchange speculation. Employment in the financial sectors of foreign exchange and futures markets that engage in speculation increases, but employment in the goods-producing segments of the economy suffers.

The most fervent advocates of free trade also resist most aggressively any efforts to place public-policy boundaries around the present foreign-exchange markets. But they fail to realize that these arrangements increase the cost of internationally traded goods and thereby lower the volume of international trade. Public policy that addresses foreign-exchange volatility and speculation is also trade policy in the best tradition of an open trading system—one that is shorn of the ideologically driven mantra of "free trade."

## Currency Speculation

Foreign-exchange speculation feeds off interest-rate differentials among the industrial countries. Even small differences in interest rates, after adjusting for inflation and the risk associated with future exchange-rate changes, can trigger large movements of foreign exchange. Such a development can then take on a life of its own, magnify whatever differentials started the process, and end up destabilizing the structure of interest rates in the currencies that are in play. For example, when interest rates were lower in Great Britain than they were in Germany in 1993 (after taking account of risk and expected inflation) capital moved from Great Britain to Germany. This differential had arisen because of domestic policy decisions taken in each country. Capital moved from England to Germany, as speculators took advantage of the higher returns on the German mark.

Under ordinary circumstances, relatively small movements of currencies out of sterling and into marks would be of no consequence. But if the movement becomes a stampede, then both the mark and sterling will face destabilization. A large rush out of sterling will lower the pound's exchange rate vis-à-vis the mark. If it cannot be contained by intervention, pressure will be placed on British interest rates. First, the market will signal a drift upward in British interest rates to attract and retain capital. Eventually, it [the upward drift in interest rates—Ed.] will have to be ratified by the central bank, thereby forcing a change in policy inside the British domestic economy. This scenario is not fiction. It happened to Great Britain in the summer of 1993.

The Bretton Woods arrangements were constructed,

in part, to allow nations to follow their own domestic economic policies without having them distorted by foreign-exchange speculation. John Maynard Keynes, whose influence transcended all others at Bretton Woods, sought to take the price of money out of the play of the market. He did not believe the government should set prices. His one exception was the price of money, which has an internal and an external price. Its internal price is the interest rate, and its external price is the foreign-exchange rate—one nation's price of money in terms of another's.

Keynes's *The General Theory*, published in the mid-1930s, focused on the internal domestic economy. It ignored, for the most part, external economic relations in the international economy. Central to this work is the interest rate (the internal price of money)—its function, and how it should be determined. Keynes presented a persuasive case that the interest rate should be established by the central bank in order to achieve the objectives of high levels of employment. He insisted that the interest rate be taken out of the play of market forces and that it be one of the instruments of policy retained by the government. In *The General Theory*, this one price (and just this one price!) is set by government.

Keynes extended this reasoning at Bretton Woods. If the external price of money (the foreign-exchange rate) remained within the play of market forces, the domestic interest rate would be affected. It would be dragged into the market, be subjected to its influences, and would undermine the centerpiece of *The General Theory*. The creation of fixed exchange rates, established among governments in international accord, was designed to remove the external price of money from market forces, in order to promote international trade and quarantine domestic interest rates from external market forces.

The designers of Bretton Woods saw the two prices of money linked. If one were set free on the market, inevitably the other would be as well. This would not be a terrible fate, if one believed the market was more astute at setting the internal and external prices of money. But that is not what Keynes believed; nor was it the consensus of those who accepted fixed exchange rates at Bretton Woods.

All this collapsed between 1971 and 1973, when the fixed exchange-rate regime fell under its own weight. It was caused by the absence of imagination on the part of the industrial economies which, for more than a decade, had put off treating the fractures in the Bretton Woods fixed exchange-rate system. When a market-determined exchange-rate system replaced the fixed exchange-rate regime, external prices of money began to gyrate more widely with each cycle of exchange-rate fluctuations. By the end of the 1970s, domestic interest rates were pulled into this maelstrom and were used to stabilize exchange rates. One policy instrument—the domestic interest rate—cannot simultaneously stabilize foreign-exchange rates and achieve domestic macro policy objectives.

Just as Keynes had predicted, once the external price of money was left to float freely on the market, governments began to lose control over their domestic interest rates. In the 1980s and 1990s, the two prices of money have become linked more closely by technology and institutional changes in money markets. Policy managers have absorbed the lessons of the 1970s. They now try to calibrate domestic interest rates to foreign-exchange rate movements.

## A New Policy

The answer to this conundrum is to create a new exchange-rate regime that combines the best of the fixed and market floating systems—one in which the exchange-rate bands are wide enough to accommodate the market, but not so wide as to destabilize domestic interest rates. To make this work, however, a new policy instrument must be created—the coordination of interest-rate policies among the G-3, the United States, the European Union, and Japan. This will enable countries to pursue their own domestic interest-rate objectives, but not at the expense of the potential destabilization from other nations' interest-rate policies that is induced by the foreign-exchange rate-transmission mechanism at this time.

The important factors in the movement of short-term financial capital are the relative interest rates in any two countries. Their level is inconsequential. It should be possible, therefore, to engage in policy coordination over relative interest rates while slowly moving downward the absolute level of interest rates. Today, no one government can lower interest rates too much without threatening a run on their currency and capital flight. But coordination, which can be shown to be in the interest of each of the G-3 members, could restore government's policy capabilities.

The difficulties of such a new policy thrust should not be minimized; nor should the obstacles be seen as insurmountable. The coordination need only occur among three countries—the United States, Japan, and the European Union (with Germany and France being the two major players in the Union). This is not a large group; nor is it one that does not already have formal and informal venues in which consultation goes on continuously. The key actors know each other very well and share a common financial culture and set of interests.

Nations have not pursued this collaborative interest-rate policy because they have jealously guarded what they continue to believe is their exclusive franchise over the value of their money. But this has been only partially valid for nearly two decades. The more quickly countries abandon this fiction, the sooner will they be able to ask the appropriate questions about financial policy in the last decade of the twentieth century.

## At the Crossroads

The problems posed by this new supranational economic order extend beyond the boundaries of economic stability. Political stability is also threatened by a global regime in which the nation-state has been weakened in its influence over economic performance. This is true for the old as well as the new parliamentary democracies. The new parliamentary democracies in the post–cold war era are in conflict with a supranational economic order that leaves scant room for economic improvement and imposes a unified ideology of free markets on an historical setting to which it is ill-suited. For the established market economies, a government that cannot control the internal value of its money—the interest rate—when its currency is under stress, or direct its economic destiny, has limited call on the public for support. In both instances, abstract forces emanating from the global economy appear to exercise more influence over personal economic futures than do elected governments.

The fragmentation of modern society and its accompanying resurgence of nationalism (seen most acutely in Europe) are, in no small measure, a result of the weakened economic influence of governments. Economic insecurity, rising levels of unemployment, and fear of the future all converge to destabilize political systems. They are seen to be ineffective in dealing with the erosion of economic vitality. Blaming others, hunkering down, and replaying old tapes of ethnic hatred are the result of governments having allowed the untamed forces of economic supranationalism to have their way with national economies.

Globalism begets tribalism. Governments no longer exercise dominion over their economies. The minutiae of nationalism's regression coexists with the grand scope of globalism's modernity. Tribal rituals have filled the security void left by public inaction. The threats to social stability spawned by the global economy, therefore, cut more deeply into society than the threat merely to economic stability. In the post–cold war period, this threat has become translated into nationalism and its predilection to the balkanization of societies. By not attending to economic globalism, governments are encouraging the incubation of a nationalism that confronts them with a new security threat.

DAVID FELIX

# *Financial Globalization and the Tobin Tax*

The global turnover of foreign exchange has reached a trillion dollars per day. Only about 5 percent, however, is for trade financing. About another 5 percent represents official transactions and private long-term debt and equity placements. Most of the turnover is devoted either to defending against the volatility of exchange and interest rates that has characterized the global economy since the demise of the Bretton Woods system in the early 1970s or to speculating on that volatility. Transnational corporations hedge against exchange- and interest-rate risks by spreading their liabilities across currencies and time. Banks and brokerage firms aggressively market hedging instruments and move their funds between currencies to exploit interest-rate differentials. But volatility and speculation feed symbiotically on each other. Volatility enhances the opportunities for lucrative but risky international bets on asset price movements. The hedging instruments enable speculators to leverage their bets further. And the speculative flows increase volatility.

## *The problem*

Since the 1960s, the shift from fixed to floating exchange rates and the deregulation of financial markets (notably the lifting of restrictions on cross-border capital flows) have been the chief causative factors of financial globalization. Electronic communications has been a secondary factor. It has speeded up the transaction processes. But as the period between the two world wars demonstrates, global financial bubbling can occur even with a less rapid means of communication.

The dark side is that the ballooning of global finance in the past three decades has been paralleled by slackened growth in the volume of world trade and output, greater unemployment, increased income concentrations, and a dramatic rise in the frequency of global financial crises and near crises. Fearful of capital flight, governments around the world have been subordinating their commitment to full employment and distributional equity to the need to pacify the volatile financial markets. The immense volume of global transactions is, moreover, undermining the effectiveness of pacification through conventional central-bank intervention. Speculative runs can now swamp the financial resources that central banks (*even jointly*) can mobilize to counter such runs.

These adverse trends disprove the predictions of economists who had urged the major capitalist economies to shift to floating exchange rates and decontrolled

DAVID FELIX is Professor of Economics Emeritus, Washington University, St. Louis. Reprinted from *Challenge,* May–June 1995, pp. 56–59.

financial markets. Floating rates, they had argued, would act as shock absorbers. They would insulate each economy from international monetary shocks and thereby increase the scope of countries to pursue independent monetary and fiscal policies. Liberated markets would adjust nominal exchange rates so speedily that they would discourage hot-money flows and would move exchange rates and price levels in offsetting directions. Thus they would minimize the volatility of real exchange and interest rates. Increases in long-term capital flows would improve global resource allocation by bringing about a worldwide convergence of real interest rates.

Since none of this has come to pass, a yearning for stable exchange rates à la Bretton Woods is displacing the earlier enthusiasm in international policy circles for floating exchange rates. The yearning, however, lacks as yet an adequate appreciation of the analysis that had shaped the original Bretton Woods Articles of Agreement and of the circumstances that allowed its exchange-rate regime to succeed.

The architects of Bretton woods believed, not only that floating exchange rates damaged multilateral trade and long-term foreign investment, but also that a stable exchange-rate regime required constraints on international financial mobility. The current yearning accepts only the first proposition, not the second. Thus, the International Monetary Fund (IMF) now acknowledges that "exchange-rate volatility hinders international trade and investment." But it also wants "to lock in the freedom of capital movements already achieved and encourage wider liberalization" by amending the Articles of Agreement of the IMF to require all members to make their currencies fully convertible for all capital transactions.

The Bretton Woods system, which pegged the dollar to gold and other currencies to the dollar, depended on the ability of the United States to fulfill its formal commitment to sell gold at a fixed dollar price and its informal commitment to be global lender of last resort. Its job was to supply emergency liquidity to sustain weaker currencies when their controls against capital flight were being breached. That all ended when the United States, overburdened by its outlays on *Pax Americana*, was no longer willing or able to fulfill these commitments. Cognizant that the United States is no longer the world economic hegemonic power, the IMF proposes instead a sort of hegemony by committee to support the return to exchange-rate stability. The G-3, G-5, or G-7 (which of the Gs is not clear) are to coordinate their monetary, fiscal, and social policies in order to sustain the confidence of the liberated financial markets—these to be the chief suppliers of international liquidity. But this amounts to assigning the fox to guard the chicken coop. Financial markets, with their propensity to overshoot, cannot be relied on to eliminate the volatility and systemic crises of which they are a root cause.

## A solution

The Tobin Tax on foreign-exchange transactions would partly finesse these problems. Proposed by economist and Nobel Laureate James Tobin in 1978, the tax would "throw some sand in the well-greased wheels of the global financial markets." In Keynes's well-known phrase, it would thereby help "to mitigate the predominance of speculation over enterprise."

It would accomplish this because a small transactions tax (e.g., 0.5 percent) on foreign-exchange transactions would cut deeply into the yield from "short-term financial round-trip excursions into another currency." The expected return on these transactions is usually a modest percentage of the highly leveraged funds put in motion. But it would have a lighter impact on trade and long-term investment with their higher percentage yields and delayed financial round-tripping. Moreover, while speculators, saddled with both the tax bite and less exchange volatility to exploit, would be clear losers, exporters, importers, and long-term investors would benefit from more stable exchange rates and a lesser need to incur hedging costs as a *quid pro quo* for their tax bites.

The tax would also give governments more scope to implement employment and social-equity programs. For example, a 0.5 percent tax would allow domestic interest rates on 90-day paper to deviate an additional 4 percent from foreign rates without sparking capital flows to exploit the interest differences, thereby setting off exchange-rate turbulence. The revenue from the tax would also allow substantial funding of such programs without arousing a major instigator of capital flight— worsening of the fiscal deficit.

Tobin's tax proposal, however, evoked little interest when it was published in 1978. FOREX transactions were then a small fraction of today's global volume. Explaining away the intensified exchange- and interest-rate volatility as merely the transitional adjustment of financial markets to new stable equilibria following the

OPEC oil shocks was then somewhat plausible.

In addition, his contention didn't sit well with most mainstream economists. It was that, because "goods and labor moved in response to international price signals much more sluggishly than fluid funds, and prices in goods and labor markets moved more sluggishly than prices of financial assets, including exchange rates," slowing the reaction time of financial markets in a *sine qua non* for stabilizing the real economy. Many of these economists were then adherents of "the efficient market hypothesis," which asserts that financial markets are efficient information-processing institutions. When allowed to operate freely, their continual revaluation of asset values produces the best possible price signals on which to base long-term resource allocation. Hence, contrary to Tobin's contention, the more quickly financial markets react, the better it is for the real economy. It has taken a decade of scholarly probing and real-world experience with financial bubbles and crises to expose the unreal theoretical premises of the hypothesis and its misreading of the actual behavioral dynamics of financial markets.

The Tobin Tax is now an idea whose time has come. Its objective—to curb international financial volatility—is now widely shared. Its Bretton Woods theoretical perspective on financial-market dynamics is once again gaining mainstream status among economists. The prospective revenue from a globally uniform Tobin Tax has risen to a very interesting order of magnitude. When Tobin first proposed it, global exchange-rate transactions were small enough for him to suggest putting all the tax revenue in a central fund for relending to Third World countries, as an offset to the "foreign aid fatigue" of the 1970s. Today, a 0.5 percent tax on exchange transactions would, along with reducing them to a more stable size, augment government revenues globally by as much as $300 to $400 billion per annum. Devoting merely 10 to 20 percent of that revenue to a revolving fund for long-term lending to Third World countries would be a healthy substitute for the hot money on which some have become disastrously overdependent.

## Banquo's ghost

Still, the Tobin Tax merely hovers, like Banquo's ghost, over official conferences on the stabilization of the global monetary system. It is because of technical unfeasibility? The problems of defining the scope of transactions to be taxed, the optimum tax rate, and enforcement procedures are tractable. Their solution makes far fewer demands on the regulatory skill and wisdom of governments than would a return to direct controls. The technical problems cannot explain why the Tobin proposal gets the silent treatment, rather than full assessment, at the policy confabs. The proposal does require a uniform tax rate to be applied by at least the major financial-center countries to minimize evasion through the booking of transactions in the least-taxed financial centers. But this would be far less demanding than the international coordination of monetary, fiscal, and social policies which have been the standard recommendation of the conferences.

The main obstacles to the adoption of the Tobin Tax lie, therefore, in the realm of political economy. An obvious one is the resistance of financial sectors around the world to being taxed. That resistance is understandable, since some of the side benefits of the Tobin Tax would be shrinkage of financial sectors and the release of skilled human capital to more socially productive activities. Less obvious is why the productive sectors, who would benefit from the tax, have been unwilling to break ranks with the financial sectors.

The answer, I suggest, is that elites of the two sectors are now bonded by a common objective—made more politically feasible by the cold war victory of capitalism. That objective is to shrink, perhaps even to liquidate, the welfare state. The ability of financial capital, with its instant international mobility to terrorize governments, makes it a valued ally in the effort. Its disruptive behavior raises capital costs and instability for the productive sectors, but coordinated crisis management by the governments of the major capitalist economies will suffice, they hope, to contain the instability without undermining their broader objective. The Tobin Tax, on the other hand, though a more effective way of containing the instability, would undermine the attainment of that objective.

The chief barriers to the adoption of the Tobin Tax are thus ideological and political, rather than technical. Those to whom a return to the free-wheeling barbaric capitalism of yore is ethically repugnant, therefore, should see in the tax an essential weapon in their struggle to give capitalism a human face.

INTERVIEW WITH C. FRED BERGSTEN

# A New Big Three to Manage the World Economy

*Q* With the collapse of communism in Eastern Europe, the end of the cold war, reunification of the Germanys, and now the outbreak of a new Persian Gulf crisis, the world is sailing precariously into very uncharted waters. From your vantage point at the Institute for International Economics, how do you see these changes?

A. We are witnessing three historic transformations. One is the change in the global security situation triggered by the end of the cold war, German unification, and radical political and economic changes in Eastern Europe. Now the Middle East crisis has demonstrated to us that global collective security arrangements, as originally envisaged under the UN Charter, have become possible. That, along with the end of the cold war, raises major implications for new military arrangements, alliance structures, and the very nature of a nation's defense establishment.

Second, although the Middle East crisis is a reminder that you can't forget security issues, it is clear that the relative importance of security matters is declining as compared with economic issues. The status of countries will be determined in the future much more by their economic capacities than by their military prowess. That dramatically enhances the role of Japan and an economically united Europe and sharply reduces the role of the Soviet Union. The United States is an interesting case because it is the only superpower in both military and economic terms. So whereas U.S. military prowess becomes perhaps less important, the fact that it is both an economic and a military superpower and can marry those two capabilities, as it has in the Middle East crisis, certainly gives the United States a major continuing role.

A new era of burden sharing may already be emerging, as we cope with the Middle East crisis along with European developments. Just this week we saw three fascinating bits of news: West Germany paid the Soviet Union $8 billion to withdraw its troops from East Germany; the Arabs paid the Americans $6 billion to $12 billion to defend them in the Gulf crisis; and the Japanese have put up $4 billion for the frontline countries to help maintain the embargo against Saddam Hussein. Thus, the countries that can afford it—Germany, Japan, and some Arab lands—are essentially paying for global security arrangements, increasing their clout and role in the whole process. In this fashion, economic capabilities will become much more important in dividing up global financial responsibility.

The third transformation is the change in the under-

C. FRED BERGSTEN is Director of the Institute for International Economics, Washington, D.C., and former Assistant Secretary of the Treasury for International Affairs, 1977–81. This interview was conducted by Richard D. Bartel, Editor of *Challenge*, on September 13, 1990, in Washington, D.C. Reprinted from *Challenge*, November–December 1990, pp. 17–25.

lying economic capabilities that the payments I just mentioned also reflect. By the end of this decade, and maybe sooner, a truly tripolar world economic structure will emerge, with a sharing of burdens and responsibilities among a unified Europe, Japan, and the United States. America will no longer dominate. A united Europe will become the world's largest market and biggest international trader. Japan is already the world's largest creditor nation and a leader in many key technologies. The Big Three of economics will displace the Big Two of nuclear power.

Q. Your vision of the future hinges on the economic foundations. But are the economic Big Three of tripolar leadership dealing effectively with their internal economic problems to meet the challenge?
A. As always, countries are dealing with their problems only partially and some have blinders on. The trick in putting together the new world economy is for the Big Three to maintain strong, competitive domestic economies, while at the same time they contribute to a cooperative, effective global economic system.

Q. Are they making progress?
A. First, look at how they are putting their domestic economies in shape. The Japanese have done that and are continuing to do that. I don't worry about Japan making the adjustment, though its population is aging and it still depends on external natural resources. Japan has demonstrated an ability to deal with such problems and to defend itself from a world that might try to gang up on it through trade protection.

Looking at Europe, we tend to forget that it was suffering only a decade ago from Eurosclerosis and Europessimism. But the Europeans have pulled their socks up. Europe is now benefiting from a new burst of integration in the western part of the continent in the Europe 1992 initiative. Plus they're getting inspiration from the East that is now spurring an investment boom and more rapid growth than anyone expected a few years ago.

Q. Maybe the diagnosis of Eurosclerosis ten years ago was not a very accurate appraisal of reality.
A. Maybe it wasn't, but European unemployment rates were very high by both their own historical and global standards. Their growth rates were sub par. It took Europe a long time to recover from the recession of the early '80s. So there were definitely indicators of weakness.

But the United States faces the biggest problems in achieving an appropriate internal adjustment to the needs of the newly emerging international order. The American economy still suffers from the twin deficits—budget and trade. We still have very low productivity growth and a low domestic saving rate. Even more fundamental for our economy, we have persistent problems with our education system, the motivation of our work force, and the short-term focus of our business managers. This country still has a long way to go to gear up for this new world in which international economic issues are the centerpiece of global affairs and key to domestic prosperity, and in which Japan and a united Europe will be tough competitors.

*Q* You have quoted the Japanese politician, Shintaro Ishihara, who predicted that "the twenty-first century will be a century of economic warfare." Do you think that the disappointment or, to use your word, disdain of some Europeans and Japanese over the apparent inability of the United States to solve its domestic economic problems has already become a point of contention that undermines the kind of cooperative, tripolar management you envision?
A. I think it makes it more difficult, but I don't think it is at a crucial point yet. People in those countries do express dismay about the long time it is taking the United States to get its act together. It's close to ten years now and our economic problems are growing more serious. At the same time, there are three offsetting factors. One is the enormous goodwill around the world toward the United States, and I think a genuine desire that we make the necessary adjustments. It's not as if in most quarters they're gloating about America's problems. They're basically wringing their hands and saying they need a strong America.

The second offsetting factor, which is really part and parcel of the first, is the continued need for U.S. leadership and support in the area of global security. The Middle East crisis underscores that need. Our allies want us to be strong and they don't wish us ill, even as they compete with us.

The third positive factor is that there are now indications of a resurgence of American competitive capabilities. U.S. productivity growth in manufacturing has improved very impressively during the course of the 1980s. We've cut the gap between ourselves and the Europeans and even the Japanese. Our productivity growth in manufacturing has been considerably faster in the '80s than it was in the '70s or '60s. Since the dollar came down in 1985–86 we have had a continuing export boom, and we've been able to expand the U.S. world market share and, with continued progress in penetrating foreign markets, again become the world's leading exporter. The United States can compete internationally; it's not a weak, uncompetitive economy.

All of which has led observers in most parts of the world, and in thoughtful quarters here in the United States, to conclude that we continue to have a policy problem, particularly with national fiscal policy, but that this country is not in the kind of long-term fundamental decline that many would say the British experienced for much of this century. The United States is suffering from a temporary aberration: we let our guard down, we got lazy, we got sloppy, both in public policy and private corporate management, but those things are remediable. Of course, it's up to us whether we ratify that view or waste another decade; if the latter, the result might be a much more negative and much more abiding judgment against us around the world.

*Q* Turning now to Europe's internal problems, do you see that they will be able to keep a global perspective in spite of the drive toward Europe '92, the unification of the two Germanys, and the opening up of Eastern Europe?

A. This is the European dimension of the new global order I see—the unification and integration of Eastern and Western Europe. The big question is whether European leaders can maintain a global outlook as they focus on the difficult issues of their new internal and regional arrangements. I am sympathetic to their lack of attention to the global dimension, but frankly it has also disturbed me. Take, for example, the two main blueprints for economic and monetary union (EMU) in Europe—the original Jacques Delors [president of the European Commission] committee report of April 1989, calling for a three-stage economic and monetary union, and Karl Otto Pöhl's [president of Germany's Bundesbank] speech in January of this year in which he detailed a European Central Bank System (ECBS) within an EMU. Neither of those blueprints says anything about the impact on the rest of the world, and I regard that as a shocking omission. I raised that problem with both Delors and Pöhl, and they conceded the accuracy of my observation with a little embarrassment.

The preoccupation with internal European affairs and the neglect of the consequences for the rest of the world are not malevolent, I think. But the rest of the world does have a very legitimate right to ask the Europeans how their activities will fit with an effective, cooperative global economic system. There needn't be any inherent conflict between what the Europeans are doing and what we want to achieve for the world system. But we ought to be looking at the movements toward both systems simultaneously.

Q. How do you want to proceed toward compatible systems?

A. I have proposed that we launch a new global negotiation for monetary reform. That negotiation should proceed in parallel with the European discussion of EMU, just as we now have an Uruguay Round on global trade liberalization going on in parallel with the European trade negotiations for Europe 1992. It is dangerous to permit such an important regional development to proceed without simultaneously fusing it into a global system. We risk winding up with a regional organization that is incompatible with the effective, cooperative global system that we're aiming for.

The United States has always taken the lead in trying to mesh European trade development with an open global system. The Dillon and Kennedy rounds of trade negotiations in the 1960s and '70s were really a response to the creation of the European Common Market itself. The Tokyo Round of the '70s was, to an important degree, a response to the broadening of the Common Market to include Great Britain and some other countries in the 1970s and already some broadening of those trade agreements. Now the Uruguay Round is very much about issues that are similar to those being discussed by the Europeans in their preparations for 1992. These include negotiations on agricultural trade, services, and the elimination of subsidies. The Europeans are ironing out some of these issues in their effort to harmonize a wide range of practices that also have global implications. So the Uruguay Round is a mechanism in the trade area for trying to ensure that the European regional developments are compatible with the global system.

Today, given the emerging tripolar structure of the world economy, it's not as easy for the United States to take the lead unilaterally. We saw that coming even in the '80s when the United States failed in its initial efforts to get the Uruguay Round going. Bill Brock tried in '82, when he was the U.S. Trade Representative, but the GATT ministerial meeting failed miserably. So the United States offered bilateral deals with Israel and Canada. Only four years later, in 1986, did the Uruguay Round get on track. Looking ahead, the United States can't drive the negotiating process by itself. There will have to be a more collective tripolar management to make sure that the world does not devolve into regional blocs. That might lead to an inwardly focused European EMU that would be detrimental to a broader and more open world system.

Q Haven't the annual economic summits helped to keep the policy discussions relevant to the larger global system and its needs?
A. Some have, to greater or lesser extents, but this year's Houston summit was the first that failed to discuss at all the issues of international monetary or macroeconomic cooperation. That was a major mistake in the face of this pell-mell rush in Europe to do things on a regional level. We need to get back to global negotiations on a new world monetary system, as well as on trade, international investment, and policy cooperation.

Q. You have actually proposed calling a conference to launch a round of talks on global monetary reform in 1991, haven't you?
A. That's right. The Europeans have agreed to start their EMU negotiations in December of this year, and they have talked about moving to stage two of that process by the start of 1993 or 1994. Somewhere during that period, there should be launched a parallel global negotiation toward what I would call GMU—global monetary union—to parallel European monetary union.

Q. Isn't Margaret Thatcher trying to slow that down and hasn't she succeeded this week in an agreement that was made in Europe?
A. It's not clear yet what their timetable will be. The British have tried to slow it down, and so have the least developed members of the EC—Portugal, Greece, and maybe Spain. Of late, even the Germans seem to have second thoughts, given the uncertainties involved in unifying the two Germanys. In the end, we may see a two-track, two-speed process, and Pöhl actually allowed for that quite explicitly in his blueprint back in January.

Q You have raised some serious questions here. On the one hand, regions and individual nations have internal requirements to make important progress; on the other hand, there are potential conflicts among the three blocs and their leading nations—Japan, the United States, and Germany. Will the twenty-first century be a century of economic warfare?
A. Recent history leads one to be fairly optimistic that a tripolar world can evolve in a cooperative and harmonious way. But the longer sweep of history leads to a pessimistic outlook. A pessimist might observe that the world has never been managed successfully by a committee of nations. In the past, more or less balanced power structures have tended to break down into conflict.

When you have three players, game theory indicates a very strong tendency for two countries to ally against the third. Each tends to perceive itself as weaker than the others, seeks an ally, and the two tend to gang up against the strongest nation at the moment. In the nineteenth century the British played a balancing role, actually shifting from one alliance to another to try to maintain a balance. In some ways that worked reasonably well. But a stable, ongoing collective management has never really worked. There were some efforts toward collective management between the two world wars, but the system broke down into economic conflicts and ultimately war.

More recent history, however, leads to a fairly optimistic outlook. The three economic powers have been close allies for over forty years. They all have democratic political systems, so they are like-minded in terms of their fundamental political roots. They certainly have a history of cooperation on economic issues, although not necessarily one of putting together a stable system. At least they got together to avoid crises and total breakdown. As we begin the '90s, markets, companies, and financial institutions are highly integrated on a global scale, and it would be very costly to allow conflict between nations to break up this market interpenetration.

Q. But doesn't the end of the cold war remove one of the major reasons for cooperation, even on economic issues?

A. Yes, I do worry about possible perverse effects stemming from the change in military security arrangements. The end of the cold war is obviously a good thing, but it removes the security blanket that has tended to moderate some of the economic disputes among the three big areas. In the face of the Soviet threat, Europe, Japan, and the United States did tend to submerge economic disputes in order not to disrupt their overall strategic relationships. On many occasions the United States, Japan, and Germany made concessions on economic conflicts in order to avoid jeopardizing the overall security structure. As the cold war security arrangements decline in importance and economic issues become more weighty, economic disputes could rise to a much higher level of tension, and conflict could emerge. Many Americans look to our disputes with Japan and argue that we no longer need to coddle our allies, or to "pay for their defense."

Q. Except at the outset you cited acts that are encouraging: multibillion-dollar transfers made by our allies with large external surpluses to pay for some of the costs of the current Persian Gulf intervention. This suggests that countries are willing to share the burden of the common defense and this may well be a precedent for sharing the responsibilities of multilateral economic policy.

A. That is an interesting case, because a new kind of security blanket is being pulled back over the economic disputes, particularly for the Arab states in the Gulf that are willing to pony up for their defense. As the Japanese and the Europeans face the prospect that congressional pressure here might keep the United States from defending the sea lanes and protecting Saudi Arabia and the Persian Gulf oil fields, I think they'll pony up too. Or we might simply withdraw our troops from Western Europe and from Japan. Or not even go to the next hot spot to protect the interests of the world economy.

The current Middle East crisis is essentially a replay of the earlier period when U.S. troops were essential to deter the Soviet Union. Now they are essential to deter Saddam Hussein. Just as the Europeans and the Japanese subsumed some of their economic disputes with us in the earlier period and made concessions in order to keep us on the front line militarily, they're going to do the same in order to keep us out front in the Persian Gulf.

Q. This is the third oil price crisis since 1973–74, and we shall probably see increasing imbalances among the oil-consuming and oil-producing countries with all the economic adjustments and policy changes that requires. That means a widening U.S. trade deficit on top of a budget deficit that is already approaching $300 billion for fiscal 1991. Are the United States, Europe, and Japan better able to handle those problems now than in the earlier two crises?

A. I would not be too confident about an improved ability to handle these problems. The problems of trade imbalances, and the volatility of the dollar and the other currencies were really quiescent for the last year or two. The severe imbalances of the middle '80s have come down both in absolute terms and even more so as a percentage of GNP. The trend seemed to head in the right direction as a lagged response to the Plaza Agreement on exchange rates in September 1985. Both the U.S. budget and external deficits, measured as a share of GNP, were cut by half or more, and that contributed to greater stability in the financial and currency markets and easier financing. The Japanese surpluses have also come way down.

In response to the new oil price jump, the trends could move in the wrong direction again, and renewed volatility could hit the markets. However, this time around our problems could be a blend of the problems of the '70s and the problems of the '80s. In the '70s, all of the oil-importing countries experienced rising trade deficits—the United States, Japan, most of Western Europe, and the oil-importing LDCs. The countries that benefited were the oil-producing Gulf states, and also Mexico, Venezuela, and a few others. The remedy of the consuming countries in the '70s was probably correct. There was no conflict among the United States, Europe, and Japan; they didn't try to cut each other's throats or foist off the trade deficit upon each other. Instead, they mounted a collective response to recyle petrodollars to finance the deficits. That initiative clearly went too far for a number of LDC debtors that should have undertaken more adjustment. Their excessive borrowing led to the debt problems of the early '80s. But the basic strategy in the industrial countries was probably correct.

Q. But isn't the problem more serious since the U.S. budget deficit may shoot into the $200–400 billion range?

A. Then the Japanese surplus would indeed start rising again. In addition to the oil-induced problems, we'd experience a replay of the problems of the '80s, with growing imbalances among the industrial countries leading to exchange-rate volatility and increasing sentiment for trade protection. The 1990 crisis could be more severe, because the economic imbalances, particularly the U.S. deficits and Japan's surplus, would loom large in the context of the Persian Gulf military operations. Americans would demand a more equitable sharing of burdens and press Japan to pony up. You would have to add together the oil concerns of the '70s with the trade imbalances and protectionist demands of the '80s, on top of the concerns for burden sharing of the '90s.

Q. Taken all together, would that stimulate in a positive way the evolution that you see toward a new international monetary system that started off with the Plaza Accord, then the Tokyo Summit, and more recently the Louvre Accord?
A. You have to consider both the short- and the long-run dimensions. In the short run, any renewed crisis makes it difficult to talk about reforming the global monetary system, partly because systemic reform takes a long time. Second, if you talk systemic reform, it can actually exacerbate a crisis because it raises more uncertainty: What's the role of the dollar going to be, for example?

In the long term, it certainly becomes clearer that this new world requires a basic new framework for managing monetary and macroeconomic policy. But policy makers face a dilemma. In the crisis mode, people are worried about the immediate problems and are unhappy about the inadequacies of the system. But they spend all their time fighting brush fires and trying to avoid worsening the conflicts, so they have no time to work toward systemic reforms. Then, once they get past the crisis, governments tend to forget about the systemic inadequacies and limp along with the patched-up system. Farsighted leadership is required to cope with the short-run crises while moving simultaneously toward long-run reform. That leadership will have to be on a tripartite basis; we can't just return to a Bretton Woods-style framework with the United States at the helm.

Q. Since Japan and Germany were growing at a pretty good pace before the outbreak of the Persian Gulf crisis, they are not likely to fall into recession. The United States, in contrast, was already at the brink of recession by midsummer and the oil crisis is likely to push us into a downturn. The Germans can now offset the deflationary impulse from the rise in oil prices by refocusing their external surplus on investment in the unification process. How do you see these adjustments?
A. In that scenario, continued growth in Germany and Japan will help mitigate the risk of a truly global economic crisis with a severe worldwide recession. This time we probably won't have, as we did in the '70s and the '80s, synchronized, double-digit inflation among the major economies followed by a synchronized global recession. This time it's likely to be an unsynchronized global cyclical situation, and that is desirable from a global perspective, because the overall economic shock from the Middle East oil price rise will not be as great as in the earlier two episodes.

Q. But won't that create conflicts among the three economic superpowers?
A. There is that potential stemming from the differential impact of the oil price jump, and therefore differing degrees of concern. Germany and Japan will be able to take this episode in stride, with continuing modest growth. Some there might even welcome it as a means to take off a little excess demand pressure and prevent overheating.

The United States may complain that we're out there defending the world oil supply, putting American lives on the line, spending all the defense monies, yet the United States has an economy in recession while Germany and Japan are still prospering. These attitudes may add to the volatility of the U.S. political response and create pressures to force other countries to pay more. Some Americans may press Congress to take trade protectionist measures against them if they don't cooperate fully in both the military and the economic arenas. So this crisis could either galvanize some of the new forms of cooperation that are needed in the global system or lead to the new conflicts that I fear. In any case, it is a test for leadership in the United States and abroad to make sure the Persian Gulf crisis does not lead to a deterioration of global economic arrangements.

Q. You have elsewhere alluded to the evolutionary process toward a new international monetary system, tracing the steps from the Plaza and Louvre accords and the Tokyo Summit. Let's zero in more closely on what has happened and where we're headed on international monetary reform.
A. That evolution comes into sharper focus when placed in historical perspective. During the first twenty-

five years after World War II, the world operated on an adjustable peg version of a fixed rate system—the Bretton Woods regime. It began to erode in the early 1960s, and it soon became clear that Bretton Woods was unable to carry out the kind of exchange-rate changes and other adjustments that were necessary to achieve a stable international economy. The system collapsed in the early 1970s when the dollar became overvalued by about 20 percent, and protectionist pressures arose as a result. The international regime could not cope with those pressures. So there is a clear record of failure of that version of fixed exchange rates.

Q. That's when the experiments with floating began?
A. From March 1973 until September 1985, we had a system (or nonsystem) of largely unmanaged flexibility of exchange rates. That system, too, has failed. In its extreme version, during 1980–85, it permitted the dollar to become overvalued by 40 to 50 percent, more than twice the misalignment that brought about the collapse of Bretton Woods. It failed to keep trade open. Protectionism has been growing, and the world trading system is threatened. The system failed to have any meaningful impact on national economic policies and therefore failed to achieve the most rudimentary objective of any international economic system, namely, promotion of needed internal adjustments.

Consequently, national leaders have been groping for new monetary arrangements since 1985. At the New York Plaza Hotel in September of that year, they stated explicitly that the old system had failed. At the Tokyo summit in May 1986, they began the indicators exercise as one track toward monetary reform. At the Louvre in Paris in February 1987, they installed a system of reference ranges. The world's monetary authorities were proceeding with a two-track program, based on exchange-rate reference ranges and economic indicators, in an effort to find a new regime.

Q. Where is this evolution taking us?
A. As I have emphasized, we can't go back to a rigid Bretton Woods version of fixed exchange rates. But unmanaged flexibility is also untenable, because it was so unstable and produced massive and costly misalignments of exchange rates. We are steering toward a middle road: avoiding the excessive instability of flexible rates and the excessive rigidity of fixed rates. We need a system that makes sure the major economies adopt policies that are consistent on a global basis and therefore sustainable over time. I'm referring here to sustainable current account and government budget balances.

Unfortunately, in practice the two tracks haven't really meshed very well. One school of thought preferred to focus on exchange-rate coordination with intervention in the exchange markets to manage rates. Another school argued that exchange rates are only derivative from economic fundamentals, and therefore the authorities have to worry about coordinating fiscal and monetary policies. Tension over those issues was never really reconciled before the process petered out some time in 1989 and now clearly in 1990. At present, that embryonic two-track reform process has fallen into abeyance.

Q. But why has interest faltered?
A. As I mentioned earlier, when the brush fires are extinguished, and national leaders make progress in narrowing current account and domestic budget imbalances, the leadership tends to relax. Governments feared a "hard landing" in 1987, but that was averted. Financing has seemed to take place in a fairly stable way, and heavy official intervention has not been needed. Indeed, in 1988–89, the dollar was too strong, not too weak. And far from having to intervene and defend the dollar as in '87, when central banks basically financed the whole U.S. current account deficit, they had to intervene to restrain the dollar from getting too strong and undermining the adjustment process that had been set in train earlier at the Plaza. So, the nature of the problem changed, the concerns that triggered the adoption of this two-track system faded, and the governments, I would argue, did not have the wisdom to build on what they had done to prepare for the next crisis. The successful experience in managing our recent imbalances reinforces my view that we must put in place a new system to manage international monetary relationships.

Q. Do you see that as taking place within some version of the IMF structure?
A. Any fundamental reform in the monetary system has to be based on the IMF. Just as the IMF managed the Bretton Woods system, it has to manage any new target zone system or any global exchange-rate regime. There is one big change, however, that is needed within the IMF: the steering committee in the future will have

to be the three poles—the United States, a united Europe, and Japan.

Q. What's the state of the steering committee now?
A. Right now there's not much of a steering committee. To the extent there is one, it is the Group of Seven (G7), and within that the main members are the United States, the several Europeans, and Japan. The Big Three need to begin acting as an informal steering committee for the world economy. At times the system has been led by a G2, namely, Japan's finance minister working with U.S. Treasury Secretary James Baker. As the Europeans coalesce into a single economic entity, with a single representative, they'll carry a lot more weight, but right now there are policy differences among the Germans, the French, and certainly the British. The European voice will grow stronger as it becomes more coordinated. This indicates the direction in which management must move, in contrast to the Bretton Woods arrangement, when the steering committee boiled down to a G1, the United States. That era has ended forever. In the transition period from the Plaza to the Louvre accords the United States did take the lead, but with increasing frequency Japan joined the leadership, for example when reference ranges were hammered out. But we are now clearly moving to a future in which a stable system will be managed formally and on a day-to-day ongoing basis within the IMF, using a tripolar management committee effectively steering a global policy course.

Q. Does that mean a formal institutional arrangement?
A. It is not necessary to formalize the tripolar part of the steering committee. But we do need to formalize the target zone system and the criteria for managing it, perhaps amending the articles of agreement in the IMF accordingly. But just like steering committees in legislatures, in political parties, or in the local community club, those things can be kept informal, maybe in the form of an informal G3 that meets much more regularly, without a formal constitution.

Q. How would it have any authority to enforce certain guidelines that require the surplus or deficit country to make changes in domestic policy to narrow persistent imbalances in the current account or government budget?
A. I see this as working through the formal organization of the IMF. For example, the IMF had the "scarce currency clause" on the books, but never used it. The GATT machinery incorporates retaliation clauses in trade relations. But much of the adjustment among major countries can come from G3 peer pressure among the Americans, the Japanese, and the Europeans. I can imagine that two of these could approach the third, saying, "If you want us to cooperate on policy X, you must cooperate on Y." That's where the decision power will reside and how actual political and economic steps will be taken. The formal constitution would set up the global institutional organization, with formal boards of directors and the secretariat, but the Big Three can make the key decisions informally. The challenge for the 1990s is to get something like that to work.

Q. You have ambitious goals for the international monetary system. What about the threats to an open global trading system?
A. The immediate test is, of course, the Uruguay Round. Despite all this far-reaching talk about a new tripolar world economy with a collective management structure, nations seem to be having great difficulty in taking what by comparison are baby steps in achieving the objectives of the Uruguay Round—getting rid of agricultural barriers, phasing out textile quotas, reducing subsidies that distort international trade. If we can't even complete those negotiations, it will be a pretty negative harbinger of things to come on the more ambitious and complex policy issues. Our first task is to succeed in the goals of the Uruguay Round. That boils down mainly to a U.S.-European battle over agriculture, among a few other things.

Q. What about Japan and its rice farmers?
A. Yes, I think Japan, as usual, will be dragged along kicking and screaming, but it can be counted on to do its bit, if the other countries provide the framework. Japan has to do that and some other things to make the round succeed. But the major determining issues must be decided by the United States and Europe. The real test is whether a newly self-confident, regionally oriented Europe will be ready and willing to cooperate on a global basis. If the agricultural talks fail, and especially if the Uruguay Round as a whole were to fail as a result, it would be a negative indicator of Europe's ability and readiness to cooperate in managing global economic policy.

After the Uruguay Round, we should be preparing for a major trade negotiation every decade. The Uruguay Round is really the negotiation of the '80s, though it won't be finished until 1990–91. The agenda for the '90s is to complete the half-century of trade liberalization since World War II. The postwar period traces out a historic record of such negotiations, from the Dillon and Kennedy rounds which succeeded in cutting down most tariff barriers, to the Tokyo Round which began to come to grips with the nontariff barriers; and now to the Uruguay Round which is addressing the new areas of services and intellectual property, plus agricultural trade. The final push will be toward the complete elimination of all tariffs on industrial trade, a total ban on quantitative trade barriers, including "voluntary" export restraint agreements, and a much stronger mandate given to the GATT to police the trading system. The agenda for the 1990s should also include a new initiative in the investment area—the creation of a "GATT for Investment."

Q. Global management of money, trade, and now investment too?
A. Sure. Industry, like international finance, is now increasingly global. Japanese firms have joined the globalization pattern. European firms are now merging to prepare for the world's biggest internal market after 1992. Those powerful trends feed an inherent tension between private-sector enterprise and national governments. Governments are inherently forced to focus on what happens within national boundaries. They must worry about the value of the national currency, and that means exchange rates, trade balances, capital flows. Governments can't ignore these economic forces as the apostles of economic globalization would have us do. They also have to worry about internationally immobile factors of production. Most of the world's labor force consists of unskilled workers, who are not globally mobile. And there is the concern for national defense, with its economic implications. Many decisions by national governments at the national level may inherently clash with the interests of industry and finance, which are now working at the global level. We have to reconcile the national interest with the private-sector interest that operates on a global scale, often beyond the reach of national governments. That leads me to favor some internationally agreed rules of the game to govern the global investment process in the same way we have had rules in place now for forty years to govern international trade and monetary relations.

Q. What, for example, would you advocate?
A. International agreements to eliminate or sharply limit the scope for governments to distort the investment process by offering incentives, such as tax relief, in order to lure production from one country to another. We also need to limit performance requirements that governments set that distort what investors do once they enter a country: for example, export requirements, local content requirements, value-added requirements, and the like. In 1974 I wrote an article called "Coming Investment Wars," that anticipated these problems. Conflicts over the location of investment—not just among countries but even between states in this country—are becoming more intense in this new world of globalized production organized by multinational firms.

The GATT for Investment would round out a three-pronged agenda for the '90s that the new tripolar management must address to maintain a stable world economy in the twenty-first century.

Q. It's a great long-term vision, but will it be overshadowed by the current Persian Gulf crisis?
A. It doesn't have to be. The Mideast oil crisis could even help promote Big Three negotiations and management, which are essential. The model for an international security arrangement that has now emerged under UN auspices is putting new light on strategies for cooperation, burden sharing, and recognition of new and common responsibilities. That is a very hopeful sign for the future.

WILLIAM M. BURKE

# Rising Sun . . . Falling Dollar

*If the United States kept its current-account deficit below one percent of its total output, and if Japan kept its current-account surplus below two percent of its total output, the books would balance better. Until that situation develops, the balance wheel—the exchange rate—will probably keep slipping against the dollar.*

The dollar has lost three-fourths of its value against the yen over the past quarter-century. Early last year, a progressive ex-governor of a small southern state went to Washington to discuss economic issues with another progressive ex-governor of a small southern state. The talks collapsed in full view of the TV cameras, and one former governor (Prime Minister Hosokawa) dropped into political oblivion upon his return to Tokyo. Then, after another turn of Tokyo's political merry-go-round, the top spot went to a man with strong support in Japan's Korean community—the source of the billions of hard cash that North Korea uses to finance its nuclear-weapons program. Ah, the law of unintended consequences!

As we saw from the failure of the Clinton–Hosokawa talks, esoteric foreign-trade problems can seriously affect our politics and our economic life as well. Perhaps the best single indicator of these problems is the rising yen/falling dollar syndrome. Of course, this change in the exchange rate means that American households will pay considerably more dollars for Japanese cars and electronic goods, and that Japanese investors will receive considerably fewer yen in earnings from their investments in Rockefeller Center and other upscale American properties. More basically, the change in the exchange rate represents history's cold-blooded evaluation of the relative financial strength of these two nations. The change may seem imperceptible at times but, eventually, we all feel the effects of Japanese frugality and American profligacy—especially with the precipitous fall of the dollar against the yen in the last twenty-five years (see Table 16).

A currency's exchange rate provides a useful shorthand measure of a host of supply/demand factors that affect the economy. For the dollar, these factors include: (1) the volumes and prices of U.S. imports and exports; the short-term financial flows that are always searching the world for higher interest rates; and the long-term capital flows invested around the world in stocks, bonds, factories, and real estate. In addition, there are the foreigners' ever-changing needs for dollars to buy goods priced in dollars (e.g., OPEC oil) or to use as backing for their own currencies. Interestingly, we've recently seen that the dollar can grow stronger against, say, the Mexican peso and Canadian dollar, even while it declines against the yen and German mark.

WILLIAM M. BURKE, a retired Federal Reserve economist, worked in Tokyo during the post–World War II occupation of Japan by U.S. military forces. Reprinted from *Challenge*, July–August 1995, pp. 46–51.

| Table 16 | Yen/Dollar Exchange Rate and Inflation Differential | |
|---|---|---|
| | Exchange rate | Japan–U.S. Inflation differential[1] (percent) |
| 1970 | 358 | 1.8 |
| 1971 | 348 | 1.8 |
| 1972 | 303 | 1.7 |
| 1973 | 271 | 5.5 |
| 1974 | 292 | 12.2 |
| 1975 | 297 | 2.6 |
| 1976 | 296 | 3.8 |
| 1977 | 269 | 1.7 |
| 1978 | 210 | −3.4 |
| 1979 | 219 | −7.6 |
| 1980 | 227 | −5.7 |
| 1981 | 221 | −5.6 |
| 1982 | 249 | −3.4 |
| 1983 | 238 | −1.4 |
| 1984 | 237 | −2.0 |
| 1985 | 238 | −1.6 |
| 1986 | 168 | −1.2 |
| 1987 | 145 | −3.6 |
| 1988 | 128 | −3.3 |
| 1989 | 138 | −2.6 |
| 1990 | 145 | −2.3 |
| 1991 | 135 | −1.0 |
| 1992 | 127 | −1.3 |
| 1993 | 111 | −1.2 |
| 1994 | 102 | −2.0 |

Source: *Business Cycle Indicators, Survey of Current Business*, U.S. Dept. of Commerce.

[1] Difference between changes in consumer-price indexes.

## Road to Pearl Harbor

The present tangled relationship between Japan and the United States can be traced back to events in Berlin in 1918. Imperial Germany, which previously had dominated Europe like a colossus, suddenly felt the weight of wartime shortages. It collapsed into a state of chaos and famine. With Germany as an object lesson, Japan's leaders persuaded themselves that national security depended on a policy of self-sufficiency at all costs. That meant political and economic control over the resource-rich Asian mainland. But the military buildup associated with such a policy had important consequences. Japan relied on the printing press to pay for an expanding economy and an expanding empire. The yen, which had been worth two to the dollar at the beginning of the 1930s, proceeded to lose almost half its value over the ensuing decade. Moreover, the new policy forced Japan to become economically dependent on the one country that was bound to contest its military buildup—the United States. By the late 1930s, the United States was providing nearly 75 percent of Japan's scrap iron and 80 percent of its petroleum imports.

Paradoxically, events in Europe eventually settled the Japanese–American debate. Hitler's smashing European triumphs made orphans out of the French and Dutch possessions in Asia, and endangered Britain's possessions as well. Japan's naval strategists saw an opportunity to gain rapid control over the raw-material riches of the Indies. They persuaded army leaders to join them in a southward drive, instead of following the original plan for a northward march against Soviet forces. But Japan's war plans forced her into an even greater dependence on American supplies at a time when the U.S. itself was scrambling for materials. In response to Hitler's European triumphs, the United States too had begun its own rearmament program. Leon Henderson and his colleagues in the rearmament effort pushed hard for export controls on American materials. They supported the efforts of the hawks—such as Treasury Secretary Henry Morgenthau, Jr.—who had long fought for sanctions against Japan. At a crucial cabinet meeting on July 18, 1941, FDR agreed to impose export controls and freeze all Japanese assets in this country. Supposedly, the system had some flexibility—with a two-tier licensing system for purchases. But it soon hardened into a full-scale embargo on all trade with Japan. The next move was up to Japan, as the events of December 7, 1941, demonstrated.

Now, scroll forward to September 2, 1945—the point at which the mighty American economy stood astride the world, while Japan lay flat on its back. During the war, Japan suffered almost three million dead, the destruction of almost all major cities, and the loss of half its empire's land area. It lost roughly 40 percent of its entire capital stock, including 90 percent of its merchant marine. Meanwhile, it had to provide for more than six million citizens who had returned home from the old overseas possessions. This further aggravated acute shortages of food, clothing, and housing.

## Missionaries' arrival

Into this difficult situation marched the energetic Americans. They represented every shade of political coloration—from true-blue to parlor-pink. Proconsul Douglas MacArthur sent out a call for Christian missionaries to create in Japan "a natural base from which in time to advance the cross through all of Asia." In addition, he unleashed a horde of New Deal reformers upon the defenseless Japanese people. But the occupation leaders' early attempts at social engineering were swamped by the problems of economic recovery. The Japanese bureaucrats tried to solve these problems with the printing press. They thereby caused the general price level to soar to 300 times its prewar level within four years of their surrender.

Japan's currency had practically no international value during this turbulent period. Indeed, American cigarettes were a common means of exchange. For domestic transactions, occupation authorities originally imposed a 15-to-1 yen/dollar conversion rate. Afterwards, they raised the rate several times as the postwar inflation worsened.

The authorities tried to jump-start the economy with an export-promotion program that was based on massive producer subsidies and multiple exchange rates. At one point, the yen/dollar rates ranged between 66 to 1 for canned bamboo shoots and 600 to 1 for lacquerware. By contributing to severely unbalanced budgets, the system only worsened the severe inflation. American statesmen, led by Dean Acheson and John Foster Dulles, warned Congress that Japan would remain a perpetual basket case. But by the late 1940s, they became determined to bring both Japan and Germany onto the side of the angels in the growing cold war with the Soviet Union. Somewhat to the dismay of proconsuls Lucius Clay in Germany and Douglas MacArthur in Japan, the Pentagon sent out teams of advisers to administer shock treatment to the flattened economies of the two former enemies. Both teams were led by the Detroit banker Joseph Dodge—a devotee of traditional "root canal" economics.

When Dodge arrived in Tokyo in 1949, he instituted the nine-point Dodge Line. It included a balanced budget, credit cutbacks, and an end to the system of producer subsidies and multiple exchange rates. In addition, he imposed a single exchange rate of 360 yen to the dollar—a rate that held steady for almost a quarter-century. With the help of Dodge's stabilization plan and a bonanza of American military orders (Japan's Marshall Plan) that followed the outbreak of the Korean War a year later, Japan managed to bounce back into the international financial system. The United States, the world's only economic power at the time, dominated this system—a gold-exchange standard, whereby the United States based its currency on gold, while foreign countries held their exchange reserves mostly in the form of U.S. dollars which were convertible into gold. Under this system, however, the United States flooded the world with dollars for several decades. It invested in overseas businesses, supported cold war allies, and financed the reconstruction of its war-damaged allies and former enemies. At first, the recipients were grateful for this flood of dollars. But the sorcerer's apprentice act eventually got out of hand.

## Collapse of U.S. hegemony

The gold-exchange standard then fell apart. The leading financial powers adopted a system of floating exchange rates in March 1973. Nobel laureate Milton Friedman had been advocating floating rates for several decades. Actually, "dirty" floating may be a better description, because central bankers have frequently intervened in the market (for example, several times in early 1995) to limit exchange-rate fluctuations. Headline writers went wild in August 1971, when President Nixon bludgeoned the nation's trading partners into accepting a 10-percent devaluation of the dollar. But in the ensuing decades, exchange rates have frequently fluctuated over much broader ranges for the United States and all the other actors in the world marketplace.

For most of the period, however, the dollar has deteriorated against the yen. It has declined from the long-established 360-to-1 exchange rate to the recent figure of about 80 yen to the dollar. Within a single quarter-century, in other words, the dollar has lost more than three-fourths of its value against the yen. Clearly, that reflects the financial world's dyspeptic view of U.S. economic policies, as compared with Japan's. Financiers in London, New York, Frankfurt and Tokyo—always fearful that inflation will reduce the value of their portfolios—cannot have missed the fact that prices have risen faster in the United States than in Japan in every one of the past seventeen years.

Admittedly, Japan has suffered several periods of yen weakness. One occurred during the 1973–74 oil crisis, when it experienced a rare bout of raging inflation because of the soaring price of its one crucial import. Then again, the yen sank sharply against the dollar during the 1981–85 period, as U.S. interest rates soared after Federal Reserve chairman Paul Volcker sharply tightened monetary policy in an attempt to offset the Reagan era's massive budget deficits. This odd coupling of American monetary and fiscal policies, which sent interest rates and the dollar into the stratosphere, undermined the export potential of many

American industries. But it created a bonanza for Japanese and other foreign firms that supplied the American market. Recognizing the threat to the domestic economy, Volcker later eased Fed policy. He did it first to combat the severe 1982 recession, and then to overcome the collapse of the nation's export prospects that was engendered by the expensive dollar. Despite occasional fluctuations in later years, Volcker and his (1987) successor, Alan Greenspan, subsequently presided over a decade-long decline in the dollar's value against the yen and other major currencies.

## Strange consequences

The historical record shows that financial actions have consequences—many of them unintended. For a decade and a half before 1945, Japan adopted a policy of military Keynesianism. The emperor's men rampaged throughout Asia. We have all seen the consequences. Then, in later decades, America adopted a policy of military Keynesianism. The president's men rampaged throughout Asia. We have witnessed the negative consequences of those actions as well.

Underlying today's tangled Japanese–American relationship is a paradox: The Japanese have mastered the principles of "root-canal" economics prescribed by a Detroit banker fifty years ago. In contrast, the Americans have long forgotten such principles.

C. Fred Bergsten and Marcus Noland describe the situation in these terms (in *Reconcilable Differences? United States–Japan Economic Conflicts,* Institute for International Economics, 1993):

> The United States set out to create the world's greatest consumer society and, within a single generation, attained a standard of living for most of its people beyond anything history had seen before. Japan, in contrast, set out to create a production machine that would restore both its economic security and its respectability in the family of nations. It has succeeded beyond all historical precedent—the formidably competitive manufacturing sector that emerged is the envy of the world.

As a result of these conflicting priorities, the books don't balance in the international marketplace, which handles roughly a trillion dollars' worth of transactions every day. Japan is now the world's largest creditor nation, and the United States is the largest debtor ($1,048 billion, net). It lost its place as the largest creditor during the borrowing binge of the Reagan years. But frugal Japan and profligate America find it difficult to change the behavior patterns that were once essential to their well-being—however counterproductive now. Newspaper columnists and TV talking heads make the problem sound even worse than it is, when they point with alarm every month to the latest merchandise-trade figures. They ignore the fact that our international accounts include not only farm and factory merchandise but also all types of services and financial transactions. Even worse, they always highlight the continued imbalance in bilateral trade between Japan and the United States—an almost meaningless concept.

Japan would almost certainly continue to run a bilateral surplus, even if both countries achieved complete balance in their global accounts. This is partly because Japan's trade pattern is triangular. It imports vast amounts of primary products from countries such as Saudi Arabia (oil), Australia (coal), and Brazil (soybeans). Then, it pays for these net imports by exporting large amounts of manufactured products to higher-income countries in Europe and North America. Moreover, much of the bilateral U.S.–Japan trade consists of high-technology products that don't respond to price changes. Much more of it consists of consumer and industrial products that are not even produced by American firms.

## Mercantilism triumphs

When operating in world markets, all major nations use the age-old mercantilist tactics that Adam Smith tried so hard to discredit in *The Wealth of Nations*. In this mercantilist world, national governments use their powers to the utmost to rig markets. They employ the usual expedients of export subsidies and import tariffs, plus stultifying red tape (beloved of Japanese bureaucrats), or numerical quotas for exports and imports (beloved of American bureaucrats). Modern-day mercantilists utilize a number of micro measures that are designed to help or hinder trade in specific products or industries. They describe their efforts with acronyms and esoteric jargon—VER, VIE, TQI, STA, Super 301. All of these are measures designed to undermine the sacred acronym GATT (General Agreement on Tariffs and Trade) that all have sworn to defend to the death. Typically, these micro measures simply protect certain domestic producers—such as Japanese rice farmers (even though their product costs several times as much as imported rice), or American auto producers (even though they put the steering wheel on the wrong side for Japanese drivers).

Most economists argue that the Japanese–American impasse can be solved better through a macro approach than through micro means. After all, macro measures affect the fundamentals of every economy. In fact, a mathematical identity is involved: A country (Japan) whose households, corporations, and governments save more than they invest will export that excess in the form of capital outflows and goods; a country (the United States) whose institutions invest more than they save must import savings and goods from abroad to make up the shortfall. The books would balance better if the United States kept its current-account deficit (covering trade in goods and services plus financial transactions) below one percent of its total output (GDP). The same result would ensue, if Japan kept its current-account surplus below two percent of its total output. Recent figures, in both cases, have been almost twice those levels. Until the situation improves, the balance wheel—the exchange rate—will probably keep slipping against the dollar.

Harvard's emeritus professor Raymond Vernon, searching for signs of American profligacy and dollar decline, provides a specific list of evils: "... credit cards, home-equity loans, the political rallying cry 'no more taxes,' and sheer gluttony, reinforced by a demographic bubble and by the international role of the dollar as an international currency." The last of these items may be the crucial one. Like Great Britain in the first half of the century, America may not be able to sustain the role of economic superpower, as she shifts from creditor to debtor status. *The Economist* argues; "When they were big creditors, both America and Britain naturally had a keen interest in low inflation and price stability. A debtor, by contrast, may be tempted to allow inflation to nibble away at the real value of its debt and to use devaluation to reduce its external deficit—hardly desirable properties for a reserve currency."

Despite the constant shift out of dollars during the last two decades, roughly one-half of all private-sector wealth held in foreign currencies remains in dollars today. Given the existence of this dollar overhang, and given the constant edginess of financial markets, any sign of an acceleration in the pace of dollar devaluation could change a long-term trend into a short-term stampede. And in any such currency crisis, the Federal Reserve would almost certainly raise interest rates to stratospheric levels. That would bring on a severe recession.

There is much of the 1990s that resembles the 1930s. The leading economic power (Britain then, America today) was (and might be) unable to continue as the reserve-currency country. The rising powers (America then, Japan and Germany today) were (and appear to be) unwilling to take up the burden. The United States could regain its international position, and thereby stop the decline in the dollar's value, if it truly got the nation's books in order. President Clinton tried to do that with his 1993 budget legislation. It passed without a single Republican vote. But the world's bankers apparently didn't think he went far enough. Perhaps the only cure will be the rise of a latter-day Joseph Dodge, who will be ready to apply to the U.S. economy the same "root canal" treatment that worked so well in Japan a half-century ago. Or perhaps not. The macro changes that have been imposed on the Japanese economy by the cheap dollar/expensive yen syndrome might already have ensured a better balance in the two nations' books in the waning years of the twentieth century. But many experts have refused to see the growing signs of Japanese weakness. They reverse the attitude of those who, at midcentury, saw Japan's economic future as hopeless.

## How weak is Japan?

In common with the United States and other advanced industrial countries, Japan's rate of economic growth ratcheted down two decades ago. It has yet to match its earlier performance. In the early 1970s, futurist Herman Kahn and others predicted that Japan's economy would continue to grow more than 10 percent annually. But subsequent forecasters were much more modest. Most recently, they suggested no more than 3.5 percent annual growth. Even that figure ought be questioned, now that Japan is struggling through the worst recession of the past half-century. Japan can no longer count on the "latecomer" benefits that helped it profit from all the technological advances developed by the first countries that went through the industrial revolution. Besides, slow labor-force growth now clouds its prospects. Greater labor-force participation by women boosted the economy during the 1980s. But even if that trend continues, it won't be enough to offset a sharp (55 percent) decline in labor-force growth expected in the present decade. Moreover, in the twenty-first century, Japan's aging population will not only dry up the nation's labor supply. It should also bring about a major decline in the savings rate, as the elderly spend their accumulated resources. Then, those changes will reduce the nation's ability to invest in profitable new industries.

Still, in another example of unintended consequences, Japan's economy should benefit to the extent that the nation's leaders bow to American pressures for market-opening measures. Increased competition in Japanese agriculture, manufacturing, trade, finance, and government procurement could bolster the economy—in good textbook fashion. It could make Japan an even stronger competitor than before.

In any event, the "convergence" so often praised by American trade negotiators, and the role of the declining dollar in that shift, may also create problems in the years immediately ahead. Over the past decade, Japanese firms investing abroad have suffered exchange-rate losses of about $320 billion when they repatriated their earnings. That fact alone would discourage Japanese from putting more money into capital-hungry America, thereby supporting the dollar. Besides, the collapse of Japan's "bubble economy," which had helped provide the money for the nation's massive capital exports, has sharply depleted Japan's stock of investable funds. Those funds will be sorely missed. At its peak in 1987, Japan supplied more than 80 percent of all the long-term capital exports in the world economy.

Finally, the exchange-rate drama promises to affect Japan's place in the world's political and military equation. Some analysts believe that Japan, frustrated by Washington's heavy-handed attempts to pry open Japanese markets, will gradually turn its back on the West and concentrate on becoming East Asia's superpower.

Within the past decade, Japan has doubled the proportion of its funds allocated to Asian projects—from 10 percent to 20 percent of its total investments. Moreover, by reducing its investments in heavily indebted America, it could force the United States to adopt a very tight, high-interest-rate policy to meet its copious financial needs. We've already seen evidence of this Japanese withdrawal. Enticed by wily Yankee traders into buying American commercial property and golf courses at the top of the boom a decade ago, Japanese businesses recently found themselves in the worst possible situation. They have been forced to liquidate these properties at the bottom of the market, in order to meet desperate needs for cash in a recession-beset economy at home.

Meanwhile, in the process of creating a modern-day Greater East Asia Co-Prosperity Sphere, Japan might well feel compelled to match the nuclear arsenals of its neighbors in China and North Korea. As noted above, Prime Minister Murayama is supported by those elements in Japan's Korean community that have funneled billions in hard currency to North Korea's nuclear program. Future negotiations with Washington should then be even more interesting than they are today.

Economist John Makin of the American Enterprise Institute recently said: "America's insistence on trade measures that hurt an already severely weakened Japanese economy sends a clear message to Japan's leaders that their economic and strategic dependence on the United States must be reduced as rapidly as possible.... The Clinton administration and subsequent American governments should consider seriously whether it is the outcome they desire."

Remember Pearl Harbor?

INTERVIEW WITH C. FRED BERGSTEN

# *Freer Trade: Breaking Out All Over the Globe*

*Policy makers have to face two kinds of problems. There is policy error—such as Reaganomics in the early 1980s—and there is market error—such as the case of the speculation against the French franc eighteen months ago. The remedy for both types of problems is the same: Put in place a target-zone system for exchange rates.*

Q Fifty years have now passed since the Bretton Woods agreements established a system for managing the international monetary system and trade under the leadership of the International Monetary Fund (IMF), the World Bank, and a couple of years later, the General Agreements on Tariffs and Trade (GATT). The community of nations (including both the advanced and developing economies) has continued to reach new agreements on trade in the North American Free Trade Agreement (NAFTA), the latest GATT round, and the Asia Pacific Economic Cooperation (APEC) group that you led. But the international monetary system seems to lack leadership and an institutional framework that can effectively deal with the problems of exchange rates, capital flows, and economic policy coordination in the broader framework of both the developed and developing economies. My first question is: Where do we stand at present in the international monetary system? And where are we likely to go as we move into the next century?

A. There is a tendency to look to the past as a "golden age"—to look back to Bretton Woods as a framework for international economic growth and the evolution of a stable international monetary system. Some observers may even go so far as to believe that we need only restore a fixed exchange-rate system under the old arrangements of the IMF, in order to get us back on track for stability and growth. According to the conventional wisdom, the world economy under the leadership of the IMF prospered during the first quarter-century of the post–World War II period. The rapid growth of the global economy was widely distributed across countries. Inflation was relatively low. Trade was steadily liberalized, and it expanded rapidly. International investment and capital flows increased substantially in volume. Nevertheless, payments imbalances were modest and exchange rates were relatively stable.

The IMF stood at the center of the international institutional structure. Countries sought currency con-

This interview was conducted with C. Fred Bergsten, Director, Institute for International Economics and Chairman of the APEC Eminent Persons Group by Richard D. Bartel, editor of *Challenge*, on January 6, 1995, in Washington, D.C. Reprinted from *Challenge*, March–April 1995, pp. 5–11.

vertibility within that arrangement, and the Fund functioned as the lender of last resort that came to aid even the largest countries in periods of balance-of-payments disequilibrium. The Fund's rules for macroeconomic management were generally accepted and faithfully implemented.

Q. Yes, I must confess that I look back to that golden age with some nostalgia. I wonder why we cannot rebuild it.
A. The reality was not so rosy a picture. The advanced countries in Western Europe took almost fifteen years to achieve convertibility. That task was not simple to achieve. There were sterling crises—systematically important because the pound was still the world's second key currency. And those sterling crises occurred frequently throughout the 1960s. The gold markets produced widespread disruptions. Even the dollar—already the leading currency—came under periodic attacks after 1960. These led to capital controls in the United States—the world's largest creditor nation at the time. There were obvious inadequacies in the adjustment process by the middle 1960s. For example, France sought to "dethrone the dollar" by buying gold, and American balance-of-payments policies even played an important role in bringing down a German chancellor.

Q. But didn't the advanced countries enjoy an extraordinary two decades of growth and stability?
A. No doubt, the world economy was robust. Real output and international trade grew rapidly. But much of this expansion was simply a catch-up from the devastation of World War II. It had little to do with the new policy regime established under the Bretton Woods system. Remember, the United States as the dominant economy of that time grew very slowly in the late 1950s and early 1960s. By the end of that period, inflation began to creep up almost everywhere. Eventually, that resulted in the oil price shocks of the 1970s. Meanwhile, scores of developing countries—even those that have now come to be known as economic miracles—adopted strategies of import substitution and even comprehensive socialism in some cases that eventually produced stagnation.

Q. But we did make great progress in liberalizing international trade through the GATT, didn't we?
A. You're right, but even trade policy presented a mixed picture, despite the rapid expansion of trade flows. Protectionism was already on the rise, and the failure of the Bretton Woods System to correct growing currency misalignments of the 1960s triggered an outbreak of American import controls. The United States and the United Kingdom—the key currency countries at the time—even resorted to import surcharges that blatantly violated the rules of both the IMF and the GATT. These two countries were violating the basic rules that they had worked so hard to create within the Bretton Woods System.

The institutional arrangements coming out of the 1940s and the 1950s were much more complex than the conventional wisdom would lead us to believe today. The IMF, for example, was totally bypassed by the Marshall Plan and other intergovernmental lending arrangements in the initial reconstruction period. The "golden period" of the 1960s actually relied heavily on the newly created Group of Ten countries for managing economic crises. They did so through frequent weekend meetings to rescue sterling or the dollar. They arranged frequent supplementary financing agreements via the General Arrangements to Borrow, and through bilateral swap lines of the participating countries. It was the Working Party No. 3 of the OECD, not the IMF, that was the chief institutional arrangement for discussing economic adjustment among the industrial countries. So, the real story of Bretton Woods, and the IMF in particular, is much more complex and nuanced in history than our nostalgic recollections.

Q. So, are we now standing in the rubble of the IMF and Bretton Woods?
A. Contrary to the conventional wisdom, we might even argue that the IMF reached new institutional heights during the last dozen years. That's a long time after the collapse of the Bretton Woods exchange-rate system in the early 1970s. It is a long time after the Fund had conducted its last program in a major industrial country. Look at how the IMF indisputably played a more central role in managing the Third World debt crisis of the 1980s than in managing the global monetary system of the 1960s. And today, the Fund is probably playing a larger role in managing the transformation of the former command economies than it did in the reconstruction of Europe after World War II.

Q. So, where does this leave us in rebuilding an international monetary system and a larger institutional structure for managing trade, payments, growth, and adjustment?

A. Neither nostalgia for the "golden age" of the past nor the desire to restore the monetary role of the IMF can be a credible basis for the future reform of the international monetary system. A case for reform has to be made in substantive terms and must relate to the need to remedy the weaknesses of the current monetary regime and its institutional underpinnings. An IMF of the twenty-first century should become the steward of a system of currency target zones that could evolve over time into an effective regime of macroeconomic policy coordination among at least the European Union, Japan, and the United States.

Q. In managing the world economy, the leading nations are moving along two broad fronts: ongoing progress toward liberalizing international trade and governing fair trade on the one hand, and managing international monetary and the financial relationships and the exchange-rate system on the other. The Mexican peso crisis underscores the urgency confronting our arrangements for dealing with currency crises and adjustment issues in large developing economies, as well as in advanced countries. There are tremendous flows of finance capital moving across the borders. Some of them are related to speculation—especially in so-called emergent markets in the Third World. Central banks trying to cope with these problems are carrying out "anti-inflationary" policies that dampen productive real investment and slow down output and employment growth. Are we caught in a policy trap in which the monetary tail is wagging the domestic-economy dog—so to speak?

A. I wouldn't be nearly so apocalyptic. On the whole, exchange rates are pretty stable. Therefore, I don't see many cases in which exchange-rate movements are disrupting national anti-inflationary or other policy efforts. One place they do is where a government sets an exchange rate at a clearly unsustainable level, in light of its underlying competitiveness. That's reflected in that country's current account position—an excessive deficit or surplus. In another case, under the flexible-rate regime, as in the early 1980s, an exchange rate may respond to an underlying disequilibrium in the national economy. Such an example was the huge U.S. budget deficits in the early 1980s, leading to sky-high real interest rates and the soaring dollar.

They've priced even our most competitive firms out of international markets.

Q. These are the problems I'm talking about.

A. Policy makers have to face two kinds of problems. There is *policy error*—such as Reaganomics in the early 1980s—and there is *market error*—such as the case of the French franc eighteen months ago, when there was speculation against the French franc that had no basis in economic fundamentals. In the latter case, French authorities widened the margins around which the franc fluctuated. The franc weakened a little bit. Then, lo and behold, it went right back into the old narrow trading zone. And it's still there.

The remedy for both types of problems—policy error and market error—is the same: Put in place a target zone system for exchange rates. The target zone system would help correct the market error because, if the zone around a particular currency were credible, and if the exchange rates were set at the proper levels appropriate for the economic fundamentals (and those are two big ifs), then private capital flows would become stabilizing, not destabilizing. If the monetary authorities are credible in setting the exchange rate correctly and in maintaining the margins, when the rate starts to get close to one of the margin limits, it signals to the markets that the central bank or finance authorities are going to come in and intervene to protect the margins. The speculators in the markets won't be able to make much more money pushing the rates to the extreme limit. According to their reasoning, they will see the opportunity to make a lot of profit by pushing the rate in reverse direction. The tendency then is for stabilizing speculation to regress toward the middle of the exchange-rate band. That's been shown theoretically by Paul Krugman. It's also worked out in practice in many cases in the foreign-exchange markets. So, that would take care of the market error—defined as markets driving rates far away from underlying equilibrium in part because they had no guidance from governments as to what the exchange rates ought to be.

Q. What about policy error—particularly of so great a magnitude as Reaganomics?

A. The target zone system would help protect governments against their own policy mistakes. But you cite one of the most difficult cases in Reaganomics. No international regime can be counted on to keep governments from all their foolishness. All you can do is put an international regime in place that tries to tilt a nation's internal policy debates that aren't constructive back toward a sustainable position. The international regime would give support to those people who want to maintain a more responsible policy. In the case of the Reagan administration, all those officials involved in policy making were pretty much a party to the foolishness. Maybe there would have been no way to turn it around.

But in most cases, there would be more diversity of opinion—making the ultimate decision a much closer call within governments. If it is clear that a particular macroeconomic course—a particular monetary-fiscal policy mix—is going to drive the exchange rate outside the acceptable band, and thereby force the country to violate its international commitments, the exchange regime helps build a strong argument against the dangerous policy course.

*Q* This sounds like your strategy for trade policy.
A. There is an analogy with trade policies. GATT doesn't work perfectly. We know that. But the GATT rules provide a strong argument for free traders within governments to resist protectionist pressure. They can quite sincerely say: "We're sympathetic to the problem with an industry now suffering with excess imports. But if we give them protection, we are violating our international obligations." That carries a price. The government, by law, might be required to grant tangible compensation for injury to another country. Failure to grant compensation might risk trade retaliation by the injured country.

In my own experience, time after time, I have seen that argument determine the outcome of a trade-policy decision within the U.S. government. Federal officials do respond constructively to the threat of retaliation. Violating an international commitment that falls in the category of unlawful behavior is cause for consideration. The United States, after all, is a world leader. We believe in the rule of law, and we abide by our international commitments. Second, there may be a price to pay. Innocent bystanders have to pay that price—either in terms of compensation to others or the threat of retaliation against our exporters. The whole nexus of international rules, obligations, and self-denying ordinances has been quite important in helping responsible governments to resist their own political tendencies to make policy errors.

This is an important support for responsible policy in the area of monetary policy. One can sometimes hear officials say that a system of target zones, or even some more ordered system, causes a loss of policy flexibility. According to their argument, the authorities may have to focus monetary policy on the exchange rate, rather than on domestic targets of full employment and growth.

Q. How do you answer that?
A. Two ways: First of all, that doesn't happen very often. If the authorities set the zones correctly, stabilizing help will come from private capital movements, as opposed to destabilizing transactions. Second, we now know that intervention (even sterilized intervention) is quite effective. There are two major studies of the experience with intervention in the last ten years that provide pretty persuasive evidence. Intervention (even just by itself) can often help turn the tide. For those two reasons primarily, I do not think there will be many cases when policy must be devoted to the exchange rate, and shifted away from domestic goals. Intervention has worked. The yen–dollar rate has been stabilized at about 100 for the last eight months. The dollar–mark rate has moved between 1.4 to 1.8 DM per dollar. In the very short run, intervention doesn't stop a rate movement dead in its tracks. But that's rarely the goal. There have been two careful studies—one by Jeff Frankel and another published by Banca D'Italia. They show very persuasively that even sterilized intervention can work, particularly if it is widely publicized and signals to the markets where the officials want the rates to be.

Q. Clearly, you don't share the view that capital movements are so large these days that central banks are unable to cope with them.
A. To the contrary. First of all, it's a ridiculous argument that there are trillions of dollars in the exchange market today and the officials can't cope because they just have these few tens of billions to counter speculation. There are a trillion dollars of transactions in the exchange markets every day. On most days, dollar exchange rates move very little—if at all. By definition, the market is self-balancing. What central bankers have to worry about is the difference between ex-ante supply and ex-ante demand. On some days, intervention can affect a rate movement with a few hundred million dollars in the market. On other days, the central bank cannot defend a rate if a hurricane is blowing through

the market. But, in that case, the existing rate must be inappropriate, relative to the underlying economic fundamentals. So, to summarize, I would say target zones can correct market error.

Q. Let's move on to consider policy error.
A. In the first place, the central bank and the treasury authorities will need to devote domestic policy to the exchange rate only rarely. Second, when intervention is inadequate, and policy must be shifted from domestic objectives to the exchange-rate goals, in almost every case, that is the appropriate policy in the country's best interest for the long term—given the economic fundamentals. This clearly constrains short-term policy flexibility.

If there had been effective international monetary restraints back in the early 1980s when Reaganomics was launched, this policy error would not have been so massive. I had predicted the result would be a huge rise of the dollar and massive U.S. trade deficits. Three years later, editorialists acknowledged publicly that I had the picture right and they had it wrong. Even so, my forecast of a $100 billion U.S. trade deficit turned out to be optimistic, since it actually peaked at nearly $160 billion in 1987. At that time, I believed the exchange rate would correct the trade flows sooner than they actually did. But, if there had been a regime in place to manage currencies and coordinate national policy adjustments, the U.S. Treasury Secretary could have gone into the president's office and said, "Well now, wait a minute. I know you want this huge tax cut, but it's going to blow our exchange rate way out of what we are committed to do internationally. That's going to cause a lot of broken crockery."

My second point is that if he had said that, he would have done this country a service, because then we would not have gotten the massive explosion of deficits and debt that we got from Reaganomics. So it would have been a good thing for the United States in the longer run, if our short-term policy had been constrained.

The Japanese case in the late 1980s is also instructive. After the yen doubled in value, following the Plaza and Louvre agreements, contrary to what some people had predicted, Japan's trade surplus came way down. It came down from over 4 percent to 1 percent of their GDP in 1990. Because their external surplus came down so sharply, it adversely affected the domestic economy and plunged Japan into recession. The policy issue then became: how to fight recession by expanding domestic demand—fiscal or monetary stimulus? They chose to cut interest rates and expand money and credit. As a result, Japan's financial sector fueled a bubble economy. The yen *depreciated* enormously, and the dollar climbed from 120 to 160 yen at a time when Japan's competitive position was getting stronger. That, in turn, triggered the huge renewed growth in Japan's trade surpluses in the early 1990s. In response, the United States and other countries came down hard on Japanese trade policy. That, in turn, led to a rapid turnaround in the yen—rising back to 100 yen per dollar. That sent Japan's economy into deep recession, as the financial bubble collapsed. Japan's economy took a double hit, as the yen fluctuated through wide swings. If a target zone system had been in place, the yen–dollar rate would have fluctuated around the 125 yen-per-dollar level, plus or minus 10 percent, from 1987 onward. That would have constrained them from letting the yen weaken too much, and would have discouraged them from easing interest rates too much. Japan would have been persuaded to use the better alternative by stimulating domestic demand through fiscal policy, not monetary policy. That choice would have been better for Japan's economy, and for the world as a whole.

*Q* What have we learned from these two examples?
A. The existence of a currency regime would have reduced their short-term policy flexibility. In doing so, it would have done them a huge favor for the longer term. The target-zone exchange-rate system would be of substantial help in addressing both the market error and policy error. Would it be perfect? No. No international regime is perfect or can be relied on to solve all problems. The League of Nations didn't prevent World War II, but that did not deter us from creating the United Nations. Our international institutions are changing to meet the needs of an evolving world—whether economic or political. The two extreme systems of fixed and flexible exchange rates failed. Therefore, we should try out an intermediate system of the kind I was talking about twenty years ago—a target-zone system.

*Q* Are we headed for another policy error, with the new Congress?
A. Could be. So far, every politician says he is going to pay for a tax cut at least one for one (maybe even more than one for one) to bring the budget deficit down. If Congress does that, that's fine. But I doubt it will

happen, because the tax cuts are easy and the spending cuts are difficult. Therefore, I testified before Congress to support the balanced budget amendment. It's the third time I've done that. I do it, not out of any love for the balanced budget amendment, but because it is absolutely critical to get the national saving rate up, and because other remedies have failed.

Q. Will the balanced budget amendment work?
A. I think there's a chance, because it would give politicians an excuse. When they cut their constituents' favorite program or raise their taxes, they can protest: "We're being pilloried. But I have to uphold the constitution." And that seems to me to be a pretty substantial boost to the courage of politicians who otherwise don't show much courage.

*Q* Back in the early 1980s, when the Reaganomics program was debated, there were many fairly respected economists who supported those tax cuts. Do you see that kind of support coming from mainstream economists today?
A. I don't think so. There was an amazing lack of criticism of Reaganomics in its early days by the mainstream profession. I remember only two people who really stood up at the outset and really criticized it. One was the late Otto Eckstein—on the grounds of crowding out domestic investment. The other was me—on the grounds of what would happen on the international side. Otto was wrong, because he didn't carry it far enough. He thought it wouldn't work to stimulate the economy because of crowding out. He forgot the rest of the world as a source of savings. The world could and did finance U.S. deficits for a while. I went on to say: "Yes, the world will finance it, but the result will be an enormous overvaluation of the dollar that will fuel massive trade deficits and trigger a surge of trade protectionism." Now, ten to fifteen years later, after the long string of deficits and the huge debt build-up, the obvious fraudulent nature of so-called supply-side economics has been revealed. The American people are much more cautious about going down this tax-cut road again.

So far, the president and his top people have all said exactly the right things. They will not sign on to any tax cuts that are not fully financed. The White House does not seem eager to give up on their strategy of the first two years, which will essentially bring the budget deficit down and get the country's fiscal house in order. If they stick to it, that'll be fine. But you obviously have to worry about the political competition for popular tax cuts. The defense against that is the result of Reaganomics in the last fifteen years. The public does worry about deficits and debt. There was a *Washington Post*–ABC poll report (January 5th) that asked the responders to rank the problems the country faced in the order they thought were most important. At the top of the list was the budget deficit. Fifty-five percent said it was a critically urgent issue. So maybe it's not so politically popular to ignore it anymore.

*Q* Let's shift to the trade side of U.S. international economic relations. We've made some fairly broadly scaled moves now with GATT, NAFTA, and the APEC initiatives that you led. What are the prospects for these arrangements, when the U.S. government seems to want to do less and less in the way of trade adjustment assistance and economic policy that would motivate domestic adjustment in response to trade liberalization?
A. What is really striking about U.S. trade policy is how, despite what you just said, we have eliminated practically all U.S. trade barriers—quotas, orderly marketing agreements, and export restraints. They're all gone. Ten years ago, the United States had all those barriers in place. Under the Reagan administration, as Treasury Secretary Baker has stated, the United States put up more trade protection than under any other American president in this century.

Q. How do you explain that?
A. Reagan's overvalued dollar caused it. For twenty years, I have argued that the exchange rate is by far the best leading indicator of U.S. trade policy. As it turns out, that indicator is also the best for Europe. The more overvalued a country's currency, the more protectionist it becomes. The World Bank has now provided econometric evidence that confirms the hypothesis. After 1985, and on into the Bush administration, as the dollar came down from its peak, U.S. trade barriers crumbled. The quotas on autos, steel, and machine tools all came off. The only remaining quotas apply now to textiles and apparel, and those will be eliminated under the Uruguay Round. A few quotas for agricultural products have been converted to tariffs under the Uruguay Round. The Institute for International Economics published a study just a year ago that quantifies the cost of protection to U.S. consumers and to the economy as a

whole. The consumer burden amounted to about 1.0 percent of GDP, and the results of the Uruguay Round will cut that in half. What will remain, essentially, is an average 3 percent tariff on the whole range of U.S. imports and a few tiny things in peculiar sectors. Consumer costs of only 0.005 percent of GDP and welfare losses of less than $10 billion in an economy of $7 trillion are really quite negligible. So, despite all the lack of adjustment programs and the like, the U.S. has gotten rid of practically all of its protection.

Q. Where do we go from here?
A. The next interesting thing, I think, is the new U.S. initiatives toward further trade liberalization beyond the GATT. The APEC forum had its first summit in November 1993. It was hosted by President Clinton in Seattle, with a follow-up meeting in Indonesia in November 1994. The eighteen countries there comprise one-half the world's economy. They made the stunning commitment to achieve free trade within the Asia Pacific region over the next fifteen to twenty years. They account for more than one-half of world trade. Three weeks later in Miami, at the Summit of the Americas, the thirty-four heads of state of the Western Hemisphere committed to a free-trade area covering all the Americas—to be launched in 2005. The two most dynamic regions of the world—Asia Pacific and the Western Hemisphere—have committed to eliminate all trade barriers. That is a dramatic next step in global trade liberalization.

Inevitably, these steps will lead to the next global trade negotiations under the GATT. These regions very likely will extend their benefits to one another on a reciprocal basis. Liberalization is breaking out all over—on a global scale.

Q. What is this going to do to the problems of industrial restructuring between the advanced industrial countries and the developing world?
A. It clearly accelerates the pace of adjustment. The big question is whether its fruits can be fairly equitably shared within countries. The well-trained, internationally competitive sectors of each economy, of course, benefit enormously from this. The problem is with the lagging sectors—those that are not internationally mobile, and even those that have trouble adjusting to the accelerated pace of change.

Q. What about Mexico, now in the limelight? Will Mexico be compelled to erect defensive mechanisms against capital flight and surges of imports?
A. What's interesting in the Mexican case is the lack of any new restraints or defensive measures—such as import barriers. In fact, Mexico has accelerated its deregulation and privatization process to try to pull up its competitive socks. Mexico is adjusting to the new NAFTA situation. Obviously, it has devalued the exchange rate to eliminate the lack of price competitiveness that it got itself into over the last several years.

If Mexico were to impose new, temporary import restraints, they would make their crisis worse. Then people would say: "Mexico is retreating from the whole strategic change of the last decade—back to the bad old days." Loss of confidence would cause the peso to depreciate even further, and their standard of living would decline even more. The Mexicans can credibly say that their currency crisis of today is dramatically different from their debt crisis of the early 1980s. Now, they are an open, liberalized, largely deregulated economy that can adapt structurally. This inspires confidence to potential foreign investors who are committing $7–8 billion to direct investment each year. That's pretty impressive. Unfortunately, it is not enough to finance Mexico's entire current account deficit. Therein lies the country's problem.

CHAPTER 10 | MANAGING THE GLOBAL DEBT CRISIS

# Debt Reschedulings, Credit Securitization, and the "Emerging Markets"

ROBERT GUTTMANN

The issue dominating international economic affairs during the 1980s was the global debt crisis of less-developed countries (LDCs) which had broken into the open with Mexico's announcement of imminent default in August 1982. That crisis had such a huge impact on the world economy because it was the first financial crisis in the postwar period that had reached systemic-risk proportions of a global nature. Within a year of Mexico's startling announcement, over fifty LDCs could not meet their debt-service obligations and had to be assisted to prevent default. The world's leading money-center banks, in the meantime, faced the distinct possibility of bankruptcy, if actual defaults forced them to write down their LDC loans as bad-debt losses.

These dire consequences did not materialize, however, thanks to a complex, yet reasonably effective international lender-of-last-resort mechanism set up in 1982 to deal with such a global debt crisis. This mechanism gradually eased the problem, and by the late 1980s the worst of the crisis had passed. The world community started to focus on other issues, relieved that the LDC debt problem finally seemed over. But, as Mexico's botched devaluation attempt in late December 1994 and the ensuing global panic demonstrated, the ghosts of the "lost decade" (as the crisis is referred to in Latin America) are still haunting us. If the latest peso crisis is a harbinger of things to come, then it behooves us to understand how the current situation of instability evolved from the crisis context of a decade ago.

## Origins and management of the global debt crisis

The origins of the LDC debt crisis date back to 1973. At that point the quadrupling of oil prices by the Organization of Petroleum Exporting Countries (OPEC) set in motion a massive recycling of OPEC's surpluses via the Euromarket to developing countries running large current-account deficits. OPEC countries had nowhere else to go with their suddenly exploding surpluses, since the industrial nations did not want to see those funds invested directly in their own economies for fear of losing control over their domestic resources to a presumed adversary. The LDCs needed massive funds to cover intensifying external imbalances and budget deficits. Since many of the LDCs exported a lot of raw materials, their borrowing capacity increased with anticipated increases in global commodity prices during the inflation-prone 1970s. Banks liked to make Euromarket loans to LDCs, because they were not subject to regulatory constraints, seemed at the time quite safe, and carried variable rates, which transferred the price risk to debtors. The doubling of oil prices by OPEC in 1979 triggered renewed massive recycling of petrodollars from OPEC via the Euromarket to LDCs, even though many of the latter had already accumulated considerable amounts of debt in the years between the two oil-price shocks (i.e., 1973–79).

Only six months after the second oil-price shock, at a time of massive borrowing activity by LDCs in the Euromarket, the Federal Reserve set U.S. interest rates free to slow down rapidly accelerating inflation and save the dollar's status as world money.[1] This tightening move by the U.S. central bank hit the already heavily indebted LDCs with a double whammy. Suddenly their Eurodollar loans, whose variable interest rates were tied to U.S. rates, all became a lot more expensive. But just when their debt servicing charges exploded, their ability to carry this rising burden deteriorated sharply as a result of falling export earnings from the global recession triggered by the doubling of U.S. interest rates in just three months. That squeeze became worse in 1981 when the U.S. dollar started its spectacular appreciation. A more expensive dollar tended to aggravate the debt-servicing burden of LDCs, since it now took more in local currency or nondollar export earnings to generate the same amount of dollars. Mexico's announcement of imminent default in August 1982, at the bottom of the global downturn, brought this brewing debt crisis to the fore. The banks panicked, and their sudden lending cutbacks threw other overextended debtor nations, notably Argentina and Brazil, into a liquidity crisis a couple of weeks later. At that time the nine largest U.S. banks had lent more than their entire bank capital to just those three Latin American countries alone. Actual default by one of them—Mexico, Argentina, or Brazil—could easily have set off a ripple effect and paralyzed the entire global banking system.

At the time the world was ill-prepared for such a debt crisis of global proportions. While lender-of-last-resort mechanisms existed on a national level, no such intervention capacity had been set up for international financial crises. Therefore, when the threat of LDC defaults spread across the globe in the fall of 1982, a new mechanism had to be set up in a hurry. As José Angel Gurria Treviño, Mexico's secretary of foreign affairs in the new Zedillo administration, recounts below, his country's imminent default prompted the international banking community to introduce a three-part lender-of-last-resort mechanism that soon was extended to deal with all LDC debt-servicing problems on a case-by-case basis. First, Mexico was given short-term "bridge" loans by the industrialized countries (e.g., U.S. Treasury's Exchange Stabilization Fund) or by the Bank for International Settlements (BIS), a sort of central bank's central bank based in Basle (Switzerland). These funds would halt the threat of imminent default and provide breathing space until a more lasting solution could be found. Then the country in question would negotiate an agreement with the IMF which would provide it with some additional funds in exchange for committing itself to an adjustment program that would presumably leave the debtor in a stronger financial position over time. The agreement with the IMF in turn would signal a "green light" for creditor banks, represented by an advisory committee with negotiation authority, to work out a deal with the debtor country in question aimed at rescheduling or restructuring the maturing debt.

This three-pronged strategy of crisis management was, as Benjamin Cohen points out (see below), heavily weighted toward favoring the private banks. Its institutional characteristics, centered on the IMF as a sort of monetary police and coordinator of overall assistance, were tantamount to a *creditor's cartel* that imposed solutions on a case-by-case basis. Debtor countries, which together could have had some bargaining power by threatening a moratorium on debt-servicing payments, were thus precluded from ever organizing such a collective threat.[2] The leading industrial nations in control of the IMF's policy decisions (i.e., United States, European Community) were at that point interested above all in keeping their major banks from taking large losses that could threaten their solvency. The debt reschedulings, aided by permissive and flexible regulatory accounting principles (RAPs) for banks, basically preserved bank income from LDC debt and stretched out any loss provisions.[3]

The principal burden of the crisis was thus placed predominantly on the debtor nations. Cohen shows how the IMF-led management of the crisis basically imposed most of the adjustment burden on the LDCs. These were forced, through drastic austerity measures, to squeeze enough income out of their domestic economies to sustain a stretched-out servicing of their foreign debt. The mechanisms most often used to achieve these income transfers were large currency devaluations, cuts in social spending programs, and lower real wages amidst rapidly rising domestic inflation rates. Many LDCs managed in this way to finance their net outflows of capital with current-account surpluses, but only at the expense of suffering depression-like conditions frequently coupled with hyperinflation.

This crisis-management strategy left the LDCs deeper in debt, since they had to take on new debt to service the old debt and had their interest arrears added on to principal. At the same time it weakened their ability to operate with such a high debt burden because of depressed demand and lower investment activity. For this reason the LDC debt crisis soon became a long-term solvency problem (instead of just a short-term liquidity problem) which had to be addressed differently, in more balanced fashion. The structural nature of the crisis manifested itself in sudden recurrences of acute debt-servicing problems, posing a renewed threat to the solvency of the global banking system, followed by adjustments in the crisis-management mechanism to deal with the situation. Each time, the crisis adjustment process centered on Mexico, the largest LDC debtor and "best pupil" of the IMF. Gurria Treviño shows us how the LDC debt crisis evolved by giving us the details of Mexico's different agreements with the creditor cartel.

• In 1984 Mexico negotiated the first *multi-year rescheduling agreement* (MYRA) with creditor banks. Such MYRAs stretched out debt maturities, eliminated bank commission charges in reschedulings, and lowered the risk premium that LDCs had to pay on their debts. While MYRAs made sure that banks would not fail, they still required continuous and costly income transfers from LDCs to creditor nations.

• In October 1985 the U.S. Treasury announced that Mexico and fourteen other LDCs worthy of that consideration should receive new funds in exchange for adopting structural reforms and comprehensive new macroeconomic policies. This so-called *Baker Plan,* which was followed in 1986 by a model agreement between Mexico and its lenders for new funds at low interest rates coupled with policy reforms, eventually failed, due to the refusal of commercial banks to provide new funds at an adequate scale. Some of the slack created by the disengagement of commercial banks was taken up by the multilateral institutions (i.e., IMF, World Bank) whose relative importance as suppliers of funds to LDCs consequently increased.

• By early 1987 commercial banks in the United States and elsewhere (e.g., Britain) finally had built up their capital base after five years of recovery sufficiently to write down much of their LDC debt to market value.[4] This step marked a decisive turnaround in the crisis, showing that the worst was over. The banks had finally managed to absorb the bad-debt losses from their sovereign loans to LDCs without being thrown into bankruptcy. In addition, the massive set-aside of loss reserves made it easier for the banks to pursue various financial innovations designed to reduce their LDC exposure (e.g., loan sales, debt swaps, debt-for-bond swaps, debt-for-equity swaps).[5] These market-based programs of debt reduction also benefited borrowers who otherwise had little prospect of reducing their debt burdens in the near future.

• In 1989 Mexico's new Salinas administration won approval for a new strategy to reduce its debt and debt-servicing burden. This strategy, later ratified by the U.S. government and extended to other LDCs as the so-called *Brady Plan,* centered on mobilizing additional international resources to serve as collateral for new debt instruments issued by LDCs. Better collateralized, those new instruments would carry lower yields than the old loans they replaced and induce lenders to reduce the amounts they were owed. Commercial banks were allowed to choose among reducing debt principal, agreeing to lower interest rates, or providing LDCs with new funds that were secured by government backing from industrial nations. The Brady Plan thus provided for a simultaneous reduction in LDC debt levels and debt-servicing charges. With this breathing room the global debt crisis was thought to be finally on the way to a durable resolution.

Benjamin Cohen is quite correct when he points to an important shift in crisis management after the Baker Plan, which was extended with the Brady Plan. Throughout the 1980s, the LDC debt crisis was shaped by two questions, namely how to socialize private losses or risks (to banks and their shareholders) and who to burden with those socialization efforts. In the first phase of the crisis (1982–87) the socialization channels engendered accounting relief and even fictitious gains for banks while putting the populations of the LDCs, most of them already poor, through a tremendous squeeze and burdening those societies with even more debts. This unequal distribution of pain between debtors and creditors did not in the end offer a way out of the crisis and for this reason could not go on for very long. The turning point, which came in 1987 and was not least in response to Brazil's go-it-alone confrontation with the creditors, led to institutional changes in loss-socialization channels and pain distribution. The private banks took a fairly large, but still ultimately limited, one-time hit, which gave them greater freedom to disengage from the crisis more rapidly with only limited losses by selling and swapping their loans. The burden placed on LDCs eased somewhat, while structural reforms and policy adjustments undertaken in those countries after 1984 began to show the first signs of progress and thus provide a glimmer of hope for long-term improvements. With banks disengaging and LDCs preoccupied with their restructuring efforts, the burden shifted more to the governments of the creditor banks and, through them, to the populations of the industrial nations. When, for instance, the IMF expands its official assistance or our government extends guarantees for LDC debt (e.g., U.S. backing of Mexico's bonds after 1989), American taxpayers pick up contingent liabilities that may or may not involve actual payments in the future. This shift in risk socialization is one of the reasons why government officials in the United States and elsewhere wanted the public to forget about the LDC debt crisis with the introduction of the Brady Plan in 1989.

## Assessing the role of the International Monetary Fund

The global debt crisis propelled the IMF to the core of the world economy. As the coordinating center of a newly created worldwide lender-of-last-resort mechanism, the Fund had to extend its original mandate of providing short-term funding assistance to countries with temporary payments disequilibria in return for policy corrections. As the global debt crisis unfolded during the 1980s, IMF involvement in LDCs became longer term and more oriented toward fundamental structural reform programs. It is with this extension in mind that we would like to assess the role of the IMF in managing the LDC debt crisis of the 1980s.

Such an assessment is offered here by Harvard's Richard Cooper. After evaluating the post-1982 performance of those fifty-plus LDCs in need of debt reschedulings, Cooper concludes that countries did better when they established good fiscal and monetary control over their economies, managed to maintain reasonably stable real exchange rates, and had access to external financial resources while pursuing stabilization programs at home. These are precisely the prescriptions followed by the IMF. Judged from that perspective, the IMF did very well indeed. Widespread criticisms of the Fund as a repressive institution willing to impose pain and misery on billions of already poor people miss their mark. Governments in developing countries will be inclined to blame the message of pain on the messenger, the IMF, even though they brought much of that pain on by themselves through past mismanagement of resources. Even with regard to that aspect of its responsibilities, as a convenient scapegoat for bitter medicine, the IMF has been remarkably successful in providing debtor governments with some political cover when having to take tough and painful measures.

Yet not all is positive in our evaluation of the IMF. One can, as Cooper does, criticize the Fund's staff justifiably for its excessive zeal concerning inflation, which underestimated potentially useful effects of moderate price increases (on domestic profits and budgets) and resulted in overly harsh macroeconomic policy adjustments. I might add that imposing such brutal "competitive devaluation" and fiscal austerity programs in so many countries all at once put a heavy burden on the world economy's overall growth capacity, but that was, I guess, in the nature of the crisis. Cooper also faults the IMF for excessive detail in the provisions and conditions it prescribed for LDCs to adopt. This propensity made it easier for political leaders in different LDCs to depict the IMF as invading their nation's legitimate sovereignty. At the same time it was sometimes necessary for the IMF to spell out so much detail in its conditions to make sure that reluctant politicians would be committed to a specific course of action.

## Turning some LDCs into "emerging markets"

The global debt crisis left many debtor nations in the southern hemisphere more indebted than before, destabilized by intense inflationary pressures, and subject to years of depression. As resources had to be squeezed out of any given LDC's domestic economy in fairly massive proportions for resource transfer abroad to that country's creditor institutions, income disparaties widened in what were already highly unequal societies. With real wages declining precipitously and unemployment spreading, very large numbers of increasingly impoverished households were forced to work longer hours in more marginal or casualized labor-market conditions. Public and private investment activities were sharply curtailed for an entire decade, leaving the LDC economies with a smaller capital stock for future growth.

Amidst such economic depression, the governments of LDCs were finally forced in the course of their debt-crisis adjustments to abandon their long-standing development strategies based on public ownership of key industries, import-substituting industrialization, and protection of domestic markets. The IMF's macroeconomic and structural adjustment programs played a crucial role in this regard, both in terms of enforcing and legitimating dramatic changes in the policy traditions of the LDCs. Deficit-reduction plans forced LDC governments, for example, to reduce their overblown bureaucracies, restrain their militaries, cut subsidies, deregulate prices, and improve tax administration. Such budgetary economies were typically accompanied by a shift to positive "real" interest rates and deregulation of the domestic banking sector to encourage capital inflows from abroad. These changes in turn prompted much of the deficit-financing of LDCs to shift from bank loans to the issue of marketable securities. Such *securitization* of government debt was further encouraged by the rapid spread of debt-for-bond swaps and other derivatives negotiated under the Brady Plan after 1989. In addition, LDC governments lowered trade barriers, exposed long-protected local monopolies to foreign competition, privatized public enterprises, set up stock and bond markets, and invited foreign capital into the country.

These free-market reforms reinforced stabilization policies based on deficit reduction and tight money by countering inflationary pressures with more competition. Greater price stability and market-opening reforms finally prompted foreign investors to reconsider the LDCs. Even some of the national capital, which had fled earlier, came back.[6] Renewed influx of capital, so far confined for the most part to only a dozen of relatively large and/or resource-rich LDCs (e.g., Mexico, Argentina, Brazil, Malaysia, Thailand, Indonesia), revived targeted economies in terms of increased investment, job creation, technology transfer, and world market integration. Those improvements in turn attracted even more foreign capital. Multinational corporations began to invest more there because of their cheap resources, future market potential, and generous investment incentives. Financial investors, most notably such institutional investors as mutual funds and pension funds, also found those countries very attractive due to their high real interest rates and booming securities markets. By the early 1990s, some of those restructured LDCs had turned into newly industrializing countries (NICs) which are nowadays often referred to as *emerging markets*.[7] In December 1994, however, the global euphoria surrounding the emerging markets turned sour when the Mexican peso suddenly collapsed.

## The Mexican peso crisis of 1994–95

As Gurria Treviño describes it, Mexico under Salinas benefited greatly from successful macroeconomic stabilization, market-opening reforms, and debt relief under the Brady Plan. This combination soon began to attract capital from abroad and in the process revive our neighbor's long-depressed economy. Much of that influx involved U.S. institutional investors, in particular mutual funds, buying dollar-denominated government securities (so-called *tesobonos*) that were backed by Mexico's substantial dollar reserves and carried double-digit yields often exceeding 15 percent.[8] Such massive capital imports caused the peso to appreciate considerably during 1993 and early 1994. Currency appreciation in turn prompted Mexico's current-account balance to deteriorate rapidly into a sizable deficit, a process reinforced throughout 1994 by relatively high domestic growth rates and implementation of trade liberalization under the North American Free Trade Agreement (NAFTA), both of which sucked a lot of imports into Mexico. It was at this point that Salinas, nearing the end of his term, should have devalued the peso. But he failed to take that step.[9]

By late 1994 it had become obvious to the incoming Zedillo administration that macroeconomic imbalances had intensified to the point of requiring urgent and dramatic action. Throughout the year Mexico had financed its rapidly growing current-account deficit by issuing increasingly short-term dollar-denominated government securities with rising yields at times exceeding 20 percent. Increasingly short-term and expensive financing to retire old debt and cover growing deficits, a classic example of what Hyman Minsky (1982) has referred to as *Ponzi financing*, usually does not take long to throw a debtor into a debt-servicing squeeze. Toward the end of 1994, $23 billion of tesobonos were coming due, a sum large enough to use up most of Mexico's dollar reserves should investors decide not to renew those bonds. Frightened by that prospect, Puche Serra, Zedillo's choice of finance minister in lieu of the more reassuring Pedro Arce, decided that the peso had to be devalued to reduce the current-account deficit and lower interest rates. But he blew the devaluation effort by announcing it first on television, thus inadvertently giving traders watching TV at that moment a huge information advantage over those not watching. Realizing his mistake, Puche Serra then tried to reverse his decision. But it was too late to undo the damage. Foreign investors refused to roll the maturing notes over and instead cashed in their dollars as an expression of lack of confidence. Mexico's dollar reserves declined sharply as a result, putting the country on the brink of imminent default.

The phenomenal speed of capital flight, once investors had made up their collective mind to pull out of tesobonos and cash in their dollars, compares in stark contrast to the slow-motion unfolding of the first Mexican peso crisis twelve years earlier. This difference is primarily due to a fundamental change in the nature of credit between then and now. Then, in the early 1980s, LDC debt took the form of bank loans. Unable to get rid of their illiquid loans and unwilling to write them off, bankers were generally inclined to help their troubled debtors through their debt-servicing problems in order to protect their impaired assets. This willingness was reinforced by government insurance of bank liabilities and accounting rules that allowed banks to carry their loan assets at book value. For this reason the first LDC debt crisis could be worked out over a seven-year period. By 1994, however, most of the LDC debt had been changed into securities held by institutional investors, in particular mutual funds. These institutions carry uninsured liabilities and invest in assets that have to be booked at market value. That combination necessitates much more rapid reaction to any crisis. At the same time, institutional investors, such as mutual funds and pension funds, are in a much better position to respond speedily, because their assets are tradable and the sociotechnological infrastructure of their information-processing and trading capacity is highly advanced. Their immediate and massive response to Puche Serra's botched devaluation attempt evaporated Mexico's $30-plus billion in dollar reserves, painfully built up over years, in a matter of days. Moreover, the panic of institutional investors spread like wildfire to other emerging markets (e.g., Argentina, Malaysia), suffering from similar disequilibrium conditions of speculative capital inflows, currency appreciation, and sharply deteriorating current-account balances.

In today's world of securitized credit and computerized trading, time is short and the contagion effect much more virulent. In contrast to loan officers of banks building long-standing relations with their clients around illiquid loans, today's suppliers of funds are institutional investors engaged in constant portfolio adjustments to maximize returns and/or minimize losses. Their portfolio managers move funds in and out of tradable securities at great speed and volume in response to new information on a computer screen. These actions/reactions are communicated to other market participants immediately through price signals that are constantly reevaluated. Nowadays, therefore, both time and speed are much more compressed than they used to be even just a decade ago, during the first LDC debt crisis. This new reality of global finance calls for new mechanisms of crisis management. The old go-slow, case-by-case approach introduced in 1982 cannot contain a crisis such as the massive capital flight out of the Mexican peso in December 1994.

Even though the monetary authorities of emerging markets responded to the worldwide capital flight triggered by the peso crisis of December 1994 by jacking up their interest rates, the crisis was bound to get out of hand unless Mexico's imminent default could be prevented with an effective international rescue operation. But there was no ready-made mechanism to deal with such a crisis that bypassed the banking system, the traditional locus of intervention for lender-of-last-resort assistance. Clinton tried to offer U.S. loan guarantees, but the new isolationist Republican majority in Congress did not want to go along with this bailout plan. While Washington argued, the cash needs of Mexico mounted rapidly. In the face of increasingly pronounced declines in stock, bond, and currency markets, Clinton had to bypass Congress and authorize a $20 billion package of loans and loan guarantees from the U.S. Exchange Stabilization Fund (ESF), accompanied by an $18 billion package from the IMF and several additional billions from the BIS and other central banks for a total of $50 billion in assistance—a sum much larger than ever expended on Mexico by the creditors' cartel during the 1980s. Having exhausted the ESF reserves normally used to defend the dollar instead on a rescue of the peso and at the same time angering allies by pushing through the IMF package without proper consultation, the Clinton administration soon faced an unusually pronounced attack on the U.S. currency, whose value against the other key currencies sank by over 10 percent within a month. In the meantime, Mexico had to undertake yet another brutal adjustment program, which reduced the real wages of the average Mexican worker by 12 percent in one year alone. Recessionary adjustments were somewhat less violent in other emerging markets, yet still very pronounced.

Clinton's effort to bail out Mexico, necessitated both by NAFTA and U.S. obligations stemming from the world-money role of the dollar, almost failed by becoming enmeshed in domestic U.S. politics. The crisis held other valuable lessons as well. For example, the temporal dimension of the speed-up and spatial extension of the contagion necessitated a much more rapid and potentially far more massive assistance response. The United States and other industrial nations have already begun to heed some of those lessons. In the summer of 1995 the G-7 countries agreed to a significant expansion of the IMF's emergency assistance capacity. If this initiative proves sufficient, then the peso crisis of 1994-95 will have proven a serious, but ultimately useful crisis that prepared the monetary authorities for future incidences of instability. The crisis may also help in the long run inasmuch as it prompts emerging markets and institutional investors to pursue a more gradual and better-balanced approach to the accelerated industrialization of LDCs and its financing.

## Notes

1. By early October 1979, efforts were under way across the globe to shield the world economy from a rapidly depreciating dollar. The Europeans had just introduced their mark-dominated European Monetary System, the IMF was contemplating a "substitution account" to remove some of the world's excess dollar reserves, and OPEC announced that it would like to get paid in currencies other than the dollar. It was in this context that the international banking community, at the annual IMF meeting in Belgrade, told the new Fed Chairman Paul Volcker to do something "drastic" or risk losing the dollar's world-money status. Two days later Volcker announced that henceforth the Fed would focus on slowing the growth of monetary aggregates and abandon its policy of keeping interest rates below inflation. Three months later U.S. interest rates had doubled across the entire spectrum of their term structure.

2. The only countries that dared to take on this creditor cartel (Peru early on, Brazil in the mid-1980s) had to do so alone. They were immediately ostracized from international financial markets to the point where they could not even get short-term trade credits. This, together with heavy political pressure from industrialized countries and multilateral organizations, forced each to abandon its lonely struggle and comply with creditor requests.

3. As I have indicated elsewhere (Guttmann, 1989), those RAPs allowed the banks to keep even obviously impaired LDC debt on their books as performing, list them at book value (rather than lower market value), and book additional income gains from reschedulings.

4. The process started early that year when Citibank announced that it had set aside a large loss provision of $2.5 billion for doubtful LDC debt. Its competitors soon followed suit with similar announcements, and by the end of the year U.S. banks had increased their loss provisions by $31 billion.

5. Banks, for example, had established a secondary market where LDC loans could be sold off at discounted market-values. In debt swaps banks would exchange titles of debt to different countries with each other in order to reduce their risk exposure to specific individual countries through diversification. In debt-for-bond swaps new marketable bonds carrying lower coupon yields replaced old loans. And in debt-for-equity swaps debtors would gain equity positions in the debtor country's resources in lieu of old loans.

6. At the height of the LDC crisis, in the early 1980s, an estimated capital flight of $220 billion out of Latin America to the United States and Europe had greatly contributed to the triggering and deepening of the global debt crisis.

7. The concept of "emerging markets" extends beyond revived LDCs of Latin America (e.g., Argentina, Brazil, Chile, Mexico) to a new group of rapidly growing East Asian economies (e.g., Malaysia, China), Israel, and some of the more promising new nations emerging out of the collapse of the Soviet empire (e.g., Czech Republic, Hungary).

8. The emergence of U.S. mutual funds as key investors in the world's securities markets was a byproduct of their spectacular growth at home during the last decade at the expense of commercial banks. The Mexican government's practice of issuing bonds denominated in dollars had its origins in the "dollarization" of the local economy during its hyperinflation period in the early 1980s and the Brady Plan's linkage of Mexican bonds and zero-coupon bonds from the U.S. Treasury.

9. It is not clear why Salinas defied long-standing Mexican tradition and did not administer a currency devaluation near the end of his presidency to give his hand-picked successor a clean slate. He may have been constrained by an explosion of political instability at home (i.e., civil wars in Chiapas and within his own party), by the need to make NAFTA popular through an import boom of artificially cheapened U.S. consumer goods, or by his own personal ambitions to head the newly created World Trade Organization (WTO).

BENJAMIN J. COHEN

# What Ever Happened to the LDC Debt Crisis?

*For a decade, creditor banks rescheduled debt-service and built up loan-loss reserves to avert catastrophe. Meanwhile, the real economic adjustments still go on, with Third World debtors and taxpayers of the creditor nations footing the bill.*

For years, following Mexico's financial near-collapse in the summer of 1982, nothing in international economic relations seemed more compelling than the problem of Third World debt. Would developing countries be forced into default? Would commercial banks be forced into bankruptcy? Would the industrial nations or multilateral organizations be able to organize a rescue in time? All the ingredients of a classic melodrama were there—heroes and villains, winners and losers, innocent and guilty—with the added spice that this was the real world we were talking about. LDC debt dominated a good part of the agenda of international economic negotiations in the 1980s. For many analysts, the serious as well as the sensationalist, it was the story of the decade.

Now, however, we are in a new decade, and attention has seemingly moved on to other stories. The debt problems of developing countries no longer feature prominently in international communiqués. The number of scholarly books or articles on the subject has rapidly declined. Journalistic coverage has receded to the inner pages of the business section and diminished sharply in intensity. A survey of four key news sources in the United States reveals a drop of more than 50 percent in the frequency of articles devoted to LDC debt issues over the last two years. Interest in the problem has clearly faded. Remarkably, this seems true even in many of the indebted countries themselves.

## Why has interest in the question faded?

It could be that interest has faded because there no longer is a problem: the debt crisis is solved or, at least, is well on its way toward a more or less satisfactory resolution. Attention, in other words, could have moved on simply because the bulk of the job is now done. Unhappily, that does not appear to be the case.

From the beginning it was understood that the debt crisis had not one but two dimensions: internal as well as external. The immediate goal, for most of those

BENJAMIN J. COHEN is William L. Clayton Professor of International Economic Affairs at Tufts University. Reprinted from *Challenge*, May–June 1991, pp. 47–51.

involved, was to ease substantially the cash-flow strains on struggling debtors in a manner consistent with continued stability of international financial markets. But that was hardly the whole story. For the problem to be genuinely resolved, all agreed it would also be necessary to achieve a sustained renewal of economic growth and development in debtor countries (often referred to as a "return to creditworthiness"). In practice, achievement in this respect has fallen far short of aspiration, with most LDC borrowers remaining mired in persistent stagnation at home while continuing to labor under heavy debt-service burdens abroad. Indications of progress, though not insignificant, have been spotty at best.

Consider, for example, the trend of such familiar indicators as the debt–service ratio or debt–export ratio. For the entire group of 107 developing countries covered in the World Bank's most recent debt report (1990), both ratios improved in 1989–90 from peak levels in 1987–88. However, most of the apparent improvement was in fact accounted for by LDCs without debt-service difficulties—countries whose financial health has never really been in serious question. For the so-called severely indebted countries (SICs), the numbers are far less encouraging. Among the score of debtors classified by World Bank statisticians as "severely indebted middle-income countries" (SIMICs), located mainly in Latin America, only two—Chile and Costa Rica—have so far been able to reduce their debt ratios sufficiently to be graduated to the ranks of the merely "moderately indebted."

For many other SIMICs, recorded improvements were made possible only by increased recourse to arrears on scheduled interest payments. In 1990, the stock of arrears in the SIMICs passed $35 billion, up from less than $20 billion in 1987 and only $11 billion in 1985. Yet not even such desperation measures have succeeded in overcoming the stagnation of most of the middle-income economies. In a recent survey of Latin America and the Caribbean, only five countries could be labeled as "growing" at the end of the 1980s (Barbados, Chile, Colombia, Costa Rica, and Paraguay), as compared with eleven that were labeled as "stagnating" and five as "declining."

Even worse is the situation in the more than two dozen debtors classified as "severely indebted low-income countries" (SILICs), meaning most of sub-Saharan Africa, where stagnation is almost universal. For most SILICs, debt burdens proportionately weigh even more heavily than they do for SIMICs. On average, scheduled debt service presently exceeds 50 percent of exports—a daunting level of obligations which, as among the SIMICs, has increasingly gone unpaid. Indeed, in recent years less than half of the SILICs' scheduled debt service has actually been transferred to creditors, the rest being added to arrears. Yet for the majority of these countries, too, the development process remains stubbornly stalled. In fact, with few exceptions, per-capita incomes and living standards across sub-Saharan Africa have not stopped deteriorating since the debt crisis began.

## Rescheduling LDC debt

Perhaps most discouraging has been the failure of the leading financial powers and multilateral agencies (including, in particular, the World Bank and International Monetary Fund), despite repeated efforts, to have much impact on the problem. Initially, under the so-called multilateral strategy conceived after Mexico's rescue in 1982, great stress was placed on *rescheduling* existing obligations to ease the difficulties of borrowers. For SILICs, whose debt is owed primarily to official creditors, this was organized through the established procedures of the Paris Club. For SIMICs, who owe more to private creditors, the rescheduling was done through *ad hoc* negotiations with commercial banks. Subsequently, increasing stress was placed on a *reduction* of existing obligations too, private as well as official. In the Paris Club the turning point came in 1988 with adoption of the so-called Toronto terms for debt rescheduling. These terms permit creditor governments to choose from among three alternative concessional options (partial cancellation, extended maturities, or reduced interest rates) designed to create cash-flow savings for debtors. For commercial lenders the turning point came in 1989 with adoption of the so-called Brady Plan, calling on banks to agree to debt and/or debt-service reductions for selected borrowers in return for various forms of financial support from the International Monetary Fund (IMF) and World Bank or creditor governments. Unfortunately, the net gains from either approach have been marginal at best.

For Paris Club countries, cash-flow savings since adoption of the Toronto terms have proved to be especially meager. For the nineteen debtors that rescheduled under these terms in the program's first two years (October 1988–September 1990), total savings have been estimated at about $100 million a year—a not insignificant sum, to be sure, but still no more than 1 percent of these countries' exports and only 1.5 percent of their scheduled debt service. Of the fifty LDC debtors that have rescheduled with the Paris Club since 1976, only five had managed to reestablish normal debtor–creditor relations as of early 1990.

Gains for middle-income debtors have not been much better. After two years, the Brady Plan has produced formal debt-reduction agreements in just four countries—Costa Rica, Mexico, the Philippines, and Venezuela—yielding modest cash-flow savings ranging from an estimated $1.8 billion a year for Mexico to $460 million for Venezuela. As a percentage of projected exports, these benefits vary from about 6 percent for Mexico to some 2.5 percent for Venezuela. Only in Mexico has domestic economic performance clearly improved in conjunction with its Brady program; in the Philippines, at the other extreme, growth has once again ceased, leading to renewed appeals for debt relief. And, of course, servicing difficulties continue to plague many other SIMICs as well, including some of the largest (such as Argentina and Brazil) that have yet to strike a bargain with their commercial creditors. The Brady Plan may be "beginning to work," as *The Economist* recently suggested (January 5, 1991, p. 62), but clearly it is, so far, just a beginning.

In short, the bulk of the job is not yet done. Interest in the debt problem may have faded. The problem itself—the problem of interest, one might say—plainly has not.

## Perceptions at odds with reality

We are confronted, then, with what appears to be a rather striking case of cognitive dissonance: an outright incongruity between relevant facts and prevailing impressions. This suggests that to gain a satisfactory answer to our question of why interest in the problem has faded, the issue cannot simply be addressed in terms of empirical evidence or rational analysis. The answer lies at a deeper level of ideas and cognition, where perception interacts with reality to shape underlying attitudes and opinions. What influences, psychological or otherwise, might help to explain why views of a still very serious problem have become increasingly benign over time?

One possibility could be sheer exhaustion: the parties concerned, quite understandably, might simply have grown tired of—not to say bored with—the subject. The LDC debt story has been running for an awfully long time, after all; and familiarity does tend to breed, if not contempt, certainly a good deal of fatigue. Many scholars, after having dissected the problem in so many ways, do appear to have decided that there are few new intellectual challenges to be met. Officials in the public sector and commercial banks, after having dealt with the problem for so long, seem to have become numbed by the routine and repetitiveness of it all. Journalists, after so many headlines and bylines, appear to have concluded that there is little more glamour to be squeezed out of the subject. Tedium clearly seems to have taken its toll.

But exhaustion alone is hardly a sufficient explanation. A good melodrama need not lose its grip on its audience simply because it has been around for some time. As the author of any soap opera knows, even a very long-running saga can be made to seem fresh and fascinating if its basic dramatic ingredients are kept intact. Something vital in the debt drama itself must also have changed to allow attention to drift away as much as it has. The story must have lost some of its underlying, essential *theatricality*.

That "something," I would argue, is the key element of *threat* in the debt problem: the eruption, after Mexico's crisis in 1982, of serious risks to the safety and solvency of the world's largest commercial banks. Prior to the Mexican crisis, banks had expanded their lending to middle-income developing countries with what seemed like almost reckless abandon, raising the level of their exposure, as measured by standard capital–asset ratios, to unprecedented levels. For the nine largest U.S. banks, for example, in 1982, claims on just the three largest borrowers in Latin America alone—Argentina, Brazil, and Mexico—added up to more than 135 percent of total capital. The vulnerability of commercial creditors to the possibility of default was acute. Major banks were teetering on the brink of bankruptcy. What could have been more theatrical? For years, the audience was riveted by possible scenarios of financial collapse or global depression. "The Dangers of Debt: The Serial" seemed even more gripping than "The Perils of Pauline."

The travails of debtors in all this were not neglected, of course. Indeed, their frustrations and hardships, as they struggled to cope with onerous debt-service burdens, were also viewed as a vital part of the melodrama. But for most of the audience, the importance of debtors as characters in the saga appeared to lie not in themselves but mainly in what their tribulations might mean for creditors. LDCs have always struggled with poverty, after all; nothing new or exciting in that. What was new and exciting after 1982 was the grave harm that LDCs seemingly could do to the financial community, or even to the wider global economy, by a failure to meet their outstanding contractual obligations. The real story, it seemed, lay in the travails of lenders.

Today, by contrast, few private lenders are still considered to be in serious jeopardy because of their LDC exposure. The direct threat to the banking community has largely receded, in part because of a gradual reduction of outstanding claims on developing countries, but mainly because of sharp increases in the amount of loan-loss reserves set aside in recent years to guard against any future disruptions of debt service. In the United States, bank provisions against LDC loans rose from a derisory 5 percent in 1986 to an average of about 50 percent as of June 1990; in Britain, from a range of 6–10 percent to 52–84 percent; in France, from 33–45 percent to 56–61 percent; in Germany, from 35–70 percent to 50–78 percent; and in Japan, from 5 percent to 25–30 percent. Commercial banks still have their problems, of course, including especially the deteriorating quality of their real-estate portfolios and loans for so-called highly leveraged transactions. But to the extent that any threat remains today to their continued safety and solvency, it no longer comes from the direction of the Third World.

This, in turn, has largely drained the LDC debt issue of its core audience appeal—the central dramatic tension provided by the vulnerability of rich banking Goliaths to the adversities of middle-income Davids. Once creditors succeeded in building up their shield of loan-loss provisions against the possible slings and arrows of debtor misfortune, "The Dangers of Debt: The Serial" began to seem less exciting than merely repetitious. No wonder that views of the problem have become increasingly benign.

## Burdens of cost-of-adjustment

Does all this matter? It most certainly does, so long as the problem itself resists satisfactory resolution. At the core of the debt issue has always been a very simple, albeit highly controversial, question: Who should bear the necessary burden of adjustment? That question has not gone away just because attention has now drifted on to other stories.

Until now the distribution of the burden of adjustment, as determined by the multilateral debt strategy, has been remarkably favorable to commercial creditors, who after nearly a decade still have not been obliged to make many really expensive concessions to debtors. True, sizable losses have had to be recorded in bank income statements when reserve provisions have been increased. But these are paper losses only, mere bookkeeping formalities, and cost nothing at all to the balance sheet of institutions unless or until such time that claims are actually written down, converted at a discount, or forgiven. In practice, comparatively few genuine "hits" have been incurred by the banking community, apart from the four debt-reduction programs negotiated to date under the Brady Plan (and an earlier, essentially similar program for Bolivia). Even in these instances, it can reasonably be argued, the quantitative shrinking of balance sheets was at least partially compensated by a qualitative improvement in the paper remaining in their portfolios. Not too many lenders have in fact been eager to accept formal losses of any significant magnitude via write-offs or sales in the secondary market. Most still insist, to the extent possible, on holding LDC debtors to their full contractual obligations while continuing to carry claims on their books at 100 percent of face value. Most, therefore, have been able to keep their own pain well within the range of the tolerable.

The obverse of the favorable outcome for commercial creditors under the prevailing strategy is, unfortunately, a larger measure of pain for other key actors in the story. In reality, most of the costs of adjustment have tended to fall not on lenders but on debtors, plus increasingly on the taxpayers of creditor countries.

That there would be severe costs to debtors under the prevailing strategy has of course long been understood, even if not publicly proclaimed. To protect lenders from losses, borrowers obviously would have to be compelled to do everything possible to avoid default— hence the strategy's heavy stress on IMF-sponsored or -monitored domestic "stabilization" programs, complete with tough policy conditionality and rigorous enforcement of internal and external performance criteria. In simplest terms, an obligation to pay foreign debt service requires a corresponding reduction of expenditures at home in order to release real resources for transfer abroad. In reality, for many developing countries, this has meant becoming enmeshed in a kind of "debt trap": not just persistent stagnation in the present but, worse, sacrifice of much of the capital investment needed to raise productive capacity and accelerate growth in the future. The costs to debtors have been abundantly evident in the continuing deterioration of living standards in Third World nations.

What has been perhaps less well understood is the extent to which, in addition to the costs to debtors, there would be increasing costs to taxpayers in the creditor countries as well. Most obvious are the budgetary impacts of debt cancellations or other concessions under programs like the Paris Club's Toronto terms. The counterpart of any cash-flow savings for debtors is a loss of receipts for creditor governments that over time must be matched, if expenditures are not to be reduced, by offsetting increases of fiscal revenues from other sources. The burden of official debt for many developing countries, especially among the SILICs, still remains heavy, despite recent relief measures; and pressures continue to build for greater and greater generosity. At present the Paris Club is considering a proposal made last September by John Major, then still Britain's Chancellor of the Exchequer, for a doubling of benefits available under the Toronto terms (the so-called Trinidad terms). So long as the development process remains stalled in so many low-income countries, ever more radical—and expensive—remedial proposals can undoubtedly be expected in the future.

Potential taxpayer costs are also implicit in the prevailing strategy *vis-à-vis* middle-income debtors, which has functioned incrementally to transfer a growing portion of the risk and exposure in these countries from commercial lenders to creditor governments and the multilateral agencies. While bank claims on SIMICs have declined, debts to official creditors have more than tripled since the early 1980s. In part, this reflects continued lending along traditional lines by the governments of capital-market countries as well as by the IMF and World Bank (whose obligations, of course, are backed primarily by those same capital-market countries). Less traditionally, it reflects also the impact of the Brady Plan's emphasis on public-sector support of debt or debt-service reduction by the private sector. Over the last two years more than $6 billion of government money has been provided in support of programs negotiated under the plan, to assist in direct buybacks of bank debt or to collateralize the principal or "enhance" (guarantee) interest payments on new debt-reduction instruments. As a result of these developments, official debt service (paid) by SIMICs has nearly doubled, from 5.2 percent of exports in 1982 to 9.7 percent in 1989, even as the ratio of private debt service (paid) to exports fell by nearly half, from 27.2 percent to 16.5 percent. Increasingly, it is the governments of the creditor countries—and through them, ultimately, their taxpayers—rather than private lenders that are becoming the most vulnerable to the difficulties of middle-income debtors.

## Strategy benefits banks

The resulting distribution of the burden of adjustment, skewed so much in favor of commercial creditors, is no accident—quite the contrary, in fact. It is an inherent corollary of the prevailing strategy's underlying design, which has always tacitly accorded highest priority to the interests of private lenders: specifically, to minimizing any serious risk of bank failures or financial-market instability. That priority, though not explicitly stated as such, was evident in the first organized responses to the troubles of Mexico and others in 1982–83; it has remained evident in all subsequent adjustments of the strategy as well—including the Baker Plan in 1985 and the so-called menu approach in 1987 as well as the Brady Plan in 1989. All along, the clear aim was to end any threat to commercial creditors from the cash-flow difficulties of debtors, and to minimize potential pain to the banking community itself. In this respect the framers of the strategy—the creditor governments and multilateral agencies—have been eminently successful.

In turn, one index of that success is the great extent to which interest in the problem has faded as the direct threat to banks—the central dramatic challenge that held everyone's attention—has receded. Once it was clear that the Goliaths were no longer at risk from the Davids, views were bound to grow more benign despite the continuing seriousness of the issue for debtors (and growing costs for taxpayers). The resulting cognitive dissonance, however, is more than merely an incidental by-product of the prevailing strategy's success. It is in fact an essential condition for that success to endure. For the strategy as conceived cannot continue to prevail unless the skewed pattern of adjustment burdens can be preserved; and the skewed pattern of adjustment burdens cannot be preserved if discontent is allowed to fester. Concerned parties must be persuaded that there is no longer a problem: the audience must truly believe that the long run of "The Dangers of Debt: The Serial" has indeed closed. They cannot be permitted to linger over the thought that it is they who may be paying the price.

In short, at the level where perception interacts with reality to shape underlying attitudes and opinions, more has been going on than merely the end of an exciting melodrama. The psychology of the audience's response to the easing of dramatic tension is clearly relevant. But even more salient is the manner in which that response has been exploited and cultivated by creditor governments and the multilateral agencies to reinforce the prevailing strategy's high priority for private creditor interests. Much as in a shell game, the eye has been kept sufficiently distracted to win the players' money. Cognition, in effect, has served as an instrument of public policy.

There is no need to invoke insidious conspiracy theories to account for the crucial importance traditionally attached by capitalist governments to the continued viability of their largest financial institutions and markets. Objective analysis does suggest that more open debate of the prevailing strategy might well now be in order, to review priorities and reconsider alternatives. There is nothing inevitable or preordained about the current distribution of adjustment burdens; there are still serious questions here of efficiency as well as equity. Perceptions notwithstanding, the LDC debt crisis is not yet over.

RICHARD N. COOPER

# *External Adjustment: The Proper Role for the IMF*

The past decade has not been a good one for developing countries as a group. During the 1980s, per capita incomes grew by 1.7 percent a year, less than half the rate attained during the 1960s. But the anomalies within the group have been enormous, ranging from minus three to nearly nine percent. Since all these countries have been part of the same world economy and have participated to some extent in the same world events, what can we say by way of explanation for this considerable statistical disparity?

## *Disparity between developing countries*

First, we can offer some negative lessons, useful because they address some common views of the matter. The growth of developing countries was *not* significantly related to the size of external shocks; indeed, there were several during the 1970s and the 1980s: (1) two substantial increases in oil prices (in 1974 and 1979–80), followed by a sharp drop (in 1986); (2) a sharp rise in coffee and cocoa prices (in 1976–77), followed by a fall; (3) a sharp increase in world interest rates (in 1980–82); and (4) a host of disturbances of lesser magnitude.

What is especially surprising is that performance is not even related to the *sign* of the shocks. Countries that experienced positive shocks did not, on average, do better than countries that experienced negative shocks. To put it bluntly, many countries squandered the potential created by favorable external developments.

Second, performance is not correlated with political system—whether democratic or authoritarian, liberal or illiberal in civil rights. It is true that some of the best performers were authoritarian (for example, Korea), giving rise to the view that authoritarian countries perform well; but some of the worst performers (for example, Argentina) were also authoritarian during the relevant period. The democratization of both countries occurred later—during the course of the 1980s.

Third, variations in growth do not seem to be related to rates of inflation, except where inflation reaches above several hundred percent a year and becomes highly disruptive of normal economic activity. Indeed, moderate inflation has certain fiscal advantages, raising revenue for the government (through seignorage) with

RICHARD N. COOPER is Maurits C. Boas Professor of International Economics at Harvard University. Reprinted from *Challenge*, May–June 1993, pp. 53–56.

less distortion and less evasion than many other taxes. It also stimulates the use of interest-bearing financial assets when interest rates are market-determined.

On the positive side of the ledger, countries that maintained good fiscal control, which in developing countries usually also implies good monetary control, performed noticeably better than countries whose governments lost control of their budgets—something that frequently occurred during economic booms. "Good fiscal control" means good administrative control over the budget combined with an ability to keep expenditures within range of revenues from all sources, thus requiring limited financing from the central bank amounting to a few percentage points of GDP.

Furthermore, maintaining reasonable steadiness in the real exchange rate (the country's exchange rate adjusted for differences between domestic and foreign inflation) contributed to good economic performance. Posited another way, countries that experienced substantial fluctuations in their real exchange rates tended to perform badly.

Further, countries that had access to external resources, particularly in the context of a stabilization program, tended to perform better than those that had a more difficult time getting financial inflows from abroad. While inflows of financial resources cannot assure good economic performance (indeed, such inflows sometimes permitted countries to pursue careless economic policies), financial assistance can help spread out difficult adjustments and avoid drastic curtailment of investment and other growth-enhancing activities.

## The role of the IMF

The International Monetary Fund and (in its structural adjustment loans) the World Bank have played an important role in encouraging fiscal discipline and reasonable steadiness in real exchange rates. They also, of course, have provided financial resources to assist adjustment, both directly through their own lending, and indirectly through "cofinancing" (conditioned on IMF programs) by aid donors and commercial banks. In short, the IMF should be seen as a helpful institution, one that can ease the pain of necessary adjustment to adverse external shocks or reversal of unsustainable domestic policies.

But the IMF is not seen as a helpful institution. On the contrary, it has developed a reputation as a repressive and growth-throttling institution, bearing heavily on the poor countries, and requiring them to do abhorrent things. It is perceived somewhat as a monetary policeman of the world economy, or more accurately, as a harsh schoolmaster who administers corporal punishment to those who fail to execute their lessons adequately.

What explains the contrast between the reputation the IMF should have and that which it actually has? Partly, the IMF is wrongly criticized for the adverse conditions that exist in countries it is trying to help. It brings the unpleasant message, already known to the government officials who have called on the IMF, and who know that the *status quo ante* cannot continue, that some kind of squeeze on resource use is necessary to achieve a sustainable condition. But many, often including the local financial officials, find it convenient to use the IMF as a scapegoat—to blame the message on the messenger.

Also unfairly, the IMF is criticized for not carrying out an agenda it was neither designed for nor commissioned by its articles to carry out. It is *not* designed to eliminate poverty, *nor* to assure democracy, *nor* to improve the environment. It *could* advance these worthy objectives modestly, but it is not well designed to do so, and its current objectives are themselves important and quite absorbing.

It is useful to recall the original conception of the IMF, reaffirmed when last amended in 1978. Basically, it boils down to three considerations:

• encouraging member countries to integrate themselves into the world market, insofar as currency arrangements are concerned, by requiring convertibility of currencies for current account transactions, and by prohibiting discriminatory currency practices;
• discouraging actions that are taken at the possible expense of other countries, such as currency restrictions on imports or competitive depreciation to stimulate domestic employment by reducing imports;
• granting loans to countries in order to tide them over periods of temporary payments disequilibrium, and providing them "with an opportunity to correct maladjustments in their balance of payments without resorting to measures destructive of national or international prosperity" (Article I of IMF's Articles of Agreement).

In short, the interest of the international community, as reflected in the IMF Articles of Agreement, is to limit the antisocial financial behavior of states toward other states, and to help their fellow states that are temporarily in distress.

This fundamental conception is still valid. It is necessary to have a harsh schoolmaster, but only to hold member countries to the (relatively modest) rules, and to help them during temporary periods of difficulty. Permanent aid was not envisioned, nor is it possible, given the capital structure of the IMF. The key analytical problem lies in distinguishing whether an observed disequilibrium is temporary or fundamental, and evaluating the policy measures necessary to eliminate that which is fundamental.

That task involves both analytical skill and seasoned judgment. There is room for disagreement on both, but nearly all agree that the relevant instruments involve the overall stance of monetary and fiscal policy and, of course, exchange rate policy—given the commitment in the articles (too often ignored in practice) for all member countries to strive toward full convertibility of currencies for current account transactions. They need not involve, however, myriad details of tax, expenditure, and social policy.

The IMF is open to valid criticism for having made two generic mistakes. First, in the early 1980s it embarked upon a crusade against inflation, not only in making its global pronouncements (which were appropriate at the time) but also instituting programs in individual countries. It is a wise policy to restrain inflation in most countries, although, as noted above, modest inflation has some useful fiscal effects—especially in countries with poorly developed tax and financial systems. But the issue for the IMF—which represents the interests of the international community in the policies of each of its member countries—is not whether the policy is wise but whether the world community has a strong legitimate interest in each country's rate of inflation.

The answer is negative for most countries, provided gross distortions in international payments are avoided. The IMF should, of course, stand ready to assist governments wishing to reduce inflation as part of their adjustment to external or internal shocks; but that should be each government's initiative, not the IMF's. The IMF should keep its eyes on the distortions to trade and payments, not on the rate of inflation per se—each country legitimately choosing that for itself.

## Does the IMF overstep its bounds?

It may be asked that if the world community has a legitimate interest in preventing each country from exporting its unemployment through restrictions on trade (part of the historical rationale for the IMF), does it not also have a legitimate interest in preventing countries from exporting their inflation?

The answer may well be affirmative in principle; but there is an intrinsic asymmetry between the two. A country can export its unemployment by restricting imports and making its exports artificially competitive, for example, through undervaluation of its currency. Most countries can export inflation only insofar as they can acquire financing from the rest of the world to cover their import deficits. The major exception was the United States, whose deficit before 1973 was "automatically" financed by foreign central bank acquisition of U.S. Treasury bills and other liquid dollar assets. Halting that process was a major reason for the switch to floating exchange rates in 1973. So most countries' ability to export inflation is intrinsically limited; it does not need additional reinforcement from the IMF. Appropriate exchange-rate adjustment can complete the separation between domestic inflation and the inflationary impetus a country transmits to the world economy.

The second generic mistake made by the IMF is that it has come to stipulate national policy actions in great detail. A recent IMF draft letter of intent, for instance, stipulated what the country's urban property tax rates should be. This practice is at once extremely intrusive into the domestic political process and unnecessary for the IMF to perform its essential functions. It creates much resentment in any society, but especially in democratic societies where decisions with respect to the structure of public expenditures and taxation go to the heart of the democratic political process.

The IMF may of, course, be giving excellent advice in the details that it stipulates. That is not the issue. Why should the world community be interested in urban tax rates in any country? It has a legitimate interest in the country's overall monetary/fiscal stance, and in its exchange rates, since these determine its financial interactions with the rest of the world. Energy prices were added to this list following the large oil shocks of the 1970s, since oil price subsidies were so large in some countries that they determined the country's fiscal position and influenced its demand for oil and its overall import bill.

But urban property tax rates? Meddling in that level of detail is highly intrusive and builds resentment against an institution that should be seen as supportive.

Two nuances need to be introduced into this criticism. First, the IMF has lots of experience in many countries, and can often bring useful new ideas and policy advice to a country's officials. Such valuable accumulated experience can be made known to them in the form of technical advice, however, rather than as conditions for financial assistance.

Second, a country's finance minister may need some reinforcement in dealing with his public, his legislature, and even other members of his cabinet, who are less well versed in the economic facts of life (for example, a government cannot for long spend more than it earns without borrowing). The finance minister may therefore *welcome* some policy details in the commitments that are made to the IMF as a condition for a loan.

But this critical *political* judgment should be made by the government, not by the IMF; and the government should take full public responsibility for having made the commitments. That is quite different from the IMF's pressing a reluctant government into specific actions. Such undertakings are unlikely to stick if the key officials of the government are not fully committed to them. Of course, if the government does not agree even on the basic actions required, the IMF should not lend to the country; no degree of detail will evade that problem.

I would go further to suggest that, if a country does not subscribe to the basic principles of the IMF, it should not be a member. It is not essential, after all, to be a member of the IMF. Switzerland remained outside for over forty years, although that will soon change. One basic rule is a commitment to current account convertibility. Article XIV permits postponement of convertibility from the date of initial membership in the IMF, but this exception is clearly to be transitory. Some countries have invoked this provision for thirty or forty years—surely a gross abuse of the term "transitory." It is puzzling that, for example, India remained in the IMF (and was allowed to remain) for decades when it was openly hostile to convertibility—not as a temporary expedient, but as a matter of fundamental philosophy. Cuba is properly excluded on those grounds, as were most other communist countries. India has recently changed its official stance on this important issue. It is desirable for the IMF to be open to all countries that subscribe to its club rules, but there is no compelling reason for it gratuitously to be a universal institution for its own sake.

## Conclusion

The IMF is an extremely useful institution for countries in balance-of-payments difficulty, and, with proper guidance, its lending can ease the pain of adjustment. It does not *cause* the need for adjustment, and is unjustly blamed for doing so. But it should keep its eye on the ball—namely, the desire of the international community to maintain its members' prosperous and open economies. It should refrain from pressing countries into policies that do not meet these requirements, for, in the long run, that will undermine political support for the IMF—not only in borrowing countries, but in lending countries as well.

JOSÉ ANGEL GURRIA TREVIÑO

# *The Mexican Debt Strategy*

*Mexico is well aware that, with negotiations behind it, its efforts must remain focused on the generation of a "virtuous circle" that will utilize continued economic reforms to fuel further improvements to the economy, and will build on the critical foundation of reform that it has already established.*

On August 22, 1982, Mexico's official debt crisis began. On that day, the Mexican government requested a three-month extension for all Mexican public-sector debt that was scheduled to come due within the next ninety days.

In the main, the need for an extension was the result of the extraordinary rise in Mexico's cost of financing this debt and a deterioration in the terms of trade for Mexican exports. Specifically, in the early 1980s, oil prices (on which Mexico depended as a major source of income) dropped precipitously. At the same time, tightened U.S. and British monetary policies led to a sharp rise in international borrowing rates.

A miscalculation on the part of both Mexico and its foreign lenders that the spike in oil prices in the 1970s would be sustainable had led forecasters on both sides of the equation to project Mexico's balance of payments for 1981 and 1982 in excessively optimistic terms. Consequently, Mexico was able to overextend itself in both spending and foreign indebtedness. Moreover, a lack of early intervention in exchange-rate policy by Mexican officials resulted in a distortion of an array of other macroeconomic variables.

Rather than respond to these economic forces with changes in the Mexican macroeconomic infrastructure, the government of Mexico determined that its economic difficulties were temporary, and that the remedy was to obtain further commercial capital from overseas lenders. Because of the increased risks that resulted from Mexico's economic difficulties, foreign banks raised the borrowing rates for Mexico and shortened the maturities of the new loans that they made. In the process, commercial banks loaned Mexico another $2.5 billion.

But, by mid-1982 it had become clear that Mexico's economic difficulties were not temporary. Commercial banks stopped lending. From that year until 1989, Mexico was forced to service its debt with internal capital. It didn't receive any new, voluntary funding from foreign banks. As a result, each year between 1983 and 1988, Mexico had to transfer about 6 percent of its GDP to other countries. This transfer made Mexico a new capital exporter, and compounded its pre-existing problem of being "over-leveraged," thereby sharply limiting its capabilities for domestic investment and consumption.

The solution to this crisis was achieved only through four separate rounds of debt negotiations. In the first

JOSÉ ANGEL GURRIA TREVIÑO is the Secretary of Foreign Affairs of Mexico. Reprinted from *Challenge*, March–April 1995, pp. 34–38.

round, Mexico sought additional foreign capital, as well as a postponement of the maturity of the principal amounts of all existing foreign debt. However, Mexico promised to continue to make scheduled interest payments.

## *Early negotiations*

August 1982 marked the beginning of talks between the Mexican government and the U.S. Treasury to arrange a package of emergency loans for Mexico. While a solution was difficult to reach, Mexico ultimately received two separate loans. The first, effectively, was a $1 billion "advance" by the U.S. government on its future oil purchases from Mexico. For these funds, then Treasury Secretary Don Regan proposed that Mexico pay an implicit rate of interest of 38 percent. The second loan (also for $1 billion) was granted to Mexico by the U.S. Commodity Credit Corporation. Separately, Mexico was able to obtain a third loan (for $1.85 billion) from the central banks of major industrialized countries through the Bank of International Settlements (BIS).

On August 20, 1982, Mexican officials met in New York with representatives of its most important commercial creditors. As a result of that meeting, the banks agreed to permit Mexico to defer repayment of $8.1 billion in principal. They also agreed to create an advisory committee to coordinate the debt rescheduling process. The establishment of this committee was indispensable for Mexico, because it permitted negotiations through a single entity, rather than through each of the more than 530 lenders worldwide who had extended credit to Mexico.

The final step in the first round of negotiations was to obtain the support of the International Monetary Fund (IMF). That support was crucial in gaining further assistance from the commercial banks. Through negotiations, the IMF agreed to give Mexico a $4.5 billion "Extended Fund Facility" that would be disbursed over a three-year period. But, before it would approve the facility (and in an extremely novel move), the IMF insisted that Mexico's commercial lenders had to commit themselves to lending another $5 billion to Mexico. In addition to these new funds, Mexico was allowed by the banks to reschedule $23.1 billion in pre-existing debt payments.

## *Subsequent rounds*

In early 1984, when Mexico's "breathing room"—its postponement on principal repayments—began to run out, a second round of negotiations was initiated. Prior agreements with commercial lenders directed that major principal repayments would have to begin in 1985. But Mexico still had inadequate resources to fund these repayments. As a result, Mexican authorities began work on a comprehensive restructuring program to reschedule $48 billion in public-sector debt that would mature between 1985 and 1990.

Through the second round of debt restructuring, "Multi-Year Rescheduling Arrangements" (MYRAs) were introduced. The MYRAs extended the maturities of commercial loans, eliminated bank commissions, and reduced interest rate spreads paid by Mexico from 2.25 percentage points to between 0.875 and 1.5 percentage points. While this new schedule ensured that foreign commercial lenders would not go bankrupt, it still did not address the problem that Mexico faced in its continuing transfer of wealth abroad. Though the debt schedule was more manageable for Mexico, the cost of repayment was still extremely high. To service its debt, Mexico had to generate large surpluses in its trade and current account balances.

## *The Baker plan*

In October 1985, a third approach began when U.S. Treasury Secretary James Baker announced that Mexico's debt crisis could be resolved by spurring Mexican economic growth with new financial resources from abroad. The so-called Baker Plan included the following three-part strategy:

• Mexico (and other Latin American debtor countries targeted by the plan) would adopt comprehensive new macroeconomic policies;
• the IMF would continue to play a central role in debt management, and multilateral institutions would support the adoption of new, market-oriented economic policies through increased and more structurally adjusted lending;
• commercial banks would further support these adjustment programs with additional lending.

Secretary Baker asked multilateral institutions and commercial banks to increase their lending significantly between 1985 and 1987. While some new funds were made available, economic conditions in Mexico and in the overseas commercial banking sector once again hindered efforts to restructure Mexico's foreign debt in a manner that was productive for Mexico and its creditors.

## The crisis of 1986

The year 1986 marked the climax of Mexico's worst economic crisis in the postwar period. Oil prices plummeted by more than 50 percent. That, in turn, cost Mexico 6 percent of its GDP and 20 percent of all public revenues. The government of Mexico responded to the crisis by tightening both fiscal and monetary policies. It devalued the peso and again sought new, more favorable debt-repayment terms with foreign lenders.

Once again, Mexico obtained more and more manageable debt. After considerable negotiation, Mexico reached an agreement with the IMF in September 1986. Commercial banks responded with new loans of $6 billion, and with even lower interest rate spreads. This time they were just under 0.875 of a percentage point. But, even at such low borrowing costs, the assumption of new debt still did not help Mexico resolve the fact that a large portion of the wealth it created was needed to pay back its overseas creditors.

Furthermore, commercial banks ignored Secretary Baker's request. Gradually, they stopped participating in new financing packages to Mexico and other debtor countries. The banks had survived the debt crisis and avoided bankruptcy. They were eager to reduce their existing debt exposures by increasing the extent to which they had reserved capital relative to outstanding loans (so-called loan-loss reserves). To do this, the banks marked down the value of the loans on their books. Citibank, for example, marked down its loan portfolio for debtor countries by 25 percent. Several banks also sought to exchange the loans on their books for new assets in the emerging secondary and derivatives markets.

For several months after the IMF deal was negotiated, Mexico's only sources of new funds were multilateral institutions. Thus, Mexico was taking in institutional funding to pay the debt service on commercial bank loans. By 1987, the world economy was strong enough to permit Mexico to pursue market-based programs to reduce its debt. Moreover, with no improvement in Mexico's long-term ability to overcome its debt overhang, such a strategy was a necessity. Furthermore, there was a growing consensus among debtor and creditor countries alike that any solution to the problem of debt overhang must be permanent. And it must permit Mexico and other debtor nations to obtain resources sufficient to resume sustained economic growth.

## A permanent solution?

The beginnings of Mexico's permanent solution emerged in early 1988 when, in an effort to lessen Mexico's overall debt burden, the Mexican government worked with the firm of J. P. Morgan to carry out a massive debt-for-debt swap. Through this offer, lenders could exchange the loans they had already given to Mexico for twenty-year bonds, the principal of which was guaranteed with U.S. Treasury zero-coupon bonds. As a result of the swap initiative, $3.6 billion of old debt was canceled and exchanged for $2.5 billion in new bonds. Mexico's debt balance was thereby reduced by a net $1.1 billion. The novel, market-based approach of this initiative was a watershed in the area of voluntary debt reduction. It influenced later multilateral efforts to alleviate Mexico's debt crisis further.

In the fall of 1988, Carlos Salinas de Gortari was elected president of Mexico. In his inaugural address that December, President Salinas outlined four objectives of Mexico's continued debt-restructuring program to reach a permanent solution to the country's economic turbulence. Salinas stated that these goals were:

• The conclusion of a multi-year debt arrangement that would eliminate uncertainty in long-term economic planning;
• a reduction in Mexico's net transfers of wealth to a level that permitted the resumption of national economic growth;
• a reduction in Mexico's total external debt balances;
• a reduction in the ratios between Mexico's total GDP and the costs of paying and servicing the national debt.

Toward these ends, the Salinas administration set out to reach agreements with Mexico's official, multilateral creditors, including the IMF, the World Bank, and the governments of major, industrialized countries. It was an attempt to ensure that these creditors would provide both political and economic support during anticipated negotiations between the Mexican government and its commercial lenders. In early 1989, in discussions between Mexico and its institutional lenders, it was agreed that Mexico must both eliminate its debt overhang and restore economic growth, in order to ensure against future debt crises.

## The Brady plan

Mexico presented an external debt reduction/management strategy to its institutional lenders. It requested continued international resources to help the country reduce its debt and its debt-service costs. Shortly after this strategy was presented, the U.S. Treasury secretary, Nicholas Brady, developed a new plan for addressing the debt crisis in Mexico and similar crises in other developing countries. The "Brady Plan" supported Mexico's request for debt and debt-service reduction—specifically, through the use of international resources that would "enhance" the collateral on new debt instruments issued by Mexico. The improved collateral would lower the risk associated with lending to Mexico, thereby reducing the interest costs to the Mexican government of taking on new debt. With this type of security, the collateral would also provide a guarantee to lenders that they would be repaid. In turn, they might be willing to reduce the amounts that were owed.

With the Brady Plan in hand, Mexico secured support from its most critical institutional creditors for a restructuring program on a scale that had never before occurred in the world credit market. The IMF and the World Bank agreed to set aside a portion of their programmed lending to support the reduction of Mexico's debt and debt-service costs. The IMF committed $1.7 billion to guarantee Mexico's principal and interest payments, and the World Bank put up slightly more than $2 billion. In addition, the government of Japan pledged nearly $2.1 billion to be committed through the international Export-Import Bank. Finally, the Mexican government set aside $1.3 billion of its own reserves, bringing the total collateral pool available to $7 billion.

With this new collateral secured, Mexico began discussions with commercial lenders in April 1989. After four months of intense negotiations, an agreement-in-principle (AIP) was announced. Through this agreement, a total of $48.2 billion in Mexican debt became available for restructuring. Each of the commercial lenders of these funds could choose one of the following options:

- *It could reduce the principal amount of Mexico's debt.* Banks could swap their eligible debt for thirty-year, floating-rate bonds whose principal value was 35 percent less than the value of the original debt. The bonds featured a bullet payment, and bore an interest rate equal to 13/16ths of a percentage point over international bank overnight lending rates.

- *It could reduce the interest rates on Mexico's debt.* Banks could swap their eligible debt for thirty-year bullet bonds whose principal value was "at par" with the value of the original debt. These bonds would bear a fixed interest rate of 6.25 percent.

- *It could provide new, secured funding to Mexico.* Banks could lend Mexico new money equal to 25 percent of existing eligible debt holdings over a period of three years.

For banks that selected either of the first two options, the principal amount of the new bonds they received were guaranteed by thirty-year zero-coupon bonds, with an additional guarantee equal to eighteen months' worth of interest payments of those bonds. Based on the choices they were given, 46.5 percent of the banks chose a debt-service reduction plan, 42.6 percent chose principal reduction, and 10.9 percent chose new funding. A massive restructuring had taken place. Since the negotiation of this deal, Mexico has put into effect additional voluntary debt-reduction initiatives through direct buy-backs of its debt from commercial banks.

The success of the Brady Plan has been incontrovertible. Mexico's debt overhang has been diminished. It has fallen from an astounding 76.3 percent of GDP in 1986 to 33 percent of GDP last year. As a result, there now exists in Mexico an environment for investment, stability, and growth.

Not surprisingly, domestic interest rates declined considerably after the restructuring was completed. Both Mexican and foreign investment in Mexico have risen precipitously. Capital has been repatriated. And public finances have been consolidated. Once-legendary Mexican inflation has plummeted from triple-digit rates in the early 1980s to single-digit rates today. Consumer prices rise each year at a lower rate than they did on a monthly basis only five years ago. Mexico has switched from being a net exporter of its wealth to being a net importer, taking in capital flows each year since 1989 worth about 4 percent of its GDP.

On June 1, 1992, Mexico canceled nearly 9 percent of its total outstanding public sector (external) debt. The country has also regained voluntary access to international capital markets, and has taken in sizable capital inflows. It has accomplished this principally through direct and portfolio investment of the private sector, rather than through additional bank lending. Mexico's public-sector entities have achieved financing through the placement of many types of well-received bond issues in the European and U.S. markets. The bonds have provided these organizations needed capital access without creating further indebtedness to the world's commercial-banking sector.

After eleven years (and with considerable work), Mexico has achieved remarkable economic progress. Today, Mexico is the thirteenth-largest economy in the world, and has one of the world's most open economies. It has diversified its export structure considerably over the last decade, boosting nonoil exports by 400 percent and manufacturing exports by 500 percent.

## Lessons learned

The lessons that Mexico learned during the years marked by its debt crisis are numerous. It knows now that it cannot substitute external debt management for sound economic policy. It knows that packaging strategies for "debtor clubs" can only result in lowest-common-denominator solutions. It knows that negotiated financial packages must be as ample, simple, and flexible as possible. It knows that a timely agreement is better than an optimum, albeit extemporaneous, solution. It knows that progress must be measured using a number of different gauges. And it knows that, because each country has different circumstances and needs, what has worked for Mexico might not work elsewhere.

The Mexican experience over the past decade has proven that the best reforms utilize deep, structural programs, and that these reforms have an impact that will far outlast the terms and conditions obtained through the final round of restructuring negotiations. By freeing additional public resources that have become available through the restructuring and follow-up initiatives, Mexico can achieve continued reform and progress. It is well aware that, with negotiations behind it, its efforts must remain focused on the generation of a "virtuous circle" that will utilize continued economic reforms to fuel further improvements to the economy, and will build on the critical foundation of reform that it has already established.

## The present turmoil

As this issue was going to press, Mexico again found itself in economic turmoil. A constant inflow of foreign resources from 1989 to 1993 caused gradual appreciation of the currency and a widening of the current-account gap to almost 8 percent of GDP. Exacerbated by political events, uncertainty turned into a loss of confidence and fueled a 50 percent devaluation in the last days of 1994. A financial package of $50 billion—put together by the U.S. government, the IMF, the BIS, and some commercial banks—was being used to refinance short-term debt and stabilize markets. The fundamentals are still strong and sound. But two new lessons became clear: (1) Don't rely too much on foreign savings—especially if they are short-term; and (2) keep a close eye on your exchange rate.

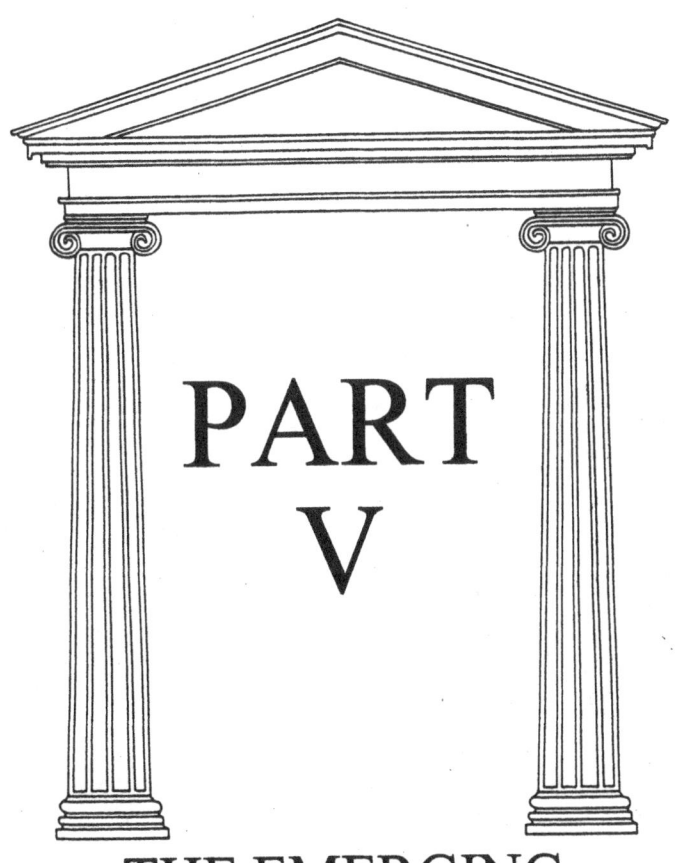

# PART V

## THE EMERGING MONETARY REGIME

CHAPTER 11 | TRANSITION TO A NEW MONETARY REGIME

# *Defining Monetary Regimes*

ROBERT GUTTMANN

This last chapter attempts a synthesis by pulling the various themes of the preceding chapters together into a coherent story. That story is about a financial system in a state of transition. Gone is the tightly regulated, strictly segmented, and predominantly national credit system of yesteryear. In its place has emerged a largely deregulated, increasingly integrated, and essentially global credit system. The qualitative differences between the kind of credit system we used to have until the early 1970s and the one that has evolved since then are dramatic and have important implications for the performance of our economy.

## *Conceptualizing the strategic role of money and credit*

We have to understand that money plays an absolutely crucial role in our cash-flow economy in which all our economic activities (e.g., consumption, production) are mobilized as *monetary circuits*. These take the form of interdependent cash flows, either between market participants (i.e., exchange) or over time (i.e., investments in income-producing assets). Money is the glue that keeps this cash-flow economy together. Its different forms and the modalities of its circulation thus play a major role in the organization of economic activity.

Since Roosevelt's monetary reforms, which replaced the destroyed gold standard in the mid-1930s, the issue of money has been fundamentally linked to credit extension in the banking system (see chapter 1). Such a system of *credit-money* allows individual agents (i.e., households, businesses, government organizations) to spend at any time more than their current income levels by taking out bank loans (or tapping into lines of credit) through which new money gets created by private banks with central bank backing.[1] This *monetization* of debt, involving the automatic creation of new liquidity with which to back that portion of debt-related cash-flow commitments tied to bank loans, has allowed credit to become a much more central force in our economy by providing for continuous financing of excess spending.

Credit gives borrowers temporary access to someone else's income. This allows producers to cover the cash-flow gaps of their investments and consumers to buy large-ticket items (e.g., homes, cars, college education). Economic activity depends therefore on a continuous supply of credit at affordable terms. Moreover, the level and structure of interest rates in the credit system have a powerful influence on investment demand, determining the minimum rate of return required by investors (i.e., the "hurdle rate") and their time horizon. In addition, the transfer of funds in the credit system mobilizes capital for different investment uses and thereby plays a crucial role in the allocation of our resources. On the macroeconomic level, credit stimulates faster growth by turning otherwise unspent funds into an additional source of demand, while at the same time providing savers with opportunities for income gains. Yet credit is at the same time a destabilizing force in our economy, since it exacerbates industry's inherent overproduction tendency by an equally pronounced propensity of lenders for credit overextension (see our discussion of the "credit cycle" in chapter 2). Lenders, just like corporations in their investment activities, are induced by the profit motive into cyclical behavior. First they are driven by greed and optimism into excessive pursuit of income gains; then, when difficulties arise, they cut back too much out of fear and pessimism.

These features of our cash-flow economy necessitate state management of money and credit. For example, if certain private consumers or producers were able to create their own money for payments, they would have an undue advantage over others not able to do so. This is one reason why money creation has been placed in the banking system—that is, outside the marketplace for goods and services and subject to government regulation as a public good. Moreover, the inherently cyclical nature of economic growth has engendered various stabilization efforts by government institutions, including measures to contain financial crises. Even though recessions are nothing but the market economy's mechanism to correct underlying imbalances, they have to be kept within bounds. Not only are they very painful episodes, but they may also under certain circumstances (such as a collapsing banking system) turn into much deeper depressions. Finally, the strategic role of the credit system, coupled with its tendency for overextension, has convinced policy makers time and again of the need to regulate the behavior of financial institutions.

## The elements of the postwar regime of credit-money

When analyzing how the government manages money and credit, it is useful to introduce the concept of *monetary regime*. This concept comprises all the institutional arrangements pertaining to money creation and the structure of our credit system. More specifically, a monetary regime is typically made up of the following policy dimensions:

*(1) Monetary Policy* Governments all over the world have set up central banks and empowered them to regulate the process of money creation. This responsibility entails several central bank activities, including the issue of its own paper currency, the operation of the nation's payments system, the guarantee of automatic convertibility among different money forms, and the implementation of controls over the issue of private bank money. In addition, the central bank has to define the operating targets it wishes to use when determining its policy objectives.

*(2) International Monetary Arrangements* Central banks must also administer whatever multilateral agreements their respective governments have concluded to regulate cash flows among countries. This area of responsibility may involve the central bank in maintaining the convertibility of the domestic currency, managing its exchange rates, meeting the country's international payments obligations, and facilitating or restricting capital transfers between the domestic economy and the rest of the world.

*(3) Financial Regulations* Financial institutions and markets are subject to regulatory restrictions by the state's monetary authorities. Some of these regulations are an integral part of monetary policy, especially the ones defining which types of deposits count as money and who is allowed to issue them. Others, relating to the structure of the finance sector, try to keep different institutions apart by specifying their respective assets and liabilities and by other controls. These structure regulations limit potentially destabilizing competition among different institutions and at the same time manipulate credit allocation in favor of specific uses (e.g., thrifts offering mortgages for real estate transactions). Another group of regulations aims to enhance the safety of financial institutions by controlling their propensity for overextension (e.g., minimum capital requirements for banks).

*(4) Lender-of-Last-Resort Mechanisms* These provide failing institutions with emergency assistance and thus prevent financial crises from spreading out of control.

This concept of monetary regime implies that monetary policy tools, international monetary arrangements, financial regulations, and lender-of-last-resort mechanisms are interrelated and hence need to be properly integrated within an institutional framework. Their effectiveness depends on the degree to which they form a coherent entity. Moreover, each component of such a monetary regime is subject to possible adjustments or extensions. In normal times the monetary regime is changed only in a very gradual manner, requiring at most an occasional correction here and there. But there have always been exceptional periods, usually triggered by war or depression, when the entire monetary regime disintegrates and needs to be reorganized.

One such period occurred during the Great Depression of the 1930s, when the collapse of the gold standard and thousands of banks prompted a series of reforms by the Roosevelt administration to create an entirely new monetary regime. The abolition of the gold standard in 1933–34 and the strengthening of the Federal Reserve's monetary policy tools (i.e., discount loans, open-market operations, reserve requirements) under the Bank Act of 1935 completed a gradual transition of our economy toward a state-managed inconvertible paper standard. The Glass–Steagall Act of 1933 gave our banking system a new regulatory framework and introduced the FDIC as lender of last resort to cope more effectively with bank failures. The securities markets and their participants came under increased supervision and had to follow a code of behavior under laws passed in 1933, 1934, and 1940. Finally, the Bretton Woods Conference in 1944 created a new international monetary system, based on a gold-backed dollar, fixed exchange rates, and new international monetary authorities (i.e., International Monetary Fund, World Bank).

Elsewhere (Guttmann, 1989, ch. 11; 1994), I have analyzed in greater detail how this regime of credit-money instituted by Roosevelt in the 1930s and 1940s contributed to the postwar boom of the 1950s and 1960s. Briefly, that postwar monetary regime provided for an *elastic currency* whose issue responded endogenously to aggregate liquidity and credit needs in the economy. Ample credit at low interest rates was available for all major sectors of the economy to finance excess spending on a continuous basis. This provided the institutional underpinnings for the main pillars of the long boom period after World War II—consumer purchases of large-ticket items (i.e., suburban homes, cars), which provided large positive multiplier effects for the rest of the economy; the formation of large corporations using the most modern mass-production technologies; deficit spending by the government in support of income maintenance programs and infrastructure investments; and, finally, orchestrated capital transfers from the United States to the rest of world, which allowed other industrial nations to catch up through export-led growth strategies.

That postwar monetary regime supported economic growth by keeping exchange rates stable and interest rates low. Its government-operated payments system guaranteed the automatic convertibility and smooth circulation of its various constituent forms of paper-money, thus greatly encouraging monetary stability. Most of the credit was channeled through banks acting as intermediaries between ultimate lenders and borrowers, and this dominance of indirect finance gave the central bank relatively effective control over money creation and/or interest rates. The banking system was tightly regulated and, at least in the case of the United States, institutionally separated from the rest of the credit system (i.e., other financial institutions, securities markets). Financial crises were contained with relative ease due to effective lender-of-last-resort mechanisms supplying emergency funds to troubled banks. On an international level, the postwar regime of credit-money provided for a stable world-money standard and ample global liquidity supplies conducive to rapid industrialization across the globe.

As successful as this monetary regime was during its first twenty-five years in promoting rapid worldwide expansion, it did not prove long-lived. Stagflation conditions during the 1970s eventually destroyed or undermined each of its key components. First came the collapse of Bretton Woods in August 1971 which ushered in an era of flexible exchange rates (see chapter 3) and moved us from a dollar-dominated international monetary system to a less stable multicurrency system based on three competing key currencies (dollar, yen, mark). Then came the Fed's reversal of its low-interest policy in October 1979, followed by broader price deregulation of banks and other depository institutions.[2] Many of the structure regulations, which have kept commercial banks apart from each other and separated from the rest of the financial-services industry, have become largely obsolete in the new era of global computer and communication networks. Financial crises intensified throughout the 1980s and early 1990s and could be managed only by substantial extensions of existing lender-of-last-resort mechanisms. But such bail-out extensions produced their own negative side effects, in particular the encouragement of excessive risk taking by banks in the knowledge that they would be rescued by the government if risky investments turned out a failure (the so-called moral hazard problem).

## Deregulation, securitization, and globalization

Ever since the early 1980s we have moved at an accelerated pace toward a new monetary regime. Its principal characteristics—deregulation of banking, securitization of credit, globalization of financial markets and institutions—are analyzed in this concluding chapter by Henry Kaufman, one of the leading Wall Street economists of our time. His speech to Fed officials reprinted here argues that these three features of the emerging monetary regime, especially when combined in their mutually interacting dynamic, have already profoundly altered how our economy operates in the following ways:

*(1) Deregulation* Ever since the introduction of the Euromarket, a globally organized private banking network dealing in currencies outside their respective countries of issue, the world's leading banks have been able to operate a credit system in truly stateless currencies beyond the reach of any national central bank. This parallel banking system forced the deregulation of exchange rates in the early 1970s and of interest rates in the early 1980s. Freed of government regulation and instead determined by market forces, these two prices of money have become much more volatile. This volatility has contributed to the slow-growth pattern of our economy while at the same time boosting financial transactions, especially those of a primarily speculative nature. The viability of the emerging monetary regime depends not least on finding effective ways to stabilize exchange and interest rates.

Financial deregulation has more recently extended to the form(s) of money itself. Following the deregulation of interest rates in the early 1980s, banks have developed a whole new generation of private bank money in the form of variable-rate deposits with (usually limited) check-writing privileges, such as NOW accounts, money-market deposit accounts, or money-market fund shares. Since these new money instruments typically combine transaction and investment purposes, it is very difficult to predict how they will behave in terms of interest elasticity or turnover time. Central banks have therefore had to give up trying to target monetary aggregates and develop alternative monetary policy strategies that assure price stability. The monetary authorities have tried to incorporate the anti-inflationary bias of Monetarism by keeping inflation-adjusted interest rates well above zero.

The conduct of monetary policy is further complicated by yet another aspect of money's deregulation, the gradual privatization of the payments system. Once directly and completely controlled by the Fed as a monopoly supplier, payment services have become increasingly run by private bank consortia who are competing with the central bank for business.[3] The precise mix between private and public elements of the payments system will be decided not least by market forces. But the Fed is both competitor and regulator of the private payments services whose commitments it has to back up in any emergency situation. This dual role gives the central bank a good deal of influence over the future shape of the payments system. The issue of the proper private-public mix regarding the payments system will come to a head with the introduction of an entirely new form of money, *"cybercash"* transactions on the Internet. Central bank control over such *electronic money* depends on how these computerized payment flows are routed through the banking system and whether their settlement procedures involve reserve transfers between banks.

The third dimension of deregulation, besides money's prices and the payments system, involves the operations of banks. Many of the prevailing regulations, which have limited the product variety, geographic diversification, and ownership of banks, have become obsolete. Technology makes many of these restrictions easy to circumvent. To the extent that they are still effective, these structure regulations have in recent decades more often than not tended to weaken banks by making them less diversified and less capitalized than they need to be. Assuming that electronic banking technology will eventually provide major economies of scale and scope, we can expect a gradual tendency towards *universal banks* engaging in a large variety of products and financing mechanisms.[4] Smaller banks can survive against these giants by specializing in a lucrative market niche or dominating regional markets.

*(2) Securitization* The precise shape of the future banking industry will greatly depend on one of the most significant trends transforming our credit system, the growing importance of securities at the expense of loans. It is obvious that more and more borrowers, in particular corporations and governments, have come to prefer the liquidity and convenience of financial markets. While the postwar regime of credit-money centered on loans as the primary form of credit and indirect (intermediation) finance as the principal credit relation, the new regime will be dominated in contrast by securities and direct finance. This qualitative change erodes

the market share of banks and other depository institutions specializing in deposit-taking and loan-making while boosting institutions organizing the securities markets (e.g., investment banks, mutual funds).

The banks have responded to this long-term threat by joining the trend. Besides increasing their own securities holdings, they have actively engaged in the repackaging of loans into securities (e.g., mortgage-backed securities) and in financial derivatives tied to securities portfolios for hedging or speculation purposes. They have also set up their own mutual funds and are now lobbying for regulatory permission to expand their investment banking operations. These responses by commercial banks will only accelerate the securitization of our credit-system.

*(3) Globalization* The third crucial feature of our emerging monetary regime is its global nature. Money and banking have become essentially transnational institutions of our economy that operate outside and beyond the reach of national monetary authorities. The very form of contemporary money, combining currencies circulating outside their respective countries of issue in the Euromarket and electronic fund transfers, physically transcends national borders. The removal of capital and exchange controls during the last decade has greatly facilitated cross-border flows of funds. As our largest corporations evolve into globally organized production networks, they tap the capital markets of many countries at the same time. In this they are helped by bankers who try to provide their best corporate clients with cash-management and investment-advice services across the globe. Institutional investors, in particular mutual funds, organize themselves increasingly as global investment portfolios. Finally, computer technology has made it easier for national financial markets, in particular the stock market, to get connected through cross-listings and settlement procedures for trading in each other's markets. When taken together, these trends illustrate clearly the extent to which the credit system is rapidly becoming globally integrated.

Kaufman concludes below that these three trends—deregulation, securitization, and globalization—do not necessarily make for a stable monetary regime. On the contrary, he views these trends as potential sources of heightened financial instability and as possible barriers to vigorous economic growth. The question is how to assure a more effective balance between market-driven and government-regulated elements determining the organization of financial markets and institutions. Only then, with such an effective balance between the private-commodity and public-good aspects of money, will we have a viable new monetary regime.

## Notes

1. In the postwar system of credit-money, most of the money has taken the form of checking deposits which commercial banks and other depository institutions create when they lend out their reserves. This private bank money is backed by the central bank through its automatic convertibility with government-issued currency, deposit insurance, and a payment system for the transfer of funds. This state management of money and banking supposedly guarantees money in its quality as a *public good,* whose accessibility and use by everyone provides our society with very large social benefits that cannot be captured by the profit-dominated market mechanism alone.

2. Other depository institutions, besides commercial banks, are mutual saving banks, savings and loans institutions, and credit unions.

3. These private payments services (e.g., electronic funds transfers routed through automated clearinghouses, integrated transfer networks between banks to link their automated-teller machines) have been spurred by computer technology and given added impetus by deregulation. In the DIDMCA of 1980 Congress decided to encourage private competition to the Fed's payments services. The largest private payments system, the so-called Clearinghouse Interbank Payments System (CHIPS), came into existence much earlier with the emergence of the Euromarket.

4. This tendency toward universal banking is most clearly expressed in the European Commission's Second Banking Directive of 1989 which, as part of the European Community's "single market" initiative, adopted precisely such a model for Europe's banking institutions of the next century.

HENRY KAUFMAN

# Structural Changes in the Financial Markets: Economic and Policy Significance

Over the recent weeks, we have gotten an eye-opening, though relatively brief, preview of how profound changes in the structure of world financial markets have magnified the potential for extreme market volatility that can reverberate across the global financial system. Today, I want to speak to you about those structural changes, the new financial risks they will almost certainly spawn, and how these serious financial risks should be contained. For it is undeniable that we have moved into a more hazardous environment in which new financial excesses are practically unavoidable. The reason is that certain defects are already deeply imbedded in the genes of our financial condition. These defects will contribute to progressively greater fluctuations in the prices of stocks, bonds, and currencies, to bouts of turbulence in the credit markets, and possibly to a plunge in financial asset values that will dwarf what we have experienced so far this year.

Indeed, from a longer perspective, the latest swings in bond and stock prices are likely to be merely a prologue to much greater volatility in the years ahead. This potential for financial trauma is a by-product of radical changes in the structure of financial institutions and markets that over time are leaving the system without an adequate institutional buffer and, therefore, more susceptible to sharp oscillations in the flows of investment and credit.

While new financial excesses cannot be totally prevented, proper action can mitigate their adverse consequences to some extent. To accomplish that, however, we must be willing to acknowledge the risks that lie ahead, to take them into account in the formulation of monetary policy, and to make some fundamental changes in the structure of official oversight and regulation of financial institutions and markets.

HENRY KAUFMAN is president of Henry Kaufman & Company, Inc. Reprinted from Federal Reserve Bank of Kansas City, *Economic Review,* 2nd Quarter 1994. This speech was delivered to the Board of Directors of the Federal Reserve Bank of Kansas City on March 9, 1994, and to the CS First Boston Global Banking Conference, New York City, on April 25, 1994. The views expressed in this speech are those of the author and do not necessarily reflect the views of the Federal Reserve Bank of Kansas City or the Federal Reserve System.

I suspect that to many it seems incongruous that market volatility has burst forth in a dramatic way at the very time when the financial positions of American households, corporations, and financial institutions themselves were on the mend. Financial rehabilitation in the United States has, in fact, proceeded at a very good pace. Debt burdens have been reduced sharply and capital positions have increased significantly for financial institutions and businesses.

But there is a dark side to financial rehabilitation. A sense of financial well-being—and the capacity of aspiring demanders of credit to tap into the resources of willing lenders and investors—is a necessary condition for incubating new financial excesses. Thus, it would be wrong to become complacent about what might follow as the economic expansion matures. Sooner or later, credit demands of businesses and households will begin to pick up momentum, and stronger financial institutions will be in a position to readily meet those demands. Monetary policy will switch, first, from accommodating to neutral as it has already started to do in the last few months and, eventually, toward overt restraint. Somewhere in this sequence of events, the structural changes in the financial markets will have a far more profound impact on securities values than the gyrations that occurred in recent months.

## Fundamental changes in financial institutions and markets

I particularly want to call attention to three structural changes that keep the financial system vulnerable to excess.

First, in the United States, traditional lending and investing institutions are playing a diminishing role in determining the composition of investment and the response to market developments, whereas the household sector, mainly through the vehicle of the mutual funds, is playing an enormously expanded and still unfolding role.

Second, the global financial markets are undergoing what I would call the "Americanization of finance." This encompasses (1) increasing deregulation of markets and institutions, (2) rapidly increasing securitization, (3) much greater use of new financial instruments and trading techniques, especially incorporating financial derivatives, and (4) the growing presence in the markets of an expanding group of "high-octane" portfolio managers who are free to roam throughout the financial sphere, in and out of currencies, equities, bonds, commodities, and related derivative instruments with primarily a very near-term focus and no particular loyalty to any national marketplace.

Third, both in the United States and in most of the major industrial countries, a tremendous infrastructure has been put into place to promote credit creation. Most of the newcomers operate outside the conventional banking system and therefore largely outside the purview of central banks. But conventional depository institutions, now with rebuilt capital positions, are also in a position to lend. Thus, the potential for rapid increases in credit is high. Add these three structural changes together and we have a lush environment for cultivating financial excesses.

Let me try to put some dimensions on each of these three elements.

## Mutual funds and diminished role of traditional institutional investors

For nearly three decades—that is, from the early 1960s until the beginning of the 1990s—the archetypal institutional investor was the pension fund of a major multinational corporation or of a state and local government entity. Supplanting insurance companies, which had been the preeminent institutional investor in prior decades, these funds grew over this period by almost $2 trillion, or about two-thirds of the total increase in institutional net financial assets. But by the onset of this decade, that electrifying growth had already begun to taper off, mainly as a by-product of corporate restructuring. As the corporate giants, one by one, moved to shed business lines and employees, and as defined contribution plans began to supersede the defined benefit plans of yesteryear, pension fund growth started to flatten.

By comparison, almost overnight, mutual funds boomed. One of the most interesting aspects of the mutual fund phenomenon is how long the vehicle existed before truly significant amounts of money were invested in them. As recently as the end of 1984, the combined total of equity and bond mutual funds in the United States amounted to only a little over $100 billion, less than 2 percent of total financial net worth of households. Since then, mutual funds have mushroomed and now substitute for conventional bank deposits. Of that total, $1 trillion is owned by households, representing almost 10 percent of household financial net worth.

Perhaps even more significant are the following facts: Since the stock market crash of October 1987, equity mutual funds have swelled from about $180 billion to some $700 billion through a combination of fresh inflows of funds and capital gains. What this means is that the average investor in equity mutual funds has never experienced a prolonged bear market. Neither has the average investor in fixed-income mutual funds. From the onset of the secular bull market in bonds which began in 1982, the assets of bond mutual funds increased by a factor of 35 times, from a minuscule $20 billion to over $700 billion. Up until last fall, only a minority of individuals had much personal memory as investors of what happens to bond prices—and consequently mutual fund net asset values—when interest rates start a protracted cyclical rise.

The fact is that we do not know how the ordinary investor in mutual funds will react when equity prices and bond prices continue to display spasms of volatility, instead of the highly agreeable upside volatility to which most had grown accustomed. Probably the sternest test will come as the economic expansion matures, credit demands start to lift, and short-term interest rates move persistently higher. At some point, after repeated bouts of volatility in the stock and bond markets, interest rates on CDs or other money market instruments, which will have moved higher, will no longer be looked at contemptuously by many investors, new inflows into mutual funds will dry up, and many individuals may become net sellers. The managers of mutual funds have no really viable alternative but to pass through these sales into the market. They cannot take a view apart from their investors; they cannot leverage mutual fund portfolios to take advantage of what they might think will be a temporary downward price correction. They will have to sell regardless of the impact on prices and regardless of whether other buyers of equities and bonds step forward quickly to buy.

I understand that there are valid differences of opinion on how the individual investor will behave under such circumstances. Some recall the transitory nature of the October 1987 stock market break and say that individuals generally will be slow to act, essentially riding out sharp contractions in equity and bond prices and thereby providing a buffer against more proactive traders. Perhaps. But that assumption of sluggishness on the part of the ordinary citizen proved to be conspicuously wrong in the case of the mortgage market. Homeowners were not at all sluggish in taking advantage of lower interest rates to refinance existing mortgages. On the contrary, they acted with an alacrity that utterly confounded the vast statistical models run by market professionals. As prepayments surged, holders of mortgage securities who were operating under the flawed assumption of household inertia were badly burnt.

Drawing an analogy from that episode, I conclude that it is a potentially grievous error to assume that individual investors will always be slow to react to sudden, highly visible setbacks in stock prices, bond prices, or both— certainly not in a world when all an investor has to do in order to switch from an equity or bond fund into a money market fund is to go to the telephone and push a sequence of buttons. The technology is in place for a cascade of selling by investors in mutual funds.

Consequently, I am even more seriously concerned now than a year or two ago when I began calling attention to this lurking problem—namely, that excesses originating in the mutual funds area may be the source of an economic shock should an asset price bubble suddenly burst. An abrupt, substantial drop in financial net worth can easily have a powerful impact on consumption decisions, leading to a postponement or even abandonment of spending on homes, cars, and other big-ticket items. Such a wealth effect may swamp other, more conventional determinants of household expenditure. In extreme cases, it could be large enough to precipitate an economic contraction. In principle, the central bank could offset this contractionary impact by easing monetary policy, but in practice that might be a hard thing for the Federal Reserve to do, since the shift out of equity and bond mutual funds and into money funds and bank deposits will naturally swell the monetary aggregates. Because this whole chain of events is most likely to occur at a time when the central bank is already engaged in a process of tightening money and credit conditions, it is not impossible to suppose that there will be at least some delay in making the decision to engineer such an abrupt about-face in policy.

It seems to me that not enough thought has gone into the question of how mutual funds should be regulated and supervised. This is not meant to be critical of the Securities and Exchange Commission (SEC), which is the official institution charged with overseeing the U.S. mutual fund industry. But the time has come when we have to be concerned not only with the issues of fraud and abuse, which is the conventional focus of the SEC, and consider the systemic implications of the explosion of mutual funds. We need to evaluate two things: First, the consequences for the American economy and for the financial markets of a potential sudden sell-off of mutual fund shares and, second, how to limit the impact of such shocks by putting in place a waiting period for fund sales in order to drive home to investors that equity and bond funds are not to be considered close substitutes for money funds and bank CDs. In a sense, this would be the functional equivalent of the circuit breakers installed by the stock exchanges and the futures exchanges, which were designed to introduce some delay when the market is stunned by a surge of volatility. The question of how to shield the system from a collapse of confidence in mutual funds is one more reason why comprehensive reform of financial regulation is badly needed, going well beyond the narrow industry focus of proposals now on the table.

## Americanization of global finance

The second area of profound structural change in finance is what I have earlier referred to as the "Americanization" of global finance. This involves progressive deregulation of financial markets. It means a greater access of borrowers to different types of credit products, therefore greatly expanding credit availability to both businesses and households. In addition, Americanization entails a significant extension of securitization to many other capital markets in the world. In the all-important markets for government securities it entails a gradual adoption of many of the practices that first developed in the American government securities markets, such as repurchase agreements, scheduled auctions, and increased participation of foreign investors. Greater securitization means that over a period of time, more and more financial assets will be marked to market, and fewer assets will be sheltered from potentially volatile price changes, as is the case when loans are held on the balance sheets of traditional lenders. Americanization also involves the broadening of professional portfolio management, usually with a very short-term investment horizon and the widespread use of performance measurements which more deeply ingrain this behavior.

In practical terms, the implications of Americanization are far-reaching. To begin with, virtually all major industrial countries are now living within the confines of a more or less deregulated financial system, wherein financial entrepreneurs are the principal players reshaping this system. Granted, a handful of depository institutions, particularly in Japan, but also in the United States and even in Western Europe, are operating under greater official scrutiny because the memories of recent excesses are still vivid. But a whole host of other banks, together with unregulated or lightly regulated financial institutions, are engaged in pushing their own risk taking in new directions, and sometimes to unaccustomed limits. The common denominator is to try to jump into any market niche where returns appear to be greater than average, regardless of the long-term compatibility of that line of business to the underlying experience and strengths of the firm. As a result, we can expect to see some significant missteps by at least a few of the more hard-driving competitors.

Moreover, high-octane portfolio managers are expanding in number and in the magnitude of funds they deploy. The ultimate evolution of the risk-taking financial entrepreneur is the portfolio manager who can go long or short in any market, in any currency, and on a leveraged or an unleveraged basis—and who often can do this in a tax-advantaged offshore vehicle, with minimal, if any, official supervision. When full leverage is employed by this new breed of managers, I suspect that they can command portfolios totaling upwards of $500 billion, although no official statistics are kept by any national or international agency—which itself is a matter for concern.

Why is this class of investor a potential incubator of the next round of financial excess? After all, if they make a misjudgment on the market, their contributing investors will merely lose money, and since those investors are by definition highly sophisticated, as well as wealthy, they can afford the hit. The reason has to do with human behavior. When the managers of large high-octane portfolios go into the market to build sizable risk positions, others inevitably follow, since it is practically impossible to disguise these substantial positions completely. The hangers-on have benefited handsomely when the leaders have been right. But experience teaches that no one is clairvoyant, however astute technically or financially. The leaders also get it wrong from time to time, and while their investors might tolerate the resulting losses, others may not be so fortunate.

Finally, the growing use of financial derivatives is itself another manifestation of Americanization. What are some of the concerns that this development poses? I would cite the following:

(1) The current high profitability in financial derivatives will inevitably pull in a greater number of market participants. This will eventually generate excess capacity, depressing profit margins and inducing many to move to the marginal edge of risk taking where competition is least and fees are most lucrative.

(2) Another set of concerns in financial derivatives involves the matter of exposure to credit risks. No one knows whether adequate credit evaluations are possible, especially when they relate to exposures resulting from transactions with new types of organizations, such as leveraged funds for which conventional credit ratings are inapplicable, or with subsidiaries of nonfinancial corporations which may have a complex and not entirely unambiguous relationship with the parent. This type of problem was apparent in the recent difficulties encountered by Germany's Metallgesellschaft. I, along with others, have concerns about an erosion of credit standards as competition in the marketplace increases.

(3) As for the potential for market disruption, I question whether market risks in financial derivatives can always be managed and whether any open position can always be covered before it goes hopelessly wrong. Experience has shown that whenever there is even the slightest chance of trading halts or of the abandonment of market-making by leading dealers, normal market access shrinks. As a result, new hedges cannot be put on when essentially everybody in the market is trying to do the same thing at the same time. Thus, volatility can balloon by orders of magnitudes, defeating even the best-planned hedging strategy.

(4) A related problem for hedging risks is the danger of basing hedging strategies on statistical models relying on past behavioral patterns. The structural changes alone in financial markets are bound to cause significant deviations from past relationships. There is no way these differences can be adequately incorporated in risk modeling.

(5) A final source of concern about these markets is simply this: Financial derivatives permit greater leverage in the system, allowing marginal borrowers to stay in the market longer than would otherwise be possible.

While I raise this concern in the context of financial derivatives, my worry is actually a broader one. As I mentioned in my introductory remarks, financial rehabilitation, while essential for creating the conditions for a strong revival of business activity, has a dark side. It is that the infrastructure for vigorous credit expansion has not only been rebuilt but has been enlarged in the process. Let me turn now to the implications of this development.

## Infrastructure for credit creation

I suppose that the late Sidney Homer and I, back in the 1960s, were the first to coin the term "credit crunch" to describe an abrupt discontinuity in the flow of credit that may set severe contractionary economic forces in motion. In fact, both before and since, the history of business and financial cycles has been punctuated by sharp discontinuities in the channels of credit creation. Those disruptions have had varying causes—ranging from quantitative rationing in decades past engendered by such devices as Regulation Q ceilings, to the credit quality rationing that characterized the financial crunch of the latest cyclical episode. But regardless of origin, these discontinuities had similar effects: they set in motion a sequence of events that eventually was responsible for terminating a period of economic expansion by choking off credit availability to important segments of the economy.

Today, when memories of the most recent financial crunch are still fresh in our minds, it may come as a surprise to hear me warn of the unprecedented infrastructure for *credit creation* that is now in place in the United States and soon will be in other major financial centers. Commercial banks and many thrift institutions have shifted from a position of capital insufficiency to capital surfeit. They show a renewed appetite for lending and are in a position either to issue CDs or to liquefy securities holdings to finance new lending. But the nonbank financial institutions and open credit markets, which have successfully wrested considerable market share in lending to businesses and households away from the depository institutions, are not about to disappear. Instead, they are in a position to move even more aggressively to make use of their considerable capacity to lend.

Moreover, the infrastructure in place to support extensive securitization is available for branching out into new markets. Securitization of mortgages, credit card receivables, and auto loans is just the beginning of the process, not the end of it. Domestically, home equity loans will be securitized to an increasing degree. What will probably follow will be widespread securitization of ordinary commercial loans, with or without the establishment of government-sponsored entities to lubricate the process.

Internationally, securitization is advancing quickly, with discordant results. For example, we have experienced the rather extensive securitization of Less Developed Country (LDC) debt, which has effectively transferred the great bulk of the previously outstanding bank loans by repackaging them either as conventional bonds or as debt obligations that trade like bonds. This has been the product not only of the elaborate debt restructuring exercises supported by the United States and other industrial country governments, the International Monetary Fund (IMF), and the banks, but it also reflects the substantial new issuance of securities on behalf of LDC borrowers. An estimated $75 billion of such new securitized assets have been absorbed by the public markets in the past five years, with a growing portion of the investment flows coming from the mutual funds and other commingled funds. This whole process has done a great deal to solve one problem, namely extricating the major commercial banks from their past credit misjudgments, only to introduce new and potentially formidable risks. In recent weeks, the market for the debt of emerging countries has undergone truly extraordinary turbulence, with price fluctuations averaging three to four times those of U.S. Treasuries. Consider how much greater volatility may become if one or more of the large emerging countries run into economic difficulties and cannot service the bonds. Reschedulings will turn out to be even harder to negotiate in a world of securitized obligations than they were in the bleakest days of the LDC debt crisis of the 1980s, since bondholders, with no ancillary business to protect, are unlikely to be as cooperative as bankers—and in retrospect the cooperation of those bankers was not entirely enthusiastic, either.

From a broad economic policy perspective, securitization will have far-reaching consequences. In such an evolving world, the degree of credit restraint in operation at any particular time will not be measurable by standard money supply or even bank credit indicators. Other time-honored rules of thumb, such as the notion that financial intermediaries are in the business of borrowing short and lending long, will be turned on their heads. Finance companies engaged in active securitization may be borrowing long and lending short, while hedging their exposure to interest movements through a series of transactions in financial futures and options. Surges in credit demand therefore may not have the conventional effect of flattening the yield curve; the impulses may be quickly transmitted up and down the yield curve through the actions of the new lending originators. This will indirectly impart greater volatility on intermediate and longer-term bond markets, with corresponding effects on equity markets.

As a consequence, in the emerging financial world of high-octane, high-credit-availability finance, restraint will come more from unprecedented asset price variation and less from squeezes on short-term credit availability or cost. This world will have striking implications for monetary policy, for the financial supervisors and regulators, and for various market participants, including commercial banks. Let me discuss each in turn beginning with the implications for monetary policy.

## Implications for monetary policy

Central bankers throughout the industrial world are struggling with a dilemma. On the one hand, they have achieved an extraordinary independence in the formulation and execution of monetary policy. The Bundesbank, the Federal Reserve, and the Bank of Canada already had a substantial measure of independence. But now the central banks of France, Italy, and even Japan are operating with considerably more independence than ever before. Only the Bank of England is formally subordinate to the U.K. government, but I suspect it is only a matter of time before that will change and a form of independence compatible with British constitutional traditions will be crafted.

On the other hand, there is no longer any reliable analytical guidepost on which to direct monetary policy. The vast structural changes in the financial system that I have described make it impossible for any central bank to anchor policy to any monetary or credit target. There is no alternative but to fall back on judgment. But judgment exercised toward what objective? Significant differences of view now exist on what the basic objective of monetary policy should be, especially among politicians, academics, and financial market participants, although perhaps less so among central bankers themselves.

Let me state my own view up front. I believe that the primary objective of a central bank should be to maintain the financial well-being of society in the broadest sense. That means establishing stable financial conditions by exercising careful oversight over financial markets, institutions, and trading practices, anticipating potential problems, and taking remedial action before they can do widespread damage. Thus, it means pursuing monetary policy actions that will over a period of time provide the foundation for the successful achievement of sustainable economic growth with minimal inflation, and with minimal risk of financial shocks that could disrupt the economy.

Therefore, I do not go along with the line of thinking that maintains that the central bank should have only the most single-minded of objectives: specifically the pursuit of price stability, perhaps defined as a target range for the inflation rate. In my view, the logic of enshrining such a narrow objective—namely, that an environment of low inflation is both a necessary *and* sufficient condition for economic growth and financial market stability—is flawed, and in practice such a price-stability objective will rarely, if ever, be faithfully pursued.

Indeed, I would argue that because it fails to give precedence to maintaining the financial well-being of society, it is a deceptive objective, for the following reasons:

First, low inflation, while obviously desirable in and of itself because it does contribute to a sturdy framework for a nation's economic prosperity, is nonetheless no guarantee against the emergence of financial excesses. History proves this conclusively. The classic case for the United States was the decade of the 1920s, when inflation remained low, but financial excesses developed both in the equity market and in commercial real estate. In recent times, we also have the vivid example of the mid-1980s. Inflation performance was exemplary; the rise in the consumer price index in 1986 was one of the lowest in the entire postwar period. But within the fabric of our financial markets there was developing some of the worst financial excesses of this century, a process that would lead to massive financial failures, huge taxpayer costs, and a largely unforeseen credit crunch that would aggravate the business downturn and constrain the subsequent economic recovery. Arguably, low inflation is a *necessary* condition for financial well-being, but it surely is not a *sufficient* condition for financial well-being. That requires a more complex set of economic and financial circumstances grounded not only by a central bank's monetary actions but also by its role as the institution entrusted with assuring the safety and soundness of the financial system as a whole.

Second, an obsession with achieving low inflation at all costs carries other risks. Long-lasting economic stagnation can bring about a potentially large and highly undesirable redistribution of wealth. Thus, the approach can over a period of time undermine public support for free markets. This may eventually be manifested in a swing toward a narrowly nationalistic posture on international trade and thus can do considerable damage to important principles.

Third, the alternative to a sole central-bank objective of low inflation is not indifference to the rate of inflation. Central banks that have acquiesced in, or abetted, high inflation are practicing a form of financial corruption that eventually destroys national unity and ends up in financial ruin. But for a central bank that has built up a reputation of integrity and devotion to stability, there is a powerful case for looking beyond the inflation situation at any particular time and anticipating how the inflation rate will evolve in reaction to changing economic circumstances. This means that such a central bank will be able to pursue an accommodative monetary policy even in the face of a lingering rate of inflation that is higher than the expected rate that will eventuate over a long time period. This ability to craft a policy on the basis of sound analysis of future trends, rather than moving in lockstep with available data that necessarily record only what has already happened, is a hallmark of sensible, effective monetary control.

As I see it, the proper responsibility of the central bank—assuring the financial well-being of society—requires an intimate involvement in financial supervision and regulation. In fact, I have long believed that it is only the central bank, among the various regulatory agencies that share responsibility in this area, that can represent the perspective of the financial system as a whole. This should be the central organizing principle behind any comprehensive reform of financial regulation and supervision in the United States.

## Toward a comprehensive framework for financial regulation

The danger of a new round of financial excesses presents a clear challenge to the official supervisory and regulatory structure for financial institutions. I have argued over the years for a serious effort to reform in a fundamental way the convoluted system of financial regulation we have stumbled into. I have also supported efforts to forge a better international harmonization of supervisory, regulatory, accounting, and trading standards and practices. In both realms, the domestic and the international, much work is left to be done.

Recently, the U.S. Treasury put forward a proposal for reform of one relatively circumscribed, though no doubt important, part of the regulatory structure—consolidating bank examinations in one agency so as to eliminate a good deal of duplication of effort and expense in the current system. On its face, it is a legitimate goal, but the benefits of reducing duplication need to be weighed against the costs of restricting the Federal Reserve's direct role in financial supervision and regulation. On this issue, once the public relations phase of the bureaucratic tug-of-war has run its course, I would expect a reasonable compromise can be worked out.

The main reason why I am not an enthusiastic supporter of the Treasury proposal is that it is too narrow. It misses most of the key structural changes in domestic and global financial institutions and markets that I described earlier in my talk. What is really needed is a comprehensive overhaul of regulation and supervision. That would involve a number of elements.

One, we need to bring together banking, securities, and insurance regulators to reach agreement on *standards*—accounting standards, disclosure standards, and trading standards, and on minimum capital requirements. This should also include nonbank institutions such as finance companies, which are now effectively unregulated. At the present time, there are large differences from country to country and within countries from one type of financial institution to another. They are out of touch with the realities of how markets now work and how business is being done. Harmonization is essential to ensure fairness in the marketplace and to avoid the lowest common denominator outcome, as institutions practice what is known as "regulatory arbitrage." I might add that the Internal Revenue Service and its counterparts in other countries also ought to be included in the process, so that tax considerations do not unduly influence the location and form of financial activity.

Two, in order to reduce the danger of sharp setbacks in bond and stock prices that would endanger economic growth, I propose that investors in bond and stock mutual funds be required to give sixty to ninety days' withdrawal notice. This condition would be roughly analogous to the long-standing requirement that applies to Certificates of Deposit and time deposits at banks and thrifts. It would reinforce the notion that mutual funds are not cash equivalents and should be approached as a serious investment. It would have the desirable effect of forcing investors to become more aware than they appear to be at the moment of the risks they are exposing themselves to through investment in such funds and will introduce a useful brake on exaggerated reaction to abrupt price movements. Since it is a significant departure from existing procedures, this measure should be phased in gradually beginning with net new investments.

Three, these and the many other issues that inevitably flow from the greater internationalization and complexity of finance cannot be dealt with reasonably and in a timely way without an ongoing institutional capability. I have long believed that the most promising approach would be to establish a new international institution to serve as the focal point for regulatory harmonization. A "Board of Overseers of Major International Institutions and Markets" should be established, consisting of central bank and other governmental agencies. It should also include members drawn from the private sector. It should be empowered to set mutually acceptable minimum capital requirements for all major institutions, to establish uniform trading, reporting, and disclosure standards for open credit markets, and to monitor the performance of institutions and markets under its jurisdiction.

## Outlook for financial markets and institutions

Let me conclude by highlighting seven key implications that arise from the intersection of the structural changes in financial markets and institutions and the cyclical condition of the U.S. and foreign economies.

First, volatility in financial markets is bound to increase significantly in the period ahead. The increased importance of risk "pass through" institutions, notably mutual funds, which merely transmit the investment decisions of their investors and take no risks of their own, and the diminished role of traditional financial institutions that take risks onto their own balance sheets magnify the danger of wide swings in equity and bond prices. This volatility will also be enhanced by the continued rapid growth of securitized assets and the more subdued increases in nonmarketable assets, as the practice of marking to market becomes the norm rather than the exception. Moreover, as we move from a period of secular rise in equity and bond prices to a more unsteady future, the likelihood of episodes of sudden asset price declines will increase. Financial market are better equipped to shift risk from one participant to another, especially through the use of financial derivatives. But that reallocation of risk does not materially lessen the danger of a period of disorderly trading in the event of an unforeseen shock. Those financial institutions that have been unduly complacent about their capacity to insulate themselves by supposing that they can always go into the market to hedge risks are the most vulnerable to an adverse surprise.

Second, in the new financial environment, the Federal Reserve may find it impossible to flatten the short-to-long yield curve, let alone invert it. The reason is that conventional rules of thumb about the impact of monetary policy actions on the financial markets no longer apply in a financial world dominated by mutual funds and other risk "pass through" institutions. Also of importance for monetary policy, the decline in segmented financial markets, wherein financial institutions used to be able to count on making moderate profits without straining to deal with fierce competition, combined with the move toward a mark to market requirement, will make it far more difficult for affected institutions to take the longer view that might otherwise justify holding onto long positions in stocks or bonds through a financial storm. Consequently, at the next cyclical peak in interest rates, short-term rates—such as on three-month Treasury bills—may reach close to 7 percent while the yield on long U.S. Governments may trade somewhere in the 9 percent to 10 percent range.

Third, for well-managed commercial banks involved in traditional lending and investing with floating rates of return on assets and variable rate liabilities, the persistence of a positively sloped yield curve will continue to be highly beneficial. They will also benefit from a further consolidation in banking, improving their capacity to maintain a profitable pricing structure.

Fourth, the greatest threat to the stability of the system will probably come through more aggressive and more lightly regulated participants in the marketplace or through banks that seek to exploit the new vogues.

Fifth, central banks will be compelled to move away from a strategy of gradualism and give greater weight to actual and prospective conditions in financial markets in conducting monetary policy. Gradualism gives the appearance of prudence and caution, but actually imparts considerable risks onto the economy and the financial markets. In a period of deteriorating economic conditions, when excess productive capacity emerges and the private sector faces financial difficulties, gradualism prolongs distress and inhibits economic and financial rehabilitation. The central bank must be willing to act before the inflation rate has had a chance to respond to the emergence of slack and the weakening of demand pressures in the economy. By contrast, in a period of improving economic conditions and under a changed financial system with powerful entrepreneurial participants that can breed new financial excesses, gradualism in moving toward a less accommodative monetary policy—and eventually to a policy of restraint—carries the risk of encouraging financial bubbles that will force economic setbacks. What is needed is a more flexible monetary policy that can be quickly adapted to changed circumstances, even if that means reversing course on a few occasions when false signals intrude. Giving greater weight to conditions in financial markets is a necessary ingredient of such a flexible approach, since changes in asset prices have a powerful effect on the net worth of the private sector, influencing consumption and investment decisions, and borrowing intentions.

Sixth, before the end of this decade, the financial markets of many emerging countries, which have flourished in recent years, will be hit with substantial turbulence, far beyond the gyrations that occurred in the last few months. This is because renewed economic growth in the industrial world a few years from now will generate enlarged credit demands and will reduce liquidity in the industrial countries, limiting the availability of funds for developing countries. Moreover, securitized markets and the interwoven linkages of international markets will expedite the flight of capital whenever prospects appear to deteriorate.

Finally, I am more convinced than ever that we will have a thoroughgoing overhaul of financial markets and institutions, both nationally and internationally. The question is "When?" Will such a new framework come about in an orderly manner, after an intensive and relatively expeditious discussion of alternatives? Or will it come about after a major financial crisis, in an attempt to repair the damage? No one, least of all the American administration, wants a new financial crisis, but, more important, the American economy cannot afford one. That is why I conclude that the answer to the question "When?" is right now, when there is still containable volatility in financial markets—a condition that cannot be taken for granted a few years hence, if nothing is done to improve the structure and capabilities of our official supervisory and regulatory institutions.

# Bibliography

Andrews, M. 1984. "Recent Trends in the U.S. Foreign Exchange Market." Federal Reserve Bank of New York, *Quarterly Review,* 9 (2), 39–47.

Avery, R., T. Belton, and M. Goldberg. 1988. "Market Discipline in Regulating Bank Risk: New Evidence from the Capital Markets." *Journal of Money, Credit and Banking,* 20 (3), 597–610.

Backus, R. 1984. "Empirical Models of the Exchange Rate: Separating the Wheat from the Chaff." *Canadian Journal of Economics,* 17 (4), 824–40.

Baer, H. 1985. "Private Prices, Public Insurance: The Pricing of Federal Deposit Insurance." Federal Reserve Bank of Chicago, *Economic Perspectives.* September/October, 41–57.

Bank of England. 1986. "The Market in Foreign Exchange in London," *Quarterly Review.* September, 379–82.

Barth, J., and M. Bradley. 1989. "Thrift Deregulation and Deposit Insurance." *Journal of Financial Services Research.* 2 (September), 231–59.

Benston, G., D. Brumbaugh, J. Guttentag, R. Herring, G. Kaufman, R. Litan, and K. Scott. 1989. *Blueprint for Restructuring America's Financial Institutions.* Washington, DC: The Brookings Institution.

Benston, G., R. Eisenbeis, P. Horvitz, E. Kane, and G. Kaufman. 1986. *Perspectives on Safe and Sound Banking: Past, Present, and Future.* Cambridge, MA: MIT Press.

Benston, G., and G. Kaufman. 1986. "Risk and Failures in Banking: Overview, History and Evaluation." In *Deregulating Financial Services: Public Policy in Flux,* ed. G. Kaufman and R. Kormendi. Cambridge, MA: Ballinger.

———. 1988. "Risk and Solvency Regulation of Depository Institutions: Past Policies and Current Options." *Monograph Series in Finance and Economics.* New York: New York University.

Berger, A., K. Kuester, and J. O'Brien. 1989. "Some Red Flags Concerning Market Value Accounting." In Federal Reserve Bank of Chicago, *Proceedings from a Conference on Bank Structure and Competition.* May, 515–46.

Buser, S., A. Chen, and E. Kane. 1981. "Federal Deposit Insurance, Regulatory Policy, and Optimal Bank Capital." *Journal of Finance,* 38 (1), 51–60.

Caliguire, D., and J. Thomson. 1987. "FDIC Policies for Dealing with Failed and Troubled Institutions." Federal Reserve Bank of Cleveland, *Economic Commentary,* October.

Campbell, C., and H. Minsky. 1987. "How to Get Off The Back of a Tiger, or, Do Initial Conditions Constrain Deposit Insurance Reform?" In Federal Reserve Bank of Chicago, *Proceedings from a Conference on Bank Structure and Competition,* May, 252–71.

Canto, V., D. Joines, and A. Laffer. 1983. *Foundations of Supply-Side Economics: Theory and Evidence.* New York: Academic Press.

Cates, D. 1989. "Market Discipline: The Key to Deposit Insurance Reform." Paper presented before the American Bankers Association's Deposit Insurance Task Force, Washington, DC, July 27, 1989.

Corrigan, G. 1987. "Financial Market Structure: A Longer View." Federal Reserve Bank of New York, *Annual Report,* January.

Diamond, D., and P. Dybwig. 1983. "Banking Runs, Deposit Insurance, and Liquidity." *Journal of Political Economy,* 91 (2), 401–19.

Dornbusch, R. 1976. "Expectations and Exchange Rate Dynamics." *Journal of Political Economy,* 84 (6), 1161–76.

Downs, A. 1957. *Economic Theory of Democracy.* New York: Harper and Row.

Ely, B. 1985. "Yes—Private Sector Depositor Protection is a Viable Alternative to Federal Deposit Insurance," In Federal Reserve Bank of Chicago, *Proceedings from a Conference on Bank Structure and Competition,* May, 335–53.

———. 1989. "Privatizing Depositor Protection: More Feasible than Ever." Ely and Company, Washington, DC, May 2.

Federal Reserve Bank of Cleveland. 1988. "Banking Deregulation: Examining the Myths." *Annual Report.*

Federal Reserve Bank of Minneapolis. 1988. "A Case for Reforming Federal Deposit Insurance." *Annual Report.*

Frenkel, J. 1976. "A Monetary Approach to the Exchange Rate: Doctrinal Aspects and Empirical Evidence." *Scandinavian Journal of Economics*, 78 (2), 200–24.

Friedman, M. 1953. "The Case for Flexible Exchange Rates." In Friedman, M., *Essays in Positive Economics.* Chicago: University of Chicago Press.

———. 1967. "First Lecture." In *The Balance of Payments: Free versus Flexible Exchange Rates*, ed. M. Friedman and R. Roosa. Washington, DC: American Enterprise Institute, 1–24.

———. 1968. "The Role of Monetary Policy." *American Economic Review*, 58 (1), 1–17.

———. 1985. "The Case for Overhauling the Federal Reserve." *Challenge*, July–August, 4–12.

Friedman, M., and A. Schwartz. 1963. *A Monetary History of the United States, 1867–1960.* Princeton, NJ: Princeton University Press.

Giddy, I. 1979. "Measuring the World's Foreign Exchange Markets." *Columbia Journal of World Business*, 14 (4), 36–48.

Gorton, G., and D. Mullineaux. 1987. "Joint Production of Confidence: Endogenous Regulation and the Nineteenth Century Commercial-Bank Clearinghouses." *Journal of Money, Credit, and Banking*, 19 (3), 457–68.

Gorton, G., and A. Santomero. 1990. "Market Discipline and Bank Subordinated Debt." *Journal of Money, Credit, and Banking*, 22 (1), 117–28.

Guttentag, J., and R. Herring. 1986. "Disaster Myopia in International Banking." *Essays in International Finance.* No. 164, Princeton, NJ: Princeton University.

———. 1988. "Prudential Supervision to Manage Systemic Vulnerability," *Proceedings from a Conference on Bank Structure and Competition.* Federal Reserve Bank of Chicago, May, 602–33.

Guttmann, R. 1984. "Stagflation and Credit-Money in the USA." *British Review of Economic Issues*, 6 (15), 79–119.

———. 1989. "The Socio-Economic Foundations of Financial Accounting." *British Review of Economic Issues*, 11 (24), 75–102.

———. 1989b. *Reforming Money and Finance: Institutions and Markets in Flux.* Armonk, NY: M.E. Sharpe.

———. 1990. "The Regime of Credit-Money and Its Current Transition." *Economies et Sociétés*, 24 (6), 81–105.

———. 1994. *How Credit-Money Shapes the Economy: The United States in a Global System.* Armonk, NY: M.E. Sharpe.

Hoskins, L. 1989. "Reforming the Banking and Thrift Industries: Assessing Regulation and Risk." 1989 Frank M. Engle Lecture in Economic Security, presented to the American College, Bryn Mawr, PA, May 22.

Jensen, M., and W. Meckling. 1976. "Theory of the Firm: Managerial Behavior, Agency Costs and Ownership Structure." *Journal of Financial Economics*, 3 (2), 305–60.

Jensen, M., and C. Smith. 1985. "Stockholder, Manager, and Creditor Interests: Applications of Agency Theory." In *Recent Advances in Corporate Finance*, ed. E. Altman and M. Subrahmanyam. Homewood, IL: Richard Irwin.

Johnson, H. 1962. "Monetary Theory and Policy." *American Economic Review*, 52 (2), 335–84.

———. 1972. "The Monetary Approach to Balance-of-Payments Theory." In *Further Essays in Monetary Economics*, ed. H. Johnson. London: Allen & Unwin, 229–49.

Jordan, J. 1969. "Elements of Money Stock Determination." Federal Reserve Bank of St. Louis, *Review*, October, 10–19.

Kane, E. 1977. "Good Intentions and Unintended Evil: The Case Against Selective Credit Allocation." *Journal of Money, Credit, and Banking*, 9 (1), 55–69.

———. 1983. "A Six-Point Program for Deposit-Insurance Reform." *Housing Finance Review*, July, 269–78.

———. 1985. *The Gathering Crisis in Federal Deposit Insurance.* Cambridge, MA: MIT Press.

———. 1986. "Confronting Incentive Problems in U.S. Deposit Insurance: The Range of Alternative Solutions." In *Deregulating Financial Services: Public Policy in Flux*, ed. G. Kaufman and R. Kormendi. Cambridge, MA: Ballinger, 97–120.

———. 1987. "No Room for Weak Links in the Chain of Deposit Insurance Reform." *Journal of Financial Services Research*, 1 (1), 77–111.

———. 1988a. "Adapting Financial Services Regulation to a Changing Economic Environment." In *Advances in the Study of Entrepreneurship, Innovation and Economic Growth*, vol. 2, JAI Press, 61–94.

———. 1988b. "How Market Forces Influence the Structure of Financial Regulation." In *Restructuring Banking and Financial Services*, ed. W. Haraf and R. Kushmeider. Washington, DC: American Enterprise Institute, 343–82.

———. 1989a. "How Incentive-Incompatible Deposit-Insurance Funds Fail." National Bureau of Economic Research Working Paper No. 2836, February.

———. 1989b. *The S&L Insurance Mess: How Did It Happen?* Washington, DC: Urban Institute Press.

———. 1989c. "Defective Regulatory Incentives and the Bush Initiative." *Independent Banker*, November, 30–35.

———. 1989d. "Changing Incentives Facing Financial-Services Regulators." *Journal of Financial Services Research*, 2 (3), 265–74.

———. 1989e. "The High Cost of Incompletely Funding the FSLIC Shortage of Explicit Capital." *Journal of Economic Perspectives*, 3 (1), 31–47.

Kaufman, G. 1988. "The Truth About Bank Runs." In *The Financial Services Revolution: Policy Directions for the Future*, ed. C. England and T. Huertas. Boston, MA: Kluwer Academic Publishers, 9–40.

Keehn, S. 1989. "Banking on the Balance, Powers and the Safety Net: A Proposal." Federal Reserve Bank of Chicago.

Keynes, J.M. 1930. *A Treatise on Money.* London: Macmillan.

———. 1936. *The General Theory of Employment, Interest and Money.* London: Macmillan.

Kindleberger, C. 1978. *Manias, Panics, and Crashes.* New York: Basic Books.

Kondratieff, N. 1926. "Die langen Wellen der Konjunktur." *Archiv für Sozialwissenschaft und Sozialpolitik*, 56 (3).

Litan, R. 1987. *What Should Banks Do?* Washington, DC: Brookings Institution.

Luckett, D. 1980. "Approaches to Bank Liability Management." *Economic Review*, Federal Reserve Bank of Kansas City, March, 11–27.

McCulloch, J., H. and M. Yu. 1989. "Bank Runs, Deposit Contracts, and Government Deposit Insurance." Unpublished Manuscript.

Meade, J. 1966. "Exchange-Rate Flexibility." *The Three Banks Review*, no. 70, 3–27.

Meese, R. 1986. "Testing for Bubbles in Exchange Markets: A Case of Sparkling Rates?" *Journal of Political Economy*, 94 (2), 345–73.

Meltzer, A. 1986. "Financial Failures and Financial Policies." In *Deregulating Financial Services: Public Policy in Flux*, ed. G. Kaufman and R. Kormendi. Cambridge, MA: Ballinger, 79–96.

Mengle, D. 1989. "The Feasibility of Market Value Accounting for Commercial Banks." Working Paper 89–4, Federal Reserve Bank of Richmond.

Merton, R. 1977. "An Analytic Derivation of the Cost of Deposit Insurance and Loan Guarantees: An Application of Modern Option Pricing Theory." *Journal of Banking and Finance*, 1 (1), 3–11.

———. 1978. "On the Cost of Deposit Insurance When There Are Surveillance Costs." *Journal of Business*, 51 (3), 439–452.

Miles, M. 1984. *Beyond Monetarism: Finding the Road to Stable Money*. New York: Basic Books.

Minsky, H. 1964. "Longer Waves in Financial Relations: Financial Factors in the More Severe Depressions." *American Economic Review*, 54 (3), 324–35.

———. 1982. "Can 'It' Happen Again?" *Challenge*, 25 (3), 5–13.

Moore, B. 1983. "Unpacking the Post Keynesian Black Box: Bank Lending and the Money Supply." *Journal of Post Keynesian Economics*, 5 (4), 537–56.

Mundell, R. 1971. *Monetary Theory: Inflation, Interest and Growth in the World Economy*. Pacific Palisades, CA: Goodyear.

Passell, P. 1989. "Economic Scene: Are Banks Broke, Too?" *New York Times*, August 23, 1989.

Pennacchi, G. 1987. "Market Discipline, Information Disclosure, and Uninsured Deposits," *Proceedings from a Conference on Bank Structure and Competition*, Federal Reserve Bank of Chicago, May, 456–472.

Randall, R. 1989) "Can the Market Evaluate Asset Quality Exposure in Banks?" *New England Economic Review*, Federal Reserve Bank of Boston, July/August, 3–24.

Revey, P. 1981. "Evolution and Growth of the United States Foreign Exchange Market," *Quarterly Review*, Federal Reserve Bank of New York, 32–44.

Ronn, E., and A. Verma. 1986. "Pricing Risk-Adjusted Deposit Insurance: An Options-Based Model." *Journal of Finance*, 41 (3), 871–95.

Rousseas, S. 1986. *Post Keynesian Monetary Economics*. Armonk, NY: M.E. Sharpe.

Saunders, A., and I. Walter. 1987. "Are Banks Special?" *Journal of International Security Markets*, Winter, 171–76.

Schulmeister, S. 1983. "Exchange Rates, Prices and Interest Rates." Economic Research Reports, New York: New York University.

———. 1987. "An Essay on Exchange Rate Dynamics." Discussion Papers, Berlin: Wissenschaftszentrum Berlin für Sozialforschung.

Schwartz, A. 1987. "The Lender of the Last Resort and the Federal Safety Net." *Journal of Financial Services Research*, 1 (1), 1–17.

———. 1988. "The Effects of Regulation on Systemic Risks." *Proceedings from a Conference on Bank Structure and Competition*. Federal Reserve Bank of Chicago, May, 28–34.

Tallman, E. 1988. "Some Unanswered Questions About Bank Panics." *Economic Review*, Federal Reserve Bank of Atlanta, November/December, 2–21.

Thomson, J. 1986. "Equity, Efficiency, and Mispriced Deposit Guarantees." *Economic Commentary*, Federal Reserve Bank of Cleveland, July 15.

———. 1987a. "FSLIC Forbearances to Stockholders and the Value of Savings and Loans Shares." *Economic Commentary*, Federal Reserve Bank of Cleveland, 3rd Quarter, 26–35.

———. 1987b. "The Use of Market Information in Pricing Deposit Insurance." *Journal of Money, Credit and Banking*, 19 (3), 528–32.

———. 1989. "Economic Principles and Deposit Insurance Reform." *Economic Commentary*, Federal Reserve Bank of Cleveland, May 15.

Thomson, J., and W. Todd. 1990. "Rethinking and Living with the Limits of Bank Regulation." *The Cato Journal*, no. 9, Winter.

Tobin, J. 1978. "A proposal for international monetary reform." *Eastern Economic Journal*, 4.

Todd, W. 1988a. "Lessons of the Past and Prospects for the Future in Lender of Last Resort Theory." *Proceedings from a Conference on Bank Structure and Competition*, Federal Reserve Bank of Chicago, May 1988, 533–77.

———. 1988b. "No Conspiracy, but a Convenient Forgetting: Dr. Pangloss Visits the World of Deposit Insurance." Cato Conference Paper, November 2.

Trigaux, R. 1989. "Isaac Reassesses Continental Bailout." *American Banker*, July 31.

Wall, R. 1989. "A Plan for Reducing Future Deposit Insurance Losses: Puttable Subordinated Debt." *Economic Review*, Federal Reserve Bank of Atlanta, July/August, 2–17.

Williamson, J. 1987. *Targets and Indicators: Blueprint for the International Coordination of Economic Policy*. Washington, DC: Institute for International Economics

Wolfson, M. 1994. *Financial Crises: Understanding the Postwar U.S. Experience*. 2nd edition, Armonk, NY: M.E. Sharpe.

# *Index*

Accounting practices of banks, 97–98, 99, 101–102, 109, 115, 124, 125, 127, 129, 130, 131, 153–154, 160, 180
   Generally Accepted, 97, 98, 109, 115, 117, 118, 144
   Regulatory, 97, 100n, 141, 142, 144, 229, 234n
   of Bank Insurance Fund, 132
Asia Pacific Economic Cooperation (APEC), 192, 195, 197n, 226

Baker Plan, 19, 230, 239, 246
   *See also* Global debt crisis; Lender of last resort, international
Bank deposits, 4, 6, 8, 9, 11, 13n, 28, 30, 46, 55, 75, 78n, 96, 98, 100, 115, 125, 163, 166, 187, 199, 254, 257n
   runs on, 6, 120, 127, 139, 140, 146n, 152, 156
   "near-money" deposits, 11, 12, 30, 163–164, 166, 256, 259
Bank failures, 4, 6, 7n, 12, 84, 97, 102, 104, 107, 108, 115, 120, 122, 124, 125, 127, 134, 135, 139–140, 141, 146n, 155, 164–165, 177, 239
Bank holding companies, 9, 12, 13, 110, 119, 123–124, 136, 143, 146n, 165, 167, 168, 174
Bank Holding Company Act of 1956, 9, 13, 13n, 110
Bank Insurance Fund, 97, 98, 101–102, 112, 113, 116, 123, 124, 126, 127, 130–131, 132
   *See also* Federal Deposit Insurance Corporation; Financial Institutions Reform, Recovery, and Enforcement Act
Bank Merger Act of 1966, 9, 12
Bank reserves, 5, 6, 7n, 18, 28, 29, 30, 33n, 35, 153, 256, 257n
   loan-loss, 19, 110, 111, 115, 124, 157, 161, 230, 235, 238, 247
   pyramiding of, 28
   requirements, 6, 9, 12, 28, 123, 135, 150, 162–164, 165, 166, 180, 186, 194, 196n, 199, 255
Bank supervision, 7, 9, 18, 96, 102, 115, 133, 136, 145, 147n, 151, 152–153, 172, 174, 175, 176–177, 181, 186–187, 198, 264–265
Banking Act of 1935, 7, 9, 28, 78, 255
Basle Agreement of 1988, 135, 136–137, 153, 166, 173, 178
Bond-market view, 22, 32, 40, 61, 65–66
Borrowed liabilities, 11
   *See also* Commercial banks, liability management of
Brady Plan, 19–20, 230, 231, 232, 234n, 236, 237, 238, 239, 248
   *See also* Global debt crisis; Lender of last resort, international
Brazil, 18, 19, 229, 231, 232, 234n, 237
Bretton Woods, 14–15, 30, 158, 192, 193, 195, 200–201, 204, 212, 213, 217, 221, 222
   demise of, 15–16, 192, 193, 201, 212, 217, 255
Britain, 7n, 16, 38, 151, 194, 196, 200, 208, 209, 213, 219, 222, 230, 238, 239, 263
Bush, George, 32, 53, 60, 87, 98, 114, 145, 226

Capital, 8, 9, 47, 93, 253
   financial, 16, 191, 192, 194, 205, 223
   flight of, 17, 18, 19, 20, 22, 32, 194, 200, 201, 203, 204, 227, 233, 234n

Capital *(continued)*
   international flows of, 15, 16, 17, 19, 20, 191, 193, 203, 204, 221, 224
   internationalization of, 14, 191
   shortage of, 66, 106
   short-term movements of, 16, 20, 191, 193, 201
   transfers of, 14, 19, 254
   U.S. exports of, 15, 199, 255
   U.S. imports of, 21, 22, 32, 92, 196
Carter administration, 16, 194
Central bank, 4, 8, 14, 16, 30–31, 32, 33n, 34, 36, 40, 41, 150, 186, 203, 253, 255, 257n, 260, 266
   control over bank reserves, 4–5, 11, 199
   coordination, 33, 41, 194, 223
   exchange-rate management of, 15, 194, 195–196, 212, 217, 223–225
   as lender of last resort, 18, 20, 77–78
   in monetary theory, 5, 29, 30, 201, 264
   role of, 27, 36, 47, 176, 180, 187, 254, 256, 263–264
   structure of, 27, 28–29
Check-clearing mechanism, 5, 7n
   *See also* Payments system; Bank reserves
Clearinghouse Interbank Payments System (CHIPS), 191, 257n
   *See also* Euromarket; Foreign exchange markets
Clinton, Bill, 22, 38, 53, 54, 57, 60, 128, 215, 219, 220, 227, 233–234
Commercial banks, 4, 7n, 11, 12–13, 14, 28, 32, 40, 46, 88, 90–91, 96, 97–98, 98–100, 110, 114, 119, 120, 121–123, 133–135, 136, 139–140, 142, 146n, 148, 150, 151–152, 158–159, 162, 174, 177, 182–183, 253, 255, 256–257, 261
   branching restrictions of, 8, 11, 12, 95, 98, 110–111, 112, 114, 150–151, 159, 161
   capital requirements of, 7, 9, 18, 54, 75, 91, 94, 99, 103, 105, 107–108, 109, 110, 111, 117–119, 129, 131, 133. 135, 136, 142, 151, 153, 166–167, 168, 173, 179, 187, 254, 265
   and the global LDC debt crisis, 17, 18–20, 23n, 106, 111, 162, 228–232, 234n, 236, 237–238, 239, 245–246, 263
   and investment banks, 8, 9, 13, 98, 151, 156–158, 162, 178
   liability management of, 11, 13n
   loss-accounting rules of, 18, 19, 98, 102, 106, 111, 125, 127, 229, 231
   market-share erosion of, 59, 84, 98, 102, 105–107, 115, 133, 149, 256–257
   "narrow bank" plan for, 95, 100, 108, 111, 119–120
   1991 crisis of, 32, 35, 97, 101–102, 123–125, 133, 161–162
   recapitalization of, 75, 78, 95, 111–112, 124–125, 127, 128, 132, 135, 143, 154, 161, 165, 166, 169, 259, 262
   "spread banking" practice of, 21, 76, 78n, 123
   "trade-off" dilemma of, 6, 142
Commercial paper, 7n, 37, 54, 97, 102, 106, 122, 124
Commodity money, 3–4, 6, 15
Competitive Equality Banking Act of 1987, 97, 116
Computerization, 51, 62, 64, 63, 65, 66, 105, 107, 191, 198, 233, 255, 257, 257n

Consumer credit, 8, 10, 13n, 98
Credit, 32, 150, 154, 156, 180, 191, 233, 253, 254, 255, 256, 257, 259, 261, 262–263
  link to savings, 84
  securitization of, 20, 59, 98, 102, 105–106, 107, 132, 148, 149, 150, 170, 182, 187, 232, 233, 256–257, 259, 261, 262–263, 265
Credit controls, 8, 29, 30, 33n
Credit Control Act of 1969, 8
Credit crunch, 7, 54, 75, 76, 79, 96, 157, 262, 264
Credit cycle, 5–6, 75, 254
Credit money, 4–5, 253, 255, 256, 257n
Crowding out, 32, 77, 82, 226
Cybercash, 256

Debt, 9–10, 21, 34, 36, 37, 43, 45, 46, 60, 63, 72, 76–77, 78n, 80–82, 85, 86, 88, 89–91, 95, 148, 169, 226, 259
  deflation, 6
  of developing countries, 17–20, 107, 111, 210, 227, 228–229, 235–239, 263
  external, 22
  monetization of, 253
  overhang, 77, 79, 81, 98, 154
  refinancing of, 55, 75
  reschedulings, 18, 230, 236–237, 246
  short-term, 10
Debt economy, 9, 10
Demand deposits, 4, 5, 11, 13n, 163–164, 166
  See also Credit-money; Private bank money
Depository Institutions Deregulation and Monetary Control Act of 1980, 7, 12, 96, 116, 257n
Deposit insurance, 6, 78, 86, 94–95, 96, 102–103, 108, 118, 120, 124, 127, 130, 139, 140–141, 146, 147n, 155, 156, 180, 257n
  reform of, 95, 99, 108–109, 110, 114–118, 119, 125, 132, 133, 143, 151, 159–160, 160
Depression, 6, 10, 17, 19, 30, 77, 168, 230, 231, 232, 237, 254, 255
Deregulation, 170, 193, 256, 257, 257n, 259
  of banks, 12–13, 30, 99, 110–111, 121, 125, 134–135, 145, 178, 192, 232
  of currency prices, 16, 256
  of financial markets, 40, 203, 261
  of interest rates, 12, 32, 76, 105, 116, 192, 255, 256
  of thrifts, 12, 96, 134
Derivatives, 50, 52n, 71, 85, 98, 100n, 191, 196n, 232, 247, 257, 259, 261–262, 265
Discount loans, 5, 6, 7, 7n, 8, 28, 133, 143–144, 255
  See also Federal Reserve
Disintermediation, 11, 54, 76, 96, 187
Dollar, 22, 38, 41, 48, 57, 71, 72, 84, 158, 196, 199, 208, 210, 211, 215, 217–218, 222, 224, 233
  overvaluation of (1968–73), 15, 212
  revaluation of (1981–85), 21, 212, 223, 226, 229
  as world money, 14–15, 156, 192, 204, 217, 219, 220, 229, 234, 234n

Economic and Monetary Union, 192, 197n, 208, 209
Emergency Banking Act of 1933, 4, 9
Emergent markets, 20, 22, 223, 232–234, 234n
Employment Act of 1946, 71
Exchange rates, 16, 23n, 30, 67, 146n, 158, 192, 200–201, 203, 214, 215, 223, 226, 242, 254, 256
  in the Bretton Woods system, 14–15, 193, 204, 212, 221, 255
  flexible, 16, 30, 193–194, 200, 203–204, 217, 243
  under gold standard, 3
  realignment in Smithsonian agreement, 15
  target zones for, 194, 195–196, 196n, 201–202, 212–213, 223–225
Euromarket, 11, 15, 16, 17, 18, 167, 191–194, 196n, 199–200, 228–229, 256, 257, 257n
European Community/Union (EC/EU), 22, 32, 111, 135, 173, 174, 178, 192, 195, 201, 208, 223, 229, 257n
European Monetary System (EMS), 192, 193, 234n

Federal Deposit Insurance Corporation (FDIC), 6, 9, 29, 35, 97, 98–99, 102–103, 109, 110, 112, 117–118, 120, 123, 124, 125, 130, 132, 135, 143, 146n, 155, 156, 162, 164, 165, 168, 175, 176, 186, 255
  See also Bank Insurance Fund; deposit insurance, Federal Deposit; Insurance Corporation Improvement Act of 1991; Savings Association Insurance Fund
Federal Deposit Insurance Corporation Improvement Act (FDICIA) of 1991, 99, 114, 117–118, 127, 128–130, 131, 133, 179, 180

Federal funds, 13n, 33n, 41, 50, 140
  "pegging" the rate of, 30, 31, 33n
  rate, 41, 55, 56, 78n
  See also Monetary policy (U.S.)
Federal Reserve (Fed), 4, 5, 6, 7n, 9, 10, 21, 38, 41, 54, 60, 70–72, 75, 95, 133, 135, 140, 143, 150, 162, 163, 164, 166, 180, 199–200, 219, 255
  as bank regulator, 13, 18, 27, 29, 136–137, 153, 174–176, 178, 185–187, 256
  as book-keeper in check-clearing mechanism, 5
  control erosion of, 59, 60, 76, 200, 266
  control over payments system. 33n, 256, 257n
  credibility of, 31, 34, 41, 50
  influence on interest rates, 29–30, 31, 32, 33, 33n, 34–35, 40–41, 47, 56, 75
  membership of, 12, 28
  notes, 4, 28
  open-market operations of, 5, 6, 29, 30, 35, 78n
  operating targets of, 5, 11, 27, 30, 33, 47, 55, 56, 67–70
  policy switch in 1979, 17, 30, 67, 229, 255
  Regulation Q, 9, 11, 12, 21, 54, 75–76, 78n, 163
  soft-landing strategy of, 31, 32, 51–52, 61, 66, 67, 76
  strategic (post-1982) comprise of, 31, 41, 51–52
  structure of, 28–29
Federal Reserve Act of 1913, 4, 5, 28
Federal Reserve–Treasury Accord of 1951, 30, 70
Federal Savings and Loan Insurance Corporation (FSLIC), 7, 97, 100n, 116, 126, 127, 129, 130
Financial crisis, 6, 7, 75, 78, 78n, 96, 115, 136, 171, 193, 203, 205, 228, 229, 254, 255
Financial fragility, 32, 76–77, 78, 85
Financial innovation, 11, 19, 84, 98, 230
Financial instability, 6, 9, 10, 51, 75, 79, 82, 86, 96, 168, 198, 240, 257
Financial institutions, 6, 8, 10, 13n, 29, 34, 35, 40, 43, 60, 72, 84, 100, 102, 139, 144, 149, 153, 170, 182, 192, 209, 258, 265–266
  product extension of, 12–13, 107, 145, 146n, 163
  special role of, 8, 142, 150, 151
Financial Institutions Reform, Recovery and Enforcement Act (FIRREA) of 1989, 97, 102, 116, 127, 138, 142–143, 144, 145
Financial regulation, 8–9, 11, 13n, 145, 170–178, 179–181, 183–188, 192, 254, 261, 264–265
First Bank of the United States, 27
Fiscal stabilizers, 20, 22, 60
Foreign exchange markets, 16, 23n, 41, 191, 196, 200–201, 203
Fractional-reserve banking, 5, 6
France, 16, 39, 194, 196, 202, 222, 223, 238, 263
Friedman, Milton, 5, 16, 27, 119, 193, 217
Futures, 196n, 261, 263
  currency, 16, 191, 192, 196n, 200

Garn–St.Germain Depository Institutions Act (DIA) of 1982, 12, 13, 96, 116
General Agreement on Tariffs and Trade, 23n, 195, 197n, 209, 213, 214, 218, 221, 222, 224, 226, 227
Germany, 15, 39, 59, 169, 192, 196, 199, 206, 209, 211, 213, 216
  banking in, 135, 151, 158–159, 173–174, 176–177, 186–187, 238
Glass-Steagall Act of 1933, 6, 8, 9, 11, 78, 78n, 133, 142, 156, 172, 173, 185–186, 187, 255
Global competition, 51, 57, 62, 63, 64, 98, 156, 173
Global debt crisis of developing countries, 17–18, 111, 228–229, 235–239, 245–249,
  management of, 18–20, 229–232, 246–249, 263
Globalization, 31, 63, 121, 135, 178, 191–192, 203, 214, 257
Gold Reserve Act of 1934, 4, 9
Gold standard, 3–4, 7n, 9, 29, 253, 255
Great Depression (1929–1938), 4, 5, 6, 7n, 9, 28, 96, 97, 108, 139, 255
Greenspan, Alan, 31, 33, 53–56, 58–60, 65, 67–70, 71, 72, 107, 109, 111, 123, 187, 218
Group of Seven (G–7), 196

Humphrey-Hawkins Full Employments and Balanced Growth Act of 1978, 46, 56, 71.

Inconvertible Paper Standard, 4, 9, 255
  See also Credit-Money
Inflation, 4, 15, 16, 17, 21, 22, 29–30, 31–32, 33, 34, 36–38, 40, 41–42, 44–45, 47, 49, 55, 56, 57, 59–60, 61, 62–64, 68, 71, 72, 75–76, 89, 105, 154, 156, 169, 211, 219, 222, 229, 230, 232, 234n, 241, 243, 264, 266

Inflation *(continued)*
  debt-inflation spiral, 10–11, 20, 162
  early-warning signals of, 31, 51
  expectations, 21, 31, 38, 41, 44, 48, 51, 56, 57, 58, 61, 65, 67, 68, 70, 72
  measure of, 65, 71
  Interest rates, 10, 11, 15, 21, 22, 35–36, 38, 40, 43, 44, 45, 48, 50, 54, 62, 65, 72, 80, 84, 85, 89, 95, 96, 99, 129, 166, 192, 199, 204, 217–218, 253, 255
  and budget-deficit reduction, 45, 54, 66
  on debt, 9, 80, 82
  and global debt crisis, 17, 18, 229, 239
  as monetary policy target, 29, 31–32, 33, 35, 40, 47, 50–51, 54, 55, 56, 67–71, 72, 194, 199, 201, 255
  and security prices, 33n, 51, 52n
  *See also* Deregulation of interest rates
International Lending Supervision Act of 1983, 18
International Monetary Fund, 14, 204, 212, 213, 221, 234n
  as lender of last resort, 18, 20, 222, 229, 231, 234, 242–244, 246–248, 263
Italy, 39, 196, 263

Japan, 14, 15, 22, 32, 33, 34, 36, 39, 57, 59, 72, 86, 135, 192, 196, 199, 201, 211, 213, 215–220, 225, 261, 263
  banking in, 158, 238,
J-curve effect, 16, 196n
Johnson, Harry, 5, 16

Keynes, John Maynard, 5, 7n, 33n, 85, 86, 194, 201, 204
Keynesianism, 5, 16, 21, 29, 31, 52, 218

Lender of last resort, 6–7, 7n, 9, 10, 20, 51, 72, 77, 86, 96, 134–136, 140, 144, 153, 175, 185–186, 254, 255
  international, 18, 20, 204, 222, 228–231, 233–234
  moral-hazard problem of, 7, 107, 115, 116, 141, 255
Leverage, 9, 10, 52n, 76, 77, 89–90, 94, 95, 97, 105, 117, 204, 261
Leveraged buyouts, 80, 85, 88, 97, 98, 144, 156
Limited services banks, 12, 13, 13n, 135, 137
Long waves, 76, 77, 78n, 96
Louvre Agreement of 1987, 196, 211, 212, 213, 225

McFadden Act of 1927, 8
Merger wave, 60, 77, 80, 85, 86, 88
Mexico, 17, 18, 19, 20, 112, 192, 223, 227, 228–234, 234n, 235–239, 245–249
  *See also* Global debt crisis; North American Free Trade Agreement (NAFTA)
Minsky, Hyman 76, 77, 78n, 86, 232
Monetarism, 5, 7n, 16, 21, 29, 30–31, 52, 193, 256
  Federal Reserve's abandonment of, 30, 31
  growing influence of, 30
Monetary aggregates, 5, 30, 33, 33n, 34, 37–38, 46–47, 55, 67, 72, 164, 234n, 256, 260
Monetary policy (U.S.), 4, 7n, 8, 9, 10, 12, 29–31, 41, 43, 45, 47, 48, 49, 50, 54, 56, 67–72, 95, 103, 136, 150, 153, 163, 175–176, 180, 185, 187, 254, 259, 263–264, 266
  central bank tools of, 5, 9, 28, 56, 67, 119, 224, 255
  debate over, 5, 7n, 27, 29, 31–32, 36, 52, 62, 72
  and fiscal policy, 38, 39, 59–60, 71, 95, 217
  limits of, 6, 11, 32, 33, 34, 39–40, 59, 65, 152, 187, 256, 266
  in the post-1982 recovery, 21, 30, 51–52
  in the post-1991 recovery, 34–35, 43–44
Monetary regime, 254–257
Money, 3, 162, 166
  creation of, 4, 5, 6, 8, 11, 21, 27, 96, 134, 162, 254
  forms of, 3–4, 254, 256, 257, 257n
  functions of, 3, 163
  as public good, 257, 257n
  as social institution, 3, 253
  supply of, 5, 6, 7n, 12, 29, 30, 33n, 38, 198, 199, 263
  velocity of, 21, 47, 164
  *See also* Credit-money; Private bank money
Money-market mutual funds (MMMFs), 8, 11, 13n, 30, 46, 55, 78n, 96, 98, 105, 122, 149, 150, 187, 260, 261
Money multiplier, 5, 7n

National bank notes, 4, 28
National Banking Acts of 1863/64, 4, 9, 28
Nationwide banking, 12, 95, 111, 125, 134, 136, 150–151, 161
Nixon, Richard, 15, 59, 217
North American Free Trade Agreement (NAFTA), 192, 195, 221, 226, 232, 234, 234n

Office of Thrift Supervision, 97, 116, 153

Payments system, 5, 16, 33n, 96, 139–140, 142, 146n, 186, 254, 255, 256, 257n
  *See also* Federal Reserve, control over
Plaza Agreement, 210, 211, 212, 213, 225
Private bank money, 4, 5, 6, 8, 27, 30, 192, 254, 256

Reagan, Ronald, 7n, 20–21, 29, 91, 97, 223–226
Reconstruction Finance Corporation, 78
Regulatory forbearance, 97, 98, 99, 101, 102, 105, 109, 111, 117–118, 130, 132, 134, 135, 162, 164, 166
Resolution Trust Corporation, 97, 116, 127, 164, 165, 168
Roosevelt Administration (New Deal), 4, 9, 21, 54, 78, 96, 253, 255

Savings Association Insurance Fund, 97, 116, 126
  *See also* Federal Deposit Insurance Corporation; Financial Institutions Reform, Recovery, and Enforcement Act
Second Bank of the United States, 28, 33n
Securities Act of 1933, 9
Securities Exchange Act of 1934, 9
Securities and Exchange Commission, 9, 136, 159, 181, 260
Seigniorage, 15, 22
Speculation, 8, 10, 60, 77, 78n, 79–80, 80–81, 84, 85–86, 89, 97, 100n, 128, 131, 193–194, 196n, 200, 257
  in currencies, 15, 16, 192–194, 198, 200–201, 203–204, 223
Stagflation, 10, 15, 96, 255
  *See also* Inflation
State bank notes, 4
Stock market, 8, 33, 42, 51, 77, 80, 90, 112
  circuit breakers in, 261
  crash of 1929, 9, 96
  crash of 1987, 7n, 20, 31, 89, 140, 196, 260
Supply-side theory, 7n, 20, 21, 29, 226

Tax Reform Act of 1986, 95
Thrifts, 7, 7n, 10, 12, 13, 13n, 32, 54, 96–97, 98, 100n, 102, 103, 105, 106, 107, 111, 115, 116, 127, 130, 142
  bailout of, 95, 97, 99, 108, 116, 120, 127, 130, 138, 145
Tobin tax, 85, 204–205
Trade, 57, 64, 191, 195, 196, 198, 200, 203, 204, 210
  postwar liberalization of, 14, 23n, 195, 208, 214, 221–222, 226–227
  restrictions of, 40, 211–213, 218–219
Treasury's Bank Reform Proposal of 1991, 98–99, 100, 110, 116–117, 118, 133–136, 148, 150–154, 155–158, 161–162, 174–178, 184–187, 265–266

Unemployment, 51, 59, 61, 65, 67, 72, 87, 198, 202, 231, 243
  in Europe, 207
  natural rate of, 51, 61, 64, 87
United States, 15, 33, 34, 35, 49, 50–52, 55, 57, 58, 61, 64, 66, 67, 70, 72, 76, 77, 85, 87–90, 92–93, 97, 106, 112, 135, 150, 158, 159, 168, 173, 177, 183–183, 192, 195, 200, 204, 206, 208, 216–217, 259, 264
  budget deficits of, 20, 32, 38, 45, 57, 58, 60, 66, 77, 83, 88, 91–92, 94, 226
  capital exports of, 15, 199, 222, 255
  as net debtor, 22, 32, 92, 156
  productivity performance of, 51, 57, 58, 64, 66, 67, 72, 77, 80, 81, 90, 92, 93, 207–208
  trade deficits of, 16, 21, 32, 72, 83, 92, 196, 207, 210, 225, 243
Uruguay Round, 195, 198n, 208, 213–214, 226

World Bank, 14, 206, 230, 236, 242, 248, 255
World Trade Organization, 135, 195, 197n

Yield curve, 30, 31, 32, 33, 35, 40, 41, 47, 50, 68, 123, 154, 266

# *About the Editor*

Robert Guttmann is a professor of Economics at Hofstra University. He studied at the University of Vienna and the Free University of Berlin before receiving advanced degrees in economics from the University of Wisconsin and in London. Professor Guttmann has written widely on issues in money and banking in a global setting and on industrial policy. His works include *How Credit-Money Shapes the Economy: The United States in a Global System* (M.E. Sharpe, 1994), winner of *Choice Magazine's* "Outstanding Book in Economics" award of 1995.